Palgrave Studies in Prisons and Penology

Series Editors
Ben Crewe
Institute of Criminology
University of Cambridge, Cambridge, United Kingdom

Yvonne Jewkes
School of Applied Social Science
University of Brighton, Brighton, United Kingdom

Thomas Ugelvik
Criminology and Sociology of Law
Faculty of Law, University of Oslo, Oslo, Norway

D1489789

This is a unique and innovative series, the first of its kind dedicated entirely to prison scholarship. At a historical point in which the prison population has reached an all-time high, the series seeks to analyse the form, nature and consequences of incarceration and related forms of punishment. Palgrave Studies in Prisons and Penology provides an important forum for burgeoning prison research across the world. Series Advisory Board: Anna Eriksson (Monash University), Andrew M. Jefferson (DIGNITY - Danish Institute Against Torture), Shadd Maruna (Rutgers University), Jonathon Simon (Berkeley Law, University of California) and Michael Welch (Rutgers University).

More information about this series at
http://www.springer.com/series/14596

Peter Scharff Smith • Thomas Ugelvik
Editors

Scandinavian Penal History, Culture and Prison Practice

Embraced By the Welfare State?

Editors
Peter Scharff Smith
Department of Criminology and Sociology
of Law, University of Oslo
Oslo, Norway

Thomas Ugelvik
Department of Criminology and Sociology
of Law, University of Oslo
Oslo, Norway

Palgrave Studies in Prisons and Penology
ISBN 978-1-349-84408-1   ISBN 978-1-137-58529-5 (eBook)
DOI 10.1057/978-1-137-58529-5

Library of Congress Control Number: 2016949750

Cover illustration: Simon Whaley/Alamy Stock Photo

Printed on acid-free paper

This Palgrave Macmillan imprint is published by Springer Nature
The registered company is Macmillan Publishers Ltd.
The registered company address is: The Campus, 4 Crinan Street, London, N1 9XW, United Kingdom

Contents

Contributors

R. Andersson Institute of Police Education, Linnaeus University, Växjö, Sweden

A. Bruhn Department of Social Work, Örebro University, Oslo, Sweden

H. J. Engbo Former Chief Executive, Correctional Service of Greenland, Denmark

A. D. Fisher Department of Public and International Law, University of Oslo, Oslo, Norway

P. Fransen The Danish National Archive, Copenhagen, Denmark

T. E. Fredwall Center for Care Research, University of Agder, Kristiansand, Norway

T. Kolind Centre for Alcohol and Drug Research, Aarhus University, Aarhus, Denmark

T. Langelid Former National Coordinator of Prison Education, Bergen, Norway

M. Langford Department of Public and International Law, University of Oslo and Co-Director, Centre on Law and Social Transformation, University of Bergen and Chr. Michelsen Institute, Oslo, Norway

O. Lindberg Department of Social Work, Örebro University, Oslo, Sweden

I. R. Lundeberg University of Bergen, Bergen, Norway

C. Mathiassen Aarhus University, Danish School of Education, Campus Emdrup, Copenhagen, Denmark

L. K. Minke Department of Law, University of Southern Denmark, Odense, Denmark

R. Nilsson The Department of Historical Studies, Gothenburg University, Gothenburg, Sweden

P. Å. Nylander Department of Social Work, Örebro University, Oslo, Sweden

A. Olesen Department of Law, University of Southern Denmark, Odense, Denmark

F. Pareus Norwegian Centre for Human Rights, University of Oslo, Oslo, Norway

G. Ploeg Directorate of the Norwegian Correctional Service, Oslo, Norway

K. Reiter Department of Criminology, Law & Society and at the School of Law at the University of California, Irvine, USA

J. K. Schaffer Norwegian Centre for Human Rights, University of Oslo, Oslo, Norway

L. Sexton Department of Criminal Justice and Criminology at the, University of Missouri-Kansas City, Missouri, USA

V. L. Shammas Department of Sociology and Human Geography, University of Oslo, Oslo, Norway

P. S. Smith Department of Criminology and Sociology of Law, University of Oslo, Oslo, Norway

A. B. Smoyer Department of Social Work, Southern Connecticut State University, New Haven, USA

J. Sumner Department of Public Administration, California State University, Dominguez Hills, California, USA

T. Ugelvik Department of Criminology and Sociology of Law, University of Oslo, Oslo, Norway

T. Vander Beken Department of Criminologie, Criminal Law and Social Law, Faculty of Law, Universiteitstraat, Ghent, Belgium

List of Figures

List of Tables

Part I

Introduction

Introduction: Punishment, Welfare and Prison History in Scandinavia

Peter Scharff Smith and Thomas Ugelvik

Imagine a prison. What does it look like? Who live inside? How are they treated? Ask these questions of children, and they will tend to give you a pretty straightforward answer based on what they have learned from adults and quite often what they have seen in movies, TV series and on the Internet: "The windows are very small and it's dark," "you wear a blue uniform—or orange," "the guards are strict because you are criminal" and so on.[1] Many learn from childhood that if a person does something very wrong the police will come and get you, and if you are a "criminal" you will go to prison. This pretty much sums up

---

[1] Danish fifth-graders interviewed by Janne Jakobsen (Smith 2014, p. 68).

P.S. Smith (✉) · T. Ugelvik
Department of Criminology and Sociology of Law, University of Oslo,
Oslo, Norway
e-mail: p.s.smith@jus.uio.no; thomas.ugelvik@jus.uio.no

© The Author(s) 2017
P. Scharff Smith, T. Ugelvik (eds.), *Scandinavian Penal History,
Culture and Prison Practice,* Palgrave Studies in Prisons and
Penology, DOI 10.1057/978-1-137-58529-5_1

some of the most basic definitions of what a prison is—or at least is supposed to be: a building where people found guilty of committing a crime are forced to live for a time as punishment for what they have done. What actually goes on inside these facilities tend to be much more unclear and the common knowledge about how prisons actually operate is typically rather limited. Prisons have in fact been described as "the last great secretive institutions in our society" (Coyle 2005, p. 6). Indeed, the very basic and common quality of these facilities—the fact that they are designed to lock up people out of sight of the rest of society—has arguably shaped these places in a rather uniform way and made it difficult to escape the historical and architectural origins of these institutions. Certainly, as anyone who has visited prisons in different parts of the Western world will know, prisons often resemble each other across geographical borders. In other words, one could argue, substantial prison reform is apparently not an easy task. In a way, this makes the differences that actually *do* exist much more interesting and relevant to discuss, especially when you sometimes run into institutions or prison practices which seem unique or at least very different from the usual way of doing things:

> Denmark doesn't treat its prisoners like prisoners—and it's good for everyone. (Reiter et al. 2016)

> The Radical Humaneness of Norway's Halden Prison. The goal of the Norwegian penal system is to get inmates out of it. (Benko 2015)

> Why Scandinavian Prisons Are Superior. "Open" prisons, in which detainees are allowed to live like regular citizens, should be a model for the U.S. (Larson 2013)

As these quotes show, it has been claimed that prisons in Scandinavia exhibit significant differences when compared to institutions elsewhere. For this reason alone, study of the penal arrangements in these countries is important. If truly different prisons have been created and if they actually are more humane than other such institutions, should we not try to discover how and why? After all more than 10 million people are locked up in penal institutions throughout the world (Walmsley 2016, p. 2), and if there are positive lessons to be learned from the Scandinavian experience, we should try to identify them and share them with the world. On the other hand, it is important to ask whether the almost fairy tale-like images conjured by the international headlines really constitute a true representation of prison conditions in this northernmost corner of Europe. Is such a thing as a humane prison even possible? And if it is, is there any particular reason to assume that it is a uniquely Scandinavian phenomenon?

Visiting Prisons with Prison Visitors—Experiencing the Foreign Eye on Scandinavia

We, the editors of this book, have studied prisons for many years and are used to visiting and researching the various types of penal institutions in our home countries of Norway and Denmark.[2] During years of such work we have also on many occasions had the pleasure of entering "our own" local Scandinavian prisons in the company of foreign visitors such as researchers from different countries or participants in criminal justice or human rights courses from different parts of the world. The former (the international research colleagues) have often been directly interested in Scandinavian prisons and the question of their possible exceptional character, while the latter group have typically visited prisons—along with other local institutions such as the Police academy and the Ombudsman's office—to learn about the allegedly high human rights standards and good practices in Scandinavia. We have both found that these visits can be a very interesting experience in themselves. On such occasions we have often had the benefit not only of gathering empirical evidence—something a prison researcher will inevitably always do when visiting a prison regardless of the purpose—but also of witnessing the reactions of our fellow visitors. In a sense, our role on these occasions has been to observe not only the penal institutions but our international colleagues reacting to them.

---

[2] We have even visited several prisons in Sweden and for that matter studied some Swedish prison practices.

Visiting Scandinavian prisons together with foreign prison visitors has shown us that everything is not simply black and white and that differences are sometimes perhaps more a matter of cultural context and background. Even visitors working with penal reform in their home countries may be unaccustomed to restrictions that are normal and seem obvious from a Scandinavian perspective. We have also experienced prison researchers reacting primarily with recognition perhaps especially when visiting old 19th-century panoptical prisons of which there are also several still in operation in Scandinavia—a situation and context which will be familiar to many a prison scholar from most other European countries. Finally, we have observed foreign researchers react with a certain disappointment after visiting progressive, seemingly exceptional and initially very humane-looking Scandinavian institutions, when discovering that, after all, these places are still prisons; places of detention where people are deprived of their liberty and subjected to strict rules and regulations.

Nevertheless, many visitors clearly also react with surprise when visiting Scandinavian prisons. A very specific practice which tends to draw a lot of attention during such visits are the knives in the common kitchen areas which accompany the self-catering regimes that allow prisoners to cook their own meals; a very uncommon and visually striking sight from the perspective of most foreign visitors. Another visually striking practice is that of open prisons where a number of specific institutions are based in old farm buildings, barracks, etc. sometimes lacking a surrounding perimeter fence or wall. Hence these institutions appear *very* open and very different from the archetypical Western prison. The initial experience visiting such places is in some ways not very prison-like at all. These and other practices can cause raised eyebrows during visits and give the sensation that something quite special is going on here. Another example is foreign visitors encountering imprisoned women and men together in Danish penal institutions. Many outsiders perhaps would not give this much thought, but a prison researcher would know that this is rather special and perhaps even unique in a Western context. Finally, many prison visitors from abroad clearly feel that staff welcome them openly and perhaps also get a sense that they treat prisoners with a certain level of respect and kindness.

But do these different examples truly reflect some sort of different (or even exceptional) Scandinavian way of doing things? If yes, then how should we go about explaining it? So far a popular line of thought has been to connect Scandinavian prisons to another seemingly unique Scandinavian arrangement, namely the wider welfare state context. Does it make sense to say that Scandinavian prisons are uniquely welfare oriented? If yes, then how and with what consequences?

Social Control in a Scandinavian Welfare State

It is often said these days that we are living in a neoliberal age. Taking Bourdieu's (1998) analytical distinction between a left hand and a right hand of the state as a starting point, Wacquant (2008, 2009), for instance, describes how the neoliberal condition is characterized by a development where the left hand—the hand that typically takes care of "social functions" like public education, health, housing, welfare and labour law—withers, while the right hand—the member responsible for enforcing budget cuts, fiscal incentives, economic deregulation, as well as managing the courts, the police and the prisons—is stronger than ever.

In comparative analyses, the Scandinavian countries are often used to exemplify well-functioning welfare states. They are described as among the most egalitarian societies in the world, with a narrow field of class differences (Moene and Barth 2004), factors which help them to consistently do well on the UN Human Development Index.[3] This has allegedly made it possible for the Scandinavian countries to resist the turn from "welfare" to "workfare" (and further on to "prisonfare") and thereby avoid many of the punitive policies and practices characteristic of the neoliberal era, according to Wacquant (2008).

Other scholars (Lacey 2008; Pratt 2008a, b; Pratt and Eriksson 2011, 2012a, b) also see the Scandinavian countries as exceptions to the

---

[3] In the 2015 report, Norway is ranked 1, Denmark 4, and Sweden 14 out of the 188 countries listed. See http://hdr.undp.org/sites/default/files/hdr15_standalone_overview_en.pdf. Accessed 29 April 2016.

international rule of convergence towards the increasingly punitive neo-liberal model characteristic of the Anglophone countries. In contrast to these countries, where a focus on penal rather than social measures and workfare rather than welfare has been the trend, the Scandinavian countries all combine a high level of equality with government efficiency, a relatively stable employment market and generous welfare schemes in a way unparalleled elsewhere in the world (Witoszek 2011, p. 10). The safety net available to citizens is strong and wide. One will find comparably low levels of unemployment backed up by generous unemployment benefit schemes, liberal social welfare schemes, a universal right to secondary level education, a free public health care system, free and easy access to higher education and so on.

States are more or less ambitious when it comes to welfare policies and their intended impacts. According to Esping-Andersen and Korpi (1987), the Scandinavian model in the 1980s was comprehensive, institutionalized and universal, and this image is still very much alive today in much of the international scholarship. Since the 1980s and 90s it has been customary to talk about a *Nordic Model* of public and social policy and the egalitarian "social democratic welfare state regime" which is often associated with these states (Kautto et al. 1999, p. 1; Brochman and Hagelund 2010). The array of welfare state responsibilities has widened drastically with this *Nordic Model* and in contrast to earlier regimes and those in operation elsewhere. In the words of Esping-Andersen and Korpi: "The welfare state is meant to integrate and include the entire population rather than target its resources toward particular problem groups" (1987, p. 32). In other words, the welfare schemes in such states are (in principle at least) available to all irrespective of social or geographical position. The level of what Rugkåsa (2011) has called "welfare ambitiousness"—the scope of responsibilities that the state assumes for the welfare of its citizens and the extensiveness of the welfare system—is apparently second to none. Compared to almost everywhere else, the Scandinavian countries have high hopes when it comes to their goals of modifying and engineering social conditions in a way as to create a just and healthy society for all citizens, regardless of background.

Understood, following Rugkåsa (2011), as a constellation of (1) political ideals about a well-functioning society, (2) institutional mechanisms and (3) principles for the allocation of resources, the welfare state can be said to constitute a sort of general social frame in these countries. In Denmark, it has been called a secular religion (Brochman and Hagelund 2010); in the current Norwegian context, it can according to some be understood almost like a total social phenomenon in the Maussian (1954) sense: The welfare state is to be found almost everywhere, and very often it is trusted and regarded as benevolent. It is a source of Norwegian pride and identity and, as a national symbol and rhetorical trope, all-important for the legitimacy of many state initiatives. "The state" may be criticized, but "the welfare state" is in a sense beyond reproach.

Nevertheless, there is also general agreement in the literature that times have changed for these Scandinavian welfare states and that crisis and Neoliberal ideology have transformed the original egalitarian social democratic model to a greater or lesser extent. Some Scandinavians talk about not only the rise but also the "fall of the welfare state," with Nordic model countries suffering from "increased poverty" as well as "greater social and economic inequality" (Wahl 2011, p. 13).

Regardless, it seems safe to argue that the welfare ambitions of Scandinavian states are still very high compared to most other countries. These ambitions are driven by, among other things, strong states with high tax level, which are willing and have the power to initiate schemes to normalize and civilize its citizens. In other words, states with high welfare ambitions will arguably tend to interfere in citizens' (and non-citizens') lives more readily and more profoundly than states with lower ambitions. Furthermore, following this logic, ambitious welfare states have also been called Janus-faced (Barker 2012), meaning that generous care and intrusive social control are often two sides of the same coin. This tendency is part of a culture and intimate relationship between the state and its individual citizens which prompted Huntford (1972) to describe Swedish society in the 1960s and its Swedish members as *The New Totalitarians.*

This book is about Scandinavian prisons and their possible relationship with the Scandinavian welfare states and their associated values. One can argue that there exist multiple strong connections between the welfare and the penal systems in all these countries. It has even been claimed that it makes sense to call Scandinavian prisons welfare state institutions (Ugelvik 2015). On the other hand, one could perhaps say that all public institutions, including schools and hospitals, by nature are closely connected to the welfare state. If that is the case, however, then what is unique or even especially interesting about the relationship between prisons and welfare states in Scandinavian societies? Or to ask in another way, are Scandinavian schools, hospitals, etc. especially humane and well functioning compared to those in other countries, thanks to the Scandinavian welfare state model? It is not a question which will be answered nor researched in this volume but the hypothesis seems somewhat unlikely. But why then have welfare ambitions been found to be relatively high in Scandinavian prisons and how does that possibly reflect the quality, values and presence of the welfare state?

In any case, if such a thing as welfare-oriented prisons does exist, there is no reason to believe that they are exclusively benevolent and constructive places. Rather, it means that the penal systems in these countries (to various degrees perhaps) are shot-through with welfare- oriented social technologies, logics and optics. In other words, one could argue, when made to serve a custodial sentence in these countries, you are grasped by the left and the right hands of the state simultaneously. In this book, we explore the particulars of this powerful penal-welfare embrace and the degree to which it might (or might not) constitute an important element in Scandinavian prisons.

Scandinavian Prison History in the Eyes of International Observers

In 1777 famous philanthropist and prison reformer John Howard published his ground-breaking study *The State of Prisons* after having visited prisons all over Europe and beyond. Howard's travels also brought him to Sweden and Denmark, but unlike many of the internationally oriented penal observers of today he did not particularly like what he found in Scandinavia. After visiting Denmark he went on to Sweden and noted the following:

I observed the houses to be much cleaner than those in Denmark; and this led me to hope I should find the same difference in the prisons (. . .) But I was disappointed, for I found them as dirty and offensive as those in Denmark. (Howard 1929, p. 71)

In Denmark Howard had visited the "Stockade prison" in Copenhagen, a facility for slaves,[4] where he described the treatment of the inmates as "shocking to humanity" (Howard 1929, p. 71). The slaves wore ankle or neck chains and received new clothing only once every two years. "I did not wonder to find many of them the almost naked" wrote Howard, and further remarked that each visit gave him a headache (Howard 1929, p. 77 f.).

Howard was not the only traveller who left Scandinavia with such an impression. Little more than a decade later—in 1788—the Venezuela-born Spanish-American world traveler Francisco de Miranda also visited prisons in Copenhagen and recorded all his impressions carefully in his diary. On the one hand, he was impressed by the short but intensive period of reforms in Denmark under the brief reign of the King's physician (and the Queen's paramour) Johann Struensee, who was beheaded in 1772 for the crimes of lèse-majesté and high treason. On the other, Miranda visited different Danish prisons and was appalled by what he saw. In the "Blue Tower prison" Miranda was met by putrid air caused by the fact that the barrels used as toilets were only emptied five or six times a year. In the previously mentioned "Stockade prison", the responsible governor, who clearly misread his visitor's agenda, proudly displayed all his whips and torture instruments and even demonstrated how to most effectively use the former against the prisoners to force them to confess crimes and misdeeds: "this fool demonstrated with great zeal how to handle the whip (. . .) as if it was a grand and very valuable talent", Miranda lamented (Smith 2003, p. 110).

Regular prison visits by philanthropists and prison reformers continued well into the 19th century and during this time Scandinavia was on the receiving end of harsh criticism. It was frankly not a place travellers

---

[4] Slavery was made illegal in Denmark in 1848.

went for penal reform inspiration. In 1818, for example, Akershus fortress and Christiania prison in Oslo, which both held sentenced slaves, were visited by the Quakers Stephen Grellet and William Allen, en route from London to Sweden and later to Russia. Allen and Grellet were very interested in prison reforms and clearly critical of the conditions in the Norwegian institutions (Schaanning 2007, p. 67). Both Grellet and Allen knew another Quaker, Elisabeth Fry, who went on to become one of the most influential philanthropist prison reformers of her time. Fry also showed an interest in Scandinavian prisons and as late as 1841 she came to Denmark, together with her brother John Gurney, in order to visit prisons. Once again, severe criticism was the result (Smith 2003, p. 144 ff.). In general, foreign visitors were rarely impressed by the standards of the early Scandinavian prisons.

Early Scandinavian Prison Reform

There was however a certain willingness among Scandinavian royalty to listen to the critique from the travelling philanthropists. There are even examples of specific and very sincere early interest in the issue of prison reform (Nilsson 1999; Smith 2003). Public interest in prisons was apparently also on the rise and in the early decades of the 19th century, extensive prison reform seemed to move closer in Scandinavia as was the case in several other European countries at the time. But the days of international interest in progressive Scandinavian practices were still far away and it was the Norwegians, Swedes and Danes who directed their attention outwards to other European countries for inspiration. In 1819, the Norwegian doctor Fredrik Holst visited prisons in Germany and France. He did not find the model prisons he was looking for until he came to England the year later, however (Larsen 2001; Schaanning 2007, p. 67). A few years later the momentum of prison reform had moved from England to the USA, where the Auburn and Pennsylvania prison models were created during the 1820s. These two models came to set the agenda for international prison reform to quite a remarkable degree. In 1840, the Swedish crown prince anonymously published a book on prisons, known as "the yellow book", in which he advocated for extensive prison reform based on the Pennsylvania model (Nilsson 1999). In fact the Pennsylvania model and thereby the more strict form of solitary confinement won increasing support all over Scandinavia. In 1840, a Danish prison commission was formed which sent a delegation to the USA, in the footsteps of Tocqueville and other influential thinkers and penal reformers of the time (Beaumont and Tocqueville 1979; Crawford 1834), to study the two famous American prison models. The majority of the Danish prison commission favoured the Pennsylvania model although a minority preferred the Auburn model. After the commission delivered a report in 1842 it was decided to reform the Danish prison system according to both models (Smith 2003). In Norway a prison commission was also formed during the same years and like in Denmark it approached the matter of reform as a choice between the two American models. In 1841, the Norwegian commission decided in favour of the Pennsylvania model (Schaanning 2007, p. 101). Finally, in Sweden reforms also began during the 1840s mainly along the lines of the Pennsylvania model and to some extent the Auburn model (Nilsson 1999).

From Import to Export—Modern Scandinavian Prisons in International Context

To cut a long story short, the result of the Scandinavian interest in the US models was importation especially of the Pennsylvania (or Philadelphia) and (to a lesser extent) the Auburn prison models. As a result, a system of large-scale solitary confinement was created. In fact, the entire prison systems in Scandinavian were to a greater or lesser extent reformed after the American models. Furthermore, these isolation regimes proved long lived in Scandinavia and were resilient to substantial change well into the 20th century. The single-cell system and strict solitary confinement even spilled over into remand practice in Norway, Sweden and Denmark. This meant that the vast majority of prisoners—remand and sentenced—were subjected to intense solitary confinement throughout much of the latter half of the 19th century and way into the 20th century. For sentenced prisoners a progressive system was introduced already during the 1860s which allowed prisoners who behaved well to progress through a number of stages and thereby gain privileges, which could include being allowed to read more books, write more letters and even get more out of cell time (Schaanning 2007, p. 181 ff.; Smith 2003). Nevertheless, this still amounted to very limited contact with other people, and the basic prison experience was still solitary confinement (Berggrav 1928; Smith 2003). In other words, large-scale isolation of prisoners continued often for several years in a row, and although serious health problems and cases of insanity quickly arose the systems were not abandoned as such (Nilsson 1999; Smith 2003). In all of Scandinavia sentenced prisoners were subjected to variants of Pennsylvania model solitary confinement during much of the first half of the 20th century, and while this principle was abandoned in Denmark during the 1930s, decisive change in Sweden had to wait until 1945 and legally the principle of isolation for sentenced prisoners was not abandoned in Norway until 1958 (Nilsson 1999; Smith 2003; Hjelm 2011; Horn 2015).

In all three countries large-scale solitary confinement of remand prisoners, however, continued unabated for many years. Today there are, however, large differences between the Scandinavian countries when it comes to the use of court ordered pre-trial solitary confinement. Reforms have all but ended this particular use of remand isolation in Denmark and less than one percent of all remand prisoners were placed in court-ordered solitary confinement in 2014. In Norway, similar reforms have significantly (albeit to a lesser degree than in Denmark) decreased the use of isolation. About 12.2 % of remand prisoners in Norway spent any time in solitary confinement at all in 2014. In 92 % of these cases, isolation ended within a month (Kriminalomsorgen 2015). In Sweden, however, the vast majority of remand prisoners are still kept in strict solitary confinement (Åklagarmyndigheten 2014).

The fact that serious reforms of the regimes for sentenced prisoners had to wait until the 1930s and 40s (and came decades later for remand prisoners) is a likely reason that these countries apparently did not attract much attention as places of progressive prison reform earlier in history. In any case, the international picture of Scandinavian prison practice certainly appeared to change around that time. When American criminologist Negley K. Teeters published his study on "World Penal Systems" in 1944 he claimed that in Scandinavia one found "one of the most enlightened penal philosophies in Europe" (Teeters 1944). This was in fact one year before the Swedes finally chose to abandon solitary confinement for sentenced prisoners ("Ensamhetsstraffet") although reform of the Pennsylvania system of strict isolation had been gradually introduced since 1906 (Hjelm 2011, p. 238). Teeters himself made a point of the significant changes Scandinavian penal practice had experienced since the time of John Howard and even offered an explanation for the earlier brutal and punitive behaviour:

> As we survey these countries today, noting their progressive concepts in every realm dealing with the welfare of humanity, we can scarcely understand that these same people, during the time of John Howard, were meting out the most barbaric forms of corporal and capital punishments to the wayward. True, this was prevalent all over Europe, but the Scandinavian countries were doubtless even more bloodthirsty and severe. This may be accounted for by the fact that the old Norse traditions of blood vengeance merely reflected the harsh climate they had to withstand. (Teeters 1944)

As far-fetched as that particular interpretation sounds, there is little doubt that Teeters' positive view of Scandinavian penal practice was gaining ground. Although the history of how outsiders have perceived Scandinavian prisons and justice systems has not been written, a reasonable hypothesis seems to be that important changes took place especially after the Second World War, and not least during the 1960–70s, which caught the international eye. One such thing was the opening of Ringe State prison in Denmark in 1976, apparently the first prison in Europe (and perhaps the world) where women and men were allowed to mix and serve time together and also the prison which introduced a self-cooking regime for prisoners with a prison grocery and communal kitchens placed in each wing in a college-dormitory like fashion. In 1977 a Californian newspaper reported about Ringe: "Denmark's newest prison already has a few unusual firsts: two of its inmates recently married, contraceptives are on sale at the prison supermarket, inmates must buy their own food and do their own cooking, and wardens and prisoners alike wear blue jeans and shirts" (*Lodi News Sentinel*, 17 March 1977). While the idea of mixed gender prisons never really spread to the other Scandinavian countries, Scandinavian correctional systems continued to exhibit many common elements, including a significant amount of open prison spaces and the strong focus on the principle of normalisation.

The latter, the principle of normalisation, is often highlighted as a Scandinavian ideal although it is actually a European and international principle, which to varying degrees is reflected in international and regional human rights standards. This principle is for example clearly stated in the European prison rules and hence part of the regional European human rights framework where it consists of two related key elements: (1) Prisoners retain all their rights when imprisoned except those which are taken away by necessary implication of the deprivation of liberty; and (2) conditions in prison should resemble conditions in the free community as much as possible (European Prison Rules, Basic principles 2, 3 and 5). But the principle of normalisation can also be a matter of national law, and is, for example, part of prison law and prison service rules in Norway and Denmark. There is indeed little doubt that the principle of normalisation has enjoyed a very strong standing in Scandinavian law and related policy documents. Scandinavian prisoners may, for example, vote in elections and they have the same right to secondary education as other citizens. When it comes to legal status, prisoners are in fact not in a fundamentally different situation from other people (see Engbo, this volume).

The mounting international attention towards Scandinavian prison practice was not, perhaps, just a matter of outsiders being drawn to some of these qualities and practices. Scandinavians had also started to actively market their correctional services and principles internationally. Nilsson (2012), for instance, describes how the international image of Swedish prisons and penal polices as humane and modern was at least partly the result of a successful marketing campaign. Still, Scandinavian practice in the 1960s and 70s did not impress all outsiders. We find a colorful example of a more critical stance in the writings of Roland Huntford who in 1972 described the Swedish welfare state (including its penal practices) as a real-life example of Huxley's terrifying *Brave New World*. According to Huntford, the Swedes had created a powerful omnipresent state and were "the first of the new totalitarians" (Huntford 1972, p. 11). In this welfare state Huntford found that the "Swedish totalitarians" had created a system of law and punishment where the ultimate crime was to deviate from the norm: "That norm is innocent of ethics and morality, and decided on grounds of expediency alone. The situation is already a doctrine of Swedish law. Gone is the idea of right or wrong, or the moral content of an action. Crime is now defined as social deviation" (Huntford 1972, p. 12).

Scandinavian Penal Exceptionalism?

Whether one agrees with Teeters or Huntford, there is little doubt that Scandinavian penal practice has continued to evoke widespread international interest. In recent decades the debate over Scandinavian penal practice has by no means been only a matter for media and casual observers. International criminological interest in Scandinavian punishment and prisons has been on the rise and resulted in several research projects, debates and publications. There is in particular a growing Anglo-American literature arguing that the Scandinavian countries, Denmark, Norway and Sweden, often along with the two other Nordic countries Finland and Iceland, exhibit egalitarian welfare policies, low rates of poverty, humane social and penal policies, and human rights oriented agendas. Similarly, the Nordic countries are frequently used in the field of comparative penology as an exception to the general rule. Within this tradition the Nordic countries are described as exhibiting a specifically Nordic penal culture, resulting in what has sometimes been termed a Scandinavian or Nordic penal exceptionalism (Pratt 2008a, b; Pratt and Eriksson 2012b). Especially, two factors have been central in these discussions: the low rate of imprisonment in the Scandinavian and Nordic countries and the allegedly humane prison conditions—but other factors such as, for example, trust in the police and the criminal justice system have also been highlighted and analysed (Lappi-Seppälä 2007, 2012; Pratt 2008a, b; Pratt and Eriksson 2012b; Cavadino and Dignan

2006). For some, Nordic prisons have been seen as beacons of humanity in a time of increasing penal populism and hence as an example the rest of world should follow (Pratt and Eriksson 2012a, p. 256).

Members of the Nordic societies have to some extent grown accustomed to this type of story. When documentary filmmaker Michael Moore decided to "invade" Norway in his most recent film *Where to invade next* (2016), it was because of his deep admiration for the Norwegian prison system. The Star-Spangled Banner was raised as he sailed the Oslo fjord, his eyes firmly set on the small island of Bastøy, ready to take over what has in recent years arguably become the world's most famous open prison. Scandinavian prison systems have in recent years on several occasions experienced this kind of more or less uncritical praise from international visitors in international media. Also in the human rights field, the three Scandinavian states in particular have been highlighted repeatedly as leading international examples by international commentators. On the one hand, Scandinavian stakeholders have taken up this cue and have to some extent turned human rights into export goods for an advanced Scandinavian "Human Rights industry." On the other hand, human rights principles and human rights-based critique have historically been applied to domestic policies and practices much less frequently (Christoffersen and Madsen 2011).

The notion of penal exceptionalism seems to fit well with Scandinavian self-perceptions in general. Representatives of the Scandinavian ministries of justice and prison systems have certainly applauded this concept. In 2012 the then Norwegian Minister of Justice, Grete Faremo, simply concluded, "We are administrating the world's best prison service (. . .) We have good reason to be proud."[5] A former Danish Minister of Justice, Lene Espersen, made a similar, although slightly more modest, claim in 2007 when she stated that the Danish prison service was "one of the best in the world."[6] Along the same

---

[5] The Norwegian Minister of Justice, Grete Faremo, in *Aktuelt for kriminalomsorgen*, no. 1, 2012, p. 14.

[6] Lene Espersen quoted in "Referat fra Dansk Fængselsforbunds 3. Ordinære kongres 23.-25. Maj 2007 på Hotel Nyborg Strand."

lines the former Director of the Danish Prison service explained to his employees that "the Danish prison service is considered to be among the best in the world."[7] When it comes to Sweden there is little doubt that, as already mentioned, a positive self-image and self-understanding has played a role in marketing Swedish penal practice internationally (Nilsson 2012).

While Scandinavian penal practices are clearly interesting in a number of ways and while it is safe to say that these societies sometimes exhibit exceptional (and perhaps peculiar) tendencies and practices, Nordic prison researchers have nevertheless been more reluctant to agree entirely with the exceptionalism thesis (Smith 2012; Barker 2012; This volume). Several Nordic prison practices and penal policies have been seen to challenge such an understanding, and researchers have pointed at a number of theoretical challenges with regard to the comparative approach and the very concept of Nordic exceptionalism (Mathiesen 2012; Smith 2012; Barker 2012). A more nuanced image of the very centralistic and strong Nordic states has similarly been put forward within other fields of research. One influential analysis argues that the powerful Swedish state has created free and individualistically minded citizens partly through limiting the rights of the individual (Berggren and Trägårdh 2013). This theory seems to fit well with the strong tradition for granting extensive powers to, as well placing a great deal of trust in, the police and other agents of state power in Scandinavian societies, as well as the well-known Scandinavian history of forceful state interventions in the private sphere of their citizens. Aspects of any state structure which would normally awaken scepticism and a critical approach from criminologists and those interested in the sociology of law. Indeed, David Garland showed us three decades ago how a "penal welfare strategy" involves an "extended apparatus of control" which does not necessarily reform offenders but manage and administer criminality "in an efficient and extensive manner, while

---

[7] William Rentzmann quoted in "Godt arbejde hos os. Medarbejdere af rette støbning," Kriminalforsorgen (without year), p. 11.

portraying that process in terms which make it acceptable to the public and penal agents alike" (Garland 1985, p. 260).

Another current development which clearly seems to challenge the whole idea of Scandinavia being especially humane and egalitarian is the recent political response to immigration in especially Denmark and Norway. Recently, for example, a new Danish bill requiring the police to confiscate jewellery and valuables from newly arrived refugees, so they could pay for their own humanitarian stay in Denmark, went around the world press and prompted reactions of disbelief and outrage. In the British newspaper *The Guardian* the Danish Prime Minister was portrayed as a Nazi leader, and US media also made parallels to Nazi policies. Similarly, the Norwegian response has been, quite explicitly, to try to make Norwegian asylum regulations the strictest in Europe (e.g. making family reunification much more difficult). While the Swedish response to the refugee crisis was very different (at least initially) these events clearly tell us that the values normally associated with the Scandinavian welfare states—solidarity, inclusiveness and egalitarian policies—are not necessarily so "universalist" in nature as some would like to think.

Regardless, there is little doubt that while sometimes lacking in nuance and empirical depth, international research focusing on Scandinavian penal practice has inspired a very interesting comparative debate and also pointed to a thought-provoking possible relationship between welfare state values and penal practices and principles.

Scandinavian Exceptionalism and Scandinavian Prisons—What We Need to Know

Criminologists have for some time looked towards the Scandinavian social democratic welfare state, and the values traditionally associated with this welfare model, in an attempt to explain the low rates of imprisonment and prison practices that they claim to have found in these countries. There are good reasons for looking in that direction but it is still open for debate whether or not an actual causal relationship between these different entities has actually been found.

As already touched upon, positive values often associated with Scandinavian and Nordic welfare state regimes include their universalist and egalitarian policies along with the aim to create solidarity and being inclusive (Esping-Andersen 1995; Hilson 2013; Lappi-Seppälä 2007). If Scandinavian prison practice truly is more humane, then it would make sense to look for such values in an attempt to find an explanation. But a number of important questions remain. For example, to what degree is there still a specific Nordic or Scandinavian welfare state model? There is little doubt that the Scandinavian social democratic welfare state model with a high level of decommodification (Esping-Andersen 1995) has been challenged severely during recent decades and has changed in a more neoliberal direction. Furthermore, even if such a welfare model state still exists to what degree and in what way is there a causal relationship between its underlying culture on the one hand and penal policy and prison conditions on the other hand? What are, in other words, the essential elements of the Scandinavian welfare state and how and to what degree can we find these reflected in Scandinavian prison policy and practice (Smith 2012)?

In addition, it would be fair to say that a truly comparative study of Scandinavian prison practice has never been made. This certainly goes for prison practices and prison culture, but also when it comes to the general conditions found in these prisons. In fact, even the numerous comparisons of prison population rates, where the Nordic countries always score low, lack nuance in the sense that they always compare stock and not flow numbers (i.e. the number of people imprisoned at any one time, not the number of people being sent to prison over the course of a year, for instance). While it is certainly true and clearly important that "stock" prison population rates are always low in Scandinavia and the Nordic countries, in general this does not mean that few people are sent to prison in these countries. Flow statistics tell a different story. Such statistics are much more difficult to obtain but are available for 2011 from he European Institute for Crime Prevention and Control (HEUNI). In that year, based on data from 46 European jurisdictions, Sweden, Norway and Denmark all had "stock" prison population rates below 80 per 100,000 inhabitants, with Sweden having the fourth lowest prison rate (72 per 100,000), Norway claiming sixth place (76 per 100,000) and Denmark sharing the seventh place with Switzerland (77 per 100,000) (Aebi et al. 2014). Such comparative "stock" statistics and the continuing low Scandinavian scores are well known from many other reports. But the European Institute data include "flow" statistics which show that among the 46 European jurisdictions surveyed Estonia was the country where most people—measured per citizen—went through the national prison system in 2011 (991 per 100,000). However, on that list Sweden was no. 5 in Europe (414 per 100,000), Denmark no. 13 (290 per 100,000) and Norway no. 15 (221 per 100,000). At the opposite end of the scale were Romania (no. 45 with 76 per 100,000) and Portugal (46 with 59 per 100,000) (European Sourcebook of Crime and Criminal Justice statistics 2014).

This fact—a result of the large number of short sentences being meted out by Scandinavian courts—adds an important dimension to the story about the allegedly modest use of imprisonment in these countries. In fact, Sweden, Denmark, and Norway all use imprisonment and deprivation of liberty in a quite liberal and relatively extensive manner—although frequently only for very short periods of time. Under all circumstances this means that we are dealing with states that are quite willing to imprison the people who fall under their jurisdiction—not something typically associated with penal welfare aims (Garland 2001, p. 35).

Furthermore, it can certainly be discussed theoretically and methodologically how such a comparative study should be done. Instead of simply comparing selected practices more or less irrespective of their different local contexts (which seems to have been the preferred method so far), should one not also compare the quality of prison conditions with the national quality of life and economic standard and thereby seek to know what you lose by being imprisoned in a given country? Would this not make for a much more meaningful basis for international comparison of penal practices and penal values?

To sum up, the question still remains whether or not (a) Scandinavian prisons in general are more humane or in some other sense "better" than similar institutions in other countries, (b) if they are, in what ways exactly this is the case, and how can we explain those differences and (c) what role, if any, do Scandinavian welfare state values and models play in that equation? Trying to answer these questions could help us identify in a more refined and useful manner exactly where, how and to what degree Scandinavian penal practice might serve as an example to other countries, prison practitioners and policy makers, and it could also potentially tell us something about where the Scandinavians states can learn from international policies and practice. In any case, we believe that we need to get empirically close to Nordic prison practice and recent prison history to understand and discuss these issues further. Accordingly it seems to us that it is now time to attempt a more thorough empirically based analysis and discussion of Scandinavian penal practice and to make the results of such an undertaking available for an international readership. This book therefore aims to discuss different aspects of the Scandinavian prison systems in great detail and in that process examine in what way these systems might relate to the Scandinavian welfare state models and their associated values.

With thorough historical and cross-disciplinary studies we hope to achieve a more nuanced picture of Scandinavian penal practices, their causes and the surrounding culture. We will look at prisons' historical conditions in the Scandinavian countries, its relationship with the Scandinavian welfare state and the trajectory that Scandinavian penal policy and prison practice has taken during the last two centuries in general and during the last two decades in particular. This involves looking not only at the positive and empowering qualities of these societies but also demands an analysis of the darker, coercive and more intrusive aspects of welfare policies, ideologies and social control in strong centralistic states. In what ways are the prisons and their associated values and practices the results of the Scandinavian welfare state model and its underlying culture and ideologies of equality, universality and homogeneity? Under what conditions can the values of these welfare states exist in harmony, and when will the logics of welfare and punishment clash and create conflicts, or will they in fact sometimes strengthen and support each other? Finally, do the strong and powerful Nordic states always give sufficient priority to protecting their most marginalized citizens in order to keep their penal powers in check? In other words, is it always liberating and constructive to be "embraced" by a powerful welfare state with an altruistic self-image? Is the "Big Mother" state—the welfare oriented sister of the notorious Big Brother society—empowering or controlling its citizens?

The Structure, Scope and Content of the Book

Scandinavia is a geographical area consisting of Denmark, Norway and Sweden. These countries have a common cultural heritage and can understand each other's languages reasonably well. The Nordic countries on the other hand also include Iceland and Finland. Although part of the same linguistic family, most Scandinavians cannot understand Icelandic. And Finnish, being part of a totally separate family of languages is, as the proverb goes, like Greek to Scandinavians, although Greek is actually a closer linguistic relative. In common English usage, however, the difference between Scandinavia and the Nordic countries is often blurred. In this book we limit ourselves to studying the three Scandinavian countries and thereby not all the Nordic countries. This is not because we find these countries irrelevant in this context—on the contrary both the Icelandic and perhaps especially the Finnish case is clearly relevant in a discussion of the existence of a possible Nordic penal exceptionalism.[8] But all projects have their limitations and this particular one is born out of the Scandinavian Studies of Confinement network where scholars from Norway, Sweden and Denmark have cooperated and exchanged ideas, knowledge and research on Scandinavian prison practices for more than a decade. Although we cannot claim to cover all the Nordic experiences we, depart from a unique position as members of a network which for many years has focused not broadly on criminology, punishment or sociology of law but exclusively on Scandinavian institutions of confinement and especially prisons. Through numerous workshops and conferences we have evolved discussions and research on these institutions, and this book is the latest result of these efforts. It is also the only recent publication focusing in

---

[8] See, for example, the extensive research done by Tapio Lappi-Seppälä (2007, 2012).

depth on prison conditions, cultures and practices in Norway, Sweden and Denmark. Furthermore, all contributions are based on new or recent empirical studies. In addition, this is the first volume to combine thorough empirical research in all these three countries with a discussion of prison practice, culture and Scandinavian welfare state values.

Following this introductory chapter (Part I), the remainder of the book is structured into four substantive parts (Parts II–V) focusing on different aspects of the question welfare and punishment in the Scandinavian countries, as well as a short concluding part (VI) in which it is attempted to pull together some of the lessons learned throughout all the previous chapters.

Part II consists of four chapters all of which adopt a historical perspective. Nilsson ("First we build the factory, then we add the institution': Prison, Work and Welfare State in Sweden c. 1930–1970") studies the moral and practical role of work and vocational training in the Swedish prison system in the context of industrialization. Shammas ("Prisons of Labor: Social Democracy and the Triple Transformation of the Politics of Punishment in Norway") describes the historical development of the current correctional philosophy in Norway in three distinct stages. Fransen ("The rise of the open prisons and the breakthrough of the principle of normalization in Denmark from the 1930s until today") provides a rare insight into the development of the open Danish prison model. Andersson ("A Culture of Intervention – Vagrancy and Drug Treatment in Sweden from the late 19th century until today") studies what he calls a correctional "culture of intervention" through the lens of vagrancy and drug treatment in Sweden.

Part III collects eight chapters that discuss different links and contrasts between welfare and punishment-oriented practices and policies in the Scandinavian countries today. Smith's analysis of Scandinavian remand imprisonment ("Punishment Without Conviction? Scandinavian Pre-trial Practices and the Power of the 'Benevolent' State") looks at perhaps the least "exceptionalist" of all Scandinavian prison policies. Fredwall ("Guarding, Guiding, Gate Opening. Prison Officer Work in a Norwegian Welfare Context") analyses different prison officer ideals in Norway and shows how punishment and welfare can be mixed in quite different ways in the self-image of prison officers. Bruhn, Lindberg and Nylander ("Treating

Drug Abusers in Prison: Competing Paradigms Anchored in Different Welfare Ideologies. The case of Sweden") and Kolind ("Prison-drug Treatment as Welfare Service?") discuss the tension between punishment and care in drug treatment schemes in correctional settings in Sweden and Denmark, respectively. Langelid ("The Development of Education in Norwegian Prisons") describes the development and current role of prison education, while Lundeberg ("Exceptional Procedures? Offenders' Experiences of Procedural Justice in Re-entry Work") examines prisoners' experience of procedural justice in the context of re-entry work, both of them in Norway. Olesen's chapter ("Exceptional Procedures? Offenders' Experiences of Procedural Justice in Re-entry Work") targets the Danish release process and asks whether the welfare state is good enough at reintegrating and including newly released prisoners. Finally, Ploeg ("Scandinavian Acceptionalism? Community Sanctions in Norway") examines Norwegian non-custodial penal sanctions and asks where the strong acceptance these alternatives enjoy in the Norwegian public come from.

Part IV consists of four chapters that focus in particular on the principle of normalization, a core principle in all three Scandinavian correctional systems. All four chapters explore the limits of normalization in different ways. Engbo ("Normalisation in Nordic Prisons: from a Prison Governor's Perspective") discusses the very principle itself and looks at how it has been conceptualized slightly differently in the three Scandinavian countries. Minke and Smoyer ("Prison Food in Denmark: Normal Responsibility or Ethnocentric Imaginations?") asks whether the different food regimes in Danish prisons really result in food and meal situations that are "normal" in the eyes of prisoners. Mathiassen ("Being a Woman in Mixed Gender Prisons") describes the practice of gender-mixed prisons in Denmark, while Ugelvik ("The Limits of the Welfare state? Foreign National Prisoners in the Norwegian Crimmigration Prison") looks at normalization and welfare-oriented policies in Kongsvinger prison, Norway's only prison designed to hold foreign national prisoners only.

Several scholars (Dullum and Ugelvik 2012; Mathiesen 2012) have observed the difference between internal analyses of Scandinavian prison policies and practices conducted by Scandinavian prison researchers, and the external analyses of prison scholars from other parts of the world writing about Scandinavia from a comparative perspective. Part V of the book collects three chapters that all in different ways add an external perspective to the discussion. Vander Beken ("In Search of Norwegian Penal Exceptionalism. A Prison Tourist's Perspective") describes his impressions of Norwegian prisons following a comparative project where he has travelled to several countries from all over Europe and beyond in the footsteps of 18th-century prison reformer John Howard. Langford, Schaffer and Fisher ("The View from Elsewhere: Scandinavian Penal Practices and International Critique") look at the external human rights-based criticism directed at the three Scandinavian prison systems by international monitoring agencies, while Reiter, Sexton and Sumner ("Negotiating Imperfect Humanity in the Danish Penal System") discuss their impressions after a thorough empirical exploration of life in Danish prisons.

Finally, in the concluding chapter (Part VI, "Punishment and Welfare in Scandinavia"), we revisit the previous chapters and put them in dialogue with each other. The aim is to condense important insights from each chapter and connect the dots between them in order to try to answer perhaps the most fundamental questions raised in this book: Is there a specifically Scandinavian way of doing state punishment? Are Scandinavian prisons welfare oriented, and if they are, in what ways, and with what limitations?

References

Aebi, M. F., Akdeniz, G., Barclay, G., Campistol, C., Caneppele, S., Gruszczyńska, B., Harrendorf, S., Heiskanen, M., Hysi, V., Jehle, J.-M., Jokinen, A., Kensey, A., Killias, M., Lewis, C. G., Savona, E., Smit, P., Þórisdóttir, R. (2014). *European sourcebook of crime and criminal justice statistics*. Helsinki: HEUNI.

Åklagarmyndigheten. (2014, January). *Häktningstider och restriktioner*. Stockholm: Åklagarmyndigheten.

Barker, V. (2012). Nordic Exceptionalism Revisited: Explaining the Paradox of a Janus-Faced Penal Regime. *Theoretical Criminology* 17 (1), 5–25.

Beaumont, Gd., & Tocqueville, Ad. (1979/1833). *On the penitentiary system in the United States and its application in France*. Illinois: Southern Illinois University Press.

Benko, J. (2015, march 26). The Radical Humaneness of Norway's Halden Prison. *New York Times.* http://www.nytimes.com/2015/03/29/magazine/theradical-humaneness-of-norways-halden-prison.html?_r=0.

Berggren, H., & Trägårdh, L. (2013). *Är svensken människa? Gemenskap och oberoende i det moderna Sverige.* Stockholm: Norstedts.

Berggrav, E. (1928). *Fangens sjel—og vår egen. Erfaringer og iakttagelser fra Botsfengslet i Oslo.* Oslo: Forlaget Land og Kirke.

Bourdieu, P (1998). *Acts of resistance: against the new myths of our time.* Cambridge: Polity.

Brochman, G., & Hagelund, A. (2010). *Velferdens grenser: Innvandringspolitikk og velferdsstat i Skandinavia 1945–2010.* Oslo: Universitetsforlaget.

Cavadino, M., & Dignan, J. (2006). *Penal systems. A comparative approach.* London: Sage.

Christoffersen, J., & Madsen, M. R. (2011). The end of virtue? Denmark and the internationalisation of human rights. *Nordic Journal of International Law, 80*(3), 257–277.

Coyle, A. (2005). *Understanding prisons: key issues in policy and practice.* Glasgow: Open University Press.

Crawford, W. (1834). *Report of William Crawford, Esq. On the Penitentiaries of the United States Adressed to his Majesty's Principal Secretary of State for the Home Department,* British Parliamentary Papers. Crime and Punishment—PRISONS. No. 2, Session 1834.

Danish prison life just like being home. (1977). *Lodi News Sentinel.* March 17.

Dullum, J., & Ugelvik, T. (2012). Introduction: exceptional prisons, exceptional societies? In T. Ugelvik and J. Dullum (Eds.), *Prison exceptionalism? Nordic prison policy and practice.* Abingdon: Routledge.

Esping-Andersen, G. (1995). *The three worlds of welfare capitalism.* Cambridge: Polity.

Esping-Andersen, G., & Korpi, W. (1987). From poor relief to institutional welfare states: the development of Scandinavian social policy. In R. Erikson (Ed.), *The Scandinavian model: welfare states and welfare research.* Armonk: Sharpe.

Garland, D. (1985). *Punishment and welfare. A history of penal strategies.* Aldershot: Ashgate.

Garland, D. (2001). *The culture of control. Crime and social order in contemporary society.* Oxford: Oxford University Press.

Hilson, M. (2013). *The Nordic model: Scandinavia since 1945.* London: Reaktion Books.

Hjelm, A.-C.P. (2011). *Fängelset som välfärdsbygge.* Stockholm: Institutet för rättshistorisk forskning.

Horn, T. (2015). *Fullstendig isolasjon ved risiko for bevisforspillelse.* Oslo: Det juridiske fakultet, Universitetet i Oslo.

Howard, J. (1929). *The state of prisons.* London: Everymans Library.

Huntford, R. (1972). *The new totalitarians.* New York: Stein and Day.

Kautto, M., Heikkilä, M., Hvinden, B., Marklund, S., & Ploug, N. (Eds.) (1999). Introduction: The Nordic welfare states in the 1990s. In *Nordic social policy. Changing welfare states.* Abingdon: Routledge.

Kriminalomsorgen. (2015). *Kriminalomsorgens årsstatistikk 2014.* Oslo: Kriminalomsorgens sentrale forvaltning. http://www.kriminalomsorgen.no/statistikk-og-noekkeltall.237902.no.html. Accessed 5 September 2016.

Lacey, N. (2008). *The prisoners' dilemma: political economy and punishment in contemporary democracies.* Cambridge: Cambridge University Press.

Lappi-Seppälä, T. (2007). Penal policy in Scandinavia. *Crime and Justice, 36,* 217–295.

Lappi-Seppälä, T. (2012). Penal policies in the Nordic Countries 1960–2010. *Journal of Scandinavian Studies in Criminology and Crime Prevention, 13,* 85–111.

Larsen, Ø. (2001). Fredrik Holst og Fengslene. *Tidsskrift for den norske legeforening, 121,* 3556–3560.

Larson, D. (2013). Why Scandinavian prisons are superior. In *The Atlantic,* September 24, 2013. http://www.theatlantic.com/international/archive/2013/09/why-scandinavian-prisons-are-superior/279949/. Accessed 5 September 2016.

Mathiesen, T. (2012). Scandinavian exceptionalism in penal matters: reality or wishful thinking? In T. Ugelvik and J. Dullum (Eds.), *Penal exceptionalism? Nordic prison policy and practice.* London: Routledge.

Mikko, K., Heikkilä, M., Hvinden, B., Marklund, S., Ploug, N. (Eds.) (1999). Introduction: the Nordic welfare states in the 1990s. In *Nordic social policy. Changing welfare states.* Abingdon: Routledge.

Mauss, M. (1954). *The gift: forms and functions of exchange in archaic societies.* London: Cohen & West.

Moene, K., & Barth, E. (2004). Den skandinaviske likhetsmodellen. *Plan* [Volume not specified] (3), 30–35.

Nilsson, R. (1999). *En välbyggd maskin, en mardröm för själen. Det svenska fängelsesystemet under 1800-talet.* Lund Lund University Press.

Nilsson, R. (2012). The most progressive, effective prison system in the world. The Swedish Prison System in the 1960s and 1970s. In T. Ugelvik and J. Dullum (Eds.), *Penal exceptionalism? Nordic prison policy and practice*. Abingdon: Routledge.

Pratt, J. (2008a). Scandinavian exceptionalism in an era of penal excess: part I: the nature and roots of Scandinavian esceptionalism. *British Journal of Criminology, 48*(2), 119–137.

Pratt, J. (2008b). Scandinavian exceptionalism in an era of penal excess: part II: does Scandinavian exceptionalism have a future? *British Journal of Criminology, 48*(3), 275–292.

Pratt, J., & Eriksson, A. (2011). "Mr. Larsson is walking out again": the origins and development of Scandinavian prison systems. *Australian and New Zealand Journal of Criminology, 44*(1), 7–23.

Pratt, J., & Eriksson, A. (2012a). In defence of Scandinavian exceptionalism. In T. Ugelvik and J. Dullum (Eds.), *Penal exceptionalism? Nordic prison policy and practice*. Abingdon: Routledge.

Pratt, J., & Eriksson, A. (2012b). *Contrasts in punishment: an explanation of anglophone excess and Nordic exceptionalism*. London: Routledge.

Reiter, K., Sexton, L., Sumner, J. (2016, February 2). Denmark doesn't treat its prisoners like prisoners — and it's good for everyone. *Washington Post*. https://www.washingtonpost.com/posteverything/wp/2016/02/02/denmark-doesnt-treat-its-prisoners-like-prisoners-and-its-good-for-everyone/.

Rugkåsa, M. (2011). Velferdsambisiøsitet, sivilisering og normalisering: Statlig velferdspolitikks betydning for forming av borgeres subjektivitet. *Norsk antropologisk tidsskrift, 22*(3–4), 245–255.

Schaanning, E. (2007). *Menneskelaboratorier: Botsfengslets historie*. Oslo: Spartacus.

Smith, P. S. (2003). *Moralske hospitaler. Det modern fængselsvæsens gennembrud 1770–1870*. København: Forum.

Smith, P. S. (2012). A critical look at Scandinavian exceptionalism: welfare state theories, penal populism, and prison conditions in Denmark and Scandinavia. In T. Ugelvik and J. Dullum (Eds.), Penal exceptionalism? Nordic prison policy and practice. Abingdon: Routledge.

Smith, P. S. (2014). *When the innocent are punished. The children of imprisoned parents*. Basingstoke: Palgrave.

Teeters, N. K. (1944). *World penal systems. A survey*. Pennsylvania: Pennsylvania Prison Society.

Ugelvik, T. (2015). Prisons as welfare institutions? Punishment and the nordic model. In Y. Jewkes, B. Crewe, J. Bennett (Eds.), *Handbook on prisons*. Abingdon: Routledge.

Wacquant, L. J. D. (2008). *Urban outcasts: a comparative sociology of advanced marginality.* Cambridge: Polity.

Wacquant, L. J. D. (2009). *Punishing the poor: the neoliberal government of social insecurity.* Durham, NC. Duke University Press.

Wahl, A. (2011). *The rise and fall of the welfare state.* London: Pluto.

Walmsley, R. (2016). *World prison population list* (11th edn). ICPS. http:// www.prisonstudies.org/sites/default/files/resources/downloads/world_ prison_population_list_11th_edition.pdf. Accessed 30 May 2016.

Witoszek, N. (2011). *The origins of the "regime of goodness": remapping the cultural history of Norway.* Oslo: Universitetsforlaget.

Part II

The Development
of Scandinavian Prison Practice

"First We Build the Factory, Then We Add the Institution": Prison, Work and Welfare State in Sweden c.1930–1970

Roddy Nilsson

Labour and the Swedish Welfare State

Labour in different forms has been a central tenet in most carceral systems from the early modern houses of correction and up until today.[1] At the same time, the central feature of the welfare state that developed during the post-Second World War decades was labour or, to quote one of Sweden's most well-known political economists, "work has been the cement of the

---

[1] The most important historical exception to this rule is the late 18th and 19th century penitentiaries in the United States and some European countries where, instead, the organization and architecture were modelled with the goal of the inmate's inner transformation in solitary confinement. The type of labour carried out in these institutions were mostly of a pre-modern handicraft character. For a discussion of Scandinavian 19th century penitentiaries (see Nilsson 1999; Scharff Smith 2003).

R. Nilsson (✉)
The Department of Historical Studies, Gothenburg University,
Gothenburg, Sweden
e-mail: roddy.nilsson@gu.se

© The Author(s) 2017
P. Scharff Smith, T. Ugelvik (eds.), *Scandinavian Penal History,
Culture and Prison Practice,* Palgrave Studies in Prisons and
Penology, DOI 10.1057/978-1-137-58529-5_2

Swedish welfare state."[2] In the following I will discuss the connection between labour and the Swedish prisons in the post-Second World War decades. More precisely, I will argue that the real character of the much-talked-about Swedish prison reforms in this period cannot be understood unless one takes into account the central role given to labour. Furthermore, a closer look at the role given to labour will also contribute to a more general discussion about whether we can talk about a special Swedish (or Scandinavian) model for penal reform.

In the political discourse, Sweden, sometimes together with the other Scandinavian countries, has been seen as the archetypical welfare state (Esping Andersen 1990; Baldwin 1990; Wilensky 2002; Christiansen et al. 2006; Hilson 2008). Although the empirical descriptions as well as the theoretical understandings of this concept have varied considerably, there is relative unanimity regarding its distinctive features: a large public sector, a strong and well-organized labour movement, strong and centralized labour and employers' federations on the labour market aiming at resolving conflicts through collective bargaining, far-going insurance schemes and/or welfare benefits financed primarily by taxes and built on the principle of universalism and a general striving to promote high levels of social equality (Christiansen and Markula 2006, pp. 11–29; Hort 2014, p. 111).[3] It could be argued that the central feature of the welfare state is labour—most evidently manifested in the emphasis put on productive labour and the full employment strategy (Schön 2010). Work, i.e. rationally organized work, could be seen as the main vehicle for the delivery of social security, if not for all, at least for the many. This means that work has an economic, social and moral value. Yet another central feature associated with the welfare state is its programmatic social reformism, primarily associated with the

---

[2] www.government.se/articles/2015/05/work-is-the-cement-of-the-swedish-welfare-state.

[3] However, it must be underlined that the Swedish welfare state was not something that came out of a grand design or some master plan. It was rather the result of several determining factors: a special balance of power between the social classes, a favourable economic situation, parliamentary compromises, a step-by-step reformism as well as close political, economic and administrative cooperation with the labour movements in the other Nordic countries. See, e.g. Christiansen and Markula (2006).

Social Democrats but in some cases also with other parties. Soon after coming into power in 1932, and especially after an agreement was made with the Agrarian party the following year, the Swedish Social Democrats began to launch an ambitious reform policy.

When it comes to penal reform the development in Sweden from the 1930s to the 1970s, as in some other countries, could be described as a period of transformation from a punishment-centred penal system to a treatment-oriented one.[4] However, this general characterization contains a wide array of ideological shifts, legal discussions and measures as well as changes in penal practices and governmental techniques. Thus it is reasonable to talk of a general prison reform movement sweeping across most of the countries in Western Europe as well as parts of the United States during this period (see for example Franke 1995; Hammerlin 2006; Blomberg and Lucken 2008).[5] However, in the 1960s Sweden had acquired the reputation of being the country where prison reform perhaps had gone further than anywhere else in the world (Nilsson 2011).

Prison Work

Thomas Mathiesen discusses prison work—together with schooling, discipline and moral influence—as one of four key elements in a rehabilitative ideology that goes back at least to the *tuchthuisen* and bridewells of the 17th century. Mathiesen argues that this ideology—which he sees as a version of Max Weber's famous Protestant ethic—has been remarkably constant through the centuries (Mathiesen 2000, pp. 31–42). This may very well be so but more interesting is how these different elements have been transformed as well as the relative weight that has been ascribed to each of them during different periods and in different prison systems.

---

[4] It is, however, important to note that the same characteristic can be given to the period when the above-mentioned penitentiaries were established. See, for example Nilsson (1999) and Scharff Smith (2003).

[5] There is a considerable amount of literature dedicated to what can be loosely described as "prison reform". However, prison reform is a problematic concept given its positive connotations among politicians and prison administrators as well as among great many scholars. See Murton (1976) and Rotman (1990).

The strongest link between work and punishment in general and prison in particular is to be found in the Marxist and neo-Marxist hypothesis that penal practices are connected to the dominant relations of production in any given society, succinctly expressed in Max Horkheimers and Theodor Adornos *The Dialectic of Enlightenment* where they state, "the prison is the image of the bourgeois world of labour taken to its logical conclusion" (Horkheimer and Adorno 1972, p. 227). However, the most famous elaboration of this hypothesis is found in *Punishment and Social Structure* by two other German scholars, Georg Rusche and Otto Kirchheimer, first published in 1939. In this seminal work they developed a history of Western penal systems on materialistic grounds where the key variable that determined the character of punishments was the supply of labour. According to Rusche and Kirchheimer every system of production "discovers" punishments that correspond to its productive relationship so that punishments tend to become harsher, i.e. longer and more exploitative, when there is a surplus of labour and milder, i.e. shorter and less exploitative, when the situation is the reverse (Rusche and Kirchheimer 2003, p. 5; cf. De Georgi 2006). This also means that the system of punishment plays a role as a regulator when it comes to the supply of labour.

It is not my intention to put up this hypothesis to some empirical test against the Swedish case.[6] Rather, by placing prison work in the context of the welfare state I will argue that work was given a central but partly different meaning in the new institutional setting characterizing the emerging welfare state. Most importantly, prison work was included in the labour policy of the welfare state, a policy characterized by strivings to create large production units organized in a "modern," efficient, rational and highly mechanized way at the same time as it was associated with a strong work ethic. Thus work should discipline the untrained and recalcitrant inmates but also—and this is one of its new elements—create responsible, loyal and active welfare state

---

[6] However, in a review of research following the Rusche-Kirchheimer thesis, Alessandro De Giorgi concludes that there are some positive correlations from different national contexts, at the same time as he underlines the need for a more complex model that opens up for including political, sociological and ideological factors. See De Georgi (2006, pp. 19–33).

citizens. Furthermore, the pivotal role given to productive work in the prisons must be seen in relation to the relative failure to develop a system built on individual treatment (Petersson Hjelm 2002; Nilsson 2013).

The Beginning of a New Penal Policy in Sweden

The Social Democratic government that came into power in 1932 initially concentrated most of its energy on solving the unemployment crisis but subsequently began to prepare for a comprehensive penal reform (Nilsson 2013). The post as Minister of Justice went to Karl Schlyter, a senior judge from one of Sweden's courts of appeal, who almost immediately began to draw up proposals for a grand penal law reform as well as for a transformation of the prison system. In several ways Schlyter was the catalyst of the reform movement. But it must be kept in mind that the offensive launched by Schlyter and his collaborators in the penal area was only a small and quite subordinate part of the Social Democrats' much more extensive reform programme, which aimed at developing what has become labelled "a people's home" and later on the welfare state (Björk 2008). Thus, it is important to have in mind that penal reform became a less prioritized area in the Social Democrats' general policy (Eriksson 1977, p. 42; Sundell 1998, p. 72). However—perhaps somewhat paradoxically—the relative lack of interest in penal questions seems, at least in the initial phase, to have opened up some space for Schlyter and the group of reformers he gathered around him.

After a period of preparation inside the Department of Justice and the Prison Administration, Schlyter in 1934 presented his plan for a new penal code as well as for considerable changes in the prison system. Later the same year he gave a famous public speech in front of a big labour movement audience with the provocative title "Depopulate the Prisons" (Schlyter 1935). The title of the speech alluded to the on-going debate over the population question in Sweden, where there was talk about a "depopulation" of the nation (Myrdal and Myrdal 1934). In his speech Schlyter put forward a programme that rejected retaliatory punishments as well as large-scale use of imprisonment. Instead, the general aim of punishment should be to protect society, something that was most effectively done through individual preventive measures and social prophylaxis. Penal policy could not, as in the past, be left to the juridical professions and courts alone. Also other experts and professionals as psychiatrists, psychologists, pedagogues and sociologists must be involved. Schlyter's speech was a skilled tactical move. By turning to the public in this way Schlyter and his associates drew attention to penal questions and signalled that the time was ripe for a new policy in this area. From now on penal policy should be an important part of the new welfare-oriented policy in the interest of the people. Schlyter's speech soon became integrated into the narrative of penal reform that developed during the following decades and since came to function as a major source of inspiration for the following generation of penal reformers (Eriksson 1967, 1976, 1977; Rudstedt 1993).

The centre for the reform work became The Penal Law Committee, a governmental select committee led by Schlyter which included a long line of reform-minded experts, jurists and parliamentarians. From the start in 1938 to 1956, when the final proposal for a new penal code was presented, The Penal Law Committee produced a large number of reports and public investigations that laid the ground for the on-going reforms. Another important channel for penal and prison reform was the close cooperation maintained with other Nordic jurists and prisons administrators both through formal meetings under the auspices of the Nordic Criminalist Association and through more informal contacts (Sundell 1998).[7] These kinds of inter-Nordic contacts in different policy areas were a central feature of the policy formation in the Nordic welfare states (Christiansen et al. 2006). Nevertheless, as a result of a government re-construction in 1936 Schlyter had to step down from the post of Minister of Justice, the rumour being that the more down-to-earth Prime Minister Per Albin

---

[7] But another more informal association perhaps better describes the character of the penal reform work. This was the *Criminal Policy Society* founded by Schlyter in 1945 as an informal meeting place for a wide array of penal reformers, jurists, psychiatrists, physicians, social workers, prison bureaucrats as well as politicians and other laymen in the penal arena. The existence of this association mirrors the widening of the penal reform field to include a broader group of professionals that was characteristic of the emerging welfare state. See Sundell (1998).

Hansson saw Schlyter as *too* reform minded and impulsive (Eriksson 1977, pp. 84–85; Sundell 1998, pp. 84–88).[8]

Although the explicit task of the Penal Law Committee was to present a proposal for a new Penal Law, a considerable amount of time and energy was dedicated to prison reform. One of the first results of the reform process was the development of a new Implementation of Sentence Act of 1945. The new law stressed the prisons' character of treatment facilities on individual preventive basis at the same time as it abolished the practice of solitary confinement that had been the backbone of the Swedish prison system since the second half of the 19th century (Nilsson 2003). Of more interest here is the central role the law dedicated to productive work. Although the new Implementation of Sentence Act did not come into force until 1945, the preparation had started immediately after the Social Democratic government took office in 1932, and the first sketch to new prison rules had been produced already the following year. Here it was stated, "it was the task of the Prison Administration to accustom the prisoner to work and order and through moral influence and educative measures arouse his inclination to work", thereby enabling him to live an honest life and procure his own subsistence after release.[9] We can see that this first document described work as strongly morally charged and connected to order and the living of an honest life. Two years later a more elaborate proposal was presented that became the basis for the prison instructions of 1938. The text in general had now taken a clear turn towards adopting individual preventive ideas and stated, "the prisoner shall receive such care and treatment that is likely to raise him to a law-abiding and socially useful life" and furthermore, "due respect should be given to his age, mental and physical development, character, work ability, aptitude and previous education".[10] However, prison work was

---

[8] However, as chairman both of the Law Committee in the Swedish parliament and, above all, of the Penal Law Committee, Schlyter came to occupy a key position in Swedish penal policy for another two decades.

[9] Draft for a Regulation on general rules for prisoner treatment and care, 18 October 1933. Penal Law Committee Acts 33:1. Quoted from Petersson Hjelm (2002, p. 136, my translation).

[10] Prison Instruction 1938:34. Quoted from Petersson Hjelm (2002, p. 141, my translation).

not yet given any special prominence and was only subsumed under other treatment measures (Petersson Hjelm 2002, p. 141). However, this instruction was only a complement to the older laws regulating the prison area and a more profound revision was under way that resulted in the Implementation of Sentence Act of 1945. During the final preparations for this act the importance of work came to be emphasized more and more as the members of the Penal Law Committee underlined that work was the primary means for correcting criminals at the same time as they distanced themselves from the idea of legitimizing work with effective arguments. Thus, the committee stated that prison work in the future must resemble work on the "open" labour market, i.e. it should be "rational, productive, profitable and meaningful" as well as an incentive for the prisoners (Petersson Hjelm 2002, p. 174).[11]

Work as the Principal Treatment Method in the Welfare State Prisons

So, if medically or psychologically oriented treatment methods gained limited influence in the post-war era, what instead came to determine the character of the prison system in these decades was the concentration on productive work in a such a way that work came to be *the* principal treatment method. By upholding productive work as the central part of prison life—besides the loss of freedom—punishment was connected to a dominating societal value in post-war Sweden. Hence, work—and, admittedly, compulsory work—became not only a form of punishment in the traditional sense but also an expression for and symbol of this value (cf. Lacey 2003, p. 187). It has also been pointed out that the Lutheran inheritance in the Nordic states contributed to a certain understanding of work ethics and equality so that daily work became the fulfilment of a vocation given by God corresponded to the principle of full employment (Christiansen and Markula 2006, p. 10).

---

[11] See also *Svensk Författningssamling* 1945:872 Lag om verkställighet av frihetsstraff m. m. §§ 24, 52, 53, 58 and 65.

But to understand the role given to productive work in prisons it is necessary to look at the general societal and economic context in Sweden in the decades after the Second World War. The decades after the Second World War was the "golden age" for Swedish industry, mainly due to strong foreign demand for industrial products, something that resulted in an unprecedented economic growth but also in labour shortage, above all in the industrial sector (Schön 2010, pp. 321–326). The goal for the labour policy became the full employment strategy, which meant that all hands in society—also those of the prisoners—were needed. Given the prisoners' class background it was logical to connect their chances of rehabilitation with their willingness and ability to adapt to this situation. The "role model" in these years was the loyal and conscientious working class man who contributed to the welfare of the whole of society.

During the 1950s several select committees emphasized the role of prison work stressing the need for an extensive rationalization and streamlining of prison production. It was argued that the time spent in prison must be used to become accustomed to working discipline and being prepared to function in the modern industrial production. In line with this a committee report delivered in 1952 recommended that work should be arranged so that the inmates quickly could get the opportunity to make a productive contribution, something that could be achieved in a specialized production of "not too complicated objects in reasonably large series" (*SOU 1952, 21*, p. 26). The central role given to productive work continued to be expressed also in other committee reports in the 1950s where it was emphasized that inmates must be employed with "appropriate work" and that it was important that the Prison Administration could arrange training for the prisoners in key occupational areas, especially "those areas in which it on the free labour market is a strong demand for skilled labour" (*SOU 1959:15*, p. 15; *SOU 1959:18*, p. 89). Further, it was pointed out that the working environment in the prisons should be stimulating with "bright, large rooms and modern equipment." Here prisoners were supposed to form a positive attitude to work and learn to adapt to the routines of modern working life. It was underlined that work intensity in the prisons could and should be increased, notably through the introduction of piecework and other incentives (*SOU 1959:18*, pp. 12–16, 18). By organizing prison work after the model of industrial series production, divided into various easy moments, one could achieve that also less good workers could be quite effective and get job training (*SOU 1959:18*, pp. 16–17). It was now emphasized that the new institutions would be "industry prisons" with a modern factory organization as the dominant element, and that treatment in these institutions should be based on the motto *work at the centre* (*SOU 1959:18*, p. 19, italics in original). The Prison Administration must therefore also in production terms be equated with a commercial company that has as efficiently as possible used its productive apparatus (*SOU 1959:15*, pp. 134–135).

An important prerequisite for establishing the central role of productive work had come in 1952 with the introduction of the normal day schedule (Rolfsson 1989, p. 147). The so-called "principle of normalization", which underlined that life in prison was to resemble life on the outside as much as possible, had been a central element already in the Implementation of Sentence Act of 1945 which also included a furlough system, possibilities to get visits from relatives, extended rights to send and receive letters as well as the right for prisoners to associate freely during leisure time (Petersson Hjelm 2002, p. 128). The normal day schedule was part of the aim to organize life in prison in the same way as for the industrial worker, i.e. with clear differences between working hours, leisure time and rest. The inmates were supposed to be trained to live a regulated and ordered life, which besides work included planned and organized leisure activities like sport, hobby work, collective study circles and self-studies. Strongly connected to the discourse of normalization was the idea that regular wage work was a sign of normality and thus that it was "normal" to be engaged in this kind of activity and "abnormal" not to be. The adjective "normal" was a key concept in the prison discourse during this period. Thus, the majority of the prisoners where labelled the "normal clientele", contrasting this group to those in need of special treatment and security arrangements.

Another step in the introduction of the works programme was the inauguration of a new regional prison organization in 1955. From this time on prison work should be organized with geographical regions as the basic treatment and productive units. At central level the Labour Division of the Prison Administration became responsible for the planning and organization of prison work. To meet the demands for new and larger production units in 1956 a special building committee was set up inside the Prison Administration. The committee existed for nearly fifteen years and played a central role in the designing of the "industrial prisons" or "factory prisons" that was erected during this period.[12]

During the 1950s and 1960s the prisons step by step was integrated into the industrial sector and the prison industry was more and more seen as a "natural" part of national industrial production. For every year the prison production rose, most notably in the first half of the 1960s. In 1971 the Swedish Prison Administration declared—not without a certain amount of pride—that the workshops in the new institutions were "fully comparable in every respect with their counterparts in civilian life" (*Kriminalvården 1971*, p. 9). During these decades more organized cooperation also began both with private companies and with national unions and in the 1960s also with the National Labour Market Board[13] that began to organize special employment courses for prisoners. Later on several bodies aimed at increasing the cooperation between the prisons and different associations on the labour market where founded, including the so called Industry Board for Treatment Institutions[14] and, at the local level, councils for labour market and union issues (*Kriminalvården 1971*, pp. 41–42).

The Man in the Middle

The man who more than anyone else came to personify the amalgamation of the working imperative of the welfare state with prison policy was Torsten Eriksson, Governor General for the Swedish Prison Administration from 1960 to 1970. If Schlyter was the most important individual at the start of

---

[12] During this period seven new prisons, including two youth prisons, equipped with modern machinery parks were erected. To this could be added the modernization of the largest of the security prisons. In 1971 these facilities housed approximately 1,500 prisoners of a total number of 4,000 held in closed institutions. Although serving their sentences in older prisons also the large majority of the remaining 2,500 prisoners worked with industrial production. See *Kriminalvården* (*1971*, 60–62, 80).

[13] Sw. Arbetsmarknadsstyrelsen.

[14] Sw. Vårdinstitutionernas industrinämnd.

the prison reform movement, Eriksson was the one who carried on this task during the following decades and thus represented the continuity in the movement (Sundell 1998). Coming into the prison administration as a young man in the early 1930s, he soon became Schlyter's protégé and later reform collaborator. From the 1930s to the 1950s Eriksson took part in a series of select committees dealing with questions of penal matters besides holding various posts on the Swedish National Social Board before subsequently becoming Director Governor of the Prison Administration.

Eriksson became a well-known figure on the international penological scene delivering reports and short articles to international meetings and conferences (Nilsson 2011, p. 83). In the 1960s, as part of his growing international engagements, he travelled widely abroad giving lectures on Swedish prison policy. In 1961 he was elected chairman of United Nations advisory committee on penal policy. During the years 1966 to 1969 he held the same position in the European Committee on Crime Problems (CEPC) a committee inside the European Council (Eriksson 1967, pp. 348–357). In a characteristic description Schlyter called Eriksson "the soul in Swedish penal policy reform" (Sundell 1998, p. 220). Although educated in jurisprudence Eriksson during his career became a severe critic of this profession's rule-bound rigidity, conservatism and inability to depart from the punishment model.

Immediately after taking office Eriksson made clear that he saw work as the primary method of treatment and that an efficient and well-organized working division was the primary sign of a rationally functioning prison administration (Nilsson 2013, p. 143). The priority given to productive work by the Prison Administration stood out most clearly in his often repeated slogan: "First we build the factory, then we add the institution" (Eriksson 1962a, p. 168, 1965, p. 60). Already in an article published some years earlier he had emphasized that modern society required the contribution from all societal forces and that there was no reason to allow one group, i.e. the prisoners, to work at "half speed".[15] On the contrary, everybody's interest was best met

---

[15] It should be emphasized that "prisoners" in this context refers to those serving sentences, which means that remand prisoners are excluded.

by *demanding a hundred per cent effort.* It was of the "utmost importance" that the inmates learnt to work "hard and energetically" because modern society demanded that everybody contributed to the general welfare. This was no degradation of prison work, Eriksson underlined. Instead, he argued, by taking the prisoner's role as a worker seriously society showed respect for his value as a human being (Eriksson 1956, pp. 100–101, italics in original).

In an interview shortly after his appointment as head of the Prison Administration he told a journalist that the most important issue was that "the prisoners should work as hard as everybody else" and that it was not fair to them, nor to society, if they were allowed to be idle in prison. He furthermore underlined that it was as a worker that the prisoner had the chance to show that he wanted to contribute to economic prosperity and thus gain admission to society (Gerdes 1961). In the Prison Administration's annual report for 1961 the readers were told that the works programme since the middle of the 1950s had been aimed "as far as possible at *industrial mass production* in factories and workshops, which both technically and organisationally are fully comparable with civilian installations of corresponding size" (*Kriminalvården 1961>*, p. 13). And further:

> Swedish corrections operate according to the full employment policy. The inmates have an obligation to work, and all able-bodied do work. No idleness may occur [...]. The inmate serving prison time shall have the opportunity to acclimatise to a modern working environment and get used to the fast pace in the production that now prevails in the business world. (*Kriminalvården 1961*, p. 54, my translation)

The report included a description of the organization and aims of the working activities in Swedish prisons. The readers were told that work was carried out in modern workshops and that the prisoners during working hours now were instructed by specially trained foremen, including engineers. The inmates usually worked in small teams with different types of machine work (*Kriminalvården 1961*, p. 17).

During the 1960s the annual prison reports contained plenty of discussions, tables and figures showing the growth of the prison industry, but very little about other forms of treatment or activities in the prisons. By the middle of the decade the goal of full employment had been nearly reached in the prisons, at least nominally, and Eriksson emphasized that instead of talking about 5,000 inmates it was now time to talk about 5,000 workers (Eriksson 1962b, p. 38). The 1965 annual report expressed in a succinct way the essence of the role that was given to prison work:

> The inmate shall be given the opportunity to improve or to maintain his working capacity. Experience shows that this objective is best attained through orderly and productive work, at which the inmates have a chance to adapt themselves to a modern working environment with up-to-date methods and to become accustomed to order, discipline and a satisfactory pace of work (*Kriminalvården 1965*, p. 13, my translation).

The 1960s—The Height of Prison Work in Sweden

The introduction of new and improved production units and methods together with the large increase in the number of prisoners led to a sharp rise in production during the 1950s and 1960s. Measured in fixed monetary value, the increase in the decade from 1952/53 to 1962/63 was more than 3½ times. Related to the number of inmates the efficiency had more than doubled (*Kriminalvården 1963*, p. 33, *1966*, p. 44). The concentration on work inside the prisons was complemented by a so called free-labour system, introduced in the Implementation of Sentence Act of 1945, which meant that prisoners could get permission to work for employers outside prison at daytime while spending the night in prison (e.g. *Kriminalvården 1965*, p. 25).

During the 1960s the Swedish way of organizing prison work also attracted attention abroad. After a visit to Swedish prisons in 1963 the English prison administrator Mr Ogier said that the most characterizing feature about the Swedish prison system was "its practical and spacious workshops" (En engelsman 1963, p. 1). In the 1960s the Swedish works programme also became a source of inspiration for progressive American scholars (Morris and Hawkins 1970, pp. 130–135). In 1965 the United

Nations Congress for the Prevention of Crime and the Treatment of Offenders was held in Stockholm. Here Torsten Eriksson delivered a keynote speech in which he presented the Swedish prison system as well as parts of the penal policy. He emphasized that Sweden now had introduced a new up-to-date Penal Code that aimed at a "sensible, effective and humane treatment of all offenders." In the following he described the "open" character of the Swedish prison system with a large number of open facilities of a colony type, frequent use of furloughs, lack of censorship and generous possibilities to receive visits from relatives and friends. However, the real pride of the Swedish correctional system was the works programme. The goal was, according to Eriksson, to adapt the working conditions in the prisons as closely as possible to conditions in civil society (Eriksson 1965, p. 53). From the beginning of the 1960s Eriksson and the Correctional Administration was also successful in using the media for spreading the message about the central role dedicated to productive work in the prisons (Nilsson 2013, p. 143). However, this picture of a well-planned and effective prison work organization must equally be seen as a normative account as a correct description of the factual situation. Eriksson had clear reasons for describing the Prison Administration as a rational and modern organization in line with the general tendencies of the welfare state. Being an active Social Democrat and married to a woman who represented the party in parliament, he had strong political and ideological interests in presenting such a picture.

The pride that can be discerned in the annual reports from the Prison Administration and particularly in statements delivered by its Governor General of a constantly developing and ever more efficient prison work division thus corresponded to the much talked-about success of the Swedish (and Nordic) welfare model (Nilsson 2011). The investment in the expansion of work activities within prisons must also be seen against the background of the traditional problems with organizing meaningful, continual and efficient prison work that practically all prison system suffered from. In many countries with similar prison systems there were huge problems when it came to organizing work for the prisoners who instead often spent their time in idleness or in extremely inefficient and unprofitable types of work. Hence, as Governor General for the Swedish

Prison Administration and the leading advocate of the works programme, Eriksson appeared both as a vigorous and able prison administrator and as a dedicated welfare state ideologue.

Prison work could have many functions, from pure punishment and control of the prisoners to a sort of therapeutic activity. In the case of Sweden in the post-second World War years the goal was to organize prison work in the same rational and efficient way as the civil labour market, aiming at maximizing profit for the state and thus in the end contributing to the general welfare. Contemporary research has discussed whether, and in that case, to what extent, post-release work has a rehabilitative effect, first of all in reducing recidivism. Although the findings are somewhat ambivalent they nevertheless point to a positive correlation (see for example Skardhamar and Telle 2012). However, one of the variables that are hard to catch is the quality of the work carried out in prison before release and how this "match" with the labour market. Prison work in the welfare state aimed not only—as in the classical liberal political economy—at inculcating a general physical work discipline but also educating the prisoners in one specific kind of work: industrial work in large productive units organized in the form of piecework. It was at the same time embedded in an inclusive ideology that assigned prison work the role of changing the inmates in accordance with the image of the ideal worker as a subject characterized by industriousness and loyalty both to his working companions and to society as a whole. During the post-Second World War decades prison work gradually turned into a matter of rationalization, effectiveness and productive capacity. This also meant that the prisoners' working efforts became the prioritized measure when it came to determine whether they would get furloughs, visits from friends and relatives, permission to be part of the free-labour system as well as his actual security classing and, ultimately, how the prison administration judged the possibilities for the individual prisoner to be rehabilitated.

After the expansion phase into the latter half of the 1960s the conditions for productive work within the prisons changed during the following decade (*Kriminalvården 1969*, p. 40). Prison production stagnated and from the beginning of the 1970s the belief in productive work as the central component in the rehabilitation of criminals began to vanish.

The reasons for this change must be sought both in the terms of the strong criticism in Sweden and several other countries against prisons and other institutions for being "inhumane," repressive and undemocratic (Nilsson 2013, pp. 163–192) and in the worldwide economic stagnation that at the time also hit Sweden with rising unemployment as the result (Schön 2010, pp. 376–378).

Prison Work and the Welfare State Citizen

During the period that has been discussed here Sweden carried through a series of considerable legal changes, culminating in the introduction of the new Penal Code in 1965. The preceding three decades were characterized by a step-by-step penal reformism that resulted in a number of changes, primarily aiming at a more treatment-oriented legal system.

However, earlier research has shown that prison reforms in Sweden in the post-Second World War decades failed in the sense that the medically or psychologically oriented care- and treatment-oriented system that the reformers had envisaged never materialized (Petersson Hjelm 2002; Nilsson 2013).

My main argument in this article is that prison reform in post-Second World War Sweden can be best understood, not in relation to the introduction of advanced care- and humane treatment methods on a large scale but instead in relation to the central priority given to productive work, both as a source of general welfare and as a meta-ideology with deep roots in Swedish culture. In his article concerning Scandinavian penal exceptionalism John Pratt argues that the road taken by these countries in the penal area must be understood in the light of a deep egalitarian tradition that subsequently became institutionalized and embedded in the social fabric of the welfare states (Pratt 2008). But the fact that Pratt hardly mentions, let alone problematizes, the role played by work in the Scandinavian post-war prisons results in a partly inaccurate description of the character of the prison systems, at least when it comes to Sweden. Even though the Swedish (and Scandinavian) prison system in comparison with most other systems perhaps *was* more humane and less punishment-oriented it was *not*, first of all, a system characterized by humanism and tolerance and individualized medical, therapeutic and psychological treatment as Pratt argues (Pratt 2008, pp. 129–132). It was a prison system organized with collective compulsory labour as the core of the treatment model.

One of the reasons for this outcome was a lack of definitions and regulations concerning how more exactly individual treatment should be carried out in combination with the insufficient resources that were allocated to such activities created a space that was filled by productive work. On a more structural level the outcome must be seen in the light of certain elements in the Swedish (or Scandinavian) welfare ideology that besides emphasizing on equality, included a strong leaning towards pragmatism and practical solutions, a strong work ethic, and the view that fairness and security is something the citizens deserved through "pulling their bits" to society.

Moreover, the prioritizing of productive factory work was a strategy for constructing a prison system with the capacity to function inclusively and thus overcoming the stigmatizing mechanisms of life in prison. Thus, the prisoners were supposed to work, not because they were forced to do it, but out of a sense of duty to society. Work was seen as an instrument by which the contact with the community could be restored. Still, work was also supposed to function as a form of self-help for the prisoners to gain acceptance in the community. Anyone who proved himself and showed loyalty to society had a moral right to inclusion in the same society. Correspondingly, this right was questioned for the groups that did not live up to these standards (e.g. Hilson 2008, pp. 95, 101). To become a real citizen in the welfare state the prisoner, as well as the alcoholic, vagrant, prostitute etc. had to change their status from a receiver of welfare services to the status of worker and thus a contributor of the same welfare. Here the state, in this case the prison authorities, had an important role to play by encouraging and supporting the strivings of individuals or, if necessary, coercing those unwilling to conform. Neither was it right for society and its loyal and hard-working members that prisoners did not work for their subsistence. Ultimately, the prisoners should have the *right* to work—guaranteed by the welfare state—and the opportunity to help themselves.

Thus, the Swedish welfare state in the first post-Second World War decades was very much built on the idea that social values transcend individual preferences and that the highest form of well-being shows itself when individual needs are congruent with the total harmony of society as a whole. Consequently, in such thinking there was no conflict between the interest of society, the common good and the interest of the offender. At the same time, the logic of social intervention resulted in certain groups being looked upon as in need of treatment and re-adjustment. These were the groups that had broken the "contract" between the society and its subjects. Anyone who "abstained" from a job or a useful employment belonged in a deeper sense, not to the society. In exchange for the promise to build an inclusive society with economic and social security for everybody, the welfare state expected loyalty and conscientiousness from its subjects. From this perspective crime and other forms of deviance turn into signs of either disloyalty or abnormality. In both cases the cure became work and vocational training or, for youths, schooling, measures that at the same time were supposed to function as a method for imprinting norms in accordance with the dominating social and moral values of the welfare state. Hence, to understand the role of the prisons in the decades around the middle of the 20th century it is important to have in mind that these institutions were expected to be a tool in a larger project for constructing a better society and maintain national unity and harmony, the latter being something that was threatened by those unwilling, or unable, to conform to.

At the same time it has been claimed that the modern prisons right from their emergence during the 19th century have played a role in transforming criminals to workers, and thus functioned as an element in the class-formation process in the bourgeois society. The prison, according to this idea, managed to create, not free and independent citizens, but workers, i.e. "disciplined subjects," out of prisoners (Foucault 1995; Melossi and Pavarini 1981). With this in mind we can say that the welfare state prison still aimed at creating disciplined subjects but this time in a slightly different form, not only as law-abiding workers but also as conscientious and industrious, "respectable" citizens loyal to the welfare state, its laws and moral underpinnings. Only as such a subject could the ex-prisoner be deserving of his re-admission into society. This means a qualitatively different form of subject compared to the worker-subject in the pure liberal capitalistic economy. So although the welfare state is a modified or "checked" form of capitalism—and a model for managing the capitalist economy—it builds on a different conception of labour that holds that the worker not only works for (the capitalist) employer and for his own subsistence but also for the benefit of the whole. This gives work a further significance as a sort of duty to society, also for the prisoners.

References

Baldwin, P. 1990. *The politics of social solidarity: Class bases of the European welfare state, 1875–1975.* Cambridge: Cambridge University Press.

Björk, H. 2008. *Folkhemsbyggare.* Stockholm: Atlantis.

Blomberg, T. C., Lucken, K. 2010. *American Penology: A history of control.* (2nd ed.). New Brunswick and London: Aldine Transaction.

Christiansen, N. F., et al. 2006. *The nordic model of welfare: A historical reappraisal.* Copenhagen: Tusculanum Press.

Christiansen, N. F., & Markula, P. 2006. Introduction. In N. F. Christiansen, et al. (Eds.), *The nordic model of welfare: A historical reappraisal* (pp. 11–29). Copenhagen: Tusculanum Press.

De Georgi, A. 2006. *Re-thinking the political economy of punishment: Perspectives on post-fordism and Penal Politics.* Aldershot: Ashgate.

1963. En engelsmans syn på svensk kriminalvärd, *Tidskriftfor kriminalvard,* 1,12.

Esping Andersen, G. 1990. *Three worlds of welfare capitalism.* Princeton: Princeton University Press.

Eriksson, T. 1956. Straff eller bättring. In A. söner (Ed.), Text och bilder nr densvenska arbetarrörelsens saga. Del IV. Nydaningens tid (pp. 100–101). Stockholm: Steinsvik.

Eriksson, T. 1962a. Kriminalvärden och dess klientel. *Sodala meddelanden* 1-2, 166–174.

Eriksson, T. 1962b. Den svenska kriminalvärdens framtid. Förhandlingar vid Svenska kriminalistföreningens årsmöte i Stockholm den 3 maj 1962, i *Nordiska kriminalistföreningamas cirsbok 1962* (Stockholm), 34-44.

Eriksson, T. 1965. The Correctional System of Sweden. *Third United Nations Congress on the Prevention of Crime and the Treatment of Offenders.* Stockholm 9–18.8.1965, 58–72.

Eriksson, T. 1967. *Kriminalvård. Idéer och experiment.* Stockholm: Norstedts.

Eriksson, T. 1976. *The Reformers.* New York: Elsevier.

Eriksson, T.1977. *Politik och kriminalpolitik.* Stockholm: Tiden.

Foucault, M. 1995. *Discipline & Punish: The Birth of the Prison.* New York: Random House.

Franke, H. 1995. *The Emancipation of Prisoners*: A socio-historical analysis of the Dutch prison experience. Edinburgh: Edinburgh University Press.

Gerdes, T. 1961. Fångvårdens nya giv är att lära interneraa jobba. *Aftonbladet* 610403.

Hammerlin, Y. 2008. *Om fangebehandling, fange- og menniskesyn i norsk kriminalomsorg i anstalt 1970–2007* Oslo Det juridiske fakultet.

Hilson, M. 2008. *The nordic model. Scandinavia since 1945.* London: Reaktion Books.

Horkheimer, M., & Adorno T. 1972. *Dialectic of Eenlightenment.* New York: Seabury Press.

Hort, S. E. 2014. *Social Ppolicy, welfare State, and civil society in Sweden. Volume 1. Histoiy, politics, and Institutions 1884-1988.* Lund: Arkiv Academic Press.

Kriminalvärden 1961 (Kriminalvårdsverket, 1962).

Kriminalvärden 1963 (Kriminalvårdsverket, 1964).

Kriminalvärden 1965 (Kriminalvårdsverket, 1966).

Kriminalvärden 1969 (Kriminalvårdsverket, 1970).

Kriminalvàrden 1971 (Kriminalvårdsverket, 1972).

Lacey, N. 2003. Penal theoiy and penal practice: a communitarian approach. In Séan McConville, (Ed.), *The Use of Punishment* (pp. 175–198). Cullompton: Willan.

Mathiesen, T. 2000. *Prison on trial.* Waterside Press: Winchester.

Melossi, D., & Pavarini, M. 1981. *The Prison and the Factory: Origins of the Penitentiaiy System.* London Macmillan.

Morris, N. M. & Hawkins, G. 1970. *The honest guide to crime control* Chicago: Chicago University Press.

Murton, T. 1976. *The dilemma of prison reform* New York: Praeger Press.

Myrdal, G. & Myrdal, A. 1934. *Kris i befolkningsfrågan.* Stockholm: Bonniers.

Nilsson, R. 1999. *En välbyggd maskin, en mardröm för själen: det svenska fängelsesystemet under 1800-talet.* Lund: Lund University Press.

Nilsson, R. 2003. The Swedish Prison System in Historical Perspective: a Story of Successful Failure? *Journal of Scandinavian Studies in Criminology and Crime Prevention,* 4(1), 1–20.

Nilsson, R. 2011. 'The most progressive, effective correctional system in the world': The Swedish prison system in the 1960s and 1970s. In T. Ugelvik and J. Dullum (Eds.), *Nordic prison practice and policy – Exceptional or Not?* (pp. 79–99). London: Routledge

Nilsson, R. 2013. *Från cellfängelse till beteendeterapi. Fängelse, kriminalpolitik och vetande 1930–1980.* Malmö: Egalité.

Petersson H. 2002. *Ann-Christine,* Fängelset som välfärdsbygge. Tre studier om behandlingstanken i svensk fångvård. Uppsala: Uppsala universitet.

Pratt, J. 2008. Scandinavian exceptionalism in an era of penal excess. Part 1: The nature and roots of Scandinavian exceptionalism. *British Journal of Criminology* 48, 119–137.

Rolfson, M. 1989. *Den svenska kriminalvården under 1900-talet. En rättssociologisk analys mot rättshistorisk bakgrund.* Lund. Rättssociologiska institutionen, Lunds universitet.

Rotman, E. 1990. *Beyond punishment: A new view on the rehabilitation of criminal offenders.* Westport: Greenwood Press.

Rudstedt, S. 1993. *Ifängeiset. Den svenska fångvårdens historia.* Stockholm: Tiden.

Rusche, G., & Kirchheimer, O. 2003. *Punishment and social structure.* New Brunswick: Transaction Publishers.

Schlyter, K. 1935. *Avfolkafängelserna.* Stockholm: Tiden.

Schön, L. 2010. *Sweden's road to modernity. An economic history.* Stockholm: SNS Förlag.

Svensk Författningssamling 1945.

Skardhamar, T., & Telle, K. 2012. Post-release employment and recidivism in Norway. *Journal of Quantitative Criminology* 28, 629–649.

Smith, P. S. 2003. *Moralske Hospitaler: Det moderne fængselsvcesens gennombrud 1770–1870.* København: Forum.

SOU 1952:21 Räjongplan för fångvården.

SOU 1959:15 Fångvårdsstyrelsen.

SOU 1959:18 Fånges arbetserättning.

Sundell, J.-O. 1998. *Karl Schlyter – en biografi.* Stockholm: Norstedts Juridik.

Wilensky, H. L. 2002. *Rich democracies.* Berkeley: University of California Press.

Prisons of Labor: Social Democracy and the Triple Transformation of the Politics of Punishment in Norway, 1900–2014

Victor L. Shammas

Introduction

This chapter charts the structural transformation of the Norwegian welfare state and attendant shifts in the modality of punishment over the course of the 20th century and beyond. Between 1900 and 2014, the Norwegian welfare state embodied three distinctive forms: first, a residualist, minimally decommodifying regime of Bismarckian welfare politics; second, a comprehensive, universalist regime of social democracy that was broadly redistributive and decommodifying along Fordist-Keynesian lines; third, a hybridized semi-neoliberal regime that maintained important elements of social democracy while implementing marketized logics of state governance, relying increasingly on private providers to deliver core state services and witnessing accelerating

V.L. Shammas (✉)
Department of Sociology and Human Geography, University of Oslo, Oslo, Norway
e-mail: victor.shammas@gmail.com

© The Author(s) 2017
P. Scharff Smith, T. Ugelvik (eds.), *Scandinavian Penal History, Culture and Prison Practice,* Palgrave Studies in Prisons and Penology, DOI 10.1057/978-1-137-58529-5_3

socioeconomic disparities. Three modalities of penality arose out of and in conjunction with these stages of transformation of the welfare state in this period (see also Hauge 2002): first, *penality as paternalism*, mobilizing prisons to act as warehouses for the poor and disreputable, particularly the unemployed, vagrants, thieves and alcoholics; second, *penality as treatment*, entailing the medicalization of social pathologies and the resurgence of prison labor schemes, paving the way for a reintegrative system of treatment and work that was fundamentally aimed at bringing wayward social agents back into the fold of the citizenry through gainful employment; third, *penality as dualization*, in which the prison system diverged along lines of citizenship, giving rise to a rehabilitation-oriented track increasingly reserved for national insiders and slowly mounting a residual, punitive wing to be mobilized vis-à-vis foreign outsiders and non-Norwegian citizens. In this third and last period, incarceration rates slowly crept upwards to levels not seen since social democracy's apex at mid-century.

More generally, there exists a nexus between *social policy* and *penal policy*, and understanding changes in the latter domain mandates attending to transformations in the former. In teasing out the myriad ways in which the political economy of the state—more traditionally the provenance of economists political scientists—impacts the objects of study held to be the preserve of criminologists, penologists, historians of the prison, and sociologists of punishment, this historical account of transformation of welfare and penality in Norway throughout the 20th century and beyond underscores the importance of "bringing the state back in," to use Theda Skocpol's phrase, in studies of the politics of punishment. Admittedly, while there is a *covariation* between the structure and logic of the welfare state and the modality of the penal state, the latter is not reducible to the former (Wacquant 2009); the penal field is relatively autonomous, and the contours of punishment adhere in some measure to a principle of autochthony in which agents internal to the field determine policy agendas that are not immediately translatable to transformations in the wider state (e.g. Goodman et al. 2015). While detailing the totality of mechanisms underpinning the coevality of social policy with penal policy remains beyond the scope of this chapter, for the purposes of a macrohistorical account of systemic evolution over the *longue durée*, a "state-centered approach" offers an initial, parsimonious mapping that would otherwise threaten to be as large and unwieldy as the terrain it purports to describe.[1]

Three Faces of Penality

Penality as Paternalism (1900–1945)

At the outset of the 20th century, Norway was a poor, underdeveloped, and largely nonindustrialized member of the European periphery. Despite its backward economic condition and subservient membership in a political union with Sweden (lasting until national independence in 1905), a series of early attempts at constructing an embryonic welfare state had started in the 1880s which had resulted in a series of carefully circumscribed, moderately protective social policies. This constituted the second half of Polanyi's (2001 [1944]) famed "double movement," the first being the institution of *laissez-faire* capitalism across large parts of the industrialized and industrializing world, revolving around the fantasy of the "self-regulating market," the second being the counterreaction that saw a movement towards growing "collectivism" across the advanced world. This latter "movement" entailed a form of primitive welfarism, including policies like workers' safety legislation to deal with decrepit conditions of life in factories and mines, sickness insurance, public housing, healthcare, sanitation, and public education. On Polanyi's account, this collectivist reaction to the dream of market society was not the outcome of a "conspiracy"; rather, it was the natural and expected counter-reaction to the visibly harmful effects of the self-regulating market—of excessive inflation, rampant unemployment, and squalid living conditions.

---

[1] For alternative mappings and periodizations of the history of imprisonment in the Scandinavian countries, see Nilsson's (2013) account of Swedish incarceration in the mid-sections of the 20th century; Søbye's (2010) micro-level account of the historical transformation of a prison in Oslo, Norway; Pratt and Eriksson's (2013) comparative analysis of incarceration in three Nordic and three Anglophone societies; and Smith's (2003) study of the rise of the modern prison in Denmark over one century.

In Norway, excessive commodification and marketization were counteracted by policies that were, as Bjørnson (2001) notes, limited in scope and aimed at preventing only the most destitute and impoverished elements of society from falling off the cliff of social risks into abject misery. In this age, "it was accepted that the authorities would take care of the elderly, disabled and indigent if 'utter impoverishment threatened'" (Bjørnson 2001, p. 199). As part of the wave of moderately decommodifying Bismarckian welfare reforms that began in the 1880s on the European continent (Briggs 2006, pp. 20–23), a series of social policies and legislative reforms were enacted that sought to protect the poor, sick, and elderly as well as injured or disabled workers, including such legislation as the Factory Inspection Act of 1892, the Accident Insurance Act of 1894, and the Sickness Insurance Act of 1909 (Bjørnson 2001). In this period, as Esping-Andersen and Korpi (1986) note, social insurance was of a clasically *liberal* kind, in part because of the fact that these legislative reforms were enacted by non-socialists. Norway implemented a voluntary scheme for unemployment insurance, operated by unions, and mandatory insurance policies for low-income laborers, but would not see universal and compulsory forms of accident, sickness, and unemployment insurance or universal old-age pensions introduced until mid-century. This was, then, a "predominantly liberal era" (Esping-Andersen and Korpi 1986, p. 46).

In the first half of the 20th century, Norway's prison system was to fulfill one central function: to control and contain problem populations and their attendant social pathologies and perceived vices. At the outset of the century, more than one-half of all convicted persons—some 2,231 persons out of a total of 3,951 convicted persons in 1900—were punished on charges of theft (Det Statistiske Centralbureau 1903, p. 107). Nearly three-quarters of incarcerated men in Oslo's central prison, Botsfengselet, between 1920 and 1939 were classified as manual laborers or precariously employed by contemporary observers (Møglestue 1962, pp. 172–173). But this was also a period of liberal reform. It was a period that was deeply self-conscious of its own perceived liberality. "There has been a momentous development, particularly in a milder and more humanitarian direction, in the domain of penal policy," wrote a group of state statisticians on the period lasting from the closing decades of the 19th century to the first years of the 20th century (Det Statistiske Centralbyraa 1913, p. 8). A new penal code was introduced in 1902, widely lauded in Europe for being in the vanguard of legal reform; it abolished the use of the death penalty in times of peace, raised the age of criminal responsibility from 10 years to 14 years, and would allow convict laborers to be considered for release after 6 months of hard labor (see Heivoll and Flaatten 2014; Hauge 2002).

This was an era of liberal-paternalist concern with the socially deleterious effects of punishment. Particularly among legal elites there was a growing belief that corporal punishment would not fulfill its aims. "We all know that bodily infliction of pain and corporal punishment have not helped," said Andreas Urbye, a state prosecutor, at a meeting of Nordic legal experts in 1899, "and that they have been repealed not only on account of their inhumanity, but also—and first and foremost—because of their futility" (Den Norske Bestyrelsesafdeling 1899). There were efforts to curb the imposition of penal constraint. On 22 January 1925, a 32-year-old man, Hjalmar Sigvard Olsen, was sentenced to 60 days in prison for vagrancy (Ministry of Justice 1925). Olsen was a renowned recidivist, a man who had "previously been sentenced on 10 separate occasions" for breaking the law against vagrancy and committing an act of violence against a public official, and who had accumulated in excess of 40 fines during his rootless wanderings. A pardon was sought for his sentence. Olsen's petitioners—four character witnesses, all respectable members of conventional society, including the chief of police in Olsen's hometown, his employer, and a representative of the *Fattigstyre*, a public agency tasked with providing for the indigent—noted that Olsen was gainfully employed as a gardener and able to provide for his wife and three children. Incarceration would cancel his terms of employment, and his wife and children would consequently be cast into deeper poverty. One of the petitioners noted that he was "under the impression that Olsen would make amends"; his employer remarked that Olsen had been sober and dutiful throughout the period of his employment, and that he had "lately not been seen to be intoxicated"; the police chief was more hesitant, noting in qualified terms that "there may possibly be reason to hope that the applicant . . . will quit his inebriated lifestyle." Nevertheless he supported

Olsen's request for pardon. There was room for contrition within the confines of the system, especially when the crimes were considered to be broadly social in origin: Olsen was pardoned by the Ministry, which had observed that a previous court had noted that Olsen's inebriation had been of a "relatively innocent character."

Indeed, all across the penal system there were signs that an incipient humanitarian transformation of criminal justice was under way. There was a growing concern with the problem of ensuring that conditions of confinement were "rational," a notion that was thought to entail incarceration in a single cell under conditions that were not to be excessively austere with the possibility of engaging in meaningful work. In 1927, the Ministry of Justice circulated a memo to a number of other government ministries emphasizing that a wide range of artisanal and semi-industrial products would now be manufactured in prisons around the country, permitting prisoners to work as bookbinders, carpenters, cobblers, painters, and saddle makers in the hire of the state (Fengselsvesenet 1936, p. 5). Certainly, such work had already been ongoing in some penitentiaries since the late 18th century, but by the end of the 1920s, skilled work activities became the norm for prisoners at the nation's central prisons (*landsfengsel*): on average, inmates in Oslo's two largest prisons spent some five-and-a-half days per week in gainful employment (Fengselsvesenet 1936, pp. 24–25). The desire for a rationally ordered prison also made the administrators of the prison wary of collective living quarters, overcrowding, and the formation of a hardened society of captives. In a missive to the Ministry of Justice, the warden of the penal colony (*tvangsarbeidshus*) at Opstad observed that the colony was filled to excess, that inmates were being housed in overfull dormitories rather than in solitary cells, and that overcrowding would create a criminogenic environment. Conditions would not improve, the warden complained, until a series of new cells could be constructed, but no money was forthcoming from the government to carry out its mission; more satisfyingly, it was noted that primitive forms of coercion, such as using irons and straitjackets, had not been in use at Opstad for a full year (Fengselsvesenet 1929, pp. 13–14).

Just as the risks facing the newly formed industrial proletariat in the course of their labors were to be collectivized and mitigated by the proto-welfare state, so too did the state consider laboring inmates as deserving some modicum of social protection. One 39-year-old inmate who was held at Akershus Landsfengsel in 1918 lost the use of four of his fingers while laboring in the prison sawmill (Ministry of Justice 1918). After reviewing the facts of the inmate's case, the Ministry of Justice declared that the incident "must be characterized as an accident, which now and then will take place in any industrial enterprise." Inmates were laborers, and prisons were industrial enterprises: the overlapping sociodemographic characteristics of the industrial proletariat and the prison populations revealed a vision of the prison as an industrial enterprise. For the inmate, compensation for his injuries was to be calculated following the procedures that were used to allocate compensation in ordinary "private enterprise," the Ministry observed. The National Insurance Administration was consulted, and the agency calculated the inmate's invalidity to the preposterously precise figure of "16 and two-thirds percent," which should have afforded the inmate an annual compensation of "10 percent of annual wages." But such precise metrics only gave rise to further problems of computation, for what was the *value* of the inmate's labor? In a firm, the value of labor was represented by the laborer's wages. Inmates, however, received only the most minimal remunerations. Cutting a clear path through such metaphysical quandaries, the Ministry simply decreed that the inmate's annual salary "under the present circumstances" was to be pegged to the wholly artificial level of 1,200 Norwegian kroner. An insurance payment of 120 kroner per annum was therefore to ensue upon his release. In light of the inmate's record of theft and recidivism—the man had previously been convicted 12 times for "crimes of theft" (*tyvsforbrydelser*) and once for robbery—the Ministry stipulated that compensation should not be permitted to accumulate "if he were to be placed in prison for forced labor" in the future or "in any other way be placed under public or municipal supervision for any considerable duration."

This was also an age of ascendant biopolitics, of the medicalization of correctional expertise, and of scientistic schemes of prisoner classification (see Schaanning 2007; Søbye 2010). In a letter to the prison warden of Oslo Central Prison, the institution's chief medical officer, the renowned psychiatrist and eugenicist Johan Scharffenberg, requested that all inmates that were to be released and who had been classified as "expressly abnormal," should be noted as such in their criminal records

(Ministry of Justice 1924). Taking the example of one of his inmate-patients, who had exhibited "groundless delusions of persecution" and "elevated self-confidence," Scharffenberg recommended that an annotation be added to the man's files that this man should be categorized as a "homosexual, paranoid psychopath." Such classificatory designations were to be used in the probable event of any future dealings with the criminal justice system. The other face of a seemingly progressive and high-minded project of social engineering found its legal expression in a 1934 law that permitted both quasi-voluntary and explicitly compulsory sterilization on the basis of eugenic grounds (Haave 2007, p. 46). Unlike most other European societies, the Scandinavian turn to eugenics took place under the auspices of democratic governments in relatively egalitarian societies and were "linked to a liberal movement for social reforms rather than a politically conservative agenda" (Dikötter 1998, p. 469). The intrusive nature of liberal paternalism found its dual expression in incipient rehabilitationism within the correctional apparatus and, more broadly, in concerns with reproductive suitability in wider society; it was a movement that was supported by broad sections of the Scandinavian social-democratic parties (Roll-Hansen 1989).

This was a time of contradictions, then, characterized by a strengthened belief in the possibility of the rational and utilitarian treatment of persons liable to be categorized as incorrigible in the previous century, the advent of medical-psychiatric instruments of classification and assessment, and growing rehabilitative ambitions that were constricted by narrow fiscal means. A wave of liberal-humanist sentiments confronted the continuing material austerity of penal confinement and servitude as well as the extrapenological functions of social control directed against the unemployed, destitute, homeless, morally outrageous, and related constitutents of the "dangerous classes." At the heart of the primordial welfare state there existed a tension between the growing recognition of the need to relieve the plight of the burgeoning industrial proletariat and the desire to maintain the essential balance of power within the framework of the conventional social order, a tension that was made visible in the structure and operation of the penal state in this era.

Penality as Treatment (1945–2000)

While the social-democratic Norwegian Labour Party had formed its first durable cabinet government in 1935, it was not until the postwar years of national reconstruction that the project of erecting a universal, generous, and strongly decommodifying welfare state began to gain ground. After 5 years of occupation under Nazi rule between 1940 and 1945, the Norwegian social democrats, taking a cue from the British Labour Party, urged that a "people's war" of popular and partisan resistance should be followed by a "people's peace" of fervent restoration and modernization. In a flourish of Marxist phraseology, the party noted that its goal was to construct a "socialist Norway" wherein "broad masses of the people" would secure the right to work, leisure, education, and gender equality "in all areas of social life" (Norwegian Labour Party 1945).

With a program for vibrant postwar reconstructionism, the party secured some 41 % of the vote for the national assembly, laying the foundations for a stable period of governance—interrupted by two short-lived center-right coalition governments and a more long-lasting center-right coalition government from the mid-1960s to the mid-1970s—by a (nominally) social-democratic party for decades to come. Facing weak opposition from conservative parties, the Norwegian Labour Party, allied with a strong trade union movement, took advantage of this "golden age" of social democracy to roll out a series of Keynesian welfare reforms with an aim of full employment (Esping-Andersen 1990, pp. 167–169). With absolute parliamentary majorities in the immediate postwar decades and a strong neo-corporatist model of wage setting, the Norwegian Labour Party was able to secure historically low levels of unemployment: an average of 2 % between 1950 and 1960(Esping-Andersen 1990, p. 170). A series of universal, protective social policies were implemented in the postwar era: universal and compulsory accident, sickness, and unemployment insurance as well as universal, state-financed flat-rate old-age pensions were rolled out in the second half of the 1950s (Esping-Andersen and Korpi 1986, p. 48).

Crime control was not of great concern for the architects of the Norwegian welfare state at mid-century. The prison remained an inconspicuous institution: on average, around 1,375 inmates were held in confinement on any given day in 1902, and by 1952, this figured had crept marginally upwards to 1,587 persons (Statistics Norway 2015). To the reigning Norwegian Labour Party, building a universal healthcare system, constructing public housing, establishing social security programs, and securing full employment were the primary objectives of postwar reconstruction: a strategic plan for the country for the years between 1953 and 1957 does not so much as mention the criminal justice system with a word (Norwegian Labour Party 1953). Crime was viewed as a pathology whose causes were largely social in origin; it was to be combated indirectly by building a more just social order. Macroeconomic policies were criminal justice policies in disguise. An all-embracing welfare state was the best bulwark against offensive acts of crime and the attendant need to punish, a view that was fully in evidence by the time the postwar social democrats published their first major white paper on crime policy in the late 1970s. "Crime and community are connected," observed the authors, noting that a respect for the law was simultaneously a vote of confidence for the "key political lines" governing the social order, and "in this respect, a just distribution of goods is of central importance"; furthermore, crime was to be viewed as something of a social construct because of the way in which society categorized acts as deviant (Ministry of Justice 1978, p. 5). While such statements echoed the logic of penal modernism sweeping across the Western world in the postwar era, their publication in a 1978 white paper on criminal justice policy produced widespread criticism of the apparent naïvete of penal modernism, finally resulting in the early departure of the Minister of Justice, Inger Louise Valle. Such controversies were a symptom of the continuous ebb and flow of supportive and critical sentiment surrounding penal modernism in the second half of the 20th century.

A series of counterpunitive policies and legislative acts were implemented throughout the period. The scope of conditional sentencing was expanded by legal reform in 1955, young offenders between 14 and 17 years old were largely not imprisoned but had their criminal sentences dropped (*påtaleunnlatelse*) by the early 1960s, and an extrapunitive option of "hard time" (*skjerpet fengsel*), which included the option of sentencing offenders to a barebones subsistence diet of "bread and water," was dropped in the Prison Act of 1958 (Hauge

2002, pp. 53–54). The crime policy architects of the late 1970s emphasized the importance of preventing the commission of crimes, developing a "humane" system of punishment that was in accord with the nation's "culture," and a criminal justice apparatus that made effective use of available resources (Ministry of Justice 1978, p. 6). Obviously, these were woolly notions that did not immediately translate into definite policies. But there existed a prevailing notion that prisons should restrict the pains they imposed on their institutional charges and that rehabilitation was a moral, sensible, and cost-effective course of action: the criminal age of responsibility was raised to 15 years, crimes of theft were to be met with alternative sanctions besides imprisonment, persons who could not pay their fines were not to be incarcerated, a form of preventive detention (*forvaring*) was to be abolished, and life imprisonment was also removed (Ministry of Justice 1978, pp. 169–170).

The period started with an exception. The immediate postwar trials against Nazi collaborators exhibited a veritable penal rampage. Nowhere else in Western Europe were such large proportions of collaborating members of the population subjected to legal punishment: all 55,000 members of the Norwegian pro-Nazi party, *Nasjonal Samling*, and an additional 40,000 citizens were set to be tried in the postwar proceedings (Judt 2007, p. 45). Around 9,000 persons were sentenced to prison, an additional 9,000 individuals were sentenced to forced labor, 48 persons were sentenced to a "loss of public trust"—a novel punitive option that entailed, among other things, permanent disenfranchisement and the loss of right to hold public office—and 25 individuals were executed (Central Bureau of Statistics of Norway 1954). From mid-1945 to mid-1946, nearly 23,000 persons were incarcerated, suspected of collaborating with the Nazi occupying powers (Fengselsstyret 1954, p. 16), a remarkable figure for a relatively low-incarceration society.

Some accounts of punishment policies in Norway avoid mention of such proceedings (see e.g. Pratt and Eriksson 2013, p. 212, footnote 12). But there is no sound basis for excluding a deviant case simply because it is deviant. In the postwar proceedings, retributivist sentiment were activated and mobilized by the social-democratic builders of the welfare state, suggestive of the fact that social democracy did not necessarily or intrinsically entail counterpunitive practices. What obtained for an unusual situation was suggestive of trends that were ongoing, if less pronounced, during periods of relative normalcy, captured by the notion of a "Janus-faced" exclusionary dimension in the ideology and practices of social democracy (Barker 2013). Indeed, despite progressive practices and rhetoric, there was still a definite class dimension to the deployment of punishment in this period: in 1960, for instance, one-third of all inmates were in prison for theft, alcohol consumption, or vagrancy (Statistisk Sentralbyrå 1962, p. 8). And it was the moral opprobrium generated by the visibly austere conditions of incarceration that led the prominent Norwegian writer Jens Bjørneboe to engage in a series of scathing public commentaries of penal practices in the late 1950s, revealing a profound disbelief in the promise of rehabilitation and resulting in the formation of a radical prison reform group, the Norwegian Association for Penal Reform (KROM), in the late 1960s.

Throughout this period there was a growing realization that prisoners would be returned to society. Man was condemned to live in society, and that society would contain former convicts. The 1958 Prison Act paved the way for a series of "open," minimum-security prisons and a furlough program that granted prisoners the possibility of home leave. Rehabilitation was humane but seemed also to be rational. To take a mundane example, in 1980, fully one-fourth of all "long-term prisoners" were let out on home leave for annual Christmas celebrations (Verdens Gang 1980). Penal modernism (Garland 2001) found its doctrinal expression in the "principle of normalization"; inmates were in the main to "maintain all their rights during the term of incarceration" (Ministry of Justice 1988, p. 301): it was the mere loss of freedom that was to constitute the central deprivation of criminal confinement. From this it followed that conditions of confinement should be made to mimic conventional life in the community as far as would be possible within the strictures of a correctional environment. But even this formula, apparently concrete and definite, concealed a pragmatic open-endedness, and the principle contained a greater latitude of possible interpretations than its proponents would admit. Ethnographic accounts of maximum-security incarceration in this era suggest that imprisonment was not particularly exceptional or humane relative to the rest of the Western world (Mathiesen 1965). But if penal modernism had limited institutional effects in these decades, its political-economic manifestations were considerable: a sturdy social safety was constructed that prevented social pathologies from flourishing, prisoner populations remained small, and the very need for a prison system remained limited due to the existence of a protective and generous state.

Drugs did not sit quite so well with the apparent lenience of this political-economic modality of punishment. Alcohol was already sufficiently dubious to merit censure: "When a large proportion of crime is committed in a state of intoxication, each individual must take responsibility for limiting the consumption of alcohol in society," the Ministry of Justice (1978, p. 6) emphasized. If the tone was timid, the policies were comprehensive: alcohol distribution was subject to comprehensive regulation through a state monopoly on its sale. As drug use increased during the 1960s, Scandinavian social democrats envisioned a society that was to be "drug-free" (Tham 2005). A "drug paragraph" was introduced into the national penal code in 1968 that stipulated a maximum length of imprisonment of 6 years for drug offenses; gradually, upper sentencing limits inched upwards, and by 1984, serious drug offenses were punishable by up to 21 years in prison (Shammas et al. 2014, pp. 593–594). While this legislative agenda was part of a broader, global coalition against drugs, a horror at the specter of unproductive hedonism or costly pathologies associated with the consumption of illicit substances also fed off a distinctly social-democratic impulse: the very normative order seemed at stake as the project of constructing and maintaining a generous, comprehensive system of social provision helped elevate the role of labor to a position of sacrality; work was instrumental in securing the reproduction of the welfare state. Drugs undermined the tight reciprocal bonds between citizens and the state under social democracy and were consequently criminalized and penalized at levels that seemed conspicuously disconnected from a wider regime of penal moderation (Pratt 2008, p. 285). Between 1968 and 1998, the number of drug offenses investigated by the police rose more than 150-fold from around 200 cases per year to more than 30,000 cases per year (Statistics Norway 1999). By the late 1980s, nearly 60 % of inmates in the nation's district prisons were locked up for drug offenses

(Ministry of Justice 1988, p. 35). On the occasion of the publication of a Ministry of Social Affairs white paper that took a prohibitionist stance toward drug use, one newspaper commentator noted that "a drug-free society" had become the state's "key objective in the field of drug policy." It was a "goal that is strongly anchored in public opinion, in all political parties, and in the remainder of civil society," and there existed, according to this observer, a broad "agreement that we cannot accept drug abuse in any form" (Verdens Gang 1985).

Penality as Dualization (2000–2014)

By the late 1970s, the "golden age" of the Fordist-Keynesian social compact had run into severe difficulties and sustained political opposition across the Western world. Starting in this decade, a transition from the Keynesian state to a Schumpeterian "competitive state" was initiated in many of those countries where social democracy had previously produced a virtuous circle of sustained levels of economic growth, low levels of employment, rising productivity, growing incomes, and high levels of aggregate demand (Jessop 2002). So too in Norway. With the formation of Kåre Willoch's Conservative government in October 1981, the near-hegemonic status of Keynesian, universalist decommodification in the postwar era drew to an end.

Riding on the wave of post-Keynesian, Reaganite-Thatcherite "market revolutions" in the early 1980s (Harvey 2005), a series of Conservative governments or Conservative-led coalition governments traded off with the Labour Party in holding the reins of power throughout the 1980s. What is more, the Labour Party governments formed in the 1990s were largely modeled on the "New Labour" model of Blairite centrism, based on the one hand on the conviction, fueled by the "median voter theorem," that centrists were the only viable means of securing electoral victory, and, on the other hand, that under novel conditions of post-Fordist global competitiveness, the renewal of social democracy along a "Third Way" was an ineluctable necessity. National enterprises were privatized starting in the 1990s. Healthcare remained firmly universal and public, but a growing reliance on private general practitioners, rising co-payments for consultations, and the proliferation of private alternatives to state health-care meant that one of the pillars of Keynesian welfare state was looking increasingly unstable. Workfare policies proliferated (Kildal and Kuhnle 2005, pp. 26–29). Tax reforms were initiated in the 1980s that over the next decades generated increasingly inegalitarian distributions of wealth (Aaberge and Atkinson 2008). While union membership—the plinth of leftist state capitalism in the postwar era—remained strong, its semantic meaning had transitioned from serving as a fount of radical agitation to functioning as an instrument of macroeconomic corporatist management and providing inexpensive benefits, such as home insurance policies, for individual members. As a result of widening socioeconomic inequalities, a "New Nordic Model" (Hansen 2014, p. 478) had arisen that was neither fully neoliberal nor recognizably social-democratic in the sense suggested by that term in the immediate postwar years.

By the start of the new millennium, Norway had made a circum-scribed turn towards increasingly punitive politics (Shammas 2015): the incarceration rate increased by more than 25 % between 2000 and 2012;[2] legislative changes raised maximum sentencing levels for violent offenses throughout the 2000s; post-9/11 counterterrorist legislation increased the maximum penalty for offenses considered acts of terrorism from 21 years to 30 years in prison; penal expenditures grew by 80 % between 2005 and 2012; a novel and intrusive mode of criminal sanc-tioning like electronic monitoring of non-incarcerated offenders using ankle bracelets may in the long term contribute to a widening of the penal dragnet, even as it may in the short term have had a counter-punitive effect on the system as a whole by replacing prison sentences with the possibility of serving time at home. A new penal sanction of "incarceration under preventive detention" introduced the theoretical possibility of life imprisonment in a country that at the beginning of the

---

[2] The incarceration rate for Norwegian citizens remained relatively stable over the period; the growth in criminal confinement should be viewed in conjunction with targeted police action aimed at arriving citizens from postcolonial developing countries in and around the Middle East following American military incursions in Iraq and Afghanistan as well as the eastwards expansion of the European Union that attracted tens of thousands of migrants through the increased mobility offered by a widened Schengen Area.

21st century had capped prison terms at 21 years. Prison construction failed to keep apace with the growing number of prison sentences generated by the court system, so that by 2014 some 1,300 persons with unconditional sentences were waiting to begin their sentences, the pretrial remand system was overflowing, and some prisons began housing two inmates per cell in formerly single-occupancy cells—a move that was considered a departure from an important constituent pillar of penal welfarism. Taken as a whole, the penal field underwent a moderate rightwards tilt in this period, a transformation that was accelerated and catalyzed by competition between the previously predominant Labour Party and the newly ascendant right-wing, neoliberal Progress Party over the right to "stage sovereignty" by taking a "tough on crime" stance toward perceived social pathologies. The fundamental axis of transformation in Norway's penal field in this period stretched between the Labour Party and the Progress Party as both parties entered into a cyclical and punitive arms race, each attempting to outbid the other in adopting stricter measures to respond to the perceived interconnections between crime, immigration, and "permissive punishment"—and thereby demonstrating that parties of both the left and right remain susceptible to the perceived attractions and symbolic profits stemming from the politics of penal austerity (e.g., Tham 2001).

Emblematic of this struggle was the growing deployment of surveillant and punitive energies trained on foreign citizens.[3] In 2005, some 12 % of

---

[3] The police trained its gaze on "foreign" criminals in this period. "Norwegians constitute the majority of registered criminal offenders responsible for less serious drug crimes, while foreign citizens are responsible for most serious drug offenses," observed a Norwegian police report in 2014 (National Crime Investigation Service 2014, p. 9); the report enumerates a panoply of "criminal networks" presumed to be stratified along ethnonational or ethnoracial lines and organized by social agents hailing from the Baltic states, Poland, the Balkans, Vietnam, Morocco, Somalia, Kurdish regions, and West-African nations. The report notes, "Statistics show a tenfold increase in the number of drug cases where west-Africans were suspected, accused, and convicted [of drug crimes] between 2000 and 2009." And yet it remains unclear whether this "explosion"—the term used by the police, enclosed in quotation marks, to characterize the outsized prevalence of "West-African" offenders in the commission of drug offenses—is a function of disproportionate commission of crime by definite social groups or rather an *ethnoracially targeted police surveillance* aimed at uncovering drug offenses by those already presumed to be primarily responsible for the importation of cocaine and heroin into Norwegian society.

new entrants to prison were foreign citizens (Norwegian Correctional Services 2005, p. 6), but by 2013, this figure had grown to 29 % of new entrants, and a full one-third of the prison population was now composed of non-Norwegian citizens (Norwegian Correctional Services 2013, p. 7). For leading politicians on both the left and right of the political spectrum, this seemed to spell crisis for the penal order; the alleged influx of roving bands of predatory criminals from Eastern Europe, rapacious sex offenders, and exploitative drug dealers of African or Middle Eastern origin, was seized upon by politicians from both the Labour Party and right-wing populist Progress Party (Shammas 2015). Through a more aggressive application of the provisions of Norway's Immigration Act, foreign citizens suspected of a crime while residing in Norway could be subject to deportation, sometimes even in the absence of a legal conviction due to the lower evidentiary standards required for deportation to occur (as with asylum seekers suspected of providing false information about their true identity); a veritable boom in the number of deportations of foreign citizens followed, operated largely under the auspices of the immigration bureaucracy and therefore not considered a bona fide legal sanction; the number of such deportations grew from 190 orders in 1991 to nearly 2,500 orders by 2014 (Aas and Mohn 2015).

Declaring that foreign citizens would not be sufficiently deterred from committing criminal acts due to the elevated standards of the Norwegian correctional system, the deputy leader of the Progress Party, Per Sandberg, contended that "foreign criminals are a big problem, and mild sentences and high-quality facilities aren't helping" (Progress Party 2011). Defying the reigning "principle of normalization," Sandberg proposed a 10-point plan for prison reform aimed at making conditions of confinement more austere: Norwegian inmates were to have their prison wages cut in half and foreign inmates were not to receive any wages whatsoever; foreign citizens were to be placed in penitentiaries with "lower standards" than those inhabited by Norwegian citizens; the names of pedophile sex offenders were to be publicized in the mold of a US-style Megan's Law; parole opportunities for early release were to be curtailed; and work programs were to be made mandatory, reducing the opportunity to pursue educational programs. The proposal, put forth at a national party congress and given to rousing rhetoric and grandstanding, was ridiculed by the Labour Party Minister of Justice, Knut Storberget, who called the proposals "unspeakably poor" and observed that "the countries that try to worsen inmates' conditions, struggle the most with crime" (Verdens Gang 2011).

And yet only a few months later, one of the Progress Party's proposals had become official government policy: Ullersmo Prison in eastern Norway was set to house foreign citizens in an ethnonationally segregated cell block. A year later, it was announced that a 97-bed prison in eastern Norway, Kongsvinger Prison, was to be converted into a segregated facility for foreign citizens (Ministry of Justice 2012). While political elites promised that this prison was to offer tailor-made rehabilitative programs for offenders who were destined for extradition to other national cultures upon release, this was also a rhetorical strategy that served to reap dual symbolic profits. On the one hand, it assuaged supporters of penal modernism who would not accept the wholesale degradation along ethnonational lines of one of the core pillars of the rehabilitative regime of criminal justice, namely the principle of normalization; on the other hand, it signaled to those sections of the electorate that were increasingly given to ecstasies of denunciation of allegedly crime-prone asylum seekers and stigmatized, mobile economic migrants that toughened measures were being taken.

Punishment is one of the core functions of the state. However, the twin pressures of a growing prison population and a declining willingness to invest rehabilitative energies in stigmatized foreign offenders within sections of the penal field, placed even the most fundamental functions of the state under pressure.[4] Arguing that the Conservative Party and Progress Party coalition government had inherited a deficit in

---

[4] A growing number of political agents in the Norwegian penal field believe that rehabilitative functions should be reserved for a privileged core of national insiders by reducing correctional standards for non-national offenders. In 2010, the Conservative Party expressed a desire to establish a "differential treatment" of foreign inmates by "moving foreigners out of ordinary Norwegian prisons and into separate, more basic prison wings." The party's spokesperson on criminal justice issues believed it would be desirable to construct "separate wings for foreign criminals with somewhat lowered standards in regards to amenities and rehabilitative services" (Conservative Party 2010). Similarly, the Progress Party's manifesto notes, "The proportion of foreign convicts is approaching 40 percent [of the inmate population], and high standards in

public spending on prison construction, efforts were made in 2013 to lease spare prison space in neighboring countries. The newly elected Progress Party Minister of Justice, Anders Anundsen, contacted his Swedish counterpart, requesting permission to lease unutilized space in one of Sweden's correctional facilities. After some delay, the Swedish Ministry of Justice rejected the request, noting the troubling issue of ceding sovereignty to another state: "Either Sweden would take on the exercise of authority on behalf of the Norwegian government, or representatives of the Norwegian state would exercise such authority in Sweden" (Svenska Dagbladet 2014). Both options were viewed as deeply problematic.

Not to be deterred, the Progress Party minister sought assistance from the Netherlands. Having housed some 500 prisoners for Belgian authorities under a similar program in 2010 and successfully reduced the use of criminal confinement over the previous decade, the Netherlands accepted the Norwegian request. Gradually, the terms of public debate shifted from moving prisoners per se to the Dutch prison to moving *foreign* prisoners who would be extradited following the completion of their sentence. Rehabilitation would be made more difficult by the great distance between Norway and the Netherlands. Visits from friends and family would not be possible to the same extent as before. But this was considered a less salient issue when the inmates were foreign citizens, who, it might be supposed, would lack such social bonds and affiliations. A Conservative Party spokesperson contended that the Norwegian-Dutch prison would be modeled on the ethnonationally segregated section of Kongsvinger Prison. "We have a situation in Norwegian prisons where one-third of the prisoners are foreign citizens," said the spokesperson. "This will first and foremost be an initiative aimed at inmates who will be extradited, and who will therefore not be remaining in Norway" (NRK 2014). By October 2014, the Dutch-Norwegian prison housed 153 inmates and around 80 % of the inmates were non-Norwegian citizens; while it was not a facility reserved for incarcerating foreigners, it was disproportionately deployed to this end.

Norwegian prisons are not having a deterrent effect on these criminals. We must establish separate prisons for foreign criminals" (Progress Party 2011).

In a period of a transformation of the logic of service provision by the state where core capacities from elderly care to asylum housing were increasingly subcontracted to private providers, and the offshoring and mass migration of manufacturing capacities to low-cost countries, it seemed only a slight stretch of the imagination to combine these dual transformations and to outsource yet another central capacity of the state—the power to punish— to an extraterritorial entity. Penal modernism had increasingly become the preserve of the national citizenry.

Conclusion

The history of punishment in Norway between 1900 and 2014 can be understood as a series of struggles over the state. The social state was transformed from a minimally decommodifying liberal welfare state, followed by a generous and expansive Keynesian-Fordist regime of social democracy, which finally culminated in a semi-neoliberal regime of state capitalism. To each of these welfare state regimes belonged, with some measure of contingency and variation, a definite stage of penality, shifting from a regime that can be described as *penality as paternalism*, wherein humanitarian and liberal reforms imposed a minimal set of constraints on punitive austerity, followed by *penality as treatment* that saw the ramping up of social policies and rehabilitationist sentiment, and replaced by *penality as dualization* that witnessed a growing bifurcation along ethnonational lines at the core of the criminal justice system. Certainly, the exertion of force from the structure of the social state to the operation of the penal state is far from unmediated or unidirectional. Exigencies intervene, scientific expertise and the media impose their own logic of autonomy, and global trends transmute the operation of the bureaucratic field by forcing it into a condition of heteronomy. However, the structure of the social state remains vitally important, and it is here that all accounts of penality must begin.

Throughout the modern period, the prison has been a riveted, conflict-ridden institution, both from within and beyond its jealously guarded perimeter. There has been a constant labor of imagination revolving around the fevered fantasy of *alternatives*, of additional ways of arranging entities in penal space, of novel sanctions and instruments, of dealing with the "immense task, [the] extreme ambiguity of the prison" (Petit 1990, p. 10). Perhaps no other institution has been quite so haunted by the perpetual desire, even from within its professional core, to imagine other ways of ordering and practicing the art of punishment. The prison has always been a remarkably recalcitrant institution, proving resistant to reform and modification at nearly every turn. Even during the course of its apparently smooth operation, it has always generated more pathologies, vices, and problematics than it has been able to quell or resolve. Even when the prison has done what it has nominally been tasked with accomplishing, it has generated more discord than contentment.

References

Aaberge, R., & Atkinson, A. B. (2008, July). Top incomes in Norway. Statistics Norway Discussion Papers, no. 552.

Aas, K. F., & Mohn, S. B. (2015). Utvisning som straff? Om grensesnittet mellom strafferett og utlendingskontroll. *Tidsskrift for strafferett, 15*(2), 154–176.

Barker, V. (2013). Nordic exceptionalism revisited: explaining the paradox of a Janus-faced penal regime. *Theoretical Criminology, 17*(1), 5–25.

Bjørnson, Ø. (2001). The social democrats and the Norwegian welfare state: some perspectives. *Scandinavian Journal of History, 26*(3), 197–223.

Briggs, A. (2006). The welfare state in historical perspective. In C. Pierson (Ed.), *The welfare state reader* (pp. 16–29). Cambridge: Polity Press.

Central Bureau of Statistics of Norway. (1954). *Statistics on treason and collaboration, 1940–1945*. Oslo: Central Bureau of Statistics.

Conservative Party. (2010). Vil forskjellsbehandle innsatte. http://www.hoyre.no/nb-no/aktuelt/arkiv/vil-forskjellsbehandle-innsatte. Accessed 31 August 2016.

Den Norske Bestyrelsesafdeling af Nordisk Juristmøde. (1899). *Forhandlinger Paa Niende Nordiske Juristmøde i Kristiania*. Kristiania: Aktie-Bogtrykkeriet.

Det Statistiske Centralbureau. (1903). *Statistisk Aarbog for Kongeriget Norge*. Kristiania: H. Aschehoug & Co.

Det Statistiske Centralbyraa. (1913). *Oversigt over de vigtigste resultater av kriminalstatistikken for aarene 1886–1904*. Kristiania: H. Aschehoug & Co.

Dikötter, F. (1998). Race culture: recent perspectives on the history of eugenics. *American Historical Review, 103*(2), 467–478.

Esping-Andersen, G. (1990). *The three worlds of welfare capitalism.* Cambridge: Polity Press.

Esping-Andersen, G., & Korpi, W. (1986). From poor relief to institutional welfare states: the development of Scandinavian social policy. *International Journal of Sociology, 16*(3/4), 39–74.

Fengselsvesenet. (1929). *Fengselsstyrets årbok, 1925.* Oslo: H. Aschehoug & Co.

Fengselsvesenet. (1936). *Fengselsstyrets årbok, 1926–1930.* Oslo: H. Aschehoug & Co.

Fengselsstyret. (1954). *Report of the prison administration, 1931–1950.* Oslo: Fengselsstyret.

Garland, D. (2001). *The culture of control.* Chicago: University of Chicago Press.

Goodman, P., Page, J., & Phelps, M. (2015). The long struggle: An agonistic perspective on penal development. *Theoretical Criminology, 19*(3), 315–335.

Haave, P. (2007). Sterilization under the Swastika: the case of Norway. *International Journal of Mental Health, 36*(1), 45–57.

Hansen, M. N. (2014). Self-made wealth or family wealth? Changes in intergenerational wealth mobility. *Social Forces, 93*(2), 457–481.

Harvey, D. (2005). *A brief history of neoliberalism.* Oxford: Oxford University Press.

Hauge, R. (2002). Utviklingslinjer i straffelovgivningen i det 20. århundre. In Norwegian Ministry of Justice (Ed.), *Ny straffelov: Straffelovkommisjonens delutredning VII (NOU 2002: 04)* (pp. 41–77). Oslo: Justis- og politidepartementet.

Heivoll, G., & Flaatten, S. (Eds.) (2014). *Straff, lov, historie: Historiske perspektiver på straffeloven av 1902.* Oslo: Dreyers Forlag.

Jessop, B. (2002). *The future of the capitalist state.* Cambridge: Polity Press.

Judt, T. (2007). *Postwar: a history of Europe since 1945.* London: Vintage Books.

Kildal, N., & Kuhnle, S. (Eds.) (2005). The Nordic welfare model and the idea of universalism. In *Normative foundations of the welfare state: the Nordic experience* (pp. 13–34). London: Routledge.

Mathiesen, T. (1965). *The defence of the weak: a sociological study of aspects of a Norwegian correctional institution.* London: Tavistock.

Møglestue, I. (1962). *Kriminalitet og sosial bakgrunn.* Oslo: Statistisk Sentralbyrå.

National Crime Investigation Service. (2014). *Den organiserte kriminaliteten i Norge: Trender og utfordringer, 2013–2014.* Oslo: Kripos.

Nilsson, R. (2013). *Från cellfängelse till kognitiv beteendeterapi. Fängelse, politik och vetande, 1930–1980.* Malmö: Égalité.

Norwegian Correctional Services. (2005). *Kriminalomsorgens årsstatistikk 2005*. Oslo: Kriminalomsorgen.

Norwegian Correctional Services. (2013). *Kriminalomsorgens årsstatistikk 2013*. Oslo: Kriminalomsorgen.

Norwegian Labour Party. (1945). Det norske Arbeiderpartis Arbeidsprogram, 1945. http://arbeiderpartiet.no/file/download/5350/60954/file/Arbeidsprogram% 201945.pdf. Accessed 1 September 2015.

Norwegian Labour Party. (1953). Arbeidsprogrammet for stortingsperioden 1953–57. http://www.nsd.uib.no/polsys/data/filer/parti/10045.rtf. Accessed 1 September 2015.

Norwegian Ministry of Justice. (1918). *1050/1918D. Nr. 6. Statsråd Blekr. [Justisdepartementet D del 2—RA/S-1043/A/Aa/L0017]*. Oslo: National Archives of Norway.

Norwegian Ministry of Justice. (1924). *Brev fra Lægen ved Botsfengselet, Johan Scharffenberg, 3. juni 1924 [Justisdepartementet D del 2—RA/S-1043/D/Da/ L0142]*. Oslo: National Archives of Norway.

Norwegian Ministry of Justice. (1925). *J. nr. 1423-25 D. Statsråd Holmboe. Nr. 35 [Justisdepartementet, Fengselsstyret D del 1—RA/S-1043/A/Aa/L0018]*. Oslo: National Archives of Norway.

Norwegian Ministry of Justice. (1978). *St.meld. nr. 104 (1977–78). Om kriminalpolitikken*. Oslo: Justis- og politidepartementet.

Norwegian Ministry of Justice. (1988). *NOU 1988/37: Ny fengselslov*. Oslo: Justis- og politidepartementet.

Norwegian Ministry of Justice. (2012). Kongsvinger fengsel: Ny avdeling for utenlandske innsatte. https://www.regjeringen.no/no/aktuelt/kongs vinger-fengsel-ny-avdeling-for-uten/id709573/. Accessed 10 December 2012.

NRK. (2014). Ap vil ha svar fra Anundsen om fengselsplasser i Nederland. http:// www.nrk.no/norge/ap-vil-ha-svar-fra-anundsen-om-fengselsplasser-i-neder land-1.12070610. Accessed 29 November 2014.

Petit, J.-G. (1990). *Ces peines obscures: La prison pénale en France, 1780–1875*. Paris: Fayard.

Polanyi, K. (2001 [1944]). *The great transformation*. Boston: Beacon Press.

Pratt, J. (2008). Scandinavian exceptionalism in an era of penal excess. Part II: does Scandinavian exceptionalism have a future? *British Journal of Criminology, 48*(3), 275–292.

Pratt, J., & Eriksson, A. (2013). *Contrasts in punishment: an explanation of anglophone excess and Nordic exceptionalism*. Abingdon: Routledge.

Progress Party. (2011). Sandberg strammer inn. http://web.archive.org/web/20110519082142/http://www.frp.no/Sandberg+strammer+inn.d25-TxlDK5S.ips. Accessed 1 September 2016.

Roll-Hansen, N. (1989). Geneticists and the eugenics movement in Scandinavia. *British Journal for the History of Science, 22*(3), 335–346.

Schaanning, E. (2007). *Menneskelaboratoriet.* Oslo: Scandinavian Academic Press.

Shammas, V. L. (2015). The rise of a more punitive state: on the attenuation of Norwegian penal exceptionalism in an era of welfare state transformation. *Critical Criminology, 24*(1), 57–74.

Shammas, V. L., Sandberg, S., Pedersen, W. (2014). Trajectories to mid-and higher-level drug crimes: penal misrepresentations of drug dealers in Norway. *British Journal of Criminology, 54*(4), 592–612.

Smith, P. S. (2003). *Moralske hospitaler: Det moderne fængselsvæsens gennembrud 1770–1870.* Copenhagen: Forum.

Søbye, E. (2010). *En mann fra forgangne århundrer: Overlege Johan Scharffenbergs liv og virke 1869—1965. En arkivstudie.* Oslo: Forlaget Oktober.

Statistics Norway. (1999). Kraftig økning i narkoforbrytelser. http://www.ssb.no/sosiale-forhold-og-kriminalitet/artikler-og-publikasjoner/kraftig-okning-i-narkoforbrytelser. Accessed 1 September 2015.

Statistics Norway. (2015). Population of penal institutions. https://www.ssb.no/a/histstat/tabeller/8-8-12t.txt. Accessed 1 September 2015.

Svenska Dagbladet. (2014). Inga norska fångar i Sverige. http://www.svd.se/inga-norska-fangar-i-sverige. Accessed 5 February 2014.

Statistisk Sentralbyrå. (1962). *Kriminalstatistikk: Domfelte innsatt i og løslatt fra fengselsvesenets anstalter i 1960.* Oslo: Statistisk Sentralbyrå.

Tham, H. (2001). Law and order as a Leftist project? The case of Sweden. *Punishment & Society, 3*(3), 409–426.

Tham, H. (2005). Swedish drug policy and the vision of the good society. *Journal of Scandinavian Studies in Criminology and Crime Prevention, 6*(1), 57–73.

Verdens Gang. (1980, December 23). Hver fjerde langtidsfange hjem til jul, p. 10.

Verdens Gang. (1985, September 26). Narkotikapolitikken, p. 2.

Verdens Gang. (2011, May 13). FrPs fengselsreform (mest for utlendinger): Hard og simpel soning, pp. 4–5.

Wacquant, L. (2009). *Punishing the poor: the neoliberal government of social insecurity.* Durham, NC: Duke University Press.

The Rise of the Open Prisons and the Breakthrough of the Principle of Normalisation from the 1930s Until Today

Peter Fransen

The use of imprisonment in open prisons is considerable in the Danish penal system. Accordingly, the open prisons have attracted a lot of international attention. In the past few years, this has especially been reflected in the literature about "Nordic Penal Exceptionalism" (Ugelvik and Dullum 2012; Pratt and Eriksson 2013). The open prison institution is considered an example of the allegedly humane conditions in the Nordic/Scandinavian countries, which has been explained, among other things, as a result of the Nordic countries' egalitarian and humane policies. But is this assumption correct? Part of the answer to this question is to be found in the history of the open prisons in Denmark.

In 1933, Denmark opened a youth detention centre (Borstal)—a prison that offered freer conditions than in existing prisons. The prison was almost a carbon copy of the British Borstal prison system.

P. Fransen (✉)
The Danish National Archive, Copenhagen, Denmark
e-mail: pf@sa.dk

© The Author(s) 2017
P. Scharff Smith, T. Ugelvik (eds.), *Scandinavian Penal History, Culture and Prison Practice*, Palgrave Studies in Prisons and Penology, DOI 10.1057/978-1-137-58529-5_4

81

Another important shift in Danish penal practice was the open prisons, which were established by the end of the 1940s. With these new institutions the dogma gradually developed that prisoners should serve their sentence in an open prison, unless matters dictated otherwise. An open prison is characterised by a low level of static security, i.e. there is little guard against escape and considerable freedom of movement within the prison area.

Why did this development take place, who were the driving forces behind the development, and where did the inspiration come from? Were there specific Danish circumstances that encouraged this development, or was it foreign trends that primarily determined the process? The conclusions can be seen in an overall context of the development of the modern welfare state.

The Introduction of the Open Prison Model in Denmark

It is tempting to say without further ado that it is in the 1930s we must look for the seeds of the open prisons. The open prisons could then be linked to the extensive social legislation of the 1930s, which has been described as one of the cornerstones of the Danish welfare model. However, this is an overestimation of the youth detention centre institution. The youth detention centre was a special measure for young men between the ages of 15 and 21 who were described as budding repeat offenders. They were given a partially indeterminate sentence of long duration, which had to be combined with education and served under freer physical conditions than in traditional prisons (Fransen 2011, pp. 122–145). These types of youth detention centres in Denmark existed right up until 1973 and were later replaced by Youth Criminal Justice Act which make it possible to put young offenders in secure residential youth care institutions. But the Youth detention centres seem to have had only a limited impact on the development of the open prisons. The same may be said of the open Work house program, which was for older non-dangerous repeat offenders. In this institution, education was replaced with work training in open-air work, and imprisonment took place in an open institution based on a pavilion system.

The youth detention centre and the workhouse were both results of the Danish penal code of 1930, which came into force in 1933. In comparison with the previous penal code, there were new rules both in terms of prisons and in terms of prisoner differentiation. Unlike in the past, far-reaching rules were introduced for special treatment of offenders according to age, character and mental condition. In order to handle the new prison forms, a whole range of new institutions had to be provided, or at least units in the existing prisons that could meet the requirements for special treatment (Kampmann 1933, pp. 1–55). According to the law, the state was obliged to provide the following prison structure:

- State prisons for periods of imprisonment exceeding 6 months
- Prison for psychopaths
- Custodial institution for psychopaths
- Youth detention centre
- Institution for sentence in workhouse
- Institution for preventative detention

Experience with special prisons—Youth detention centres and Workhouses—did not give rise to experimentation with similar freer conditions within the ordinary state prisons. In fact, the establishment of the Danish open prisons was closely associated with the horrors and human sacrifice resulting from the Second World War and had no direct relation to the penal code of 1933 and the treatment ideology which it supported. During the German occupation of Denmark 1940–1945, the number of inmates rose from about 2,000 in the period before the occupation to 6,000, which meant that the traditional prisons lacked sufficient capacity (Henze 2010, p. 62). The result was that the Danish prison service had to rent or acquire buildings which were not suitable as traditional cell prisons, and where the security measures and treatment of the inmates was of a different character compared to that in the big closed prisons. However, it was not until after the occupation that freer prison forms were combined with more humanistic perceptions of conditions for the large prisoner population.

On the ideological level, the ideal in the post-war period was to strengthen the position of the individual in relation to the law. These were efforts which could be described as novel on an organisational level, and which were a reaction against the totalitarian regimes' contempt for humanity. The development also affected the perception of prisoners. Seeing the prisoners as individuals, who apart from their imprisonment had rights as citizens, began to trickle down slowly from the top through the prison hierarchy (Henze 2010, pp. 62–152).

However, the ideological aspect should not be overestimated in comparison with the more mundane and acute problems faced at the end of the Second World War, namely the confrontation with the collaborators. Those who had helped the Germans during the occupation of Denmark 1940–1945 were pursued with demands for prosecution. About 40,000 people were arrested, and more than 13,000 convicted (Christiansen and Hyllested 2011, pp. 8–10). Although releases came quickly, the large numbers sentenced led to a tremendous pressure on the existing prisons.

This pressure resulted in the creation of special penal camps. There was political consensus that collaborators required different treatment than that previously received by convicts. Added to this, the resistance fighters who had experienced the Danish prison system also pressed for the general prison system to be changed. The sentence should promote the prisoners' adaptation to society upon release.

The Principle of Normalisation

In 1945, the resistance movement delivered through Free Denmark a report, "On the Principles of Enforcement of Imprisonment for Treason and other Subversive Activities" (Om Principperne 1945). The prison service was well represented on the committee. The work was continued in the committee that the Ministry of Justice set up in February 1946 under the leadership of the Director of Prisons. The committee issued a preliminary report in 1946 on the enforcement of prison sentences, etc. There were completely new tones that were being struck here. The sentence should promote the prisoners' adaptation to society upon release. With regard to the general preventive purpose—that is, the threat of imprisonment as a deterrent from committing crime—the deprivation of liberty itself and the resulting social consequences were sufficient. It was not necessary to maintain all of the interventions hitherto connected with the sentence, which had emphasised the nature of the suffering of the punishment. It was important to organise the imprisonment in such a way that it came to resemble life outside prison as much as possible so that the prisoner in prison was neither physically nor mentally degraded. What had started as a premise for re-education of collaborators had now become an entirely new set of principles for the treatment of all prisoners. This was a revolt against and a clear criticism of the previous line within the prison service. The idea of the normalisation of prison life was thus enshrined as a principle for the prison service's work in the future. The fact that the idea of normalisation had a hard time breaking through in practical terms is another matter, and a real breakthrough did not come until much later. Indeed, it could be argued with some justification that the principles have never been fully implemented.

The inspiration came from Sweden, which in 1945 had a new enforcement of punishment act, where it was precisely these ideas that played a decisive role (Nilsson 2013, pp. 99–100). In addition, the fact that many of the political prisoners who had been imprisoned during the war demanded prison reform, and finally the large influx of new political prisoners, that is the collaborators, meant that the traditional image of a prisoner could not be maintained. These prisoners were not significantly different from us, as Carl Aude-Hansen, prison governor at the open prison in Møgelkær in Jutland, put it in 1948 (Jyllands-Posten 1948).

The report led in 1947 to the adoption of a new provision for enforcement of imprisonment in state prisons with associated regulations for prisoners in state prisons (Anordning 1947). Just as in Sweden community treatment was now the rule, and thus solitary confinement was finally abandoned as the leading treatment principle. There was also a change of the progressive system so that the sentence which in the 1932 provision was made up of the reception stage, the general stage and final stage, but without the four classes that the general stage had been divided into. This meant that the intricate system for the allocation of privileges was greatly simplified. The framework was thus laid out for a new treatment of prisoners. Prisoners should be treated with firmness and seriousness with a view to supporting their adaptation back into society.

With regard to the general preventive purpose, the deprivation of liberty itself and the resulting social consequences were sufficient. It was important to organise the imprisonment so that it came to resemble life outside prison as much as possible, so that the prisoner in prison was neither physically nor mentally debilitated.

A Different Prison—Kragskovhede Open Prison

How complex the development actually was can be illustrated by looking at the country's largest open prison—Kragskovhede in Northern Jutland. Kragskovhede was set up during the economic crisis of the 1930s as a voluntary camp for the young unemployed. In 1943, the camp was taken over by the German occupying forces to house troop transports, supplies and prisoners of war. In 1945, the camp was taken over by the Danish prison system under the name Penal Camp at Kragskovhede and was primarily used for placement of collaborators. In the hectic months after the country's liberation in 1945, it was planned to accommodate 2,500 collaborators, but by the following year this number had been reduced to 400. At the end of 1947, the last collaborators left the camp and there were voices proposing to close down Kragskovhede. However, the directorate of the prison service had no wish to close down the prison. On the contrary, here is where the ideas for a large open prison for ordinary prisoners could be realised. It was emphasised that for the open prisons it had been possible to find qualified idealistic and competent staff, who had shown great enthusiasm in taking care of the special educational and cultural tasks that were specific to this institution (1. betænkning 1947, p. 170). There was a clear distancing from the old closed state prisons, and it was emphasised that the staff were cast from a different mould to those in the closed prisons, where strict military discipline reigned and where there was also a desire to return to the conditions in place before the occupation. The person who headed Kragskovhede since 1945 was Candidate of Law, Carsten Rafael, who had himself "escaped" in a very dramatic way from a closed prison and subsequently came to construct an open prison and ended his career as a governor in the closed prison he had escaped from! From 1943 to 1945, Rafael served as deputy head of the closed state prison in Nyborg, but after his active efforts to free the political prisoners in

Nyborg, he sought exile in Sweden to avoid being arrested by the Germans (Fransen 2013, pp. 105–110). As soon as Denmark was liberated, Rafael wrote to the Directorate of the Prison Service from his exile in Stockholm and volunteered his services. He was then put in charge of the penal camp at Kragskovhede, which later became the Kragskovhede State Prison. This was an institution he came to have great influence over for the next 20 years, until 1966 when he again returned to Nyborg to try to reform the closed prison. He died, however, the following year. In 1954 he published *Programme for Treatment Work with the Inmates of Kragskovhede State Prison*, in which he paints a picture of what the framework of a Danish open state prison was. Rafael had a free hand to organise treatment activities. Rafael did not hide the fact that he was inspired by the ideas emerging in the United States and which were laid down in the Handbook on Classification in Correctional Institutions, as well as by the information he had received about the Swedish prison service during his exile. Drawing inspiration from these two countries was quite characteristic of the Danish state administration in the years after 1945 (Hansen and Jespersen 2009, p. 533).

A drive towards "scientific truth," rationality, methodological rigour and top-down planning were characteristics of the public sector in the 1950s, while the institutional as well as the financial framework placed restrictions on what could actually be realised. The prison service was not at the forefront of this development, but it is clear that the influence was also felt here and was adapted to the special Danish conditions among the new and progressive prison administrators (Hansen and Jespersen 2009, pp. 295–368). At Kragskovhede, imprisonment was organised almost as if it was an overseas penal colony. The main building was surrounded by a barbed-wire fence and included a reception section with 26 single rooms and a building complex that was used as a school with its own library, cinema, hobby room and sports facilities. The main building also had a farm property with adjacent land of 10 hectares. A few kilometres north of the main building workshops were arranged and outside the workshop sections stretched the institutions' moorland, of which 1,000 hectares could be cultivated. On the northern outskirts of the moorland area was a so-called advance section, which was also a former camp for the young unemployed, and here there was a fully open section accommodating 72 inmates, 12 of whom were in a separate building with single rooms, which was run totally without staff. The entire large area covered by the institution, consisting of units scattered all over the area, was linked together by a narrow gauge railway system which had been set up by the institution itself. There was indeed a world of difference from the country's old closed prisons with their physical confinement behind high walls. Now ordinary prisoners who were not sentenced to youth detention centres or the workhouse could also serve their time in an open prison.

Treatment Philosophy for Open Prisons

The institution had to rely on the experiences that had been made in social and educational work in the broadest sense—the starting point for treatment was the conviction that it was possible to awaken a person's desire for assistance, and gone was the pathological perception of criminals as degenerate individuals (Rafael 1954, p. 10). Rafael stressed that a powerful and lasting sense of lack of freedom could be detrimental to self-respect and restricts initiative. In the open institutions, this sense could be offset by showing the prisoner trust, as the maintenance of the deprivation of freedom rested on the prisoners voluntarily remaining in place until legal release took place. Among other measures that can be mentioned was the introduction of a weekly home day, where the prisoner could go to school in the morning and in the afternoon had the possibility of contact with the staff member who was responsible for his treatment, as well as the payment of wages and practical tasks such as changing clothes and bathing. The other 5 days were working days with the work primarily in agriculture and heath cultivation, as well as in the workshop. In each unit, spokesmen were chosen from among the prisoners, and these spokesmen negotiated with the institution's leadership on issues of a general nature concerning the institution's organisation and rules. A student council was also elected and this had to negotiate with the school's management on the educational and leisure activities (Rafael 1954, p.42). In comparison to most of the country's prisons, this was a completely new approach. That this was possible was due to the fact that individual prison governors had a large degree of autonomy to organise "their" prison as they wished.

No systematic studies have been made of how the prisoners assessed the first years of the open prisons, but the prison service proclaimed that they had been a success. In the mid-1950s, the Director of the Prison Service, Hans Tetens concluded that as the collaborator issue was settled, the prison service would be able to allow a number of these institutions to transfer to open or semi-open institutions, and he described the open institutions as the most significant achievement in the state prison system. In the mid-1950s, there were three large open institutions with between 100 and 350 prisoners each, and four smaller ones which each had fewer than 100 prisoners (Tetens 1956, p. 5).

Denmark had thus become a pioneer when it came to open prisons. Internationally there was also an increased focus on a freer form of imprisonment. Since the beginning of the 20th century, work had been ongoing through the International Commission Pénale a Pénitentiare to establish minimum rules for the treatment of prisoners, work that was promoted by the League of Nations and from 1945 continued under UN auspices. Ten years later, the open institutions also became a part of this codex. From here on, an open institution could be characterised by the fact that there were no material or physical barriers to escape and that there was an attempt to build self-discipline and the prisoners' sense of responsibility for the group they lived in. In accordance with each country's prison system, a prisoner could be sent to an open institution either immediately after sentencing, or after they had served part of their sentence in an institution of the other type. Emphasis was placed on the fact that the selection of prisoners for an open institution should not be due to their belonging to a special group and neither should it depend on the length of the sentence. What was crucial was whether the prisoner would be suited to being in an open prison. Suitability was defined as the prisoner's social reintegration after the sentence being increased by this kind of imprisonment. As far as possible, selection should be based on a medical-psychological test and a social investigation. The resolution was completed with high-flying aspirations for the open prisons, which according to the UN congress represented an important step in the development of modern prison systems and an expression of one of the most successful applications of the principle of individualisation of punishments with a view to social reintegration (Aude-Hansen 1959, pp. 175–177).

Knowledge of the UN resolution was promoted in Denmark by the then chief operating officer for work within the prison system, Carl Aude-Hansen, who had been superintendent of the open prison in Møgelkær from 1945 to 1949. With a good deal of worldly wisdom, he stated that the real progress is obviously not made by the adoption of the reforms—what was crucial was whether the actual practice changed. For many countries that officially endorsed the resolution, the reality left much to be desired. Aude-Hansen himself thought that in the majority of cases the stated requirements were fulfilled in the Scandinavian countries. The human spirit and the rational vision that bears the regulatory framework should be an inspiration to the practitioners who wanted to measure their prison system. It might sound like wishful thinking, but it was not without basis in reality. The desire to experiment characterised the Danish open prisons, and Governor Carsten Rafael continued to look for inspiration in Sweden and the USA. For example, after a study visit to the Highfields institution in the state of New Jersey, he introduced a trial with group therapy for a group of repeat offenders (Rafael 1960, pp. 189–193).

In 1965, Rafael could look back on the first 20 years of running open prisons in Denmark. This he did with considerable pride. The experiment had made satisfactory progress. He stressed that there were no theoretical considerations behind it, and that the development took place in line with the lessons learned along the way. An open prison conflicted with the traditional preconceptions of detention of those involved in the prison service, and he stated that the transition process was far from being complete. He thus clearly saw the open prison as a more humane form of detention, which went hand in hand with the humanisation that had taken place in society. He claimed that through the experiments that had been made with the open institutions, it was documented that a significant portion of the country's state prison population could be housed in open institutions, even inmates who had committed serious crimes. What he saw as just as important was that the practice had developed where long-term prisoners from closed prisons were transferred to open prisons in the final months or years of their sentence, although experience was still lacking with regard to persons convicted of severe violent crime, sexual offences and other acts of a dangerous nature. He also pointed out that the traditional forms of treatment—order and discipline, work, education, welfare work, the impact of discussion and learning by example—did not necessarily have a greater effect in open institutions than they did in closed ones. However, the open institutions were not hampered by the traditions of the older institutions and thus could better adapt to novel experimental conditions. He boldly stated that the open prisons were only at the beginning and that they represented prison society of tomorrow. The open prisons were still hampered by excessive monitoring and control of prisoners. And the prisoners' helplessness in many ordinary activities of everyday life could surely be remedied in the future by simply leaving practical tasks to the prisoners (Rafael 1965, pp. 21–24). Here were perhaps the seeds of the reforms of later decades, where prisoners in Danish prisons could themselves carry out tasks such as cooking and washing clothes.

At Kragskovhede, starting in 1947, the first systematic attempts had been made with the open prison and its possibilities based on its own terms. It was a forerunner of the democratisation process, which would really hit the prison system at the end of the 1960s. Sandwiched between the chaotic 1940s and the rebellious tendencies of the late 1960s were the 1950s. The debate on the prison service was strongly influenced by the conceptual world of the 1930s with its re-education and the desire for expansion and diversification of the system of institutions. Seeing the prisoners as individuals, who despite their imprisonment, had rights as citizens, began to trickle down slowly from the top through the prison hierarchy. In the 1950s, the prison service remained an area for specialists—it was criminologists, lawyers and often prison governors who set the agenda. In the post-war period and up until the end of the 1960s, a high degree of consensus prevailed about the performance of prison tasks. In a paradoxical way, developments in the open prisons were hampered by the development that was to take place in the youth detention centres. The emergence of a modern treatment system populated with social workers and psychologists gained ground both in youth detention centres and open prisons in the 1950s, but the approach to the prisoners in the 1950s was more progressive in the open prisons. While youth detention centres retained the rearing philosophy, though it was increasingly undermined, it was possible to act more freely in the open prisons. While youth detention centres still were a paternalistic institution the open prisons focused more on normalisation which from the 1960s paved the way for discussions about prisoners' rights as citizens. But the focus in the 1950s was on expanding the youth detention centre structure. This changed at the end of the 1960s, when there were more critical players in the field who wanted to have direct influence on the debate on the penal code and prisons (Hansen and Jespersen 2009, pp. 352–356). Doubts were raised about whether the youth detention centres really had the greater specific deterrent effect they had been ascribed to and which should be their justification. Above all, a fierce criticism of the indefinite term element arose. In 1967, the Directorate of the Prison Service acquired a new director, Lars Nordskov Nielsen, and he reformed the service. He also had his own clear perception of youth detention centres versus the open prisons. When youth imprisonment was introduced, assumptions were different—prison was prison, but youth detention centres was something significantly different. It was this that made both the long term and partially indefinite terms defensible. Now the assumptions had changed. The terms of specified sentences had been lowered, but above all, a large part of these were now served in open institutions. In open institutions, prisoners were also offered treatment programs just as in the youth detention centres—though with the restrictions that followed from the shorter period of time. According to Nordskov Nielsen, it could come as no surprise that this development had now led to the question of the complete elimination of youth detention centres as an indefinite sentence (Henze 2010, p. 88) The entire Danish prison service came under general attack in those years, and this gave rise to a group consisting of critical journalists, young criminologists, and even an interest group of inmates and former inmates (Fransen 2013, pp. 125–126). In addition to youth detention centres, the criticisms applied in particular to the rigid closed state prisons. It would not be wrong to argue that the tone of operation and conditions in the open prisons were held up as a comparison to conditions in the closed prisons.

Prison Reforms and the Danish Open Prisons

On 7 August 1969, Nordskov Nielsen gave a talk to members of parliamentary committees regarding drug abuse and pornography. The talk dealt in general with the enforcement of criminal penalties and put the open prisons in the current criminal justice context (Nordskov Nielsen 1969). In a larger perspective, his talk substantiated the view that prisons and thus the prisoners had not benefited enough from the explosive developments which the Danish welfare state had undergone.

Nordskov Nielsen pointed out that custodial sentences were only a very limited part of the total set of sanctions. Every year 300,000 fines were imposed for criminal offences. The number of dropped charges for criminal offences was about 4,000, of which about 1,500 were dropped charges for young people on condition that the young person should be subject to child and youth welfare services. Among the custodial penalties, short prison sentences were the most numerous with more than 7,000 a year. Mitigated imprisonment was a mild form of imprisonment which was previously used in Denmark. It was intended for "persons who are outside the actual criminal circles." It was introduced into the Penal Code of 1930 and abolished in 2001. These punishments were usually 20–30 days in duration, and almost 90 % of these sentences were for drunk-driving. The unconditional fixed-term prison sentences were around 3,000 per year, while the partially indeterminate sanctions were distributed with 200–250 sentences for youth detention centres and around 20 to psychopath detention and 20 to the workhouse.

Despite the fact that numerically speaking the number of prison sentences was not huge, in recent years it had been these that had attracted almost all the attention. This was natural, as prison was not only society's last resort in terms of choice of sanctions in its efforts to ensure respect for the legal system but also because imprisonment was a violation of human freedom that seemed to bring it in contrast to the attitudes, judgements and values in which Nordskov Nielsen believed, "we would otherwise deem to be essential values in our contemporary cultural perception." This was a view of prison sentences which he thought had developed in the Nordic countries. He elaborated the viewpoint by stating that the function of the prison service was to ensure that detention took place in a decent way, a way that was consistent with the cultural norms of humane treatment. The Danish open prisons played an absolute key role in this. At the end of the 1960s, criminological research especially in the Anglo-Saxon countries had made it clear that specific knowledge of which sanctions or forms of treatment worked, was severely limited. In other words, the risk of the potential harm of keeping people in prison was considerable. In this perspective, treatment needs and treatment possibilities should primarily work towards mitigating the risk of harm and only secondarily be means of having a positive effect on making the prisoner more suited to leading a non-criminal life following release. Prison policy should be determined just as much by an attitude of humane responsibility as by utilitarian treatment perspectives. What was Nordskov Nielsen's response to this challenge? It was systematic reform work that aimed to expand and secure the protection of the prisoners' legal rights and the change of the prison system into a welfare institution. This work had already started in the open prisons. He pointed out that more than probably any other country with which Denmark could be compared in terms of criminal policy, Denmark had succeeded in abolishing placement in closed prisons in favour of placement in open institutions. Rules were put in place for exit permits allowing family visits as well as education and training. This was just the start of the reform wave which Nordskov Nielsen let roll over the prison system.

The following year, the Directorate of Prison Services stated that prisoners should be placed in open institutions unless such placement was inadvisable for specific reasons. This could be that the person was dangerous, suspected of being an escape risk, had shown poor adaptability when serving former sentences, or there was the risk of adverse influence on other inmates. What stood out was that the length of the sentence did not in itself preclude placement in an open institution. The general guidelines were that for a sentence of 3 years or less, prisoners as a rule were placed in an open institution. Between 3 and 5 years, a more detailed investigation would have to be made, while persons sentenced to more than 5 years would as a rule be placed in a closed unit. With the decriminalisation that had already taken place and which continued through the 1970s, especially with regard to practice in enrichment crime cases, it was quite evident that the majority of Danish prisoners served their time in open institutions (Lokdam 1977).

However, the Nordskov Nielsen period is particularly characterised by his persistent struggle for the protection of prisoners' legal rights. The old attitude that prisoners could obtain privileges through good behaviour was hard-fought, while the principle that prisoners had (human) rights was promoted very forcefully and permeated the whole of the reform agenda (Smith, forthcoming). It happened at a pace which led to many employees—from prison governors to prison guards—having trouble keeping up. How would things go, for example, when a pilot scheme was introduced with regard to letter censorship at Kragskovhede? Now letters that the prisoners received or sent were only to be read when there was a reason for suspecting that the correspondence would be abused. The following year, the system, with some changes, was made permanent in all Danish prisons. Around 1970, the Danish journalist Erik Nørgaard pointed out that the consequence of a complete normalisation and human rights policy would be that the open institutions would become redundant. However, this did not come to pass (Aude 1972, p. 170).

In 1971, Danish prisoners were given the right to vote in parliamentary elections, and in 1973 the Directorate of the Prison Service became the Directorate of Prison and Probation Services, by which its area of responsibility was greatly expanded. In the same year a new penal code was passed, which abolished the system of special prisons including youth detention centres, and in the Executive Order on the Enforcement of Custodial Sentences in 1973, it was established that "the inmates have the right to exercise their ordinary civil rights to the extent that detention does not in itself prevent these" (Executive Order 1973).

In addition to the rational ideas that might lie behind it, the integration between prison services and welfare services could also be seen as the prison service's attempt to finally climb aboard the wagon of public prosperity. Looking at the prison service in 1969, Nordskov Nielsen was complaining that in financial terms there was a discrepancy between the official policy and its desire for rehabilitation and the welfare and prison work which was actually being carried out in the prisons. A comparison of the rates of growth in funding paid into the prison system, on the one hand, and child and youth care, care for those with learning difficulties, rehabilitation and state hospitals, on the other hand, showed a significantly weaker rate of increase in the prison system than in the other social sectors. This is a key element in the assessment of the prisons and the welfare state. Why had it not been possible to provide prisons and prisoners with the same increase? This was most strikingly apparent in the possibilities for new construction work. Here there had been no success in realising the plans that had been on the drawing board since the 1950s.

Whereas countries such as Norway and Sweden had managed to raise funds to replace outdated institutions or parts of them, the funding of the Danish prison service would have to be raised to a whole new level in order to realise the desired new buildings. In an analysis of the state's social planning in Denmark in the 1950s, it has been argued that with the economic growth that followed in the 1960s, it might have been expected that there would also be room for newly built prisons with improved physical conditions for the country's inmates. However, this was not the case (Hansen and Jespersen 2009, p.352). Furthermore the costly construction and improvement plans for the existing prisons were also only realised to a limited degree (Betænkning II 1965). There are many indications that the Ministry of Justice and the Directorate of Prison Services lacked influence and contacts with the new rush of political graduates in the ministerial finance committees that had the task of coordinating funding. The reforms that the management of the prison service managed to push through—often first tested in open prisons, led to increased funding, but not at the level of the health, education and social sectors.

When conditions in the prisons changed, it was arguably a sign that society's norms had been turned upside down. There was an end to many more or less moral and authoritarian views, which was a natural consequence of society's general and more open-minded development in the 1960s and 1970s—but not because the welfare state architects paid special attention to prisoners. The irony was that when in 1973 the prison service became criminal care, the explosive growth in the state sector was already over. The weaker economic conditions now set their limitations. One area did undergo explosive expansion, and that was the Probation Service. There was a widespread realisation that the concentration of people in prison was followed by increasing asociality. In other words, it was about developing systems where the sentence was just as off-putting as prison, but at the same time did not have the asocialising impact on those affected. It was also established that crime was a typical young person's phenomenon, and the judicial system and the social system refused as long as possible to bring in the use of inappropriate detention. When it finally happened, it had the character of being something like a powerlessness treatment conditioned by the desire to bring the activities to a close for a time—even though one was aware from a slightly more long-term view that it was a risky measure. It could hardly be a more clear formulation of the fact that the treatment optimism in the 1930 Penal Code had finally been abandoned. Detention could no longer be legitimised for therapeutic reasons.

The Open Prisons Lose Their Momentum

Back in 1965, Rafael said that prisons were just like doors: they can only be either open or closed. While the task of the closed prison from the perspective of security is to ensure the prisoners' presence throughout the sentence to be served, then "security" in the open institution consisted only of the ability to ascertain a possible escape in the shortest possible time after it had occurred. He added that it had not been easy to realise this, as it seemed to run counter to all conventional notions of prisons and the very concept of deprivation of liberty.

When the open state prison in Jyderup in Zealand became operational in 1988, many of Raphael's thoughts and visions could be seen in the way the prison operated. One of the first prisoners, coming directly from a local jail, asked when it was time for exercise in the yard—only to be told that in an open prison prisoners could move relatively freely both inside and outside. Similarly, the custom was that when a prisoner received a visit, this could take place in the entire area of the prison, not only in the living rooms or in a special visitor section. In terms of building history, Jyderup followed the same tradition as the country's first open prisons (Engbo 2008, pp. 29–64). Plans to create a totally new open prison from the ground remained a dream. The welfare society did not want to sacrifice the funds needed to build a new prison, so the prison in Jyderup was housed in buildings that consisted of an old factory complex that had subsequently been adapted as a boarding school. Despite the poor housing the treatment of prisoners could naturally take place in a humane manner. The prison made a slight correction to the bias in the distribution of prison capacity in relation to the principle of geographical proximity, which was made at the end of the 1970s. One of the tasks of the Directorate is to allocate the prisoners to the Directorate's institutions, and sentenced men were generally placed as near to home as possible and in prisons with mixed populations. Most open prison places were in Jutland, but most prisoners came from the Zealand area.

From the late 1980s, the political signals in the area of penal policy began gradually to change. It was no longer the case that the agenda was set by liberal experts and officials. The fact that the number of prison places had not been expanded since the end of the 1970s ensured that Denmark did not jump on the spiral in prison numbers that flooded large parts of the Western world, whether governments were right-wing or not. Those days were over. Both right-wing as well as socialist/radical governments had followed this path. There was a tightening up in particular on violence, drugs and gang crimes, and there had been the political will to find funds for new prisons. The change that had taken place was expressed by Niels Kløve Larsen, then prison governor of the open prison in Nørre Snede in Midtjylland, who in 2004 stated, "We have of course long got over the debates that we had in the 1970s and 1980s, where it was argued that prison sentences were just trash. We now use prison more and at the same time it is honestly admitted that it is not because we think people become better people by going to prison, but we consider it necessary for reasons of the public's sense of justice" (Information 2004). The dubious notion of sense of justice has been used both by politicians and the public alike, whether it was in regard to the old closed prisons, which struggled with higher populations due to harsher sentences for hard gang crime and the related violence and drug trafficking, or the 90 % or so of all prison offenders who were now being placed in open prisons.

Whereas the more experimental parts of the prison service were previously carried out in the open prisons, the momentum now moved over to the Probation Service. Denmark focused on using alternative forms of punishment, and it is the Probation Service which oversees the large group of offenders who are found to be suited to serving their sentences in freedom. With inspiration from the UK, this has particularly involved community service—introduced in Denmark as a trial in 1982 and made permanent in 1992, as well as electronic tagging from 2005, where the sentence is served at home. Here, the model was copied from the Swedish system, which had been running since the mid-1990s. Electronic tagging was primarily associated with convictions for drink-driving and the under-25s. From mid-2008, the scheme was extended so that everyone with a sentence of up to 3 months could be considered to serve their sentence with a tag, and now the scheme has been increased to include sentences of up to 6 months. These initiatives have not led to open prisons being abolished in Denmark, but it is fair to say that they have again changed their character and moved in a different direction compared to Raphael's open prisons. The degree of openness is now qualified in any case. In 2006, it was stated that the Prison Service had acquired many new fences, nets, cameras and other items to strengthen security in open institutions. It has become much more difficult to smuggle in such items as alcohol, drugs and mobile phones. The open prisons have also been fenced in with the creation of semi-open spaces and for example remand prison units established within the open prisons—with large fences, tight security and small "cages" for short spells of outdoor yard time. The State Prison in Jyderup now has a fence around the whole prison. Raphael's vision of open prisons did not come to fruition, but much has indeed been changed in the Danish prisons.

In 1995, differentiation was again the keyword and the then Deputy Director and later Director of the Directorate, William Rentzmann, at the time, had an ambivalent attitude to the differentiation concept.

> When we are now discussing greater differentiation of prisoners, more special units and perhaps special institutions, it is more out of necessity than any desire. Because we still believe that the normalisation principle and the resulting mixture of prisoners is the right starting point. (Rentzmann 1995, p. 170)

Since then, there has been the creation of special sections for members of biker gangs as well as drug rehabilitation sections. The development was based on the fact that prisons on one hand had more drug addicts, the mentally ill and other vulnerable groups than in the past, and on the other hand, a number of very powerful inmates, including criminal motorcycle gang members, who were able to dominate the other inmates (Esdorf 1998, p. 4). In a comprehensive review undertaken by the Directorate, it was stated that the principles of being placed in close proximity to family and dilution (mixing people) were important, but not essential principles (Placering af indsatte 2000). The open prisons—or perhaps it would now be more correct to say the not fully closed prisons—are struggling today with many of the same challenges that the closed prisons face. These include the widespread use and smuggling of illegal drugs and problems with gang-related prisoners who demand protection money from their fellow prisoners.

From a welfare state perspective, the new millennium has seen the open prisons being put on performance contract—an offshoot of the modernisation process in the state part of the public sector. The inspiration for this has come from New Public Management, and a variety of control and management tools from the private sector were introduced into the public sector, and there was a "marketisation" of the production of public services. The focus of the prisons has been on efficiency and improved security, combined with cost control.

The Probation Service is still populated with employees who clearly acknowledge their spiritual debt to Nordskov Nielsen, but for how long is this going to continue? Both the open and closed prisons have also received a comprehensive catalogue of treatment initiatives, and individual action plans have been set up for all inmates, but from an overall perspective there has been a failure to drive the liberal and humanistic treatment of prisoners beyond that of the 1970s. It could also be argued that the rights of prisoners have come under pressure now that there is a greater degree of political micromanagement and with politicians' subservience to the diffuse concept of sense of justice.

References

1. betænkning fra Forvaltningskommissionen af 1946. [First report of the Executive Commission of 1946]. (1947). København: J.H. Schultz A/S.

Anordning angaaende Fuldbyrdelse af Fængselsstraf i Statsfængsel 10. maj (1947). 1947 og Reglement for Fanger i Statsfængsel ligeledes fra 10. maj [Provision concerning Enforcement of Imprisonment in State Prisons 10 May 1947 and the Regulations for Prisoners in State Prisons also from 10 May 1947.] Direktoratet for Fængselsvæsent.

Aude, C. (1972). Fra fængsel til frihed. [From prison to freedom]. København: Det danske forlag.

Aude-Hansen, C. (1959). Standard minimumsregler for behandling af fanger. [Standard Minimum Rules for the Treatment of Prisoners] *Nordisk Tidsskrift for Kriminalvidenskab*, (vol. 47, pp. 149–177). København: GAD.

Betænkning II vedrørende fængselsvæsenets anstaltsorganisering. [Report regarding prison measures organization] Betænkning nr. 385. (1965).

Christiansen, S. B., & Hyllested, R. (2011). *På den forkerte side* [On the wrong side]. Aarhus: Aarhus Universitetsforlag.

Engbo, H. J. (2008). Hovsa!—et åbent fængsel i Jyderup [Oops! -an Open prison in Jyderup]. (pp. 29–64). Fængselshistoriske Selskab.

Esdorf, A. (1998). Ændret placering af de indsatte i Nyt fra kriminalforsorgen 4/5. [Modified placement of inmates, News from the Prison Service 4/5].

Executive Order. (1973). 423 of 21 June 1973 on the Enforcement of Custodial Sentences Section 19 par. 1.

Fransen, P. (2011). Ungdomsfængslet på Søbysøgård og baggrunden for oprettelsen i 1933. [Borstal prison – sentenced to an indefinite period of upbringing] *Fynske Årbøger*, (pp. 122–145). Odense: Historisk Samfund for Fyn.

Fransen, P. (2013). Borgen med de mange ansigter. Statsfængslet i Nyborg 1913–2013. [The fortress with many faces. Nyborg State Prison 1913–2013]. Nyborg.

Hansen, E., & Jespersen, L. (Eds.) (2009). Samfundsplanlægning i 1950'erne. Tradition eller tilløb [Planning in the 1950s. Tradition or attempt] (including Peter Fransen: Ungdomsfængsel—dømt til opdragelse på ubestemt tid, [Borstal prison – sentenced to an indefinite period of upbringing]. pp. 295–368). Museum Tusculanums Forlag.

Henze, M. (Ed.) (2010). Direktoratet for Kriminalforsorg 1910–2010 [Directorate of Prison Services 1910–2010]. (Including Peter Fransen: Altid en noget urolig etat, [Always a somewhat uneasy state] pp. 62–152). Fængselshistorisk Selskab.

Information. (2004, June 24).

Jyllands-Posten. (1948, January 4).

Kampmann, E. (1933). Fængselsvæsenet i Danmark efter den nye straffelov [The prison system in Denmark in accordance with the new penal code]. *Nordisk Tidsskrift for Strafferet*, (vol. 21, pp. 1–55). København: GAD.

Lokdam, H. (1977). Nedkriminalisering: Rapport om udviklingen i domstolenes praksis i berigelsessager i perioden 1970–1974. [Decriminalization!: Report on developments in court practice in enrichment cases in the period 1970–1974]. Justitsministeriet, kriminalpolitisk forskningsgruppe.

Nordskov Nielsen, L. (1969). Direktoratet for fængselsvæsenet 4. kontor journalsag 998-4. The Danish National Archives. [Directorate of Prisons, 4th office journal 998–4].

Nilsson, R. (2013). Från cellfängelse till beteendeterapi: fängelse, kriminalpolitik och vetande 1930–1980 [From prison cell to behavioral therapy]. Malmö: Egalité.

Om principperne for fuldbyrdelse af frihedsstraf for forræderi og anden landskadelig virksomhed. [On the principles of enforcement of imprisonment for treason and other subversive activities]. Betænkning afgivet af udvalget af 18. oktober 1945, nedsat af Frit Danmark. 1945.

Placering af indsatte. Indstilling afgivet af Differentieringsudvalget. Bind 2. [Placement of inmates]. Differentieringsudvalget. (2000).

Pratt, J., & Eriksson, A. (2013). *Contrasts in Punishment. An explanation of Anglophone excess and Nordic exceptionalisme.* Oxford: Routledge.

Rafael, C. (1954). Program for behandlingsarbejdet med de indsatte i Statsfængslet på Kragskovhede [Programme for treatment work with the inmates of the State Prison at Kragskovhede]. Direktoratet for Fængselsvæsenet.

Rafael, C. (1960). Gruppeterapi anvendt i et dansk statsfængsel over for et klientel af recidivister [Group therapy used in a Danish state prison with a group of repeat offenders]. *Nordisk Tidsskrift for Kriminalvidenskab* (vol. 48, pp. 189–193). København: GAD.

Rafael, C. (1965). De åbne anstalter [Open prisons]. *Fængselsfaglige Meddelelser.* Nr. 1-2, pp. 21–24. Direktoratet for Fængselsvæsenet.

Rentzmann, W. (1995). Differentiering, [Differentiation] Nyt fra kriminalforsorgen nr. 6.

Smith, P. S. (2016). Prisons and human rights—past, present and future challenges in Weber, Fishwick and Marmo, *The Routledge handbook of criminology and human rights.* Oxford: Routledge.

Tetens, H. (1956). Nogle hovedlinjer i fængselsvæsenets udvikling. [Some of the main strands in the development of the prison service] *Fængselsfaglige Meddelelser.* Nr. 1. Direktoratet for Fængselsvæsenet.

Ugelvik, T., & Dullum, J. (Eds.) (2012). Oxford: Routledge.

A Culture of Intervention—Vagrancy and Drug Treatment in Sweden from the Late 19th Century Until Today

Robert Andersson

The Swedish social democratic welfare state seems to be the result of some unique historical set of circumstances. A vital condition seems to be that reform instead of revolution became the king's way to changing society. In practice this meant that a certain set of *problematizations* were put to use which pointed toward the welfare state as a political solution. My interest here is how the welfare state was opened as a political arena. For Vanessa Barker the social democratic welfare state is not the solution to "(...) a more just and equal penal order" (2013, p. 21). On the contrary, due to ethno-nationalism and weak constitutional traditions regarding individual rights, the Swedish welfare state has a tendency toward repressiveness against individuals deemed as "others." But if liberal constitutions in themselves could counter punitiveness and lower imprisonment rates then the Anglo-Saxon world would not be where it is today in the realm of penality. Instead of using normative concepts such as repression

R. Andersson (✉)
Institute of Police Education, Linnaeus University, Växjö, Sweden
e-mail: robert.l.andersson@lnu.se

© The Author(s) 2017
P. Scharff Smith, T. Ugelvik (eds.), *Scandinavian Penal History, Culture and Prison Practice*, Palgrave Studies in Prisons and Penology, DOI 10.1057/978-1-137-58529-5_5

103

or humaneness, I am more interested in what kind of governance is entailed in the Social democratic welfare state. As I see it, there are no two sides to the coin, lenient/repressive, but rather different practices of governing set on the same target, producing welfare.

Using a constitutional cookie cutter model, i.e. an ideal conceptualization of state power framing it as limited by a body of fundamental law, on the Swedish welfare state misses out on central aspects of it. For Michel Foucault (2003) constitutionalism was the work of the sovereign against the historical rights of the nobility. Constitutionalism is a way of writing history that places law as the main "actor" in the process of making up nations. In *Society must be defended* Foucault instead shows how a blood and history rationale is much more present in the making of nations. Nations are not built on a law rationale, but a rationale of blood and history wherein the race war, i.e. race as heritage not as biology, against external threats is pivotal in the creation of the nation. What I want to show in this paper is how the Swedish welfare state opens up as a political arena by way of a blood and history rationale. Instead of limiting myself through normative assumptions concerning the workings of the welfare state I intend to analyze how a certain way of governing is rationalized and made possible. I use two case studies to show this: drug treatment in prisons and vagrancy policies. I will in each case analyze the problematizations underpinning governing. Problematizations are ways in which a (political) question is caught and described, i.e. it is analyzing the framing of problems and their solutions. Analyzing problematizations is not about finding the representation of a pre-existent object, nor a discursive formation of an object that does not exist. It is rather the set of discursive or non-discursive practices that makes an object of thought into something that can enter into the game of true and false, whether this game takes the form of moral reflection, scientific knowledge production, or political analysis (Foucault 1994, p. 670).

I have elsewhere (Andersson 2012) tried to understand the workings of the Swedish welfare state in terms of what I labeled *a culture of intervention.* Good intentions turned to punitiveness by way of a wish of conformity. I believe that an essential part in understanding the welfare state is to understand what problematizations helped giving birth to the social democratic welfare state.

The purpose of this paper is to do a genealogy of the culture of intervention. My intent is to trace factors and conditions facilitating the intervening welfare state, i.e. how a field for policy is opened up. This is done by way of two examples, the vagrancy law of 1885 and the drug law of 1968.

Part I—Vagrancy and the Culture of Intervention—The Social Question

The celled prison, the public school, as well as the modern police are products of the 19th century. All three of them are also reactions to the so-called social question, i.e. the political interest concerning the social conditions of the underclass (Petersson 1983). As the genesis of the social question urbanization, population growth, industrialization and rationalizations of farming, is often given (Nilsson 2003, p. 110). However, the social question, at least as it evolved during the late 19th century in Sweden, could be understood as a result of the needs of a capitalist economy (Davidsson 2015, pp. 37–39). Until the mid-19th century, life for wage-labors, farmhands and the like was highly controlled (Junestav 2008, p. 101). Being unemployed was criminal and poor relief was only accessible for persons deemed as deserving poor, i.e. unable to sustain themselves due to an impaired work capacity (Nilsson 2003, p.125; Junestav 2008). In practice this meant that poor relief was only for children, the handicapped and the elderly. Another aspect of this control was that wage-laborers were highly stationary, tied to the municipal they lived in. Being caught without an employment outside one's municipal meant that one could be sent to a work-house. However, such a social order did not function in a capitalist mode of production since capitalism demands access to a mobile labor surplus. The vagrancy law of 1885 can be seen as a way of de-criminalizing unemployment (Nilsson 2003, p. 219). The law changed the focus from the question of employment to the question of the willingness to work. Looking for work everywhere possible was being rightfully mobile, while drifting, unwilling to sustain oneself by wage labor, was anti-social and thus forbidden (Edman 2008, p. 131).

The "unregulated" society that faced the social question was thus a liberal society that had produced the working class, the masses, the crowds, the unemployed as means and part of a new social order—market economy. At the same time it was a society that spent much effort on demonizing the working class. With the vagrancy law a new problematization was put in action, focusing not on unemployment as the core problem, but rather focusing on how one conducted one's life thus making anti-social living into something forbidden.

The Teleological History of the Social Democratic Welfare State

A spirit of agreement and a will to compromise are said to be the foundation upon which the social democratic welfare state is built—a welfare state that is also depicted as the manifest destiny of a social democratically ruled Sweden. This teleological interpretation has framed many readings of the Swedish welfare state (Nyzell 2009, pp. 358–359), especially so when it comes to the history writing of the social democrats themselves (Linderborg 2001). The trajectory of the Swedish welfare state is depicted as one free from conflict and with a destiny that is unfolded by the social democrats (Nyzell 2009). Nevertheless, the "will to compromise" and "spirit of agreement" that are claimed to be pivotal for the welfare state's genesis are better understood as historical constructs used to hide the conflicts that actually ran through Swedish society from the mid-19th century and onwards (Nyzell 2009, p. 396). The fact that Sweden during the first decades of the 20th century was a country with numerous strikes and labor conflicts seems to have been written out of history along with the fact that the social democrats were neither the first socialist workers movement nor the only one (Nyzell 2009, p. 364). It is, however, crucial to recognize that the social democrats within just a few years went from being first contenders to state power becoming instead primary defenders of state power (Nyzell 2009, p. 358). The supposed inevitability of the welfare state and the alleged causes behind it, "the will to compromise" and "the spirit of agreement," are thus what legitimatize a social democratic gain of power and the resulting ruling of Sweden. Through the "people's home" ideal the "spirit of agreement" and "the will to compromise" were put into play.

The People's Home—Giving Up Class Struggle

In 1928 the leader of the social democrats, Per-Albin Hansson, held his famous *people's home speech*. The conservative political scientist Rudolf Kjellén originally launched the concept, but by highlighting the democratic features of the social democratic notion of it, Hansson used the concept to form the party's future policies. The concept was used for broadening the social democrats support base, transforming the party from a workers party, i.e. a class party, to a "peoples" party (Zander 2001). This was however not a move into the political middle, but a broadening of the party built on the notion that the middleclass and farmers' interests also were threatened by the capitalistic system (Nyzell 2009, p. 356). It was nonetheless a calculated move based on the analysis that if social democrats wanted to become the ruling majority party, it would only be possible if they broadened their electorate beyond the working class (Dannefjord 2009, p. 245).

The concept was launched at a time when nationalization of private industries as a political strategy was being questioned.[1] It marked the party's abandonment of the notion of class struggle, an idea that had been fundamental to the early Social Democratic movement. Substituting class struggle and revolutionary socialism

---

[1] The social democratic government of 1920 appointed a nationalization committee to look into how industries and natural resources could be nationalized. The project was, however, more or less abandoned from the start; still the committee kept working until 1936, primarily as an alibi for not nationalizing.

was a reform socialism that sought the transformation of society by democratic means, a political strategy where businesses were to be controlled not by government ownership, but by regulation. This also facilitated a central aspect of the Swedish model: the principle that it was the parties of the labor market, i.e. the trade unions and the employers' associations, that were to regulate the labor market by means of agreements, making it unwarranted for the government to regulate by law.

The concept opened up new fields of policy for the social democrats and became the anchor of the whole social democratic welfare project. As such the concept meant the abandonment of a class perspective and class struggle, an abandonment that became indispensible to the social democratic welfare state in the making since it enabled a social democratic social policy. The social democratic interest in social policy had prior to this been more or less nonexistent (Qvarsell 2008, p. 75). As long as a class perspective framed the social question, poverty and unemployment had been nothing more and nothing less than the effects of the capitalistic class society—and the solution to it had been the abandonment of the class society by revolution. Adopting reform socialism also, apart from enabling a social democratic social policy, paved the way for social engineering—soon to become the primary technique for reform in the social democratic welfare state. Accordingly, this also produced a new problematization, replacing a revolutionary rationale for one built on reforming deviant individuals deemed in need of improvement. In the case of the vagrancy law, this is visualized in how the law, from the social democratic rule in the 1930s and onwards, lost its relevance for the regulation of the labor market, becoming instead a demarcation on responsible living.

Looking at this social democratic reframing of the social question from a governmentality perspective and as a form of problematization it becomes obvious how a liberal governmentality, a governing of freedom that focuses on the abilities and merits of the individual as well as the fabric of the population, was adopted. Social engineering, with its pedigree in Keynes's liberal economic theory and Roosevelt's new deal, is a liberal policy built on transforming the individual either directly or indirectly thus improving the stock of the population as a means of furthering the nation's interests.

The Work Strategy and the Conscientious Worker

The struggle against poverty was the primary social policy question in Sweden from the 1890s and onwards (Lundberg and Åmark 2000, p. 26), and the solution to it was *the work strategy* (arbetslinjen). The content of the strategy evolved over time, but its primary denotation, i.e. that those capable of sustaining themselves through work should do so, remained intact. The solutions to the social question and poverty that had developed during the 19th century had a conservative as well as a liberal answer: the conservative was charity to the deserving poor and punishment of the pauper, while the liberal was help to self-help. In both cases the worker was portrayed as a threatening and dangerous character. Opening up for policies toward unemployment, the social democrats needed to frame the social question in line with their political rationale. But the demonization of the entire working class, common to conservative and liberal framings of the social question, was not an option open to the social democrats; they needed a framing of their own, transcending previous conceptualizations, while still keeping misbehavior and deviation as an open question to be corrected by way of state intervention. *The conscientious worker* (den skötsamma arbetaren) became the solution to this problem.

Hard working, advocating sobriety, assiduousness and cleanliness, the conscientious worker became an ideal used as a demarcation against "the dangerous" part of the lower classes.[2] Conscientiousness became a central feature to the social democratic labor movements making of the working class in terms of means for self-disciplinization and the making up of oneself (Ambjörnsson 1988). At the same time it was also something used as a way of countering what was framed as the bourgeois' egoism, class vanity and double standards (Nilsson 2003, p. 195). It can also be seen as a social democratic formulation of the reason why

---

[2] This was also used as demarcation toward other parts of the labor movement, such as communists and syndicalist, framing them as dangerous and irresponsible and not conscientious workers (Jansson 2012).

the working class should and could rule society. When the liberal market economy was introduced, the bourgeoisies claimed the right to lead on the basis of personal competence, high moral standards, reason and effectiveness, i.e. they deserved to be the governing class as a result of their industriousness and ability (Frykman and Löfgren 1979, p. 34). The conscientious worker can thus be seen as a social democratic meritocracy that enables the working class to rule society.

As will be shown, the social democrats came to redefine the work strategy, a reframing that, I will argue, is best understood as a conditional social contract—a contract that in consequence regulates if and how the welfare state will intervene in peoples' lives or not.[3] The work strategy rationalizes the culture of intervention. As long as one fulfills one's part of the contract by sustaining oneself through work—the state will stay out of one's life and instead support it as much as possible by means of different forms of welfare support. If one neglects to fulfill one's part, the state will have the right to intervene in the life of the misbehaving subject.

Transforming Unemployment

As pointed out earlier, the struggle against poverty can be seen as the dominant question in Swedish social policy from the 1890s to the 1950s. But in the social democratic reframing of the work strategy in the 1930s, and thus also the poverty question, lies, as I see it, a fundamental shift that enabled the Swedish welfare state (Junestav 2008, p. 104).

The work strategy was the solution to the poverty question, but the risk of unemployment was a real threat for all those dependent for their livelihood on wage-labor. Prior to the social democratic reframing of unemployment in the 1930s unemployment was seen as brought on by individual shortcomings such as unwillingness to work, incompetence or

---

[3] The conscientious worker ideal is pivotal in understanding social policy in Sweden during the 20th century (Ambjörnsson 1988; Tydén 2000), and it is also decisive in understanding the use of involuntary treatment (Björkman 2001).

unwillingness to move. It was also because jobs were not really lacking, it was just that the demands on wages were set too high. (Junestav 2008, p. 103). However, the inter-war period saw mass unemployment on a scale that was hard to explain in this way.

The social democrats were in power in periods during the 1920s, but always in a minority. The long, and for 45 years unbroken, social democratic rule began in 1932.[4] The soon adopted economic policies, inspired by Keynes ideas, came to reframe and transform unemployment from a question of poverty and social policy, making it instead part of economic policy and an economic rationale (Junestav 2008, p. 104). Transforming unemployment also meant reframing the work strategy. The basic understanding that one had to work to eat remained[5]—but the right to work as a fundamental part of the social order was something new. In the social democratic work strategy the right to work was a key aspect, and full employment became the fundament of the Swedish welfare state.[6]

I believe this transformation of the social question also "caused" an altered approach to the vagrancy law—the law went from being a tool to structure and order the mobile labor force needed by a capitalist system, becoming instead a marker separating out the good and conscientious worker from the misbehaving one. As I see it, making work into a right also transformed work avoidance. It went from being about individual's shortcomings, becoming instead about the individual's solidarity to the new welfare state, the people's home, which the social democrats were building. Unwillingness to

---

[4] The social democrats came to power by striking a deal with the farmer's part, the so-called cow-deal. The social democrats were in power until 1976.

[5] In 1919 Sweden adopted general suffrage, but there was still restriction. The most important one was the so-called poverty line, i.e. losing the right to vote due to having upheld poor relief. A restriction not lifted in practice until the 1947 election.

[6] Sweden's route to a neo-liberal political economy started with the social democrats being re-elected in 1982 and the deregulation of the banks and the so-called financial market. But it was the replacement of the full employment goal by inflation regulation policy in the mid-1990s that marked the final downfall of a Keynesian political economy and the victory of Friedman's monetarism.

work became a moral beacon that signaled an unwillingness to contribute to the new society that was to be built.[7]

Reframing the Social Question

One argument in this paper is that the social democrats, rather than extinguishing the social question by way of terminating the class society, instead produced the welfare state as a solution to the social question. But this also meant that a culture of intervention was adopted and used against those breaking the social contract of the welfare state, i.e. the work strategy. As I see it, this shift can be visualized by way of the transformation of the vagrancy law. Between 1923 and 1965 six public inquiries dealt with the law, and even though most inquiries were negative toward the law it was still not abolished. With the social democratic stand that work was a right, the law lost its original intention and, as an obvious class law, should have been repealed. Instead it seems to have become essential for the new state bearing party. I think this was partly due to the character of the law: The vagrancy law was an administrative law, a police law to be used for maintaining public order. The warnings and the detentions[8] that the law facilitated were decided not by courts, but by the county administrative board or by local police chiefs or, in large cities, by the police chambers (Nilsson 2003, p. 297). The law was in other words a powerful instrument in the hands of a state that wanted to intervene relatively freely into the lives of its misfits.

An important aspect of the law was thus its usefulness. Since the vagrancy law was an administrative law, the need for proof of "crime" in a criminal law sense was non-existent. The act of vagrancy was an act of omission. Accordingly, the law came to be handy when there was not enough proof for a criminal conviction (Nilsson 2013a, p. 300). During

---

[7] Jenny Björkman (2001, p. 236) sees the period between 1932 and the late 1960s as permeated by the idea that everyone and everybody at heart wanted to, or at least should want to, be conscientious, normal, and well adapted, thus making the opposite grounds for forced measures.

[8] Vagrancy could be met by 2 years of forced labor, sometimes even 3 years.

the inter-war years the vagrancy law came to function as a detention law for criminals, anti-social and generally unwanted elements of society. Having such measures at ones command seem to explain the unwillingness to dispose of the law, but it also rationalizes why the law was not abolished until a new social law was adopted in 1982—a law that also made away with any forms of forced measures, placing forced actions against drug-abusers or the young in separate laws. The vagrancy law was in the last decades of its existence thus used as an instrument for the state in dealing with those disturbing the social order that was beyond the reach of the penal law (Nilsson 2013a, p. 316).

Another interesting aspect of the law was also the transformation of the clientele over time. In the beginning the law was used against vagabonds and others threatening the mobile work force. The vagrant was the remainder, what was left over when the deserving poor and those unable to work had been distributed amongst the emerging social security systems, what was left when those convictable according to the criminal law were locked up and when the alcoholic institute had taken its share (Edman 2008, p. 135). During the 1920s the expanding field of psychiatry began to make its mark on the vagrancy question, analyzing the etiology of vagrancy, thus a medicalization of the vagrant commenced, a medicalization that would reach its full bloom with the 1939 committee report (SOU 1939:25). The clientele of the law consisted of persons with many prior convictions. A study in the 1920s showed that more than 70 percent of those sentenced according to the law had previous prison conviction and/or forced labor. A follow-up study in the 1930s showed that the clientele had become even more burdened since 80 percent had priors (Nilsson 2013a, p. 299). From the first years top number of 1,444 incarcerated, the numbers dropped over time (1901, 1,287, 1911, 1,000, 1925, 607 and in 1951, 364, 1954, 474 and 1959 437) (Edman 2008, p. 134, SOU 1962:22, p. 120). Gender aspects were also revealingly obvious since the numbers of convicted women related to how prostitution was handled over time (Svanström 2006). In the 1930s a more intrusive alcoholics law was adopted, a law that made forced measures up to 4 years possible (the vagrancy allowed 2 years' incarceration, sometimes 3 years). What followed was a redefinition of vagrants, administratively transforming many vagrants into alcoholics, thus enabling their incarceration (Edman 2008, p. 135; Nilsson 2013a, pp. 303–305).

A fundamental aspect to the latter use of the law is found in the concept of stationary vagrancy. The concept as such, apart from being a contradiction in terms, points to how the law from the 1930s and 40s primarily came to be used against persons living on the margins in the large Swedish cities. The law was used to police those living in slum areas sustaining their livelihood by an assortment of petty crimes, prostitution, and the like. Even though we are talking about a heavily burdened clientele that was aging, the laws preventive gains still were emphasized in terms of a deterrent on the young, a group that was seen as easily led astray by indolence (SOU 1962:22, p. 198). The rise in crime that had started after World War II was in part framed as a youth problem, and amongst the factors that could lead to a life of crime was prostitution among both boys and girls (SOU 1958:34, p. 39).

Another interesting aspect of how the vagrancy law was argued for in the 1940s and 50s is visualized in the concept *social policing* (SOU 1958:34). Defining the polices' surveillance of vagrants and prostitutes as social prevention, the government wanted to develop what was called a social police, thus countering social problems such as vagrancy, prostitution, vice and abuse by means of the police. Since the police had better admission to persons deemed to be in need than the social and medical authorities, they could also be used in establishing care.[9] It was the police's right to take persons into temporary custody that was to facilitate it, since a detention could lead to the detainee being given social or medical treatment. An intensified surveillance of anti-social elements by the police thus was framed as a vital part of crime prevention (SOU 1958:34, p. 9 f.).

This assumption that coercive measures can lead to rehabilitation can be seen as a bridges between the vagrancy law and the narcotics law. In both cases, the somber, assiduous and productive life can be forced upon both the vagrant and the drug-abuser alike. Another

---

[9] This was to be done by using the laws concerning vagrancy, childcare, sobriety, and insanity (SOU 1958:34).

bridge is that work-avoidance and/or an inability to work becomes the defining character mark of both the vagrant and the drug-abuser. The subject of the vagrancy law as well as the narcotics law is a subject escaping the commandment of work in favor of a life of idleness thus breaking the social contract consequently squandering their liberty.

When the law finally was abolished in 1981, it was not due to the anti-social problem being seen as solved; on the contrary, it was rather that new laws had made it obsolete. The need to intervene was still there, but this could be done by way of other means (SOU 1977:40, pp. 829–830).

Part II: Re-Inventing a Culture of Intervention— Drug, Sobriety and Temperance

The underlying rationale of the social policies of the social demo-cratic welfare state that had emerged since the 1930s was individual prevention—by means of experts the state had set about transform-ing individuals deemed as deviant. In the late 1960s this so-called rehabilitative ideal came under fierce criticism, a critique that in the 1970s would lead to it being deemed as scientifically unsupported. Questioning also the benevolence of the welfare state, the downfall of the rehabilitative ideal also meant the demise in the penal sphere of the culture of intervention. Apart from losing the scientific rational of crime and social policy, the social democrats also lost their long-standing rule in the 1977 election. At the return to power in 1982 they faced the task of re-opening crime policy as a political arena (Andersson 2002, pp. 128–129). A major key in this re-opening was the framing of drugs as a crime problem (Andersson and Nilsson 2009, pp. 171–172).

Sweden came to choose a punitive path concerning drugs. In just 4 years from the enactment in 1968 the punishment for drug-crime rose from a maximum of 2 years to a maximum of 10 (Victor 2007). Originally the law targeted the so-called drug-shark—an exceedingly dangerous criminal preying on the poor drug-abuser, utilizing abuse to make riches. The drug-user on the other hand was to be met with rehabilitative measures aiming at sobriety; thus possession to use was not prosecuted. In 1980 all this changed. Due to new directives from the Swedish prosecution authority, drug-use became a target for the police, thus turning Swedish drug policy into a hunt of the drug-user (Andersson and Nilsson 2009). A shift that was accentuated in 1988 when drug-use was criminalized and again in 1993 when a prison sentence was made possible for using drugs.

The chosen drug policy path has a historical heritage within the Swedish social democrats. The close relationship between the social democratic labor movement and the Swedish temperance movement is a strong one. The temperance movement had, due to the fact that it recruited many of its followers amongst the working class, played an important part in the struggle for general suffrage (Nilsson 2003, pp. 198–199). According to Leif Lenke (2009) there are also other important aspects to the temperance movement—its influence on drug policy. Lenke discerns two types of movements, a moderate and a radical. A moderate movement developed in Germany, Holland, Belgium, France and Denmark. These movements were expert driven, initiated and lead by physicians and politicians. Committing themselves to the liquor question, the goal of the moderate movements was not the abolishment of alcohol, but the reduction of the consumption of liquor as a means of public health, thus framing temperance as a medical question. The radical movements were, on the other hand, often of a popular movement kind. Not differentiating between forms of alcohol, framing all alcohol as equally bad, temperance and sobriety became a question of morals (Lenke and Olsson 2003). In Sweden, the connection between the workers and the temperance movement became instrumental in establishing the conscientious worker and the goal was to achieve an absolute abolishment of alcohol.

Lenke's (2009) argument is that of a path-dependency—the path taken by the temperance movement spilled over onto the drug policy.[10]

---

[10] The temperance movement has long held an un-proportionate high number of members amongst Swedish members of parliament that far overreach its number in the common population (Lindblad and Lundkvist 1996). The movement has thus had far greater impact on policy than expected due to popular support.

Among the Scandinavian countries, Sweden and Norway decided on a radical path whilst Denmark chose a more moderate course. Norway and Sweden have in the same fashion preferred a punitive drug policy aimed at the "drug free society" and in both countries drugs are considered a moral question and combatting drugs is the path of the morally righteous (Lenke and Olsson 2003). The Danish on the other hand have chosen more of a harm reduction approach to drugs in society.[11] Differentiating between the Scandinavian countries is thus the choice of policies on alcohol and drugs.

Apart from re-inventing a culture of intervention, the punitive and moralizing Swedish drug policy[12] has a historical pedigree common to the welfare state's treatment of deviators like vagrants. It is a pedigree aligned to the work strategy—drug use undermines the work ability of individuals and thus threatens the social contract of the welfare state and its proponent—the conscientious worker.

The Work Strategy as Rehabilitation

The work strategy as a social contract has also come to permeate penal policy and in particular the Swedish version of the rehabilitative ideal.[13] Accordingly, the Swedish prison and probation services came, during the 1950s and 60s, to make great investments in new and large prison facilities fitted with modern workshops. An often-used quote from the head of the services said, "first we build the factory, then we place the prison beside the factory." This quote gave high hopes that installing a healthy work ethics would have a beneficial effect on a culprit (Andersson and Nilsson 2009, p. 95). However, in the late 1960s the Swedish prison and probation services got what was framed as a *new*

---

[11] http://www.emcdda.europa.eu/country-data/harm-reduction/Denmark (160201).

[12] In the latest government report on drug treatment the committee conclude that addiction is generally seen by the health and social services as self-inflicted and that the solution to it is by way of education, to strengthen the character of the individual.

[13] Roddy Nilsson (2013b, pp. 138–139) shows, how during the 1930s, work and work training were framed as basic conditions for rehabilitation.

clientele. The key character flaw of the so-called new clientele, a flaw that is claimed to have changed the situation in Swedish prisons, was the inability to work (Nilsson 2013b, p. 140). This new clientele of cause consisted of drug-abusers.[14]

The political downfall of the rehabilitative ideal in Sweden is one question; its downfall within the prison and probation services is another. The so-called new clientele that, due to narcotics, appeared in the 1960s and 70s seemed of great importance. It is commonly assumed that the arrival of drugs changed how and what could be done inside the prison walls. The new problem comprised the drug-abusers' inability to work (Nilsson 2013b, p. 149).[15]

An Alien Threat

A chief argument for keeping the vagrancy law was its assumed deterrent effect on work aversion—a line of reasoning that spilled over on drug policy since one aspect that made drugs so dangerous was that drug-use implied escapism (Edman 2012, p. 99). Just as vagrancy had been seen as a threat against the strivings of the conscientious worker, did drug-abuse pose a similar threat since it implied a will to escape or avoid the humdrumness of the working man's everyday life. The problematizations of the drug-user thus came to share common features with the vagrant: work aversion and/or an inability to work. And just as the vagrant was alien to the Swedish society and culture, so too were drugs and drug-users something alien. Narcotics was not only something alien to Swedish culture, it was also framed during the 1970s and 80s as a threat against the nation and the Swedish welfare state (Edman 2012, pp. 404–405).

---

[14] The treatment programs in Swedish prisons that were started during the 1970s were directed at drug-abuse. See Bruhn et al., in this edition.

[15] Work training had been an essential part of the rehabilitative work with alcoholics since the early 20th century. Learning to labor became important when it came to drug treatment as well (Edman 2012, pp. 183–185).

Drug Policy as Social Policing

What I want to capture with the culture of intervention concept is a process that facilitates the development of a just and egalitarian welfare society, while at the same time assenting to the use of invasive, coercive and intrusive measures against those who break the conditional social contract. As pointed out above, social policing was framed as a means of reaching those who did not voluntarily submit to the corrective techniques of the welfare state.[16] This rationale has come to permeate Swedish drug policy after 1980, making a punitive policy both a viable as well as a reasonable means to reach the overarching ideal of the drug-free society (Edman 2012 Victor 2007; Lenke and Olsson 2003).

Harm reduction has just about no proponents within Swedish politics.[17] The drug-free society is the goal and a zero-tolerance policy is the means (Linton 2015). The repressive handling of the drug-user gets its rationale not only from the assumed effect of decreasing the recruitment of new drug-users—equally important seems to be the "idea" of social policing, where the harassment of the drug-user is meant to make him/her stop their abuse and seek help. This tough love, this embracement of the Swedish welfare state has led to situations where drug-users let their friends die of overdoses—since calling an ambulance also means that the police will show up.

The Swedish prison is a place where drug-abuse is a common theme, and some 70 percent of the culprits have an addiction (SPPS 1). Of the ones serving prison time more than 50 percent serve time for drug related crimes (SPPS 2). Interestingly enough: the tendencies toward alternative treatment forms, however weak, that allow for substitute drugs, has not made its way into the prison. According to Nylander et al., harm reduction is not much of a topic within the Swedish prison

---

[16] According to Björkman (2001, pp. 282–284) not subordinating oneself to care deemed appropriate by the authorities became proof of negligent living, thus necessitating forced measures.

[17] While writing this UN's High Commissioner for Human Rights have has just criticized Swedish drug policy for violating basic human rights. (SR 2015).

and probation services (Nylander et al. 2012, p. 571).[18] Nylander et al. conclude that the politically all embraced hard lined Swedish drug policy "(. . .) is even more restrictive in Swedish prisons" (p. 572).

The Welfare State—A Liberal Project?

When Barker summarizes that the social democratic welfare state is not the road to a just and equal penal order, her argument rests on an ideological understanding of liberalism—an understanding that is essential to liberalisms self-understanding. Liberalism depicts itself as a restriction on government—a sound government is not to infringe upon the freedom and liberties of its subjects. As Foucault (1997) and those following and developing his concept of governmentality (Rose et al. 2006) has shown, liberalism is better understood as a practice of governing. Instead of freedom and liberties being something essential that liberalism protects, freedom and liberties becomes means of governing—governing through freedom. In this sense the social democratic welfare state is also a liberal project. In the social democratic welfare state freedom becomes being free to work and support oneself. Not doing so, however, is misusing ones freedom—thus opening up for state intervention in the name of freedom. However, there seems to be something more at play here. It is neither saving nor reintegrating the vagrant or the drug-addict for the conventional society that is at stake here—but the building of a social democratic Sweden. The welfare state is a nationalistic project and the people's home concept also became the social democrats road from internationalism to nationalism. Consequently, the vagrancy law and Swedish drug policy became part of a public health perspective that placed the care of the population at the heart of matters. The individuals rights are overridden by a greater good—that of the people. Society must be defended against any threats against its existence. What we have here according to Foucault is thus a race-struggle rationale that that overrides the law rationale.

---

[18] According to Bruhn et al. (this edition) treatment programs also facilitate an increased control of the prisoners.

Law vs. History

Liberal democracies rest on the assumption that the law and the courts are neutral means for conflict-resolution. This rationale is thought to permeate the actions of the state and as means of legitimization it make transgressions of it into troublesome normative questions like: How come that most former colonial states seems to have an un-proportionate high number of ethnic minorities in prison? Questions like this cannot, I think, be answered by scrutinizing the manifest legitimacy of democracies, i.e. that the rule of law prevails. In *Society must be defended*, Foucault instead traces the legacy of the democratic nation state to a race struggle. Instead of accepting the history writing of the sovereign, a history in which the nation is founded by a lawmaker, Foucault shows, by way of the race war, how the idea of the nation is instigated by way of a struggle between different groups. In France it's the Gaul's against the Frank's, in England it is the Normand against the Saxon (Foucault 2003).

Instead of asking how a seemingly just and lenient democratic state, such as Sweden, can come to use such repressive means to further its ends, I think it more constructive to ask: what kind of rationalization facilitates a social democratic culture of intervention? My answer is that it is a historical legacy based on a notion of "race struggle" that does this. What are the vagrants and the drug-abusers? They are something alien to Swedishness. What is drug-use and what is idleness? They are threats against a sound Swedish youth, potential corrupters of the heirs of Swedishness. The social democratic adoption of the people's home meant a nationalization of socialism, consequently transforming socialism from something alien to Swedish society, becoming instead an essential part of the manifest destiny of Sweden.[19] The conscientious worker and the teleological history writing of the Social democrats are ways of transforming class-war into race war, and the social democrats into the defenders of a historical legacy tied to the birth of the nation—Swedish society must be defended.

---

[19] Communism, with its internationalism, on the other hand is something utterly alien to Swedish society. It is thus no surprise that it was not the Nazis but the communists that were detained in camps in Sweden during WW II.

Final Remarks

Sweden has decreased its prison-population the last 5 years. Both the numbers admitted to prison and the numbers serving at a given time (1 October 2014) is down.[20] The reduced admittance-rate seems to, in part, be due to a crime-drop, whereas the reduction in serving at a given time seem to be caused by a changed courts praxis.[21] In both cases drug crime stands out. The number admitted due to drug crime is up, reflecting the effort the police put on drug crime (Bruhn et al., this edition), whereas the numbers serving at a given time for drug crime is down due to the changed court praxis.[22] Both the prior and the acting minister of justice view the decreased prison-population as failure for Swedish crime policy and the drug war Swedish style does not seem to have an end in sight. Facilitating all of this is, as I see it, a culture of intervention based on a race war rationale. Drugs are alien to that which is Swedish and the war on drugs seems to have no end due to it being fought to keep the nation safe and to protect the future generations.[23]

References

Ambjörnsson, R. (1988). *Den skötsamme arbetaren: idéer och ideal i ett norrländskt sågverkssamhälle 1880–1930*. Stockholm: Carlsson.

Andersson, R. (2002). *Kriminalpolitikens väsen*. Diss. Stockholm: Stockholms Universitet.

---

[20] Admission to prison is down 16 % whereas serving at a given time is down 22 % since 2005, according to the Swedish crime prevention council. Sveriges officiella statistik. Kriminalvård: slutlig statistik för 2014.

[21] In 2011 the Supreme Court changed the praxis concerning drug crime and lowered it considerably.

[22] Kriminalvård: slutlig statistik för (2014, p. 10).

[23] The success of Swedish drug policy is measured in terms of numbers of new drug-users. Keeping the number down is what it is all about. This line of reasoning is, however, built on the assumption that drugs produce a new group of people—the drug abuser. Lenke shows that this is built on a misconception since drugs rather mean a change of substance from alcohol to drugs.

Andersson, R (2012). A blessing in disguise – The ADHD-diagnoses and Swedish correctional treatment policy in the 21st century. In T. Ugelvik, & J. Dullum, (Eds.), *Penal exceptionalism? Nordic prison policy and practice.* London: Routledge.

Andersson, R. & Nilsson, R. (2009). *Svensk kriminalpolitik.* Stockholm: Liber.

Barker, V. (2013). Nordic Exceptionalism revisited: Explaining the paradox of a Janus-faced penal regime. *Theoretical Criminology, 17*(1), 5–25, February 2013.

Björkman, J. (2001). *Vård för samhällets bästa: debatten om tvångsvård i svensk lagstiftning 1850–1970.* Diss. Uppsala: Uppsala Universitet.

Dannefjord, P. (2009). *Organisationspraktiker och målförändring: exemplet svensk socialdemokrati.* Diss. Växjö: Växjö universitet.

Davidsson, T. (2015). *Understödets rationalitet: En genealogisk studie av arbetslinjen under kapitalismen.* Diss. Göteborg: Göteborgs universitet.

Edman, J. (2008). Lösdriverilagen och den samhällsfarliga lättjan. In H. Swärd, & M.A. Egerö, (Eds.), *Villkorandets politik – Fattigdomens premisser och samhällets åtgärder – då och nu.* Malmö: Egalitet.

Edman, J. (2012). *Vård & ideologi: narkomanvården som politiskt slagfält.* Umeå: Boréa.

Faubion, J. (Ed.). (1997). *Ethics,subjectivity and truth: Essential works of Foucault 1954–1984,* vol. 1. New York: New Press.

Foucault, M (1994). *Dits et écrits: 1954–1988. 4, 1980–1988.* Paris: Gallimard

Foucault, M. (1997). Security, territory and population. In J. Faubion, (Ed.), *Ethics, subjectivity and truth: Essential works of Foucault 1954–1984,* vol. 1. New York: New Press.

Foucault, M. (2003). *Society must be defended: lectures at the collège de France, 1975–76.* New York: Picador.

Frykman, J. & Löfgren, O. (1979). *Den kultiverade människan,* 1. uppl., LiberLäromedel, Lund.

Jansson, J. (2012). *Manufacturing consensus: the making of the Swedish reformist working class.* Diss. Uppsala: Uppsala universitet.

Junestav, Malin. (2008). Arbetslinjen i sociallagstiftningen – från nödhjälp till aktivitetsgaranti. In H. Swärd, & M.A. Egerö, (Eds.), *Villkorandets politik – Fattigdomens premisser och samhällets åtgärder – då och nu.* Malmö: Egalitet.

Kriminalvård: Slutlig statstik för 2014.

Lenke, L (2009). Dryckes mönster, nykterhetsrörelser och narkotikapolitik. In von H. Hofer, (Ed.), *Leif Lenke in memoriam: valda skrifter.* Stockholm: Kriminologiska institutionen, Stockholms universitet.

Lenke, L. & Olsson, B. (2003). Den narkotikapolitiska relevansen av narkoti-karelaterade dödsfall. In H. Tham (Ed.), *Forskare om narkotikapolitiken.* Stockholm: Kriminologiska institutionen, Stockholms universitet.

Lindblad, H. & Lundkvist, S. (1996). *Tusen nyktra: 100 år med riksdagens nykterhetsgrupper.* Stockholm: Sober.

Linderborg, Å. (2001). *Socialdemokraterna skriver historia: historieskrivning som ideologisk maktresurs 1892–2000.* Diss. Uppsala: Uppsala Universitet.

Linton, M. (2015). *Knark: en svensk historia.* Stockholm: Atlas.

Lundeberg, U. & Åmark, K. (2001). Social rights and social security: The Swedish welfare state, 1900–2000. *Scandinavian Journal of History, 26*(3), 157–176.

Nilsson, R. (2003). *Kontroll, makt och omsorg: Sociala problem och socialpolitik i Sverige 1780–1940.* Lund: Studentlitteratur.

Nilsson, R. (2013a). Parasiter i folkhemmet: Svartsjöanstaltens sista lösdrivare. In S. Holmlund, & A. Sandén, (Eds.), *Usla, elända och arma: samhällets utsatta under 700 år.* Stockholm: Natur & kultur.

Nilsson, R. (2013b). *Från cellfängelse till beteendeterapi: fängelse, kriminalpolitik och vetande 1930–1980.* Malmö: Égalité.

Nylander, P-Å., Holm, C., Jukic, E. & Lindbergd, O. (2012). Drug treatment in Swedish prisons – moving towards evidence-based interventions? *Nordic Studies on Alcohol and Drugs, 29*(6), 561–74.

Nyzell, S. (2009). *Striden ägde rum i Malmö: Möllevångskravallerna 1926: en studie av politiskt våld i mellankrigstidens Sverige.* Diss. Lund: Lunds universitet.

Qvarsell, R. (2008) De fattigas vård i 1910-talets Sverige. In H. Swärd, & M.A. Egerö, (Eds.), *Villkorandets politik – Fattigdomens premisser och samhällets åtgärder – då och nu.* Malmö: Egalitet.

Petersson, B. (1983). Den farliga underklassen: studier i fattigdom och brott-slighet i 1800-talets Sverige = ["The dangerous classes": studies in poverty and crime in nineteenth-century Sweden]. Diss. Umeå: Umeå Universitet.

Rose, N., Valverde, M. & O´Malley, P. (2006). Governmentality. *Annual Reveiw of Law and Society, 2*, 83–104.

SPPS 1 https://www.kriminalvarden.se/forskning-och-statistik/statistik-och-fakta/narkotika-och-missbruk/ (2015-09-04). Om andelen missbrukare inom kriminalvården.

SPPS 2 https://www.kriminalvarden.se/globalassets/publikationer/forskningsrap porter/langtidsdomda-man-och-kvinnor-i-sverigepdf. (2015-09-04) Andelen dömda för narkotika – straff över fyra år.

SR 2015 http://sverigesradio.se/sida/artikel.aspx?programid=2054&artikel=6299618 (visited 2015-11-12).

SOU 1939:25. *Betänkande med förslag till lag om arbetsfostran m. m.. 1937 års lösdriverilagstiftningskommitté.* Stockholm: Nord. Bokh.

SOU 1958:34. *Socialpolis och kvinnlig polis: betänkande.* Polisverksamhetsutredningen. Stockholm: Esselte.

SOU 1962:22. *Samhällsfarlig asocialitet: betänkande.* Stockholm: Esselte.

SOU 1977:40. *Socialtjänst och socialförsäkringstillägg: lagar och motiv: Socialutredningens slutbetänkande.* Stockholm: Liber Förlag.

Svanström, Y. (2006). Prostitution as Vagrancy: Sweden 1923–1964. In *Journal of Scandinavian Studies in Criminology and Crime Prevention, 7*(2), 142–163.

Tydén, M. (2000). *Från politik till praktik: de svenska steriliseringslagarna 1935–1975: rapport till 1997 års steriliseringsutredning.* Stockholm: Fritzes.

Victor, D. (2007). Narkotika brottslighetens gärningsmän och offer. In H. von Hofer, & A. Nilsson, (Eds.), *Brott i välfärden: om brottslighet, utsatthet och kriminalpolitik: festskrift till Henrik Tham.* Stockholm: Kriminologiska institutionen, Stockholms universitet.

Zander, U. (2001). *Fornstora dagar, moderna tider: bruk av och debatter om svensk historia från sekelskifte till sekelskifte.* Diss. Lund: Lunds Universitet.

Part III

The Scandinavian Model:
From Remand to Release

Punishment Without Conviction? Scandinavian Pre-trial Practices and the Power of the "Benevolent" State

Peter Scharff Smith

It is August 2015 and I am sitting in East Jutland prison in Denmark in the middle of a focus group interview with long-term prisoners several of who have sentences running in double digits. This is one of the most modern high-security facilities in all of the Danish penal estate and the prisoners we talk to have generally been imprisoned for many years. I am together with two American research colleagues who are asking the prisoners about how they experience punishment in the Danish penal system.[1] The prisoners respond by talking about two things: the lack of contact with their families and, especially, their experiences sitting in a remand prison awaiting their

---

[1] I helped Keramet Reiter, Lori Sexton and Jennifer Sumner plan and conduct this research visit as part of their study of imprisonment in Denmark. They write about this and other prison visits in Denmark elsewhere in this volume.

P.S. Smith (✉)
Department of Criminology and Sociology of Law, University of Oslo, Oslo, Norway
e-mail: p.s.smith@jus.uio.no

© The Author(s) 2017
P. Scharff Smith, T. Ugelvik (eds.), *Scandinavian Penal History, Culture and Prison Practice*, Palgrave Studies in Prisons and Penology, DOI 10.1057/978-1-137-58529-5_6

trial. Directly questioned "what is punishment?" one prisoner simply answer "B and B", which refers to the special restrictions on visits and correspondence which the Danish legal system allows during pre-trial (field notes 2015).[2] The reason is not that these inmates have recently left remand imprisonment; it is simply because they seem to have had their worst and toughest prison experience there before they were even sentenced. Their current stay under maximum security conditions feels much less like punishment to these prisoners.

Such a reaction comes as no surprise to me after having surveyed and interviewed numerous prisoners and prison staff in the Danish system—during remand, as sentenced prisoners, and later post-release—and after having studied Danish remand practice for several years. As one Danish remand prisoner simply concludes, "Those, who have not yet been sentenced, they live under very poor conditions—much worse than those, the sentenced prisoners live under" (Interview, remand prisoner). In the words of a former Danish prison governor, "we cannot begin to understand the humiliation, which it is [remand imprisonment]. One has to ask permission for everything, even to be allowed to go to the bathroom."[3]

As I will show in this chapter remand imprisonment is in fact the toughest and most restrictive prison experience in Denmark save for what is offered in a very limited number of special isolation units, most notably the small 24-cell prison called "Politigårdens fængsel" (the "Police station prison"[4]) and the "E unit" at East Jutland,[5] which could be termed as the closest we come to anything resembling Supermax conditions in a Danish context. As will be described later, there are in fact several important examples of Scandinavian pre-trial practices which seriously challenge the notion of Scandinavian penal exceptionalism. At first glance such practices seem to

---

[2] B and B means "Brev- og besøgskontrol" which translates into "control/surveillance of correspondence and visits."

[3] Ole Hansen cited in "Remand imprisonment is a punishment before conviction"; in: *Bladet Kriminalforsorgen*, no. 8, June 2011, p. 9.

[4] Although bearing such a name the facility is *not* for police detention—it is a prison administered by the Danish Prison and Probation Service which happens to be physically located in the same building as the Police headquarters in Copenhagen.

[5] Along with even smaller isolation units at other prisons.

have little to do with the "welfare" logic of Scandinavian welfare states but they illustrate the relatively far-reaching social control efforts inherent in these strong, ambitious and powerful states.

The purpose of shedding light on a number of Scandinavian pre-trial practices is by no means to criticize Scandinavian prison practice in general nor is it meant as an attempt to roll back the entire literature on Nordic penal exceptionalism. But it is an important empirical corrective to a literature which has generally ignored the fate and conditions of up to 1/3 of the Scandinavian prison populations and it is a way of highlighting aspects of Scandinavian practice which lie very far from the values and ideologies often associated with penal exceptionalism. These pre-trial interventions also make for an interesting case where punitive practices appear without any clear connection to the allegedly egalitarian logic of the welfare state. I could also have chosen to focus on several other Scandinavian prison practices which reveal much more liberal and humane intentions and practices than those described in this chapter. Some of these practices are addressed in detail elsewhere in this volume like, for instance, the principle of normalization (Engbo), the importance of open prisons (Fransen), the system of self-catering (Minke and Smoyer), and the ongoing attempt to balance "hard" and "soft" prison policies and practices (Reiter, Sexton and Sumner). In fact, I have myself worked extensively with reform projects together with the Danish prison service and have thereby become directly involved in influencing and creating Scandinavian prison practices—especially in connection with projects aimed at improving the situation and treatment of children of imprisoned parents. These projects might very well have been supported and enhanced by Scandinavian penal culture and are themselves interesting case studies in that regard. But that is a different story which I have discussed elsewhere (Smith 2014, 2015).

Scandinavian Exceptionalism and the Forgotten Remand Prisoners

Although remand prisoners suffer from poor conditions in many parts of the world one would perhaps expect that advanced and rich welfare states with inclusive and expansive social policies would have a different approach. Indeed, the problems associated with Scandinavian pre-trial practices are unlikely to be a product of insufficient resources or bureaucratic inefficiency as is the case in countries where criminal justice systems often suffer from a number of very basic flaws and structural problems (Open Society Justice Initiative 2014). In any case, empirical research has uncovered several peculiar examples of how Scandinavian pre-trial practices grant authorities very significant powers and routinely restrict the rights of the accused in ways which look quite remarkable also when compared with other jurisdictions.

It seems important if seemingly benevolent Scandinavian states routinely restrict the rights of untried citizens even more than those of sentenced prisoners. The principle of "presumption of innocence" is after all a very basic rule of law and human rights principle which is firmly rooted in a tradition going back to 18th-century enlightenment philosophy (see for example Beccaria 1998). European human rights standards in this area clearly underline that in "view of both the presumption of innocence and the presumption in favour of liberty, the remand in custody of persons suspected of an offence shall be the exception rather than the norm" (COE, Recommendation Rec(2006) 13, §3.1). This means that "remand in custody shall only be used when strictly necessary and as a measure of last resort; it shall not be used for punitive reasons" (COE, Recommendation Rec(2006)13, §3.3). This approach means that there should always be a presumption in favor of release during pre-trial which has been confirmed in several judgments by the European Court of Human Rights (ECHR) (Havre 2014, p. 5). Indeed, national criminal codes in democratic countries will often have provisions designed to limit the use of remand custody.[6] Furthermore, several European countries have not only ratified but also incorporated the European Convention on Human Rights into national law, which is the case in Norway, Sweden and Denmark. In reality, however, it can be very difficult for a judge to decide against the police in such matters and

---

[6] Concerning Denmark see the Administration of Justice Act §762, para. 3 and §765. Regarding the Norwegian case, see Havre (2014, p. 12 ff).

say that, for example, the risk of flight is not present as argued by the prosecution and, in any case, there is no guarantee that Scandinavian court practice actually follows the European human rights guidelines in this area. As I will return to below the result is that remand imprisonment is a routine practice used extensively in Denmark and by no means only as an "exception" or as a "last resort". In a thorough legal analysis and discussion of the Norwegian use of remand imprisonment, it has similarly been found that Norwegian court practice is out of sync with European human rights principles. According to this study, Norwegian courts simply "overlook" that the individual right to freedom and to human rights protection should be the main rule and that intervention and restrictions in the form of remand imprisonment should be the exception (Havre 2014, p. 318), a critique which seems to fit well with the argument that "limited" and "weak individual rights" might characterize Scandinavian states (as Barker argue in the case of Sweden; Barker 2012, p. 15 f.).

Nevertheless, most of the existing international literature has almost completely ignored the way that Scandinavian states allow police, courts and correctional services to operate before a sentence is passed. One illustration of this is the way that "out of cell time" in Scandinavian prisons has been praised as an example of humane prison practices. In one account it is for example argued that "prisoners in the Nordic countries [. . .] are likely to be out of their cells considerably longer than those in Anglophone systems" (Pratt and Eriksson 2013, p. 13). The homepage of the Swedish Correctional Service is used as a source to document this (a very trustful approach to scrutinizing prison conditions one might add) as it states that prisoners are woken at 7.00 am and lockdown is not until 8.00 pm in closed prisons and 10.00 pm in open prisons. But is this really the case throughout the Swedish prison estate? In fact, one quarter of the entire Swedish prison population—the remand prisoners—are left completely out of this equation although around two-thirds of these are subjected to "restrictions" which generally means solitary confinement and staying alone 22–24 hours in the cell (Åklagarmyndigheten 2014; Smith et al. 2013). This in other words means that around 1/8 of the entire Swedish prison population is kept in solitary confinement as I will return to below. A remarkable situation which of course cannot simply be ignored if one wants to meaningfully compare out of cell time and quality of prison life across jurisdictions.

In Norway, by contrast, the general situation is very different since many remand prisoners are treated just as sentenced prisoners and are often allowed to mix on the wings. This very likely means that untried prisoners generally have much better and more liberal conditions in Norway than they do in Denmark and Sweden—although the practice of mixing sentenced and untried prisoners actually run counter to the general human rights standards in the area.[7] Regardless, although the use of pre-trial solitary confinement has been brought down significantly in Norway, around 12–15 % of all remand prisoners are still placed in solitary confinement for the purpose of protecting the police investigation (Smith et al. 2013, p. 11). Importantly, this severe "Scandinavian way" of treating untried prisoners is not found in most other European countries. Still, a thorough study among remand prisoners in Oslo prison describe how these inmates have access to communal areas and activities although, nevertheless, "remand prisoners are locked up alone in their cells much of the day" (Ugelvik 2011, p. 48). An ambitious project at Oslo prison called "Quality in remand work" ("Kvalitet i varetektsarbeidet") was carried out some 10 years ago and clearly aimed at improving that particular problem. Nevertheless, the National Preventive Mechanism under the Norwegian Ombudsman confirm that this problem still exist and describe how prisoners—especially in the first phase of their imprisonment—often risk being locked up alone 22 hours or more in their cells. Such prisoners are in other words effectively in solitary confinement despite not being officially placed in any form of segregation or isolation (The Ombudsman, 5 April 2016[8]).

---

[7] See for example the European Prison Rules (CoE, Committee of Ministers, Recommendation Rec(2006)2), rule 18.8a, which clearly state that states "need to detain (...) untried prisoners separately from sentenced prisoners" (concerning possible exceptions see rule 18.9). Concerning living conditions for Norwegian remand prisoners, see Ugelvik (2014).

[8] https://www.sivilombudsmannen.no/aktuelt/aktivitetstilbud-og-tiltak-for-a-motvirke-isolasjon-article4346-2865.html

While it is certainly true that many Nordic prisons have very open regimes (exemplified especially by the widespread use of open prisons) this is not at all the case when it comes to remand imprisonment in Sweden and Denmark—and in Denmark 34 % of the entire prison population was made up by remand prisoners in 2015.[9] Empirically speaking, it is a significant shortcoming in much of the literature on Scandinavian exceptionalism that up to around 1/3 of the national prison populations and the conditions they are subjected to have been left out of consideration. Perhaps this lack of interest has something to do with the fact that the welfare state perspective has been important in much of this research (Cavadino and Dignan 2006; Pratt 2008a, b; Pratt and Eriksson 2013; Lappi-Seppälä 2007). One could argue that focusing on the welfare state (in a positive light) might turn attention towards sentenced prisoners where one would expect to find values and practices associated with the egalitarian and universalist welfare policies found in Scandinavia—such as a focus on rehabilitation and treatment as part of the process from sentence to release instead of purely punitive rationales with accompanying bleak and austere prison conditions.

Remand Practice and Welfare State Values

The positive values and practices often associated with Scandinavian and Nordic welfare state regimes are their *universalist* policies—that is benefits for all citizens (e.g. insurance for everyone and not only "means tested" interventions); their *egalitarian* policies and attempts to create *equality*; and along with that a focus on *solidarity* and being *inclusive*, thereby not excluding or marginalizing specific groups or individuals from mainstream society (Esping-Andersen 1995, p. 27 f.; Hilson 2013, p. 87; Lappi-Seppälä 2007, pp. 8 and 13; Kautto et al. 1999, p. 10 ff.) As discussed elsewhere in this volume it has been argued by several observers that these Scandinavian and Nordic welfare state values and

---

[9] The official 2015 statistics are currently not available, but the author has been supplied this information in an e-mail from the Danish Prison and Probation Services 26 January 2016.

policies have helped secure and maintain low prison population rates, humane prison conditions and a general commitment to rehabilitating and reintegrating offenders into society (see Smith and Ugelvik, this volume). In other words, such research suggests that "social and economic security, equality in welfare resources and generous welfare provision should contribute to lower levels of punitivity and repression" (Lappi-Seppälä 2007, p. 8).

If we are looking for inclusiveness, equality and solidarity in penal systems one could argue that it makes sense to focus on how and to what degree *sentenced* prisoners are treated and reintegrated into society, while the primary concern with *untried* prisoners would normally be to establish whether they are guilty or not. In legal terms, one could even argue that untried prisoners fall completely outside the field of penology since they have not been subjected to punishment, a sanction or a penalty (Morgenstern 2013, p. 193). In rights based terms, one could also argue that submitting remand prisoners—who have not yet been found guilty of a crime—to rehabilitation and treatment for criminal behavior would be unjust and perhaps even abusive (this is for example why remand prisoners in Denmark are allowed but not required to work, whereas sentenced prisoners have a duty to work or take an education). In other words, why look for rehabilitation, attempts at social re-integration, or punitive intentions for that matter, at this stage of the criminal justice system? However, the problem with such a line of reasoning is that it does not take actual remand prison conditions and other pre-trial practices into consideration including the way that these are sometimes misused by authorities and often perceived as punishment by those on the receiving end (Morgenstern 2013, p. 194). In fact, the time spent in remand imprisonment will often constitute some or even all of the prison sentence which many receive after their trial and thereby pre-trial imprisonment becomes de facto punishment, something which seems to be a significant problem in Denmark and Norway (Havre 2014, p. 177 f. and 318 f.; Smith and Jakobsen, forthcoming).

From a legal point of view, there certainly is a significant difference between remand imprisonment and the imprisonment of sentenced prisoners. In Denmark the latter is regulated through the Act on the Execution of Sentences ("Straffuldbyrdelsesloven"), while remand imprisonment is regulated by the Administration of Justice Act ("Retsplejeloven"). Apart from the ever-present security aspect the Act on the Execution of Sentences stipulate rehabilitation of offenders as an important objective and so does the "Program of Principles" of the Danish Prison and Probation Services (Engbo 2005, p. 46). Both these sources of law clearly state that sentenced prisoners should receive help and support in order to be rehabilitated and reintegrated into society—but this is not an objective in the same way when it comes to remand prisoners. The reasons for depriving the latter of their liberty are primarily based on the logic and rationale that the police will need to detain and restrict the communication of accused individuals in order to investigate their possible crimes and secure the pursuit of justice.

This does not mean that the welfare provisions of the Scandinavian welfare states are invisible during remand. The administrative Remand Imprisonment Regulations (known as "Varetægtsbekendtgørelsen") states that the Prison and Probation Service shall support remand prisoners in order to reduce the negative impact of imprisonment (§30), and remand prisoners of course have access to medical treatment (§31). The extent to which the latter is sufficiently available given the frequency of (mental) health problems among prisoners is, however, a discussion in itself. One area where significant ground has been gained in remand prisons is drug treatment which can clearly be understood as being part of a general welfare policy—although prison-based drug treatment can also be perceived as being part of a disciplinary discourse aimed at criminalizing social problems rather than empowering individuals (Kolind, this volume. See also Bruhn, Lindberg and Nylander, this volume). In any case a Danish remand prisoner has a right to receive drug treatment (§32) and an impressive 1,069 remand prisoners completed a so-called pre-treatment program for drug abusers in 2014 (Løppenthin 2015, p. 21). But despite such initiatives the reality is that most of a remand prisoners' day is typically spend locked up in the cell. With the notable exception of especially drug treatment there is generally very little focus on rehabilitative interventions. However, another well-known but sometimes downplayed trait of the Scandinavian welfare state regimes is clearly present pre-trial, perhaps especially so in Sweden and Denmark: that is the extensive willingness of these states to intervene deeply and with great strength into the lives of their citizens.

Scandinavian Pre-sentence Practices—A Few Examples

There are several examples of how Scandinavian state power can be deployed with significant force and somewhat limited regard to rule of law and human rights principles even before a pre-trial detainee is placed in a remand prison. We see this with certain police practices and the legal context within which they take place. For example, and quite interestingly, the history of the Danish police complaints mechanism illustrate how the Danish state has been extremely reluctant to introduce basic democratic and rule of law principles into the complaints handling process. In fact, it was up until 1996 the case that all complaints over police conduct had to be delivered to a police station, and while the State Attorney in 1996 took over complaint handling from the local Police Commissioner, it was in practice still often police officers who investigated colleagues and complaints over police conduct still had to be handed in at a police station (Amnesty International 2008, p. 13 ff.). After decades of discussions and criticisms, a new system with an independent complaints handling mechanism was introduced in 2012, although this model and its decisions has already been criticized for lacking a critical approach.

Another example of extensive police powers in Scandinavian states is the use of police detention cells in Norway. Here solitary confinement is automatically used during police custody—before and very often also after the detained person has been before a judge. The cells, which are used for all kinds of police detention, are typically more or less similar to security and observation cells in prison—that is strip cells with no real furniture, no accessible light source for the prisoner etc.—and are sometimes even without windows. In principle, people detained by the police should be transferred to a regular prison within 48 hours, but this deadline does not apply if there is a shortage of prison space. As a result,

20–40 % of those who are later transferred to remand imprisonment have been in solitary confinement for more than 48 hours in police custody and occasionally for periods up to 10 days (Smith et al. 2013, p. 12). There is no warrant for solitary confinement and no assessment is made of the need for isolation—it is simply the way that the system works when the police take a citizen into custody. This particular use of solitary confinement likely involves systematic violations of the ECHR and indeed the Norwegian state was in 2014 found in breach of article 14 (ad art. 8) in the ECHR in a case about the effects of solitary confinement in police detention in Oslo (*Stamnes v. Norway* 2014). In comparison, the use of solitary confinement during police detention seems to be an unknown problem in Denmark, where suspects are normally put before a judge and transferred to a regular remand prison within 24 hours (Smith et al. 2013, p. 12). In Sweden however, solitary confinement also regularly occur during police custody normally for up to 4 days. This practice routinely involves even detained children (Barnombudsmannen 2013).

Historically the use of solitary confinement in remand prisons during pre-trial has been widespread in Norway, Sweden and Denmark and has been termed a "peculiarly Scandinavian phenomenon" (Evans and Morgan 1998, p. 247) which since the 1990s has attracted significant international human rights criticism (Smith 2012). The official purpose of this practice is to avoid collusion—that is to prevent the detainee from influencing the investigation. I have described this practice and its history in detail elsewhere (Smith 2006, 2011; Smith and Koch 2015). The purpose of the following paragraphs is to briefly describe the current magnitude of this practice in Sweden where solitary confinement during remand imprisonment continues to be used with a very high frequency.

In 2014 the office of the Swedish prosecution for the first time gathered thorough statistics on the actual use of restrictions during remand. The result was astonishing and revealed that 70 % of all remand prisoners during 2013 had "restrictions" and these inmates where thereby typically locked up in solitary confinement (6,558 out of 9,415 remand prisoners). Among the 15–17 years old, the percentage was 82 and thereby even higher (Åklagarmyndigheten 2014, p. 91). Remand prisoners make up around 25 % of all prisoners in Sweden and as already mentioned this means that around 1/8 of the entire Swedish prison population is placed in solitary confinement (and then we haven't even begun to count all the other forms of solitary confinement used for sentenced prisoners). I wonder if it is possible to find a similar situation in any other prison system in the world?

We are, however, not dealing with a new phenomenon but rather a very old practice which has historical roots in the 19th century (Smith 2005, 2006; Horn 2015). That children are subjected to these methods have also been publicly known for some years. When the CPT visited Sweden and went to Gothenburg remand prison in 2009, for example, they were "particularly concerned by the fact that all juvenile prisoners interviewed (. . .) had been subject to restrictions (in particular no association with other prisoners and no visits) for two to three months". CPT described such practice as "draconian" and observed that prisoners were damaged by the effects of solitary confinement (CPT 2009). Furthermore, in 2013 the Swedish Children's Ombudsman described in a report how children are routinely put in solitary confinement, both during police custody and during remand imprisonment in Sweden, and that they are treated in a "completely unacceptable" manner that denotes a "systematic and far-reaching failure to observe detained children's basic human rights" (Barnombudsmannen 2013).

Danish Remand Practice

Like Sweden, and Norway for that matter, Denmark has had a history of extensive use of solitary confinement during the remand phase—that is, solitary confinement used according to the Administration of Justice Act in order to protect the ongoing police investigation (there are several other forms of solitary confinement used in prisons). But unlike in Sweden this has been a heavily debated issue nationally since the late 1970s and during the last four decades this practice has been gradually reformed in Denmark. Accordingly, the Administration of Justice Act has been changed in this specific regard four times during this period—in 1978, 1984, 2000 and 2006. The reforms have had a very gradual but significant impact and while more than 40 % of all remand prisoners were placed in solitary confinement during the latter part of the 1970s this percentage has recently dropped below one (Smith 2005; Smith and Koch 2015). Accordingly, in 2014 a mere 0.7 % of all remand prisoners were placed in this particular kind of court ordered solitary confinement (to protect the police investigation) with an average duration of 19 days.[10]

Seen from the point of view of creating humane Scandinavian prison practices this development is a very significant achievement. But the question of course remains which remand regime you will actually find if you go beyond these figures and traverse the walls into a Danish remand prison. In fact, and in spite of the above-mentioned reforms, there is still a significant probability that you as a pre-trial prisoner will sit in your cell for up to 23 hours a day and sometimes alone. There is in other words still a lot of isolation in the Danish remand prison system. In reality prisoners are not guaranteed much more than an hour of social interaction with other prisoners during the daily exercise (unless they are in court ordered solitary confinement where exercise is solitary). Work, education and exercise can for some remand prisoners result in social contact with the other inmates but this is far from always the case. Thanks to the work of private entrepreneurs and a sufficiently flexible attitude within the Danish Prison and Probation Service there are a number of very innovative initiatives in this area, including for example a cooking school at Vestre prison (remand), which has been very well evaluated (Minke and Balvig 2015). Typically, however, to the degree that any work is available at all it will often be solitary and take place in the cell. In some places and for some remand prisoners an hour or so of indoor exercise will allow contact with one or two other inmates but often this will not be the case. In some of the big remand prisons there are more available activities with somewhat better opportunities for social contact but a typical day for many remand prisoners will be spent mainly alone in the cell. A contributing factor is the remand prison buildings which are typically constructed as isolation prisons—due to the above-mentioned history of this practice—why they simply do not have proper facilities for communal activities. Furthermore,

---

[10] See: http://www.anklagemyndigheden.dk/nyheder/Sider/Fald-baade-i-antallet-af-langvarige-var etaegtsfaengslinger-og-i-antallet-af-varetaegtsfaengslinger-i-isolation.aspx

if you compare the situation of remand prisoners with sentenced prisoners the access to meaningful activities and possibilities for making future plans are extremely limited. No "sentence plans" with rehabilitative and/or re-integrative interventions will be prepared during this phase and most remand prisoners have little idea of when their case will be settled and when they will get out or get a sentence.[11]

The primary tool for social interaction in the Danish remand prisons which keep the majority of inmates from ending up in outright solitary confinement is the possibility of time-limited cell community—that is spending some time in a cell together with a fellow prisoner. In this regard, the Danish Prison and Probation Service do a significant job in quite difficult circumstances to ensure that a lot of prisoners are allowed a limited amount of social contact. The concept of cell community is however practised in different ways with very diverse results. First of all, there is a large group who are not at all part of a cell community—according to a survey of 230 remand prisoners this group constitute between 27 % and 30 % of all remand prisoners. Those who are allowed cell community have an average of 3.3 hours community. If one compares these figures with the remand prisoner's opportunities for access to social interaction outside the cells (which *can* include work, exercise, yard time, education and other program activities), then it is possible to estimate the overall level of isolation experienced in Danish remand prisons. In the survey of 230 remand prisoners such an analysis revealed that 6 % were in de facto solitary confinement (22–24 hours of solitude in the cell), while nearly 18 % would spend 20–24 hours alone in the cell each day—regardless of whether or not they are placed in any kind of official isolation (court ordered solitary confinement, disciplinary solitary confinement or other forms of administrative isolation). Mainly due to the practice of time limited cell community the rest of the remand prisoners would have access to a bit more social contact but the vast majority would still experience being locked up in their cell for the major part of the day. In addition a

---

[11] The above is based on information gathered during an ongoing research project on remand imprisonment in Denmark (by Peter Scharff Smith and Janne Jakobsen), which is based on surveys, interviews (prisoners and staff) and other field work.

large quantity of the inmates at some point or another during their remand imprisonment actually experience being officially placed in solitary confinement in the form of disciplinary sanctions, other forms of administrative isolation or even so-called voluntary isolation. In the above survey, 31.7 % had experienced on average 31 days in various forms of official solitary confinement during their current remand imprisonment.

Taken together, the relatively high levels of isolation, the lack of meaningful activities and the uncertainty of the whole situation creates anxiety and place remand prisoners in a kind of limbo. Accordingly, boredom and lack of agency are recurrent themes when inmates are asked.[12] One remand prisoner simply state that "to little happens and you are locked up to much of the time" (Survey, respondent no. 83). A remand prison officer agrees and states that "too many sit behind a closed door 23-hours a day" (Survey, prison staff). A female remand prisoner in her 30s vividly describe the complete lack of agency and feeling of helplessness which she experience every day on remand: "Everything is taken care off instead of you being able to do it yourself. You are not supposed to do anything at all and you do not have a say in anything. You have no responsibility—you have no agency. Your identity is being peeled off" (Interview, remand prisoner).

Contact with Relatives and the World Outside

The worst part of being in remand prison is definitely the social violence, the social isolation. You are torn away from everything. You can't keep in touch with your family—the visits are rare and under surveillance, the letters take forever to arrive, you can't make a phone call. You are isolated from the life you had before. It is of course the same in a prison, but it is on completely different scale when you are in a remand prison. It is more absolute. (Interview, former remand prisoner)

---

[12] Survey and interviews conducted 2013–15 by Peter Scharff Smith and Janne Jakobsen.

The possibilities for remand prisoners in Denmark to keep in contact with their relatives and with people on the outside are extremely poor. They may write letters but do not, as a rule, have access to telephones and they have a right to receive visits for only half an hour a week (minimum). Most prisoners also experience great trouble in communicating via ordinary mail because they are subjected to special restrictions. For the majority of remand prisoners, visits can only take place once a week and will last for up to an hour or only the 30 minutes that they have a right to. In addition, a majority of the remand prisoners are subjected to special restrictions which mean that visits are conducted under surveillance of a police officer (or occasionally a prison officer) and often only allowed during mid-day, when most people work and children attend school. Taken together, these circumstances result in a very low overall frequency of visits. According to a 2011 survey study from the Danish Prison Service, 41 % of remand prisoners had never received visits from their family and 74 % had not received visits from friends. Furthermore, data covering 1,164 remand prisoners revealed that they had received on average only 1.6 visits from their family during, on average, 116 days in remand prison. A small group of 14 % had received visits from their family 4 times or more, while the rest had received less or no visits at all from their family (Clausen 2013, p. 147, table 4.68).

Special Restrictions—The "Correspondence and Visit Control" Regime

I was subjected to Correspondence and Visit control the first year. It does something to you, mentally. It is difficult to recover from. (Interview, remand prisoner)

Besides the few and short visits, the only method of communication with families and friends which remand prisoners in Denmark have a legal right to, is sending and receiving letters. However, remand prisoners can be subjected to "Correspondence and Visit control" (Bekendtgørelse om ophold i varetægt § 44 og § 62; Administration of Justice Act §§ 771 og 772). This type of control is very restrictive but is nevertheless being applied without any official statistics being produced regularly. Figures obtained from the Prison Service in 2010 and in 2013 show that around 70 % of all prisoners in the category "custody before sentence" (i.e. remand prisoners) were subjected to this type of control on the specific dates where the data was gathered. In the above-mentioned survey of 230 remand prisoners, 84 % of the respondents who answered this question (4 % did not answer) claimed that they were or had been subjected to correspondence and visit control during their current imprisonment on remand. These remand prisoners had on average been subjected to such control in 141 days. Significantly lower, but still very high, percentages are found in a recent dataset from a different source, namely the police, which state that 2.567 remand prisoners were subjected to correspondence and visit control during 2015, which corresponds to 45 % of all remand prisoners.[13] In any case, we are clearly *not* dealing with a tool, which the police only use in particularly substantial or difficult cases—it is a routinely applied measure.

When a remand prisoner is subjected to correspondence and visit control, it means that all visits will be conducted under close surveillance by a police- or prison officer who will be present in the visiting room, during the entire visit. The police officer shall ensure that the remand prisoner does not speak about his or her case, which means that the remand prisoner may not tell the visitor what has happened and what he or she is accused of, which can be very frustrating for both prisoner and family. In the survey of 230 remand prisoners, 84 % (of those who answered) responded that they find these types of visits uncomfortable and an even higher percentage responded that adult visitors and visiting children found the situation uncomfortable. According to a female relative, most of the police officers controlling the visits "are ok. They just sit and read and the like. They just look up from the newspaper if

---

[13] The Ministry of Justice (Retsudvalget 2015–16, L80 endeligt svar på spørgsmål 4), 26 January 2016.

they think that you are talking about something they don't want you to. I had to adjust to it. They hear everything you say. And some of them look at you in a strange way, like: why do you bother with that fool?" (Interview, remand prisoner's relative). Lasse, a 24-year-old remand prisoner, recounts: "Some of the police officers keep a distance, don't interfere. Others sit at the end of the table and meddle in the conversation. And there is not any physical contact at all. Not even when people have children. That's sick, if you're not allowed to give your kid a hug" (Interview, remand prisoner).

Correspondence will also be subject to a special control regime if you are subjected to "B and B". This means that the prisoners' letters will be read by the police, something which many of the remand prisoners experience as very uncomfortable. Furthermore, this control regime means that letters will often be delayed for around three weeks, which obviously makes this type of correspondence extremely problematic and typically completely inadequate in a stressful situation of emotional and often economic crisis for prisoners and their families. A woman, whose husband was held in remand, recounts: "The most frustrating thing about the letters is that it takes such long time, before you receive an answer, when you write. You think: has he received the letter? Why haven't I heard anything?" (Interview, prisoner's relative).

Remand prisoners are for the most part subjected to correspondence and visit control in order to protect the police investigation while in a few cases the risk of flight or new crimes being committed are listed as motivation for the restrictions. Like the reasons for using remand imprisonment, we are dealing with methods, motives and mechanisms which have nothing to do with any kind of welfare provisions or welfare logic. Nor is the logic punitive as such although the result is. It is simply a matter of granting the police power to conduct its business without interference. Whether or how these restrictions work as a police investigation tool has never been studied or evaluated and the Danish state has so far showed little interest in applying a serious principle of proportionality and balancing act in this area. When asking prisoners, they often do not understand why restrictions should be necessary in their case and there is a common understanding that the use of these measures is merely a matter of harassment or outright pressure. One remand prisoner even recounts that he experienced being teased with a possibility of having more contact with his family if only he would confess: "The police use Correspondence and Visit control as a way to break me. Because then I can have more visits. The police officer who is connected to my case—I told him that I think that it is poor manners to keep the children away from me for so long. What I am told is: 'confess, and it will get easier' " (Interview, remand prisoner). The prisoners are quite often supported in this criticism by both prison staff and defence lawyers. A high-ranking Prison Service staff member for example states that "Correspondence and Visit control is used as leverage by the police" (interview). If that is the case we are not dealing with welfare ideology, nor rule of law principles or modern power technology in a Foucauldian sense for that matter, but simply traditional sovereign state power applied against an often weak and vulnerable group of citizens. The Danish police has never admitted using restrictions coercively during remand, unlike in Norway where a senior police officer in 1993 in fact acknowledged "the use of such psychological pressure" in front of a visiting delegation from the CPT (CPT/Inf(94)11 pkt 13; Horn 2015).

Telephone Access

A remand prisoner in Denmark does not have a right to telephone his or her family or friends unless ordinary mail correspondence is impossible for one reason or another (Bekendtgørelse om ophold i varetægt § 72). In practice this often translates into a complete ban regardless of whether or not the remand prisoners are subjected to "B and B" restrictions. For many remand prisoners this means that they can sit on remand sometimes more than a year without ever being allowed to make or receive phone calls to/from family and friends. However, the rules are interpreted somewhat differently from one remand prison to another and there seems to be a certain regional difference in this area. A prison officer working in a remand prison in Jutland describe that "the rules are clear here: no phone calls before sentencing and the enforcement order has been received—meaning up to numerous months after the verdict has been delivered. Phone cards can be purchased when the sentence has been received, and the phone can be used for 10 minutes a week." The same prison officer has worked in a remand prison on Zealand, and explains that back then the prisoners were "simply given a hands-free extra phone and were allowed to sit and talk for a longer duration without surveillance and without having to pay" (Interview, prison staff). Since then, tighter rules have been implemented in the remand prisons on Zealand as well, but there are still differences and some remand prisons allow a few phone calls to family members to some of the prisoners who are not subjected to correspondence and visit control.

In interviews and surveys, remand prisoners support the above—that it is typically not possible to use the phone and that it is sometimes allowed in certain places. One remand prisoner describe that she can call her children once a week, while another explains "NEVER IN REMAND" (Survey respondents no. 138 and 40). The latter, an 18-year-old remand prisoner, describe that he was not even allowed to call his parents, when he was imprisoned on remand. Prison officers explain that prisoners are very frustrated by this policy. One staff member "believe that we risk forcing remand prisoners to choose not to appeal their verdict or confess to something they haven't done, in order to start serving their sentence faster and thereby gain the right to phone privileges" (Interview, prison staff). A manager in the Prison Service does not at all believe, that there is a constructive explanation to the restrictive phone policy: "Why aren't they supposed to be allowed to make phone calls, especially those who aren't subjected to Correspondence and Visit control? It is a political question. They just aren't allowed to make phone calls!" (Interview, prison staff).

Remand Imprisonment and Prisoner Rights in Different Jurisdictions

It "has been observed that living conditions in pre-trial detention facilities throughout Europe are often worse than those in prisons for sentenced prisoners" (Morgenstern 2013, p. 195). In that sense it comes as no surprise that remand prisoners in Denmark also face worse conditions than sentenced prisoners. But although we lack proper comparative empirical research in this area there seems to be a culture and tradition of applying especially strict and arguably quite radical restrictions during remand in the Scandinavian states. The Scandinavian history of pre-trial solitary confinement is a well-known example of this (Smith 2012) which has clearly not been addressed adequately especially in Sweden. That a democratic country choose to place 70 % of its remand prisoners in strict isolation and thereby at least around 1/8 of its entire prison population is remarkable to say the least. Although Norway seems to be a rather different case in some ways (remand prisoners are allowed to use a phone and are often allowed to be with sentenced prisoners) we still see clear and significant remnants of the Scandinavian isolation heritage also here exemplified by 12–15 % of all remand prisoners being subjected to pre-trial solitary confinement (to protect the police investigation) as well as the previously mentioned practice of solitary confinement in police detention. As shown in the above, despite the extensive Danish reform of the system of pre-trial solitary confinement remand prisoners still face high levels of isolation and minimal contact with the outside world.

Although remand prisoners in many parts of the world are often treated badly, this Danish (and certainly also Swedish) obsession with restricting the communication of remand prisoners—and thereby their rights to for example privacy and family life—seems to differ from what one will find in many other western countries. In England and Wales, the "Prison service order No. 4600" stipulate that unconvicted prisoners have "a number of special rights and privileges" and are entitled to for example: (a) Having "items for cell activities and hobbies handed in by relatives or friends, as well as to purchase them from private cash or pay"; (b) "Carry out business activities"; (c) "Send and receive as many letters as he/she wishes"; (d) "Receive as many visits as he/she wishes, within reasonable limits." In addition, remand prisoners are allowed to use a phone. There is no scope in these rules for restricting a remand prisoner's contact with the outside world like what we find in Denmark and Sweden.[14] We know from the monitoring work of HM Inspectorate of Prisons that remand prisons "are

---

[14] Special rules and regimes can apply in certain cases involving terrorism—but that goes for a minority of prisoners.

afforded considerable discretion" when "implementing the 'mandatory requirements' in PSO 4600" which "risks diluting the entitlements of unconvicted prisoners to the extent where they can be treated much the same as convicted prisoners" (HM Inspectorate of Prisons, thematic report, p. 25). In practice, remand prisoners in England and Wales are allowed a minimum of three visits per week, and in some establishments a daily visit, and while 37 % of the remand prisoners in a survey had "problems accessing phones" (HM Inspectorate of Prisons, thematic report) this is still a very different situation from simply not being allowed to phone anyone at all. In other words, the problem in England and Wales seems to be that while remand prisoners have special rights and privileges they are in practice sometimes being treated just as sentenced prisoners. In Denmark, on the other hand, remand prisoners long to be treated as sentenced prisoners and receive the same privileges, rights and benefits as those who have already been found guilty of a crime.

Forceful State Interventions—Individual Rights, Trust and the Power of the Welfare State

Conditions for sentenced prisoners in the Scandinavian countries and especially the use of open prisons have often been praised by foreign criminologists and other visiting observers. The conditions for, and the treatment of, remand prisoners is however often forgotten when the Scandinavian penal and criminal justice systems are put under scrutiny by criminologists despite the fact that they account for up to 1/3 of all prisoners.[15] As shown in the above, a careful study of Danish remand practice along with examples from especially Sweden and to some extent Norway, illustrate that a number of important pre-trial practices are still often characterized by strict isolation and very limited contact with the outside world in a way, which has very little to do with the typical image of

---

[15] Human rights mechanisms have been more critical and more aware of *some* of the problems in this area.

Scandinavian or Nordic penal exceptionalism. But these practices arguably reveal another common trait of the Nordic welfare states, namely their willingness to intervene extensively into the private lives of their citizens. In the words of Henrik Stenius "all the doors are open" to state intervention in the Nordic countries: the doors "to the living room, the kitchen, the larder, the nursery, not to mention the bedroom—and they are not just open: society marches in and intervenes, sometimes brusquely" (Stenius quoted from Hilson 2013 p. 88).

In my opinion, the willingness to use significant and very intrusive state power against those who we are supposed to "presume innocent" should be understood alongside other well-known examples of extensive social control and social engineering in Scandinavia and the Nordic states. This includes, for example, the eugenic policies which in many ways were spearheaded by the Social democratic Scandinavian countries. Denmark was the first European nation to introduce a eugenic sterilization law in 1929 and in Sweden preventive eugenic social policies were championed by welfare state reformers in order to create "a better human material" (Smith 2014, p. 29 f.). Such policies were not motivated by punitive intentions but illustrate how the strong Scandinavian welfare states are willing to deploy state power very forcefully against their own citizens as long as it is done with a welfare agenda that promise securing a path towards a better society. History has shown us the obvious dangers of such policies and the way they tend to ignore individual rights. Indeed, as suggested elsewhere in this volume these countries might exhibit a special "culture of intervention" (Andersson). In that sense, Scandinavian states may not be *Big Brother* but rather *Big Mother* states which want to create good citizens and rich societies and are not afraid to wield considerable power to do so.

The question and role of individual rights and the culture surrounding such rights is likely to be a key issue in this context. In an analysis of Swedish history and the Swedish welfare state it has for example been argued that one of the prices paid for creating a strong welfare system with a capacity to free citizens of their social bonds, and in that sense create an impressive level of individual autonomy, has been to subordinate the individual to society in a way which make people vulnerable to state intervention. According to this interpretation, the increased level of individual autonomy secured *through* the state has not corresponded with a similar development of strong individual rights securing citizens *against* the state (Berggren and Trägårdh 2013, p. 368). Along the same lines Vanessa Barker argue that in Sweden "weak individual rights compounded by an ethno-cultural basis of belonging create the conditions that make individuals, particular those cast as outsiders or 'others,' vulnerable to intrusive uses of state power" (Barker 2012, p. 16). The practices described in this chapter are clearly examples of how the rights of individuals are restricted in significant ways which, for example, allow the use of solitary confinement (a radical and harmful intervention) and other isolation-like regimes, as completely normal practices which the strong Scandinavian welfare states routinely apply against individuals not yet found guilty of any crime.

One can speculate whether or not the Scandinavian states are sometimes able to make these powerful interventions and shows of force more or less unquestioned because of the high levels of trust in the police and the justice system exhibited in these states (Justitsministeriet 2014; Lappi-Seppälä 2012, p. 105), and because of their own self-understanding as being predominantly humane, democratic, benevolent and fair (Christoffersen and Madsen 2011; Engbo and Smith 2012, p. 42 ff.; Nilsson 2012). This is not to say that the high levels of trust are primarily a negative penal force —on the contrary there is very good reason to believe that trust in fellow citizens and authorities can be a strong force in creating and maintaining relatively peaceful societies and relatively mild penal arrangements (of which there are clearly also many and important examples in the Scandinavian countries). But too much trust is not necessarily a good thing and sometimes there is a danger of "trusting without testing"—for example by continuing problematic practices instead of scrutinizing them. In any case, when assessing Scandinavian penal practice we clearly have to incor-porate remand and other pre-trial practices into our analysis as a reminder of what these states are capable of and as an important part of the penal, welfare and criminal justice cultures they have created.

References

Åklagarmyndigheten. (2014). Häktningstider och restriktioner, report January 2014. Stockholm: Åklagarmyndigheten.

Amnesty International. (2008). *Behandlingen af klager over politiet i Danmark*. Copenhagen: Amnesty International.

Barker, V. (2012, December). Nordic Exceptionalism revisited: Explaining the paradox of a Janus-faced penal regime. *Theoretical Criminology, 17* (1), 5–25.

Barnombudsmannen. (2013). From the inside. http://www.barnombudsman nen.se/om-webbplatsen/english/our-work/thematic-annual-reports/from-the-inside/. Accessed 5 September 2016.

Beccaria, C. (1998). *Om forbrydelse og straf*. Copenhagen. Museum Tusculanum Press.

Berggren, H., & Trägårdh, L. (2013). *Är svensken människa? Gemenskap och oberoende i det moderna Sverige*. Stockholm: Norstedts.

COE, Recommendation Rec (2006) 13. http://pjp-eu.coe.int/documents/3983922/6970334/CMRec+(2006)+13+on+the+use+of+remand+in+cus tody,+the+conditions+in+which+it+takes+place+and+the+provision+of+safe guard+against+abuse.pdf/ccde55db-7aa4-4e11-90ba-38e4467efd7b. Accessed 5 September 2016.

CPT visit report Norway 1994, CPT/Inf(94). http://www.cpt.coe.int/docu ments/nor/1994-12-inf-eng.pdf. Accessed 5 September 2016.

CPT visit report Sweden. 2009. http://www.cpt.coe.int/documents/swe/2009-34-inf-eng.pdf. Accessed 5 September 2016.

Cavadino, M., & Dignan, J. (2006). *Penal systems. A comparative approach*. London: Sage.

Christoffersen, J., & Madsen, M. R. (2011). The end of virtue? Denmark and the internationalisation of Human Rights. *Nordic Journal of International Law, 80*, 257–277.

Clausen, S. (2013). *Klientundersøgelsen 2011*. København: Direktoratet for Kriminalforsorgen.

Engbo, H. J. (2005). *Straffuldbyrdelsesret*. København: Jurist- og Økonomforbundets forlag.

Engbo, H. J., & Smith, P. S. (2012). *Fængsler og Menneskerettigheder*. København: Jurist- og Økonomforbundets forlag.

Esping-Andersen, G. (1995). *The three worlds of welfare capitalism*. Cambridge: Polity Press.

Evans, M. D., & Morgan, R. (1998). *Preventing torture*. Oxford: Oxford University Press.

Havre, M. (2014). *Den store balansetesten—varetekt etter en proporsjonalitetsmodell*. Oslo: Det Juridiske Fakultet, Oslo Universitet.

Hilson, M. (2013). *The Nordic model: Scandinavia since 1945*. London: Reaktion Books.

Horn, T. (2015). *Fullstendig isolasjon ved risiko for bevisforspillelse*. Oslo: Det juridiske fakultet, Universitetet i Oslo.

Justitsministeriet. (2014). Tryghed og holdning til politi og retssystem. http://justitsministeriet.dk/sites/default/files/media/Arbejdsomraader/Forskning/Forskningsrapporter/2014/ESS%20rapport%202014.pdf. Accessed 5 September 2016.

Kautto, M., Heikkilä, M., Hvinden, B., Marklund, S., Ploug, N. (Eds.) (1999). Introduction: the Nordic welfare states in the 1990s. In *Nordic social policy. Changing welfare states*. Abingdon: Routledge.

Lappi-Seppälä, T. (2007). Penal policy in Scandinavia. *Crime and Justice, 36*, 217–295.

Lappi-Seppälä, T. (2012). Penal policies in the Nordic countries 1960–2010. *Journal of Scandinavian Studies in Criminology and Crime Prevention, 13*, 85–111.

Løppenthin, N. (2015). Årsrapport for 2014 vedr. Misbrugsbehandling. Kriminalforsorgen. https://www.google.dk/url?sa=t&rct=j&q=&esrc=s&source=web&cd=1&ved=0ahUKEwi4r8Kvu_jOAhVjMJoKHTJlDQsQFggnMAA&url=http%3A%2F%2Fwww.kriminalforsorgen.dk%2FAdmin%2FPublic%2FDownload.aspx%3Ffile%3DFiles%252FFiler%252FPublikationer%252Frapporter%252F%25C3%2585rsrapport%2B2014%2B-%2BMisbrugsbehandling.pdf&usg=AFQjCNFLCUT29HCx8v1t3QWLdwT_HqaS5A&sig2=hXIHzkE-FCPPtEJ3ddOQkg&bvm=bv.131783435,d.bGs&cad=rja

Minke, L., & Balvig, F. (2015). *Kokkeskolen: Evaluering af de foreløbige erfaringer*. København: Direktoratet for Kriminalforsorgen.

Morgenstern, C. (2013). Remand detention in Europe: comparative and pan-European aspects as elements of a wider European penology. In T. Daems, D. van Zyl Smit, S. Snacken (Eds.), European Penology? Oxford: Hart Publishing.

Nilsson, R. (2012). The most progressive, effective correctional system in the world? The Swedish prison system in 1960s and 1970s (pp. 79–99). In T. Ugelvik and J. Dullum (Eds.), *The Nordic model—exception or not?* Abingdon: Routledge. 79–99.

Open Society Justice Initiative. (2014). *Presumption of guilt. The global overuse of pretrial detention.* New York: Open Society Foundations.

Pratt, J. (2008a). Scandinavian exceptionalism in an era of penal excess. Part I: the nature and roots of Scandinavian exceptionalism. *British Journal of Criminology, 48,* 119–137.

Pratt, J. (2008b). Scandinavian exceptionalism in an era of penal excess. Part II: Does Scandinavian exceptionalism have a future? *British Journal of Criminology, 48,* 275–292.

Pratt, J., & Eriksson, A. (2013). *Contrasts in punishment.* Abingdon: Routledge.

Smith, P. S., & Jakobsen, J. (forthcoming). *Varetægtsfængsling—Danmarks hårdeste straf?* København: Jurist- og Økonomforbundets forlag.

Smith, P. S. (2005, June). Varetægtsfængsling i isolation—en besynderlig Skandinavisk tradition? *Social Kritik,* no. 99, 4–17.

Smith, P. S. (2006). The effects of solitary confinement on prison inmates: A brief history and review of the literature. In *Crime and justice,* Vol. 34, No. 1. Chicago: The University of Chicago Press.

Smith, P. S. (2012). A critical look at Scandinavian exceptionalism: welfare state theories, penal populism, and prison conditions in Denmark and Scandinavia. In T. Ugelvik and J. Dullum (Eds.), Penal exceptionalism? Nordic prison policy and practice. Abingdon: Routledge.

Smith, P. S. (2014). *When the innocent are punished. The children of imprisoned parents.* Basingstoke: Palgrave.

Smith, P. S. (2015). Children of imprisoned parents in Scandinavia: their problems, treatment and the role of Scandinavian penal culture. *Law in Context, 32,* 147–168.

Smith, P. S., Horn, T., Nilsen, J., Rua, M. (2013). Isolation i skandinaviske fængsler—der er ikke tilstrækkeligt fokus på den omfattende brug af isolation i skandinaviske fængsler. *Social Kritik,* no. 136, 4–20.

Smith, P.S. & Koch, I. (2015). Isolation – et fængsel i fængslet. In Vestergaard J., Holmberg L., Kyvsgaard B. ands Elholm, T. (Eds.), *Kriminalistiske pejlinger - festskrift til Flemming Balvig.* København: Jurist- og Økonomforbundets forlag.

Ugelvik, T. (2011). *Fangenes friheter. Makt og motstand i et norsk fengsel.* Oslo: Universitetsforlaget.

Ugelvik, T. (2014). *Power and resistance in prison. Doing time, doing freedom.* Basingstoke: Palgrave.

Guarding, Guiding, Gate Opening: Prison Officer Work in a Norwegian Welfare Context

Terje Emil Fredwall

Introduction

Anne A is a prison officer, and for years, she has been working behind the walls—in low-security and high-security wings, with remand and sentenced prisoners. She says:

> We are there fifty per cent in order to keep an eye on them, to ensure that they stay here [in prison]. The other fifty per cent we are trying to help them. They may be drug users or have other problems, and it's just as much our duty to help them as to watch them. And when we help, this contributes to security just as much as a locked door or an alarm.

T.E. Fredwall (✉)
Center for Care Research, University of Agder, Kristiansand, Norway
e-mail: terje.e.fredwall@uia.no

© The Author(s) 2017
P. Scharff Smith, T. Ugelvik (eds.), *Scandinavian Penal History, Culture and Prison Practice,* Palgrave Studies in Prisons and Penology, DOI 10.1057/978-1-137-58529-5_7

The professional work of prison officers is complex and multi-faceted (Arnold et al. 2007; Fredwall 2015b; Johnsen et al. 2011; Liebling 2011; Liebling et al. 2011; Mjåland and Lundeberg 2014; Nylander 2011). In a Norwegian context, the officers are on the one hand to deprive convicted persons of their liberty, as well as to keep remand prisoners where the court or prosecuting authority has decided that they should be. On the other hand, they are expected to take care of, support and motivate the prisoners during their prison stay, as well as to lay a foundation for rehabilitation and change, reintegration and improvement of living conditions (Norwegian Ministry of Justice and the Police 2000, 2008). Prisons, in the words of Ben Crewe (2007, p. 123), thus become "a potent symbol of the state's power to punish and its failure to integrate all its citizens into its systems of norms", and the confinement could be staged as an opportunity for doing something about this failure. A growing body of studies, however, indicate how challenging this task of integration and rehabilitation could be, describing how the time in high-security prisons also may lead to social stigmatization, cause both physical problems and psychological sufferings, increase the chance of relationship challenges and often deteriorate the prisoner's financial situation (Hammerlin 2015; Kolind 1999; Liebling and Maruna 2006; Smith 2006).

In this chapter, I will offer some observations and reflections on imprisonment, welfare services and prison officer work in Norwegian high-security wings. Based on a reading of two key policy documents, I will first show that the political and professional leadership of the Norwegian Correctional Services position high-security prisons as arenas of welfare-oriented work. The ambition is that the door into prison also should be a way out to heightened welfare and a life without crime. I will then turn to Anne A, one of the prison officers whom I interviewed for a larger study on professional ethics (Fredwall 2015b), describing how she encourages the prisoners to make use of the prison's health services and educational facilities and how she tries to help them to get a job and/or a proper housing to go to after release. Both the leadership and the prison officer are thereby highly concerned with welfare services and the period after prison release, but they have different reasons for the importance of this. While the two key documents primarily express an expectation that the offer of welfare services will yield a gain—measured in recidivism rates, Anne A regards the enabling process primarily as a benefit for the prisoner as an individual. And while Anne A emphasizes the importance of giving the prisoners an opportunity to live good and meaningful lives, with themselves and others, after release, the social utility is used as the primary reason in the policy documents. In the final part of the chapter, I will locate these differences within what I will term a transformational and a guiding officer ideal (Fredwall 2015b, pp. 366–395), appending some short reflections concerning the values represented by each of these ideals.

Materials and Method

The first of the two key policy documents, selected for analysis in this chapter, is the White Paper *Punishment that works—less crime—safer society* (Norwegian Ministry of Justice and the Police 2008). This document, which was the first White Paper on the subject of Norwegian Correctional Services for a decade, is partly a descriptive account of the activities of the Correctional Services, and partly a normative approach focusing on the future direction of penal implementation policy desired by the Ministry. Thus, it could also be read as an instruction to the Norwegian Correctional Services.

The second key document is *The Norwegian Correctional Services' strategy for professional activity* (Norwegian Directorate for Correctional Services 2004). According to the Directorate (2004, p. 2), important reasons for issuing the professional strategy included creating a common professional identity for all employees and establishing good support for decision-making in relation to further professional development.

Further, I will draw on the qualitative interview material collected for the study *Murer og moral* (*Walls and Values*) (Fredwall 2015a, b). During a period of about one and a half years, between January 2009 and August 2010, I interviewed nineteenth prison officers in Norwegian high-security wings (which is the highest security level normally adopted in Norway) about their everyday work and their reflections on the officer role. We talked about good work moments and the challenging days, time pressure and security, discretion and rules, humour, boundary setting and belief in change. In the course of these interviews, we often touched upon welfare-oriented services as well as challenges relating to the prisoners' living conditions, but it is first in this chapter that these topics are the main focus in my research. The interviews lasted between 2 and 3 hours and were later fully transcribed and analysed.[1]

For the purposes of this chapter, the prison officer whom I have named Anne has been selected as case due to her clearly marked focus on the future in her role description. In the interview, she expresses a clear attention to the inmates' future, on how things will be for them when they are released from prison. At the same time she is concerned with the present: with showing care, helping and enabling in the actual circumstances of the prisoners during their time in prison. This type of role understanding was also expressed by other officers I interviewed, but Anne's descriptions and reflections were presented with a clarity and animation that make them particularly suited to the topic of this text. According to Bent Flyvbjerg, the value of case studies are by some scholars labelled as arbitrary or a method of producing anecdotes, but as he argues (with a quote from Hans Eysenck): "Sometimes we simply have to keep our eyes open and look carefully at individual cases—not in the hope of proving anything, but rather in the hope of learning something" (Flyvbjerg 2006, p. 224). In this chapter, I follow Flyvbjerg in his recognition of case studies' closeness to real-life situations and wealth of details.

In the end of the chapter, I will place her role interpretation, as it is described here in the text, along with the descriptions presented in the two policy documents, within what I have identified in *Walls and Values* as different moral ideals for the officer role in Norwegian high-security prisons (Fredwall 2015b, pp. 365–395). In the study, I identify altogether five such moral ideals,[2] basing the identification on

---

[1] Quotes from key documents and interviews are translated from Norwegian by the author.

[2] Two of these ideals will be presented in the final part of this chapter. The other three ideals are *the order-protective ideal, the correctional ideal* and *the supportive ideal*. In short, *the order-protective ideal* is characterized by values such as control, order and predictability. The position of having a stable and orderly existence in the prison wing is here viewed as being valuable in itself. *The correctional ideal* is characterized by the expectation that the officers practice their role with a

descriptions presented in three key policy documents issued by the leadership of the Norwegian Correctional Services, in a recruiting brochure from The Prison Staff Academy (which trains all prison officers in Norway) and through interviews with nineteenth prison officers and five members of the Admission Board (which is responsible for interviewing and selecting applicants for prison officer training). In this ideal-typical analysis (Weber 1949, pp. 90–92), a moral ideal is understood to be a picture of a better or higher way of performing in the role of a prison officer (see: Taylor 1992, p. 16). Anne's role interpretation, as presented in this chapter, can be located within a guiding officer ideal, while the descriptions given by the political and professional leadership can be located mainly within a transformational officer ideal.

The Political and Professional Leadership—Better Out than In!

As already noted in the introductory chapter, a core feature of the Scandinavian welfare state is a clearly expressed understanding and expectation of a public, collective responsibility for health and care, education and social security for all legal residents in the country (Halvorsen and Stjernø 2008). In my view, it is also reasonable to read Norwegian high-security prisons into this type of welfare state framework. This is apparent not least in the White Paper, in which prisons are explicitly tied to a public welfare responsibility. Indeed, the primary task of the Correctional Services is to enforce remand orders and sentences in a manner that reassures society. "The Norwegian Correctional Services", the Ministry (2008, p. 8) emphasizes in the White Paper, "shall implement penalties in such a way that new

---

conscious intention of transmitting a set of values, attitudes and skills to the inmates, while *the supportive ideal* is characterized by the values of care, support and autonomy. The officers are here challenged to see each inmate as fellow human beings that the officers—within the framework of the imprisonment—have a moral responsibility for (Fredwall 2015b).

offences do not occur during the penal implementation". This task is regarded as particularly important in the case of "acts of such severity or extent" that the court has determined imprisonment (Norwegian Ministry of Justice and the Police 2008, p. 19). However, incapacitation is, still according to the Ministry, far from enough to protect public safety. At some point the prisoners will be released, and the best way of preventing the loss of health and life, saving society from large costs and creating a safer society is through rehabilitation and improved reintegration into society after release. In fact, the key issue is to get inmates into a rehabilitation track during the course of the sentence—irrespective of its length: "The goal", writes the Ministry (2008, p. 7), "is punishment that works—that reduces the likelihood of new crime. . . . The punishment must be of a nature that recidivism is reduced":

> If the penalty is to work, reintegration work must be satisfactorily planned and addressed. It matters less how good the Norwegian Correctional Services is in its rehabilitation work, if released prisoners are not followed up after the end of the penal implementation. . . . The objective of the Norwegian Correctional Services' professional activity is a convict who has served the sentence, is drug-free or has control of his drug use, has a suitable place to live, can read, write and do basic mathematics, has a chance on the labour market; can relate to family, friends and the rest of society, is able to seek help for any problems that may arise after his release, and can live an independent life. The Government considers that a good point of departure on release increases the probability of inmates succeeding in living a life without crime. (Norwegian Ministry of Justice and the Police 2008, pp. 9–10)

The last two sentences of this quote originally formed part of the professional strategy, a document that establishes a clear rehabilitation framework around the execution of sentences. The mission of the Correctional Services, it is emphasized here, is "to provide a better chance for those who have taken a wrong path": "Once the sentence has been served, the convict should be better equipped to face a life without crime. *Everything* we do should be measured up against this.

The sentence is to be a turning point" (Norwegian Directorate for Correctional Services 2004, p. 4).

In other words, everything a prison officer does—every conversation, each activity and any provision that is established in the prison— is to be measured up against this principle: that the prisoner should be better equipped on release than at the time of committal. In this way, considerations of reoffending and rehabilitation legitimate the work training and cultural arrangements, the educational provisions and interaction between inmates and officers. And as such, important threads are woven between welfare work and the role of a prison officer. The prison stay should have an impact on the inmates, offenders are to be rehabilitated, lives are to be changed—and within this task, the officers are referred to as the very "backbone of the work of change and reintegration that is carried out in the prisons" (Norwegian Directorate for Correctional Services 2004, p. 8). This significance relates particularly to the system of personal contact officers, which since 2002 has included all the prison officers in Norway. Here, the personal contact officers were given a responsibility to follow up individual prisoners during their time in prison, and they were instructed to assist the inmates with their sentence plan, to help them in their approaches to the Labour and Welfare Administration (NAV) and to support and motivate them to work constructively during their time in prison (Norwegian Directorate for Correctional Services 2002). In this way, the work of the contact officer constitutes an important part of the prison officer role.

The professional strategy was issued in 2004. The following year, the Soria Moria Declaration—a government manifesto by the Norwegian governing coalition parties—introduced a social reintegration guarantee, which subsequently was clarified and laid out in the White Paper (Stoltenberg's 2nd Government 2005, p. 68; Norwegian Ministry of Justice and the Police 2008, pp. 173–189). This social reintegration guarantee was meant to provide inmates with help in accessing the rights that they already have as Norwegian citizens, such as adequate housing and educational opportunities, help with accessing the work market, treatment for physical ailments and help with their drug addiction. It represents the intentions that the government recognizes an obligation to help convicted persons to access the rights they already possess as Norwegian citizens, but, as the Ministry (2008, p. 174) emphasizes, the reintegration guarantee is political in character, not legal. The public bodies that otherwise exercise this responsibility in society are responsible for "carrying out their services in relation to the convicted persons in such a way and such place that they can have a reasonable opportunity to make use of them", while the Correctional Services is to ensure that this can happen (Norwegian Ministry of Justice and the Police 2008, p. 174). In this way, the Ministry (2008, p. 8) points out, crime policy is "insolubly connected with" welfare policy. And furthermore, the reason given for this work—as in the rest of the White Paper—is primarily anchored in recidivism and social utility. A punishment that works, the White Paper says, entails that the offender reduces or ceases criminal actions as a result of the punishment:

> The responsibility of the Norwegian Correctional Services can well be described with the slogan chosen by its Swedish counterpart [Kriminalvården]: "Better out than in!" (Norwegian Ministry of Justice and the Police 2008, p. 183)

> Reduced recidivism demands many different measures. It is necessary both to do something about the living conditions and to offer measures *that help transform the convicted persons themselves*. (Norwegian Ministry of Justice and the Police 2008, p. 11, my italics)

> Both an improvement in living conditions and behaviour influence should assume a key role during the execution of a prison sentence. It is important to form an overall picture of the inmate and to direct rehabilitation initiatives in accordance with this. . . . Given the right measures at the right time for the right participant, it is possible to limit the risk of reoffending. (Norwegian Ministry of Justice and the Police 2008, pp. 78, 68)

It is reasonable to regard both the social reintegration guarantee and the formulation of the Correctional Services' professional goals as an attempt to ensure that other public bodies in the welfare state should take a greater responsibility for the convicted persons' living conditions.

It can also be regarded as an emphasis of the import model, a way of organizing prison work, which means that those public bodies that are responsible for these services outside prison walls also have a responsibility for them within the prison (Norwegian Ministry of Justice and the Police 2008, pp. 22, 33, 174–175). It can further be read as reinforcing the principle of normality: the ambition that life inside the prison will resemble life outside as much as possible (Norwegian Ministry of Justice and the Police 2008, pp. 22, 108–109), as well as the notion that condition of confinement should be viewed in relation to the general standard of living in the country as a whole (Jewkes 2015). It can be interpreted as a recognition of the fact that personal contact officer work does not always function in accordance with its intention: that staff work rotas, sickness and holidays can complicate regular meetings between officer and prisoner, and that it is challenging for officers to maintain an adequate overview of the complex and comprehensive field of welfare provision—to mention but a few aspects (Fredwall 2015b, pp. 261–364). And finally, it expresses an understanding of the complex web of circumstances surrounding each individual (Nussbaum 1999), a web of circumstances that for many prisoners can relate to poor psychological health, lack of employment and housing before committal, a low level of education, interrupted schooling and/or drug addiction (Bukten et al. 2011; Hetland et al. 2007; Revold 2015).

In the wake of the parliamentary consideration of the reintegration guarantee, a service market was introduced into many prisons in 2010. These service markets are a physical meeting place at which the prisoners themselves were intended to have direct contact with representatives of the various public bodies. The following year a number of so-called reintegration coordinators were employed, given the responsibility of leading these markets and coordinate the collaboration between the various professional groups. The coordinators, however, were not intended to work individually with the prisoners (Norwegian Directorate for Correctional Services 2012; Falck 2015).

The personal contact officers' responsibility for informing, conversing with, guiding and motivating prisoners regarding their release is therefore still a very important element of the prison officer role.

Anne A—The Prison Officer Who Became Tired of Saying No

Anne A is one of these personal contact officers, and in the interview I conducted with her, she articulated a role interpretation that in my view could be understood as a guiding officer ideal (more about this ideal later). For her, the most meaningful moments at work are essentially those connected to welfare-oriented work: to situations in which she experience that she has "managed to sort something out", as she puts it. After a while, and for this reason, she applied to the prison governor to work as much as possible with the convicted persons. This was a well-thought-out choice, she explains: "It was not satisfying just to lock and unlock doors. I never much enjoyed the work in the remand unit," she says, elaborating this phrase by referring to what she meant was a limited scope of action. At the end of the day, she would reflect on what she had achieved during the hours at work, and generally the answer revolved around refusals, escort duties and to lock and unlock doors:

> At that time there weren't any toilets in the cells, and they [the inmates] said to me: "I want the toilet". That was the only chance they had to see another human being. "No, there's a queue for the toilet now, so you'll have to wait. There are four others before you". You ran and unlocked the door, and then they didn't want to go back in. They walked as slowly as they could in the hope of getting to speak with someone else in the corridor. "No, go in, you have to go in there". So you were very no-oriented when you got home. And I was so very tired of saying no. So I thought: "I've got to do something else, something that's more valuable. Otherwise I won't be able to cope with this".

In the convicted prisoners unit it was different. There, she explains, she had the opportunity to contribute to "putting something together" for the prisoners: something in relation to the dreams and desires that they spoke of for their lives. And in this wing, she was able to do something that could have an impact on their future—not just there and then during their prison stay, but after their release as well. She says:

We [prison officers] work year after year, but we very rarely encounter anyone who stands there and is pleased about the work we're doing: "Yee, that's great". The exception is if you've put something together for someone. You can see it is working. We've sent them off for drug addiction treatment. They've got somewhere to live. We've found them a job. They have got help. You have at least managed to get a result in that respect. And that, I believe, is something we need as human beings.

According to Anne, the work thus becomes meaningful if she has the opportunity to carry out tasks that engage her, that interest her and at the same time that mean something for the prisoners' future. This dimension of meaning is also other-oriented. By means of her work with the convicted persons, she can see that her contribution makes a difference to how life can be after release. She has been able to "do something for someone", as she puts it, and this makes the work itself important and interesting, meaningful and rewarding.

In this way, Anne's interpretation of the role as a prison officer is highly related to welfare provisions as health care and education. The heart of this work lies, as I interpret it, in revealing opportunities and to motivate the prisoners to put in an effort themselves. It's a matter of pointing to the positive aspects, to let them realize that life is not over even though they have been given a custodial sentence, Anne says. She refers here to a talk she regularly has with the prisoners for whom she is the personal contact officer: "You are perhaps only 22, and you've got the whole of your life ahead of you. And even though you've had a bad time up to now, you don't need to have a bad time for the rest of your life," she might say to them—before continuing: "But you have to do something yourself. We can't work magic, like everything will turn into happiness for you. But you can make a start yourself. You can begin to look to the future—after release."

Thus, Anne wants to be an involved enabler, a gate opener who makes people aware of their opportunities. One way in which this can happen is by being present. She can sit down for a chat about this and that, she can attempt to find out how people are coping and she can point to positive aspects of their lives. She can also encourage them to do something constructive about their confinement.

Many prisoners have a drug addiction, health problem or both, and during their stay in prison they can be given an opportunity to do something about this. "Over the years we have brought new life to many people," she says. "They have come in—and we have a pretty strong health service here—and they've received medical help and supervision."

Many of the inmates also lack education, and the prison can provide an opportunity for them to get a craft certificate, complete their schooling or begin higher education. This, she explains, seems over and over again to do something for their self-esteem and self-understanding (see also Hetland et al. 2007; Manger et al. 2008). According to Anne, many prisoners gain a new focus: They experience that they can move into another role than as a criminal or an inmate; they can be a student as well, a man who gains a craft certificate, a woman who can get herself a job. This kind of activity can make the prison stay easier to deal with, and it can provide them with hope and new prospects, Anne says:

> We have had so many people here who have gained basic study qualifications when they leave. And suddenly a whole new world has opened up for them. They've suddenly got many opportunities. They can become just like every other student, with a study loan and a student flat. "Then you no longer have anything to do with prison life any more", when I suddenly say this—"now you can move wherever you like, now you can call your mother and say 'I'm now starting at the university', How would that be?". "No, she would faint". "Yes, it'll be fun when she faints" (laughs). "Really, is it true? Can I?" "Yes, you can"—I don't think they would ever in their wildest fantasies have believed that they could.

A central part of Anne's work, as she describes it, is therefore related to giving them hope, making their prison stay as meaningful as possible and motivating them to make use of the welfare services in prison. At the same time it relates to their practical everyday life after release: to motivating and helping them to make sure that they have a job and/or an adequate housing after the end of their sentence. "You've sat down and listened to their stories, heard what they desire, what they've dreamed of," she says. "After all, most of them in here are dreaming of a better life when they get out—even though they perhaps won't manage it. But it's a matter of trying to put something together that relates to their dreams, to their desires."

At the same time, she relates this closely to the work of maintaining control, order and security in the prison. This becomes apparent when she describes prison officers who do a poor job. In her opinion, such officers try to spend as much time as possible sitting in the duty room. They indicate that they are tired of the prisoners. They have little time, avoid conversations with the inmates, don't keep their promises and say no to most things—without giving any reason. This kind of behaviour is a problem, she says. Not only does it demonstrate a lack of respect for colleagues ("everyone else has to make up for what they really out to be doing"). It also indicates little respect for the prisoners as human beings, it has an impact on the convicts' quality of life and it affects prison security. If the staff don't get to know the prisoners, and if the prisoners do not "get the feeling that you have their interests at heart", Anne claims, these officers will be more vulnerable if any fighting or conflicts arise on the wing. She says:

> The day on which there is real trouble, if the person in question is out on the wing, he's the first one they'll get. They've no relationship with him. They've got nothing. All they know is that he says "no". But those of us who've helped them, we'll be protected.

The growing literature about security, order and staff–prisoner relationships emphasizes that order and control are to a considerable degree based and dependent on the relations between staff and inmates. Such relationships, it is claimed, are at the very heart of the prison system, in which control and security "flow from getting that relationship right" (Great Britain 1984, p. 6; see also: Sykes 1958; Sparks et al. 1996; Crawley 2004; Liebling et al. 2011). The way in which prison officers communicate with the prisoners, how they handle the regulations and the extent to which the prisoners feel respected and fairly treated is stressed as extremely important—not only for security, but also for the prisoners' well-being (Arnold et al. 2007; Liebling and Arnold 2004;

Liebling et al. 2006; Johnsen et al. 2011) and the officers' ability to get their job done in an adequate manner (Sparks and Bottoms 1995; Sparks et al. 1996). As Alison Liebling puts it: "Staff–prisoner relationships—or the way prison staff use their authority—contribute disproportionately to prisoner evaluations of the fairness of their treatment":

> What made one prison different from another was the manner in which prisoners were treated by staff, how safe the prison felt and how trust and power flowed through the institution. Prisoners' well-being was to a large extent a consequence of their perceived treatment. (Liebling 2011, pp. 533–534)

Such perspectives are, in my understanding, also apparent in Anne's narratives of everyday experiences as a prison officer. She is concerned with helping the prisoners within the situation in which they find themselves—here and now, during the prison stay, as well as motivating, enabling and advising them in their use of welfare services. The manner in which she interacts with the prisoners, the tone in her actions and her willingness to contribute in a constructive manner can, according to Anne's descriptions, in this way make a difference in terms of care, respect and security. The main perspective for creating positive relationships with the prisoners is other-oriented, but order and control within the wing is also deeply tied to the empathy and care, recognition and respect she shows towards the prisoners.

Different Ideals, Different Values

The descriptions Anne gives of an everyday life in a Norwegian high-security wing are apparently close to the emphasis found in the professional strategy and the White Paper: the focus on improving prisoners' living conditions. As noted in the introduction to this chapter, there are, however, also important differences. The White Paper and professional strategy present considerations towards social utility and recidivism as the primary reason for improving the living conditions, while Anne emphasizes the significance that education, employment, housing and contact with family can have for the lives *of the prisoners themselves*—here and now, as in the future after release. Her work is thereby not primarily a matter of ensuring that the prisoners will live a crime-free life after imprisonment; value is attributed to those individuals she meets and has a relation to inside the prison: that they are given the opportunity to have a good and meaningful life after the prison stay. In this sense, the opportunity for inmates to learn a trade or earn an education is primarily not seen as an instrument for living a law-abiding life; instead, it is seen to have value in and of itself. And interacting with the prisoners is meaningful not only because it leads to less crime or increased prison security; it has a value in and of itself.

In my view this constitutes two different ways of interpreting the role of the prison officers in a welfare-oriented framework. In the following, I will attempt to locate these two approaches within what I in *Walls and Values* have identified as a guiding and a transformational ideal for prison officers (Fredwall 2015b).

However, let me first dwell on some of the expectations that the two ideals have in common. Both ideals are emphasizing that the primary responsibility of the prison officers is to ensure that inmates are kept where they are supposed to be. If a prisoner escapes, it may threaten the public's perception of safety, threaten the security of the society and/or reduce the public's trust in Correctional Services. Another important common trait is the expectation that the officers must have a certain ability to balance things in order to do an adequate job. The profession of prison officer is here presented as a persistent balancing between too much and too little: the officers should have the ability to show concern for others' situations, yet not so much that it comes at the cost of security; they can be personable, yet not in a manner that the inmates can use against them later; they can be humorous, yet not tactless or flippant; they can be trustworthy, yet not naïve; tolerant, yet not without boundaries; friendly, yet not buddies. The expectations placed on the prison officers to guard and to balance are therefore something that characterizes each of the two ideals (Fredwall 2015b). The difference lies in how the officers are challenged to combine these characteristics with other values and attitudes.

Anne's interpretation of her role, as presented in this chapter, can be located within a guiding officer ideal (Fredwall 2015b, pp. 385–388). This ideal is characterized first and foremost by the way the representatives combine a future orientation with the everyday life in prison wings (right here, right now). Within this ideal, the officers are encouraged to serve as conversation partners and guides to the prisoners towards release. The utility to society is not the primary reason for showing care, in giving help or in making arrangements for work, education or housing. Instead, the attention is on the prisoners' future, on how life will be for them when they are released: if, for example, they will have an education or a job to go to. At the same time, the importance of the present is emphasized. Getting to know the prisoners, talking with them and listening to them, is viewed as important, since the inmates—within the framework of their prison stay—are to have as good a life in prison as possible. This means, among other things, that the officer is to set boundaries when necessary, yet showing care and helpfulness as often as possible.

In this way, the individual is placed in the centre; the prisoners are to be regarded as fellow humans for whom the officers carry a moral responsibility for—and autonomy is seen as an important value. Representatives of this ideal carefully emphasize that the prisoners themselves must first want to receive the help and assistance that officers can offer them. Interaction with the prisoners is here seen as a benefit in and of itself, but is given a clear secondary meaning in that the officers may gain insights into how they should relate to and guide the individual inmates. Through conversations and personal presence, through care and recognition the officers may be able to sow a seed of optimism for change: that it might in fact be possible to do something about how life has been so far.

The descriptions given by the political and professional leadership, as presented in this chapter, can mainly be located within a transformational officer ideal (Fredwall 2015b, pp. 388–390). This ideal is partly characterized by the desire to change the prisoners' course of life and living conditions in order to contribute to less crime, and partly of the view that the officers are to be the decisive and initiating agent in this process of change. It is strongly stressed within this ideal that the officers are to prepare the prisoners to live a law-abiding life after release from prison. Such measures may have an effect on recidivism, and it is therefore important that the prisons offer work experience and education, cultural arrangements and recreational activities to the inmates. Within the framework of imprisonment, representatives for this ideal value and legitimize programmes that have a measurable effect on the likelihood of recidivism. There are, however, at least two different approaches within this ideal. Representatives of the first approach—a society-centred one—are mostly concerned that the change process will contribute to a safer society, improved protection of society (since the individuals do not commit new crimes) and a strengthened social economy (since crime generates certain costs to society). Whether the change seen within an individual will lead to the inmate living a better and more meaningful life after release is regarded as less important. Representatives of the second approach—an individual-centred one—are mostly concerned with the significance the process of change has for the individual prisoner. While these representatives also stress that bringing change to the inmates will work towards building a safer society, better protection for society and a strengthened social economy, they also emphasize that improving the prisoners' living conditions in order to live a future, law-abiding life is primarily in the best interest of the individuals themselves. In my interpretation, it is the society-centred transformational ideal that is most strongly expressed in the White Paper and the strategy for professional activity.

Closing Remarks

The differences between these two officer ideals, a guiding and a transformational approach, raise important moral questions about the legitimation of the role of prison officers and the welfare-oriented work within high-security prisons. Does it form part of the officer's role to change people for the better, to improve them, to correct their values and attitudes? Where are the moral boundaries to be drawn for how far officers should go in terms of doing "something about the living conditions and [. . .] offer measures that help transform the convicted persons themselves", as the White Paper puts it (Norwegian Ministry of Justice and the Police 2008, p. 11)? Is it possible to improve the conditions of confinement without strengthening the idea of an expanded use of prisons (Giertsen 2015; Mathiesen 2007)? These questions are complex and require much further investigation and discussions, but in this preliminary contribution, Anne A's descriptions provide, in my view, an important and engaging insight into how she, as a prison officer in a Norwegian high-security context, is motivated by and attempts to resolve the difficult task of supporting, influencing and enabling in an institutional context of control, asymmetry and deprivation of liberty.

References

Arnold, H., Liebling, A., & Tait, S. (2007). Prison officers and prison culture. In Y. Jewkes (Ed.), *Handbook on prisons* (pp. 471–495). Devon: Willan Publishing.

Bukten, A., Skurtveit, S., Stangeland, P., Gossop, M., Willersrud, A. B., Waal, H., . . . Clausen, T. (2011). Criminal convictions among dependent heroin users during a 3-year period prior to opioid maintenance treatment: A longitudinal national cohort study. *Journal Substances Abuse Treatment, 41*(4), 407–414. doi: http://dx.doi.org/10.1016/j.jsat.2011.06.006.

Crawley, E. (2004). *Doing prison work: The public and private lives of prison officers.* Cullompton: Willan.

Crewe, B. (2007). The sociology of imprisonment. In Y. Jewkes (Ed.), *Handbook on prisons* (pp. 123–151). Cullompton: Willan publishing.

Falck, S. (2015). *Tilbakeføringsgarantien som smuldret bort: Mellom kriminalomsorg og kommunale tjenester: Tiltaksbro, systematikk eller tilfeldighet?* Oslo: Statens institutt for rusmiddelforskning.

Flyvbjerg, B. (2006). Five misunderstandings about case-study research. *Qualitative Inquiry, 12*(2), 219–245.

Fredwall, T.E. (2015a). 'Alle de som sitter her, har en ny mulighet': Perspektiver på påvirkning og utvikling av fengslede i norske høysikkerhetsavdelinger. *Psyke & Logos, 36*(1), 28–49.

Fredwall, T.E. (2015b). *Murer og moral: En bok om straff, verdier og fengselsbetjenter.* Oslo: Cappelen Damm akademisk.

Giertsen, H. (2015). Abolitionism and reform: A possible combination?: Notes on a Norwegian experiment. In T. Mathiesen (Ed.), *The politics of abolition revisited* (pp. 286–296). London: Routledge.

Great Britain. (1984). *Managing the long-term prison system: The report of the Control Review Committee*. London: Home Office.

Halvorsen, K., & Stjernø, S. (2008). *Work, oil and welfare: The welfare state in Norway*. Oslo: Universitetsforlaget.

Hammerlin, Y. (2015). Å bryte livet i fengsel – og når livet og fengselslivet blir en livtruende byrde. *Psyke & Logos, 36*(1), 174–194.

Hetland, H., Eikeland, O.-J., Manger, T., Diseth, Å., & Asbjørnsen, A. (2007). Educational background in a prison population. *Journal of Correctional Education, 58*(2), 145–156. doi: 10.2307/23282733.

Jewkes, Y. (2015). Abolishing the architecture and alphabet of fear: Afterword. In T. Mathiesen (Ed.), *The politics of abolition revisited* (pp. 321–327). London: Routledge.

Johnsen, B., Granheim, P.K., & Helgesen, J. (2011). Exceptional prison conditions and the quality of prison life: Prison size and prison culture in Norwegian closed prisons. *European Journal of Criminology, 8*(6), 515–529. doi:10.1177/1477370811413819.

Kolind, T. (1999). Den betingede accept: Løsladtes identitetsproblemer i mødet med den "normale" verden. *Nordisk Tidsskrift for Kriminalvidenskab, 86*(1), 44–61.

Liebling, A. (2011). Moral performance, inhuman and degrading treatment and prison pain. *Punishment & Society, 13*(5), 530–550. doi: 10.1177/1462474511422159.

Liebling, A., & Arnold, H. (2004). *Prisons and their moral performance: A study of values, quality, and prison life*. Oxford: Oxford university press.

Liebling, A., & Maruna, S. (Eds.). (2006). *The effects of imprisonment*. Devon: Willan.

Liebling, A., Price, D., & Schefer, G. (2011). *The prison officer*. (2nd ed.) Abingdon: Willan.

Liebling, A., Durie, L., Stiles, A., & Tait, S. (2006). Revisiting prison suicide: The role of fairness and distress. In A. Liebling & S. Maruna (Eds.), *The effects of imprisonment* (pp. 209–231). Devon: Willan publishing.

Manger, T., Eikeland, O.-J., & Diseth, Å. (2008). Norge. In O.-J. Eikeland, T. Manger, & A. Asbjørnsen (Eds.), *Utdanning, utdanningsønske og -motivasjon: Innsatte i nordiske fengsler* (pp. 117–138). København: Nordisk ministerråd.

Mathiesen, T. (2007). Fra "Nothing works" til "What works": Hvor stor er forskjellen? In H. Von Hofer & A. Nilsson (Eds.), *Brott i välfärden: Om brottslighet, utsatthet och kriminalpolitik: Festskrift till Henrik Tham* (pp. 277–287). Stockholm: Kriminologiska institutionen.

Mjåland, K., & Lundeberg, I. (2014). Penal hybridization: Staff-prisoner relationships in a Norwegian drug rehabilitation unit. In H.S. Aasen, S. Gloppen, A.-M. Magnussen, & E. Nilssen (Eds.), *Juridification and social citizenship in the welfare state* (pp. 183–202). Cheltenham: Edward Elgar.

Norwegian Directorate for Correctional Services. (2002). *Retningslinjer for kontaktbetjentarbeidet: Rundskriv nr. 2.* Oslo: The Directorate.

Norwegian Directorate for Correctional Services. (2004). *Strategi for faglig virksomhet i kriminalomsorgen 2004–2007.* Oslo: The Directorate.

Norwegian Directorate for Correctional Services. (2012). *Tilbakeføringsgarantien (TG): Kort og godt.* Oslo: The Directorate.

Norwegian Ministry of Justice and the Police. (2000). *Ot.prp. nr. 5 (2000–2001): Om lov om gjennomføring av straff mv. (straffegjennomføringsloven).* Oslo: The Ministry.

Norwegian Ministry of Justice and the Police. (2008). *St.meld. nr. 37 (2007–2008): Straff som virker – mindre kriminalitet – tryggere samfunn (kriminalomsorgsmelding).* Oslo: The Ministry.

Nussbaum, M.C. (1999). Equity and mercy. In M.C. Nussbaum (Ed.), *Sex & social justice* (pp. 154–183). Oxford: Oxford university press.

Nylander, P.Å. (2011). *Managing the dilemma: Occupational culture and identity among prison officers* (Ph.D.), Örebro: Örebro universitet.

Revold, M.K. (2015). Innsattes levekår 2014: Før, under og etter soning (Vol. 2015/47). Oslo: Statistisk sentralbyrå.

Smith, P. S. (2006). The effects of solitary confinement on prison inmates: A brief history and review of the literature. *Crime Justice, 34*, 441–528.

Sparks, R., & Bottoms, A. (1995). Legitimacy and order in prisons. *British Journal Sociology, 46*(1), 45–62.

Sparks, R., Bottoms, A., & Hay, W. (1996). *Prisons and the problem of order.* Oxford: Clarendon Press.

Stoltenberg's 2nd Government. (2005). *Plattform for regjeringssamarbeidet mellom Arbeiderpartiet, Sosialistisk Venstreparti og Senterpartiet 2005–2009.* Retrieved from https://www.regjeringen.no/globalassets/upload/smk/vedlegg/2005/regjeringsplatform_soriamoria.pdf.

Sykes, G.M. (1958). *The society of captive: A study of a maximum security prison.* New Jersey: Princeton university press.

Taylor, C. (1992). *The ethics of authenticity.* Cambridge, MA: Harvard University Press.

Weber, M. (1949). *The methodology of the social sciences.* New York: Free press.

Treating Drug Abusers in Prison: Competing Paradigms Anchored in Different Welfare Ideologies. The Case of Sweden

Anders Bruhn, Odd Lindberg,
and Per Åke Nylander

Introduction

The number of prisoners in Sweden categorized as drug abusers have increased substantially in the last 20 years according to the Swedish Prison and Probation Service (SPPS). Drug abusers are defined by SPPS as those who have used illicit drugs during the previous 12 months (Ekbom et al. 2011). In 1970 about 20 % of the prisoners could be classified as drug abusers, while they made up 28 % of the prison population in 1997 (Amilon and Edstedt 1998). In 2010 the number of prisoners with drug problems had risen to 60 % (Ekbom et al. 2011). One reason for this increase may be the sentencing policy. Between 1995 and 2004 the number of persons indicted for drug offences went from 10,250 to 17,670 (Swedish National Council for Crime Prevention 2008, p. 23).

A. Bruhn (✉) · O. Lindberg · P.Å. Nylander
Department of Social Work, Örebro university, Oslo, Sweden
e-mail: anders.bruhn@oru.se; Odd.Lindberg@oru.se; per-ake.nylander@oru.se

© The Author(s) 2017

177

P. Scharff Smith, T. Ugelvik (eds.), *Scandinavian Penal History,
Culture and Prison Practice,* Palgrave Studies in Prisons and
Penology, DOI 10.1057/978-1-137-58529-5_8

According to this report the increase is explained by changes in the legislation and application of law, but also because of increasing resources allocated to the police and customs to fight drugs. It is not likely though that the number of drug abusers has increased accordingly during this period (Swedish National Council for Crime Prevention 2008, p. 23).

As a result of the development sketched the number of treatment programs in prison has grown, and so has the number of prison officers that work with these programs. Kolind et al. (2013, p. 10) states that this development... "reflects a broader criminalization of social problems...," and it should be put in context of heavy cost-savings and a decrease of alternative treatment methods in Sweden. An interesting reflection here is that prisons now seem to have become major institutions for treatment of drug abusers. Similarly Smith (2015, p. 34) highlights such a course of criminalization in a Danish context, and sees tendencies toward an unfortunate development when stating, "As part of this process, the prison and the criminal 'other' gradually risk becoming alienated and dislocated even further from the allegedly respectable society."

When the first drug-related programs were implemented during the 1970s and 1980s these were the sole type of treatment programs in Swedish prisons. A fundamental idea was that the program should be integrated with daily life in a special treatment wing, and run by the officers working there. The overall treatment ideology was that treatment is relational round-the-clock work (Holm et al. 2014). Quite the opposite the recent trend is that treatment programs are run in isolation from other day-to-day activities in prison. Today most prison-based treatment consists of psychopharmacological drugs, complemented by programs based on Cognitive Behavioral Theory (CBT). Ever since the first program of this type was introduced—Cognitive Skills in 1990—there has been a claim that these must be held by specially trained program leaders. These do not take part in the other day-to-day activities in the wings (Andersson 2004).

The two treatment approaches mentioned have existed in parallel in different parts of the prison organization since the 1990s. We hold that this situation is a manifestation of an ongoing ideological transformation of the welfare state. However, the latter is a non-linear process marked by institutional and organizational inertia, as well as ideological struggles between different parties of interest. Such a multi-facetted process admits different welfare policies to live side-by-side for long periods of time. Depending on the strength of different actors involved, welfare models on retreat like the "relational approach" here mentioned can reside in different pockets of authorities and organizations.

In this chapter we will on the basis of two "case studies" of treatment programs for drug abusers illustrate the content of and differences between the two treatment ideologies existing in parallel in today's Swedish prisons. Further, we will discuss how the increasing dominance of "What works" in prison policy, what we may call the Evidence-Based Practice (EBP)-movement in Swedish society relates to today's methods of governance in public sector, as well as neoliberal values about how to handle crime and crime prevention, that is the contamination of the welfare state by neo-liberal ideology.

Four research questions guide this study:

- Which are the central features of the treatment methodology behind these programs?
- How do the programs work in practice, and how do they relate to daily prison life?
- How are they affected by the ongoing trend of enhanced security measures in prisons?
- How do the growing dominance of the EBP-trend relate to ongoing changes in the Swedish welfare regime?

Methods and Data

This chapter is based on data retrieved from a Nordic research project concerning drug treatment in prison (see Holm et al. 2014; Kolind et al. 2013, for detailed information about methods and data). In the Swedish part of the project a purposive sample was used where three prisons were included, all with special drug treatment wings. The sample consisted of two prisons for men, security classes 1 and 2, and one prison for women, security class 2 (the highest for women). Here we will use the data from the women's prison and the male cat. 1 prison. In the women's prison we interviewed the prison governor, four prisoners in the treatment wing and six prison officers working in the wing on a daily basis, one chaplain, one external therapist and one nurse. In the male prison we interviewed the prison governor, five prisoners in the treatment wing, four program leaders (specially trained prison officers including the head of the team) and two staff working in the treatment wing on a daily basis but not involved in programs. The interview guides used consisted of several themes related to the motivation for and content of treatment, institutional settings, cooperation with other staff in prison, relations between program leaders and prisoners, relations between prisoners and wing officers working on a daily basis, and the conflict between rehabilitation and control. The researchers also did about two weeks observations in each treatment wing.

The qualitative data analysis is basically performed via meaning concentration and categorization (Kvale 1996). We are aware that it is not always easy to compare climate, culture, relations, attitudes, and formal and informal rules in men's and women's prisons. Other studies have shown that prisons for women often can be characterized as having better relations between prisoners and prison officers than male prisons (Lindberg 2005). This points toward the importance of gender aspects (Bruhn 2013). However, the fact that these two cases represents two different treatment models does not have to do with gender (the third case, the category 2 male prison does in fact practice the same type of model as the women's prison). And, our point of departure in this paper is to compare the general structure of the treatment, its ideological basis, and how they relate to and affect the immediate prison context.

The Swedish Prison System—Some Short Facts

In Sweden there are 47 prisons with about 5,000 beds. Some 5,500 prison officers are working in the prisons. They are by far the largest occupational group in the prisons. Prisons in Sweden are divided into three different security categories. The two highest categories are closed prisons. Category 3 are open prisons. The majority of the prisons belongs to category 2.

There are five prisons for women. Here category 2 is the highest security level. About 93 % of the prisoners are men. Men and women are, with one exception, not placed in the same prison in Sweden.

A Growing Impact of Neo-liberal Policy, and a "Security Turn"

A permanent dilemma that permeates penal and prison policy is how to strike a balance between society's conflicting objectives of punishing convicted offenders, protecting ordinary citizens from criminals, and to rehabilitate prisoners to lead a normal life after sentences served (Griffin 2002; Hemmens and Stohr 2000; Foucault 1977; Sykes 1958). How this dilemma is balanced is closely related to fundamental values of the state's welfare regime. In Sweden neo-liberal values about economism and the small state, and the New Public Management (NPM) doctrine of governance (Power 1997) started to gain ground in politics and public service already in the late 1980s. However, as mentioned in the introduction above this process has not been a linear one. On the contrary it has been quite fragmented. NPM in itself, for instance, contains several sometimes quite contradictory currents (Hood 1991). All in all though a focus on cost-savings in the area of treatment and social care, and later on combined with extensive tax reductions, has led to a dismantling of available alternatives for social interventions. Less alternatives here can be as mentioned in the introduction expected to trigger an increase in the amount of treatment efforts offered in prisons.

Another central element of change is the growing impact of deterrence and punitive thinking on criminal policy. This became increasingly manifest when a new right wing government took office in 2006. The preferential right of interpretation has now been concurred by a world-view that sees committing crime as profoundly a matter of choice. The deviant, the criminal, is here first and foremost driven by instrumental rationality, the *economic man* choosing criminal acts on the basis of calculations about risks and benefits. Therefore, crime prevention is about making crimes too costly, and avoiding risks in different societal contexts. The opportunity structure must be reduced, and "crimino-genic" factors and situations prevented (Nilsson 2013).

Even if Swedish social policy started to became increasingly influenced by a harshening social climate in other social and criminal policy areas already in the 1990s, for example tougher young offenders sentence (LSU) and more restricted drug treatment opportunities in society (Kolind et al. 2014), the prisons were not immediately affected by this development. A number of spectacular prison escapes in 2004 however, came to strongly push Swedish prison policy in this direction. The great political turbulence in the aftermath of these incidents led to a rapid "security turn." An official committee report (SOU 2005) triggered several changes in the prison system, for example the installation of new electric fences impossible to break through around all closed prisons, the creation of segregated high-security units in three category 1 prisons, an increasing number of specialized security officers, and a general change of rules and routines in all prisons. In addition we find an extensive increase of urine tests and sniffer dogs (Bruhn et al. 2015). Risk assessment and different control tasks are now influencing almost all activities in Swedish prisons. A similar development can be seen also in other Nordic countries (see Smith 2015). Heavy investment has also been made into electronic control devices such as cameras, remote-controlled locks and metal detectors.

All in all we may expect that the security measures introduced in the aftermath of 2004 have had a strong impact on rehabilitative efforts. Most of them facilitate distance between prisoners and prison staff. Together they add to a stigmatization of prisoners and counteract efforts of motivational work built on nearness and personal relations between staff and prisoners (Bruhn et al. 2015).

Two Cases—Two Treatment Models

In Swedish prisons drug treatment programs follows either of two different approaches: the principle of therapeutic community (PTC) in our case with the Twelve-step model (Alcoholics/Narcotics Anonymous; AA/NA) included, or CBT treatment. In the first of our cases the Twelve-step model is practiced, in the second only CBT programs are offered. The first model is not uncommon; it is still in use in some prisons today. However, the second one—CBT-programs is without doubt the dominating treatment model of today. It is used to treat criminality as well as drug abuse.

First Case: Milieu Therapeutic Principles and a Twelve-Step Program in a Women's Prison

This prison is a category 2 prison and has around 100 prisoners serving medium and long sentences. Besides a National reception unit and five regular wings, it has a treatment wing—a prison therapeutic community (PTC) for treatment of drug addicted prisoners. The prison is surrounded by two barb-wired high fences but no concrete walls.

The PTC started in the 1980s and has since been running a Twelve-step Facilitation Therapy Program by the help of external drug therapists. The faith-based Twelve-step ideology comprises daily group-therapy sessions. It has a collectivistic approach building on intense group support in and between activities. Staff in this PTC wing participate in all daily activities, including the therapy sessions. The PTC model was developed locally in some prisons and on a larger long-term scale by the so-called Österåker Prison Project (see SPPS 1990).

The group sessions in the Twelve-step treatment model shall always be led by a non-uniformed drug therapist with one uniformed prison officer present. The prison officers who participate in the therapy groups (i.e., all ordinary officers in the treatment wing) must have some training in the program and a regular supervision in how to practice the program methods. All prison officers here must have self-awareness, personal maturity, and an understanding of the concept of drug addiction. The program ideology rests on an assumption that drug abuse is a lifelong disease, and that the abuser is a "slave" under the drug, that is has lost self-control. The person must accept that this means lifelong dependency. The ritualized group-therapy sessions are an important program tool. These create emotions of attachment and community between the participants. After the program the participants are expected to regularly attend AA meetings to retain the feelings of connection and community (Lindberg 1998). Another central feature is the relational work. The aim here is to create relations between participants with the same kind of drug abuse problems. Relations are expected to foster abilities to build future bonds of support and help, in other words collective solidarity in life after release.

The treatment wing is located in an old building (The Castle) in the prison area. All other wings have more recently built facilities. The Castle has a home-like interior with carpets on the stone-floors and curtains in the windows. The PTC (treatment wing) has 18 prisoners divided into a "primary therapy phase" group and a "secondary therapy phase" group. Most of the time the two phases meet and socialize together. In case of emergency though they might be separated in two different legs of the wing.

To be transferred from a regular wing to the PTC the prisoner has to apply via a personal letter. The basic condition for transfer is of course having drug problems. After application the prisoner is interviewed by the therapist and a prison officer. If approved by these and the principal officer the prisoner is transferred. An important condition for being transferred is that the prisoner is assessed to fit-in with the present group of prisoners in the PTC.

Some prisoners describe their days in the PTC as much more meaningful than those in the regular wing. A collective goal is that the wing must run smoothly and the therapy groups be balanced and built on mutual trust among the prisoners. An important aim is also to, if possible, conditionally release prisoners to some kind of treatment center outside the prison.

Some prisoners emphasize the Twelve-step program as much more involving, compared with short-term and cognitive programs that they have attended earlier. They state that they have reached the conviction that becoming drug-free is a long-term project. It is rare with indications of a personal tactic to get temporary benefits or to adjust and improve the authority's risk assessment in order to get transferred to a prison with lower security classification (which sometimes can be a motive for attending treatment among prisoners). A prisoner with some years of experience spontaneously compared the Twelve-step model with CBT programs:

> The [cognitive program name] you do in a couple of weeks. But the Twelve-steps you can continue in. It becomes a sort of a lifestyle, like Alcoholics Anonymous actually is. It is something you continue to practice daily.

Thus it is about a new lifestyle in "community" with the AA movement. But a community is also created among the prisoners in the wing, owing to the mutual therapy experiences and the deep knowledge they reach about each other. They hopefully start to support each other and care about each other in all daily situations.

Relational Work in Focus

Prisoners regard prison officers in the PTC wing in a different way than they usually regard prison officers and prisoner–officer relationships. One reason for this seems self-evident: the officer's participation in therapy sessions and the deeper knowledge about the prisoner and her special life history this brings. The therapists are also trusted and respected among the prisoners. One important reason is that all therapists have experiences of being addicts themselves. This opens up for communication and trustworthiness. But they are of course also valued for their personal skills in helping others. This trust partly seems to spread over also to the wing officers, especially their special contact among staff, their Personal Officer:

> My own attitude towards staff in the PTC is quite different than in the regular wing. Now I talk to the officers, and I get feed-back from my Personal Officer and I really feel confident with her. Earlier I did not see the meaning with having a Personal Officer, now I seek help from her.

The relational work toward mutual trust seems to have been successful for the institutionalization of a general caring approach between prisoners and officers. Of course this takes some time for new officers to adjust to. Most of them though have voluntarily chosen to work in this wing. Therefore we may expect them to be a bit "prepared" for this approach and what is expected of them. Especially in a wing like this where relational work always is on the agenda, there are situations where clashes and quarrels appear, and also some relations that are more tense and distanced. Mostly though these seem to be temporary exceptions to the general wing-atmosphere.

The weekends are often described by the prisoners as boring. The schedule then has no therapy sessions and no organized work. Often some leisure activities are planned though. Wing staff normally participate in these, be it baking or outdoor activities. A middle aged prisoner with long experience describes the caring approach in this way:

> Prison officers here care about how I feel. They come into my room, ask how I feel, and even give me a hug. And I think that's very nice.

Of importance is that officers relate to the PTC prisoners first and foremost as individuals with their own personalities as they learn to know them well. Officers regard themselves as having special tasks compared with regular wing officers. Work is experienced as a round-the-clock therapy based on a milieu therapeutic thinking. All activities shall be integrated toward the general goal of treatment:

> We work as a team, the prison officers and the drug therapist. We are always participating in the therapy sessions, one of us is always there. And then we try to uphold the "Twelve-step spirit", as we say, in the wing. It must be present all the time, not only in the sessions, but also in the wing.

The Relation Between Security and Treatment

The prison officers in the PTC wing do not seem to have problems with security measures. Urine tests are as frequent as in the rest of the prison. The same goes for other types of security routines. Officers do not seem to have a problem combining these measures with having close personal relations with their prisoners, quite the opposite:

> Our close relations [with them] actually might make it easier to explain the importance of controls, room searches, and urine tests. We're familiar with how they react.

The changing security routines after 2004 concern all wings. There are not many extra incentives for prisoners in the PTC either. Sometimes a PTC prisoner could be allowed to have some extra advantages but on the other hand they also have some disadvantages. The standard of the PTC facilities is not better than in regular wings. On the contrary the cells here are older and colder than are the regular wing cells. According to many prisoners this is weighted up by the better collective atmosphere. Prisoners in the PTC wing are also viewed in another way than are regular prisoners. Prison officers regard them first and foremost as drug addicted persons instead of traditional prisoners. They are often not regarded as fully responsible and capable (because of having a disease), for example they are often called "the girls." This should not be seen as a patronizing attitude, rather it is a sign of familiarity and concern about the prisoners.

Second Case: CBT in a Men's Prison

For several reasons the CBT programs fit extremely well with the above-mentioned fundamental values about crime and crime prevention typical of neoliberal ideology. The aim with these programs is to raise the participants' awareness of how earlier behavior patterns and cognitions have affected their social situation, that is in our case drug abuse and criminality. They contain practical exercises in how to change thoughts, feelings and behavioral patterns in different situations. The individual shall learn to replace non-functional thoughts and behavioral patterns with functional ones.

The program focus is to " . . . target a criminal's way of thinking while the social context of crime is often disregarded" (Smith 2015, p. 37). The person attending is expected to reach an insight of what is wrong and destructive with his/her former way of life. On the basis of free will the attendant shall develop ways to change and improve his/her style of living, and exercise self-control not to fall back in former behavior (Andersson 2004; Smith 2006). This prison drug treatment (PDT) is a service offered to inmates/users aiming at empowering them to govern themselves from within (Kolind et al. 2013, pp. 11–12). The recruitment to these courses in Swedish prisons is based on the internal risk assessment processes and the categorization of prisoners into "treatable" or "heinous" ones (Bruhn et al. 2015). Even if the many sessions in the programs are group sessions, the programs are clearly individual- or self-directed. The individual prisoner is supposed to, with the help of the program tools, develop self-help capabilities in a process of change.

Our case here is a category-1 prison with stipulated 406 places. It is surrounded by several layers of walls, electrified fences, and barb wires. It contains prisoners with often very long sentences all assessed as quite dangerous. The prison is permeated by a spirit of security. Security measures are manifold and applied with firm strictness. The treatment wing holds 30 places. At the time of our research only 15 of those were used. According to a senior officer this was partly because a majority of the prisoners are un-interested of treatment. He also expressed doubts about if the prison should have a treatment wing at all, probably based on a perception of the prisoners as career criminals not interested in a life without crime and drug abuse.

The leaders of the CBT program are specially trained and certified prison officers. To achieve such certification they first have to take a course in the specific program. Next step is to run it together with a more experienced leader. Last step is to run programs oneself. After having completed a number of programs in this way the applicants are assessed and approved for a certificate by the supervisor.

The treatment wing is situated in a building consisting of cells, a kitchen, and a living room. The prisoners do self-catering, that is they plan their shopping and cook their own meals. Program attendance happens in the morning or the afternoon. The program leaders have their office in another building. They come to the wing only for fetching the prisoners for sessions in a separate place. Program leaders do not take part in daily activities in the wing. They do not interact with the prisoners outside the program sessions either. They also have very sparse, if any, contact with the regular wing staff. All programs in this prison are CBT programs.

Treatment Assignment

The program unit gets its assignment fully in line with the market logic of NPM, that is short sited production goals measured by performance targets and result control. These measures do not leave much room for assessments about whether the program has had any qualitative effects when it comes to attendants' rehabilitation.

> We have some objectives to fulfill from the regional office. The objectives are based on some key figures. How many staff we have in the program team and what a program team member are expected to perform during a year. So...on the basis of what programs we deliver and what human resources (number of staff in the program team) we have, there are key figures for what we are expected to produce during a year. The problem is that the key figures does not always take into account all parameters, like sick leave or away on external training. (Head of treatment team)

The treatment team also have to report monthly the progress of the treatment operation to the regional office. All deviations from the assignment have to be reported and explained. One of the officers in the program reflects upon efficiency motives:

> I think that this approach is linked to "production" (a specialized program team, our remark). Program teams are able to deliver more programs compared to prison officers that work on a daily basis in treatment wings, they have two jobs to do. It should be effective to get many clients to go through programs. But I also think that organized this way with special program teams the programs will work better, the results or the effects on the individual prisoner will probably be better.

The Relation Between Security and Treatment

In relation to security and treatment the physical environment first of all has to be taken into account. A spatial distance is built-in in the treatment wing. The building that holds this wing was constructed after the dramatic escapes in 2004. The guard room is built on a platform. Prisoners that want to contact the officers have to go up some stairs. The officers can monitor what the prisoners are doing from above, so it is basically built like a Panopticon.

After 2004 the distance between prisoners and staff become more apparent. You were not to be alone with a prisoner, they are very dangerous. This attitude also reflect how the new buildings are constructed. The form of the guard room in the treatment wing is one example. The guard room creates distance not closeness. As soon as I take the steps up and into the guard room I have taken some steps into distance. The borders between the prisoners and the staff have become much marked (officer in the program team).

Management in this prison holds that the policy of increased security and control conduce to more and better drug treatment in prison. What are the program leaders' thoughts then? Almost all program team officers agreed that it is a good thing: control and security is here seen as a prerequisite for treatment:

> My opinion is that a good security work is a prerequisite for a good treatment and rehabilitative work. We have to know that the prisoners are drug free, we have to be aware of the prisoners risk behavior in order to be able to work properly with them. There are good and bad of course but one does not exclude the other. The basis for a good prison officer work is a god security work.

One prison officer in the program team though express some doubts about the efforts on security:

> There are problems with the rehabilitative work because security and risk assessment always come first and take a lot of time from treatment work.

Because the prison officers in the program team only meet the prisoners in group sessions the room for developing deeper relations seems rather narrow. However, the majority of them defend this organization of treatment, that is they do not see the importance of interacting with prisoners outside sessions.

Relational Work or Distantiation?

A few program leaders expressed that relational work is important for treatment though. However, one type of argument here is that not taking part in daily activities is good for relational work.

Between 2008 and 2010 I worked as both prison officer in the wing and as prison officer leading program. The problem was that in the program we work a lot with trust and confidence in each other. We open up for each other or rather the clients open up for each other. For me it was very difficult to first sit in a group session and in the afternoon do a visitation of a prisoner's cell and perhaps read the prisoner's letter, the same prisoner who had been in the session in the morning. So we all in the program team thinks that this model is much better. We go in and do our thing and then we walk away. A problem with this model could be that we in the program team will be the good guys and the prison officer in the wing the bad guys. But we work very hard trying to avoid this. We try to make our work as transparent as possible so that the prison officers' in the wing feel that they are involved.

It should be noticed that this argument—that treatment must be done in isolation from other parts of prison activities—actually contradicts the reasoning illustrated in the former section about the compatibility of control and treatment. This raises at least two questions. First, is it really unavoidable to separate treatment from daily life in this way? Some argue that it is because prisoners in high security prisons do not tell their fellow prisoners about their weaknesses or things that can hurt them. They will not show weakness in front of other prisoners. Therefore relational work has to be done in other fora. However, in this wing the same prisoners that interacts outside the program sessions also interacts inside them. Second, is it possible to develop a well-functioning relational work only in the framework of group sessions? Program team officers indicate that they work with creating trust in the group sessions. Prisoners are opening up for each other, tell things about themselves they would not do in other arenas. They do not say anything about whether also program leaders "opens up" relating the prisoners experiences with their own experiences. Such mutuality between the professional and the client is normally seen as pivotal in relational work (Bowlby 1997). One officer from the program team express critique about the separation though.

If we worked in the wing the daily interaction and rehabilitative work would be more natural. If I sit in a group session and we have trained certain skills and then in the wing I see that the prisoner acts in a way that he has forgotten what he learned in the session I can talk to him directly. I could say to him ... perhaps you should remember what we trained to day and try to use these skills in the situation. The rehabilitative work would then come more naturally.

Thus treatment work should perhaps be performed much more in collaboration with the wing staff. And this actualizes another eventual problem: the relations between groups of staff. The division between ordinary staff and program teams may trigger a distanced relation between the two groups. Such feelings of distance is also expressed by wing officers.

We do not get much information from the treatment team. I have worked with program in the treatment wing before, we were a group and there was an open climate and we informed each other of the prisoners' progress or setbacks. We were a team, it does not work like that now.

The wing officers obviously feel that they are not involved in the treatment, and only seen as guards (screws) by the prisoners. This makes it harder to uphold good relations to prisoners.

It is us (the prison officers in the treatment wing) and them (the treatment team). We are the bad guys and the treatment team are the good guys (wing officer).

Also the head of the program team admits the presence of such a distance to the wing officers. He also admits that these group sessions may start processes within prisoners that they dwell upon when being back in the wing, processes that wing staff then has to deal with. This may create conflicts. And, seen from another angle, conflicts between prisoners and wing staff often come up in program sessions. The program team seem to deal with those without really involving the wing staff. Thus, the latter are excluded from solving problems that aroused in their own interaction with prisoners.

There are of course conflicts between the prisoners and the staff in the treatment wing quite often and we in the program team are in the middle and try to be mediators. We listen what the prisoners want and interpret what we think the staff in the treatment wing meant with what he/she did or said. (Program leader)

In the backdrop of the above one may reflect on the effects of the program. Programs are supposed to lead to change of thoughts and self-control. Changed processes of thought shall lead to changes in actions, attitudes and norms. The prisoners in the case here studied explicitly express a trust in program-leaders but not in wing officers. The latter are called "screws," seen only as guards. Program attendance obviously do not have any immediate effects, any immediate changes in how prisoners think in their specific setting. They still cultivate distancing, objectifying "the other" taking stand against improved relations in their day-to-day context.

Treatment in Prisons—Institutional Change in a Changing Political Framework

Relational Work—A Methodological Watershed Between the Two Models

The two cases illustrated above obviously differ in relation to a long row of aspects. In this section we will discuss the most important ones. For the sake of simplicity we use PTC as label for the first one, and CBT for the second.

First of all, PTC is a round-the-clock treatment model, that is principally all activities in the treatment wing shall be integrated and contribute to rehabilitation. Thus, the Twelve-step program is only one part of the whole. Ideologically PTC is inspired by Milieu Therapeutic thinking (De Leon 2000). Here division of labor between staff shall be held on a minimum level. Staff must work close together, be well informed about what is happening, and how things develop. CBT, on the other hand, is sharply marked off from the surroundings. Therapists are special certified staff, and courses are held in isolation from other activities in the wing. Wing staff is not involved.

Second, the core of PTC is relational work. It is about finding strength and support in the community, in familiarity, group solidarity. It is about learning to develop emotional bonds and viable, trustful personal relations. Staff as a group has a central function, on the one hand via personal interaction help the prisoner in his/her personal development, on the other to be an example of how to handle relations in a respectful manner. Personal care is central, to be seen as a person, a subject. The group, the collective is also a key tool in PTC. Therefore recruitment of prisoners, the composition of the group, becomes very important. Quite contrary CBT focuses on self-help—to make the individual stronger and better equipped to replace non-functional thoughts and behavioral patterns with functional ones. It has no strategy for relational work, no developed strategy for using the collective as a force and support either. Group sessions are not used for building relations neither between attendants, nor between prisoners and therapists, the latter because they are not based on giving and taking. A one-sided giving from the prisoner is a weak basis for relational work. The lack of contact between program staff and wing staff further underpins the isolated context in which therapy is taking place.

Third, the Twelve-step program as therapy is based on group rituals for building solidarity and positive emotional energy. For the building of trust it is also very important that sessions are led by a therapist "that have been there," someone who "knows what his talking about" together with one who knows the attendants, that is wing staff that meets the prisoner round-the-clock. CBT courses on the other hand are run by staff with specific program competence. Manuals are developed "scientifically" and shall be followed step-by-step. Deviations jeopardizes program aims. In this way manuals stimulate objectification and distance toward the attender which contradicts relation building. The room for adjusting to unique individuals with their unique experiences and background is strictly limited.

Fourth, PTC is built on a long-term strategy. It has a clear aim of leading the attendant into a new life style after release, helping in connecting the attendant to a membership and a belonging to a special community (NA). CBT on the contrary is a short sited effort. CBT-courses are often run in quite a short time, often a couple of months, and they lack measures for long-term follow-up.

Finally, the relation of PTC to prison control and security is compatible with the concept of dynamic security. Dynamic security stresses that relational work is a prerequisite for security in prisons because it creates mutual trust between staff and prisoners. Constructive personal relations counteracts violence and outbursts of frustration—they are platforms for solving problems in a friendly manner. Advocates of CBT programs in prisons seem to be looking upon security work as a prerequisite for treatment. The two shall be held apart though, that is security and control in ordinary day prison life and treatment in special occasions and places.

To understand the differences, and the struggle for domination, between the two treatment "paradigms" illustrated above it is necessary to put them in their historical context of prison policy development. And, to understand the latter we hold it is necessary to put prison treatment and prison policy development in its social and ideological context, that is the development and change of the political welfare regime. The chapter deals with the more specific prison policy development in the next section and ends up with discussing changes in welfare regimes in the last section.

Competing Prison Treatment Paradigms in Historical Light

In the beginning of the 1970s SPPS introduced their first strategy of drug control and treatment, and started drug treatment in prisons. During the following decades, aims about treatment in prison was an important part of criminal policy (Andersson and Nilsson 2009). This strategy of rehabilitation was also in line with a pronounced government policy of a "drug free society" (Svensson 2012). One important part of the rehabilitative efforts was the Personal Officer reform in 1992. Most prison officers became Personal Officers. This meant being contact person for three to eight prisoners, responsible for doing motivational work, regular counselling and social planning for release, during time in prison. Thus, this reform stresses that the work role of prison officers shall include rehabilitative efforts, and relational work with prisoners. During the 1990s the first systematically manual-based treatment programs were also introduced, and a more systematic work with program development started. This was inspired by the "What Works debate" (McGuire 1995). In many ways the 1990s was a period of prison policy transition. On the one hand several developments anchored in the spirit of criminal politics from earlier decades relating crime to social heritage and context and so forth, where taking place, that is the Personal Officer reform, the introduction of such treatment wings as our first case above, using programs based on social-psychological insights. On the other hand and in correlation with a growing trend of a more punitive societal debate about crime and drug abuse, a new tone began to influence internal policy and governance of SPPS.

In the beginning of 2000 a Commission for The Special Anti-Drug Effort published a white paper (SOU 2000, p. 126). One chapter here was about strategies for "drug free prisons." The Commission proposals concerned mainly three areas in prisons: drug control, anti-drug treatment, and evaluation of programs (Nylander et al. 2012). By reducing drugs in prisons and separating drug users and non-users, the Commission expected to avoid violence and disturbance in wings. In this way a more secure environment in prisons was expected (Kolind et al. 2013). Within the SPPS the "scientific approach" of treatment in the framework of the What Works debate did a break-through. In Sweden this closely relates to the contemporary movement for EBP in care and social work (Nilsson 2013). Programs were now developed in areas such as drug abuse, violence, and sex offending. Inspired by Canada and the UK, an accreditation panel of researchers from different Swedish universities for assisting SPPS with expertise knowledge to assess the programs was set up in 2002. The panel was heavily dominated by psychiatrists and psychologists. The assessments of the panel came to be based first and foremost on effect evaluations built on randomized control techniques (RCT), or meta-evaluations of first and foremost several such RCT studies. This way of evaluating clearly facilitates programs based on standardized manual following, that is different CBT programs (Bergmark et al. 2011). In particular the aim of accreditation was to ensure the effectiveness of programs, making sure they were designed and delivered in accordance with an evidence base (cf. Hollin and Bilby 2007). The accreditation panel intended to guarantee professionalism and to ensure that the SPPS gets value for money (Kolind et al. 2013).

Besides increasing the number of treatment programs the authority started to train prison officers to be program leaders. In parallel, as mentioned above, security and control measures increased heavily. Heavy investments in security measures accompanied with arguments about that those (also) are necessary for successful treatment, together with the CBT treatment programs, signify that a "new" rehabilitation ideology have conquered domination.

A Step Up: Prison Policy in Its Ideological Context—Changes in Welfare Regime

The PTC model has been influenced by several different treatment approaches, international as well as Swedish ones. The central concept of alcohol as a disease has roots in the Twelve-step ideology, later developed into a treatment program starting in the Hazelden Hospital in Minnesota, US, and imported to Sweden in the 1980s under the name of the "Minnesota model" (Karlsson 2012). However, as described the treatment ideology has its emphasis on relational work and group solidarity. This in turn is rooted in sociological and social-psychological insights about the individual as a social creature belonging to a social context (Collins 1988). As such it is well anchored in theories about social heritage so dominant during the 1960s and 1970s—the era of the Nordic "social-democratic" welfare regimes (Bruhn et al. 2015; Nilsson 2013): People become criminals and/or drug addicts, at least to a great extent as a result of bad life chances and social conditions. All humans have abilities to grow under the right circumstances. Methods for rehabilitation were supposed to create better social conditions for the individual under and after treatment. As a consequence, several of the tools in PTC are about learning to develop good and trustful relations to others, building partnership and collective solidarity, but also helping to prepare for a better life after sentence served, that is not only to keep a job but also to end up in positive social networks (cf. Bronfenbrenner 1979; Scheff 1997; Bowlby 1997).

On societal level the last decades have meant a successive transformation of welfare state policy toward what may be called a neo-liberal welfare regime (cf. Garland 2013). This is clearly mirrored in how the prison and penal policy has changed, not least when it comes to theories and methods for treatment of criminal offenders. On a macro level this means a strong emphasis on *economic man* and the individual's freedom of choice at the expense of strivings toward equality and fair social conditions for every citizen (Bruhn et al. 2015; Smith 2006). And, as discussed in the section about neoliberal values above: in the field of crime and crime prevention, the natural prolongation of this neo-liberal world-view is that committing crime is profoundly a matter of choice (Garland 2001). Preventing crime becomes a question of making it "costly," of deterrence and control (Nilsson 2013). In relation to treatment in prison categorizations between "heinous" criminals (hopeless cases), and "regular" ones are today made on the basis of risk assessment. The latter, as well as the minor group who suffers from some kind of psychological or psychiatric disease are the "treatable" ones. A drug addict may have started the abuse out of choice. However, this may lead to a "disease" that needs special treatment. To treat the ill ones there are two alternatives often used in combination: psychopharmacologic drugs and specially developed treatment programs based on clinical expertise.

This ideological change on state level gives perspective to the growing repressiveness of the penal system. To fully comprehend the causes behind "the security turn" in Swedish prison policy, it is not enough to refer to some spectacular events (escapes etc.). Rather, these should be seen as triggers of an ongoing undercurrent of policy change. What may be not as obvious is the connection between the changing welfare policy and the changes in treatment ideology—the "scientific approach" (the EBP movement) that has come to dominate in later decades. The "What Works?" movement in prison policy is variant of this, at least in Sweden. According to Sackett et al. (1996, p. 71), "evidence-based practice is the conscientious, explicit and judicious use of current evidence in making decisions about the care of individuals" (cf. Morago 2006). The dominating variant of this approach in Swedish health care and social work has come to be relatively short, clear-cut programs for treatment held in isolation from their physical and social context (Bergmark et al. 2011). As also Smith highlights:

even when treatment programs and rehabilitative efforts are used in prisons today they are often focused more on the individual prisoner´s internal psychology (such as cognitive programs) and less on relations with the outside world (family, social contacts, education, work) whereby the criminal "Other" and the dangers (and risks) it allegedly presents become the focus of attention rather than a prisoner's welfare needs (2015, p. 34).

As described, programs are built on standardized treatment. Taking the individual's unique conditions into consideration then becomes a hindrance. Deviations from manual may jeopardize both the scientifically carefully worked out treatment process, and the possibilities to evaluate and secure evidence of efficiency. In this paradigmatic context the ability to evaluate via quantitative indicators is decisive. It facilitates comparisons with other programs, and marks out the status of evidence. The aim of EBP proponents is to construct such evidence status hierarchies in different areas. On top of these comes systematic reviews and meta-analysis of RCT studies. Second best are single RCT studies (Oxford Center for Evidence Based Medicine 2009).

Besides the treatment ideology in itself two aspects are of special importance in the prison context. First, the relation to security and control. A new balance of the prison dilemma between security and rehabilitation is taking place. In practice treatment and motivational work tends to be performed in complete isolation from all other day-to-day activities in prison. And, security/control represents a postulate for treatment. PDT methods are expected to contribute to a reduction of crime in society, and to uphold internal order in prisons (cf. Hannah-Moffat 2005). At the same time control is believed to contribute to better drug treatment. Treatment is prioritized not primarily because of drug users' social problems or because individual welfare can improve the inmates' self-esteem or insights, but because it links up with criminality and constitutes means to manage risk (Kolind et al. 2013, p. 11, see also Holm et al. 2014; Robinson 2008). In a way this development reflects a broader criminalization of social problems. Social policy becomes increasingly formed in relation to its crime reducing potential. When drug problems are framed as crime problems the welfare state implicitly becomes a penal mechanism (Kolind et al. 2013, p. 10).

Second, the emphasis on quantitative measuring makes the EBP-paradigm well fit to the ruling doctrine of public sector governance—NPM. NPM consists of a cluster of ideas and measures based either on a bureaucratic logic of detailed regulation, or ideas retrieved from private sector favoring market and businesslike principles (Hood 1991; Christensen and Lægreid 2007). It rests on neo-liberal values about small government and tax payers' right to know that their money "is being spent economically, efficiently, and effectively" (Power 1997, p. 44). The commission of the state is to uphold the law and the distribution of resources according to principles of cost-efficiency and equal justice, not welfarist ideals of social engineering and empowerment of "underdog" individuals or groups (Bruhn 2015). The message is embedded in a managerial rhetoric of administrative neutrality. "Whether in prison or the corporate world, mission statements make palatable and disguise that which is disturbing" (Bosworth 2007, p. 81).

Despite having their origin in different scientific disciplines, EBP and NPM share the same individualistic approach to free choice, and the use of technological knowledge. They both stress evidence and general techniques based on standardization and quantitative indicators to deal with issues independent of context (Petersén and Olsson 2014). Both emanate from an ideological context of mistrust of "the other," of top-down rationalistic views about the need to control organizational performance and human behavior (Power 1997). This fact has been beneficial to the diffusion of EBP in prisons as well as other public sector branches. The influence of both is strongly indicated, for instance, in the above referenced White Paper (SOU 2000, p. 126). When drug treatment in prison is discussed themes are expertise, evaluation, monitoring, evidence-based programs and accreditation panel. Treatment in prisons becomes clearly linked to a managerial rhetoric of measurement and efficiency (Kolind et al. 2013). And, how this way of thinking about treatment efforts in prisons have "sunk in" is mirrored in the data of the second case above when management and prison officers reduce their talk about quality and efficiency in treatment to number of courses, number of prisoners that have completed programs and so forth.

To conclude, two treatment paradigms are living side-by-side in today's Swedish prison context. Each of them basically reflects one of the two different competing ideologies of the role of the state and the public sphere in late modern society—the socio-liberal and the neo-liberal one. In the same way as neo-liberal ideology has come to dominate Swedish welfare policy in later decades the CBT paradigm has come to dominate treatment of those deviants from normality that is "taken care of" in different societal institutions. At the same time the "older" welfare ideology and models for treatment live on in different niches and spaces of welfare policy and institutions, and the struggle between these world views continues in the mundane activities of ordinary life in welfare institutions as well as on different political arenas of societal debate. This is quite obvious also when it comes to criminal and prison policy.

References

Andersson, R. (2004). Behandlingstankens återkomst—Från psykoanalys till kognitiv beteendeterapi [The return of treatment thought—from psychoanalysis to cognitive behaviour therapy]. *Nordisk Tidskrift for Kriminalvidenskab, 5.* 384–403.

Andersson, R., & Nilsson, R. (2009). *Svensk Kriminalvårdspolitik [Swedish penal policy]*. Malmö: Liber.

Amilon, C., & Edstedt, E. (1998). *Kriminalvård—insikter och utblickar [Prison care—insights and views]*. Stockholm: Norstedts juridik.

Bergmark, A., Bergmark, Å., Lundström, T. (2011). *Evidensbaserat socialt arbete. Teori, kritik, praktik [Evidence-based social work. Theory, critique, practice]*. Stockholm: Natur & Kultur.

Bosworth, M. (2007). Creating the responsible prisoner. Federal admission and orientation packs. *Punishment & Society, 9*(1), 67–85.

Bowlby, J. (1997). *Attachment and loss*. London: Pimlico.

Bronfenbrenner, U. (1979). *The ecology of human development*. Cambridge, MA: Harvard University Press.

Bruhn, A. (2013). Gender relations and division of labour among prison officers in Swedish male prisons. *Journal of Scandinavian Studies in Criminology and Crime Prevention, 14*(2). 115–132.

Bruhn, A. (2015). Changing occupational roles in audit society—the case of Swedish student aid officials. *Nordic Journal of Working Life Studies, 5*(1), 31–50.

Bruhn, A., Nylander, P. Å., Lindberg, O. (2015). Swedish "prison exceptionalism" in decline—trends towards distance and objectification of the other. In A. Eriksson (Ed.), *Punishing the other* (pp. 101–123). London: Routledge. 101–123

Christensen, T., & Lægreid, P. (2007). Introduction—theoretical approach and research questions. In T. Christensen and P. Lægreid (Eds.), *Transcending new public management. The transformation of public sector reforms* (pp. 1–16). Surrey: Ashgate Publishing Limited. 1–16

Collins, R. (1988). *Interactional ritual chains.* New York: Harcourt Brace & Company.

De Leon, G. (2000). *The therapeutic community. Theory, model, and method.* New York: Springer Publishing Company.

Ekbom, T., Engström, G., Göransson, B. (2011). *Människan, brottet, följderna—kriminalitet och kriminalvård i Sverige* [*Man, crime, consequences—criminality and prison care in Sweden*]. Stockholm: Natur & Kultur.

Foucault, M. (1977). *Discipline and punish: the birth of the prison.* New York: Vintage.

Garland, D. (2001). *The culture of control: Crime and social order in contemporary society.* New York: Oxford University Press.

Garland, D. (2013). The 2012 Sutherland address penalty and the penal state. *Criminology, 51*(3), 475–517.

Griffin, M. L. (2002). The influence of professional orientation on detention officers' attitudes toward the use of force. *Criminal Justice and Behaviour, 29*(3), 250–277.

Hannah-Moffat, K. (2005). Criminogenic needs and the transformative risk subject: hybridizations of risk/need in penality. *Punishment & Society, 7*(1), 29–51.

Hemmens, C., & Stohr, M. K. (2000). The two faces of the correctional role: an exploration of the value of the correctional role instrument. *International Journal of Offender Therapy and Comparative Criminology, 44*(3), 326–349.

Hollin, C. R., & Bilby, C. (2007). Adressing offending behavior: "what works" and beyond. In Y. Jewkes (Ed.), *Handbook of prisons* (pp. 608–628). Devon: Willan Publishing.

Holm, C., Lindberg, O., Jukic, E., Nylander, P. Å. (2014). Flera nyanser av blått. Kriminalvårdare på behandlingsavdelningar—deras beskrivningar av yrkesroller, drogbehandling och de intagna. *Nordisk Kriminalvidenskaplig tidskrift, 101*, 183–204.

Hood, C. (1991). A public management for all seasons? *Public Administration, 69*(1), 3–19.

Karlsson, M. (2012). 12-stegsbehandling—en behandlingsmetod för att uppnå nykterhet och drogfrihet [12-step treatment—a treatment method for being sober and free of drugs]. *Handbok i missbrukspsykologi—teori och tillämpning.* Malmö: Liber.

Kolind, T., Frank, V. A., Lindberg, O., Tourunen, J. (2013). Prison-based drug treatment in Nordic political discourse: an elastic discursive construct. *European Journal of Criminology, 10*(6), 659–674.

Kolind, T., Asmussen Frank, V., Lindberg, O., Torunen, J. (2014). Officers and drug counsellors: new occupational identities in Nordic prison. *British Journal of Criminology (EJC), 55*, 303–320.

Kvale, S. (1996). *Interviews: an introduction to qualitative research interviewing.* Thousand Oaks: Sage.

Lindberg, O. (1998). *Emotions, social bonds and rituals. A qualitative study on drug careers* (dissertation). Örebro: Örebro University.

Lindberg, O. (2005). Prison cultures and social representations: The case of Hinseberg, a women's prison in Sweden. *International Journal of Prisoner Health, 1*, 143–161.

McGuire, J. (1995). *What works: reducing reoffending: guidelines from research and practice.* Chichester: John Wiley & Sons.

Morago, P. (2006). Evidence-based practice: from medicine to social work. *European Journal of Social Work, 9*(4), 461–477.

Nilsson, R. (2013). From learning to labour to learning to self-control: the paradigmatic change in Swedish prison policy. *Journal of Scandinavian Studies in Criminology and Crime Prevention, 14*(S1), 24–45.

Nylander, P. Å., Holm, C., Jukic, E., Lindberg, O. (2012). Drug treatment in Swedish prisons: moving towards evidence-based interventions? *Nordic Studies on Alcohol and Drugs, 29* (6), 561–574.

Oxford Center for Evidence Based Medicine. (2009). *Levels of evidence.* University of Oxford. http://www.cebm.net/?O=1025. Accessed December 2015).

Petersén, A. C., & Olsson, J. I. (2014). Calling evidence-based practice into question: acknowledging phronetic knowledge in social work. *British Journal of Social Work Advanced Access*, pp. 1–17, doi:10.1093/bjsw/bcu020.

Power, M. (1997). *The audit society. Rituals of verification.* New York: Oxford University Press.

Robinson, G. (2008). Late-modern rehabilitation. The evolution of a penal strategy. *Punishment & Society, 10*(4), 429–445.

Sackett, D. L., Rosenberg, W. M. C., Gray, M. J. A. Haynes, B. R., Richardson, S. W. (1996). Evidence-based medicine: what it is and what it isn't. *British Medical Journal, 312*(7023), 71–72.

Scheff, T. J. (1997). *Emotions, the social bond and human reality, part/whole analysis.* Cambridge: Cambridge University Press.

Smith, P. S (2006). Fängslet og forestillingen om det moraliske hospital. Fra religös omvendelse till kognitive behandlingsprogrammer. In C. Lomholt and L. Kuhle (Eds.), *Straffens menneskelige ansikt* (pp. 93–124). Forlaget ANIS. 93–124

Smith, P. S. (2015). Reform and research: re-connecting prison and society in the 21st century. *International Journal of Crime, Justice and Social Democracy, 4*(1), 33–49.

SOU (Swedish Government Official Report Series). (2000). *Vägvalet—den narkotikapolitiska utmaningen.* SOU 2000:126. http://www.regeringen.se/sb/d/108/a/2815. Accessed 2 September 2016.

SOU (Swedish Government Official Reports Series). (2005). *Säkert inlåst? En granskning av rymningarna från Kumla, Hall, Norrtälje och Mariefred 2004* [Safely locked up]. Betänkande av rymningsutredningen. SOU 2005:6.

SPPS (1990). *The Österåker project. A further follow-up of the drug misuser treatment program at Österåker Prison.* Research Paper No 1. Norrköping: Kriminalvårdsstyrelsen.

Svensson, B. (2012). *Narkotikapolitik och narkotikadebatt.* Studentlitteratur: Lund.

Swedish National Council for Crime Prevention (SNCCP). (2008). *Behandling av narkotikamissbrukare i fängelse – en effektstudie.* Rapport 2008:18. Stockholm: Brottsförebyggande rådet.

Sykes, G. M. (1958). *The society of captives: a study of a maximum security prison.* Princeton, NJ: Princeton University Press.

Is Prison Drug Treatment a Welfare Service?

Torsten Kolind

Introduction

The intricate relation between welfare and punishment in Nordic prisons is especially noticeable in present prison drug treatment. As an institution within the institution, prison-based drug treatment programs are to deliver a welfare service to incarcerated citizens on line with what non-incarcerated citizens are entitled to. However, the larger institutional context (the prison) as well as the general criminal justice political discourse naturally interfere with and affect such service delivery. As a result of this, it becomes difficult to disentangle what is in fact a part of the welfare service (drug treatment) and a part of punishment and the related disciplinary sanctions. The questions arise whether prison disciplinary sanctions can be re-interpreted as being a part of drug treatment? Whether drug treatment is mainly to be seen as a crime-reducing

T. Kolind (✉)
Centre for Alcohol and Drug Research,Aarhus University, Aarhus, Denmark
e-mail: tk.crf@psy.au.dk

© The Author(s) 2017
P. Scharff Smith, T. Ugelvik (eds.), *Scandinavian Penal History, Culture and Prison Practice,* Palgrave Studies in Prisons and Penology, DOI 10.1057/978-1-137-58529-5_9

strategy? And can prison drug treatment programs, intended to mirror community programs, simply become enmeshed in the traditional prison control/rehabilitation conundrum? In this chapter I attempt to address these questions.

Over the last 20 years there has been a growth in prison-based drug treatment in Danish prisons. Among other things, this development can be seen as an answer to the increase in the drug-using prison population; approximately, 60 % of all prisoners report drug use before imprisonment in Denmark (Kriminalforsorgen 2014). Also, in other European countries such a development regarding prison drug treatment programs and increasing drug use within the walls has been seen (EMCDDA 2012; Frank and Kolind 2012; Seddon et al. 2012). Moreover, several studies have documented how drug-dependent prisoners and drug-related problems influence or even dictate the everyday life of many prisons (Stöver and Michels 2010). Drugs are increasingly controlled, sold, and used in prisons (Crewe 2005, 2006). Drug use and drug selling is increasingly sanctioned (Seddon et al. 2012), drug use is treated (Kolind et al. 2012), and health services are directed toward drug users (e.g., in order to prevent the spread of infectious diseases) (Levy and Stöver 2013). In Denmark a range of different drug treatment services are offered in prisons, organized by a so-called import model, implying that counselors are employed by outside private or municipal institutions and then hired to do drug treatment within the walls. In remand prisons motivational programs aim at motivating drug-using prisoners to start in a drug treatment program when sentenced or if released, and in prisons one finds treatment wings, day treatment programs (for cannabis, cocaine, or heroin users respectively), drug-free wings, and after-treatment wings. The treatment wings are closed off from the rest of the prisons and offer intensive programs including individual and group sessions and training in everyday activities, and the interaction between officers and prisoners is more relaxed and personal than in the regular wings (see, for instance, Haller 2015). The day treatment programs are less intensive, divided between cannabis-, cocaine-, and harm reduction-oriented programs, and in general they offer individual sessions once a week. Drug treatment in Danish prisons is primarily inspired by Minnesota and/or cognitive therapy methods (Storgaard 1999).

Currently, approximately 15–20 % of all prisoners are in some kind of drug treatment program (including the so-called drug-free wings) (Kriminalforsorgen 2011). Finally, Danish prisoners are covered by a drug treatment guarantee promising all drug-using prisoners access to a drug treatment program within 14 days after their first request. In sum then, we have seen a growth in drug treatment-related welfare services offered in Danish prisons over the last two decades.

At the same time however, one has also since around year 2000 witnessed a growth in drug control and disciplinary sanctions in prisons as for instance reflected in the two Governmental drug action plan (Regeringen 2003, 2010). In fact, one can speak of a dual prison drug policy characterized by increased drug treatment and increased drug control.[1] Among other things, higher fences have been built to hinder drugs being thrown into prison yards, the use of sniffer dogs have increased (also used on visitors), and it is a political demand that the Prison Service do urine tests on an average 2 % of the daily prison population (in fact, from 2006 to 2011, 2.7 % of the daily prison population was tested Kriminalforsorgen 2011b, p. 6). Also, sanctions for possessing, using or selling drugs have increased (Frank and Kolind 2008). According to a Ministerial circular (Kriminalforsorgen 2004), drug use in prisons is to be sanctioned by 3–4 days in a confinement cells, a fine, and, most importantly, for the prisoners, paroles and week-end leaves are suspended. As a consequence, many of the most addicted and heavily affected prisoners who do not manage to terminate their drug use while imprisoned are serving full time, not allowed out on weekend leaves and often also build up a drug debt to other prisoners while in prison (Kolind et al. 2010).

In conclusion, we have on the one hand witnessed an increase in the welfare services offered in Danish prisons directed toward drug-using prisoners. On the other hand, and this will be the focus of this chapter, it is important to discuss whether and to what extent such prison-based

---

[1] Such dual drug policy is also seen in other Nordic countries; Norway: Mjåland (2015); Finland: Tourunen et al. (2012, pp. 575–588).

welfare services differ from the community-based drug treatment services they are to mirror as they are much more linked up with disciplinary control and sanctions. In the following, I will outline how the existence of what could be termed a welfare hybrid in Danish prisons appears on respectively the policy level, the institutional level, and from the perspective of the prisoners. In the end of the chapter I will discuss the implications of the growth of prison-based drug treatment in a welfare state perspective.

Data

This chapter is based on data stemming from the Nordic comparative research project "Prison-Based Drug Treatment in the Nordic Countries," which compares prison-based drug treatment at the level of political discourse, institutions, and prisoners' experiences in Denmark, Finland, Norway, and Sweden. In this chapter, data from the Danish part of the research project collected from June 2011 to June 2012 will be drawn upon. These data includes policy documents and political debates and qualitative interviews with three key informants (three men with long-term experiences with prison rehabilitation), and qualitative in-depth interviews with 32 prisoners (20 men), 11 officers (5 men), and 16 counselors (11 men) in three prisons, two high-security (closed) prisons and one low-security (open) prison. In addition 1 month of fieldwork was conducted in each of the three prisons. The interviews, lasting 1–1½ hours each, were digitally recorded and subsequently transcribed. Transcripts of interviews and observational notes were then coded thematically. The thematic coding helped to develop relevant analytical concepts as well as isolate and categorize specific and contextual related themes (cf. Lewis 1995; Strauss and Corbin 1997). In previous chapters, data, method and methodology has been outlined in greater details (Kolind et al. 2012, 2014; Frank et al. 2015). The research project was funded by the Joint Committee for Nordic Research Councils for the Humanities and Social Sciences (NOS-HS).

Policy Level

The policy approach to prison-based drug treatment in Denmark has already been touched upon above. In general, the present Danish political prison drug strategy can be analyzed as a dual policy advocating for both more control and more treatment at one and the same time. As also discussed elsewhere in this volume (see Smith, this volume), the opposition between ideas of rehabilitation and punishment is built in to modern prisons. As such, one could expect that in the dual Danish drug political discourse some ambiguousness would exist. This is however not the case. In policy documents, like the Governmental drug action plan "Fight against drugs" (Regeringen 2003, 2010), and in the political discourse alike, advocacy for increase in both prison-based drug treatment and control and disciplinary sanctions goes hand in hand.

The increase in prison drug treatment has been argued as sound and legitimate for at least four different reasons. First, it has been argued as being part of the official zero tolerance strategy of the Danish Government. Having drug treatment programs, it is argued, help prisoners become drug free and will hereby lead to a diminishing of the prison drug market in prisons. Reversely, the harshening of disciplinary sanctions following the policy of zero tolerance will, it is argued, simultaneously motivate (scare) prisoners to start in treatment as they increasingly will fear the potential disciplinary sanctions following their continued drug use. Second, the general aim of Danish prisons is to help reduce crime. Hence, prison-based drug treatment is also argued as being central in achieving this strategy; the so-called drug-crime link (Duke 2006). The argument put fore is that crime and drug use/selling are intertwined. Therefore, by making people drug free they are also at the same time becoming crime free. A third and rather different kind of argument in favor of the growth in prison-based drug treatment relates to the rights of citizens to welfare state services. As part of both the Danish Prison Service principle of Normalization (see, e.g., Engbo 2005, pp. 44–45) and laws stipulating that prisoners are to be offered the same health services as the outside population, prison-based drug treatment and especially the drug treatment guarantee has been implemented on the argument that this secure prisoners the same civil rights as the general public. The fourth and final argument relates to the management of modern welfare institutions. Increasingly, new public management techniques have been introduced in modern welfare institutions (Villadsen 2004) with the overall intention that such management tools will foster well-led and well-managed public institution (Dahler-Larsen and Larsen 2001; Rieper 2004). In the Danish Prison Service and in relation to prison-based drug treatment such techniques have among other things included the mandatory accreditation of drug treatment programs, the monitoring of prisoners' drug use by use of standardized registrations, the introduction of self-evaluation manuals for counselors running the drug treatment programs, and the introduction of new software and information technology. Hence, by implementing all these management tools in relation to prison-based drug treatment, prison-based drug treatment becomes for the Prison Service a way to show itself to be a modern and well-governed institution.

These four rationales are then together put forward in the Danish political discourse on prison-based drug treatment, and, as argued elsewhere (Kolind et al. 2013), one could speculate if such envisaged outcomes of prison-based drug treatment can in fact help explain the large and relatively sudden growth in prison-based drug treatment and its popularity. That is, the growth of prison-based drug treatment relates to the fact that it has been constructed as fit-for-all purposes. It should however be noted, that the increasing intertwining of control and disciplinary sanctions in the political discourse on prison-based drug treatment differs from the political discourse on community-based drug treatment in which we over the last 10–15 years have, in fact, seen a move in the opposite direction (Frank et al. 2013). As will be discussed below, this development goes somewhat against the Prison Service's principle of Normalization arguing that welfare services, like prison-based drug treatment, are to be similar whether they are offered inside or outside the prison walls.

Institutional Level

Looking at the intuitional level, that is, the individual prisons in which the drug treatment programs are implemented, the daily practices and the experiences of the staff are more ambiguous and caught in more dilemmas than is the case in the political discourse. Also, these front workers' practices often divert from official policies; so-called street-level bureaucracy (Lipsky 1980). That is, when counselors or officers do treatment or carry out control, personal discretion is often essential in order to secure a smooth running of the everyday life in prisons and in order to uphold order and manage a large group of people *en bloc* (Liebling 2000, 2011).

The counselors and officers' discretionary practices and hence the way drug treatment is implemented in practice in Danish prison settings is very much influenced by both the structural arrangements of the prisons and by the prisoner culture. First, the structural framework in prisons differs in many ways from community-based drug treatment. Due to, inter alia, the high level of control, the frequent relocation of prisoners from one wing or prison to another, and the restricted facilities inside the prisons, drug treatment programs often have to adjust. For instance, group therapy sessions are not always feasible due to security matter, motivational counseling may suddenly be discontinued if the prisoner is moved to another institution, case management-related advocacy is restricted as movements between welfare services is restricted, and harm reduction initiatives are limited because of prison specific regulations (needle exchange is forbidden in Danish prisons as is also heroin treatment, despite the existence of these services in the community) (Michel et al. 2015). Second, the so-called inmate culture together with what has been termed the pains of imprisonment (Sykes 1958) likewise informs the drug services delivered in the prisons. Enrolment in drug treatment programs, for instance, often holds low status among prisoners. Moreover, group therapy is often experienced as risky for the prisoners as they fear that any (vulnerable) information disclosed during such sessions can and will be used against them by other prisoners at a later point, and counselors even report that group session can be used to make drug deals. Besides, many prisoners report that though they may participate in drug treatment programs because they want to become drug free, their motivation also strongly relates to the hard times they experience in prisons; for instance, the harsh prison culture, violence, drug debt, the prisons' disciplinary sanctions, loss of privacy, and the miss of family member (see below).

Considering then the counselors' delivery of welfare services (drug treatment) to the prisoners, we see that this service is different from how drug treatment is practiced on the outside. Two diversions are to be mentioned here. One the one hand, counselors tend to sympathize with the prisoners and the difficult time they often experience in prisons, and they feel that they have to somehow mitigate the prisoners' deprivations; deprivations which include both those imposed by imprisonment and by the counterproductive prisoner culture (as outlined above). In consequence, counselors often adjust the drug treatment programs, the focus of the therapy sessions, and the aim of the treatment to match the daily lives of the prisoners. That is, the content of the drug treatment programs often come to center on how the prisoner can best manage prison life. In short, prison-based drug treatment is in practice mainly about alleviating the negative consequences of imprisonment (see also Kolind et al. 2010), whereas the aims stipulated in the political discourse about crime reduction and zero tolerance turn out to be of only secondary importance.

However, the counselors also adjust prison-based drug treatment in another way when implementing this service in prisons. Though counselors generally experience that the prison environment restrict the programs in certain ways, as discussed above, many counselors also see some advantages in conducting drug treatment in a highly controlled setting. Some for instance tell that prisoners show up to scheduled appointments more frequently than compared with outside outpatient treatment simply because they are locked up and then easier to get hold of. Moreover, and maybe more importantly, some counselors not only adjust, but even integrate the drug control and the disciplinary sanctions in their drug treatment ideology and practices. As mentioned, random urine tests, urine tests on prisoners suspected of having taken drugs, cell searches, and use of sniffer dogs are part of the daily control as are also the disciplinary sanctions following illegal drug use/sale/possession. And some of the counselors perceive such control and disciplinary practices more and more as tools which can be integrated in their own work. Some counselors for instance tell that they advocate for prisoners being punished for having sniffed their legally prescribed drugs (e.g., Retalin) instead of taking it orally, as they see such practices as part of a "drug user attitude" despite such practice is not illegal. Three days in an isolation cell, for instance, would in the eyes of these counselors make the prisoner consider and reflect on his commitment to and engagement in the program and especially the program's focus on honesty, personal change, and abstinence (see also Nielsen and Kolind, 2016). In another example, some counselors tried to prevent prisoners from going on weekend leaves even though they were eligible from the officers' point of view; as the counselors argued, these prisoners were not psychologically "ready" for a leave and hence the counselors believed that the prisoners would maybe fall back in to drug use if allowed out on leave.

In sum, the counselors' practice of drug treatment in Danish prison settings focussing on alleviating the pains of imprisonment and integrating prison control and disciplinary sanctions departs from the aims stipulated in the political discourse, and it departs from how drug treatment is practiced in the outside community as a welfare service.

It should however also be mentioned, that the growing presence of prison-based drug treatment in Danish prisons may also influence the outlook and attitudes of the prison officers. In short, as counselors move toward integrating control and sanctions in their treatment approach, prison officers involved in drug treatment experience themselves as becoming more humane, considerate, and also interested in the prisoners rehabilitation. They spend more time together with the prisoners (primarily in the treatment wings) and also tell that they tend to use their discretionary power to support the running of the drug treatment program and to a larger extent than would normally be the case they support the prisoners when they are going through hard times. In sum, officers highlight the treatment ethos in their control work. As the focus of this chapter is on prison-based drug treatment, I will not go into detail on this development, however, one could speculate if such changes in officers' outlook may also influence the larger prison (see Kolind et al. 2015).

Prisoners

So far, I have analyzed how prison-based drug treatment is argued in the political discourse, and how it is implemented in daily institutional practices. In this last section I look at how prison-based drug treatment is experienced by prisoners. Especially, I will show that prisoners' motivations for entering drug treatment programs and their experiences with prison-based drug treatment though related to outside circumstance are also very much determined by the structural conditions in the prisons.

First, some prisoners tell that they value the drug treatment programs in prisons as they perceive such programs to offer them a chance to, among other things, "move on in life," begin to deal with the stress and chaos their drug use causes on the outside, and break the vicious circle of moving in and out of prisons. Second, however, many prisoners also reveal a great deal of pragmatism, and they stress motives strongly related to their present situation in prison. For many, entering drug treatment is a way for them to escape the brutal and violent life in the regular wings (see, e.g., Crewe 2005; Jewkes 2005) characterized by treats, violence, and drug debts. The treatment wings are simply a safer place than the regular wings (see also Haller 2015). Some also tell that entering a drug treatment program shows to the officers and the prison authorities in general that one is trying to constructively work on one's drug problem, which in the ideology of "something-for-something"— as it is called in the Governmental drug action plan (Regeringen 2003) —can improve one's chances of getting weekend leaves, early parole, or be transferred to an open prison. Third, some prisoners tell that they are dejected by the disciplinary sanctions related to their drug use (mainly cannabis), and they hope that the drug treatment program can help them to temporarily discontinue their use. That is, they enroll in drug treatment not because of a wish to change their live as such, but because they feel pressured or even forced by the increased control and disciplinary sanctions of the prison. This can be considered problematic because motivation for treatment is critical if clients are to become fully engaged in therapy (Rosen et al. 2004; Longshore and Teruya 2006).

Considering then the prisoners experiences with the drug treatment programs, these are often full of dilemmas caused by the structural arrangements of the prison. For instance, and as mentioned above, in the programs there is a high turnover, as when prisoners are released, transferred, discharged, or leave the programs voluntarily. As a consequence of such instability in the social environment, prisoners often do not get to learn to know each other and hence experience that rapport becomes difficult to create, which in turn inflicts on especially group sessions but also the general environment in the drug treatment wings. This situation is then further accentuated by the often highly distrustful prison environment, in which prisoners seldom open up personally vis-à-vis other prisoners or reveal any vulnerable sides of themselves as they fear that such practices will later be misused by other prisoners and turned against them. To be honest and engage in personal change and to engage in intimate relations, which is encouraged by the drug treatment counselors, are simply too risky in a prison setting (see also Frank et al. 2015; Haller 2015). Finally, prisoners also experience that the prisons' control and disciplinary environment influence their treatment by at times employing collective sanctions if individuals violate prison rules. If, for instance, a prisoner in a treatment program is detected with having cannabis in his cell other prisoners tell how they feel that every prisoner is then suspected afterward and that increased control are implemented on all. In sum, the prison environment tends to generate uncertainties, which influence the prisoners' experience of the drug treatment programs.

Discussion

Contemporary Danish prison drug policy can be analyzed as a dual drug policy characterized by a simultaneous growth in drug control and disciplinary sanctions and prison-based drug treatment services. In this chapter I have shown how this development influences the existence of prison-based drug treatment in respectively the political discourse, institutional practice, and prisoner's experiences.

In this discussion I will consider the implications of this development for our understanding of prison drug treatment as being a welfare service. In line with the Danish Prison Service's principle of normalization, implying that life inside prisons shall resemble outside life as much as possible (Kriminalforsorgen 1993), drug treatment programs have been implemented on a large scale, and a drug treatment guarantee secures drug-using prisoners a right to treatment. In this way, one can argue that the Danish welfare state encompasses or at least strongly influences Danish prisons. One might even argue that the prison to some extent can be considered to be a kind of traditional welfare state institution substitute. However, such a conclusion should be taken with a pinch of salt. Despite the fact that welfare services, like drug treatment, are offered on a large scale inside Danish prisons, I have also shown how such a service changes, and at times change considerably so, when imported in to a prison context and adjusted to a prison environment.

First, if we compare prison-based drug treatment to community drug treatment on the level of political discourse, one finds that community drug treatment is argued mainly as a welfare service which drug using citizens are entitled to in line with other services which other citizens in need are entitled to (Bjerge 2005, 2008). More and more, elements of control, punishment, and sanctions have disappeared from policy documents on community drug and alcohol treatment services, and, in general, it is argued that enrolment in drug and alcohol treatment should be based on a voluntary decision (Frank et al. 2013). Prison drug treatment on the other hand, is, as argued above, very much entangled in a discourse of control, punishment, and compulsion. Furthermore, prison-based drug treatment is in the political discourse argued to be sound mainly because it can help reduce crime and because it is seen as part of the policy of zero tolerance toward drugs; not because it helps the individual psychologically or socially (see also Robinson 2008).

Second, at the institutional level we also see how prison-based drug treatment differs from community-based drug treatment. In general, I argued that prison drug treatment in counselors' everyday practices is strongly influenced by the prison environment. Not only do we see how the aims of the treatment to a large extent get adjusted to fit the prisoners' life inside the wall by aiming mainly at alleviating the pains of imprisonment, but when implemented in practice prison-based drug treatment also tends to be more based on control and sanctioning than community drug treatment. For instance, urine test are rarely used any longer in Danish community-based drug treatment, and when they are used this is often based on a voluntary approach—something the service user assign to. Moreover, and contrary to prison-based drug treatment, in community drug treatment disciplinary sanctions are no longer issued as a consequence of continued drug use, drug diversions of substitution medicine or lack of commitment to the treatment program (compare for instance Jöhncke 1997 to Asmussen and Kolind 2005). In fact, community-based drug treatment—though heavily medicalized (Frank et al. 2013)—is in practice more and more built on case management (Kolind et al. 2009), user involvement (Frank and Bjerge 2011), trust and withdrawal of control elements (Kolind 2007). Finally, prison-based drug treatment also fails to deliver the same services as community drug treatment when it comes to harm reduction initiatives as for instance needle exchange (Michel et al. 2015) or heroin-assisted treatment (Schepelern Johansen and Schepelern Johansen 2015). In fact, as we have concluded elsewhere, it seems as though the most severely affected drug users (who would probably benefit the most from harm reduction initiatives) suffer the most under the strengthened drug control sanctions in prisons (Kolind et al. 2010). Drug users, who do not manage to discontinue their drug use, are continuously sanctioned by the prison regime with fines, isolation cells, and discontinuation of weekend leave and early parole.

Third, looking at the prisoners' motives for starting in a drug treatment program it is clear that both in community drug treatment and in prison drug treatment such motives are very much dictated by the social context of the individual. Both inside and outside the walls it can be difficult to disentangle the "sincerity" of the service users' motivation and surely an individual's motivation for embarking on a drug treatment program is very much determined by the person's social context (Koester et al. 1999; Bourgios 2000; Carr 2011). However, the prison context does differ in many ways from life outside. Importantly, I argued that prisoners' motivations for starting in prison-based drug treatment was influenced by the tough and violent prison environment, the often detrimental prisoner culture, by attempts to "improve one's papers," and by prisoners being tired of being continually affected by the prisons' disciplinary sanctions. In sum, prisoners motivations for starting in prison-based drug treatment was generated by the very structural conditions of the prison, and such motivations seems to be different from what users report when starting in drug treatment programs outside the walls (Koester et al. 1999; Kolind 2007).

In conclusion then, we see that drug treatment has become increasingly popular within the criminal justice system in Denmark. However, despite such development being in line with EU recommendations (EMCDDA 2003) and despite the introduction of drug treatment in prisons in many ways appear sound, humane, and timely, I will, based on the findings presented in the chapter, argue that one should also critically discuss such development.

First, and as concluded above, prison-based drug treatment can in several ways be seen to be a derivate or even substitute welfare service. Danish drug treatment services within the walls are simply not similar to community drug treatment; neither in political discourse, institutional implementation, nor in the experiences of the users. A study comparing Scottish prison-based drug treatment with community drug treatment services also found that drug users in community programs experienced greater improvement than prisoners in prison drug treatment programs; that the range of support in the community programs were larger, and, finally, that community drug treatment was evaluated more positively by the users than prison-based drug treatment (Neale and Saville 2004). Therefore, if we keep offering prison-based drug treatment and drug motivational programs at the current level, we should beware that we in this way operate two different kinds of welfare services toward people who use drugs, a policy which in the long term will affect a large group of drug users as imprisonment is very common especially among people who inject drugs (Stöver and Michels 2010). In principle, the Danish Prison Service is aware of this predicament as their official police states that prisoners with special needs, including those who are drug-dependent, ideally should serve whole or part of their sentence in outside treatment institutions (cf. §111); in practice however, this has seldom been the case (Kolind et al. 2012).

Second, the growth in prison-based drug treatment and the way prison-based drug treatment is framed in political discourse and institutional practice also represent what has been termed "criminalization of social policy"; that is, a situation in which social policy and welfare services are increasingly assessed in relation to their crime-reducing potential (Duke 2006). Especially in relation to arguments based on the so-called crime–drug link (arguing that drug treatment is sound mainly because it can help reduce crime), one see how control and disciplinary sanctions has taken priority over treatment, prevention, and health/harm reduction objectives. Stated otherwise, prison drug treatment services are valued politically not because such programs focus on the drug users' social problems, not because a focus on individual welfare could improve the inmates' self-esteem, and not because drug use is an important social issue in itself, but because prison-based drug treatment is a way to deal with criminality and illegal drug use. Such a development is in fact in line with the way rehabilitation has been re-legitimized in late modern penal discourse. Here rehabilitation, like for instance prison drug treatment, has, according to Robinson (2008, p. 435), "entered a new discursive alliance with punitiveness." Accordingly, it is not the prisoners in the prison drug treatment program who is to be seen as the beneficiaries of these services, but the society and the larger public. In this way, to state it somewhat polemically, the welfare state implicitly and increasingly becomes a penal mechanism and linked up with penal objectives. Such a development has clear historical antecedents, as we see a similar coupling of the welfare state and penalty employed against the poor, the unemployed, prostitutes, the mentally ill, and alcoholics from the end of the 19th century until the 1960s, when drugs became the new social ill to be treated and punished (Prestjan 2004; Spanger 2007; Kolind et al. 2013; Bjønness 2015). Moreover, one could speculate if such criminalization of social problems, the linking of drug treatment with the prison, may well (indirectly) lend legitimacy to the prison and hence support growth of the prison estate (see also Smith 2015, p. 37).

Finally, some authors have also argued that the criminalization of social problems links up to a general risk-management enterprise (Pollack 2010; Seddon et al. 2012). That is, increasingly drug counselors on the ground use their time filling in monitoring forms and databases in order to determine and classify risk populations among the prisoners and hence determine to which prisoners a "rehabilitative investment" will prove most "productive." In this way, drug treatment in the criminal justice has turned in to being a system which to a large extent administers risk in order to enhance security. Thus, prison-based drug treatment primarily becomes a valuable tool related to classification and knowledge in the (welfare) state and not primarily a service intended to help individuals who use drugs to quit their drug use. So, even though I have argued that prison drug treatment is more based on traditional paternalistic power than community drug treatment (inspired more by neo-liberal currents with a focus on self-responsibility of the users), in this respect prison-based drug treatment may resemble community-based treatment, which on a general level can also be seen to be primarily be about knowledge and power, what has also been called "treatmentality" (Jöhncke 2009).

References

Asmussen, V., & Kolind, T. (2005). *Udvidet psykosocial indsats i metadonbehandling. Resultater fra en kvalitativ evaluering af fire metadonforsøgsprojekter.* Århus: Center for Rusmiddelforskning.

Bjerge, B. (2005). *Empowerment og brugerinddragelse i praksis: mellem forestillinger og det muliges kunst. En antropologisk analyse af forestillinger om "godt" socialt arbejde i relation til praksis blandt svagtstillede metadonbrugere.* Aarhus: Center for Rusmiddelforskning, Aarhus Universitet.

Bjerge, B. (2008). The re-organisation of drug treatment in Denmark—a welfare reform as policy. In V. A. Frank, B. Bjerge, E. Houborg (Eds.), *Drug policy—history, theory and consequences* (pp. 209–232). Aarhus: Aarhus University Press.

Bjønness, J. (2015). Narratives about necessity—constructions of motherhood among drug using sex-sellers in Denmark. *Substance Use and Misuse, 50,* 783–793.

Bourgios, P. (2000). Disciplining addictions: the bio-politics of methadone and heroin in the United States. *Culture, Medicine and Psychiatry, 24,* 165–195.

Carr, E. S. (2011). *Scripting addiction: the politics of therapeutic talk and American sobriety.* Princeton and Oxford: Princeton University Press.

Crewe, B. (2005). Prisoner society in the era of hard drugs. *Punishment & Society, 7*(4), 457–481.

Crewe, B. (2006). Prison drug dealing and the ethnographic lens. *The Howard Journal of Criminal Justice, 45*(4), 347–368.

Dahler-Larsen, P., & Larsen, F. (2001). Anvendelse af evaluering?—Historien om et begreb, der udvider sig. In P. Dahler-Larsen and H. K. Krogstrup (Eds.), *Tendenser i evaluering* (pp. 211–221). Odense: Odense Universitetsforlag.

Duke, K. (2006). Out of crime and into treatment?: The criminalization of contemporary drug policy since tackling drugs together. *Drugs: Education, Prevention and Policy, 13*(5), 409–415.

EMCDDA. (2003, Januar–Februar). Behandling af stofmisbrugere i fængslerne— et kritisk område inden for sundhedsfremme og kriminalitetsforebyggelse. *Fokus på narkotika.*

EMCDDA. (2012). *Prisons and drug use in Europe: the problem and responses.* Luxembourg: European Monitoring Centre for Drugs and Drug Addiction.

Engbo, H. J. (2005). *Straffuldbyrdelsesret.* København: Jurist- og Økonomforbundets Forlag.

Frank, V. A., & Bjerge, B. (2011). Empowerment in drug treatment: dilemmas in implementing policy in welfare institutions. *Social Science & Medicine, 73* (2), 201–208.

Frank, V. A., Bjerge, B., Houborg, E. (2013). Shifts in opioid substitution treatment policy in Denmark from 2000–2011. *Substance Use & Misuse, 48* (11), 997–1009.

Frank, V. A., Dahl, H. V., Holm, K. E., Kolind, T. (2015). Inmates' perspectives on prison drug treatment: a qualitative study from three prisons in Denmark. *Probation Journal, 62*(2), 156–171.

Frank, V. A., & Kolind, T. (2008). Dilemmas experienced in prison based cannabis treatment—drug policy in Danish prisons. In V. Asmussen, B. Bjerge, E. H. Pedersen (Eds.), *Drug policy—history, theory and consequences* (pp. 61–86). Århus: Aarhus Universitetsforlag.

Frank, V. A., & Kolind, T. (2012). Prison-based drug treatment and rehabilitation in the Nordic countries. *NAD, 29*(6), 543–545.

Haller, M. B. (2015). *Spaces of possibility. The contrasting meanings of regular and treatment wings in a Danish prison.* PhD thesis, Aarhus University.

Jewkes, Y. (2005). Men behind bars. "Doing" masculinity as an adaption to imprisonment. *Men and Masculinities, 8*(1), 44–63.

Jöhncke, S. (1997). *Brugererfaringer. Undersøgelse af brugernes erfaringer med behandling i de fire distriktscentre i Københavns Kommunes behandlingssystem for stofmisbrugere 1996–97*. København: Socialdirektoratet, Københavns Kommune.

Jöhncke, S. (2009). Treatmentality and the governing of drug use. *Drugs and Alcohol Today, 9*(4), 14–17.

Koester, S., Anderson, K., Hoffer, L. (1999). Active heroin injector's perceptions and use of methadone maintenance treatment: cynical performance or self-prescribed risk reduction? *Substance Use & Misuse, 34*(14), 2135–2153.

Kolind, T. (2007). Form or content. The application of user perspectives in treatment research. *Drugs: Education, Prevention and Policy, 14*(3), 261–277.

Kolind, T., Frank, V. A., Dahl, H. (2010). Drug treatment or alleviating the negative consequences of imprisonment? A critical view of prison-based drug treatment in Denmark. *International Journal of Drug Policy, 21*(1), 43–48.

Kolind, T., Frank, V. A., Dahl, H. V., Birk Haller, M. (2012). Prison drug treatment in Denmark: a historical outline and an analysis of the political debate. *Nordic Studies on Alcohol and Drugs, 29*, 547–560.

Kolind, T., Frank, V. A., Holm, K. E. (2014). Stofbehandling og nye institutionelle identiteter i danske fængsler. *Nordisk Tidsskrift for Kriminalvidenskab, 101*(2), 116–137.

Kolind, T., Frank, V. A., Lindberg, O., Tourunen, J. (2013). Prison-based drug treatment in Nordic political discourse: an elastic discursive construct. *European Journal of Criminology, 10*(6), 659–674.

Kolind, T., Frank, V. A., Lindberg, O., Tourunen, J. (2015). Officers and drug counsellors: new occupational identities in Nordic prisons. *British Journal of Criminology, 55*(2), 303–320.

Kolind, T., Vanderplasschen, W., De Maeyer, J. (2009). Dilemmas when working with substance abusers with multiple and complex problems: the case manager's perspective. *International Journal of Social Welfare, 18*(3), 270–280.

København. (1993). *Kriminalforsorgens Principprogram*. København: Kriminalforsorgen.

Kriminalforsorgen. (2004). Circular, 21 October 2004 Om normalreaktioner på områderne narkotika, ulovlige dopingmidler og vold og trusler om vold mod personalet. Justitsministeriet, Direktoratet for Kriminalforsorgen (J.no. JUR 04-034-108).

Kriminalforsorgen. (2011). Behandlingsafdelinger og –programmer I danske fængsler. http://www.kriminalforsorgen.dk/Default.aspx?ID=98. Accessed 23 April 2012.

Kriminalforsorgen. (2011b). *Behandlingsindsatsen mod misbrug i fængslerne.* Årsberetning: Kriminalforsorgen.

Kriminalforsorgen. (2014). *Kriminalforsorgen Statistik.* København: Direktoratet for København.

Levy, M., & Stöver, H. (Eds.) (2013). *Safer prescribing of medications in adult detentions.* Oldenburg: BIS-Verlag.

Lewis, S. (1995). A search for meaning: Making sense of depression. *Journal of Mental Health, 4*(4), 369–382.

Liebling, A. (2000). Prison officers, policing and the use of discretion. *Theoretical Criminology, 4*(3), 333–357.

Liebling, A. (2011). Distinctions and distinctiveness in the work of prison officers: legitimacy and authority revisited. *European Journal of Criminology, 8*(6), 484–499.

Lipsky, M. (1980). *Street-level bureaucracy. Dilemmas of the individual in public services.* New York: Russell Sage Foundation.

Longshore, D., & Teruya, C. (2006). Treatment motivation in drug users: a theory-based analysis. *Drug and Alcohol Dependence, 81*(2), 179–188.

Michel, L., Lions, C., Van Malderen, S., Schiltz, J., Vanderplasschen, W., Holm, K., et al. (2015). Insufficient access to harm reduction measures in prisons in 5 countries (PRIDE Europe): a shared European public health concern. *BMC Public Health, 15*(1), 1093.

Mjåland, K. (2015). *Makt, legitimitet og motstand. En etnografisk analyse av rus og rehabilitering i et norsk fengsel.* PhD thesis, University of Bergen.

Neale, J., & Saville, E. (2004). Comparing community and prison-based drug treatment. *Drugs: Education, Prevention and Policy, 11*(3), 213–228.

Nielsen, B., & Kolind, T. (2016). Offender and/or client? Fuzzy institutional identities in prison-based drug treatment in Denmark. *Punishment & Society, 18*(2), 131–150.

Pollack, S. (2010). Labelling clients "risky": Social work and the neo-liberal welfare state. *British Journal of Social Work, 40,* 1263–1278.

Prestjan, A. (2004). *Att bota en drinkare. Ideer och praktik i svensk alkolistvård 1885–1916.* Örebro: Örebro University.

Regeringen. (2003). *Kampen mod narko. Handlingsplan mod narkotikamisbrug.* Regeringen (the Government).

Regeringen. (2010). *Kampen mod narko II. Handlingsplan mod narkotikamis-brug.* Regeringen (the Government).

Rieper, O. (2004). *Håndbog i evaluering. Metoder til at dokumentere og vurdere proces og effekt af offentlige indsatser.* København: AKF forlaget.

Robinson, G. (2008). Late-modern rehabilitation. *Punishment & Society, 10*(4), 429–445.

Rosen, P., Hiller, M., Webster, J., Staton, M., Leukefeld, C. (2004). Treatment motivation and therapeutic engagement in prison-based substance use treatment. *Journal of Psychoactive Drugs, 36*(3), 287–396.

Schepelern Johansen, B., & Schepelern Johansen, K. (2015). Heroin: from drug to ambivalent medicine. *Culture, Medicine, and Psychiatry, 39*(1), 75–91.

Seddon, T., Williams, L., & Ralphs, R. (2012). *Tough choices. Risk, security, and the criminalization of drug policy.* Oxford: Oxford University Press.

Smith, P. S. (2015). Reform and research: re-connecting prison and society in the 21st century. *International Journal for Crime, Justice and Social Democracy, 14*(1), 33–49.

Spanger, M. (2007). Myndigheternes köns- och sexualsyn. Lösaktiga kvinnor i 1930-talets Danmark. In A. Jansdotter and Y. Svanström (Eds.), *Sedligt, renligt, lagligt. Prostitution i Norden 1880–1940* (pp. 197–225). Göteborg: Makadam Förlag.

Storgaard, A. (1999). *Straf og misbrugsbehandling under samme tag.* Aarhus: Center for Rusmiddelforskning.

Stöver, H., & Michels, I. (2010). Drug use and opioid substitution treatment for prisoners. *Harm Reduction Journal, 7*(17), 1–7.

Strauss, A., & Corbin, J. (1997). *Grounded theory in practice.* London: Sage Publishers.

Sykes, G. (1958). *The society of captives: a study of a maximum security prison.* Princeton: Princeton University Press.

Tourunen, J., Weckroth, A., Kaskela, T. (2012). Prison-based drug treatment in Finland: history, shifts in policy making and current status. *NAD Nordic Studies on Alcohol and Drugs, 29*(6), 575–588.

Villadsen, K. (2004). *Det sociale arbejdes genealogi. Om kampen for at gøre fattige og udstødte til frie mennesker.* København: Hans Reitzels Forlag.

The Development of Education in Norwegian Prisons

Torfinn Langelid

Introduction

The industrialisation of Europe and Norway in the eighteenth and nineteenth centuries led to social unrest and widespread poverty. Prisons and penitentiaries became religious institutions where the prisoners, in addition to being punished, were to be improved through work, spiritual guidance and education. The Confirmation Act of 1736 played a decisive role in the introduction of universal education in 1739, with a strong emphasis on religious education. The improvement philosophy that dominated prisons and penitentiaries followed the same religious track. We can see how the education system and the penal system were closely allied, where the school was seen as part of the rehabilitation process.

I would like to thank Paal Chr. Breivik, Inger Marie Fridhov, Oddrun Hjermstad and Cecilie Høisæter for their valuable comments during my work on this chapter.

T. Langelid (✉)
Former National Coordinator of Prison Education, Bergen, Norway
e-mail: torfinn.langelid@gmail.com

P. Scharff Smith, T. Ugelvik (eds.), *Scandinavian Penal History, Culture and Prison Practice,* Palgrave Studies in Prisons and Penology, DOI 10.1057/978-1-137-58529-5_10

225

Prison schools did their best to keep up with developments in the education system in society at large. In 1875, teaching was provided at all the eight penal institutions in Norway. The total number of school staff was 24—including chaplains, teachers, organists and others (Beretning om Rigets Strafanstalter for Aaret 1875).

This was a transition from a brutal penal system based on corporal punishment to a system based on improvement of the soul (Foucault 1977). It was also a development whereby the State exercised greater social control by taking greater social responsibility. Until the mid-20th century, the prison service was responsible for all aspects of the execution of sentences, including education, health and chaplaincy services.

In 1969, the Ministry of Church and Education took over professional and financial responsibility for the education of convicted criminals in prisons. It was not until 2007, however, that schools had been established in all prisons. The right to education is enshrined in both the Education Act (1998) and the Execution of Sentences Act (2001). Why did it take almost 50 years for the authorities to fully accept the consequences of prison prisoners having the same right to the services of the welfare state as other members of society?

I have been involved in the development of prison education in Norway on different levels, 10 years as a teacher in prisons and as a bureaucrat in the Ministry of Education and Church Affairs, and 18 years as national coordinator of prison education in Norway (1993–2011). I was liaison officer for the Nordic network for education in prison from 2006 to 2011 and a member of the steering committee for the European Prison Education Association (EPEA) from 1997 to 2007 and was asked by the EU Commission to contribute to the development of education in prison in Europe. I was also a member of the steering committee of Forum for Education in the Correctional Services (FOKO, the national branch of the EPEA) from 1996 to 2011. From my point of view I see that politicians and bureaucrats have gradually given more attention to this area both in Norway, the Nordic countries and in Europe. That is mainly due to influenced and focused strong individuals in the correctional services and the educational services. Other important role players in this development have been researchers with their new findings concerning prisoners' educational backgrounds, preferences and motivation, as well as international conventions and recommendations.

Everyone Shall Be Included—But a Few Are Excluded

During the occupation time 1940–1945 the political parties developed solidarity and cooperation with each other, and they wanted to continue this in the reconstruction after World War II. The four big parties presented a Joint Manifesto in connection with the general election in 1945. Education at all levels free of charge emerged as an important welfare state goal. It was to be a service for and a right enjoyed by everyone (Eriksen and Lundestad 1972, pp.33–34). Education in prisons was far down the list of priorities, however. Little education was offered in Norwegian prisons in the decades following World War II. The penitentiary prison called Botsfengselet, which, with its emphasis on isolation, punishment and improvement, was presented as an innovation when it opened in 1851, was one of the prisons that still offered some education. In addition seven other prisons offered educational programmes. Most of the prisons did not offer prisoners education of any kind, only workshops or isolation in their cells. The teachers were employed by the prison service (Langelid 2015). This was part of a model based on self-sufficiency, which meant that the prison service was responsible for all activities in prisons.

It was the prison service and not the school authorities that pushed for young prisoners to be given an education on a par with other young people. In the 1960s, director Kåre Bødal of the Juvenile Prison sent one letter after another to the Central Prison Administration requesting that a satisfactory prison educational service be established that was subject to the provisions of the Education Act. Bødal advocated allowing young prisoners to benefit from the welfare policies that applied to other citizens. Initially, however, the Central Prison Administration was uncertain about whether responsibility for education in prisons should be taken over by the educational authorities. It was a matter for discussion whether the right and duty to take an education lapsed when a young person was in prison.

At a meeting in November 1967 between the Prison Service and the Ministry of Education, the Director General of the Ministry of Education and Church Affairs maintained that a person forfeited the right to education when he or she was imprisoned. He believed that the re-socialisation of those serving prison sentences fell under the remit of criminology, not educational science. The prisoner was not viewed as a member of society (Langelid 2015, pp. 122–126). This is strange because the Director General at the time, Tønnes Sirevåg, was a well-informed person both nationally and internationally as regards school matters. There was also tension between civil servants in the Ministry of Education. One said that if a student does not have the opportunity to attend school, the school must organise education in the institution.[1] Sirevåg resigned in 1968 and a new person, Johan Bjørge, took over his position, who took a positive view of this issue.

Following negotiations between the ministries, the Ministry of Church and Education issued a circular in October 1969 on education for young prisoners in the prison service's institutions. Education was to be provided for youth of school age, and it could also be provided for young people whose education had been inadequate or who for other reasons were *educationally retarded*.[2] The local school board was assigned responsibility for the teaching, and teachers were employed by the educational authorities—not by the prison. However, the educational activity had to be adapted to the prisons' need for order and security. This paved the way for conflicts between security-based and education-based philosophies. The first phase of the work to get the school authorities to take over was now complete (Langelid 2015).

Bødal convinced the prison service and the educational authorities that prisoners had the same right and duty to take an education as other young people in society. In a simple, theoretical model, criminologist Nils Christie summed up the idea that services offered in free society should also be offered

---

[1] Conversation with former adviser, Einar Nyhus, in the Ministry of Education, 11 November 1980.

[2] Circular No. As L 1969 from the Ministry of Church and Education, 24 October 1969, to the school directors and school boards.

in the prison system. In 1969, he launched the import model, a model that still stands today. He believes that this model opens up the system by placing all service functions outside prisons (Christie 1970). The model was advocated by bureaucrats and a researcher, not by the politicians. Bødal and Christie argued that the welfare state should also include prisoners. The result of this was a system where the right to an education was part of the services offered by the welfare state, but where many prisoners were denied these services. They were still excluded because the State did not allocate sufficient funds for education in prisons. Young people were given priority.

In the 1970s, the *nothing works* ideology was so predominant that it almost obliterated prisoners' right to education and training. In the prison system, education was still regarded as part of the rehabilitation process. Mathiesen (1995), one of the strongest critics of the treatment philosophy in Norway, pointed out that work, school, morals and discipline had been the four principal components of rehabilitation efforts in both the past and the present. Mathiesen claimed that the rehabilitation measures had never improved people's capacity to function (Mathiesen 1995, pp. 68–71). This view was dominant at the time. I experienced this myself when, in 1974, I started working as a teacher in a large Norwegian prison with relatively high security and helped to establish a school there. The argument that nothing works was so all-pervasive that going to the prison every day to teach gave me a guilty conscience. At the same time, however, I found that the prisoners were interested and very concerned with learning. But I also had a strong feeling of the prison as a control system where the prisoners were subjected to demanding ordeals that seemed to be both unnecessary and humiliating. The overall perspective was nonetheless that prisoners should have access to an education on a par with other citizens.

Some positive signals came from abroad. Stephen Duguid of Simon Fraser University in British Columbia had been responsible for education in four prisons in British Columbia since 1975, both upper secondary education and programmes at the university level (Duguid 1987). He had good experience of education in prisons and introduced the *model of opportunities* to counterbalance the treatment model (Duguid 2000). Criminologist Friedrich Løsel (1993) carried out an extensive meta-analysis of research on measures implemented in prison systems and found that some of them worked under certain conditions. A certain optimism began to take hold. The new and positive signals from abroad gave strength to those who believed in different treatment activities offered in prison.

Hauge regards the treatment philosophy as part of the development of the welfare state. New vocational groups and professionalisation of the work in prisons were part of this development. Prisoners were to be helped to change their lives. The treatment ideology led to less use of prison sentences in the 1950s and 1960s (Hauge 1996, p. 255).

Even though the treatment philosophy lost its popularity among researchers in the 1970s, it continued to thrive in the prison system in Norway. We will see that strong and forceful individuals, with the courage to develop the prison system based on humanistic principles, made a big mark on the development of the Norwegian correctional services in the last few decades of the 20th century. The belief in re-socialisation and that a period of imprisonment could lead to something positive lived on. Asbjørn Langås, who launched the therapeutic community, was a driving force for the development of the Norwegian prison system. Something had to be done to overcome the *nothing works* mindset. He wanted to open up a closed system to society to a greater extent (Langelid 2015, pp. 141–142). Langås underlined the importance of rehabilitation programmes and he pushed the school authorities to develop educational programmes in prisons.

The prison service opened up for imported services, but it seemed to want to have control over the new groups that entered the prisons. The prison system and the educational system have different tasks and goals. The prison system is tasked with punishing people, while at the same time rehabilitating them. Schools, on the other hand, are tasked with helping to develop independent, critical and socially aware individuals. The meeting between the two systems was destined to lead to conflict. In the 1970s, two of the teachers at the juvenile prison resigned in protest against the regime that prevailed in the prison. They found it difficult to teach in a way that was in accordance with the Education Act and pertaining guidelines (Berg et al. 1972, p. 117).

In an advertisement for teachers at a large national prison in 1974, we note that it was the laws and regulations relating to prisons that dictated conditions. The teachers had to undertake to cooperate within the framework of the prison's objective (Langelid 2015, p. 29). The advertisement led to strong reactions in educational circles, and the teachers found that the law and regulations relating to prisons took precedence over education law and educational guidelines. At the end of the 1970s, prison teaching positions were advertised on a par with other teaching positions in the municipalities. At several prisons, a person employed by the prison was responsible for administration of the educational activities. The teachers were dissatisfied with this arrangement and raised the matter with their unions. Administrative staff were later employed by the school authorities. Today, it is taken as given that it is the school authorities that advertise positions and appoint teaching staff in prisons. In one case, it was the prison authorities at a prison that decided the admission of pupils to upper secondary education. The County Governor (the State's representative) clearly stated that the county authority could not grant the prison authorities the right to make such decisions (Langelid 2015, pp. 30–32). Prison schools must comply with the provisions and regulations as set out in the Education Act.

The Import Model—A Welfare Policy Measure

The various welfare policy measures were also supposed to apply to prison prisoners. Prison schools were at the forefront of this development. Langås was concerned with developing contact between the different agencies that were responsible for education in prisons. In 1975, he succeeded in establishing a national steering committee for education in prisons. Its members came from the Ministry of Church and Education and the Ministry of Justice. The goal of the steering committee was to establish and further develop the education and training offered to prison prisoners. In 1977, the Expert Council for the Prison Service was appointed. The Council was intended to be an advisory body for the Ministry of Justice. The implementation of the import model, which entailed normalising periods of imprisonment, was an important goal (Instructions for the Expert Council for the Prison Service. Adopted by Royal Decree of 9 September 1977, Section 2). The Expert Council for the Prison Service had 10 members, and was composed of representatives from: the fields of teaching (can use school authorities instead?), culture and sports, the health service, The Norwegian Trade Unions (LO) and

The Confederation of Norwegian Enterprise (NHO), the prison service management, prison staff and the probation service.

Langås established close connections with both the national and the local media. Education in prisons was given broad and positive coverage in the press. The most important marketing of the service took place at seminars held in Oslo during the period 1975–1979. Guests from the Nordic countries were also present (Langelid 2015, pp. 141–143). Even a former prime minister, Einar Gerhardsen, who served a prison sentence in the 1920s, was invited for dinner at one conference to tell the participants about his experiences in prison.[3]

In April 1980, Langås summed up the status of the work on education in prisons in a lengthy memo addressed to the Steering Group for Education in Prisons. The status was that education at primary and lower secondary level had been established in 23 prisons, and upper secondary education in 13 prisons. An action programme was drawn up for future activities. It entailed establishing and further developing the education offered in prisons, as well as emphasising follow-up after prisoners were released. Education in prisons had gained a foothold, but many prisons still did not offer educational programmes (Langelid 2015, pp. 137–144).

At the same time the import model challenged the prison system. Even though the politicians said that prisoners had the same rights to services as other citizens, this was not always followed up in practice in the form of funding allocations. The Ministry of Justice did not take the import model seriously, and it did as it wished as regards the building of new prisons and the refurbishment of old ones. The Ministry of Church and Education was not consulted. The result was that the Ministry of Church and Education fell behind as regards allocating sufficient funding for education in prisons. This led to strong criticism from politicians and the educational authorities.

The import model was later described as an administrative cooperation, cf. the Execution of Sentences Act, White Paper No 37 (2007–2008). The schools had a central place in the development of the import model, which

---

[3] Rapport Seminar 1979 «Undervisning og opplæring i fengsel».

would later include librarians, cultural workers, chaplains, health personnel and people from the employment service. The import model was to have a decisive effect on the development of the correctional services in Norway.

Strategies for Highlighting Education in Prisons

In the late 1980s and in the 1990s the educational authorities took more responsibility for and directed the development of education in prisons. A government body, the County Governor of Hordaland, was in 1993 assigned national responsibility, on behalf of the Ministry of Education, Research and Church Affairs, for education in prisons in Norway. In 1995, educational programmes were offered in 33 of Norway's 43 prisons. The school authorities now had the leading role and implemented different strategies to highlight education and to strengthen prisoners' right to education. A focus on information was an important strategy for drawing attention to education in prisons. Conferences were held where the correctional services, the educational authorities and other relevant agencies were represented. Irritation and discord were gradually replaced by understanding between the different personnel groups. A circular played an important part in the normalisation process and in clarifying prisoners' rights as citizens: *Circular on Administrative co-operation between the Education and Training Sector and the Norwegian Correctional Services* (2008). This circular is based on the principle that prisoners have the same rights and duties as the rest of the population. The circular sets out who is responsible for the different areas at the national, regional and local level.

Another strategy was research and evaluation. In this area, the County Governor of Hordaland managed to secure a research and development agreement with the University of Bergen, which, together with educational consultants Eikeland forskning og undervisning, has carried out surveys of the prison population's educational background, needs and wishes over several years.[4] During its

---

[4] In 2004, 2006, 2009 and 2012.

consideration of the national budget for 1998, the parliament asked the cabinet to initiate a research-based evaluation of education in prison.

The evaluation covered a broad area. The research community proposed a number of measures to improve and develop education in prison. The education offered must be more differentiated and include more vocational training programmes; ICT must be part of all the education offered; cooperation between prison schools and prison workshops must be improved; women prisoners must be offered more programmes leading to formal competence, with the emphasis on vocational training; and the right of minority language prisoners to education must be clarified. Preparations for release and follow-up after the completion of sentences must be given priority. Binding cooperation must be developed between the different professions in the correctional services. The prisons' control procedures should not interfere with teaching and schoolwork (Langelid 2015, pp. 217–219).

All the reports were sent to those involved in the correctional services, to the Storting and to Nordic partners. A summary report was sent to all the ministries of education and ministries of justice in Europe.[5]

A third strategy was experimental and development work. Several national projects were initiated to follow up the white paper. One project involved validation of prisoners' prior learning. Validation of prior learning is important for the prison population, because many of them do not have formal competence, but have know-how that they have picked up in the school of life. The evaluation showed that the project succeeded in establishing validation of prior learning as a tool for mapping the competence of this group of students, which led to the students planning ahead to a greater extent after their release (Garmannslund and Meltevik 2010).

Another project involved further developing cooperation between prison schools and prison workshops. Workshops have long been the

---

[5] Report number 1 05. Research-based evaluation of education in Norwegian prisons. *Recommendations from the group nominated to monitor the evaluation of education in Norwegians prisons.* County Governor of Hordaland.

most important activity offered by the correctional services. In recent years, emphasis has been placed on the importance of normalisation, more vocational training and competence that is relevant in the ordinary labour market. Despite little research in this area, several working groups and reports have proposed improvements in workshop activities over the last 50 years (Langelid 2015, p. 230). The Ministry of Justice has done surprisingly little to follow this up.[6] Cooperation between prison schools and workshops has nonetheless developed in a positive direction. More apprenticeship contracts have been signed, more prisoners have taken craft certificate exams and there are more prisoners taking practical training (Langelid 2015, p. 233).

The cookery book *Ærlig mat i Halden fengsel* (Mathisen 2012) is a good example of good cooperation between school and workshops in a prison. Sixteen prisoners, five teachers and two workshop officers have taken part in the project. One of the students has translated the book into English—*Decent food in Halden prison.* At the prisoners' request, part of the profits goes to the rehabilitation foundation Wayback (Langelid 2015, p. 232). It is wrong, therefore, when Mathiesen (2012) claims that prison work is just as meaningless today as it was in the 1960s when he carried out his study at Ila Preventive Prison.

The development of ICT for prisoners is another experimental and development project. According to the national curricula, digital competence is necessary in order to ensure that students acquire adequate competence. Like students on the outside, the students taking education in prison must acquire digital competence by using digital tools. The use of digital tools entails some security challenges, but these challenges must be addressed by introducing technical adaptations. The security philosophy must not be so all-pervasive that it precludes good solutions. All these different projects are focusing on prisoners' right to education. The strategies that were applied—information, research, development work and national projects—were all elements that contributed to highlighting the fact that prisoners are part of society just like any other citizen.

---

[6] See, for example, Proposition No 1 to the Storting from the Ministry of Justice and the Police for 1996–1997, 1997–1998, 1998–1999, 1999–2000, 2000–2001, 2001–2002.

White Paper on Education in Prison

In light of the research-based evaluation, the government presented a separate white paper on education in prison in 2005.[7] The white paper highlighted the right to education for prisoners and, in addition to the Education Act and the Execution of Sentences Act, also referred to international conventions and recommendations such as Article 2 of the First Protocol of the European convention on Human Rights, the UN International Covenant on Economic, Social and Cultural Rights and two recommendations from the Council of Europe: *Education in Prison* and *The European Prison Rules*. This is the first ever white paper in this field, and it is unique in the European context. It is a sign that education in the correctional services is now on an equal footing with other areas of the welfare society.

Both the government and the parliament emphasised what has previously been said in many contexts, namely that prisoners have the same right to education as other citizens. This also applied to foreign prisoners, who, back in 2005, accounted for 18 % of the prison population. The objective of education in prison is the same as for all other education (Langelid 2015, p. 223).

Four Norwegian researchers strongly criticised the white paper, characterising the Norwegian correctional services as slack. Specifically, they criticised poor follow-up after release, lack of cooperation between government agencies, conflicts and power struggles between the professions and a need for more varied education and training (Langelid 2015, pp. 245–246).

Seen in hindsight, it is correct to say that the white paper represented a boost for education in prison. Relevant issues and challenges have been made clear to both politicians and the bureaucracy. Since 2007, education and training have been provided in all prisons, and budgets have shown a positive development and were more than doubled

---

[7] Short Version of Report No 27 to the Storting (2004–2005) Education and Training in the Correctional Services "Another Spring."

between 2005 and 2012 (Langelid 2015, pp. 248–249). The white paper is a manifestation of prisoners' right to education.

In the wake of the white paper, the government and the Storting were concerned with identifying how many prisoners had a right to education. Surveys show that the number of prisoners who had not completed lower secondary school was stable at around 7–10 % during the years in question. One-third of the prisoners had not completed upper secondary education (Eikeland et al. 2013). This tells us something about the drop-out rate in the ordinary education system, where many students taking vocational programmes fail to complete their education. Some of them end up in prison. Preventive measures will be of great economic benefit to society, with potential savings of billions of kroner (Rasmussen et al. 2010, pp. 5, 65–78).

The number of foreign prisoners in Nordic prisons has been increasing rapidly. There are major challenges associated with this group of a linguistic, cultural and social nature. Nordic researchers conducted a survey in which prisoners from Somalia, Russia, Poland, Iraq and Serbia were interviewed. As a whole, the prisoners of foreign nationality were motivated for education and training. The survey found that they were often not aware of their rights. The report contains a number of recommendations for improving the situation for foreign prisoners in Nordic prisons as regards education (Westrheim and Manger 2013).

They experienced many barriers that prevented them from taking an education. Even though the Ministry of Education and Research stated in the white paper "*The Ministry favours guaranteeing the right to education and training for foreign prisoners, so that they are better able to continue their education or work in their native countries*" (Short Version of Report No 27 to the Storting, (2004–2005) 2007, p. 39), some problems arose concerning foreigners' right to education. The Education Act states that it is a condition for the right to education that the applicant has legal residence in the country. This applies both to youth and adults. Høstmælingen et al. (2013) and Gröning (2014) state that, based on the sources, "*there is no basis for claiming that Norway is bound by criminal law to ensure a certain level of educational provision for either adult prisoners or for prisoners who are to be deported after serving their sentences*" (Høstmælingen et al. 2013, p. 15; Gröning 2014, p. 183).

To clarify further, they both refer to the principle of non-discrimination. The question *"is whether it is lawful under the provisions relating to the right to education to treat foreign prisoners who are to be deported from Norway after serving their sentences differently from Norwegian prisoners . . . Pursuant to the European Convention on Human Rights, it is in principle unlawful to discriminate between people in comparable situations based on nationality"* (Høstmælingen et al. 2013, pp. 15–16, see also Gröning 2014, pp. 183–188).

Gröning (2014) believes that citizens' access to education is a human right that, under international law, must apply to everyone, also people serving prison sentences. The principle argument for the import model (1969) was that prisoners should not forfeit their civil rights. The right to education is enshrined in a number of international law documents. Gröning also states that the law and international law contain a general prohibition against discrimination, whereby everyone who is in a comparable situation, such as prisoners serving a sentence in a Norwegian prison, shall have equal access to education. As a human right, the right to education applies to everyone, including those serving a prison sentence, irrespective of nationality (see also Høstmælingen 2004, p. 311). Even though criminal law scholars believe that the right to education must apply to all, also those without legal residence, some politicians question whether the welfare state shall also include groups where doubts can be raised about whether or not they have legal residence.[8]

International Cooperation

The development of education in Norwegian prisons has been influenced by Nordic and European cooperation. In 1999, the Nordic Council adopted a recommendation on education in prison in a Nordic perspective. It was a political initiative aimed at ensuring that prisoners in the Nordic countries could enjoy the same public services as

---

[8] Two Norwegian newspapers: Vårt Land 19.05.2011, Dagbladet 15.10.2011.

other members of society. The goal was that the prisoners should be included in the Nordic welfare state. A survey was conducted by the prison services and the prison education services in the Nordic countries. This resulted in the report *Nordic Prison Education. A Lifelong Learning Perspective* (Nordic Council of Ministers 2005; Langelid et al. 2009).

Even though the models on which the organisation of education in prisons is based differ between the Nordic countries, Nordic cooperation has led to mutual consolidation and strengthening of prison education. Norway and Iceland use the import model, whereby the teachers are employed by the education authorities. Denmark has a self-sufficiency model, where it is the correctional services that employ teachers and organise teaching. Finland has a threefold model. The teaching is carried out by teachers employed by the local educational institutions (the import model), teachers employed by the Ministry of Justice (the self-sufficiency model) and teachers hired on a contract basis (the contract model). Sweden has a kind of self-sufficiency model, whereby teachers are employed by the correctional services, but the educational service is under the supervision of the Swedish National Agency for Education, which monitors teaching in prisons to ensure that it is in accordance with the Education Act and national curricula.

Today, all these countries have enshrined in law that prisoners have the same right to education as other citizens. The focus has been on strengthening vocational training, including the use of digital tools in the educational programmes offered, more emphasis on creative subjects, more focus on foreign prisoners and the initiation of Nordic research in the field.

The research collaboration on education in prison in the Nordic context was something completely new. It led to the first ever Nordic survey (Eikeland et al. 2009). The report led to greater interest in the issue of education for prisoners from politicians, decision-makers, the correctional services, the educational authorities and the media.

The development of education in prisons has also been influenced by conventions and recommendations from the Council of Europe and from EU programmes. The Council of Europe's recommendation *Education in Prison* (Council of Europe 1990) came to have a great influence on education in prisons in Norway and Europe. It contained

17 recommendations and was used more or less as a textbook on how education in prisons should be organised in the different European countries. It is an overriding goal that education in prison should have the same status as education outside prison.

The EU has contributed to the development of education in prison in Europe through its education programmes. Many schools have gained a new perspective on their own teaching, while at the same time offering partners new knowledge and competence (Langelid 2015, pp. 320–322).

According to the European Commission, many different actors are responsible for education in prisons. The ministries of education and justice are responsible for it in many countries. Voluntary organisations offer education and training, and EU-funded projects play an important role in securing resources for organising and implementing education in prison. Not all countries have a statutory right to education for prisoners, as we find in the Nordic countries (GHK 2012).

The Right to Education and the Import Model Today

The administrative cooperation between welfare agencies is now enshrined in law and in circulars and agreements between the Correctional services and the "imported" agencies. There will always be challenges, and there will always be a potential for conflict between the laws and goals that apply to the individual agencies and the overarching goals of the correctional services.

Today, education and training are provided in all Norwegian prisons. Just over half of all prisoners in Norwegian prisons participate in some form of education or training. There has been a shift from programmes qualifying for higher education to vocational training. The number of prisoners taking university college and university education is also increasing.

The libraries are an important support function for prison schools and an important source of information for prisoners. The librarians are employed by the municipal library services.

Public agencies are responsible for dental and the health services in Norwegian prisons. Since the 1990s, some prisons have employed people to help prisoners to find work after release. Today, these positions are organised through the Norwegian Labour and Welfare Administration (NAV) (Langelid 2015, pp. 357–358).

The imported services have found an established place in the Norwegian correctional services. The prisoners have thereby been given greater access to the same services as other citizens are entitled to. It is probably correct to say, as Christie assumed, that the import model has opened up the prison system.

With respect to education in prison, Costelloe and Warner (2014) compare the Norwegian White Paper on *Education and Training in the Correctional Services: "Another Spring"* with the English Green Paper (2005) on the same topic (England and Wales. Ministry of Education and Skills 2005). The big difference is that the Norwegian white paper views people in prison as citizens with a right to education. The English green paper views them as criminals and is concerned with what effect measures have. The main challenge is to stop or reduce re-offending. In their opinion, this is a much narrower approach.

They observe that access to education in European prisons is being reduced, and fewer prison services take a broad approach based on the curricula in the ordinary school system. When education in prison is defined as a right for prisoners and as part of the services offered by the welfare state, education becomes a goal in itself. Otherwise, education in prison becomes a means of reducing recidivism.

Education in Prison Was Not Embraced by the Welfare State, but Has Become Part of It

The welfare state has developed over time. In different periods, the state has endeavoured to introduce measures for the few who fall outside society's normal pattern (see Midre 1995). Historically, it was the schools that were responsible for providing a religious education both in society in general and in institutions. Both citizens and prisoners had to learn to read so that they could be confirmed. Education in prison gradually came to be of a more general nature and endeavours were made to keep pace with the amendments that were adopted to education laws.

It was Sir Anthony Beveridge who gave the welfare state its modern content in England in 1942. His plan probably had a strong influence on welfare policies in many European countries after World War II (Seip 1981; Kuhnle and Kildal 2011). Seip (1984, 1994) looked at the development of the "social assistance state" in the last 200–300 years. She discussed many aspects of social assistance policy, such as work-houses, poor houses and social responsibility up until the introduction of modern welfare policies in our own time. The welfare state is charac-terised by universal benefits and an extensive public responsibility for all, including for those who, for various reasons, are placed in institutions. Education in prison is part of the services offered by the welfare state. We note that it is the groups that most need such welfare services that get them last.

Bødal and the prison service fought hard to get the Ministry of Church and Education to take responsibility for education in prison. Once it was in place, key individuals in the Central Prison Administration worked together with like-minded people in the Ministry of Church and Education to market the import model. The prison service talked about school as an important rehabilitation measure, while the education autho-rities gradually came round to the view that prisoners had a right to education on a par with everyone else.

Why is it necessary to make a special argument for why the few should have the same access to public services as everyone else enjoys automa-tically? We have seen that the few often disappear off the politicians' radar. It would seem that the political message that prisoners also have a right to education has been ignored by both the government, bureau-cracy and the municipalities. The welfare state is under pressure, it is becoming too expensive. Could it be the case that those who deviate from the norm constitute such small groups that they simply disappear from view in society's vast systems?

It is the central government's duty to ensure education for everyone. Unlike in many other countries, convicted offenders in Norway are seen as citizens with the same rights to public services as the rest of us. Everyone shall be included, but vulnerable groups do not have strong lobbyists on their side. Their interests must be looked after by the different systems and by the politicians, and they must be followed up by the bureaucracy at different levels. Society has often failed them in this respect. Even though education is now established in all prisons, there are still around 800 prisoners who have a right to upper secondary education but who do not take part in such programmes. Their right to education must be ensured on a par with that of other citizens. According to the Norwegian Parliamentary Ombudsman, prisoners must be given help to complain, so that they can exercise their right to education (Fliflet 2003).

The big shift in education in prison in Norway came in 1969, when the education authorities took over responsibility for education in prisons. Special arguments had to be made for why prisoners should be given the right they already had in law. It is not until the last few decades, however, that the politicians and bureaucrats have fully acknowledged that this group has the same right to education and to the same welfare services as other citizens. This interpretation of the law now appears to be under threat. In 2015, because of a backlog of offenders waiting to serve their sentences, the Norwegian authorities decided to transfer prisoners to the Netherlands.[9] The Dutch prison in question will not provide education in accordance with Norwegian curricula. In connection with the debate in the Storting about which prisoners could be sent to the Netherlands, it was asked whether the right to education applied to all prisoners. The reply was that foreign nationals are not entitled to the same rehabilitation measures as Norwegian prisoners.[10] This is interesting, because the school authorities and the correctional services agree on offering the foreign prisoners the same educational activities as the Norwegian prisoners.

---

[9] Proposition 92 LS (2014–2015) from the Ministry of Justice and Public Security concerning Amendments to the Execution of Sentences Act (execution of sentences in another state), consent to entering into the agreement with the Netherlands of 2 March 2015 on the use of a prison in the Netherlands and changes to the national budget 2015.

[10] Meeting of the Storting, Monday 8 June 2015, Agenda No 84, p. 34.

We have seen that Norwegian research shows that prisoners are interested in education (Eikeland et al. 2013; Manger et al. 2013). They see education as important when it comes to coping with and changing their future. For some prisoners, education in prison has helped to give them a new voice—a voice that has been liberating in a system otherwise characterised by control.

Bibliography

Berg, P. L., Johansen, S., Olaussen, L. P. (1972). *På steingrunn. Skolen i Ungdomsfengslet.* Oslo: Pax Forlag.

Christie, N. (1970). Modeller for en fengselsorganisasjon. In R. Østensen (Ed.), *I stedet for fengsel* (pp. 70–79). Oslo: Pax.

Costelloe, A., & Warner, K. (2014). Prison education across Europe: policy, practice, politics. In E. Carroll and K. Warner (Eds.), *Re-imagining imprisonment in Europe. Effects, failures and the future* (pp. 238–254). Dublin: The Liffey Press Ltd.

Council of Europe. (1990). *Education in prison. Recommendations No. R (89) 12 adopted by the Committee of Ministers of the Council of Europe on 13 October 1989.* Strasbourg: Council of Europe.

Den Kongelige Norske Regjering. (1877). *Beretning om Rigets Strafarbeidsanstalter for Aaret 1875.* Christiania: Ringvolds Bogtrykkeri.

Duguid, S. (1987). *University prison education in British Columbia. Combining academic living skills for personal growth.* Burnaby: Simon Fraser University.

Duguid, S. (2000) *Can prisons work?: The prisoner as object and subject in modern corrections.* Toronto: University of Toronto.

Eikeland, O. J., Manger, T., Asbjørnsen, A. (2009). *Education in Nordic prisons. Prisoner's educational backgrounds, preferences and motivation. Tema Nord 2009:508.* Copenhagen: Nordic Council fo Ministers.

Eikeland, O. J., Manger, T., Asbjørnsen, A. (2013). *Nordmenn i fengsel: Utdanning, arbeid og kompetanse.* Bergen: Fylkesmannen i Hordaland.

England and Wales. Ministry of Education and Skills. (2005). *Reducing re-offending through skills and employment.* Norwich: The Stationary Office: Ministry of Education and Skills.

Eriksen, K. E., & Lundestad, G. (1972). *Kilder til moderne historie II. Norsk innenrikspolitikk.* Oslo-Bergen-Tromsø: Universitetsforlaget.

Fliflet, A. (2003, November 12). Foredrag på avslutningskonferansen for "Evaluering av fengselsundervisninga" på Quality Airport Hotel Gardermoen. *Rettssikkerheten og forvaltningssamarbeidet i en lukket institusjon.* Gardermoen, Norge.

Foucault, M. (1977). *Det moderne fengsels historie.* Oslo: Gyldendal Norsk Forlag.

Garmannslund, P. E., & Meltevik, S. (2010). *Med blikket rettet fremover. Sluttrapport for evaluering av realkompetansevurderingsprosjektet innenfor kriminalomsorgen.* Bergen: Fylkesmannen i Hordaland.

GHK in association with Anne Costelloe, Torfinn Langelid and Anita Wilson. (2012). *Survey on prison education and training in Europe—final report order 23 of the DG education and culture framework contract 02/10-Lot 1.* Brussels/Birmingham: European Commission/GHK.

Gröning, L. (2014). Education for foreign inmates in Norwegian prisons: a legal and humanitarian perspective. *Bergen Journal of Criminal Law & Criminal Justice, 2*(2), 164–188.

Hauge, R. (1996). *Straffens begrunnelser.* Oslo: Universitetsforlaget.

Høstmælingen, N. (2004). *Internasjonale menneskerettigheter.* Oslo: Universitetsforlaget.

Høstmælingen, N., Steen, H., Kjeldegaard-Peders, A. (2013, February 5). *Notat om menneskerettslig regulering av rett til opplæring i norske fengsler for utenlandske fanger som skal sendes ut av landet etter endt soning.* Oslo: ILPI—International Law and Policy Institute.

Justis- og beredskapsdepartementet (Ministry of Justice). (2001, May 18). *Lovdata. Lov om gjennomføring av straff (The Execution of Sentences Act).* Hentet May 4, 2015 fra https://lovdata.no/dokument/NL/lov/2001-05-18-21.

Justisdepartementet. (1977, September 9). Instruks for Rådet for kriminalomsorgen fastsatt ved kgl.res. av 9.9.1977. Oslo, Norge: Justisdepartementet.

Justis-og Politidepartementet. (2008, September 26). St.meld. nr.37 (2007–2008) Straff som virker—mindre kriminalitet—tryggere samfunn (kriminalomsorgsmelding) Punishment that works—less crime—a safer society. Report to the Storting on the Norwegian Correctional Services. Oslo, Norge: Justis-og Politidepartementet.

Kuhnle, S., & Kildal, N. (2011). Velferdsstatens idegrunnlag i perspektiv. In A. Hatland, S. Kuhnle, T. I. Romøren (Eds.), *Den norske velferdsstaten* (pp. 15–40). Oslo: Gyldendal Akademisk.

Kirke- og undervisningsdepartementet, Justisdepartementet. (1979). *Rapport Seminar 1979 "Undervisning og opplæring i fengsel".* Oslo: Kirke- og undervisningsdepartementet og Justisdepartementet.

Kunnskapsdepartementet. (1998, July 17). *Lovdata. Lov og grunnskolen og den vidaregåande opplæringa (opplæringslova). The Education Act.* Hentet Mai 4, 2015 fra https://lovdata.no/dokument/NL/lov/1998-07-17-61.

Langelid, T. (2015). *Bot og betring? Fengselsundervisninga si historie i Noreg.* Oslo: Cappelen Damm.

Langelid, T., Mäki, M., Raundrup, K., Svensson, S. (2009). *Nordic prison education. A lifelong learning perspective. Tema Nord 2009:536.* Copenhagen: Nordic Council of Ministers.

Lösel, F. (1993). *Evaluating psychosocial interventions in prison and other penal contexts.Psychosocial interventions in the criminal justice system. Twentieth Criminological Research Conference.* Strasbourg: Council of Europe.

Manger, T., Eikeland, O.-J., Roth, B. B., Asbjørnsen, A. (2013). *Nordmenn i fengsel: Motiv for utdanning.* Bergen: Fylkesmannen i Hordaland.

Mathiesen, T. (1995). *Kan fengsel forsvares.* Oslo: Pax Forlag a.s.

Mathiesen, T. (2012). Scandinavian exceptionalism in penal matters. Reality or wishful thinking? In T. Ugelvik and J. Dullum (Eds.), *Penal exceptionalism? Nordic prison policy and practice* (pp. 13–38). London and New York: Routledge Taylor & Francis Group.

Mathisen, Y. (2012 (2.opplag)). *Ærlig mat i Halden fengsel. Decent food in Halden Prison.* Halden: Lutefiskakademiet.

Midre, G. (1995). *BOT, BEDRING ELLER BRØD? Om bedømming og behandling av sosial nød fra reformasjonen til velferdsstaten.* Oslo: Universitetsforlaget.

Ministry of Justice and the Police and Ministry of Education and Research. (2008, October 28). *Circular on administrative co-operation between the education and training sector and the Norwegian correctional services.* Oslo, Norway: Ministry of Justice and the Police and Ministry of Education and Research.

Nordic Council of Ministers. (2005). *Nordic prison education a lifelong learning perspective. Tema Nord 2005:526.* Copenhagen: Nordic Council of Ministers.

Norwegian Ministry of Education and Research. (2007). *Short version of Report no. 27 to the storting (2004–2005) education and training in the correctional services "another spring".* Oslo: Ministry of Education and Research.

Rasmussen, I., Dyb, V. A., Heldal, N., Strøm, S. (2010). *Samfunnsøkonomiske konsekvenser av marginalisering blant ungdom.* Oslo: Vista Analyse AS.

Seip, A.-L. (1981). *Om velferdsstatens framvekst.* Oslo, Bergen, Tromsø: Universitetsforlaget.

Seip, A.-L. (1984). *Sosialhjelpstaten blir til. Norsk sosialpolitikk 1740–1920.* Oslo: Gyldendal Norsk Forlag.

Seip, A.-L. (1994). *Veiene til velferdsstaten. Norsk sosialpolitikk 1920–75.* Oslo: Gyldendal Norsk Forlag A/S.

Westrheim, K., & Manger, T. (2013). *Ethnic minority prisoners in Nordic prisons: educational background, preferences and needs. A qualitative study of prisoners from Iraq, Poland, Russia, Serbia and Somalia.* Bergen: The County Governor of Hordaland.

Exceptional Procedures? Offenders' Experiences of Justice in Re-entry Work

Ingrid Rindal Lundeberg

Introduction

Inspired by perspectives and research on procedural justice, I will examine in this chapter how current and former prisoners evaluate the re-entry process they have experienced during and after incarceration. I strive to contribute to a constructive debate surrounding the possibilities and limitations of re-entry work by exploring which approaches current and former prisoners perceive as supportive and fair, and which they perceive to be offensive and unfair. I view re-entry work as series of different interventions and a social process (Maruna and Immarigeon 2004). Re-entry is most often a long-term process of transition from conviction, incarceration to the community which starts prior to release and continues well afterwards (Laub and Sampson 2001). Understanding the re-entry process

I.R. Lundeberg (✉)
University of Bergen, Bergen, Norway
e-mail: ingrid.lundeberg@uib.no

P. Scharff Smith, T. Ugelvik (eds.), *Scandinavian Penal History, Culture and Prison Practice,* Palgrave Studies in Prisons and Penology, DOI 10.1057/978-1-137-58529-5_11

249

requires a perspective on how the different correctional interventions offenders are exposed to help them change and avoid continued involvement in criminal behaviour (Maruna and Immarigeon 2004). While it has been argued that the Nordic countries maintain exceptional humane prison conditions (Pratt 2008), this "thesis of exceptionality" seems to neglect how procedural weaknesses in penal matters may contribute to patterns of misdistribution, "othering" and misrecognition. Studies investigating the *process* by which offenders have their re-entry rights realised and whether and how offenders experience these procedures as exceptional have been few. The "principle of normalization" implies that prisoners have access to the same welfare rights as all other Norwegian citizens. The "reintegration guarantee" (White paper 37. 2007–2008) emphasise the importance of individually accommodated re-entry work with the aim of reintegrating prisoners to the community with enhanced chances of living a law-abiding life. The idea of tailoring welfare services to the individual's needs may enhance prisoner's user involvement and opportunity to take active part in their own re-entry process, but it might also increase professional discretion in the decision-making and lead to paternalism. How prisoners have to behave to earn their rights, and how they experience their opportunities to participate in decision-making processes, is crucial for understanding how re-entry works. Research in other contexts shows that how we go about assisting people may be of greater consequence in the long run than the substance of the assistance we provide, and may end up carrying more substantial repercussions (Toch 2014). One of the most prominent and widely discussed topics in social justice theory is how procedural aspects—such as participation, respectful treatment and impartiality—both influence and relate to actual outcomes of distribution (Rawls 1972; Fraser and Honneth 2003). Studies inspired by procedural justice theory also show that when citizens evaluate the legitimacy of the criminal justice system, increased compliance with the law is most effectively achieved when criminal justice institutions follow principles of procedural fairness (Jackson et al. 2010; Tankebe and Liebling 2013; Tyler 1990). Based on qualitative interviews with prisoners and ex-prisoners (N = 58) in different correctional settings, and a survey among inmates in ten Norwegian prisons on re-entry work and prison conditions (N = 617), I want to discuss whether, when and how procedural justice may matter in processes of personal reform in a criminal career. Finally, I discuss whether my analysis has implications to the legitimacy of the criminal justice system.

Procedural Justice

The question of *social justice* has engaged many philosophers and social scientists and other scholars. A fundamental discussion within social justice theory is how different forms of judicial measures can help to reverse marginalisation and protect disadvantaged groups and minorities. An important argument for strengthening prisoners' rights to rehabilitative measures is the latter's contribution to reducing social differences. During the incarceration period, prisoners' rights to satisfactory accommodation, education or training, employment, health and social services, and financial advice should provide the best possible conditions for an offender to re-integrate into society after their release. This perspective on justice is often referred to as *distributive*, as justice is mainly defined as the *outcome of certain distribution patterns* (Rawls 1972). Distributive justice means that redistribution works to improve the situation for the person in the worst position more than for everyone else (Rawls 1972). The distributive understanding of justice has, however, been criticised for being more concerned with *who* is being deprived than with *how* this distribution has come about; namely, the way in which the recipient of benefits and burdens has been met, seen, heard and treated (Fraser and Honneth 2003). Injustice is more than simply a warped or improper distribution: Justice is the condition that makes it possible for all to participate in decision-making which affect them self, and to express their feelings, experience and perspective. Injustice, on the contrary, is associated with lack of decision-making power and exposure to disrespectful treatment because of the status one occupies (Fraser and Honneth 2003). Decision-making procedures can result in injustices, contribute to exclusion and stigmatisation where they degrade people and exclude them from communicating and giving their opinion, use belittling characterisations and leave the person with a sense of shame and guilt. Procedural injustice can undermine legitimacy and trust, prompting resistance and—in the worst cases—leading to an exacerbation of a disadvantaged person's circumstances, or preventing them from seeking the help they need.

In prison research, interest in procedural justice philosophy has grown in recent times (Jackson et al. 2010; Liebling and Arnold 2004; Liebling 2013; Mjåland 2015; Sparks and Bottoms 1995). There is substantial empirical evidence that shows the importance of legitimacy in achieving law-abiding behaviour and cooperation from citizens and prisoners, especially through what has been described as procedural justice. Tyler (1990) found that when citizens evaluate the legitimacy of the criminal justice institutions such as the police and courts, the perception of the *approaches* used by representatives of the criminal justice system was more important than the advantageousness of the case's outcome. The following characteristics is linked to what is perceived as processually fair approaches when law enforcement authorities make decisions: whether citizens are allowed to have their say without interruption or harassment; to be governed by rules neutrally and consistently applied and to be treated with proper respect, dignity and concern for their wellbeing (Tankebe and Liebling 2013). A central point is the inextricable link between procedural justice and legitimacy. Approaches perceived as procedurally just will improve citizens' evaluation of the legitimacy of the authorities, thereby increasing the normative willingness to follow laws and rules. The legitimacy of a criminal justice system is formed to a large extent through actual encounters with those who represent that system. The relationship prisoners have with prison staff is important both to maintaining control and executing security tasks, but also in terms of access to services and on-going work to promote law-abiding change (Liebling and Arnold 2004). Prison is a strictly rule-based interaction context, yet at the same time, the discretionary leeway given to the staff "on the floor" is considerable. Criminal justice agents, as well as being front-line bureaucrats more generally, are subject to institutional frameworks that require the creation of certain types of cases, whilst also having to live by the ideal of the unique individual's specific situation (Lipsky 1980). This relationship between individual treatment and equality of treatment poses a dilemma throughout the welfare state's service provisions generally, but gains particular significance in prison, where prisoners are in a good position to compare their own treatment with that of others (Mathiesen 1965;

Sparks and Bottoms 1995). The discretionary aspect can lead to an arbitrariness and variation which constitute a significant normative problem in correctional institutions. In what follows, I would like to throw light on how offenders perceive procedurally just correctional practises in different settings and in decision-making processes that play a crucial role in determining their rights and duties.

Methods and Data

The main research methods employed in this study involved a survey and semi-structured interviews with both prisoners (41) and ex-prisoners (17) in different correctional settings (closed wings, rehabilitation units, re-entry programs, self-supporting groups). The interviewees were identified through ethnographic fieldwork, recommended by probation officers, social workers or recruited from different self-supporting groups or suggested by ex-offenders by snowball sampling method. Interviews were conducted from January 2011 to 2015 by the author together with Kristian Mjåland. While the ex-prisoners we interviewed consisted of both men and women (8), the inmates were mostly men, typically between 23 and 45 years old, and nearly all were ethnic Norwegians. Most of the interviewee's criminal records were characterised by frequent and serious offending. The majority had considerable experience as drug users, dominated by high-frequent heroin and amphetamine use. The interviews lasted between 1 and 3 hours and took place in different settings; when inside the prison we most often had to meet at the prisoner's cell or at a room made for visitors, when possible outside of the prison the location varied from their own home, at cafes, in meeting rooms and at the author's office. The interviews were fully transcribed and coded thematically according to what the offenders recognised as the most important in the process of reintegration. General topics included pre-prison life, prison experience, re-entry program attendance and motivation for change and life after prison. Some cases provide thick examples of a process of—or meaning of—a re-entry event that could be found in the majority, but more precisely or explicitly described. The life stories of the "reformed" ex-offenders "Alf", "Alex", "Hilde" and "Gisle" provides us with such examples which in the following will be the subjects of more grounded case analyses. Our study of re-entry work also includes a survey on prison conditions and release in ten of the largest Norwegian prisons. Two of them were open and the rest were closed prisons. One was a prison for women only and another was exclusively for foreign citizens. The purpose was to get an overview of the measures and re-entry work that exist in various prisons, which inmates have access to them and how inmates themselves evaluate the help they get during their stay in prison. The questionnaires were translated into French, Arabic, Lithuanian, Norwegian, English and Polish in order to include as many foreign-speaking prisoners as possible. The prisoners were supposed to fill in the questionnaire by themselves; most of them did it in their own cell. Six hundred and seven surveys were returned which is a response rate of 45 %. Informed consent was obtained through the author's verbal recital of an ethically approved respondents information sheet. Ethical approval of the study was sought and obtained from the Norwegian social science data service (NSD).

The research methods were not designed in advance to explore procedural fairness. However, during the data collection a common feature among the prisoners became evident where procedures and decision-making processes had a crucial significance for their prison experience and perception of criminal justice. The concepts of *trust, responsibility, equal treatment, the justice of difference, respect* and *empowerment* that I try to outline and illustrate below were derived from the analyses of the prisoner's accounts of procedural issues in staff-prisoners relationship and the overall experiences of the criminal justice system.

Trust

The convicted persons in our data have had very differing experiences of the legal process, yet they also all have something in common: the way they were treated has influenced their attitude towards re-entry work. Some events in the correctional process are more symbolically charged than others. The trial in itself is a particularly important arena for the management of trust and confidence (Shover 1996). Georg was one of many prisoners we spoke to who put emphasise on the connection with earlier experiences of unfair treatment and the moral climate in prison:

This Place is in fact filled with desperation: many really believe that all that brought them here is very unfair, that the police has too much power, that the court system is a farce, that the only job the judge has is to explain that the police is right... It's not the prisons themselves that should be researched, but rather what happens in the courtrooms: if that was fine, prisons would feel much less desperate and unfair. (Georg)

Court proceedings present a transition phase that uses rituals to regulate the changing status of the individuals being sentenced (Maruna 2001). The extent to which this is performed in more or less offensive, appropriate or respectful ways can have a great impact on the prisoner's view of their prison sentence. In our data, it is evident how much prisoners' experiences of the legal process can vary. The majority of the ex-prisoners we spoke to who had succeeded in creating a new life away from substance abuse and criminality spoke of how they felt that they—during the court proceeding—had the chance to voice their own personal concerns, and that the police and the courts were acting out of a sincere desire to take their specific situation into account. However, recurring earlier negative experiences can lead to the individual gaining a sense of general mistrust. The so-called "persisters" in particular spoke of judges who seldom or never view their personal and social circumstances as mitigating or review the petitions brought by the prosecuting authorities against remand subjects. In this group, the relationship between the court and the police is perceived as being problematically close. Prisoners respond that the "system" is not neutral or impartial; neither are its representatives concerned with exercising justice. Repeated negative experiences of the police and courts create an overriding sense of opposition and unwillingness (Ugelvik 2011). Being a "victim" of extraneous painful conditions without it being seen or taken into consideration can be a contributing factor in those in question not believing in the possibility of change. The inmates try to counter the established division between "us" and "them" by pointing out how "they"—the police, the courts, prison officials, the legal process and the sanctions chain—discriminate, break their own rules and digress from their own norms, often behaving far more immorally than the inmates themselves.

Responsibility

In the survey we carried out, 42 % of respondents stated that they didn't know their rights as prisoners. Many of the interviewees described in detail how difficult it could be for them to access their rights to various re-entry measures during the course of their prison sentences. Certain prisons were perceived as being particularly restrictive and bureaucratic, and slow to respond to applications. Several of the participants discussed quite the opposite dynamic: they stated that as a prisoner, it was easier to get access to eligible services and benefits than it was as a free citizen. They felt they were treated with a respect and consideration in prison which was lacking in the outside world. Alf—like other "successful" ex-criminals in our sample—had developed a good relationship with a range of staff members in prison. The presence of imported services made it easier to negotiate the complex and bureaucratic welfare system from the inside of prison. Alf's case is an example of the potential of the wide spectrum of re-entry measures available in some prisons, where individually oriented therapeutic work is supplemented by wider welfare-oriented measures that focus on material needs and achieving social inclusion. His case illustrates how the re-entry policy concerned with activating responsibility might work successfully when the individual is *capable of having the responsibility and freedom* to be an active actor in, for instance, going back into employment. At the time of the interview, Alf is drug-free, out of prison and in what he perceived as a meaningful work. During a previous incarceration, Alf was trained as carpenter. Alf had the opportunity to go to a series of flat viewings and job interviews without being accompanied by prison staff. In addition, he was given permission to take part in "Jobbklubb", a course for job seekers held under the auspices of the Norwegian labour and welfare administration (NAV). Alf feels that "Jobbklubb" was especially useful in giving him training in how to make a reliable CV that could also cover up his many prison sentences. Although the survey showed that work-related activities were the most widespread re-entry measure used during the prison stay, and regarded by the prisoners as being amongst the most important (38 % respondents believed it was the most important), it did not necessarily help them avoid drugs and crime. Like Alf, several told that they were able to use drugs and continue to hold down a job.

How the individual manages to renegotiate their criminal past and handle their new identity in encounters with the outside world is a critical point in the re-entry process. Many of those incarcerated who openly claim to have a high drug consumption but who are nevertheless able to live a relatively normal and independent life soon become viewed as untrustworthy cases who can't be helped, suffering from a lack of responsibility and self-knowledge. Most experienced the ambivalent attitude prisons take to drug users; the drug-dependent have gained more recognition, attention and a status of patient whilst simultaneously being readily branded as inveterate criminals incapable of accepting responsibility (Mjåland and Lundeberg 2014). They are seen both responsible and irresponsible, autonomous to make choice and dependent, both deserving and undeserving of rights and rewards, both capable and incapable of personal reform.

Equality of Treatment

How the prisoners perceive their interaction and relationship with staff will have a strong influence on how they evaluate the legitimacy of the prison (Tankebe and Liebling 2013). The treatment of prisoners is a subject with many dimensions, covering everything from how they are spoken to, to how the staff make decisions on an everyday basis in the prison. An especially prominent topic was experiences of unlawful discrimination. In the survey, roughly half (49 %) of respondents stated that there is too much discrimination in the prison they served time in. Women and foreign citizens experienced this to a greater extent. They felt that they didn't have access to the same services as others, and therefore didn't have the same opportunities to progress during the sentence period:

> It's a problem that the staff did not inform about the prisoners' rights. That foreign citizens doesn't have the right to drug treatment such as "Stifinneren" in Oslo prison. If you do not have a problem with drugs one has fewer opportunities as one cannot apply for help as if one has a drug problem and thus has the possibility to seek help that could affect the

sentence because it is a way that will signal to the Court that one wishes to make a difference. (Peter, foreign prisoner)

As Peter expresses, the prison provides persons defined as "intervenable prisoners", as persons with a drug addiction problem, with more opportunities vis-à-vis other groups. Prisons' re-entry practices systematically misrecognises and disadvantage some vulnerable groups of people vis-à-vis others. At the same time, targeted groups such as drug users felt that they had to work hard on themselves and be active in order to gain access to privileges and easier prison conditions. If inmates do not follow up on their duties, for example by not taking sufficiently part in their own rehabilitation in different programs, it may have consequences for their sentence, such as postponement of parole. It is particularly the most marginalised who may suffer in a system which demands certain activities in return for receiving services. At the same time, inmates were upset that favouritism was often the primary factor in the division of goods and the imposition of sanctions (Mjåland and Lundeberg 2014). Many prisoners experienced differential treatment based on personal sentiments rather than professional, individual assessments of their needs. The definition of a need is not necessarily linked to the offenders perception of what the individual requires but rather on assessments of offenders personal attitudes, character, motivation to change and intervenability. A problem of legitimacy arises when everyday encounters and observations are used as a basis for important decisions about the individual, without the inmate necessarily being aware that they have been evaluated, what has been given weight in different situations and what has been reported further. The absence of openness, clarity and consistency left the prisoners with a feeling of being subjected of an unpredictable and unreliable power.

The Justice of Difference

Despite the fact that many of the (ex-) prisoners we interviewed had a very negative view on what they felt as arbitrary and unjust discrimination, several were sympathetic towards the principle of their particular situation being given a particular weight in decision-making processes. The criminal justice power-holders' ability to transgress discretionary boundaries and over use power when advocating—and representing—the prisoners' case in critical, determinative moments was widely recognised as good professional behaviour. As such, prisoners viewed some level of discrimination as legitimate in principle, but the *unreasonable* way discrimination was practised was often perceived as illegitimate. In our data, we have a range of examples of how special treatment can have a profound impact on the prisoners' change process.

Hilde's story is typical of many of the female offenders in our studies. Her "hyper-criminal" career began at a young age, at the same time as she developed a serious and extensive drug dependency. Over the years, Hilde was repeatedly given "new chances", receiving alternative sanctions such as being able to carry out community service and serve a sentence at a treatment centre. This continuous special treatment owed much to the fact that she was, to a large extent, portrayed as a stereotypical female victim of emotional and physical abuse, violence and social distress, where her resorting to criminality and drugs was viewed as a survival, or self-medicating, strategy. She worked on improving herself throughout the sentence periods and she followed the re-entry programmes with a relatively large engagement and openness. Hilde nevertheless took an ambivalent view on this opportunity and on the desire to live a crime and drug-free life. She experienced the correctional services' less punitive sides, but nevertheless served several sentences which didn't lead to any particularly long-term change in her criminal activities.

The last time she was arrested for fraud and serious drug crimes the police told her that she wasn't given any more chances. Even though she was completely run down, and her health was in a worse condition than on previous arrests, she understood that she had to go to prison. In a decisive moment, however, an "enthusiast" in the system played a crucial role in helping Hilde to avoid prison once more and instead made it possible for her to carry out and finally succeed with her treatment. The case illustrates how powerful encounters between offenders and professionals can develop in series of decision points over time, but it also shows how the role an individual plays in a particular situation "can make all the difference".

Hilde had developed some close relationships with people within the "system" who knew her history and who went on to serve as caring supporters, playing a considerable role at a crucial point in her life. Gender can also have a real significance in this "distinctive work". Gendered constructions of victimhood can be emphasised as a mitigating circumstance by the court because they are more likely to view female offenders as victims of bad health or social conditions than men. For Hilde, this "victimisation" served exclusively as a benefit. An unfortunate element of this gendered victimisation can, however, mean that the "victim" is deprived of the role as rational, accountable, responsible and active agents (Hannah-Moffat 2000). At the same time, Hilde's process of change demonstrates the importance of an individually accommodated decision process that takes the specific needs of the inmate into consideration. Likewise, the legal processes Hilde went through show the extent to which chance can come into play in such cases, with decisive outcomes. The processual weaknesses relate to occasions where the person has been shut out, prevented from, or is incapable of, conveying their opinions and taking part in decisions that concern themselves (Fraser and Honneth 2003). Not receiving assistance to understand or being unable to express oneself within the applicable legal frameworks means that an individual's problems may be discredited and hidden or ascribed to their own weakness of will. This can not only lead to a lack of recognition and respect, but to incorrect and unjust decisions.

Respectful Treatment

The question of equality of treatment versus discrimination is intimately linked to the way prisoners experienced being treated and met with respect in their daily interactions with officers and other staff in the correctional services (Liebling and Arnold 2004). At the same time, we see huge discrepancies between different prisons and prisoners in the evaluation of prisoner treatment. In the survey, this is shown through the fact that there is a large spread in how satisfied prisoners are with the supervision they have received from their contact officer (36 % dissatisfied; 44 % satisfied). In treatment wings the physical environment and interactions are quite different from regular wings and special security wings. Staff and prisoners interact more closely and intensively. Subcultural differences between prisons of different types, but also internally between different wings are well-illustrated through Alex's experiences. We interviewed him after his release from serving time as part of a several-year sentence for sexual offences. At the start of his sentence, Alex was moved around between different smaller prisons. He was mostly locked up at his cell, and felt that his daily interactions with prison staff demonstrated an excessive focus on security. His treatment was characterised by distance, a lack of response and condescending remarks; humiliations on a micro-scale that functioned in a stigmatising way. When he was transferred to one of the larger prisons in Norway, which has its own department and programme for sexual offenders, his life begun to change:

> So I was moved up there as a test for three days. I'd see if I enjoyed being there, and I fit right in . . . they were great, they took me in with a . . . with open arms . . . They like, were really warm to me. And there's not a damn person who has been, like, warm to me. No one . . . no one before that. I've always sat in that fucking room of mine, not wanting to go out. Suddenly you come to this warm place, and those feelings . . . (Alex).

Alex describes how he was welcomed with a genuine warmth and openness. Interactions with the supportively detached staff generated an emotional energy making program participants feel as strong and confident agents of change. The staff at the treatment unit approached Alex where he was in his process of change and as a person with individual needs and resources, not as a risky criminal. At the same time, Alex was able to take control of his own sentence plan. Being treated like a unique person with a wide spectrum of resources, abilities and potential contributed to him deciding to "give himself over", and he started a long-term process with a view to establishing a new and better life for himself after his release. Even if there are a range of factors that come into play when such choices to change are made, Alex credits the way he was treated by the prison staff with playing a central role in this. While the procedural techniques he was met with might be viewed as more "heavy", efficient and penetrative modes of penal control (Garland

2001), most prisoners acknowledged this kind of genuinely engaged interactions as supportive and respectful. The availability and visibility of prisons staff and the depth and quality of their engagement can be of great importance for prisoners' feelings of humane dignity (Crewe et al. 2014). However, to develop a personal desire for reform, the models for change that the prison worked with had to be seen as meaningful. The re-entry initiatives within prisons are built on the notion that personal change and development are an obvious goal for all inmates, a goal to which many don't aspire. Inmates with needs and wishes that stand in contrast to the institution's models were readily stigmatised as difficult, weak and dangerous individuals, or as people who lack an understanding of themselves.

Empowerment

A common feature to many of the interviews with prisoners who were satisfied with what they had managed to achieve during and after their prison sentence was the emphasis on the fact that "I did it myself". Other studies into the re-entry of offenders make a similar point of the fact that change is seen as a result of the individual's choice and ability to act (Sampson and Laub 1993; Maruna 2001). You rehabilitate yourself; the prison, correctional services, welfare state, NAV, therapists, family, job, age and time cannot change a person who doesn't make personal efforts to change themselves "from the inside". Most of the ex-criminals we interviewed, as well as the prisoners who had taken an active choice to change their way of life during their prison sentence, ascribed a decisive significance to this individual effort to go straight. Gisle empha-sised the importance of his own motivation and focus when he spoke about the change process he had gone through, from being relatively deeply involved in drug criminality to being a clean new father in a permanent job: "I believe you'll really struggle if you are not 100 % sure about or focused on getting through this." What he put particular emphasis on was partly that nobody told him what to do or think or how to solve problems; rather, they guided him to find out for himself. When you are given the chance to figure things out for yourself "[it] helps with my self-confidence and things like that, and my image of myself". In prison, prisoners are made passive: they are deprived of most of the opportunities they have to influence their own situation and everyday life. By making their story a resource and standing out as a good example, they gain a sense of self-determination and of giving something back to society as a way of showing gratitude. However, these statements should not be read as descriptions of the actual division of labour between prisoners and prisons/support systems in re-entry work. When we went into more detail about the rehabilitation process, it became clear that the prison and other external welfare actors had been crucial in different ways; for example, in job counselling, housing, implementation of responsibility group meetings, applications for medically assisted rehabilitations and more. A problem was, however, the sense that the prison didn't acknowledge the prisoners' own initiative and engagement in their rehabilitation. By not acknowledging the prisoners' efforts, and by, on some occasions, emphasising its own initiative over that of the prisoners, the prison's approach undermines one of the relationships that research now says is of great importance to successful rehabilitation (Maruna 2001). Not being recognised for the effort one devotes to the hard process of becoming a straight, law-abiding citizen, and—worse—being deprived of the credit for this, can be perceived as unfair, humiliating and degrading, and can contribute to weakening confidence in the rehabilitative ambitions and practices of the prison.

Exceptional Procedures

In this article I have discussed how the way in which the approaches used by representatives of the criminal justice system are crucial to achieving good prison conditions, trust and social recognition, and for creating participatory possibilities for particularly vulnerable groups therein. The offenders play particular value on the ability to state ones case before decisions are being made, on neutrality when authorities apply rules in an unbiased, reasoned and consistent manner, on being treated with dignity and respect and a sense of trust and openness in decision-making processes that affect them. The manner in which respondents were referred to and categorised by people who held considerable determining power within the system, and the extent to which the individual felt they were being given or deprived of self-respect, is presented as being extremely significant for the person the case concerns. This illustrates how welfare distributive regulations and self-respect must be put into context, their correlations explored in concrete practice (Fraser and Honneth 2003). The infringements offenders' experiences through their contact with the justice system relate not only to restricted freedom and revoked privileges; such infringements can also involve being exposed to interpretation and communication patterns that are both unfamiliar and oppressive in relation to their own.

Through the ex-offenders stories we have seen that the criminal justice system in Norway, to a certain extent, might be viewed as exceptional, in that *different* rehabilitative approaches are employed in which individual treatment, social inclusion efforts and the realisation of rights are all central. Our study confirms that rehabilitation in some places is deeply embedded in the penal practices and that staff at treatment wings seem committed to maintaining what can be characterised as "exceptional" humane procedures. The wide range of approaches and extensive use of discretion enable inmates to feel that their specific needs are often borne into consideration, and not their risks to reoffend. At the same time, this individualisation means that significant discrepancies arise with regard to who gains access to different measures. This *procedural arbitrariness*, as a structural feature of the welfare state, may have major consequences for the intrusive use of repressive state power against individuals. A high level of individualisation in sentence implementation is also highly problematic when considered in view of the equality ideal of criminal justice, namely that particular types of offences should be punished in the same way (Gröning 2013).

Procedural justice concerns whether the decision-making process is adapted to the abilities, needs and potential the individual possesses. The processes associated with defining needs can have profound consequences in punishment and sentencing decisions. The varying competence of prison staff, their relation to and ability to address the offenders' needs, is likely to be decisive for the determination of the individual inmate's rights and obligations and the success rate of reintegration. Misrecognition might be the case in definitional practices when a criminal justice professional categorises some needs as illegitimate targets or lacking in crimogenic potential. The available re-entry measures for some individuals and groups are restricted and are not sufficiently diverse and differentiated to match the complexity of the individual's need. This leads to unconditional outcomes of re-entry work. Re-entry measures should be better linked to the offenders' perception of what the individual requires, rather than on assessments of offenders' personal attitudes, character, chemistry, motivation to change and intervenability.

Procedural injustice arises through important decision-making processes linked to the sentence conditions being left to the whims of chance, resources, favouritism or personal characteristics. For many of the prisoners, a lack of clarity surrounds decisions made with regard to their sentence terms. Individual discrepancies between decisions that were to have serious consequences for an individual's sentence conditions were perceived as unreasonable. Convicts reacted in particular to situations where the decision-making processes did not appear to be neutral, leading to an ungrounded inequality of treatment. In order to ensure that the relationship between equality of treatment and individual treatment is recognised as reasonable in specific situations, structured interactions and clear(er) explanations are required (Jackson et al. 2010). The perception of procedural justice also concerned the extent to which the everyday interactions between prison staff and prisoners were felt to be respectful. Instances of treatment that can contribute to feelings of inferiority and powerlessness cover a wide range of situations; everything from being addressed in an offensive manner to "micro-humiliations" in everyday contexts, where staff either ignore, or are slow to respond to, the inmate's enquiries. This lack of openness, dialogue, information and co-operation leads not only to the risk of flawed or wrong decisions being made regarding sentence conditions (misdistribution), but also to a feeling of inferiority (misrecognition) and mistrust.

Despite the risk of unreasonable discrimination, inmates felt that it was equally important that the prison base its decisions regarding re-entry approaches on the prisoners' specific circumstances and needs. The majority of the inmates who felt that they had been treated respectfully and had gained support listed individual adaptations and user participation as being key to their success. Some inmates felt that prison was a good arena for being seen and making themselves heard with regard to their specific situation; they used their right to position themselves and demanded recognition as actors in their own lives, expressing their own opinions and needs. Relationships and encounters with staff members who focused on the concrete opportunities a specific individual had and which were built on personal participation, initiative and engagement, helped the individual continue to move away from criminality and improve their potential to live a law-abiding life.

Correctional interventions should better recognise the experience of a personal attained process of reform and design interventions that can enhance or complement these effects (Maruna 2001). Although many inmates receive a considerably amount of professional assistance, persons who change while in programs presented themselves as "self-changers". However, there is an underlying ambivalent assumption about agency in offender management (Steen et al. 2012). In particular, drug abusers experienced this ambivalence, which meant that at times their own ability to change their participation and viewpoint were given much weight, whereas at other times they were treated as sick, irresponsible and dangerous addicts. The value of recognition embraced by the prisoners is about being made accountable. The persons involved should be treated as independent and competent subjects, with a right to be informed about their case and being credited for the efforts one has made.

Some groups become systematically omitted and excluded from the possibility of having a rights holder status. This is partly due to a lack of good, adapted information regarding inmates' rights and the opportunities to participate in decisions about their sentence conditions. This is a significant problem for vulnerable groups and minorities—for whom learning about and asserting their rights is more difficult—who face, as a result of this shortcoming, a further risk of being discriminated against and marginalised. The judicial system's exceptionality is put to the test on occasions where a person is less able to use their voice and make their vulnerability relevant. Particularly deprived inmates can be subjected to harder punishments because they are less able to defend themselves in the correct way and make use of the opportunities available to them within the system. This inequality is reinforced through access to social benefits being conditioned by various responsibilities that the citizen has to meet. Applying the concept of misrecognition alerts us to the fact that criminal justice interventions unwittingly reassign blame to the less privileged for their individual failures and moral character deficiencies. The inherent failure of procedural "rights" to ensure justice for persons in such cases are consistent with the long-standing critique of the extension of rights to powerless groups, namely that the enforcement of these "rights" require a participatory involvement absent amongst the very groups that "rights" are supposed to aid. By identifying these procedural barriers and arbitrariness in the welfare state, this study then calls into question the progressive characterisation of the Norwegian penal order based on humane dignity and social solidarity. The discussions of justice must thus consider how lack of access to procedural rights render the needs of one person or a group invisible at the same time as they are being stereotyped and marked out as the inferior, irresponsible, incorrigible and deviant Other.

Acknowledgements I am deeply grateful to Kristian Mjåland for his contribution in the collection of data and the analyses and to Hans Tore Hansen for his insightful comments on earlier versions on this paper. I would also like to express my gratitude to the editors for encouraging comments and suggestions that have improved the chapter considerably. The research was financially supported by The Research Council of Norway, grant no. 202466

References

Crewe, B., Liebling, A., Hulley, H. (2014). Heavy-light, absent-present: rethinking the "weight" of imprisonment. *British Journal of Sociology, 65*(3), 387–410.

Fraser, N., & Honneth, A. (2003). *Redistribution or recognition? A political-philosophical exchange.* London: Verso.

Garland, D. (2001). *The culture of control: crime and social order in contemporary society.* Chicago: University of Chicago Press.

Gröning, L. (2013). Straffgenomföring som en del av straffrättssystemet: Principförklaring av fängelsestraffets innehåll. *Tidsskrift for Rettsvitenskap, 26*(1–2), 145–195.

Hannah-Moffat, K. (2000). Prisons that empower: neo-libral Governance in Canadian woman prisons. *British Journal of Criminology, 40*(3), 510–531.

Jackson, J., Tyler, T. R., Bradford, B., Taylor, D., Shiner, M. (2010). Legitimacy and procedural justice in prisons. *Prison Service Journal, 191*, 4–10.

Laub, J., & Sampson, R. (2001). Understanding desistance from crime. *Crime and Justice: A Review of Research, 28*, 1–70.

Liebling, A. (2013). "Legitimacy under pressure" in high security prisons. In J. Tankebe and A. Liebling (Eds.), *Legitimacy and criminal justice: an international exploration* (pp. 206–226). Oxford: Oxford University Press.

Liebling, A., & Arnold, H. (2004). *Prisons and their moral performance: a study of values, quality, and prison life.* Oxford and New York: Oxford University Press.

Lipsky, M. (1980). *Street-level bureaucracy dilemmas of the individual in public services.* New York: Russell Sage Foundation.

Maruna, S. (2001). *Making good: how ex-convicts reform and rebuild their lives.* Washington, DC: American Psychological Association.

Maruna, S., & Immarigeon, R. (Ed.) (2004). *After crime and punishment. Pathways to offender reintegration.* London: Routledge.

Mathiesen, T. (1965). *The defences of the weak. A sociological study of a Norwegian Correctional Institution.* London: Tavistock.

Mjåland, K. (2015). The paradox of control: an ethnographic analysis of opiate maintenance treatment in a Norwegian prison. *International Journal of Drug Policy, 26*(8), 781–789.

Mjåland, K., & Lundeberg, I. R. (2014). Penal hybridization: staff-prisoner relationships in a Norwegian drug rehabilitation unit. In H. S. Aasen, S. Gloppen, A.-M. Magnussen, E. Nilssen (Eds.), *Juridification and social citizenship in the welfare state* (pp. 183–202). Cheltenham: Edward Elgar.

Pratt, J. (2008). Scandinavian exceptionalism in an era of penal excess—Part I: the nature and roots of Scandinavian exceptionalism. *British Journal of Criminology, 48*(2), 119–137.

Rawls, J. (1972). *A theory of justice.* Oxford: Oxford University Press.

Sampson, R. J., & Laub, J. H. (1993). *Crime in the making: pathways and turning points through life.* London: Harvard University Press.

Shover, N. (1996). *Great pretenders: pursuits and careers of persistent thieves.* Boulder, CO: Westview Press.

Sparks, J. R., & Bottoms, A. E. (1995). Legitimacy and order in prisons. *British Journal of Sociology, 46*(1), 45–62.

Steen, S, Lacock, T., McKinzey, S. (2012). Unsettling the discourse of punishment? Competing narratives of reentry and the possibilities for change. *Punishment and Society, 14*(1), 29–50.

Tankebe, J., & Liebling, A. (2013). *Legitimacy and criminal justice: an international exploration.* Oxford: Oxford University Press.

Toch, H. (2014). *Organizational change through individual empowerment: applying social psychology in prisons and policing.* Washington, DC: American Psychological Association.

Tyler, T. R. (1990). *Why people obey the law.* New Haven: Yale University Press.

Ugelvik, T. (2011). *Fangenes friheter: makt og motstand i et norsk fengsel.* Oslo: Universitetsforl.

White Paper 37. (2007–2008). *Straff som virker—mindre kriminalitet—tryggere samfunn (kriminalomsorgsmeldingen).* Oslo: Justis- og politidepartementet.

Released to the "Battlefield" of the Danish Welfare State: A Battle Between Support and Personal Responsibility

Annette Olesen

Introduction

Denmark, like the other Scandinavian countries, is built on the "Nordic welfare model" where policies emerge through political dialogue and parallel decision-making (Lappi-Seppälä 2007). However, the "Nordic Welfare Model" is under pressure and the previous expert-driven and research-led strategy especially recognised within penal policy-making has been challenged and changed to a more politically ruled approach over the last decades (Lappi-Seppälä and Storgaard 2014). Nevertheless, the Scandinavian countries are still acknowledged for their stable penal policies and by some categorised as the epitome of "Scandinavian penal exceptionalism" (Pratt 2008a, b; Lappi-Seppälä 2007). The arguments for including Denmark in this "exception" are among others the country's relatively low

A. Olesen (✉)
Department of Law, University of Southern Denmark, Odense, Denmark
e-mail: aol@sam.sdu.dk

© The Author(s) 2017
P. Scharff Smith, T. Ugelvik (eds.), *Scandinavian Penal History, Culture and Prison Practice,* Palgrave Studies in Prisons and Penology, DOI 10.1057/978-1-137-58529-5_12

prison population rate trend varying from 61 to 72 per 100,000 of the national population the last 15 years; the rather stable total capacity of prisons with places for about 4,000 inmates (World Prison Brief); and the comparatively low sentences where 59 % of the sentences were 4 months or less and 8 % were 2 years or more in 2014 (The Annual Report of the Danish Prison Service 2015, p. 6). However, it is not only the (relatively mild) Danish sentences and the external prison conditions that contribute to the "exceptional" categorisation. Inside the Danish prisons, everyday life should not be reflected by hardness, instead "normalisation" and "openness" referring to the official principles of the Danish Prison and Probation Service frame the incarceration. Thus, the prison sentence should be the only loss of liberty and the aim for both the prison staff and the prisoners is to make a daily living as close as possible to the life on the outside, including educational courses; vocational training; work; unsupervised weekend accommodation with partners and children; opportunity to record bedtime stories for their children, etc. Furthermore, the Danish welfare state provides different social services to underpin the prison principles of "normalisation" and "openness" and to compensate some of the informal "penalties" faced by prisoners during incarceration. Prisoners can, for example, temporarily get their reasonable rent paid by their municipalities and are also provided with a temporary reprieve to defer repayment of their public debt during incarceration. Such protective factors as holding on to permanent housing, securing family involvement and financial stability during incarceration are suggested to ease the re-entry into society and reduce the likelihood of criminal recidivism (see e.g. Dyb et al. 2006; Skardhamar and Telle 2012; Tranæs et al. 2008).

Release from prison in Denmark is not only a reclamation of liberty but also a re-entering into society and its local authorities that offer different social services and some rehabilitative programmes, but unlike the "exceptions" in prison, life on the outside does not prescribe the ex-prisoners with special favourable legal eligibilities to secure their social, housing, and debt situation. Instead the ex-prisoners face heavy indebtedness and debt recovery enforcements from the Danish state because they as criminally convicted persons are personally liable for the necessary cost of their criminal case (legal costs) and after release they are no longer pre-approved for a temporary reprieve to defer repayment of their public debt. The situation in Denmark is rather unique; with one hand the Danish welfare state represents a low rate of incarceration, relatively humane prison conditions and rehabilitation ideals, but unlike its Scandinavian neighbours the Danish welfare state with its other hand impose criminally convicted persons to pay legal cost without taking their income level into consideration when calculating the legal costs. Nor does the Danish welfare state offer a common practice of remitting the legal costs (Olesen 2014). The dual role played by the welfare state makes the ex-prisoners a target group for both rehabilitative initiatives and intensive debt recovery strategies, and release from prison therefore frames a conspicuous struggle for power between different authorities with distinctive interests in the ex-prisoners. By approaching Bourdieu's historical sociology of the state as a power field of capital concentration, standardisation, and market construction (Bourdieu 1996, 1998a; Wacquant 1993), the struggle for power to characterise the release from prison can be examined. The fields that constitute the state or the bureaucratic field represents a variety of interests that manifest themselves in what Bourdieu analytically conceptualise as the left hand of the state (social functions and interests) and the right hand of the state (financial functions and interest) (Bourdieu 1998b, 2003; Wacquant 2001, 2009). In the specific case of release from prison, different actors, professions, and institutions are engaged in the matter and struggle to maintain their particular values and interests; the left hand of the state is mainly represented by probation officers, mentors, social workers, teachers, employers, and drug/alcohol/anger management therapists, while the right hand, in this specific case, mostly comprises the Tax Authority, bailiffs, and the police (see also Bourdieu et al. 1999).

In this chapter, I will present some observations based on a large qualitative study about released prisoners in Denmark. These observations deal with the struggle for power between the left and right hand of the Danish welfare state and how it frames release from prison. Furthermore, I wish to discuss the ex-prisoners' experiences of being placed in this core of a "welfare battlefield" post-release.

Method

The larger qualitative work of these observations and discussions builds on 77 in-depth interviews and follow-up interviews, several informal observations, conversations, email correspondences, text messages, and phone calls with 41 reoffenders. I employed four criteria to determine whether an individual was eligible to participate in the study: they should be men; 18 years of age or older; be able to speak and comprehend Danish; and be reoffenders with former pre-prison, in-prison, and post-prison experience. The age range of the participants was from 20 to 60 (median 34 years old), 25 of the participants were in a permanent relationship/married, 18 had children, seven had ethnic minority background, 14 had not completed secondary schooling, 15 had never held reported employment, and 16 were connected to (semi)organised criminal groups or outlaw motorcycle gangs. The participants' names were anonymous and replaced by pseudonyms.

I collected the data over a 36-month period. 38 of the 41 participants were recruited from an open and a closed prison in Denmark, while the remaining three participants were recruited from a drop-in-centre for ex-prisoners. Participants that were being released within a 2-year time period were asked to do one or more follow-up interviews during their re-entry period which 21 of them agreed to. The follow-up interviews were conducted in different locations, for example in the ex-prisoners' homes and cars and at coffee bars all over Denmark. Each interview lasted approximately 1–3 hours and was recorded with the participant's consent. Open-ended questions allowed the participants to identify and elaborate on domains that characterised their pre-prison, in-prison, and post-prison experiences with economy, housing, work, education, and social relations to avoid my elicit responses to structured questions. I performed an on-going verbatim transcription process of the interviews throughout the data collection, however, initially in this process I kept the data uncoded to prevent analytical bias and to enable a wide range of analytic possibilities (Bourdieu et al. 1999, pp. 607–626). During the systematic coding and analysis process, the data was categorised into conceptual domains of the interviewees' experiences of their transition back into society. In this chapter, I present the findings of the Danish welfare state's influence on how released prisoners structure their everyday life.

The Struggle for Power Between Rehabilitation and Intensive Debt Recovery

It is difficult to make a general characterisation of the released prisoners because the knowledge is very limited about who re-enters the Danish society and to which general living conditions they are assigned. The few exceptions, however, show that in general the released prisoners are financially vulnerable; highly indebted; lack a connection to the labour market; and compared with the average Danish citizens the released prisoner depends more often and for a longer time period on social security benefits (Tranæs et al. 2008; Olesen 2013a). The limited knowledge about this group could be supplemented by prison studies that over the years have shown a still more distinct social disadvantaged position of the prisoners (Kyvsgaard 1989, 1999; Clausen 2013). The latest study of the prisoners showed, among other things, that 35 % had been placed in child or youth care centres; mental health problems were rather common among the prisoners where 34 % had received psychiatric treatments; the prisoners had a relatively low level of education, as 69 % of them had primary school as their highest level of education (Clausen 2013). Taken together, the rather limited prison and post-prison studies contribute to the picture of the released prisoners being challenged on several levels compared with the average Danish citizen. In addition, it is well known that it is often the same persons that repeatedly pass through the courts, prisons, and supervision authorities making reoffenders dominate the prison population (Clausen 2013). In the last years, roughly 37 % of the released prisoners reoffended within a 2-year observation period (The Danish Prison and Probation Service 2015, p. 14).

Crime and punishment are large items of public expenditure. A cost-benefit analysis performed by Ramboll Management (2013) estimated that the total cost of crime to the Danish economy was around 10 billion DKK a year [~EUR 1.3]. Included in this estimation were the expenses to the police, courts, prisons, insurances as well as the prisoners' lost earnings. Furthermore, it has been estimated that the police approximately spend 3.8 billion DKK [~EUR 0.5] on preventing criminal activities in 2005 (The Rockwool Foundation 2006), and there are no reasons to believe that this amount has decreased over the last years. Thus, it is obvious that some would suggest a successful re-integration into society and development of pro-social behaviour to be of high priority for the welfare state, while others take a "tough on crime" approach suggesting criminal behaviour should be met with a demand of personal responsibility and therefore argues that some of the many costs of crime and punishment should be imposed on the criminally convicted persons and not be collected from the law-abiding taxpayers.

In the following, I will show how the interviewed ex-prisoners repeatedly pointed out income as a concern of vital importance in their re-entering process into society. Besides the discussion of the ex-prisoners being released to a "battlefield" of contradictory interests and how it affects their income situation, I will also briefly touch issues as the ex-prisoners' family structure and housing situation post-release.

Informally Convicted to Indebtedness Post-release

Before I open the discussion regarding the ex-prisoners' income situation I will introduce the abovementioned issue concerning the imposition of public debt directed at criminally convicted persons, because this policy is important to consider in relation to the ex-prisoners' living conditions, their strategies of action, and the effect of different welfare policies that frame their income situation.

When a person is convicted for a felony in Denmark the convicted is personally liable for the necessary costs of the criminal proceedings (Act no. 1308/2014, part 91). A clear definition of the necessary costs is not included in the Administration of Justice Act (see Rørdam 1961; Nautrup 1984; Skjødt 2004) but the costs include, among other things, the expenses to appointed defence lawyers, technical tests as DNA testing, and investigations regarding accounting data. Unlike the other Scandinavian countries, Denmark makes the convicts repay their legal costs regardless of their income level *and* without any actual opportunity for debt relief (Olesen 2013b, 2014). The imposition of legal costs, therefore, contributes to a majority of heavily indebted prisoners in Denmark (Recommendation no. 1547/2014).

No official numbers exists of the total amount of imposed legal costs or the average amount per criminal case. However, a statement from the Danish Tax Authority made on 18 January 2013 showed that the Tax Authority is owed arrears from legal costs that amounted to DKK 2 billion [EUR 0.3] at the end of December 2012. The debt was spread over approximately 60,000 debtors and 113,349 claims, which means that an average claim amounts to DKK 17,892 [EUR 2,396]. As the interviewed for this study are reoffenders (like the majority of the prison population) they have been imposed with legal costs more than once and the amount of their legal costs ranged from DKK 72,000 [EUR 9,644] to multiple millions of DKK. The majority of the interviewees' total debt burden also included other public, private, and "street" creditors who they typically owed child support, claim for damages, deposit loans, subscriptions, leasing and other personal loans, etc. To problematise the imposition of legal costs compared with other debt types, it must be taken into consideration that 38 of the 41 interviewees did not know as first-time-offenders that they were personal reliable for the necessary costs of their criminal proceedings (nor that they had to repay the expenses of their appointed defence lawyer) before they received the collection regarding legal costs. In addition, it is common practice not to break down the expenses for legal costs, which means that most of these debtors do not know which item of expenditure they are charged with covering, as they only receive a collection announcing that they repay the full amount of legal costs within 20 days. Most of the expenses are based on decisions made by the appointed defence lawyer or the police and they are not negotiable with the defendant (see also Skjødt 2004; Nautrup 1995). As it is only the persons convicted of a crime that are required to repay their legal costs, the interviewees often felt they had not received value for their money (as they were sentenced to prison). Furthermore, they pointed out that they felt tricked because according to them nobody had informed them about the government's right of recourse against them. Altogether, the interviewees experienced the legal costs as unfair and as an extra, informal punishment they only had little surplus of mental resources to deal with the problem and financially no profit to repay.

In cases were the debtor has not repaid the full amount of legal costs within six months, the recovery task is handed over from the police to the Tax Authority. Because legal costs stem from a punishable matter it is categorised by the Tax Authority as important debt to charge and recover effectively (see also Olesen 2013b). The Tax Authority can, however, provide the debtor with a temporary reprieve or negotiate an instalment agreement but they can also use enforcement actions as for example deduction, garnishing money from the debtor's bank account, registering an interest on the debtor's land, and debt recovery over gross income (The Danish Guidance and Directions for Recovery 2010). Regardless of the Tax Authority's multiple recovery strategies, the Danish Bar and Law Society (2012) estimated that less than 10 % of the full amount of legal costs is recovered.

Income: Employment, Social Security Benefit, or Crime?

With background knowledge about the released prisoners' debt position, I will now move on and discuss the Danish welfare state's influence on released prisoners' income situation by including the different policies and strategies that affect their situation and also include the first-hand experiences from the released prisoners.

This chapter will not look deeper into the Danish political transition from a Keynesian welfare national state to a Danish variant of the Schumpeterian workfare post-national paradigm (see e.g., Torfing 1999a; Dingeldey 2007). The Danish welfare state encourages its citizens to be self-supporting and this agenda also plays an important role in the prisons where work, vocational training, and education take up most of the prisoners' daily activities in an attempt to ensure they get the needed skills to (re-)integrate into the labour market and become active citizens. Employment and education programmes in prisons are, however, not only sustained to comply with the active labour market policies and activation strategies that permeates the Danish society but also to support the prisoners with qualities recognised as protective factors for criminal behaviour. The post-prison perspective included in the prison activities also recurred in my interviews with the reoffenders and it became clear that many of them invested their time in prison to be trained or retrained into a line of business they considered to be more willing to turn a blind eye to unreported or underreported payments. But what kind of future prospect do the reoffenders have since cash-in-hand jobs are of specific interest to them post-prison? The answers to this question could be many but according to my observations it is difficult to avoid the state's two competing approaches; the demands represented by the right hand and the "generosity" represented by the left hand.

Work Should Pay—But It Does Not

The right hand aims to reduce public expenses and support the viewpoint that "work should pay" and thereby stating that welfare benefits should be kept to a minimum to assure the citizens' productiveness and the state's competitive position. At the same time the actors, professions, and institutions representing the right hand advocate personal responsibility for covering any damage or costs inflicted against the state to avoid undue expenses to the public (and the taxpayers). Relating the interest of the state's right hand to the ex-prisoners' income situation results in a challenging and conflicting discussion because debt recovery of legal costs means that it does not pay to work for the ex-prisoners. A reoffender called Freddie explained from his prison cell how he previously had tried to re-establish a law-abiding lifestyle and how he experienced debt recovery of legal costs and the daily challenges living on the Tax Authority's fixed disposable amount:

> Earlier I didn't give it [the debt] a thought, but now after I've been released it became a problem, because I took an apprenticeship as a bricklayer, an adult education programme, and I think it took, well I got a temporary reprieve on my legal costs during my incarceration, but it only took a split second, 14 days or so, before it [a collection] came stating that I should repay DKK 480,000 [EUR 64,291] and at the same time I also received a financial schema that I had to complete if I couldn't [repay my debt]. And they [the Tax Authority] wouldn't accept the expenses I had in connection with the car for example. But I couldn't keep my job, well then I had to use public transportation to get to work but that would take me all day to get to work and back home. They also found my insurances to be a problem, ... From a bricklayer apprentice salary amounted to DKK 10,500 [EUR 1,406] they through and through monthly wanted more than DKK 2,000 [EUR 268] which was, which was tight, ... I completed it [the financial schema] with my girlfriend and they

[the Tax Authority] meddled in her income level,...I had absolutely no money to live for, nothing.

The majority of the participants in this study was short of money post-release and could not repay their debt to legal costs. And if they managed to find a job and receive reported income the Tax Authority invited them to accept an instalment agreement or they simply withheld a portion of their monthly income before it was paid (which is a wide-reaching method that cannot be used by private creditors in Denmark). The debt recovery process that withheld a percentage of the ex-prisoners' disposable pay to satisfy the debt meant that the ex-prisoners' take-home pay-check from working (after with-holdings) compared to receiving social security did not have any (present) effect on their financial flexibility.[1] The pay-out was calculated on the basis of a fixed disposable amount and the difference between the pay-profit and the fixed disposable amount was sent directly to cover the debt. The employed ex-prisoners experienced, like Freddie, how their pay-profit was significantly reduced by the Tax Authority's claim of an ambitious instalment agreement. And like Freddie they were often surprised when they finally made an effort to live crime-free and become taxpayers and because of this effort faced the implications of debt recovery. Moreover, the ex-prisoners were astonished when they realised that debt collection laws resulted in that they had no present financial incentive to seek employment or stay employed.

Welfare Dependency—A Way Around the Debt Problem

Simultaneously with the Danish welfare state encouraging the popula-tion to be active citizens, the state's left hand fulfil a basic founding objective by acting as a safety net for citizens in need. If the ex-prisoners experience that it does not pay to obtain reported work because of the Tax Authority's debt recovery it is evident to guesstimate that more ex-prisoners depend on public assistance and welfare. Tranæs et al. (2008) examined the unemployment rate of offenders before and after they had

---

[1] It should be mentioned that the debtors of legal costs cannot be incarcerated for non-payment; neither can the debtors repay legal costs through an alternative sentence such as imprisonment.

served a prison sentence in Denmark. Worth mentioning is that two main selection criteria were set up for the participants: they had to be first-time offenders and stay crime-free for the 5-year observation period post-release. These criteria excluded a large number from participating, especially the most vulnerable. Nevertheless, the study identified a significant increase in the ex-prisoners' dependency rate of social security benefit post-release; the dependency rate of short-term prisoners (serving ≤6 months) was approximately 100 percentage points higher than an unpunished control group, while the dependency rate of long-term prisoners (serving ≥6 months) was even higher and amounted to approximately 150 percentage points higher than the unpunished control group. These dependency rates remained remarkably high during the entire observation period. Furthermore, the study illustrated how the ex-prisoners' financial down cut post-release compared with pre-prison was dramatically reduced by the Danish welfare state's welfare services (Tranæs et al. 2008; see also Skardhamar and Telle 2012). However, the study yields no direct explanations of the ex-prisoners' high and long lasting dependency of social security benefit in Denmark but referred to general barriers for entering the labour market post-release, which among others included criminal records, lack of employment history, and poor connections to the labour market (see e.g., Pager 2003; Visher et al. 2008; Holzer et al. 2006). A more direct explanation of the high dependency rate of ex-prisoners' social security benefit could, however, be that the ex-prisoners' debt burden and the debt recovery strategies they faced post-release undermined their incentive to work and made a life as welfare-poor more "lucrative" than the life as workfare-poor. Joseph, a reoffender who served his prison sentence along with his son, described a common experience of the Tax Authority's debt repayment calculation and its negative effect on the act of looking for employment:

> Interviewer: So, you're saying that you are demotivated from working because you have a lot of debt?
> Interviewee: Yes, there's no motivation at all. It's evident when I look at David [his son]. Why the fuck should he work if he earns the same as he'll get on social security...His fixed expenses make up most of his [low] income so they [the Tax

Authority] will keep most of the money. If he works and earns DKK 5,000 [EUR 670] more they'll just withdraw 3,500 of 4,000 because there's suddenly money to withdraw. And then nobody bothers working or getting an education or anything at all. And then it's certain that... if you've been here [in prison] once you'll be back. If you don't got a job it's really easy to get tempted so it's just really important to find work.

Interviewer: So, what you're saying is that if the debt... if legal costs were limited or manageable it could be a way to motivate...

Interviewee: Yes, I would definitely try to make things work if I didn't have any debt when I'm released. But it's like when you're placed here [in prison] there is nothing else to think about than the fact that no matter what you do it'll never get any better. There is no way out.

Joseph not only expressed a common feeling among the ex-prisoners of hopelessness and a lack of incitement to change course and live a law-abiding life, he also underlined the importance of obtaining employment to avoid criminal relapse. This statement further underpins one of Tranæs et al.'s conclusions that suggests that unemployment in Denmark has a positive and significant effect on property crime (Tranæs et al. 2008). But what could not be concluded from Tranæs et al.'s study but drawn out from the interviews with Joseph and many of the other ex-prisoners was that the unemployment rate is closely connected to debt problems and a lack of financial incitement to hold a job. Most of the ex-prisoners who received social security benefits had financial latitude similar to or smaller than the Tax Authority's calculated disposable amount and they were therefore eligible for a temporary reprieve to defer repayment of legal debt. Thus, the social services provided by the welfare state's left hand head off some of the barriers faced by the ex-prisoners but being unemployed and dependent on welfare does, unlike employment, not appear to be a protective factor associated with criminal behaviour—rather the reverse applies (Edmark 2005; Tranæs et al. 2008). I will therefore argue that improving the ex-prisoners' income and employment situation is important and not just a political challenge that should be considered by looking at labour market policies or the rehabilitative initiatives during the enforcement of sentences but as a legal and financial problem that has branched off to many different areas of the welfare state, including debt recovery and welfare policies.

Sliding Out of the Activating Welfare System and into Crime

In immediate continuation of the observations of ex-prisoners' reported work that does not pay due to debt recovery and welfare dependency experienced as a way around their debt problem, it is evident to discuss whether mandatory activation programmes could be the common platform for the state's left hand and its right hand because these programmes are a rhetoric battle between obligations and rights; the "activating welfare state" demands the ex-prisoners to "be at the disposal of the labour market" while at the same time "offering" to increase the recipients' human capital through employment-creating initiatives. To support the activation paradigm for unemployment, studies have furthermore suggested activation to decrease crime (Kyvsgaard 2006; Tranæs et al. 2008). My qualitative data can neither confirm nor disconfirm whether activation programmes have served to postpone the reoffenders' relapse into crime. Nevertheless, the interviews illustrated that many of the ex-prisoners who were in line for activation refused to be at the disposal of the labour market and for this non-attendance they were met by financial sanctions. The ex-prisoners had many different explanations for justifying their absenteeism in the activation programmes; some had anger management problems and feared they would react violently if they were told by an authority to obey orders; others had social phobia and therefore feared to panic if surrounded by a number of co-workers at a workplace. The interviews nevertheless illustrated that after the ex-prisoners had faced the activating welfare system's financial sanctions they now described a rather similar reaction pattern and talked about welfare benefits in a condescending manner, regardless of their previously different forms of explanations. A reoffender called Ethan had not attended his mandatory meetings or activation activities and therefore no longer received social security benefits. When I invited him to talk about the situation he shortly pointed out:

Interviewee: "Nobody can live on welfare."
Interviewer: "How much does it affect you that you no longer receive social security benefit?"
Interviewee: "Not a damn thing (. . .) I received a text message saying that I should give them a call [the Social Services]. But I'm not fucking gonna do that. I don't bother being activated and receive 5,000 DKK [EUR 670] that's like working for 20 DKK [EUR 2.68] per hour. I don't bother doing that."

Ethan also voiced that he "made" a significant amount of unreported money which made the Social Service's financial sanctions, or their cut down of his entire social security benefit, rather unimportant in his total budget.[2] Like Ethan, some of the interviewed ex-prisoners experienced the pressure and financial sanctions from the activating welfare system and the intensive debt recovery strategies as catalysts to slip out of the system. The interviews showed how these ex-prisoners simply rejected membership and registration to the society's official institutions and instead established an alternative lifestyle that did not rely on reported incomes, official listed addresses, bank and insurance registrations, and further expunged criminal records, and so on. A reoffender called Samuel had no reported income. He provided for himself by dealing drugs and from time to time he also did cash-in-hand carpenter jobs. During one of our conversations, Samuel described how he had considered the limited options he had to improve his living conditions as an indebted reoffender and had concluded that he had to avoid reported work and reject any collaboration with the Social Services and other public authorities. Samuel preferred to give up his eligibility for welfare benefits to escape what he experienced as constant regulations and pressure from the different local authorities, including the Tax Authority. Samuel shortly compared his approach to life with a law-

---

[2] I do not report the findings of the ex-prisoners' experiences of having only unreported income and the attention it entails from the Tax Authority and the police here, but they are included in the larger work (Olesen 2013a).

abiding life and how it has saved him from facing much hardship: "Quite a few who work also struggle with the bank. And then there are others like me who doesn't have any problems because we don't bother working." According to the few interviewees who lived as law-abiding citizens post-release, Samuel and the ex-prisoners who just like him had entered a so-called "parallel society" organised by the rules of the street, experienced the consequences of their debt, criminal record and stigmatising position only to a limited degree. An ex-prisoner called Jack proclaimed that "(. . .) it is the ones that really make an effort that are punished [the hardest] (. . .)." The interviewees that were encouraged to law-abiding behaviour on release experienced how their rationality of rule-following not only unfavourably affected their financial situation but also challenged their social connections, family structure, and housing situation. The few interviewees who lived a law-abiding life therefore clearly understood why several of the other interviewees said that they felt they had no other option than to seek an unreported source of cash income from either legal or illegal activities to provide themselves (and their families) with the necessities of life.

The Battle Within the Welfare State Affects More than Income

It is not only the income situation of the ex-prisoners that is affected by the battle between the welfare state's different interests. I will briefly present two other examples where the state's left hand and its right hand are contrary to each other's practices and policies regarding release. First, the welfare state's different interests affected the attempt to stabilise prisoners' family contact and maintain their permanent housing. Various studies underpin the two focuses by indicating that support from family is of great importance to encourage anti-criminal behaviour (see e.g., Nelson et al. 1999; Naser and Visher 2006) and other studies have additionally showed that having stable housing post-prison reduce re-offending (Hickey 2002; Williams et al. 2012). Social projects in prisons have tried to establish or maintain the relationship between prisoners and their family members, while the Danish welfare system at the same time with its left hand made an effort to support the prisoners' families financially. One of the financially compensative initiatives to prisoners' families with dependent children was about providing them eligibility to subsidies supporting them in their everyday life during incarceration of a household member. The families with a provider in prison would be registered as single-parent families and the appertaining subsidy eligibility. The study showed that despite the partners' eligibility to welfare benefits they often still struggled to make all ends meet with a single-income household because only few expenses could be reduced during the incarceration of the household member (see also Smith 2014, p. 64; Wildeman and Western 2010, pp. 165–166). Therefore, the financial concern was one of the reasons why most of the separated families expected a brighter future after they became reunited post-release. Nevertheless, the findings suggested that the families' financial situation generally deteriorated after the release of the household member and law-abiding ex-prisoners elucidated how their return home often caused endless rows with their partners about financial struggles (see also Smith's discussion about the major paradox of breaking up families with dependent children due to the use of incarceration (Smith 2014, pp. 229–231). Some of the reunited families chose to officially split up and pretend to move apart in order to uphold a certain standard of living. A reoffender called Adam explained what challenges he predicted to face upon release and how he like many of the other ex-prisoners reorganised his family life because of legal and financial challenges:

> . . . she'll lose so much [money] if I put my address down with her, that's obvious. . . . She gets all sorts of kindergarten fee subsidies and all that crap. But they'll take all that away from her because they'll say that we got money enough to pay for ourselves. Then we're better off living apart . . . that's how it should appear at least.

Unofficially, however, the ex-prisoners often gave false or inaccurate information to the welfare system as they registered on a fictive address but continued to live with their family while their partner who (again) legally transformed to a single-parent household could continue claiming welfare benefits and subsidies (see also Gustafson 2011). Findings also showed another family structure that Mark and his family among others represented. After Mark's release he lived apart from his family for the welfare benefits and to avoid engaging in welfare fraud. Mark remarked on his situation that, "I don't understand why they [the public authorities] have to behave like that, being so cumbersome that a family who knows how to make things work is forced to live apart and scrape by." The welfare state supports the prisoners' families financially through welfare policies but post-release labour market policies and debt recovery challenge the same families' income level by limiting their legitimate claims to subsidies while launching them with debt recovery strategies. In addition, the findings of this study suggest that some of the consequences that can be drawn from this political contradiction between the supportive and demanding approach pre- and post-release makes the benefits of the in-prison rehabilitation initiatives concerning family short-sighted and contribute to unstable family structures post-prison.

The second example from being released to the "battlefield" of the Danish welfare state is related to the ex-prisoners challenging housing situation. During incarceration, the prisoners' (and indirectly their partners/families') permanent housing situation is supported by offering reasonable rent for up to six months to be covered by their local municipal authority if they do not have an income or fortune that could cover the costs (Act no. 90/2014, paragraph 2). In cases regarding sentences longer than six months the local municipal authority should look into the prisoners' need for housing and consider alternative possibilities to secure their housing situation post-release (Act no. 90/2014, paragraph 4). The group of interviewees who met the financial support to rent from their local municipal authority during incarceration experienced the housing support as a stabilising factor but after their release they faced similar problems as the abovementioned reunited families. Their permanent addresses were listed in the Danish national register (DNR) and this registration entailed the bailiffs to visit the ex-prisoner and collect unpaid debts, while the police could conduct a search of the home with the aim of confiscating any larger sums of money, or objects of a certain value, to cover the debt. Thus, the ex-prisoners' use of fictive addresses was not only to ensure that their partner was eligible for extra welfare benefits and subsidies, but also to avoid collections and confiscations through bailiff visits and police home searches. John, a prisoner who officially was about to be released to the street, explained the challenges many of the just-released-prisoners faced and the consequences regarding housing they experienced because of their debt due to legal costs:

I got a girlfriend and she has a place to stay but I feel like, like I don't really have a place to stay because when I get released with all that debt . . . I can't have the bailiff visiting her place all the time. (. . .) they shouldn't visit her and constantly force her to prove that I don't own a thing. I can't own anything, whatsoever.

The unpleasant experiences of bailiff visits and police searches were avoided when the ex-prisoners and their families used fictive addresses or did not have an address listed in the DNR. Some of the consequences of precarious housing, however, were undelivered mail, delayed notice of meetings with the "activating welfare system", having a disarray of personal and financial papers, and so on, which increased the ex-prisoners' instability in an already vulnerable and high-risk time period of recidivism (see also Roxell 2009; Graunbøl et al. 2010).

Discussion and Concluding Remarks

With one hand the Danish welfare state supports prisoners and ex-prisoners in developing pro-social behaviour and legally underpin protective factors as providing prisoners with stable housing, family-involvement, and acknowledgeable skills suited for (re)-integrating the prisoners on the labour market post-release, while the state's other hand performs a debt recovery strategy underlining the political ideology that every citizen should take a personal responsibility and not burden fellow citizens with expenses stemming from crime and punishment. The two different interests in and approaches to the released prisoners mean that they, for example, are encouraged to obtain employment but even before they receive their reported income, the Tax Authority has recovered a percentage of their gross income leaving them with a pay-out very similar to the pay-out received on social security benefit. The lack of financial incitement for being self-supportive blur the difference between the welfare-poor and the workfare-poor and goes directly against the political aim stating that "work should pay" while indirectly inviting ex-prisoners to live on welfare. The obligation and right to meet certain participation requirements (activation programmes) to continue to receive welfare benefits could be a way to overcome the ex-prisoners' high dependency rate of social security benefit by making their life on welfare less "lucrative". However, even though existing studies have shown that activation participation decreases crime, this study illustrated that activation programmes and financial sanctions for not participating in these programmes made some ex-prisoners struggle harder with social-phobia, anger management, etc. and in the end prefer to live of an unreported income, on an unofficial address, and without any connections to society and its institutions and registrations. Therefore, my main interest has been to demonstrate that the Danish welfare state's contradicting social and financial interests could contribute as an explanatory factor of the limited rehabilitation success and the very low debt recovery success rate of legal costs; a debt burden suggested to be one of the main factors why rehabilitation initiatives are often unsuccessful and why many (re)offenders consider a criminal lifestyle as more attractive than a law-abiding lifestyle.

The Danish welfare state, or to use Bourdieu's analytical term the "bureaucratic field", is the scene for a soundless but very intense struggle of defining release from prison and the successful re-integration strategy between the state's social interest and its financial interests. First, the many pitfalls of the release process are interesting to observe as they conflict with the "Nordic welfare model" and the "Nordic penal exception". The principles of "normalisation" and "openness" characterising the ideals of imprisonment in Denmark are challenged post-prison, as legal costs are imposed on the criminally convicted persons, which lead to that many ex-prisoners' living conditions and relations to the labour market, the education system, permanent housing, and family structure cannot be categorised as "normal". Furthermore and in addition to the observations about how the ideals of prison conditions is not advanced to include ideals for post-prison conditions, it can be added that the tradition of a relatively low sentence rate in Denmark neither reflects the situation nor the ambitions post-release, as the informal punishment of indebtedness is experienced to have wide-ranging and long-lasting consequences. Moreover, the Tax Authority consider the collection of debt from legal costs to be of high priority as this debt type stems from a punishable matter and likewise ex-prisoners experience their debt from legal costs to be of a special debt type because the only "output" they have received from the expenses, was the prison sentence and they therefore characterised their debt from legal costs as an informal punishment they had to deal with and work around after they had served their formal punishment in prison.

The consequences of the contradicting approaches towards released prisoners formed by the Danish welfare state could be summed up by pointing out that "Without employment, they were doomed to fail. But employment alone was not enough to ensure financial success, since even permanent employment did not appear to resolve the ongoing and often mounting debt (. . .)" (Pogrebin et al. 2014, p. 405). These post-prison problems, however, do not refer to released prisoners from the Danish welfare state but are identified in a study about parolees' financial obligations in the US; a country that Denmark seldom compares itself with when it comes to penal policies. Nevertheless, the findings from Pogrebin et al.'s study point out a remarkable similarity between the debt problems faced by parolees in the US and ex-prisoners in Denmark. The difference of the two countries' welfare and workfare policies, however, imply that ex-prisoners from Denmark are more dependent on social security benefits compared with the Danish population in general; while parolees from the US does not meet the same level of "safety net" but meet an obligation of employment and self-supportiveness during parole. The overall challenges of the ex-prisoners in Denmark and the US are nevertheless not that different as in both cases their indebtedness and long-term prospects of potentially improving their financial living standards may noticeably challenge their ability to successfully develop pro-social behaviour and establish a stable day-to-day living (Pogrebin et al. 2014; Harris et al. 2010; Bannon et al. 2010; Olesen 2013a; Tranæs et al. 2008).

Wacquant has argued that the police, courts, and prison regime in the US, but also in other western societies, must be included in state analysis and understood as important co-players of the state's right hand because these authorities provide regulation and surveillance of "the lower regions of the social space" (Wacquant 2001) while supporting a security discourse (Wacquant 2009). This study supported the argument of including the police in the state's right hand as it identified the police as an active player in the inter-sectorial strategies of debt recovery. The Tax Authority and the police branched out their regulation of the indebted ex-prisoners to situations that could be categorised as private affairs where the ex-prisoners were not in direct contact with officials or authorities. The ex-prisoners' debt position gave the Tax Authority "carte blanche" to reduce their pay-profit while the police and bailiffs had discretionary power to visit the ex-prisoners in an attempt to levy distress for their unpaid debt. The ex-prisoners experienced how they not only continuously were at risk of falling under suspicion for (recurring) criminal activities because of their criminal history, but also due to their debt stemming from a punish-able matter the police, furthermore, suspected them for violating the opaque rules regarding debt collection. The debt position and criminal record of the ex-prisoners involved the risk that bailiffs and the police used these registers as leads and/or legal "excuses" to unofficial surveillance of the ex-prisoners in their communities, homes, cars, and so on. On the ex-prisoners' home ground and in their private settings, the police and bailiffs could thus still question the ex-prisoners' day-to-day activities and social network, investigate their consumption pattern, assets, and potential properties and even demand their bare necessities of life to be subject to discretion while they argued for levied distress for the ex-prisoners' unpaid debt. Much of the ex-prisoners' everyday life were directly or indirectly suffused by legal regulations and barriers that left the ex-prisoners with the impression of possessing little freedom of action without falling foul of the law. In relation to Wacquant's studies, it is furthermore supported that prisons are of great importance to the state's right hand but this study identified that "the penal exceptionalism" in Denmark implied that the prisons were not a fully-fledged member of the state's right hand but consisted of a wide range of contradicting interests: the prisons both operated as "storehouses" and in the meantime attempted to preserve the aim of rehabilitation. Thus, this study does not support Wacquant's suggestion of exclusively including the Danish prisons in the state's right hand. On the contrary, Danish prisons could be studied as institutions that in different ways mirror conflicting policies and are assigned to diverse values and interests of the involved agents and professions within the prison regime.

The Danish welfare state plays an immense dual role in relation to work regarding release. The state offers a "safety net" which is of benefit to the vulnerable ex-prisoners but related to the many legal barriers faced upon release, the welfare state at the same time erodes the ex-prisoners' incitement to obtain a job, take an education, and sustain permanent housing. Thus, as long as the Danish state does not propose to change the rules regarding the imposition of legal costs, the debt recovery legislation, or the debt relief legislation, it seems like the state spends money with one hand on relatively eroded rehabilitation initiatives while it with the other hand attempts to collect debt from the ex-prisoners even though it is less than 10 % of the full amount of legal costs that is recovered. The low debt recovery success rate could be due to the ex-prisoners' challenging financial situation where many struggle to make all ends meet and because they have no economic latitude exceeding the Tax Authority's fixed disposable amount they will get temporary debt reprieve. Also, the low success rate could be affected by those ex-prisoners who are doing whatever they can to appear as unattractive as possible for the police and bailiffs but also for potentially employees. In 2005, the Rockwool Foundation estimated that the Danish state was missing out on DKK 836 million [EUR 112] annually due to the prisoners' lost earnings (The Rockwool Foundation 2006). In all probability, the downward spiral of debt faced post-prison contribute to an ongoing mounting loss of earnings from ex-prisoners who do not find reported employment financially attractive. A jointed political strategy to re-integrate ex-prisoners underpinned by law has not yet been put down thus both the left hand and the right hand of the state fall short. Consequently, the Danish welfare state's contradicting approach to release is not just a challenge for the ex-prisoners—the society as a whole will be "punished" socially and financially, and community safety will be compromised.

References

The Annual Report of the Danish Prison Service. (2015). file:///C:/Users/aol/Downloads/Kriminalforsorgens+Statistik+2015.pdf. Accessed 5 September 2016.

Bannon, A., Nagrecha, M., Diller, R. (2010). *Criminal justice debt*. New York: University School of Law.

Bourdieu, P. (1996). *The state nobility*. Cambridge: Polity Press.

Bourdieu, P. (1998a). On the fundamental ambivalence of the state. *Polygraph*, *10*, 21–32.

Bourdieu, P. (1998b). *Acts of resistance.* Cambridge: Polity Press.

Bourdieu, P. (2003). *Firing back.* London: Verso.

Bourdieu, P., Sayad, A., Christin, R., Champagne, P., Balazs, G., & Wacquant, L. J. D. (1999). *The weight of the world.* Stanford: Stanford University Press.

Clausen, S. (2013). *Fængslet ta'r (stadig) de sidste.* København: Direktoratet for Kriminalforsorgen.

The Danish Bar and Law Society. (2012). *Sagsomkostninger i straffesager.* http://www.advokatsamfundet.dk/Service/Nyheder/Nyhedsbrev/~/media/Rapporter/sagsomkostninger.ashx. Accessed 5 September 2016.

The Danish Guidance and Directions for Recovery. (2010). http://skat.dk/SKAT.aspx?oId=1617406&vId=0&lang=DA. Accessed 5 September 2016.

Dingeldey, I. (2007). Between workfare and enablement. *European Journal of Political Research, 46*(6), 823–851.

Dyb, E., Kielstrup, B., Muiluvuori, M. L., Tyni, S., Baldursson, E. S., & Guðmundsdóttir, H. (2006). *Løslatt og hjemløs.* Oslo: NIBR, Byggforsk, KRUS.

Edmark, K. (2005). Unemployment and crime. *Scandinavian Journal of Economics, 107*(2), 353–373.

Graunbøl, H. M., et al. (2010). *Retur.* Oslo: Kriminalomsorgen.

Gustafson, K. (2011). *Cheating welfare.* New York: New York University Press.

Harris, A., et al. (2010). Drawing blood from stones. *American Journal of Sociology, 115*(6), 1753–1799.

Hickey, C. (2002). *Crime and homelessness.* Dublin: Focus Ireland & PACE.

Holzer, H. J., Raphael, S., Stoll, M. A. (2006). Perceived criminality, criminal background checks and the racial hiring practices of employers. *Journal of Law and Economics, 49*(2), 451–480.

Kyvsgaard, B. (1989). *…og fængslet ta'r de sidste.* København: Jurist- og Økonomforbundets Forlag.

Kyvsgaard. B. (1999). *Klientundersøgelsen.* København: Direktoratet for Kriminalforsorgen.

Kyvsgaard, B. (2006). *Hvad virker—hvad virker ikke?* København: Jurist- og Økonomforbundets Forlag, pp. 83–108.

Lappi-Seppälä, T. (2007). Penal policy in Scandinavia. *Crime and Justice, 36*(1), 217–295.

Lappi-Seppälä, T., & Storgaard, A. (2014). Unge i det strafferetlige system. *Tidsskrift for Strafferet, 4*, 333-359.

Naser, R., & Visher, C. (2006). Family members' experiences with incarceration and reentry. *Western Criminology Review, 7*(2), 20–31.

Nautrup, J. (1984). Sagsomkostninger i retssager. *Juristen, 66*(3), 73–88.

Nautrup, J. (1995). Sagsomkostningernes behandling under domsforhandlingen i straffesager. *Fuldmægtigen, 67*(5), 79–81.

Nelson, M., Deess, P., Allen, C. (1999). *The first month out*. New York: Vera Institute of Justice.

Olesen, A. (2013a). *Løsladt og gældsat*. København: Jurist- og Økonomforbundets Forlag.

Olesen, A. (2013b). Eftergivelse af gæld vedrørende sagsomkostninger i straffesager. In H. V. G. Pedersen (Ed.), *Juridiske emner ved Syddansk Universitet 2013* (pp. 327–344). København: Jurist- og Økonomforbundets Forlag.

Olesen, A. (2014). Retlige, retssikkerhedsmæssige og resocialiserende omkostninger ved sagsomkostninger i straffesager. *Nordisk Tidsskrift for Kriminalvidenskab, 101*(3), 248–270.

Pager, D. (2003). The mark of a criminal record. *American Journal of Sociology, 108*(5), 937–975.

Pogrebin, M., et al. (2014). Employment isn't enough. *Criminal Justice Review, 39*(4), 394–410.

Pratt, J. (2008a). Scandinavian exceptionalism in an era of penal excess: Part I. *British Journal of Criminology, 48*(2), 119–137.

Pratt, J. (2008b). Scandinavian exceptionalism in an era of penal excess: Part II. *British Journal of Criminology, 48*(3), 275–292.

The Prison and Probation Service. (2015). *Reoffending statistics of the prison and probation service 2014*. https://www.google.dk/url?sa=t&rct=j&q=&esrc=s&source=web&cd=2&cad=rja&uact=8&ved=0ahUKEwjUv-egkfnOAhWD3SwKHQwtBgkQFgghMAE&url=http%3A%2F%2Fwww.kriminalforsorgen.dk%2FAdmin%2FPublic%2FDownload.aspx%3Ffile%3DFiles%252FFiler%252FStatistik%252FKriminalforsorgens%2Brecidivstatistik%2B2014%2B(november%2B2015).pdf&usg=AFQjCNGyf2svmG5hPfyVExkURPQrrqYdmQ&bvm=bv.131783435,d.bGg. Accessed 5 September 2016.

Ramboll. (2013). *Cost benefit analysis of crime preventing initiatives*. https://www.google.dk/url?sa=t&rct=j&q=&esrc=s&source=web&cd=1&cad=rja&uact=8&ved=0ahUKEwjOgOXflPnOAhUIXiwKHZflCnoQFggbMAA&url=https%3A%2F%2Fwww.kk.dk%2Ffiles%2Fsamfundskonomisk-analyse-af-kriminalprventive-indsatser-1825-rige-i-socialforvaltningen%2Fdownload%3Ftoken%3DnkxbdcLD&usg=AFQjCNGBlt2MfDywOhLSK2rN3CI8ystPnw&bvm=bv.131783435,d.bGg. Accessed 5 September 2016.

Recommendation no. 1547/2014. *Sagsomkostninger i straffesager*. http://jm.schultzboghandel.dk/upload/microsites/jm/ebooks/bet1547/pdf/bet1547.pdf. Accessed 5 September 2016

The Rockwool Foundation. (2006). Technical minute no. 15. Direct expenses to crime prevention in Denmark. https://www.google.dk/url?sa=t&rct= j&q=&esrc=s&source=web&cd=1&cad=rja&uact=8&ved= 0ahUKEwiWppaYlPnOAhVMiiwKHfRzBIgQFggdMAA&url=http%3A% 2F%2Fwww.rockwoolfonden.dk%2Fapp%2Fuploads%2F2016%2F01% 2FTeknisk-note-nr-15-1.pdf&usg=AFQjCNFr8U8w3SDBf0nSpMnM_ R8HuET_WA. Accessed 5 September 2016.
Roxell, L. (2009). Tur och retur. *Efter løsladelse*, pp. 34–43. Rapport fra NSfK's 51.
Rørdam, P. (1961). Om tilståelsessager og om sagsomkostninger i straffesager. *Ugeskrift for Retsvæsen* 327–332.
Skardhamar, T., & Telle, K. (2012). Post-release employment and recidivism in Norway. *Journal of Quantitative Criminology, 28*(4), 629–649.
Skjødt, B. (2004). Sagens omkostninger og retssikkerheden. *Lov & Ret, 14*(3), 16–19.
Smith, P. S. (2014). *When the innocent are punished*. New York: Palgrave Macmillan.
Torfing, J. (1999a). Towards a Schumpeterian workfare postnational regime. *Economy and Society, 28*(3), 369–402.
Tranæs, T., et al. (2008). *Forbryderen og samfundet*. København: Gyldendal.
Visher, C., Debus S., Yahner, J. (2008). *Employment after prison*. Washington: Urban Institute, Justice Policy Center.
Wacquant, L. J. D. (1993). From ruling class to field of power. *Theory, Culture & Society, 10*(3), 19–44.
Wacquant, L. J. D. (2001). The penalisation of poverty and the rise of neo-liberalism. *European Journal on Criminal Policy and Research, 9*(4), 401–412.
Wacquant, L. J. D. (2009). *Punishing the poor*. Durham, NC: Duke University Press.
Wildeman, C. & Western, B. (2010). Incarceration in fragile families. *The Future of Children, 20*(2), 157–177.
Williams, K., Poyser, J., Hopkins, J. (2012). *Accommodation, homelessness and reoffending of prisoners*. London: Ministry of Justice.

Scandinavian Acceptionalism? Developments in Community Sanctions in Norway

Gerhard Ploeg

Introduction

The contradiction in the work of correctional services between executing a punishment imposed by the court as a reaction to a crime, and implementing the rehabilitative element that dominates its contents is a well-known and much discussed subject. It is perhaps even more prominent in a community setting than in prison, and a perceived balance—or imbalance—between the two elements in that situation may strongly influence the level of its acceptance in society.

In this chapter, I will present a short introduction to the basic principles in Norwegian corrections and show how these permeate the development of community corrections by describing their various forms, both as a court sentence and as a way to serve a prison sentence

G. Ploeg (✉)
Directorate of the Norwegian Correctional Service, Oslo, Norway
e-mail: gerhard.ploeg@kriminalomsorg.no

© The Author(s) 2017
P. Scharff Smith, T. Ugelvik (eds.), *Scandinavian Penal History, Culture and Prison Practice,* Palgrave Studies in Prisons and Penology, DOI 10.1057/978-1-137-58529-5_13

in the community. I will then discuss the level of acceptance for the current balance on the control/rehabilitation dimension. Finally, I try to analyse whether the recent decrease in the use of the community sentence by the courts indicates a crisis in this respect. Does it mean that the sentence—or the model as a whole—has become less acceptable?

First of all, however, I need to clarify my position. I am very much a part of the system I am describing, and as a senior adviser at the Directorate of Correctional Services in Norway, I work every day with its various policies, trying to contribute to a continuously improving organisation, both in form and in contents. And I believe in the work I do. This may—will—colour the views I present in this chapter. On the other hand, I am a criminologist with a past in academic theory development and research, and I will do my best to keep the necessary distance to my day-job. I ask the reader to please bear with me and be aware of my possible bias, even where it will not be intended.

So What's so Special About Norway?

The Norwegian correctional system has often been referred to as an excellent example of Scandinavian or Nordic exceptionalism, a term coined by the New Zealand criminologist John Pratt.[1] The exceptional quality is often illustrated by pointing to some specific prisons in Norway that are presented as being representative for the whole system. Especially the human-ecological prison at the island of Bastøy[2] and 'the world's most humane prison' in Halden[3] are highlighted. Rather than being representative for the shape of the correctional system, these may be considered to be on the extreme end of what might be called the ideological dimension in Norwegian corrections. They do not give the

---

[1] Early examples are John Pratt's two articles on Scandinavian exceptionalism in an era of penal excess from 2008a, b. An attempt at explaining the origins of the system was made by Pratt and Eriksson in 2011. More recently, the argument is made in John Pratt and Anna Eriksson (2013), while the concept has been critically commented in Ugelvik and Dullum (2012).

[2] E.g. in *The Guardian*, 25 February 2013.

[3] E.g. in *The Guardian*, 18 May 2012.

general standard for prisons in Norway. Concern for the state of maintenance in a number of prisons and the high occupancy rates has regularly been voiced by management as well as staff, especially in connection with the waiting list for sentenced offenders,[4] and a considerable investment is expected in the near future in order to bring these institutions in an acceptable condition. Norway has also on several occasions been criticised by the European Committee for the Prevention of Torture (CPT) for its use of solitary confinement—or 'exclusion from company' as the Norwegian term translates—for prisoners. This concerns primarily those on remand, where such measures are administered by the police, but also during serving a sentence there are several forms of isolation possible in Norwegian prisons. Smith et al. (2013) describe 11 different forms and reasons for implementing isolation for a shorter or longer period. They conclude that there 'is no doubt that the level of isolation in Scandinavian prisons is far too high',[5] and although they do not give an indication as to what level actually would be acceptable, it is quite clear that they have a point. The establishment of a critical network on isolation in corrections in Scandinavia is therefore a valuable contribution to a continuing awareness on this issue. In the meantime, the last CPT report (2011) not only repeats the above-mentioned concerns, but also acknowledges that there has been a 'welcome development' in this respect since the previous report from 2005.

In spite of these aspects, however, the Norwegian penal system can still be viewed as exceptional, and not just for the rather unique fact that one of its prisons is currently located in The Netherlands.[6] As a result of a clear wish not to overcrowd prisons,[7] a waiting list for sentenced offenders has been a fact for several decades. Renting capacity in a country that has built

---

[4] E.g. Aftenposten, 26 June 2015.

[5] Translation by author.

[6] Since September 2015, Norway rents the 242 cells of Norgerhaven prison in The Netherlands in order to relieve the pressure on the prison system and reduce the waiting list for sentenced offenders.

[7] In its comment on the 2016 budget for the correctional services, the Parliaments Standing Committee on Justice stated that an occupancy rate of 90 % should be the target, because 'overcrowded prisons create a bad climate for education, rehabilitation and the building of relationships' (author's translation).

more than it turns out to have a need for, is in many ways an effective solution for this problem.

An important feature of Norwegian corrections that is often highlighted is the low rate of re-offending. In a report from 2010, a group of Scandinavian researchers (Graunbøl et al. 2010) found a re-offending rate of 20 % among all prisoners released in 2005, where recidivism was defined as having committed an offence within 2 years from the release date that led to a new conviction to imprisonment or community sentence. The number for those on a community sentence was 21 %. Even though these results may be and have been commented on in various ways, among others by one of the authors (Kristoffersen 2013), it was the lowest in Scandinavia in this comparative study and it may in fact be considered to be a low number by any standard. It may, in this context, also be mentioned that there are relatively few escapes or attempts to escape from prison and, for example, a rate of over 99.8 % returning from leave in 2013.[8]

One issue to take into account when looking at this low rate of re-offending is that Norway is a well-functioning, rich welfare-state with relatively low unemployment rates and little housing problems, making it easier to do rehabilitative work. In September 2015 the unemployment rate was at 4.5 %[9] and according to the International Monetary Fund its per capita annual Gross Domestic Product was fifth in the world in 2014 with $67,166, and second only to Singapore when counting only countries with over 5 million inhabitants. When considering that those who come into contact with the criminal justice system in general may be said to struggle with a number of problem areas related to social welfare factors [better known in this context as criminogenic factors (Andrews and Bonta 2006), it seems reasonable to assume that recidivism will be lower where such problems have a better chance to be managed. However, it may also be claimed that in addition to this, a number of other factors directly related to the organisation of the correctional services and the aforementioned principles and values

---

[8] Kriminalomsorgens årsrapport (Correctional Services Annual Report), 2013.

[9] Statistics Norway, 21 September 2015.

contribute to the favourable results. These specific principles in penal thinking and practice are often visible in a prominent way—like in Halden and Bastøy but they also apply in other prisons, and permeate the practice on community-based sanctions as well where they are relevant.

The question is whether the fact that the exceptional aspects of Norwegian corrections can exist and prosper is the result of the acceptance of a model that appears to pay off in terms of reduced re-offending. If so, is this because of conscious, rational positive support or do the relatively low crime rate and rates of re-offending just not generate enough energy for much resistance from within society? Are exception and acceptance linked to each other through this feature? Towards the end of this chapter, these issues will be analysed in more detail, especially by looking at the possible causes for the recent decline in the use of the Norwegian community sentence. For now, we will have a look at some of the specific principles and features in question.

Central Features in Norwegian Corrections

Discretionary Powers

The 'correctional services' have extensive discretionary authority as far as the content of the execution of a sentence is concerned. The court has three main responses to an offence at its disposition, apart from acquittal: (1) a prison sentence, either conditional or unconditional, (2) a community sentence and (3) a fine. When an unconditional prison sentence is imposed, there are a number of options for the offender to serve his sentence in the community, after applying to the correctional services and according to a set of rules. These variations of what Robinson and McNeill (2016) call 'penal technologies' in their discussion of conceptual issues around community punishment may include serving in one's own home with a curfew, with or without electronic monitoring, or serving in an institution that offers treatment for addiction or another type of rehabilitation that is deemed necessary for a successful return to society and that the prison cannot provide itself.

There is also the possibility to apply for conditional release after two-thirds of the sentence has been served. All these decisions are left up to the correctional services; the court is not involved in them. Likewise, a community sentence is imposed by the court in the form of a number of hours, but it is to a very large degree left up to the probation office how these hours are spent, depending on an assessment of what would be most relevant for preventing re-offending.

Now for some foreign readers this may all seem a bit scary. After all, there is no direct control by the judicial authorities on the decisions of the correctional services in individual cases. The sentenced offender may complain about the contents or the conditions, but that complaint goes to the regional level within the correctional services, but this is obviously not an 'independent and impartial tribunal' in the sense of the European Convention on Human Rights.[10] In addition, a complaint may be made to the National Ombudsman, but its powers to change are limited in this context.

There is, then, a potential for abuse of these powers, either willingly or by negligence. Now there is, of course, an inspection mechanism and if anything should go terribly or structurally wrong, it will be noticed, but when we talk about acceptance, 'trust' is the keyword here. There is a strong tradition in Norway to trust the authorities, from the government down to the local public service providers. This may be easier to understand when one takes into account that about one-third of the Norwegian workforce is employed in the public sector. Being the welfare state it is, these state institutions provide a large number services to the population, which may again reinforce the trust they have gained. There is a strong democratic tradition (78.3 % turnout at the latest Parliament election) that survives in a climate of high per capita income, and the value system is deeply rooted in society. The orientation is towards consensus and the level of internal conflict is low (Christensen 2003) All these factors contribute to the trust in government and state institutions. Research has also shown that trust in one state agency tends to extend to others (Christensen and Lægreid 2005).

Such factors contribute to a situation where the correctional service is trusted with the relatively extensive amount of discretionary powers it

---

[10] European Convention on Human Rights, art. 6.

has at hand. These are to a large degree made use of in incorporating the principle of normality in everyday correctional life.

The Principle of Normality

The European Prison Rules from 2007 state in Rule nr. 5: 'Life in prison shall approximate as closely as possible the positive aspects of life in the community.' This *principle of normality* is pivotal in Norwegian corrections.[11] It has three main implications:

1. The punishment is in the restriction of freedom that is imposed by the court. All other rights as a citizen are still in place. They can be claimed and, if such is the case, the correctional services will need to present arguments in case they cannot be granted. Obviously, many possible applications would be denied on the basis of security, order and organisation in the institution, or the lack of resources necessary to guarantee security for all involved. As a result, not many such applications are being filed but if they are, the prison management will need to answer with proper reasons. One is sent to prison *as* punishment, not *for* punishment. It is an old phrase, but valid as ever. Likewise, a community punishment will need to be focused on maintaining the highest possible degree of normality, and it must be geared towards optimal re-integration into society. The idea behind this, of course, being to reduce the risk of re-offending by 'producing' citizens who are motivated for a 'normal' life. The goal is that offenders refrain from committing further crimes by their own initiative, but correctional workers can act as co-producers.[12]

---

[11] It is important to distinguish between 'normality' as a condition opposed to 'normalisation' as a process, meaning 'to make normal, especially to cause to conform to a standard or norm'—Free Dictionary.

[12] See, for example, the work of Beth Weaver of the University of Strathclyde, Glasgow: https://pure.strath.ac.uk/portal/files/23068440/Weaver_final_.doc; a stunning documentation of the processes involved in desisting from crime can be found in the 38 different life-stories and articles in the special issue of EuroVista that she edited in 2013.

2. The security conditions should be the lowest possible in relation to the safety of the community. If there is no specific risk of harm or re-offending, a sentence may be started in a low-security prison.
3. Life during serving the sentence must resemble 'normal' life wherever it can. This is, of course, hard to realise when you serve your sentence in a securely restricted area along with a large number of others who are in the same situation, yet probably have very different life experiences and perspectives. Moreover, you did not choose them for company, just like they did not choose you. In addition, there is another group of people who come and go and in the meantime are watching you all the way. Still, the intention is to provide normal circumstances in as many details of everyday life as possible.

It is important to realise that this is a working principle. The actual detention situation sets clear limits for the realisation of the principle in its full form. In two words, the main goals for the correctional services are security and rehabilitation, but security considerations will always prevail. If this would not be the case, the level of acceptance for the penal system would not be where it is today.

There is also the question of whose 'normality' is the dominant one in this respect. The concept may have completely different connotations; for example, for a drug-addicted offender, a political activist or a foreign citizen than for, say, a correctional officer. People may have very different ideas about a secure existence or the right to property. The kind of normality that is supposed to be propagated is based on the reactions the offender will be confronted with in a law-abiding, non-criminal context. Staff is trained to act as role models for this type of acceptable behaviour.[13]

On another note—and first and foremost relevant for prison sentences—one might ask the question whether the principle of normality has gone through a kind of inflationary development over the last decade. Not that the extent of the idea itself has been reduced, but rather that its relationship to its surroundings has changed. What we

---

[13] See, for example, Ministry of Justice and the Police (2008).

used to call globalisation through the internet has transferred into a large number of dimensions by the rise of the many forms of—particularly social—media, other means of communication, access to streaming services for music and film, access to electronic books and so on. The idea that the punishment is only in the restriction of the freedom of movement is not really correct anymore, since all of the above-mentioned elements are for various reasons excluded from—at least a closed—prison. The reasons for not allowing such services may well be legitimate in terms of security, order in the institution or limited resources, but there is no doubt that the absolute expansion of the 'normal' world outside has added to the relative punitive character of a stay in prison.

The Import Model

A number of services that are central to the reintegration process are carried out by staff employed by external institutions, not by own prison staff: educational services, medical services, employment services and also library and clerical services are all 'imported' from outside. For example, teachers working in prison are employed by schools in the community. Apart from supporting the principle of normality, there is the advantage of a much more gradual transfer to the period after release, through the possibility to prepare a further programme and through the fact that the released person is already known to the relevant agencies and does not, for example, have to present himself as an ex-convict on his first visit to the employment agency. Also, because people from outside are involved in daily life in prison, the image of prisons becomes less threatening and the effect of the 'us-vs.-them' mechanism is reduced.

The same may be said for the community sentence. It is a well-known argument that community-based sanctions in general have a favourable effect on re-integration, for one thing because they are less likely to de-integrate in the way a prison sentence inevitably will. Doing work for the general good of the community will always be received favourably, and in the case of the Norwegian community sentence—to be described in more detail later on in this chapter—a number of other contacts through, for example, adult education institutions or employment agencies will contribute further to mutual involvement and integration. The community sentence is aimed at rehabilitation and the prevention of re-offending, and the close collaboration with various service providers as well as the resulting network that are among the consequences of the import model constitute an important tool in this process. And since these service providers actually do have something to offer because of the level of welfare in Norway, the import model pays off even better.

Employee Training

Prison officers in Norway receive a 2-year training, with a varied curriculum. Apart from obvious subjects concerning maintaining security, there is psychology, sociology, criminology, law, there are large chunks about human rights and ethics, and aspiring prison officers will need to do some essay work on those themes. Dynamic security is an important concept in this respect, meaning that staff takes the time to interact with inmates, creating a more relaxed atmosphere while at the same time having the opportunity to recognise and manage possible tensions at an early stage.

Emphasis on Reintegration Through Progression

Research on the life conditions of Norwegian prisoners has shown (Friestad and Hansen 2004; Revold 2015) that there tends to be an extensive set of—mostly combined—problematic circumstances in their existence before incarceration and a substantial risk to be returned to this situation on release if nothing is done in the meantime. If such circumstances played a part in committing the offence, as they often do, there will be a serious risk of re-offending. A gradual process of progression through the system, from high-security prison to low-security and half-way-house, or through various forms of extramural execution of the final stage before release offers the opportunity to work with this. A combination of the normality principle and the import model is employed to try and deal with difficulties in the life conditions. The various necessary services are provided by separate organisations in the community and they are coordinated for individual offenders by specifically designated staff, working as 're-integration coordinators'. Each of these is connected to a specific region and works from a prison or a probation office.

Implementing Sanctions in the Community— The Discretionary Powers of the Correctional Services

The contrast between 'normal' life and life while serving a sentence is of course larger when it concerns prison than it is in connection with community sanctions, and applying the principle of normality creates a more visible effect in the context of the former. Serving a sentence in the community offers a better opportunity for normality, and this has always been an important intended part of this type of sanction. As a consequence, there is an emphasis on punishment in the community through execution of a part or the whole of a prison sentence when possible.

There are many ways in which sanctions may be carried out in the community, some of them very creative (see, e.g. Graham and White 2015) while others are more or less generally accepted. The former ones are not to a very large degree present in the Norwegian system, but the latter ones differ somewhat from how other jurisdictions use them. A short overview may contribute to understanding how the above-mentioned principles are present in the system.

Certain community-based sanctions in Norway are the prerogative of the courts: a 'community sentence' as the 'samfunnsstraff' is usually translated, and two types of conditional prison sentences for specific cases. One of them is a specific condition to participate in a program for intoxicated drivers, and the other is a specific condition to participate in a Norwegian version of the drug-court program.

The other ways of serving a sentence in the community are to a large degree dependent on the professional discretion of the correctional services. These include various forms of extramural execution of a prison sentence. I will describe them shortly in order to illustrate the extent of the discretionary powers and then focus on the 'community sentence' since the recent negative development of the use of this type of sanction has raised some questions about the level of acceptance for it.

Conditional release may be applied for after two-thirds of a prison sentence has been served. The correctional services may impose certain conditions if this is deemed necessary. These may include a duty to report at the probation office in a sober state, or complying with instructions pertaining to place of residence, treatment, work or education and company of specific persons. The correctional services are the authority that grants or denies an application for conditional release, and decides what the type and level of conditions are within the legislative framework. However, when a serious or repeated breach has occurred, the court will decide whether this will imply re-incarceration. This decision is not placed with the correctional services, but in such a case they will act as prosecuting party.

A prison sentence may also be partly or wholly *served in an institution* that is not part of the correctional system, if the prisoner has specific needs—for example, for treatment or rehabilitation—that cannot be met in prison and that are considered to be central in the prevention of future re-offending. In most cases this implies treatment for severe addiction problems. Again, the decision lies with the correctional services. The institutions in question need to provide a 24-hour stay and the prisoner will need to be on the premises at all times, apart from the leaves that are allowed under current regulations. Here, the court is not involved in the consequences of a breach, and the correctional services have the authority to return the offender to prison.

Home detention comes in two forms, with and without electronic monitoring. Both of these forms require an application to the correctional services, although the criteria for granting are different, for example, in terms of their maximum length. After half of a prison sentence has been served, one can apply for serving the rest of the sentence in one's own home without electronic monitoring. The condition for this is that one must have demonstrated a particularly positive development during your sentence. This is obviously a factor that is both difficult to define and difficult to measure and in addition it is dependent on how good or bad one's behaviour was at the start of the sentence. Here the assessment of the correctional services of something that is difficult to standardise or quantify becomes a central element in a decision that can alter a person's existence dramatically, since half the sentence may be spent in freedom without any directly perceivable means of control—as opposed to spending it in a prison. Relatively very few people start on this type of home detention, an annual average of about 70 over the last couple of years.

Electronic monitoring started as a pilot project in 2008 and has been available nationwide since 2014. It may be granted as a replacement for an unconditional prison sentence of up to 4 months ('front door'), or for the last 4 months of a longer prison sentence ('back door'). It operates with radio-frequency, there is no GPS-solution in use yet, as is the case in a number of other countries.

Characteristic for both forms of home detention is that a full-activity schedule outside of the home needs to be in place during daytime. Work, school, programmes and so on may be included and the probation service will check whether persons are in the place where they are supposed to be. Electronic monitoring is considered more as a rehabilitative tool than as a pure means of control (Kylstad Øster and Rokkan 2013), a way to let more people serve their prison sentence outside.

Here again, breach is determined by the correctional service and it is also responsible for the decision to return—or send—the offender to prison after a serious or repeated breach.

The Community Sentence ('Samfunnsstraff'[14])

The community sentence was introduced in 2001 in the new Execution of Sentences Act.[15] The character of the reaction is described in the Penal Code. A community sentence may be imposed when a prison sentence of up to 1 year would otherwise have been appropriate, when a reaction in the

---

[14] For those who read Norwegian, the series of reports by Erlend Sand Bruer (2014) are worth paying attention to. They are available from the probation office in Oslo, for contact see www.kriminalomsorgen.no.

[15] An English version is available at www.kriminalomsorgen.no—Om kriminalomsorgen—Lover og regler.

community is considered possible and when the offender consents and lives in Norway. The length may vary from 30 to 420 hours and is associated with a subsidiary penalty in the form of imprisonment for the period that otherwise would have been imposed. It shall be executed during a period of time that as a rule will be equivalent to the length of the subsidiary imprisonment.

The Execution of Sentences Act provides more detail for the contents of the community sentence: the hours constituting the term of a community sentence shall be spent on community service—in the sense of unpaid work to the benefit of the community, programmes or other measures suitable for preventing new criminality. The correctional services will in each particular case determine the precise contents of the community sentence within the limits set by the court in its judgment. If the court has imposed a condition that the convicted person shall comply with provisions relating to residence, work, training, treatment and so forth, the correctional services shall determine the precise contents of the provisions, attaching particular importance to measures that may enhance the convicted person's capacity to rectify his or her pattern of criminal behaviour. The correctional services may alter the contents when this appears necessary in order to execute the community sentence in a manner that satisfies the need for security, or if the staff situation so indicates.

The fact that the correctional services decide on the degree in which a prison sentence can be served outside the walls is not uncommon in Western Europe. The situation around the community sentence, however, is rather less usual. There are not many countries where the court or at least the prosecutor's office is not involved in imposing or approving the activities that make up the sentence. In many countries a community sentence implies a community service, that is, unpaid work and hardly anything else. In Norway, the guidelines for probation offices, which are responsible for carrying out the sentence, state that no more than 70 % of all hours performed during a year may consist of unpaid work for the community. Since the sanction was introduced in 2002 the actual number has fluctuated between 60 and 65 %. The rest of the sentence will consist of individually tailored activities aimed at preventing further offending. An obligatory element is having regular individual conversations with probation staff on this specific topic, and this takes about 10 % of all hours on a yearly basis. Otherwise, the contents are developed at the start during an intake assessment where the offender will have to agree in order for the sentence to be implemented. The time spent during the assessment is subtracted from the total number of hours imposed.

A community sentence can in principle be completely void of unpaid work, depending on the assessment of relevant preventive measures in relation to the length of the sentence. It must be stressed that the part consisting of unpaid work will—if relevant and available—also reflect a preventive element in the sense that activities will be sought that will fit to the individuals' strengths and capacities, or that will benefit him after having served his sentence, thus reducing the risk of re-offending. The activities during the community sentence may be interpreted as intended for increasing what has been called 'offender readiness' (see, e.g. Day et al. 2010) for further treatment or rehabilitation/re-integration.

Other contents will often consist of (adult-) educational activities, work training, skills training, behavioural programmes and so on, but it is also possible to include treatment or mediation in the sentence, although these are not used to a large degree. In 2014, 65 % of all 176,000 hours on community sentence was spent on unpaid work, while 21 % consisted of various rehabilitating activities, often in collaboration with local organisations. A further 10 % consisted of various one-to-one conversations with a crime-preventing focus while behavioural programs, treatment and, mediation stood for the remaining 4 %. There has been a tendency lately to include more unpaid work than before.

Acceptance of the Community Sentence

Community sanctions may contain a large number of different things. McNeill (2013) defines them as 'a penal subfield around which it is difficult to draw precise boundaries, which is described and labelled differently in different places, and which has been characterised by the regular renaming that come with innovation, differentiation and a perennial quest for credibility and legitimacy'. The last point is important here, because it relates to the level of acceptance. One might say that the use of community sanctions has to a large degree developed without the public being aware of it. The exact number of people on this type of supervision is hard to establish, but, for example, Durnescu (2008) estimated that while some 2 million people were imprisoned in Europe on any given day, there were some 3.5 million under some form of community supervision in a penal context.

It may be said that a community sentence is exemplary for the principle of normality. The offender lives at home, may continue with his daily activities in the form of work, school, leisure and so on, and does his sentence in his spare time. He has to follow the instructions from the correctional services about the type and intensity of activities, but usually has a sufficiently long period for completion that the sanction interferes to a limited degree with his daily life. It is not hard to imagine that some might think this is a very easy way to get away with committing a crime. In other words, the way the sanction has been set up may influence the level of acceptance among various parties involved: not only the victims, the media, politics, the general public, but also the prosecution or the courts. The question is then how these experience the legitimacy of the community sentence.

Robinson et al. (2013) discuss how 'late modern' community sanctions have evolved after what they call 'the demise of the coherent meta-narrative or purpose of penal welfarism (or more specifically the "rehabilitative ideal")'. I would argue that the rehabilitative ideal is still very much alive in the Norwegian model of the community sentence, but it is worth to analyse the situation from the distinction they make between four 'visions' that have governed the development of community sanctions in general over the last few decades. These are the managerial, the punitive, the rehabilitative and the reparative view. I will now look at the Norwegian community sentence from these perspectives in order to see how they influence legitimacy and acceptance.

The *managerial perspective* implies the integration of community sanctions in a higher level system, notably its function in contributing to the overall goals of the penal system. In this view, community sanctions have a function in replacing shorter prison sentences and they are being measured more on output than on outcomes, functioning as a 'safety valve' for a correctional system under pressure. And a cheaper one at that.

There is little doubt that the introduction and increased use of community sanctions since the 1980s has had this effect, but at the same time it has created net-widening. Many people on this type of sanctions would otherwise not have been sentenced to prison, but would have received another type of sanction, for example conditional imprisonment or fines. This trend was observed in Northern America already in the 1990s, as for example reported in Phelps (2013). Based on the comparative analysis of an extensive European database (SPACE I and II), Aebi et al. (2015) come to the conclusion that community sanctions 'have become one of the instruments of an increasingly punitive approach to crime control', and over a 20-year-period (1991–2010) had 'no visible effect on prison population rates'. They note, however, that Norway seems to be one of the countries where a 'reasonable balance' has been found between the use of imprisonment and community sanctions. Ironically, Norway has introduced a new sanction in 2014 for juvenile offenders (15–18) where the responsibility for implementation lies not with the correctional services but with the 22 local offices of the—volunteer-based NGO—National Mediation Service. This sanction is meant to be used instead of imprisonment and is intensely rehabilitation- and restoration-oriented in its intention. There is a clear risk that this may result in net-widening for this age group as a result of the zeal of 'the new child savers', as Norwegian criminologist Nils Christie (2015) warned in one of his last publications.[16] If this should be the case—the sanction will be evaluated—then more young offenders will be taken over by the penal system and there is a risk that in case of breach their share in the prison-population will increase.

As we will see later on, there is a downward trend in the use of the community sentence in Norway. This is, however, contrasted by the rise of another community-based sanction, home detention with electronic monitoring. The lack of further net-widening for the community sentence may

---

[16] For those who read Norwegian, see also Christie's article on the apparent demise of the Mediation Service in its original form, becoming 'yet another powerful organ of control'. Available at: http://www.jus.uio.no/ikrs/tjenester/kunnskap/kriminalpolitikk/meninger/2014/far vel-til-konfliktradene.html

be due to the fact that the managerial aspect is warranted by this and other ways of relieving the pressure on the prison system. In any case, managerial legitimacy is first and foremost relevant for the correctional services themselves and those who are politically involved.

The *punitive aspect* seems to be of most interest for victims and—in a derived sense—the media, who thereby almost naturally involve politics. It will, by many, be viewed as juxtaposed to the *rehabilitative view*. The more the rehabilitation, the less the punitivity—*and* vice versa. In the Norwegian situation, the punitive aspect of the community sentence is definitely present, mostly in the form of community service as unpaid work for the general benefit—and in the overhanging threat of prison in case of non-compliance. At the same time, there is an overarching administrative rule that at an aggregate level no more than 70 % of all hours imposed may in its implementation consist of unpaid work—and over the years, probation has managed to keep this share around 60–65 %, other activities being of a purely rehabilitative or crime-preventing character. In addition, it may be said that probation workers will in general try to find unpaid work that will have these characteristics too.

As far *as victims* are concerned, there is little evidence of resistance. It seldom happens that victims complain about the fact that the court has imposed a community sentence or about the contents that this sentence is given. Part of the explanation for this may be that the actual content of the sanction is established out of view, and at a later point in time when victims—having experienced a relatively less serious offence—feel the need to be done with the incident. Media tend to report or write editorials in a favourable or at least neutral way about correctional work in general and the issues that may be addressed usually concern other aspects having to do with the prison queue, specific measures that have been introduced in that context (electronic monitoring at the outset, the recent rental of a prison in The Netherlands for Norwegian prisoners) or in specific high-profile cases. There has hardly been any negative attention for the community sentence since it was introduced. One reason for this may be that there have been few cases involving offences that in themselves received media attention—for example, because of their spectacular nature or because they involved public figures—having resulted in a community sentence.

Possibly correlated to this, *public opinion* seems favourable, or it may be that—as mentioned above—the public is not aware or particularly interested. At worst people may feel indifferent to sanctions in the community. A survey carried out in 2007 showed that the majority of a representative sample of the Norwegian population considered rehabilitation to be the most important goal for the penal system, as a means of preventing new offences. It received more support than retribution, deterrence, incapacitation or special prevention (Djupvik 2007).

This way of describing the goals for community sanctions is quite typical from the *rehabilitative perspective*, where the emphasis in more recent times has shifted away from rehabilitating offenders in their own interest towards re-integrating them into the community as a means of protecting the public from further criminality. 'What works'[17] means what works for the public, while also the desistance approach[18] is preoccupied with an identity change in the offender that will prevent him from committing new crimes—although this approach has far less emphasis on the instrumental aspect than 'risk-need-responsivity'. There is an interesting dimension to the apparent contrast between the punitive and the rehabilitative aspect in connection with public opinion. Studies by Balvig (2006) in Denmark and Olaussen (2013) in Norway have shown that samples of the population often have a much 'softer' attitude towards punishment than the courts have. The sanctions they proposed for actual cases were considerably milder than the ones that were in reality imposed by the judge. However, their initial statement was that the penal system in the country was far too easy on criminals. When confronted with this, they tended to emphasise that they themselves had a more understanding attitude towards offenders and the problems that may have led them to committing a crime than the general public. In short, the general public does not always know what the general public thinks.

Criminality and correctional work are only to a very limited degree 'hot' *political* topics during elections, and if they are they tend to be

---

[17] Most notably Andrews and Bonta (1994)

[18] For an impression of the diversity in this approach, see http://blogs.iriss.org.uk/discoveringdesistance/

about prison-related issues. This seems to be the case independent of the type of government. Estrada (2004) claims that crime is a social problem that is primarily placed on the political agenda by conservatives when social democrats are in power, but this is not an obvious conclusion for Norway. His contention is that 'Crime is viewed as a concrete problem that can be resolved by means of effective action—ideally with the mass media conveying an image of this vigour and efficiency to a wide audience.' This may very well be correct in other contexts, but in Norway penal policy is on the political agenda only to a limited degree, independent of the colour of the government, and it creates little dissent between parties. The discretionary powers of the correctional services may well act as 'vectors of leniency' here (Zimring and Johnson 2006), shielding penal policy from their counterpart, the 'vectors of severity'—public, media and politics—or as Ian Loader (2011) put it: 'the punitive, majoritarian tyrannies of democracy'. Probation and community sanctions especially do not seem to be a very prominent topic for politicians, maybe exactly because of the general level of acceptance or at least the lack of interest among media and general public. Community sanctions may thrive in a climate where they receive little political attention (and therewith less democratic control), according to Loader and Sparks (2011), who claim that 'opening penal policy up to democratic politics unleashes not reasoned deliberation about how societies can best govern crime, but impatient, illiberal emotions that dictate harsh penal treatment of offenders'.

Finally, the *reparative* aspect of community sanctions as a means to acquire legitimacy and acceptance is present in the Norwegian community sentence. Offenders shall do their share of unpaid work with state, state-controlled or voluntary organisations to the benefit of the community. Direct reparation towards the victims is also possible if such an agreement is made after a mediation process. This mediation process and the resulting hours are counted as a part of the community sentence as a whole. As mentioned, Norway has a good infrastructure for mediation through the chain of 22 offices of the National Mediation Service, with which many local units of the correctional services co-operate. This collaboration is also essential for the courses in conflict management for offenders that many probation offices offer as part of the sentence. Reparation as to the offenders' own situation is formulated in the Regulations to the Act on the

Execution of Sentences: 'unpaid work shall as much as possible be done in such a way that it is adjusted to the offenders' capacities, areas of interest and experiences' (author's translation).[19]

It seems as if the community sentence is sufficiently robust to survive an assessment in terms of these four grounds for legitimacy. What remains, however, is the question of acceptance by the *judiciary powers*. Are they comfortable with the fact that a large part of the impact of the sanction will not be visible for them? Does it influence the use of community sanctions? May this be a reason for the considerable decrease in the number of community sentences that have been imposed during the last 5 years? Or are there other reasons?

The Decrease in the Use of Community Sentences

So, if acceptance is high or at least not an issue almost all over the spectre, then why is there a decrease in the use of the community sentence? From the year 2003, which is the first with results over a whole year since the introduction in 2002, the number of community sentences imposed increased quickly up to 2009. After that, a decline set in that continues up to this day, as Table 1 shows. The number for 2015 is based on an extrapolation of the results until 1 December.

Does this development imply a decrease in the acceptance of this type of sanction by the judiciary? Is it may be perceived as 'soft' after all? Several alternative explanations are possible.

It has been claimed that the rise of electronic monitoring is at least partly to blame for the decrease in the use of community sentence. Since electronic monitoring is a form of executing a prison sentence at the discretion of the correctional services and a community sentence is imposed by the courts, this would imply that courts implicitly take into account that the correctional services may change a prison sentence into an execution in the community and that they therefore can leave the

---

[19] Retningslinjer til loven om gjennomføring av straff, Kap. 5, (5.1) Innholdet i samfunnsstraffen.

Table 1 Number of community sentences started in the course of a year, 2003–2015

2003	1352
2004	2093
2005	2544
2006	2684
2007	2929
2008	2812
2009	2912
2010	2647
2011	2544
2012	2437
2013	2231
2014	2246
2015	1972

consideration whether someone is fit to remain in the community to the services. Thus courts would not only accept these variants but also accept to further expand the discretionary powers of the correctional services.

Statistics, however, point in another direction. Electronic monitoring was gradually and county-wise introduced in Norway, which makes it possible to compare the development of the use of community sentences in counties that already had electronic monitoring to those who did not. There appear to be no significant differences between those two groups in the use of community sentences.[20] It is more likely that a 'competition' between various forms of executing (the final part of) a prison sentence has occurred. One might say that applying for electronic monitoring, home detention, stay in an institution, half-way house or conditional release, all imply fishing in the same pond, yet this is a matter that is beyond the scope of this chapter.

There may be a lack of potential candidates. When considering the fact that a community sentence in principle may replace a maximum of 1 year in prison and that the maximum number of hours is 420, one might say that its potential has not been fully explored. It has not replaced short prison sentences. The proportion of prison sentences of up to 6 months,

---

[20] According to an internal analysis of data from the Correctional Services Registration system KOMPIS.

imposed in the course of a year, has until recently remained at about 65 % since the introduction of the community sanction. Sentences up to the above-mentioned maximum of a year made up around 90 %. In 2014, an increase in the share of longer prison sentences occurred, changing these percentages to resp. 53 and 83 %. It is not yet clear what has caused this development or whether it will persist.

Taking into account early release, the average length of a stay in prison in Norway is around 3 months. The fact that many receive—sometimes very—short prison sentences instead of a community sentence is especially problematic from a rehabilitative point of view. There is little opportunity to do rehabilitative work with sufficient impact on reducing re-offending during such short periods. A community sentence comparable to an average prison sentence would generally lie around 100 hours, implying a follow-up period of—in general—at least 120 days. Apart from the positive—or non-detrimental—effects of a punishment in the community, it provides a longer period of possible rehabilitation.

It is not to be disputed that, when choosing a sanction to react to an offence, courts have many factors other than rehabilitation to take into consideration, like retribution, general and special prevention, social unrest etc. but it would seem fair to say that the decrease in the use of the community sentence is not due to a lack of potential candidates. The actual duration of the imposed community sentences indicates this as well, and also points in the direction of a very modest use in relation to the perceived seriousness of the offence. Of a potential 420 hours sentence, the average lies around 70 hours. Such has been the case from the beginning, so one might say that the courts have started out carefully and have not changed this attitude very much over the years. In other words, the level of acceptance was modest and remained so, in spite of a more lenient practice advocated by the Norwegian Supreme Court with respect to offenders under 18 and accomplices to an offence (Fornes 2012). Whether this is due to a prominence of other considerations in imposing the sentence or to a lack of confidence or visibility in the process following the verdict is unknown and might be a valuable object for research in its own right.

Meanwhile, the actual decrease is probably caused by other factors. For one thing, the total number of imposed sanctions has decreased during the period in question, and prison sentences have even decreased relatively more than community sentences.[21] More importantly, Norway has—as many other countries—seen a decrease in property crimes as well as in crimes by juveniles. The number of persons sentenced to a community sentence because of theft decreased by 39 % from 2010 to 2015 and the number for robbery by 44 %.[22] The number of persons younger than 25 admitted to Norwegian prisons in the course of a year decreased by 40 % over the period between 2010 and 2014, while there was a decrease of 'only' 18 % in the category over 25.[23] A similar development is visible when looking at the age categories for started community sentences. The share of juveniles under 18 in community sentences has more than halved since 2010, and the actual number went from 124 to 48 in the same period. The high number of children who are currently under the above-mentioned new sanction for juvenile offenders seems to indicate that at least part of this age category now ends up there—even though the sanction is meant to replace unconditional imprisonment. Forty-six under-18s during a period of 17 months is far more than the average number of prison sentences for this age category, so Christie's idea of potential net-widening seems to be supported by the facts for the time being.

Property crimes and juvenile offenders have from the beginning been mentioned as typical target categories for the community sentence, so it would seem probable that with their gradual decline, the number of community sentences would follow shortly after. The aforementioned slight increase in the percentage of unpaid work might also be accounted for by the fact that fewer juveniles commit offences, thus also reducing their share in the community sentences—where they often participate in other activities.

The decrease in itself is therefore probably not the consequence of a lack of acceptance. The question is justified, however, if the fact that these particular, less serious target categories that were picked constitutes a lack of acceptance that has been present from the start. If so, it would be relevant to investigate whether this is caused by the scope of the

---

[21] Data based on reports from Statistics Norway.

[22] Data from the Correctional Services Registration system KOMPIS.

[23] Data from the Correctional Services Registration system KOMPIS.

discretionary powers that have been bestowed upon the correctional services. Within the organisation itself the role of the correctional worker has always been a point of discussion and it is an important subject during the 2-year training for prison officers. No doubt the duality between the roles emerging from the security aspect and the re-integration aspect constitutes practical dilemmas that need to be solved in everyday work-life. They make the field a fascinating one and results seem to indicate that the consequences are well managed, but they may also influence the level of acceptance among other parties involved in the judicial process—especially when the discretionary powers are as exceptional as they are.

Conclusion

Central phenomena within the Norwegian penal system like the principle of normality and the wide discretionary powers of the correctional services are clearly present in the community sentence. With the role of probation in deciding on its content and a reduced emphasis on unpaid work, it reflects a form of exceptionalism of its own, compared to community sanctions in similar countries.

From a managerial point of view, its capacity to relieve the pressure on the prison system is repeatedly underlined by governments and policy makers, and although its effectiveness in this respect may be limited, it contributes to its legitimacy and acceptance. While seen from the punitive perspective, there are hardly any acceptance issues with the public, politics or media, independent of whether this element is considered to be present or not. Its rehabilitative effects are seen as positive and its restorative functions are not under any scrutiny and part of a larger feature of Norwegian society.

The only exception seems to lie with the judicial powers, where short prison sentences in many potentially eligible cases are still preferred to community sentences. The recent substantial reduction in the use of community sentence, however, does not seem to be the result of a lack of acceptance or legitimacy with the judiciary, but more of a strong reduction in the type of offences and offenders that have traditionally been linked to it.

Bibliography

Aebi, M., Delgrande, N., Marguet, Y. (2015). Have community sanctions and measures widened the net of the European criminal justice systems? *Punishment and Society, 17*(5), 577–597.

Andrews, D. A., & Bonta, J. (1994). *The psychology of criminal conduct.* Cincinnati, OH: Anderson

Andrews, D. A., & Bonta, J. (2006). *The psychology of criminal conduct* (4th ed.). Newark, NJ: LexisNexis.

Balvig, F. (2006). *Danskernes syn på straf.* København: Advokatsamfundet.

Christensen, T. (2003). Narratives of Norwegian governance: elaborating the strong state tradition. *Public Administration, 81*, 1.

Christensen, T., & Lægreid, P. (2005). Trust in government: the relative importance of service satisfaction, political factors, and demography. *Public Performance & Management Review, 28*(4), 487–511.

Christie, N. (2015). Widening the net. *Restorative Justice: An International Journal, 3*(1), 109–113.

Council of Europe. (2007). *European prison rules.* https://wcd.coe.int/ViewDoc.jsp?id=955747.

Day, A., Casey, S., Ward, T., Howells, K., Vess, J. (2010). *Transitions to better lives.* Cullompton: Willan.

Djupvik, H. S. (2007). *Advokatforeningens spørreundersøkelse om straff og straffegjennomføring.* Advokatforeningen/ TNS Gallup.

Durnescu, I. (2008). An exploration of the purposes and outcomes of probation in European jurisdictions. *Probation Journal, 55*, 273–281.

Estrada, F. (2004). The transformation of the politics of crime in high-crime societies. *European Journal of Criminology, 1*(4), 219–243.

European Committee for the Prevention of Torture. (2011). CPT/Inf 33 | Section: 17/26 | Date: 15/12/2011. http://hudoc.cpt.coe.int/eng?i=p-nor-20110518-en-17.

EuroVista Journal for Probation and Community Justice. (2013). Vol 3 # 1. http://euro-vista.org/eurovista-vol3-1.

Fornes, I. (2012). Bruk av samfunnsstraff overfor barn—nye tendenser i Høyesteretts praksis. *Lov og rett, 51*, 2.

Friestad, C., & Hansen, I. L. (2004). *Levekår blant innsatte.* FAFO-rapport nr. 429.

Graham, H., & White, R. (2015). *Innovative justice.* London: Routledge.

Graunbøl, H. M., Kielstrup, B., Muiluvuori, M., Tyni, S., Baldursson, E. S., Gudmundsdottir, H., et al. (2010). *'Retur', en nordisk undersøgelse af recidiv blant klienter i kriminalforsorgen.* Kriminalomsorgens utdanningssenter. https://brage.bibsys.no/xmlui/handle/11250/160672.

Kristoffersen, R. (2013). Relapse study in the correctional services of the Nordic countries. Key results and perspectives. *EuroVista Journal for Probation and Community Justice, 2*(3), 168–176.

Kylstad Øster, M., & Rokkan, T. (2013). Curfew as a means, not as an end— Electronic Monitoring in Norway. *EuroVista Journal for Probation and Community Justice, 2*(2), 90–96.

Loader, I. (2011). Playing with fire? Democracy and the emotions of crime and punishment. In *S.* Karstedt, I. Loader, H. Strang (Eds.), *Emotions, crime and justice.* London: Bloomsbury.

Loader, I., & Sparks, R. (2011). *Public criminology?* London: Routledge.

McNeill, F. (2013). Community sanctions and European penology. In T. Daems S. Snacken, D. Van Zyl Smit (Eds.). *European penology.* Oxford: Hart Publishing. http://www.offendersupervision.eu/wp-content/uploads/2012/10/McNeill_CSEPfinal.pdf

Ministry of Justice and the Police of Norway. (2008). *Punishment that works; less crime- a safer society.* Governmental White Paper.

Olaussen, L. P. (2013). *Hva synes folk om straffenivået? En empirisk undersøkelse.* Novus: Forlag.

Phelps, M. S. (2013). The paradox of probation: community supervision in the age of mass incarceration. *Law & Policy, 35*(1–2), 51–80.

Pratt, J. (2008a). Scandinavian exceptionalism in an era of penal excess. Part I: the nature and roots of Scandinavian exceptionalism. *British Journal of Criminology, 48*, 119–137.

Pratt, J. (2008b). Scandinavian exceptionalism in an era of penal excess. Part II: does Scandinavian exceptionalism have a future? *British Journal of Criminology, 48*, 275–292.

Pratt, J., & Eriksson, A. (2011). 'Mr. Larsson is walking out again'. The origins and development of Scandinavian prison systems. *Australian & New Zealand Journal of Criminology, 44*(1), 7–23.

Pratt, J., & Eriksson, A. (2013).Contrasts in punishment: an explanation of Anglophone excess and Nordic exceptionalism. *International Journal for Crime, Justice and Social Democracy, 2*(3), 120–134.

Revold, M. (2015). *Innsattes levekår 2014.* Oslo, Statistisk sentralbyrå rapport nr 2015/47.

Robinson, G., & McNeill, F. (Eds.) (2016). *Community punishment— European perspectives*. London: Routledge.

Robinson, G., McNeill, F., Maruna, S. (2013). Punishment in society: the improbable persistence of probation and other community sanctions and measures. In J. Simon and R. Sparks (Eds.), *The sage handbook of punishment and society* (pp. 321–340). London: Sage.

Sand Bruer, E. (2014). *Hva nytter I Norge?* http://www.kriminalomsorgen. no/rapporten-samfunnsstraffen-i-norge-tilgjengelig-paa-nett.5560552-237613.html.

Smith, P. S., Horn, T., Nilsen, J. F., Rua, M. (2013). Isolasjon i skandinaviske fengsler: skandinavisk praksis og etableringen av et skandinavisk isolasjons-nettverk. *Kritisk juss, 39*(3/4), 170–191.

Ugelvik, T., & Dullum, J. (Eds.) (2012). *Penal exceptionalism: Nordic prison policy and practice*. London: Routledge.

Weaver, B. (2013). Co-producing desistance: who works to support desistance. I. Durnescu and F. McNeill (Eds.), *Understanding penal practice*. (Routledge Frontiers of Criminal Justice Series; pp. 193–205). Abingdon: Routledge.

Zimring, F. E., & Johnson, D. (2006). Public opinion and the governance of punishment in democratic political systems. *The Annals of The American Academy of Political and Social Science, 605*, 265–280.

Part IV

The Principle
of Normalisation—Theory and Practice

Normalisation in Nordic Prisons—From a Prison Governor's Perspective

Hans Jørgen Engbo

The concept of normalisation—or normality—has been used to an ever-increasing extent in prisons policies since the 1970s in the Nordic countries, and gradually also in many other countries. It is not an unambiguous concept. In this article, I will offer my proposal for a common Nordic definition of the concept based on relevant Nordic sources of law. My approach to this subject is characterised by practical experience from my position as Prison Governor combined with my ongoing theoretical work with prisons.[1]

I am grateful to Berit Johnsen, Doris Bakken, Lone Andersen, Yngve Hammerlin, Thomas Ugelvik and Peter Scharff Smith, who have read the manuscript and made useful comments and suggestions that enriched the final text.

[1] I have more than 40 years of practical experience from serving with the Prison and Probation Service in Denmark and the Correctional Service of Greenland. For almost 30 years of this period, I have been the Prison Governor of several Danish prisons. My theoretical work comprises several years as an associate

H.J. Engbo (✉)
Former Chief Executive, Correctional Service of Greenland, Denmark
e-mail: hjengbo@gmail.com

© The Author(s) 2017   **327**
P. Scharff Smith, T. Ugelvik (eds.), *Scandinavian Penal History, Culture and Prison Practice,* Palgrave Studies in Prisons and Penology, DOI 10.1057/978-1-137-58529-5_14

Initially, I will give an account of perspectives of relevance to the concept of normalisation found in sources of law in the Nordic countries, including in relevant sources of international law. The use and perception of the concept have different nuances, and it is not a specifically legal concept. The concept is also used in sociological and crime policy discourses and as an explanatory term for the rationale of procedures of the Danish Prison and Probation Service (*Kriminalforsorgen*). Since there is no unambiguous definition of the concept, both perceptions may be equally correct. However, it may be useful for the discourse and the practical application of the concept to seek a common understanding, which I shall try to describe from a Nordic legal perspective.

What Does the Law Say?

Defensive and Proactive Normalisation

In Denmark, a prison sentence is described as a forced interference with the freedom to choose one's residence, that is, the right to move freely from one place to another (freedom of movement).[2] Similar descriptions are found in other Nordic countries.[3] In principle, no other freedoms or rights other than the freedom of movement are affected by a prison sentence, and it is therefore essential for the authorities that inmates do not experience any interference with rights and conditions of life other than the interference with the freedom of movement and the inevitable consequences of such interference combined with crime prevention measures, together referred to as security interventions. This can be termed a *defensive* requirement of normalisation, which implies that the authorities

---

professor of criminal law at the Faculty of Law of Copenhagen University and close collaboration with lawyers, criminologists and other professionals in the Nordic countries.

[2] Report No. 1181/1989 on a sentence enforcement act, etc. (*Betænkning nr. 1181/1989 om en lov om fuldbyrdelse af straf mv.*), p. 105.

[3] Sweden: The Government's Bill No. 1997/98:105, p. 6. Norway: Report to the Storting (*stortingsmelding*) No. 37 (2007–08), p. 9.

must abstain from acts interfering unnecessarily with inmates' possibilities of living a normal life (Engbo 1997, p. 103).

The requirement of normalisation may also involve a *proactive* approach, which entails an obligation on the authorities to perform acts that may lead to a particular situation or particular conditions which can facilitate 'normality'. In other words, proactive normalisation gives rise to a duty to act, whereas defensive normalisation entails a duty of non-interference.

Both defensive normalisation and proactive normalisation are reflected in legislation and in the documents of international law.

Finland

Finland is the only Nordic country that has proactively specified the requirement of normality in legislation: 'To the extent possible, prison conditions must be arranged to reflect living conditions in society.'[4]

However, the Finnish Imprisonment Act also sets out a defensive specification of the requirement of normality: 'The enforcement of prison sentences may entail no restrictions on the rights and conditions of prisoners other than those imposed by law or necessary due to the punishment itself.'[5]

Under Finnish law, the *rights and conditions* of inmates must be in accordance with normality.

Greenland[6]

The Greenland Criminal Code (*kriminallov*) specifies the requirement of normality as follows: 'During the enforcement of a measure, no

---

[4] Chapter 1, Section 3, of the Finnish Imprisonment Act (*fängelselag*) (767/2005).

[5] Chapter 1, Section 3, of the Finnish Imprisonment Act (*fängelselag*) (767/2005).

[6] Geographically, Greenland belongs to Northern America, but being part of the Kingdom of Denmark, Greenland is considered part of the Nordic countries in many contexts.

restrictions may be imposed on a person's life other than such as are prescribed by law or are a consequence of the measure itself.[7]

The Correctional Service of Greenland (*Kriminalforsorgen i Grønland*) has described the following (proactive) task in its strategic plan: 'We must organise our institutions in accordance with a "principle of normality". This means that, as far as possible, the framework for living inside an institution must be similar to the framework for living elsewhere in society.'

Life and *conditions* are the elements in focus in Greenland.

Denmark

The wording of the Danish Sentence Enforcement Act (*straffuldbyrdelseslov*) is identical to the wording of the Greenland Criminal Code, except that in Denmark reference is made to penal sanctions and in Greenland reference is made to measures.[8] Reference is made to normalisation in the Programme of Principles of the Prison and Probation Service: 'When planning the daily life in prisons and every time a specific decision is made, the Prison and Probation Service must keep in view conditions in the general society.'

In Denmark, normalisation thus focuses on *life* and *daily life*.

Sweden

In Sweden, the approach is: 'Enforcement may not entail limitations of the prisoner's liberty other than those that follow from this Act or are necessary to maintain good order or security.'[9]

---

[7] Section 172 of the Greenland Criminal Code (*kriminallov*).

[8] See Section 4 of the Danish Sentence Enforcement Act (*lov om fuldbyrdelse af straf*). The Greenland Criminal Code has traditionally had much greater focus on rehabilitation as compared with the criminal codes of the other Nordic countries. Concepts like punishment and prison are not used at all. Instead, 'measures' and 'institution for offenders' are the concepts used in Greenland.

[9] Chapter 1, Section 6, of the Swedish Act on Imprisonment (*fängelselag*) (2010:610).

Thus, the Swedish wording focuses on normalisation of the *freedom* of inmates.

Faroe Islands

On the Faroe Islands, the approach is: 'Inmates can exercise their usual civil rights to the extent that the incarceration does not, in itself, bar them from doing so.'[10] What must be protected against unnecessary interference is accordingly the inmates' *general civil rights.*

Iceland

The Icelandic Sentence Enforcement Act (*lög um fullnustu refsinga*) contains no general provision on normalisation. When it comes to health services, it appears clearly from the Act that the aim is normalisation: 'While in prison, prisoners shall enjoy health services comparable to those generally available, [...].'[11]

Norway

The Norwegian Execution of Sentences Act (*straffegjennomføringslov*) includes no express provisions on the idea of normality either. Section 2 of the Act reads: 'A sentence shall be executed in a manner that takes into account the purpose of the sentence, that serves to prevent the commission of new criminal acts, that is reassuring to society and that, within this framework, ensures satisfactory conditions for the prisoners.' What does 'satisfactory conditions' mean? The nearest we get to an answer to this question is the provision in Section 1-2 of the Regulations to the Execution of Sentences Act (*forskrift til lov om straffegjennomføring*): 'As far as is compatible with due regard for the

---

[10] Section 19 of the Executive Order on Sentence Enforcement (*bekendtgørelse om fuldbyrdelse af frihedsstraf*) of 21 June 1973.

[11] Section 22 of the Execution of Sentences Act No. 49/2005 (*lög um fullnustu refsinga*).

security of society and the general sense of justice, suitable arrangements shall be made for enabling the convicted person to amend his way of life and to prevent recidivism.'

Accordingly, satisfactory conditions seem to be conditions that make it possible for the individual inmate to change his way of life and prevent recidivism. Apparently, the Act focuses on usefulness to society rather than inmates' rights and conditions, and thereby normalisation. However, looking at the provision through Norwegian lenses, it is possible to see a link to the idea of normality as the normalisation of inmates is also called for in Norway.[12] Hammerlin (2008, p. 565) has clarified the dual Norwegian application of the concept:

Normalisation may have two different meanings in the context of the Norwegian Correctional Service:

1. One meaning is related to the creation of prison conditions and initiatives resembling the surrounding world as much as possible. [...] Inmates must enjoy the same rights as other citizens, including educational offers and health programmes.
2. The other meaning is used at the level of individuals when various methods are applied to 'normalise' a person who is considered deviant or defined as having a deviant personality.

Of course, it is possible to refer to normalisation in the latter sense, but this is not the meaning attributed to the concept in the other Nordic countries. This perception of normalisation seems to be related to words like social reintegration and rehabilitation. However, references to human normalisation give rise to serious ethical and democratic considerations. What does a state-authorised 'normal human being' look like?

A quite interesting approach to normalisation is seen in the provision of the Execution of Sentences Act setting out that the Norwegian

---

[12] As expressed by Marianne Vollan, Director General of the Directorate of the Norwegian Correctional Service (*Kriminalomsorgen*). See: http://ebladet.kriminalforsorgen.dk/default.aspx?ID=2312%26ProductID=PROD161 (25 June 2015). See also Bronebakk (2012, p. 48).

Correctional Service (*Kriminalomsorgen*) must collaborate with other public authorities to make sure that inmates receive the public benefits to which they are entitled according to law.[13] In practice, this provision means that training, healthcare, social services and cultural offers are the responsibility of the relevant authorities and not the correctional authorities (Storvik 2011, p. 39). This system, referred to as 'the import model' by Nils Christie (1993, pp. 116f.) as opposed to the 'self-sufficiency model', is also found in other Nordic countries, but the Norwegian system is far more extensive and consistent than anywhere else in the Nordic countries.

Even though Norway has not incorporated corresponding provisions on normality in the wording of the Act—as opposed to the other Nordic countries except for Iceland—the idea of normality is very widespread in both theory and practice in Norway. Kristin Bølgen Bronebakk,[14] the former Director General of the Norwegian Correctional Service, has characterised the principle of normality as 'one of the fundamental pillars of the Correctional Service' (Bronebakk 2012, p. 47). As regards normality, she has also said:

> The principle of normality entails that prisoners retain all *rights* that do not necessarily lapse because of their imprisonment.
>
> The more fundamental the human rights that are intended to be restricted, the greater the demand must be of the validity of the arguments.
>
> The principle of normality does not express a pressure on prisoners to conform; rather the opposite: to allow the same *framework for personal development* as that of citizens outside the prison.[15] (Bronebakk 2012, p. 48)

In a report to the Storting, the Norwegian parliament, the Norwegian government described the principle of normality as follows in 2008: 'It is demanding to prepare social reintegration during detention. The

---

[13] Section 4 of the Execution of Sentences Act (*straffegjennomføringslov*).

[14] Director General of the Department of the Correctional Service with the Ministry of Justice and Public Security (*Justis- og beredskapsdepartementet*) from 2003 to 2009. Worked on a PhD thesis on *The Principle of Normalisation in Norwegian Prisons* until her death in 2012.

[15] Italics added.

transition from prison to freedom is smoother the smaller the difference is from life outside the prison. The principle of normality is therefore a fundamental principle of the sentence execution policy. [...]'[16] The word 'therefore' indicates that normality is a means for social reintegration. Here it is not described as a right of the inmate or an independent aim of the authorities. The discussion paper also sets out: 'To strengthen the principle of normality, everyday life in prison must be organised to reflect the surrounding society to the greatest extent possible.'

Maybe the idea of normality is so firmly established in the Norwegian Correctional Service that the legislators found it superfluous to make a specific reference to it in the Act.

Requirements Under International Law

The European Convention on Human Rights (ECHR) protects several rights, including the right to respect for private and family life (Article 8), the freedom of thought, conscience and religion (Article 9), the freedom of expression (Article 10) and the freedom of assembly and association (Article 11). However, the individual provisions make statutory and necessary interference with these rights legitimate to safeguard particular considerations (such as national security or public safety and the prevention of disorder and crime). It was previously believed that the convention rights were to be construed with additional implied limitations for certain population groups, such as prison inmates. This idea of implied limitations was overruled in 1975 by *the European Court of Human Rights*, which said: 'The restrictive formulation used at paragraph 2 (art. 8-2) [...] leaves no room for the concept of implied limitations.'[17] The case concerned interference with the right to respect for private and family life and correspondence, but the Court's finding is deemed to apply to other central convention rights as well (Articles 8 to 11). The Court has referred to this

---

[16] Report to the Storting (*stortingsmelding*) No. 37 (2007–08), p. 9.

[17] *Golder v. the United Kingdom*, 21 February 1975 (4451/70), § 44.

judgment in numerous subsequent judgments by the phrase: 'Justice cannot stop at the prison gate.'[18]

To remove any doubt, the Court has reiterated several times in recent years: '[p]risoners in general continue to enjoy all the fundamental rights and freedoms guaranteed under the Convention save for the right to liberty'.[19] By giving this clear indication, the Court has emphasised that inmates' legal position relative to their convention rights has become normalised in the sense that inmates are fully entitled to enjoy the same rights under the ECHR as other citizens.

The ECHR has been incorporated into national law in all Nordic countries and is thus included in the legal system of the individual countries and applied like any other national legalisation.

The European Prison Rules (EPR),[20] adopted by the Committee of Ministers to the member states of the Council of Europe in 2006, include the following proactively worded recommendation on good practices: 'Life in prison shall approximate as closely as possible the positive aspects of life in the community.'[21] At first, the words 'the positive aspects of life' seem to allow ample opportunity for interpretation, but according to the comment on Rule 5, the words are intended to ensure that normalisation does not lead to 'inhumane prison conditions'.[22] What this entails can aptly be inferred from the current interpretation of Article 3 of the ECHR, which prohibits 'inhuman or degrading treatment or punishment'.[23]

---

[18] See, for example, Campbell and *Fell v. the United Kingdom*, 28 June 1984 (7819/77; 7878/77), § 69.

[19] See, for example, *Hirst v. the United Kingdom* (No. 2) [GC], 6 October 2005 (74025/01), § 69.

[20] Recommendation Rec(2006)2 of the Committee of Ministers to member states on the European Prison Rules (Adopted by the Committee of Ministers on 11 January 2006 at the 952nd meeting of the Ministers' Deputies).

[21] Rule 5.

[22] Ministers' Deputies CM Documents, CM(2005)163 Addendum, 2 November 2005. 949 Meeting, 1 December 2005. 10 Legal questions. 10.2 European Committee on Crime Problems (CDPC)—a. Draft Recommendation Rec(2005)... of the Committee of Ministers to member states on the European Prison Rules and Commentary.

[23] Reference is made particularly to the interpretation made by the European Court of Human Rights and to the European Convention for the Prevention of Torture and Inhuman or Degrading Treatment or Punishment (CPT).

The EPR also stipulate defensive requirements of normality:

Persons deprived of their liberty retain all rights that are not lawfully taken away by the decision sentencing them or remanding them in custody.[24]
  Imprisonment is by the deprivation of liberty a punishment in itself and therefore the regime for sentenced prisoners shall not aggravate the suffering inherent in imprisonment.[25]

The EPR are not legally binding. The rules are merely recommendations, but since the Nordic countries were involved in drafting them and have expressed a will to observe them, it must be possible to some extent to take the rules into account as a source-of-law factor (so-called soft law) in the legal systems of the Nordic countries.

What Is Supposed to Be Normal?

According to the sources of law in the individual Nordic countries, the focus areas of normalisation can be divided into three categories:

* Conditions and framework for prison life
* Framework for personal life and personal development
* Civil rights

All elements can be gathered under one single heading, or one common denominator for prison normality in the Nordic countries: Framework for life and civil rights.

  It appears from legislation that the aspects to be normalised include the *life, conditions* and the *everyday life* of inmates. This way of expressing it sometimes leads to the perception that the authorities have to organise a certain kind of normal (everyday) life that inmates have to fit into. However, it can hardly be the task of the authorities in such totalitarian

---

[24] Rule 2.
[25] Rule 102.2.

manner to authorise a particular way of living. The requirement of normality means that inmates must be able to form their own lives, or create their own individual norms for living—just like citizens in the free society. Accordingly, the authorities have to focus on the framework.

It is essential to keep in mind the reservation inherent in the phrase 'to the extent possible' and corresponding proactively worded provisions on normalisation. It is highly abnormal for a person to be deprived of his or her freedom of movement, and the more intensive the incarceration the more abnormal life will be merely as a consequence of the deprivation of liberty. Normality can therefore never become complete. Prison life will always be an unusual life. If the incarceration as such and the pertaining security measures are disregarded, it may make sense to talk about normality in all other aspects, and this is what the idea of normality is all about: It is not about a quite utopian and contradictory demand that *everything* must be normal for human beings who have been deprived of something as normal as their freedom of movement.

The word 'normalisation' is not particularly felicitous and is used only for the lack of a better expression. Maybe 'democratisation' would better cover the contents of the concept.[26]

Normality and Prison Security

From a modern understanding of prison security, there is no conflict between security and a normalised prison regime. Prison security is based on the fundamental culture of the correctional institution and all the pertaining elements of that culture, including a 'normal' everyday life (Engbo 1996, pp. 258ff.). Normalisation will therefore support and not work against effective security.

---

[26] 'Democracy' is a word with positive connotations used in this context in its constitutional meaning to express partly that the prison regime is governed by law and adopted by a parliament elected by the people, partly that prison inmates have the same fundamental civil freedoms as other citizens.

Of course, the incarceration as such constitutes a highly noticeable barrier to a normal life, but since exactly the restrictions on normality following from the incarceration have been taken into account, there is no conflict between security and normality.

Normality as a Principle?

It is common to talk about the *principle* of normalisation or normality. In Denmark, normalisation is described in the Programme of Principles of the Prison and Probation Service from 1993 as 'a fundamental and very wide principle'. William Rentzmann,[27] the primary author of the Programme of Principles, has subsequently said about the principle of normalisation:

> [E]very time we have to solve an issue in a prison, and every time we have to define a rule, our initial thought must be: How would we do it in the free society? Only then are we to think: Is there any particular reason for doing things differently because it is a prison? (Rentzmann 2011, p. 110)

A principle will be put to the ultimate test in marginal situations. The principle of normality is not essential in situations when normality is self-explanatory. However, the principle may be relevant as a solution in cases (of doubt) in which normality is not directly obvious, or maybe even incomprehensible or—in certain groups—offensive.

In 2004, the management of a Norwegian prison allowed the inmates to invite a female dancer to the prison to make a dance performance. When the dance developed into striptease after some time, the management interrupted the performance. It has not been told whether the principle of normality was taken into account in this decision. Striptease is a fully lawful and normal activity in the free society. Is it not so in prisons? Security was hardly an issue, and the interference may therefore seem like moralistic

---

[27] At that time Deputy Director-General, subsequently Director-General of the Danish Prison and Probation Service 1998–2013.

censorship, which is not in line with the principle of normality.[28] Apparently, the prison management found it necessary to interrupt the performance to prevent outraged and condemnatory reactions from the public (media and politicians) as are often seen in similar situations. The public opinion can be the fiercest opponent of the principle of normality, and the authorities sometimes feel compelled to yield to that fact.

The principle of normality can be regarded as an explanatory factor that can contribute to a better understanding and more widespread acknowledgement of the (proactive and/or defensive) statutory requirements of normality. The principle of normality does not, in itself, have any normative power. Legislation may be based on a principle, but legally it does not make sense to apply a supplementary non-statutory principle.

Normalisation as a Means or a Strategy?

Normalisation is not seldom mentioned as a means or a strategy, often for the purpose of contributing to the social reintegration of inmates and to the reduction of the harmful effects of the incarceration. See, for example, the following paragraph from the Programme of Principles of the Danish Prison and Probation Service: 'By establishing prison conditions which differ as little as possible from those of a daily life outside the prisons, the grounds for aggression and apathy are reduced and altogether the negative effects of imprisonment are limited, thereby creating a more fertile soil for treatment initiatives in the broad sense.'

Bronebakk has expressed that the principle of normality 'offers the best basis for a good return to society'.[29] It is highly probable that a normalised framework for prison life may offer fertile soil for social reintegration efforts and accordingly a good basis for returning to the free society. Therefore, it is hardly possible to disagree with Bronebakk.

---

[28] www.dagbladet.no/nyheter/2004/10/21/412032.html (21 October 2004).

[29] www.kriminalomsorgen.no/etikk-straff-og-fremtidens-kriminalomsorg.3127443-237613.html (4 December 2007).

However, it is important to emphasise that these effects must be seen as side effects. No requirements are made in the sources of law on normalisation cited above that normalisation must act as a means of, or a tool for, social reintegration.

Subramanian and Shames (2013, p. 19) have expressed the following perception of normalisation in a description of prison conditions in Germany: 'The rationale of normalization is to mitigate the negative effects of incarceration on prisoners and increase chances for successful offender rehabilitation and reintegration.' A reduction of the negative effects of incarceration is not the rationale of normalisation according to the predominant Nordic sources of law, but possibly useful side effects; however, that is something entirely different.

Greenland law provides a good example that normalisation is deemed to supersede social reintegration efforts:

> The fundamental view [of offers with the aim of social reintegration] is [. . .] not restricted to utilitarian views of treatment (any longer). It is an effect of the fundamental principle of normalisation and the requirement of humane treatment that convicted offenders should not be excluded from help or support if needed, no matter whether or not such help or support is specifically assumed to prevent recidivism.[30]

It would entail an obvious risk to characterise normalisation as a social reintegration tool. If it turns out that the desired effect on social reintegration does not materialise, then the main argument for normalisation no longer applies. McCorkle and Korn (1954, pp. 94–95) wrote similarly about help and treatment more than 60 years ago:

> It is the tragedy of modern correction that the impulse to help has been confused with treatment and seems to require defense as treatment. One of the more ironic difficulties with this position is that when one makes 'rehabilitation' the main justification for the humane handling of prisoners one has maneuvered oneself into a position potentially dangerous to the humanitarian viewpoint. What if humane treatment fails to rehabilitate—shall it then be

---

[30] Report No. 1442/2004 on the judicial system of Greenland, p. 1056.

abandoned? The isolated survivals of flogging and other 'tough' techniques which still disgrace American penology remain to remind us that this is no mere academic question. The bleak fact is that just as the monstrous punishments of the eighteenth century failed to curtail crime, so the mere humane handling of the twentieth century has equally failed to do so.[31]

Normality as the Aim

Normality is, first and foremost, to be seen as a statutory aim for prisons. As can be derived from the wording of statutes and other sources of law and recommendations, normality must have an impact on inmates' enjoyment of civil rights and the framework for prison life. We could turn it upside down and emphasise that it is not legitimate to create an abnormal framework, except for the (perceptible) framework put in place by the incarceration itself, and that it is therefore a duty—an aim—of the prisons to (proactively) create or (defensively) guard a regime characterised by a good framework for the individual inmate's possibility of living a normal life.

The following vision on normalised education of inmates was worded as early as 1931:

> In the prisons of tomorrow education will be taken as a matter of course, as it is now in progressive communities which seek to offer varied educational to their citizens. It will not be considered the sole agency of rehabilitation; no exaggerated claims will be made for its efficacy. It will be recognized as having the same unquestionable place in prisons that it has in the world outside, and as probably having somewhat greater value because of the unusually heavy concentration of under-educated adults presented by our prison population. The classroom and the training shop will be built into the institution with no more debate than is given to the necessity of a hospital. The teacher and the vocational instructor will have their places on the staff as surely as the doctor and the turnkey. (MacCormick 1931, p. 72)

---

[31] Quote from Korn and McCorkle (1959, p. 474).

In accordance with this vision, it has been the official aim in Denmark since 1973, as defined briefly and clearly, 'that inmates are offered education to the same extent as other citizens of the country'.[32]

Normality is not intended to 'work'. No 'evidence' of normality is required. Even though criminological studies were to reach the conclusion that normalisation does not reduce the rate of recidivism, such finding would be entirely irrelevant when it comes to the importance of maintaining normality as an essential aim and a natural core element of prison regimes based on democracy. The antithesis of such regimes is a totalitarian prison system in which inmates only have the rights and living conditions that the powerful prison management opts to bestow on them.

Who Defines Normality?

The prison authorities are to contribute to creating normality by observing inmates' civil rights and by putting in place a framework and possibilities that allow the individual inmate to the greatest extent possible to create a life in prison that is as normal as possible for him/her under the (otherwise abnormal) conditions laid out due to the incarceration. For further details, see Engbo (1997, p. 102).

Accordingly, prison authorities have to:

• reduce limitations relative to the options of the free society, and
• facilitate the individual inmate's endeavours to achieve (his or her own) normality while in prison.

However, the authorities cannot decide what the individual inmate is to consider normal (or useful). It clearly falls outside the responsibility of the prison to adopt a paternalistic approach and enforce a state-authorised normality on the inmates. I remember, to my horror, a visit

---

[32] Report No. 683/1973 on education, vocational training and leisure time activities for inmates of the institutions of the prison service (*Betænkning nr. 683/1973 om undervisning, erhvervsuddannelse og fritidsaktiviteter for indsatte i fængselsvæsenets anstalter*), p. 15.

to Sweden in 1981 when I was introduced to the substance abuse treatment at the Österåker Correctional Institution. Here they made targeted efforts to break down the inmates' identity and rebuild them as normalised 'Medium Svenssons'[33] by close-cropping their hair, dressing them in corduroy suits, forcing them to listen to Swedish pop music rather than so-called acid rock, and teaching them the blessings of an ordinary Swedish family life with a white picket fence around a red farm house (Engbo 1981, pp. 26 f.).

In brief, normality means that the individual inmates must be given the freedom to define their own (lawful) way of living and be allowed an optimum (normalised) framework for doing so. In tune with this perception, inmate spokespersons must have a voice in determining what offers are to be given to prison inmates.

Normality in Practice

When considering the prison practices in Denmark today, it is apparent that there is room for improvement in several areas when it comes to the normalisation of rights and the framework for inmates' lives. Some examples are given below. They also illustrate that it is not always straightforward to determine what is normal in a prison, which is basically an abnormal place to be forced to stay.

Voting Rights and Other Civil Rights

When it comes to the normalisation of human rights, it is mentioned as a matter of course that inmates in all Nordic prisons have long had full voting rights at parliamentary and local elections and referendums (Engbo 2005, p. 166) as opposed to the state of the law in England and Wales.[34] Also the right to education, the right to social security, the

---

[33] A Medium Svensson is the designation used by Statistics Sweden (*Statistiska Centralbyrån*) for an average Swedish citizen.

[34] *Hirst v. the United Kingdom* (No. 2) [GC], 6 October 2005 (74025/01).

right to healthcare and the freedom to manifest one's religion should be mentioned—all of which are rights and freedoms that are in principle like those of all other citizens (Engbo 2005, pp. 185ff.). However, it is proving difficult in Denmark to ensure freedom of expression; for further details see one of the following sections.

Self-Catering Schemes for Inmates

The self-catering schemes for inmates in Danish prisons have often been presented as a shining example of normalisation.[35] Maybe it is not that strange. From the outset, it seems to be normalisation that inmates are to do their own shopping and cooking like most other people in the free society, and the majority of inmates undoubtedly experience the scheme as normalisation as compared with traditional prison catering. However, not all inmates perceive self-catering as the normal way of having food. I have met several inmates to whom it would be normal to satisfy their hunger at a hot dog stand or a takeaway. Other inmates have spent a considerable part of their lives at institutions, and to them institution food service is normal. Some may think that we have a task of forcing these inmates to learn how to cook healthy food, but that would be forced social education and not normalisation. I also recall a first-time offender aged 66 convicted of bank robberies. He had been married for 40 years and had never boiled an egg. What was normal to him was to sit down at the table and eat the meal prepared by his wife. Self-catering may be the normal way of having food for some inmates, but other inmates may perceive forced self-catering as abnormal and a kind of educational paternalism. A genuine normalised catering scheme for inmates would involve different options allowing the individual inmates to choose their own 'normal' ways of satisfying their hunger. It would probably be difficult to set up such a scheme due to logistics and resources considerations, but then we have to acknowledge that and admit that full normalisation cannot be achieved by forcing all inmates into a self-catering scheme.

---

[35] See, for example, Report No. 1334/1997 on public meals in Denmark (*Betænkning nr. 1334/ 1997 om offentlig kostforplejning i Danmark*), p. 56.

Equality and Welfare

Van Zyl Smit and Snacken (2009, p. 105) argue that the requirement of Rule 5 of the European Prison Rules that life in prison must approximate as closely as possible 'the positive aspects' of life in the outside society must mean that the social inequalities of the free society should not be brought into the prisons: 'On the contrary, a certain level of equitable redistribution is an important social principle in Europe. Normalization then rather justifies guaranteeing all prisoners a good average standard of living rather than accepting extreme differences between prisoners.'

Offhand, the phrase 'the positive aspects of life in society' may seem almost synonymous with 'the good life' and accordingly a way of expressing a welfare ideal. Inmates are to be offered welfare like all other citizens. But does that involve the requirement that prisons must be organised like an (artificial) equality society with an authorised uniform welfare standard? Why should a normalised prison society not be organised in a manner that reflects the conditions of human beings in the free society, including the existing inequalities and differences in welfare standards? Such discussions are seen in connection with considerations of inmates' duty to wear prison clothes (e.g. in Sweden) as opposed to the right to wear their own clothes (e.g. in Denmark). Is it acceptable that inmates wear expensive branded clothes if they can afford it, while others have to be content with cheap second-hand clothes, or even have to make do with clothes offered by the prison? The same argumentation has been used about the consideration whether intimates may spend money brought or transferred to the prison.[36]

Unless certain adjustments of the natural social inequality among inmates can be justified for security reasons, a forced order of social equality deviating from the social order in the free society would involve a violation of the requirement of normality. Prisons may not assume the nature of ideological, totalitarian-based bubbles in a democratic order of

---

[36] Report No. 1181/1989 on a sentence enforcement act, etc. (*Betænkning nr. 1181/1989 om en lov om fuldbyrdelse af straf mv.*), p. 134.

society. The number of interventions that can be made legitimate by the phrase 'the positive aspects of life' in Rule 5 must be very limited. As already mentioned, the comment on Rule 5 specifies that the purpose of this phrase is to ensure that prison conditions do not become inhumane as a consequence of normalisation.[37] The intention seems to be that there ought to be a minimum standard of welfare for inmates and a lower threshold against 'inhumanity'. Van Zyl Smit and Snacken also narrow their suggestion to the avoidance of *extreme* differences between inmates, and such very extreme differences may, depending on the circumstances, involve security risks against which it may be legitimate to intervene.

Religious Services

It is sometimes difficult to determine what is normal. What is normal in the free society may turn out to be abnormal in a prison. When a new prison was opened in Jyderup (Denmark) in 1988, it was decided not to build a prison church as had been the tradition in the old prisons. Inmates were to be offered religious services at the local parish church together with other citizens. That was viewed as a natural realisation of the idea of normalisation. However, what inmates emphasised was that it was normal to have an unlimited right to contact the pastor at the church without being noticed and without having to apply to the authorities for permission first, and maybe having to attend church guarded by prison staff. For that reason, they wanted a prison church. They did not feel that they belonged to the congregation of the local parish church; they wanted a church of their own. The bishop became convinced by the inmates' arguments, and the Ministry of Ecclesiastical Affairs granted funds for the construction of a church in the prison. The inmates had now obtained the same direct access to their own church as

---

[37] Ministers' Deputies CM Documents, CM(2005)163 Addendum, 2 November 2005. 949 Meeting, 1 December 2005. 10 Legal questions. 10.2 European Committee on Crime Problems (CDPC)—a. Draft Recommendation Rec(2005) . . . of the Committee of Ministers to member states on the European Prison Rules and Commentary.

free citizens. They appreciated this as a welcome normalisation. It gave an additional dimension of normality when the prison church started to invite citizens from the free society to attend church services together with inmates at regular intervals. Inmates were quite proud when they could see locals flocking to their church, filling it to capacity every time (Engbo 2010, p. 166).

Digital Life

Mobile phones and Internet access are essential tools for everybody—except for prison inmates. Although it has been made possible in recent years for inmates in open prisons in Denmark to use those digital communication tools to a limited extent, and inmates in closed prisons have been allowed access to a very limited number of Internet websites for education purposes, it is not possible to use email, social media, text messages and other digital communication tools. In this respect, the conditions for inmates are far from normal. Every day, the use of digital communication tools becomes ever more widespread among citizens (Smith 2012, pp. 464ff.), and the gap between conditions in the free society and in prisons widens. *Abnormalisation* increases every day.

Is there any particular reason to maintain, and gradually increase, this abnormality?

Yes, for few inmates full Internet access entails certain security risks, such as inmates convicted of downloading child pornography. However, the stronger the interference, the stronger the reason must be for the interference, and it is difficult to find good arguments to *generally* restrict the right of a large majority of inmates to use digital communication tools.

An application from a Lithuanian citizen who was denied Internet access for education purposes is currently pending before the European Court of Human Rights.[38] The judgment is keenly awaited because it is

---

[38] *Jankovskis v. Lithuania* (21575/08).

expected to answer the yet unclarified question of whether Internet access is a human right protected by Article 10 of the ECHR.[39]

For further information about this subject, see Smith (2012, pp. 454ff.).

Public Sense of Justice and Freedom of Expression

Several provisions of the Danish Sentence Enforcement Act provide authority to limit inmates' possibilities and rights out of regard for the public sense of justice.[40] Corresponding rules apply in Norway.[41] In Denmark, for example, this applies to inmates' freedom of expression, which is restricted by the prison management's advance censorship, the purpose being to assess whether statements made by inmates to the media would involve an obvious risk of contravening the public sense of justice and in that case to prohibit the relevant inmate from making a statement (Engbo 2005, pp. 179ff.).[42]

Is it possible in the free society to interfere with civil rights on the basis of a criteria as diffuse as the public sense of justice, or maybe other feelings? No, there are hardly any such examples. As regards the freedom of expression, all advance censorship is prohibited by the constitution, but in Denmark—as opposed to Norway—the Constitution is construed to have an 'implied limitation' applicable to groups such as prison inmates.[43]

Are there any good, professional reasons to create or maintain abnormality out of consideration for other people's feelings? Can the consideration for feelings justify interference with someone's rights? It is

---

[39] See, for example, De Hert and Kloza (2012).

[40] In some connections referred to as 'law enforcement'.

[41] Section 1-2 of the Norwegian Regulations to the Execution of Sentences Act on possibilities of social reintegration (*forskrift til lov om straffegjennomføring*) and Section 3-4 of the Act on placement in open prisons.

[42] Section 59 of the Danish Sentence Enforcement Act (*straffuldbyrdelseslov*).

[43] Report No. 1181/1989 on a Sentence Enforcement Act, etc. (*Betænkning nr. 1181/1989 om en lov om fuldbyrdelse af straf mv.*), p. 123.

difficult to see that interference with the freedom of expression should be justified by the regard for the incarceration itself.

The freedom of expression has been discussed in recent years in connection with the Mohammad cartoons controversy. There is common agreement that the freedom of expression also comprises the right to violate other people's feelings—in this case their religious feelings. This also appears from the case-law of the European Court of Human Rights as the Court has found that Article 10 of the ECHR protects information or ideas that may 'offend, shock or disturb'.[44]

It is clear that the threshold of infringement has not yet been normalised in the Danish prisons and adapted to the threshold of the free society. In most of the other Nordic countries, the normalisation of the freedom of expression is considerably stronger than in Denmark; in Norway it is total:

> Inmates are entitled to give interviews and have their photo taken. The Norwegian Correctional Service must make arrangements to make it possible in practise to exercise this right. The Correctional Service may fix the time and place of the interview having regard to the peace, order and security in the prison.[45]

In Norway, it is possible to stipulate requirements as to the practical performance of an interview, but not to its contents, and advance censorship is not allowed.

Hunting and Fishing in Greenland

An example of normalisation that is probably quite spectacular from a foreigner's perspective is the Greenlander inmates' active participation in hunting and fishing. In the Greenland culture, hunting and fishing are activities performed to provide food. As opposed to many other places in

---

[44] See, for example, *Handyside v. the United Kingdom*, 7 December 1976 (5493/72), § 49, and *Yankov v. Bulgaria*, 11 December 2003 (39084/97), § 129(i).

[45] Section 24 of the Norwegian Execution of Sentences Act (*straffegjennomføringslov*).

the world, they are not luxury or gaming activities. To mention an example, reindeer hunting has a prominent position in the Greenland culture. Each year in August and September, dozens of Greenlanders head for the mountains with riffles over their shoulders to bring home reindeer meat for their deep freezers. It is therefore natural that inmates at the institutions can go reindeer hunting in groups led by correctional staff. This is also an ardent example of normalisation of Greenlander inmates—and also an activity that serves to maintain and strengthen traditional skills that are very essential in a hunting culture.[46]

A Democratic Demand and an Aim of Prison Policy

In summary, according to the predominant Nordic sources of law, the requirement of normalisation emanates indirectly from the applicable definition of a prison sentence, which implies that the only interference should be with the freedom of movement.[47] All other freedoms and rights are maintained, and it is an essential obligation on the authorities to avoid any interference with inmates' rights and conditions of life other than the restriction on the freedom of movement and the inevitable consequences of such restriction (defensive normalisation).

In supplement, the requirement of normality has a proactive approach by the requirement that prisons must create frameworks and facilities that will allow the individual inmate the possibility to live a life as normal as possible inside a prison. Proactive normalisation gives rise to a duty to act on the part of the authorities, whereas defensive normalisation entails a duty of non-interference.

Normalisation, whether defensive or proactive, is a direct obligation on the authorities. Normalisation is not something that the authorities

---

[46] To mention an example, four inmates and two correctional officers went reindeer hunting for five days in September 2014 in the mountains of Sisimiut. They brought home 14 reindeers.

[47] Report No. 1181/1989 on a Sentence Enforcement Act, etc. (*Betænkning nr. 1181/1989 om en lov om fuldbyrdelse af straf mv.*), p. 105.

may *choose* to practice. There is no alternative choice. Legislation does not provide the option not to apply normalisation in prisons. The few statutory exemptions from the principle of normality, for example when it comes to the freedom of expression in Danish prisons, is a political choice that is, in principle, contrary to the requirements and recommendations of international law.

Normalisation is not a tool or a strategy for social reintegration. The principle of normalisation is not built on speculative considerations of utility. Normalisation is an essential element of a democratically based prison regime which is opposed to totalitarian prison regimes in which inmates only have the rights and conditions of life—the 'benefits'—that the powerful prison management opts to bestow on them.

Normalisation is a democratic demand and an aim of prison policy.

Bibliography

Bronebakk, K. B. (2012). Hvis det var mitt barn [If it were my child]. In Y. Hammerlin and B. Johnsen (Eds.), *Festskrift til Inger Marie Friedhof* [Festschrift for Inger Marie Friedhof], pp. 45–53. Oslo: Correctional Service of Norway Staff Academy (Kriminalomsorgens utdanningssenter KRUS).

Christie, N. (1993). Modeller for fengselsorganisasjonen [Prison organisation models]. In T. Mathiesen and A. Heli (Eds.), *Murer og mennesker. En KROM-bok om fengsel og kriminalpolitikk* [Walls and humans. A book on prisons and criminal policy, published by KROM, the Norwegian Association for Criminal Reform], pp. 113–120. Oslo: Pax Publishing.

Engbo, H. J. (1981). Et nordisk kulturchock [A Nordic culture shock]. *Kriminalpolitik* (Crime Policy), Vol. 4–5, pp. 26–28.

Engbo, H. J. (1996). Defensiv og konstruktiv fængselssikkerhed [Defensive and constructive prison security]. *Nordisk Tidsskrift for Kriminalvidenskab* [Nordic Journal for Criminal Science], Vol. 4, pp. 257–265.

Engbo, H. J. (1997). Om behandling og anden fængselsservice. Er individualpræventiv nyttetænkning autoritær og menneskefjendsk? [About treatment and other prison services. Is individually based, preventive utility thinking authoritarian and misanthropic?] In *Fængsler: Administration, behandling og evaluering* [Prisons: Management, treatment and evaluation]. Report of the 18th Contact Seminar and the 39th Research Seminar of the Scandinavian Research Council for Criminology. Hirtshals, Denmark.

Engbo, H. J. (2005). *Straffuldbyrdelsesret* [Correction Law]. Copenhagen: Djøf Publishing.

Engbo, H. J. (2010). Fængselsfaglige udfordringer gennem 100 år: belyst gennem udviklingen i dansk fængselsret 1910–2010 [Prison challenges for the past 100 years: Illustrated by the development in Danish prison law from 1910 to 2010]. In M. Henze (Ed.), *Direktoratet for Kriminalforsorgen 1910–2010* [Danish Prison and Probation Service from 1910 to 2010], pp. 153–205. Centenary publication published by the Department of Prisons and Probation.

De Hert, P., & Kloza, D. (2012). Internet (access) as a new fundamental right. Inflating the current rights framework? *European Journal of Law and Technology*, *3*(3). http://ejlt.org/article/view/123/268. Accessed 6 September 2015.

Hammerlin, Y. (2008). *Om fangebehandling, fange- og menneskesyn i norsk kriminalomsorg i anstalt 1970–2007* [About prisoner treatment and the view of prisoners and humanity of the Norwegian Correctional Service from 1970 to 2007]. Oslo: University of Oslo, Faculty of Law.

Korn, R. R., & McCorkle, L. W. (1959). *Criminology and penology*. New York: Holt, Rinehart and Winston.

MacCormick, A. H. (1931). Education in the prisons of tomorrow. *Annals of the American Academy of Political and Social Science, 157* of Prisons of Tomorrow.

McCorkle, L. W., & Korn, R. R. (1954). Resocialization within walls. *Annals of the American Academy of Political and Social Science*, No. 293.

Rentzmann, W. (2011). *Sku' det være en anden gang?* [Maybe another time?]. Copenhagen: Nyt Nordisk Forlag.

Smith, P. S. (2012). Imprisonment and internet access. *Nordic Journal of Human Rights*, *30*(4), pp. 454–482.

Storvik, B. L. (2011). *Straffegjennomføring* [Sentence Enforcement]. Kristiansand: Høyskoleforlaget.

Subramanian, R., & Shames, A. (2013). *Sentencing and prison practices in Germany and the Netherlands: implications for the United States*. New York: VERA Institute of Justice.

Van Zyl Smit, D., & Snacken, S. (2009). *Principles of European prison law and policy: penology and human rights*. Oxford: Oxford University Press.

Prison Food in Denmark: Normal Responsibility or Ethnocentric Imaginations?

Linda Kjær Minke and Amy B. Smoyer

Introduction

All Scandinavian countries (Denmark, Norway, and Sweden) have incarceration rates below 71 per 100,000 inhabitants, with the notable exception of Greenland.[1] These rates are significantly lower than most developed countries and scholars have associated this trend with the non-punitive ideals of the Nordic Welfare Model. Indeed, the Nordic Welfare Model has been historically characterized by social cohesion and a substantial reallocation of

---

[1] Greenland - which is a semi-independent jurisdiction within Denmark - has an incapacitation rate at 208 per 100,000 inhabitants (http://www.prisonstudies.org/highest-to-lowest/prison_popu lation_rate?field_region_taxonomy_tid=All. Accessed on 15 December 2015).

L.K. Minke (✉)
Department of Law, University of Southern Denmark, Odense, Denmark
e-mail: lkm@sam.sdu.dk

A.B. Smoyer
Department of Social Work, Southern Connecticut State University, New Haven, USA

© The Author(s) 2017
P. Scharff Smith, T. Ugelvik (eds.), *Scandinavian Penal History, Culture and Prison Practice,* Palgrave Studies in Prisons and Penology, DOI 10.1057/978-1-137-58529-5_15

353

resources that perpetuates relatively small socio-economic differences between individuals (Kvist et al. 2012). In terms of criminal justice systems, these tenets suggest a system of corrections that is focused on rehabilitation and reintegration, not punishment (Pratt and Eriksson 2012; Pratt 2008).

However, in the face of global trends toward neoliberalism and the increasing diversification of Nordic society, the reality is that Scandinavian countries have begun to restructure their welfare systems in ways that reduce the "levels of security amongst their citizens" and create a "greater intolerance of and punitivism towards others" (Barry and Leonardsen 2012, p. 54; Mathiesen 2012). For example, zero-tolerance against drugs in the Danish prison system has led to an increase in the use of disciplinary punishment like solitary confinement (Scharff Smith et al. 2013). Similarly, gang problems have led to a more restrictive prison regime in Denmark. In November 2015, the head of the Danish prison staffs trade union claimed that a "throw away the key" model had been adopted to handle so-called "negatively strong" gang members. Shortly thereafter, the Danish Minister of Justice declared his support to this strategy by quoting Caesar: "one must spare the conquered and defeat the defiant" (Ritzau cited in Information, 12 November 2015). In short, contemporary Nordic penal regimes can more accurately be understood as Janus-faced: "one side relatively mild and benign; the other intrusive, disciplining and oppressive" (Barker 2012, p. 5).

This article explores the complicated character of Scandinavian corrections by describing variation in the food systems in Danish prisons. On the one hand, the benevolent, rehabilitative character is enacted through a regime that supports prisoners' autonomy by allowing them to shop and cook for themselves in circumstances that are not unlike community conditions. On the other hand, in remand centers, a centralized system of food that distributes food to prisoners in their cells is employed. In these restricted facilities, prisoners have little opportunity to cook for themselves and rely on the food prepared in the central kitchen.

To better understand these systems, we present data about prison food collected during our fieldwork and interviews with nine incarcerated women in Denmark. This analysis explores the gray areas between benevolence and punishment and seeks to better understand the extent to which food in Danish prison institutions actually reflects, or undermines, the central ideals of the Nordic Welfare Model. In addition to explicating how food is served, we describe what food is served. The fact that more than half of the remand population identify with a non-Danish ethnicity raises questions about the extent to which the menu's "traditional" Danish food is, in fact, normal for the people to whom it is served. Similarly, our data indicate that even ethnic-Danes do not find correctional food resembles regular community fare.

The disparate treatment of food in remand centers compared to prisons illustrates the assertions made elsewhere in this volume that remand facilities offer much more restrictive regimes than prisons for sentenced prisoners. Further, this data suggest that conditions are particularly harsh and unfamiliar for ethnic minorities and people with histories of substance use and addiction. These inconsistencies expose the vulnerabilities of the Nordic Welfare Model, and suggest that notions of Scandinavian Exceptionalism may be more cultural mythology than reality.

Danish Corrections: Organizing Principles

In Denmark, The Danish Ministry of Justice and the Directorate of the Danish Prison and Probation Service are charged with enacting correctional penalties. There are six central principles that inform the agency's management and operations of Danish correctional facilities. This chapter focuses on the two fundamental principles *normalization* and *responsibility*:[2]

---

[2] The other principles are *openness/transparency*, which includes that incarcerated people are giving opportunities to establish and maintain contact with their relatives and the community. The principle also includes supporting that the connection between prisons and the surrounding is strengthened. Finally, transparency is seen as the best defense against suspicion of abuse of power that might occur when a system and its staff are equipped with so much power as is the case within the prison system. The principle of *security* is to ensure the implementation of detention and to prevent inmates from committing new crimes in prison and during furloughs. The prison and probation service have to execute penalties and thus have to protect citizens against crime and inmates from abuse and harmful impacts from fellow inmates. The principle to *minimize interference* includes developing solutions which interfere as little as possible with the prisoner's life, and at the same time to ensure that the prison system is able to fulfill its task. Finally, the principle of the *optimal use of resources* includes that resources are used efficiently, flexibly, and based on need and to have a qualified staff that are able to fulfill their tasks in accordance with the principle of the program (Direktoratet for Kriminalforsorgen 1993 [Danish Prison and Probation Service]).

1. First, at every level of supervision and security, an attempt is made to ensure that prisons are organized in such a way that the conditions within the walls more or less resemble the conditions outside the walls (Danish Prison and Probation Service 1993). This principle of *normalization* reflects a human rights perspective that grants prisoners the right to autonomy and relative freedom. Normalization is reflected in several areas within the prison system and the Act on the Execution of Sentences ("Straffuldbyrdelsesloven"). For example, all incarcerated people wear personal clothing (not a prison uniform) and they maintain their voting rights during imprisonment. In several prisons, there is mixed-gender housing: Men and women live in the same housing units. Conjugal visits are permitted and incarcerated people are encouraged to work both inside the prison and in work-release to the community.

   Normalization is also enacted with the prisons' food systems that allow Danish prisoners to purchase food in a small shop located in the prison complex and prepare meals in kitchens located in the housing units, just as people do in the community. A small stipend from the State ensures that all prisoners have sufficient funds to purchase food, hygiene supplies, and personal items although, again as is typical in the community, individuals with poor budgeting skills may find themselves short at the end of the month (Minke 2014).

2. The second fundamental tenet of the Danish prison system is the principle of *responsibility*. The rationale behind this principle is that cleaning and catering services, which are often undertaken by inmate and civilian staff, actually reduce the ability of incarcerated people to manage their ordinary everyday lives after release. In order to promote individual responsibility, almost all incarcerated people are responsible for cleaning their own laundry and maintaining their housing units.

   Food and cooking are also a central piece of this equation. Incarcerated people in Denmark are responsible for cooking for themselves while imprisoned, although they may informally delegate this work to a peer in exchange for goods or services (Minke 2014). Whether the prisoner actually cooks their own food or negotiates a deal where someone else cooks for them, these culinary tasks are their responsibility. There is no cafeteria or chow hall nor staff to plan, prepare, or serve meals.

Danish Correction: Prisoner Demographics

With a prison capacity of 4,021 people, the 2014 average daily occupancy rate of The Danish Prison and Probation Service was 3,784, or 62 incarcerated people per 100,000 inhabitants. This figure includes 1,691 people (44.7 %) in remand centers, 1,213 people (32.1 %) in one of the eight open prisons, and 880 people (23.2 %) in one of the five closed prisons or closed sections in open prisons (International Centre for Prison Studies 2015; Danish Prison and Probation Service 2015). As is typical of correctional facilities around the globe, ethnic minority populations are disproportionately represented within the Danish system: While people of non-Danish origin comprise only 11.2 % of Danish society, they are 26.8 % of the prison population and are particularly over-represented in remand facilities.

As is described in Table 2, Column 5 ("Danish"), only 37.6 % of prisoners in Denmark's largest remand center in Copenhagen are of Danish ethnicity. In other words, about two-thirds (62.4 %) are of non-Danish ethnicity, compared to maximum security prisons (42.2 % non-Danish), minimum security prisons (24.3 % non-Danish), and halfway houses (12.6 %). There are several factors which can explain why the share of immigrants and foreigners are low in the less restrictive open prisons and halfway houses and extremely high in the remand centers. For one, many foreigners are individuals without any legal immigration standing in Denmark who will be deported shortly after being convicted of a crime and are, therefore, never transferred to a prison to serve a sentence. Two immigrants convicted of a crime who are legal residents of Denmark, but not citizens, are deported after the completion of their sentences. In light of their pending deportation orders, this group's risk of escape is deemed high and they are held in closed prisons. The disproportionate confinement of people of non-Danish ethnicity in the country's pre-trial remand centers reflects a systemic hesitation to release noncitizens awaiting trial because of presumed flight risks. In short, the non-citizen status on many foreign and immigrant offenders in Denmark increases their perceived level of security risk and decreases their access to less restrictive prisons. Finally, the

Table 2 Incarcerated people and people under supervision by Danish Prison and Probation Service by ethnicity on 11 November 2014[*],[**]

	Immigrant	Second-generation immigrant	Foreigner	Danish	Total	
	%				%	N
Open prisons	16.3	6.5	1.6	75.7	100	1.286
Closed prisons	18.9	8.1	15.1	57.8	100	898
Copenhagen prisons (remand centers)	13.2	9.4	39.7	37.6	100	574
Other remand centers	15.3	6.2	27.2	51.3	100	926
Halfway houses	8.6	3.3	0.7	87.4	100	151
Supervision (parole)	14.7	7.0	0.1	78.2	100	9.929
Total on 11 November 2014 %	15.0	7.0	4.7	73.2	100	
N	2.068	967	649	10.080		13.764

Note: Exclusive 42 people with a Danish *p*-number who don't have a permanent residence in Denmark.

[*]Justitsministeriet (2015, p. 2).

[**]Definitions: "Immigrants" are born outside Denmark. None of the parents are both Danish citizen and are born in Denmark. If there is no information about the parents and the individual is born outside Denmark, the individual is registered as immigrant. "Second-generation immigrants" are born in Denmark but none of the parents are both Danish citizen and born in Denmark. If there is no information about the parents and the individual has a foreign citizenship, the individual is registered as immigrant. When one or both parents are born in Denmark and get a Danish citizenship, their children will not be registered as second-generation immigrants. If Danish born parents keep their foreign citizenship, their children will be registered as second-generation immigrants. People of "Danish" origin are people who—no matter where they are born—have at least one parent who are a Danish citizen and born in Denmark. A "foreigner" doesn't have a Danish personal number and has no attachment to Denmark such as a tourist, an asylum seeker, or an individual without any legal permission to stay in Denmark.

disproportionate representation of ethnic minorities across the Danish correctional system reflects the universal role of correctional systems to confine marginal and vulnerable populations who are excluded from other systems of care and opportunity (Barker 2009, 2012; Wacquant 2008).

Danish Corrections: Description of Food Systems

As was described earlier, sentenced prisoners in Denmark purchase food from a prison shop and prepare their own meals in kitchens located in the housing units. While these self-catering systems in Denmark's open and closed prisons promote the principles of normalization and responsibility, the remand food systems do not offer the same opportunities for un-sentenced prisoners. Meals for people in remand centers are prepared in industrial kitchens either on or off site, depending on the size of the facility. The meals are then delivered on trays to prisoners in their housing units, where they eat in their cells or common areas.

The meal service in Denmark's remand centers clearly diverge from the principle of responsibility, as the confined are not allowed to shop, cook, or clean. While the incarcerated people who work in the central kitchen may be able to acquire culinary skills through this prison employment that could lead to jobs upon release, the majority of the remand population do not benefit from this opportunity. The catering mechanism undermines the principal of normalization as bedside food service is obviously uncommon in community settings. The food system's menu does, however, invoke a sense of normalization by featuring traditional Danish food. For example, in the Copenhagen remand center, the daily lunch is a typical Danish smorgasbord that is served on a cart by prisoner workers. Every prisoner is provided with slices of brown bread and then can select from several options, including sliced meats, pickled fish, cheese, pates, and sliced cucumbers or tomatoes—items which are staples of the Danish diet. Similarly, for dinner, prisoners are provided a prepared meal, usually Danish-style stew or meat and gravy, which can be warmed up in microwaves located on the housing units. Evaluation research of Danish prison systems that included several questions about food satisfaction found that there are huge differences in respondents' feedback based on type of facility (Table 3).

In this 2015 survey, more than half (56 %) of the incarcerated people within remand houses were not satisfied with the quality of prison food (Lindstad 2015). This rate of dissatisfaction was significantly higher than rates reported in the closed (32 %) and open (22 %) prisons. One explanation about the huge share of dissatisfied prisoners in remand houses may be the deprivation of responsibility and normalization. In these pre-sentence facilities, the State exercises nearly full control over prisoner food options, creating a combination of unpalatable food and a lack of autonomy that is a recipe for dissatisfaction. Smith's analysis of women's prison food experience asserts that, "Steak or spam? Prison food is prison food" (2002, p. 204), suggesting prisoners' evaluation of institutional food has less to do with the actual food than with the prison experience itself. Minkes' analysis of the self-catering system in a men prison confirmed that Danish prisoners, in general, are very pleased with the system of self-catering and that most prisoners appreciate the opportunity to prepare their own meals according to their taste and cultural diversity. Additional benefits include that prisoners' autonomy over the composition of their diets avoids complaints about prison food, which could lead to riots or other disruptions, and the tasks relating to cooking meals offer time-consuming activities in an environment often marked by boredom and listlessness (Minke 2014).

Table 3 Incarcerated peoples' opinion about quality of food in prison by facility type (Lindstad 2015, p. 15)

How satisfied are you about the quality of food?	Very satisfied/ satisfied	Not satisfied/ very unsatisfied	Don't know	Total
		%		
Closed prison	61	32	8	101
Open prison	65	22	12	99
Remand centers	41	56	3	100
Total %	53	40	7	100
N	1.229	916	160	2.305

Research about Prison Food

In addition to this country-specific research, there is a growing body of literature about prison food in Europe and North America that demonstrates how prisoners use food—in particular decisions about what, when, and where to eat—to express and negotiate power, resistance, and individual construction of self (Valentine and Longstaff 1998; Smith 2002; Godderis 2006; Brisman 2008; Earle and Phillips 2012; Smoyer 2014, 2015; Smoyer and Minke 2015; Vanhouche 2015). For example, Ugelvik (2011) conducted an ethnographic study at Norway's largest remand house in Oslo. In this facility, which houses 392 prisoners, all meals were delivered to prisoners from the central kitchen of a nearby hospital in metal food containers. Upon arrival to the remand center, the containers were wheeled to the units, where two prisoners were in charge of keeping it warm, serving it up on plates, and delivering it to individual cells. In direct violation of institutional policy, prisoners also prepared meals in their cells, using spices and homemade stoves to convert cafeteria portions into more palatable meals. Among immigrant prisoners, these cooking practices were also used to assert their ethnic identities and construct themselves as not-Norwegians (Ugelvik 2011). This strategy was interpreted by Ugelvik as an act of rebellion by incarcerated people against the remand center, the correctional authorities, and Norwegian society itself. Similarly, Smoyer (2015) describes how incarcerated women in the United States use food to resist institutional authority by hoarding food, conducting illegal food trades, and cooking in their cells, in order to be able to eat more food and a greater diversity of food, and also to restore some level of dignity and autonomy to their experience of confinement.

Methodology

Our qualitative research methodologies included participation observation and semi-structured interviews. Participant observation focuses on the meanings of human existence as seen from the standpoint of insiders and requires the researcher's proximity to the field (Spradley 1980; Wadel 1991; Denscombe 2007). The qualitative interview has the potential to gain knowledge, which is not enrolled in the researcher's pre-understanding, and to give respondents opportunity to get insight into the subjects' reality. Qualitative research interviews are thereby a well-chosen method to achieve a deeper understanding of how the world is experienced in order to interpret the meaning of the phenomena described. Prior to the interviews a guide was prepared to cover sequences of themes but the interview technique was semi-structured in order to follow up on specific answers and then change questions (Brinkmann and Kvale 2015).

Participant Recruitment, Data Collection, and Data Analysis

Data derives from a research project conducted in autumn 2014 during which time observations were recorded at three correctional facilities and nine incarcerated women were interviewed. The women were incarcerated in a remand center ($N = 1$), closed prison ($N = 2$), and an open prison ($N = 6$). Participants were identified through a process of convenience sampling. In the remand center and closed prison, the authors met with corrections officials to describe their study of prison food and then staff shared with information with incarcerated women who could volunteer, or not, to participate in interviews. In the open prison, after receiving permission from institutional administrators, the researchers spoke directly with the women about the study at a group meeting. The study was explained to the women and those who were interested in being interviewed about their experiences with prison food were asked to identify themselves to the research team. At all point in the recruitment process, it was made clear that the decision to participate in interviews, or not, would have no impact on the women's access to services or food in the prison.

All interviews were conducted inside the prison in a private space designated by the administration. All interviews were audio recorded after informed consent was obtained. During the consent process, express permission to audio-record was requested and participants were informed that if they would prefer not to be audio recorded, they could still participate in the study. All interviews were conducted in Danish by the first author. Following data collection, the interviews were transcribed and then translated into English. Also during the transcription process, all identifying information was removed including names, dates, locations, and any other information that might undermine the anonymity of the participants. Informed consent was verbal, not written, and no names or other identifying information was recorded in the course of data collection.

Using qualitative data analysis software (NVivo 9) to help manage and organize the data, thematic analysis of study data was conducted (Braun and Clarke 2006). Themes included ideas and topics that were identified in formulating the study's research questions and additional constructs that surfaced during the data collection and analysis. Thematic analysis, conducted initially by the second author, was reviewed and replicated by a graduate student research assistant in order to strengthen the trustworthiness of the findings. Both authors then discussed and explored apparent themes to construct meanings and interpretations that incorporated existing knowledge and their ethnographic observations.

Findings

All of the study participants self-identified as ethnic Danes. For the most part, their narratives about prison food reflected the results collected in previous evaluation (Lindstad 2015): Participants were decidedly negative about the catered food in the remand centers and described the self-catering systems in open and closed prisons as satisfactory. However, this qualitative data allows us to go beyond levels of satisfaction into a deeper analysis of participants' experiences with and perceptions of prison food. Specifically, these narratives complicate the idea of normal by pointing out that food systems constructed as normal are not necessarily so. Participants' descriptions of the catered meals provided in the remand centers highlight the lack of access to normal food in these environments, especially for people who identify with non-Danish ethnicities. Similarly, in prisons with self-catering systems, this food does not always represent "normal" cooking and eating, nor does it necessarily reflect the "normal" of participants' lives, many of whom have experienced irregular access to food in the community due to substance use and related income insecurity.

Remand Center/Catered Food: Not Normal

The qualitative data in this study all points to deep dissatisfaction with the catered meals provided in Danish remand centers. Taken together, these narratives describe an extremely abnormal food environment. Participants reported not eating for the first few days after arrest because the food was not appetizing and they were dope sick: "I also had withdrawal symptoms and no desire to eat" (IP5). The dirty conditions of their confinement also had an impact on their appetites:

> The walls in the cell are painted over, everything is smashed, the quilts are such ... not to criticize drug addicts, but with huge fire holes ... nothing is clean. The bed linen is filled with holes (...) At my wing we had a female prisoner from Thailand. She had a bad stomach and needed to go to toilet and she rang the bell. A prison officer opened the door and said to her she could pee and shit in her sink and she had to do so. (IP7)

Several women expressed this belief that some prisoners had used the sinks located in the cells as toilets and would not use the sinks, or drink water from the faucet, until they had the opportunity to conduct a thorough cleaning. In general, conditions in the cell, such as quilts and bedding, were described to be in a miserable state.

Unpalatable

Study participants describe the prepared meals served at Danish remand facilities in the evening hours as unpalatable. In a typical remark, one participant described the remand food in these words: "The sauce looks like pudding ... thick and flabby ... and it doesn't taste well" (IP4). Similarly, other participants described the served food as "stiff and uneatable" (IP2), reporting that the "chicken was really nasty and the pasta disgusting ... the vegetables were deep frozen" (IP5) and that the food would make them sick: "You get ulcers from them [the catered menus]. They are so spicy. It is not good food" (IP7).

The unpalatable food was largely attributed to poor preparation, including cooking food for too long and too far in advance. A participant who worked in the central remand kitchen described an extended cooking process: "The food is made and then cooled down...Sometimes it is frozen up and heated in the oven...On Sunday we get hamburgers made on Friday" (IP1). The result is that the food loses taste, emerging soggy, and perceived as lacking nutritional value. These narratives stress that incarcerated people disapprove of the readymade meals which are unappetizing after being reheated and not at all similar to what they would eat in the community.

Concerns about hygiene also made the food unappealing: claiming "you don't know how the food is prepared" (IP4), and suggesting: "those who cook spit in the food" (IP2). Because the meals are prepared in an industrial kitchen by people who they do not know or trust, participants were deeply suspicious of the food and many chose not to eat these dinners, especially when the food is unrecognizable:

> I got meatloaf with potatoes and sauce (...) and it was so disgusting (...) with gristles and lumps and the potatoes were not boiled and there was a hair in the sauce. It was so disgusting. I didn't eat anything...Throw it out...I found rubber gloves, screws and all sorts of weird things in the [catered meals] (...) The potatoes were always quite hard...all the meat was completely full of tendons and cartilage... I never touched it [catered meals]. (IP3)

This meatloaf was exceptionally bad, described by several women as the worst food served within the remand center, but even if this specific dish was atypical, the description speaks to a large sense of suspicion about the culinary system as a whole. In addition to describing the remand food as poor tasting and unclean, participants reported that the menu was comprised of food items that they would not normally eat in the community. For example, when asked to compare the meatloaf to the meatloaf eaten in the community, participants were unable to answer, reporting that meatloaf was not something that they would not typically eat on the outside.

One women described a lack of access to butter, a central staple of Danish cuisine: "You could choose from rye bread and oatmeal for breakfast (...) and no butter" (IP6). A vegetarian participant stated that she "couldn't eat the food they served such as black bread and cold cuts" (IP8). Similarly, another woman described her typical menu at home to include "tomatoes, cucumber, cottage cheese and other sorts of cheese. I never eat cold cuts" (IP1). Under these circumstances, normal could only be approximated by purchasing food from the commissary and these snacks were used to supplement the catered food.

Cell Cooking

Given their concerns about the taste, hygiene, and food selections on the catered meals, many participants reported preparing their own meals using food purchased at the prison shop and coffee makers:

> You can roast steaks on the hotplate. You can make pasta or potatoes in the kettle and make sauce afterwards. You can make everything such as pancakes...I cooked almost everything I ate outside. I had stolen an extra coffee maker, so I had two, so I could cook potatoes while I fried the meat. (IP3)

Similarly, IP4 described cooking hotdogs on the coffee plate in the remand center:

> You buy small things inside the jail that you can cook at the coffee machine like bread and sausages (. . .) You can do many things with a coffee machine like eggs and everything like that. There is even made a cookbook about how to cook on a coffee machine. (IP4)

While this cell cooking allowed women to prepare food that they felt tasted better and was safer, in terms of hygiene, preparing meals on the hot surface of a coffee maker does not reflect normal community practices.

Open and Closed Prisons/Self-Catering Systems: Normal-ish

Among the nine women whom we interviewed, reviews of the self-catering system were generally satisfactory and somewhat normal: "We get almost 900 DKR per week and that is plenty (. . .) And we get food at our working place. So it is a fairly good system. At our working place you can eat until you are full...pizza or burger and things like that" (IP7). However, their narratives about the self-catering system were not without considerable criticism. Specifically, participants raised issues about the shop, kitchen conditions, and described considerable cooking and late-night snacking in their cells. In their discussions about what they would usually eat when not incarcerated and the "outside" food that was brought to them by visitors, it becomes clear that the self-catering system is not all together normal.

The pricing and selection at the food shop was described as distinct from stores in the community. Prices were relatively high and items were never discounted or "on sale" as they often are in stores outside of the prison, and items were perceived to be of low quality or expired:

> At the small grocery store in prison, we weren't allowed to examine the groceries. It was quite stressful, you could not go and choose product, because you were behind a counter, and then you should say what you should have. You could not see the expiration dates, and it was always the last day products. We complained about it, but nothing happened. (P1)

The selection of food items was considered sub-standard, with shortages reported along with difficulties in purchasing fresh vegetables: "Often the prison grocery store are sold out of basic products such as butter, milk and eggs (. . .) but you can always have chips, candy and soda. If vegetables are not too old they are sold out. The selection of products should be healthier if they [prison authorities] want us to be healthier" (P3). So while the women appreciated their access to the store, the shop was not perceived as normal because of lacking of good and healthy products.

Similarly, preparation of meals in the shared kitchens was considered irregular. The kitchen was described as chaotic and busy, especially in mixed-gender units dominated by men: "Outside I had my own kitchen. In here...there are so many people [in the kitchen] and it causes stress in my head" (IP6). The knives provided for cooking purposes are tied to the wall for security reasons and this arrangement was perceived as unhygienic as the cord would often not be cleaned after coming into contact with raw meat.

The kitchen has everything you need. The only thing that is annoying is that the knives are stuck with wire, so it is limited where you can go. And there are so many people in here, and the wire goes in the meat. It is pretty disgusting. (IP3)

Because women felt the kitchen was dirty and unsafe, many chose to cook and eat in their cells, which considerably limited their self-catering options:

The first meal that I got when I came, was a can of tuna and a piece of rye bread because the kitchen was so disgusting, and it was so dirty that I simply could not cook . . . there was mega dirty in the kitchen. You should wash everything before you could use it. So I bought my own pans, and I even brought utensils from my home. (IP1)

As was described in the remand centers, some women used the warming plate on the coffee maker to cook eggs and meat, while others ate meals that required no preparation or cooking (i.e., bread and cheese, avocado, yogurt). While these cooking conditions may be considerably more flexible and accommodating than other prison settings (Smoyer and Minke 2015), frying hot dogs on the base of a coffee maker is far from normal Danish food circumstances. For many participants, opportunities to cook during the day—at work, church, or as part of activity programs—were their only chance to eat warm normally prepared meals.

Beyond meal times, women spoke about two different food-related circumstances. One was the evening hours in their cells. At approximately 21:00 women in the open and closed facilities reported being locked into their cells for the night. Several women, all of whom were taking medications in the evening that made them drowsy, went directly to sleep. Most women, however, stayed awake for several hours, knitting, watching TV, making phone calls to family, and eating:

I watch TV. There is not much to do. Clean up a bit. Talking on the phone. It is very sad when the door is locked. I am not so good at being alone. So if you have chocolate and other food stuff it is gone the next day.

Just to forget that you are in prison. That you cannot just go to the bathroom and things like that. The door is locked. (IP4)

Self-control and restraint regarding food was described as a challenge and many women described overeating during these evening hours. While long hours in institutionally mandated lock-down can hardly be described as normal, their activities, including late-night snacking, were not unlike what people experience in the community.

Food and Visitors

Food also played a central role in their visits from family and friends. Institutional policy allows these guests to bring homemade or "take-away" food to consume with their incarcerated kin. IP4 described sharing a much-welcomed McDonald's meal with her parents while IP1 remembered her daughter's salmon dish as the best thing she had eaten in ages.

> [In the remand centers] you sit in a visit room for three hours. It is exhausting. It is so tiring because you just sit down and talk and talk. But here [in the open prison], you can go for a walk around the lake [with visitors], or eat together in your cell. It is much more natural. (. . .) The best meal I have eaten in prison is the one my daughter brought in: salmon, avocado and lettuce. (IP1)

The distinction between the food they ate inside and what they could receive from family on the outside was clear and pronounced.

The Unfamiliar Normal

The food narrative shared by IP3 more closely approximated normal cooking and eating in large part because she was serving her sentence with her boyfriend, with whom she shared a cell and food resources.

At the time we are on a diet, but other times we snack at night (. . .) We watch movies and eat candy and have fun. (IP3)

This partnership afforded her companionship during the long evening hours and at all meal times. In addition, they were able to consistently pool their finances offering some economy of scale that expanded their resources. However normal their arrangement appeared, it was, in fact, not normal for her. IP3 described a life of food insecurity fueled by her family's poverty and her own drug addiction: "When I was outside, I took many drugs, so if it was that I was eating, it was always something quick and easy." Similarly, IP5 described growing up in a home without food and being forced to steal food as a child because her parents spent their money on drugs. Later her own substance use disorders continued this pattern of under-eating as she dedicated her resources to feeding her drug addiction: "I ate outside when I was hungry. I had a huge addiction. I had a habit of 3,000 DKR per day. Here it is very much better. I am used to not eating." IP5 appreciated the abundance of food in prison, but also found it disorientating. She didn't know how to cook and reported primarily smoking cigarettes and eating grapes and popcorn. In short, the middle-class model of shopping and preparing home-cooked meals embodied in the self-catering system did not represent the normal life experience of all participants.

Discussion

In spite of the Danish correctional system's stated goals to promote normalization and responsibility, these food narratives suggest that the correctional food systems in Denmark, especially in the remand centers, are far from normal. The meatloaf's undefinable gristles and lumps reflect the complete loss of autonomy experienced by individuals held in the remand to choose, or even to know, what they are being served to eat. This experience of not being able to choose what to eat undermines perceptions of personal responsibility as the prison assumes control over what individuals will eat. As such, remand food can be understood as a symbol of the fact that life has become restricted and independence and individualism denied.

Once the offender's case had been adjudicated and the appeal period has expired, she is transferred from the remand center to an open or closed prison to serve out their sentence. At that point, there is a shift in the narratives toward normal responsibility as the individual begins to shop and prepare her own meals within the self-catering system. This is generally a welcome change. Still, the normal that the system seeks to construct may be out of reach, especially for women living in mixed-gender housing units. Women reported being reluctant to share the kitchen with large groups of people, especially men who they perceived as dirty and unhygienic. Rather than negotiate these complicated "contact zones" (Earle and Phillips 2012), several women reported preparing simple uncooked meals in their cells and eating alone. Given this self-imposed isolation, opportunities to connect and cook with other women during the day at work and other activities, were welcomed.

The normal target was also complicated for women who had not experienced consistent food environments in their childhood or adult lives. The idea that three square home-cooked meals would represent a normal equilibrium for most incarcerated people denies the diversity and vulnerability of their lived experiences. Many women reported lives marked by poverty and drug addiction where access to food was sporadic. The Danish system ignores the reality of these lived experiences by suggesting that women require only a well-equipped kitchen to find their way back to normal. While these basic needs are an important starting point, the pathway to health and recovery requires multiple levels of intervention and support.

Those who had experienced food stability in middle-class lives on the outside also found the prison shop and cooking facilities unfamiliar. The celebration of normal food brought to them by people in the community suggests that even though they have shops and kitchens on the inside, their prison food options do not measure up to typical outside food. Their limited access to food was a constant reminder of all they had lost that served to reinforce their prisoner status and distance them from their healthy selves. In short, the prison food environment was an inadequate aberration for all participants, for many different reasons.

While the study sample did not include any people who identified with non-Danish ethnicities, these findings can still inform dialogue about the experiences of minority groups in Danish prisons, a population that is disproportionately represented among the confined. The disparate food experiences between the remand center and open and closed prisons suggest a two-tiered system is at play within Danish corrections. On the one hand, the remand centers serve as static institutions of confinement and punishment with little investment in rehabilitation. The food is neither normal nor responsible, served from a main kitchen to the prisoners' cells. On the other hand, the open and closed prisons for sentenced individuals offer an imperfect but dynamic food system that engages prisoners in the processes of acquiring and preparing their own meals. Given these two very different systems, it is worth noting that non-ethnic Danes are far more likely to be located in the remand center than the sentenced facilities. Is this merely a coincidence or does this disparity in correctional placement and food services reflect a growing division in Nordic society between those who are included in the "normal" and those who are not? If the Copenhagen remand center was 64 % ethnic Danish, instead of 64 % ethnic minority, would the conditions be the same?

This small set of data about the Danish prison experience offers a glimpse into the daily life in remand centers and prisons across the nation and the opportunity to consider the prison system's commitment to its core principals in the face of a rapidly diversifying prisoner population. If the same innovation and creativity that sparked the creation of the self-catering system 50 years ago is turned toward the remand centers, what would arise? Today, about 2.5 million people worldwide are being held in pre-trial detention in remand centers (Walmsley 2014). This incarceration is problematic for many reasons including the fact that access to health care and social services may be limited in pre-trial facilities (McDonnell et al. 2014). Resolving issues related to healthy food access in these environments is a step toward promoting wellness in these settings (Smoyer and Minke 2015).

Further, this sliver of Scandinavian life sheds light on the vulnerabilities of the Nordic Welfare Model more generally. The differences between remand centers, where most of the population identify as non-Danish ethnicities, and open and closed prisons, where the majority of the population are ethnic Danes, exemplify the growing differences between groups within Scandinavia and across Europe and challenge the equity of systems of reallocation and care among ethnic minorities and non-citizen residents. The question in a growingly diverse society is, what is normal, who has access to this ideal, and does the socially constructed normal reflect all individuals' visions of normal? This analysis encourages examination of the how normal is operationalized in corrections and other systems of social service and rehabilitation to better understand access to and perceptions of this central principal of Nordic welfare policy.

Finally, this data demonstrates that while, on the surface, self-catering prison food systems seem to exemplify claims of Scandinavian Exceptionalism, the pains of imprisonment are no less acute in these Nordic countries. The loss of personal autonomy intrinsic to the prison experience cannot be camouflaged by prison shops and open kitchens. This deconstruction of the mythology of Scandinavian Exceptionalism may offer considerable benefit by justifying prison food reforms in countries that more openly endorse the disciplinary goals of incarceration. When Nordic models are perceived as uniquely forgiving and charitable, their translation to other settings is nearly impossible. However, if they are understood as merely different strategies of confinement, if prisons with self-catering system are presented as an alternative way to punish people, then moving from catered cafeteria meals to self-cook kitchens may be more palatable to policy makers who want to improve health outcomes and expand programs of personal responsibility without sparing the rod.

References

Barker, V. (2009). *The politics of imprisonment: how the democratic process shapes the way.* Oxford: Oxford University Press.

Barker, V. (2012). Nordic exceptionalism revisited: explaining the paradox of a Janus-faced penal regime. *Theoretical Criminology, 17*(1), 5–22.

Barry, M., & Leonardsen, D. (2012). Inequality and punitivism in late modern societies. Scandinavian exceptionalism revisited. *European Journal of Probation, 4*(2), 46–61.

Braun, V., & Clarke, V. (2006). Using thematic analysis in psychology. *Qualitative Research in Psychology, 3*(2), 77–101.

Brinkmann, S., & Kvale, S. (2015). *InterViews: learning the craft of qualitative research interviewing.* Thousand Oaks, CA: Sage Publications, Incorporated.

Brisman, A. (2008). Fair fare?: Food as contested terrain in U.S prisons and jails. Georgetown. *Journal on Poverty, Law & Policy, XV*(1), 49–93.

Danish Prison and Probation Service. (1993). *Principprogrammet* [The program of principles]. Copenhagen, Denmark: Danish Prison and Probation Service.

Danish Prison and Probation Service. (2015). *Statistik* [Statistics]. Copenhagen, Denmark: Danish Prison and Probation Service.

Denscombe, M. (2007). *The good research guide.* USA: McGraw-Hill Education.

Direktoratet for Kriminalforsorgen. (1993). [Danish Prison and Probation Service] *Kriminalforsorgens princip program* [The Principle programme]. København, Denmark.

Direktoratet for Kriminalforsorgen. (2014). [Danish Prison and Probation Service]. *Statistik* [Statistics]. København, Denmark.

Earle, R., & Phillips, C. (2012). Digesting men? Ethnicity, gender and food: Perspectives from a 'prison ethnography.' *Theoretical Criminology, 16*(2), 141–156.

Godderis, R. (2006). Dining in: the symbolic power of food in prison. *The Howard Journal, 45*(3), 255–267.

International Centre for Prison Studies. (2015). *World prison brief.* Denmark: International Centre for Prison Studies.

Justitsministeriet [Ministry of Justice], Direktoratet for Kriminalforsorgen [Danish Prison and Probation Service], Koncernledelsessekretariatet [management services], Jura og statistik [Law and Statistics] (2015). *Indsatte og klienters etniske baggrund* [Inmates and clients' ethnic background]. Copenhagen, Denmark: Direktoratet for Kriminalforsorgen.

Kvist, J., Fritzell, J., Hvinden, B., Kangas, O. (2012). *Changing social equality. The Nordic welfare model in the 21st century.* Great Britain Policy Press.

Lindstad, J. (2015). *Brugerundersøgelsen 2014* [User Survey 2014]. Copenhagen, Denmark: Danish Prison and Probation Service.

Mathiesen, T. (2012). Scandinavian exceptionalism in penal matters: reality or wishful thinking? In T. Ugelvik and J. Dullum (Eds.), *Penal exceptionalism? Nordic prison policy and practice* (pp. 13–37). London: Routledge.

McDonnell, M., Brookes, L., Lurigio, A. J. (2014). The promise of healthcare reform in transforming services for jail releases and other criminal justice populations. *Health & Justice, 2*(1), 1–9.

Minke, K. L. (2014). Cooking in prison—from crook to cook. *International Journal of Prisoner Health, 10*(4), 228–238.

Pratt, J. (2008). Scandinavian exceptionalism in an era of penal excess. Part I: the nature and roots of Scandinavian exceptionalism. *British Journal of Criminology, 48*, 119–137.

Pratt, J., & Eriksson, A. (2012). In defence of Scandinavian exceptionalism. In T. Ugelvik and J. Dullum (Eds.), *Penal exceptionalism? Nordic prison policy and practise* (pp. 235–260). London: Routledge.

Ritzau. (2015). Pind vil sortere fanger i fængsler [Pind want to sort prisoners in prisons]. *Information den 15 November 2015*, p. 6.

Scharff Smith, P., Horn, T., Nielsen, J. F., Rua, M. (2013). Isolation i Skandinaviske fængsler [Solitary Confinement in Scandinavian Prisons]. *Tidsskriftet Social Kritik, 136*, 4–20.

Smith, C. (2002). Punishment and pleasure: women, food and the imprisoned body. *Sociological Review, 50*(2), pp. 197–214.

Smoyer, A. B. (2014). Good and healthy. Foodways and construction of identity in a women's prison. *Howard Journal of Criminal Justice, 53*(5), 525–541.

Smoyer, A. B. (2015). Making fatty girl cakes: food and resistance in a women's prison. *Prison Journal*. doi: 10.1177/0032885515596520.

Smoyer, A. B., & Minke, L. K (2015), *Food systems in correctional settings— a literature review and a case study*. World Health Organization. http:// www.euro.who.int/en/health-topics/health-determinants/prisons-and-health/publications. Accessed 15 December 2015.

Spradley, J. (1980). *Participant observation*. New York: Holt, Rinehart and Winston.

Ugelvik, T. (2011). The hidden food: Mealtime resistance and identity work in a Norwegian Prison. *Punishment & Society, 13*(1), 47–63.

Valentine, G., & Longstaff, B. (1998). Doing porridge: food and social relations in a male prison. *Journal of Material Culture, 3*(2), 131–152.

Vanhouche, A. (2015). Acceptance or refusal of convenience food in present-day prison. *Appetite, 94*, 47–53.

Wacquant, L. (2008 [1999]). *Fattigdommens fængsler* [Les prisons de la misère]. København: Socialpolitisk Forlag.

Wadel, C. (1991). *Feltarbeid i egen kultur* [Fieldwork within own Culture]. Seek A/S, Norge: Flekkfjord.

Walmsley, R. (2014). *World pre-trial/remand imprisonment list* (2nd ed.). London: University of Essex, International Center for Prison Studies.

International Centre for Prison Studies. http://www.prisonstudies.org/highest-to-lowest/prison_population_rate?field_region_taxonomy_tid=All. Accessed 15 December 2015.

Being a Woman in Mixed-Gender Prisons

Charlotte Mathiassen

Introduction

In this chapter,[1] I will examine the penal and mixed-gender practices surrounding female prisoners in Denmark and attempt to unfold how these practices both support and constrain the well-being and welfare of incarcerated women. I will examine the ways of how the practice of mixed-gendered prisons enables and restricts imprisoned women. In doing so, I will refer to Judith Butler (2004a) and her question: 'What, given the contemporary order of being, can I be?' (2004a, p. 58), which, in the context of this chapter, can be re-phrased as: What kinds of lives

---

[1] I want to thank Bronwyn Davies, Sebastian Mohr and Dorte Marie Søndergaard for valuable comments on an earlier draft.

C. Mathiassen (✉)
Aarhus University, Danish School of Education, Campus Emdrup,
Copenhagen, Denmark
e-mail: cham@edu.au.dk

are viable² for female prisoners in Danish prisons? Gender equality, which refers to both men and women having the same possibilities and rights to participate in societal life (I discuss this further below), is said to be a core value in advanced welfare regimes like Denmark (Bekendtgørelse 2013, https://www.retsinformation.dk/; Borchorst and Dahlerup 2003).³ However, whether and how gender equality is achieved in the Danish prison context is intimately connected to the ratio of men to women in each prison. It also depends on the professional practice in prison. It is therefore important to consider how this professional practice is co-constituted with assumptions about gender, normalcy and the reasons why women commit crime. Female prisoners in Denmark represent a marked gendered minority; so, in this chapter, I will ask what this means for the principle of gender equality in Danish prisons.

Female Prisoners—Visible in Research and Prison Practice?

It has been argued in Scandinavia and more widely that women prisoners risk being silenced in research (Smoyer 2015; Kriminalforsorgen 2011; Kriminalomsorgen 2015; Lund-Sørensen and Clausen 2014; Mathiassen 2015a, b). According to Fuentes (2013), the lived experiences of women in American prisons receive little scholarly attention, and this is also the case in several other countries. Furthermore, women have often been excluded from statistical surveys. Pemberton (2013) formulates the matter in relation to female prisoners in the United States and England as follows:

> One source of informal sex/gender discipline lies in the far smaller numbers of female than male prisoners which means that there are

---

² Butler (2004a) uses the concepts 'viable lives' and 'liveable lives' interchangeably. For the sake of clarity I primarily use 'viable lives'.

³ https://www.retsinformation.dk/Forms/R0710.aspx?id=160578.

relatively few women's prison and that female prisoners receive little attention. (Pemberton 2013, p. 166)

Apart from in Scandinavia, the number of women prisoners is increasing across the world (Moore and Scraton 2016). However, women prisoners still represent a minority compared with male prisoners (J van den Berg et al. 2011; Bosworth and Carrabine 2001; Smoyer 2015; Friestad et al. 2014, p. 1). Although the numbers vary across countries, according to Fair (2009), women prisoners usually make up between 2 and 9 % of a country's overall prison population.[4] Within Europe, the numbers vary between different jurisdictions, which is also the case in the Nordic countries. In Iceland, approximately 3 % of the prison population is female, whereas in Finland, this figure is 7.5 % (ICPS 2015). Fair (2009) suggests that this variation is the result of different policies concerning the imprisonment of women; for example, in some countries, women are given alternative punishments, such as electronic tagging or community service. In this way, the conditions and normative climate for living and becoming appear to vary considerably around the globe.

Female prisoners in Denmark have also lived a relatively invisible and silent life both in practice and in research. Until recently, there were no separate statistics on women in Danish prisons (Lund-Sørensen and Clausen 2014) and more systematic reports on the conditions and perspectives of Danish women were only released in 2011 (Mathiassen 2011; Kriminalforsorgen 2011).

According to Danish annual statistics on crime in 2014, the total number of women in prison was 87 out of a total prison population of 2,307 (3.8 %); and the total number of women on remand was 64 out of a total remand population of 1,324 (4.8 %) (Danish Annual Statistics on Crime 2014, p. 15). Therefore, in this chapter, women in Danish prisons form a minority population in a men's prison world. Given this

---

[4] In Hong Kong, Lichtenstein, the Maldives and Monaca, the proportion of women is more than 20 %, whereas in Grenada, St Kitts and Nevis in the Caribbean, the proportion is less than 1 % (Fair 2009).

minority voice, my aims are to describe how the female prisoner's living conditions are in prison and to critically discuss whether they are adequate from an equality perspective and within the frames of the welfare state.

Placement

Since there is no women's prison in Denmark, the Danish penal practice, in which men and women interact during daily prison life, can be classed as exceptional. In Denmark, there are five prisons housing women, which are named on the following map (Map 1).

Female prisoners usually serve their sentence in one of four mixed-gender prisons: Møgelkær, Horserød, Ringe or Anstalten ved Herstedvester; but, occasionally, a few women are sent to the high security prison in East Jutland. Female remand prisoners are placed in different mixed-gender remand prisons around the country, but my analysis in this chapter will focus on the four main mixed-gender prisons for convicted prisoners. Because Denmark is a relatively small country, the need for prisoners to be close to relatives or friends poses less significant challenges than in other countries in Scandinavia or worldwide; yet, despite this, as the Map 1 shows, Denmark still has a fair amount of relatively small prisons.

To inform my analysis, I will describe the four prisons in which women mainly serve time, and I will draw upon my research on the everyday life of incarcerated women in Danish prisons (Mathiassen 2011). I will also refer to continuous dialogues with prison staff and the prison and probation services as well as relevant statistics, research and websites for each prison (www.kriminalforsorgen.dk). The qualitative data in my own research comprises interviews with incarcerated women—which focus on their first-person perspective (Schraube 2013) of their experiences and observations—and interviews with staff (including civilians).[5]

---

[5] The citations from interviews are translated by me.

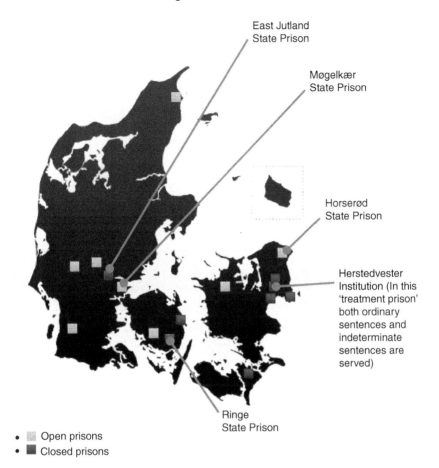

Map 1 Map of Prisons in Denmark. Arrows are added by the author

Source: Taken from www.kriminalforsorgen.dk

Mixed-Gender Imprisonment

The Danish mixed-gender practice in prisons is exceptional. In most other countries, men and women are either placed in separate prisons or women are placed in separate women's wings in men's prisons (Carlen and Worral 2004; Pemberton 2013); though, according to Carcedo et al.

(2008) and Fair (2009), there are mixed-gender prisons in Spain. There is also one mixed-gender prison in Vietnam (http://www.usp.com.au/fpss/pris-phonthong.html).[6] The literature on mixed-gender imprisonment is sparse. To illustrate the conditions in Danish prisons and to give more detail on the analysis of the possibilities of becoming women, I will now first elaborate on the rationale and/or reasons for Denmark's mixed-gender practice.

Historical Perspectives on the Danish Mixed-Gender Practice

The Danish Prison and Probation Services have fully accepted the idea of mixed-gender prisons since 2000, when the only women's prison in Denmark[7] was closed. This closure followed an inspection by the Parliamentary Ombudsman in 1998, which concluded that the state of the building was substandard (Frandsen 2011). When the prison closed, the women were distributed among the existing men's prisons. However, even before this, men and women were mixed in Danish prisons. Ringe State Prison was the first European prison to mix sexes in 1976 (Gazette 1980). The former governor Erik Andersen describes a rather liberal practice. Male and female could move freely both during work and leisure time. Intimate relationship remained a private issue for the prisoners. According to Andersen, the prison atmosphere in mixed-gender prisons was more relaxed than in the single-sex prisons and, in his opinion, these 'more natural conditions create less embittered and less neurotic prisoners, better able to adapt to society' (ibid.). So, in the mid-1970s, men and women were mixed in Ringe prison, and this was evaluated in positive terms.

However, prison conditions have changed over the last 40 years; the prison atmosphere has become more violent, and these violent incidents are being

---

[6] I do not claim that my search of electronic databases and Internet research uncovered all instances, but there is certainly little written about mixed-gender imprisonment.

[7] In Amstrup in East Jutland.

registered. Ringe prison has the highest rate of violent incidents (Lindstad 2014; Graa 2014) and prisoners are now (2015) less able to interact as freely as they did 40 years ago.[8] I shall now present some selected perspectives on gender equality in Denmark to clarify which normative powers and practices are productive in Danish society regarding rights and challenges for women.

Gender Equality in Denmark[9]

In general, the Nordic countries are known for being some of the most equal countries in the world. However, according to Borchorst and Dahlerup (2003), whilst the equality debate is continuing in other Nordic countries, it has stalled in Denmark. In a more recent analysis, Olsen (2014) argues that, until 2001, most politicians agreed that equality between men and women in Denmark had not yet been accomplished (Olsen 2014, p. 78). However, recently, right wing parties in Denmark have argued that, for the average Danish citizen, equality has—in most respects—been achieved (Olsen 2014, p. 29; 82). They have now included more groups in their equality target, namely minority women, women in prostitution and battered women. However, according to Olsen (2014), the concept of equality has historically belonged to the political left wing, and the left wing still argues that equality has not yet been accomplished and now also men and their inequality in relation to health and paternity leave, for instance, has drawn renewed attention.

The Ministry for Children, Youth and Gender Equality describe gender equality—understood as equal possibilities and rights in society regardless of sex—as a fundamental value in Danish society (http://www.uvm.dk/Ligestilling). However, according to the brief discussion presented above, it is still not clear whether equality has been achieved in Danish society. The Danish Equality Act should promote gender

---

[8] Because there are so few women in prison, the women's wing has been closed and very few women now serve time in Ringe prison.

[9] Danish women obtained the right to vote in 1915, which marks an anniversary for gender equality in Denmark. So, while writing this chapter on women in Danish prisons, we are celebrating the centenary of women's suffrage.

equality and entitle men and women to the same possibilities in all societal functions. One purpose of this Act is to prevent any kind of gender discrimination and another is '[to] counter harassment and sexual harassment' (§1). The conditions in the Danish prisons (described above) document that gender discrimination still exists in these institutions.

Gender equality contains two different dimensions. One dimension concerns securing men and women equal rights and action possibilities. The other dimension is more about *equal worth*, namely that the sexes are worth the same and should be treated accordingly. According to Udvalget (1999), this latter dimension demands a change in power relations between men and women if both sexes are to obtain the same status, because it is often assumed that women should be integrated on men's terms.

The challenge here is how to realize a concept of equality that implies equal rights and equal possibilities for women and men in mixed-gender prisons dominated by heteronormativity and where women were only 4 % of the total prison population. When it comes to sexuality, love and care, does this unequal distribution of men and women in the same institution demand that women remain abstinent in order to avoid discriminating against men? Furthermore, when the concept of equality demands equal (albeit different) worth for both sexes, how does one estimate and balance different proportions of dignity and worth? Before entering further into these challenges I will now elaborate on some theoretical concepts in order to perform a renewed analysis of my findings (Mathiassen 2011).

Active Subjects Living 'Viable Lives'?

Taking point of departure in Butler's fundamental question of which lives are viable and which lives are inviable (Butler 2004a, b; Boesten 2010),[10] I analyse the possibilities and constrains in female prisoners' everyday lives and their becoming during imprisonment. Butler urges feminists to remain vigilant against the state focusing more on sustaining its own power than on

---

[10] My reception of Butler's vocabulary and theorizing is partly inspired by Boesten (2010).

women's equality and welfare (Loizidou 2007). Furthermore, Butler argues that an understanding of women as only passive and repressed by power is a distorted understanding of how gender works. Rather, she asks us to consider women (as well as men) as gendered human beings formed by power and language (Butler 2004a). Furthermore, I argue that women participate in and are formed by concrete social practices in specific institutional arrangements, which is in line with Dreier (2008).

To a certain extent, Butler's theoretical stance which describes life as vulnerable (Butler 2004a, b) and people as active rather than passive resembles the more materialistic approach of activity theory and socio-cultural theory (i.e. Leontjev 1983; Vygotsky 1978; Valsiner and Lawrence 1997). These theoretical approaches underline humans as active participants in societal life. Authors within critical psychology (Holzkamp 1998; Dreier 2008; Schraube and Osterkamp 2013) empha-size that the human subject and institutional and socio-material struc-tures (including language and power) are intertwined. As such, people and their possibilities and constraints are intimately connected with the specific institutional arrangements in which they participate or even live. This calls for an analysis of how the human subject and her conduct of life is constrained and co-constituted with the interpersonal and social structures and dynamics in the institution—here, the prison.

Butler's work emphasizes how normative frameworks are powerful in both a constraining and an enabling way, and she asks what a person can be within a given order of being (Butler 2004a).

Norms both enable and restrict how the women in prison can live their lives and the analytical question in this text becomes: 'Which life or lives are viable for female prisoners in Danish prisons?' This question could be re-phrased as: *Which life or lives are viable within a given order or normative framework of being?*

Following Butler (2004a, p. 58), I will argue that it is necessary to understand the 'contemporary order of being' in the prison to under-stand which lives become viable for the incarcerated women. Boesten (2010) presents Butler's conceptions of normative violence, which describes that violence is produced upon the bodies that do not follow given norms and thereby excludes behaviours that do not adhere to the normative framework. In extreme cases, people who do not conform become 'non-existent' (Boesten 2010). When Butler uses the concept 'viable lives', it follows that there are boundaries of being (Butler 2004a, p. 56) and that some lives are not viable. The analytical question then becomes: *Which lives are or are not viable for female prisoners?* This gives rise to the empirical question: *How can one live a viable life in prison as a woman?* Answering this question demands a contextualized approach. It is important to consider the specific institutional conditions in prison because these conditions also define the 'contemporary order'. The theoretical frameworks mentioned above can help unpack the 'contemporary and situated normative frameworks that set the boundaries of being' (Butler 2004a, p. 56; Boesten 2010). A necessary step in establishing viable lives for women in prison is to make their lives and conditions visible and known by research for practitioners and politicians to continually reflect and develop prison practice. This chapter aims to contribute to such a step.

The Normalization Principle

According to rule 11 (a) in the 'Nelson Mandela Rules' (http://www.penalreform.org/priorities/global-advocacy/standard-minimum-rules/): 'Men and women shall so far as possible be detained in separate institutions; in an institution which receives both men and women, the whole of the premises allocated to women shall be entirely separate' (ibid., p. 8). Danish legislation does not, however, dictate that women and men be placed in different institutions. If a woman requires protection, she can be moved to a women's wing in remand facility. Such a move might not meet her general needs, but it might be necessary to protect her from sexual harassment and abuse.[11] However, often the women who are unsafe in mixed-gender regimes require services and possibilities that remand facilities cannot provide. So re-locating such vulnerable women may harm them even further. In this way, the normative decision to have mixed-gender prisons becomes a restricting condition for some

---

[11] Fieldnotes (December 2015).

women, and the problems this normative and institutional situation produces become an individual problem for individual women without any visible consequences on the structural and political level. The normalization principle, which states that, as far as possible, life inside prison should reflect life outside prison has been used both historically and recently as an argument for the Danish mixed-gender practice (Nowak 2009; Fair 2009; Frandsen 2011; CPT 2014; Mathiassen 2015a, b). The argument is that mixed-gender prisons reflect a more 'normal' (or 'natural', as Andersen says above) set-up than single-sex prisons. It is important to unpack the normative assumptions found in this argumentation.

According to Butler, '[n]orms provide the framework that guide life' (Boesten 2010, p. 4). The norms themselves imply change and to Butler gender is a norm which nobody can avoid whereby gender as a norm needs to be enacted in order for the individual to be recognizable (Butler 2004a). They enable some possibilities of living one's life and restrict others. By being performed repeatedly, norms are both produced and reproduced, and this occurs in powerful and influential ways. The individual can influence this process, but this influence should also be understood within the structural and discursive power structures. Inspired by a socio-cultural approach, one could say that the way people participate and negotiate can influence how norms are performed and changed. The so-called principle of normalization draws heavily on a heteronormative conception of 'normal' gender relations—women are supposed and expected to live with men because it is normal and reflects life outside prison—but this ignores other ways of expressing femininity and masculinity such as being gay, lesbian or transsexual. Furthermore, it affords both parties with certain ways of becoming, which are based on their individual ways of behaving but perhaps more on the (constraining) normative and institutionalized conceptions of the 'normal way' of living and doing gender. Like Butler, I do not intend to erase norms—on the contrary—but I follow Boesten (2010, p. 18) who argues that Butler 'seeks a normative commitment to equality' and that it is therefore necessary to 'expand to a normative framework that is inclusionary and nonviolent' (Boesten 2010, p. 18; Butler 2004a, p. 204). Here the conception 'nonviolent' means that norms should not enforce certain ways of living on people; norms should be without normalizations.

Even if one accepts the premise of the normalization principle, by itself, it is not an argument to support Danish mixed-gender practice. After all, forcing a gendered minority (approximately 4 %) to live in a total institution with a gender imbalance does *not* reflect life outside prison. The mixed-gender regime violates the principle of gender equality, because interventions to protect vulnerable women risk making them 'non-existent' and impede their possibilities of living viable lives.

It is also often argued that mixing genders in prison creates a more relaxed atmosphere. During my visits to Danish and Norwegian prisons, I often heard the claim: 'Women have a calming influence on the male prisoners (and female officers have a calming influence on the prison atmosphere)'.[12] On this line of argument, women are positioned as instruments to facilitate a pleasant atmosphere. It seems unlikely that using one sex as a 'tranquilizer' in this way supports the ambition of equality between the sexes. Instead, it seems to induce a certain social order in which the women are inferior, which, according to the Danish Equality Act, is an act of discrimination. Expecting women prisoners to calm down unruly individuals restricts women's scope and produces and reiterates stereotypical conceptions of both men and women. According to Butler (2004a), prisoners who do not adhere to these stereotypical gender expectations risk becoming non-existing because they violate dominant norms of how to do both man and woman in prison. I will now describe the diverse practice in the four main mixed-gender prisons in Denmark.

Women's Conditions in Danish Prisons—Diverse and Different

Danish prison practice is diverse. Each female prisoner has her own cell either in a women's wing (Herstedvester and Horserød) or either in a male or women's wing (Ringe and Møgekær). It varies between prisons on how

---

[12] I visited a number of Norwegian prisons during my employment at KRUS between 2005 and 2006.

freely women can choose their placement. In some prisons, children are allowed to stay at the prison until the age of three.[13] Some prisons also have family wings in which children can stay with their parent(s) for a period of time. Danish prisons are self-catering and the prisoners are responsible for making their own meals unless they are placed in the infirmary. They buy their food in a small grocery store within the prison. Sometimes the prisoners organize smaller groups that cook and eat together. The facilities for women-only work, craft of recreational activities—for example, sport or exercise classes—vary across prisons. Women are, in some places, employed in a laundry or (for instance) a sewing workshop on a female-only wing, but, women can also have ordinary jobs alongside other male prisoners (e.g. as a laundry worker, a gardener or a painter). Some women also attend the prison school or, if allowed, they attend school or go to work outside the prison. Some prisoners engage in heterosexual relationships and some get married. In some prisons, intimate contact between prisoners is allowed, a practice that, according to Carcedo et al. (2008), could improve the psychological health of female prisoners (an idea that I return to later in this chapter). Prisoners who were married outside prison can live together (Møgelkær) and couples who have met in prison and been together for longer than three months can apply for conjugal visits where sex is allowed (Anstalten ved Herstedvester); but this is not the case in all prisons and there is no overarching policy on how these visits are arranged.

In Ringe State Prison (closed), most women are serving sentences for drug dealing, whereas most men are serving sentences for violence and robberies. The male prisoners are typically younger than the women (the men are mainly in their 20s). Anstalten ved Herstedvester (a 'treatment prison') houses women who have been diagnosed with a severe personality disorder. Around a third of all the prisoners have been convicted of murder and around a fifth of the male prisoners have been convicted of sex crimes. The majority of prisoners are serving long—some even indefinite—sentences (http://www.anstaltenvedher stedvester.dk/Fakta-om-indsatte-2329.aspx).

---

[13] This necessitates an accept from the social authorities to secure the needs and interests of the child.

In Anstalten ved Herstedvester, more uniformed staff, psychologists and psychiatrists are employed than in any other Danish prison. In this 'treatment prison' both ordinary sentences and indeterminate sentences are served. Psychiatric, psychological, sexology and social assessment and treatment are in focus. The professionals are employed by the prison and probation service and work interdisciplinary. Prisoners are offered professional assistance in an attempt to reduce the risk of re-offending (Mathiassen 2016). Inspired by Ugelvik (2016), this offer of professional help can be viewed as the welfare state aiming to provide inclusive and ambitious treatment for all its citizens, including those in prison.

In Møgelkær open prison the women have both their own leisure and access to the rest of the prison and the different facilities. A relatively new initiative is the 'women's workshop', which is a women-only kitchen for women who do not wish to work in the mixed-gender workplaces. Here women are offered work and can study for parts of a degree course if they complete a training programme. This facility is influenced by a welfare ideology that aims to offer women assistance in an empowering process (Pollack 2000).

Diversity and Security in Mixed-Gender Regimes

Mixed-gender prisons offer different possibilities and constraints for female inmates, and politicians as well as professionals within the prison and probation services have begun to consider the standpoint that imprisoning men and women is different. The concept gender responsivity (Covington and Bloom 2006; De Cou 2002; Fair 2009) is not used in Danish penal practices, but, in recent years, a program specifically designed for women (Højdahl et al. 2013) has been implemented in the prisons where women serve. However, apart from this, women and men are offered the same programmes (e.g. cognitive skills and anger management). Different arrangements exist in different prisons for women with alcohol or drug dependency, sometimes for women-only and sometimes for mixed groups.

There have also been debates about whether Denmark should establish new institutional arrangements for female prisoners. The institutional changes (in Horserød, Herstedvester and Møgelkær) I have described above can be understood in the context of these debates. At this point, it is essential to consider the critique from the Parliamentary Ombudsman, the UN and a recent report (Lindstad 2014) which states that 25 % of female prisoners in Denmark experience harassment during their incarceration. These critiques and findings have accelerated the debate on the security of incarcerated women in Danish mixed-gender facilities.

One of the Parliamentary Ombudsman's key questions[14] was whether women were being forced into sexual relations and/or marriage by their male counterparts. Some of the males in mixed-gender prisons are, for instance, convicted of sex offences and severe violence which brings the subject of mixed-gender prisons to the fore and underlines the seriousness of the challenges associated with this practice because women who have experienced lifelong abuse often find it difficult to insist on their own right to choose (Heney and Kristiansen 1998; Kubiak et al. 2005). And women do also experience varying levels of abuse in other prisons in Denmark. The European Committee for the Prevention of Torture and Inhuman or Degrading Treatment or Punishment (CPT 2014) concluded that, in Ringe State Prison, according to both male and female prisoners, 'women prisoners were vulnerable to being exploited such as having to provide sexual favors to male prisoners in order to obtain drugs' (ibid., p. 23). The CPT report states that allowing male and female prisoners to share accommodation approximates the outside community (the 'normalization principle') and encourages prisoners to take individual responsibility (ibid.). However, they urge the prison to 're-evaluate the allocation procedures' (ibid.) and they urge the Danish authorities to 'take proactive measures to prevent sexual exploitation of prisoners' (Ringe Prison; especially those prisoners in mixed-gender wings).[15]

---

[14] He has visited Anstalten ved Herstedvester regularly.

[15] Currently (2015), the prison houses very few women and only mixes genders in a special treatment wing outside the ordinary prison.

Women as Active Participants—And Repressed Subjects

In prison, the structural arrangement is designed to exert disciplinary power over its inhabitants. In other words, it is part of the rationale of prison to rule and 'improve' subjects (Foucault 1977; Kriminalforsorgens Principprogram 1998). In Danish mixed-gender prisons, women live in this regime and handle its challenges as a gender minority. Moreover, several of the female prisoners are also burdened by a heavy social history, some are dependent on drugs (Kriminalforsorgen 2011), and Scandinavian research reveals that a considerable number of incarcerated women have suffered violence and sexual abuse (Amundsen 2010a, b), which is in line with international research (for instance Alarid 2000; Kubiak et al. 2005).

These different aspects of the incarcerated women's current and former life conduct can be understood as entwined dimensions which, in complicated ways, both enable *and* hinder the female prisoners' possibility to live viable lives. Does this mean that all women who are incarcerated in a men's prison do not act as agents but only as victims? According to the arguments presented earlier, prisoners do have some influence on their daily living and how they participate. One of the women in my research describes:

> He [her current boyfriend in prison] highjacked me rather quickly. [. . .] I know what it is like from the open prison where I served the first part of my sentence. I couldn't do anything without everybody knowing it. All the men watched you, because you were interesting, because I'm a young girl. All of them were ready to have sex with me [. . .]. But in this prison I did not experience this because the other prisoners respect my boyfriend in here. (Mathiassen 2011, p. 45)

This young woman explains that she protected herself from sexual harassment by engaging in an intimate relationship with a male prisoner who offered her protection, comfort and care. The other male prisoners, she says, respected *him*, and, through the men's mutual respect, she was enabled to live an acceptable life in prison. The normative power and social practices at work produced her as a potential sex object and she could only escape this category by accepting male protection. Furthermore, she explains that imprisoned women in general are coveted. Other women described similar experiences without engaging in intimate relationships with men.

Another woman underlines the comfort and intimacy she enjoys from her boyfriend in prison:

> I have a person with whom I can share sorrows and joys. To have a close person because you don't.... Basically you are alone in here. [When you have a boyfriend] you can get hugs. And affection. You miss that a lot, that which you can get from a boyfriend.... So.... (Mathiassen 2011, p. 42)

This woman describes how being with a boyfriend in prison enables her to live a life in which she does not feel completely isolated. She emphasizes that prison is a lonely place, which is in line with Esposito (2015), who concludes that loneliness is the most serious effect of being incarcerated (ibid., p. 154). In their own way, both the women quoted above illustrate that, by meeting a caring boyfriend, their lives become increasingly livable. In this way, they represent a type of being in prison which is both agentive and kept within the legitimacy given by the heteronormative frame—seemingly with repressive elements—because they need protection from other males and from isolation, respectively. In my earlier research (Mathiassen 2011), my general finding was that mixed-gender practices influence the everyday lives of several women because these women enjoy the affection they receive, because they get drugs for sex, or because they fear potential violence and dominance in prison.

One can ask how gender becomes productive and effective in this context? Using Butler's vocabulary, the institutional arrangements nourish a normative climate in which men to a certain extent gain access to harass women. This arrangement enables the women to live lives as 'subjects needing protection' and restricts the women's possibilities of empowerment. Women are not passive victims, but their scope of actions is structured within an influential heteronormative climate. Some of the prison officers I spoke to during my research were convinced that several conjugal visits in prison were to some extent forced sex or prostitution. They also argued that so-called loving relationships were simply a means for men to obtain easy sex in a male-dominated prison (a point also made in CPT 2014). When officers 'know about' but are not able to prevent prostitution and asymmetrical sexual relationships, this practice becomes implicitly accepted as the norm, irrespective of the Danish Equality Act. Moreover, women in Danish prisons are— by themselves and by staff—often depicted as gossiping, pleading for contact, hysterical and scheming (Mathiassen 2011). Also, when women prisoners are violent towards each other, this is sometimes portrayed as worse than the violence and harassment that occurs (or may occur) between men and women in prison. Drawing on Butler (2004a), the marginalization of women and the harassment of female prisoners cannot be combatted by only arresting men's violence towards women. It is necessary to combat normative and physical violence towards everyone who does not conform to the dominant norms (cf. Boesten 2010, p. 11)—a point that is also relevant when organizing female prison communities. In other words, normative and physical violence and harassment cannot be overcome by simply 'blaming the individual males'. If we do this, we adhere to a reproduction of the heteronormativity which itself can be described as normatively violent, and this seems to be a 'normalization of the male dominance'.

I understand why Carcedo et al. (2008) argue that allowing intimate relations in prison increases the well-being of prisoners. However, I interpret my qualitative empirical material and the other relevant cited documents in a way that calls for calm. If the prison and probations services still want to allow intimate relations in mixed-gender facilities, it necessitates a high degree of interference (CPT 2014).

I do not intend to contest that sex, love and comfort are essential parts of human life. On the contrary, it is well known that the loss of precisely these aspects is one of the several hardships of prison existence (Sykes 1958). What I have tried to argue is that, in mixed-gender prisons, several interests and repressive dynamics contest loving and sexual relationships.

Decent Life Conditions and Viable Lives?

Within the discourses of the prison and probation services, the explicit goal of activities and programmes is usually rehabilitation or successful re-entry into society (Maruna 2001; Maruna and Immarigeon 2004; Maruna et al. 2004). A successful re-entry into society means that prisoners do not relapse into criminal acts. I have chosen to adopt a vocabulary that shifts focus away from how one can improve the damaged individual or damaged individual life-skills towards how one can establish life conditions and institutional structures that facilitate women's possibilities of living viable or livable lives (Butler 2004a).

I would like to argue that the institutional and contextual conditions in the prisons described above do not support an egalitarian approach. Drawing on a relational understanding of 'empowerment' (Pollack 2000), I argue that some women in Danish prisons are unable to act as agents because they are to some extent locked in negative and exploitive relationships with men (and occasionally other women) who view them primarily as (potential) sex partners, girlfriends or people who can deliver other goods. Due to the 'non-egalitarian social conditions', some risk being arrested in their victimization instead of being offered structures and relations that would allow for other and more agential becoming. I argue that this victimization is being performed, either explicitly or implicitly, with an egalitarian ambition, namely the afore-mentioned normalization argument. Some women can live viable lives because they obtain not only comfort and intimacy but also protection. Others cannot. Knowing this one can ask, what is normal (normalizing principle) about maintaining an institutional arrangement which is not able to handle an often rather obvious need for protection among prisoners?

Returning to an idea introduced earlier, it is important to ask whether the mixed-gender practice in Danish prisons focuses more on sustaining status quo and (perhaps) the prison institution's own power than on the 'equality and welfare of the women'. If it does, then how is it possible for women to live their lives in dignity, which, according to Christiansen and Markkola (2006, p. 27), is a hallmark of the welfare state ideology?

A Women's Prison?

The majority of women in my research did not find the idea of a women's prison very attractive. One woman claims:

> I think it would be just terrible if this was a women's only prison. Because women are so mean to each other [. . .] The intrigues and so on. You cannot just sit down and have a good time. We cannot say what we need to say. It is because of envy. Maybe jealousy. (Mathiassen 2011, p. 54)

As I have argued elsewhere (Mathiassen 2015a, b), several women attribute the troubles and challenges they face to womankind. As such, they implicitly assert that male presence has a positive effect on the social climate in prisons. The woman above draws on the binary understanding of gender, which is challenged in Butlers approach but which is relatively common in the prisons I visited. As described earlier, women are often portrayed as gossiping and scheming subjects, both in a professional and a prison discourse. According to Pemberton (2013), prisoners gradually become 'self-disciplined gendered subjects' because they are continually assessed against such gendered norms which enable the women to become precisely this, and because of this understanding of gender influences the specific prison practice.

During my recent visit[16] to Horserød open prison, women described their relief that the atmosphere among the women had calmed down markedly after the prison decided to place the women in their own wing. They enjoyed being able to avoid sexual harassment and chants, and although they still faced interpersonal challenges, they described the female community in a more positive light (see also, e.g. Alarid 2000; Bosworth and Carrabine 2001; Fowler et al. 2010). This sentiment also came across in another institution:

> I think women are really nice to each other. They respect each other and communicate in a decent tone. I mean, you treat people the way you want to be treated yourself. I think it is nice [. . .]. In general every body has been nice [in the women's only wing, CM] and has told me how the rules

---

[16] December 2015.

function. Where to go to get my medicine on time. Where we were allowed to stay and where not. And how they actually thrived together. They have been so kind to inform me—all of them. (Mathiassen 2011, p. 79)

This woman was new and represented another female voice in the prisons I visited. She experienced a comforting and caring female community in the women's wing and thereby challenged the stereotypical understanding of female communities in prison. Acknowledging the challenges described in this chapter, the current arrangement produces and maintains gendered norms that do not support the ambition of equality, and it restricts the scope of possibilities for living viable lives. Following the line of argument in this chapter, it seems urgently important to design an institution and institutional practice that supports and accepts diverse ways of doing femininity and masculinity.

Following the line of argument in this chapter, it seems of urgent importance to design an institution and institutional practice which supports and accepts diverse ways of doing femininity and masculinity. Women do not 'need' males to organize their community but they do require assistance.

Following Pollack (2000), one could argue that, in a women's prison, it is possible to direct practices towards a feminist-inspired process that offers liberating positions for women. By gathering the relatively small number of women prisoners in one facility, it could be possible to offer differentiated programmes and activities. Interventions could be directed towards relational empowerment rather than individualized improvement of deficits due to earlier victimization. This requires active involvement from staff and room for different interventions and common activities where the prisoners focus on a common third (Mathiassen 2011, 2015a, b). However, having said this, some women are marked by neither victimization nor trauma, and the so-called resourceful women should also be able to find a relevant job or education during her time in prison. No female prisoner should be forced into taking a job that has no relevance other than passing the time. I argue that, if kitchen, cleaning or craft work does not meet the women's needs, then there should be other alternatives like bricklaying, carpentry or unskilled factory work.

Still one can ask: Is it even morally sound or fair to insist on offering such a marked minority special treatment in a men's facility (which represents the reality in Denmark)? Aren't male prisoners 'discriminated' against if they experience their female counterparts obtaining more favourable conditions (e.g. a lower level of security or more contact with their family and children)? Hereby, I wish to point out the sincerely problematic character of women being forced to live in facilities that do not meet their fundamental needs and which restrict their scope of viable living (Carlen 2002; Carlen and Worral 2004; Dünkel et al. 2005; Fair 2009; Moore and Scraton 2016). In mixed-gender facilities, the situation is complex, because men and women interact daily and gain a continual insight into each other's living conditions. If conditions for men and women diverge to the women's advantage, this could represent (potential) discrimination of imprisoned men.

I do not wish to suggest that segregating men and women is the only solution to conflicts, discrimination and security problems, but it seems a viable way to reduce some of the existing pressure of women prisoners, especially if it is combined with interventions and practices that focus on potential resources in female communities (Mathiassen 2011, 2005a, b). On the other hand, just segregating genders is not the most viable way to secure and accept diverse ways of doing gender. Prison is an institution regulated by relatively rigid power structures and firm norms. These can only change slowly and over time. Furthermore, women represent such a minority that it is likely to require a long and concentrated professional effort to make diverse ways of doing gender an accepted norm.

In this chapter, I have attempted to illustrate that, for women to obtain more equality in life as such and in relation to their male counterparts, it is urgently necessary to change the norms and mixed-gender practice in Danish prisons.

References

Alarid, L. F. (2000). Sexual assault and coercion among incarcerated women prisoners: excerpts from prison letters. *Prison Journal, 80*(4), 391–406.

Amundsen, M. (2010a). Kvinnelige innsatte og social marginalisering. *Spesialpedagogikk, 1*, 26–37.

Amundsen, M. (2010b). Bak glemselens slør. *Fontene Forskning, 1*, 4–15.

Beskæftigelsesministeriet, den 8. juni 2011. Inger Støjberg. Bekendtgørelse af lov om ligestilling mellem kvinder og mænd. (2013). https://www. retsinformation.dk/forms/r0710.aspx?id=160578, Accessed 1 February 2016.

Boesten, J. (2010). Inequality, normative violence and livable life Judith Butler and Peruvian Reality. *POLIS Working Papers 1.* School of Politics and International Studies, Faculty of Education, Social Sciences and Law, Leeds: University of Leeds.

Borchorst, A., & Dahlerup, D. (2003). *Ligestillingspolitik som diskurs og praksis.* København: Samfundslitteratur.

Bosworth, M., & Carrabine, E. (2001). Reassessing resistance. Race, gender and sexuality in prison. *Punishment and Society, 3*(4), 501–515.

Butler, J. (2004a). *Undoing gender.* New York: Routledge.

Butler, J. (2004b). *Precarious life.* London: Verso.

Carcedo, R. J., López, F., Begona Orgaz, M., Toth, K., Fernández-Rouco, N. (2008). Men and women in the same prison. Interpersonal needs and psychological health of prison inmates. *International Journal of Offender Therapy and Comparative Criminology, 52*(6), 641–657.

Carlen, P. (Ed.) (2002). *Women and punishment. The struggle for justice.* Cullompton: Willan Publishing.

Carlen, P., & Worral, A. (2004). *Analysing women's imprisonment.* Cullompton: Willan Publishing.

Christiansen, N. F., & Markkola, P. (2006). Introduction. In N. K. Christiansen, N. Petersen, P. Edling, P. Haave (Eds.), *The Nordic model of welfare: an historical Reappraisal* (pp. 9–30). Copenhagen: Museum Tusculanum Press.

Covington, S. S., & Bloom, B. E. (2006). Gender responsive treatment and services in correctional settings. *Women & Therapy, 29*(3–4), 9–33.

CPT/Inf (2014). Report to the Danish Government on the visit to Denmark carried out by the European Committee for the Prevention of Torture and Inhuman or Degrading Treatment or Punishment (CPT) from 4 to 13 February 2014. Strasburg: Counsil of Europe. http://www.cpt.coe.int/docu ments/dnk/2014-25-inf-eng.pdf. Accessed1 February 2016.

Danmarks Statistik. (2013). Kriminalstatistikken. DST.dk.

De Cou, K. (2002). A gender-wise prison: opportunities for, and limits to, reform. In P. Carlen (Ed.), *Women and punishment: The struggle for justice.* Cullompton: Wllan.

Dreier, O. (2008). *Psychotherapy in everyday life.* New York: Cambridge University Press.

Dünkel, F., Kestermann, C., & Zolonderdik, J. (Eds.) (2005). *International Study on Women's Imprisonment Current situation, demand analysis and 'best practice'*. Greifswald: University of Greifswald.

Esposito, M. (2015). Women in prison: unhealthy lives and denied well-being between loneliness and seclusion. *Crime Law and Social Change, 63*, 137–158.

Fair, H. (2009). International review of women's prisons. *Prison Service Journal, 184*(3), 3–8.

Foucault, M. (1991 [1977]). *Discipline and punish: the birth of the prison*. London: Penguin.

Foreign prisoner support service. Save a life. http://www.usp.com.au/fpss/prisphonthong.html. Accessed 10 January 2016.

Fowler, S. K., Blackburn, A. G., Marquart, J. W., Mullings, J. L. (2010). Would they officially report an in-prison sexual assault? An examination of inmate perceptions. *Prison Journal, 90*(2), 220–243.

Frandsen, L. (2011). Kvinder i fængsel. Folketingets Ombudsmands Beretning. http://beretning2011.ombudsmanden.dk/artikler/artikel5/. Accessed 3 February 2016.

Friestad, C., Ase-Bente, R., Kjelsberg, E. (2014). Adverse childhood experiences among women prisoners: relationships to suicide attempts and drug abuse. *International Journal of Social Psychiatry, 60*(1), 40–46. Epub 2012 Oct 8.

Fuentes, C. M. (2013). Nobody's child: the role of trauma and interpersonal violence in women's pathways to incarceration and resultant service needs. *Medical Anthropology Quarterly, 28*(1), 85–104.

Gazette Newspaper. (1980, November 13).

Graa, A. (2014). Ringe er det mest voldelige fængsel. In: *Fængselsfunktionæren*, (pp. 12–14). Copenhagen: Fængselsforbundet. www.faengselsforbundet.dk. Accessed November 2015.

Heney, J., & Kristiansen, C. (1998). An analysis of the impact of prison on women survivors of childhood sexual abuse. In J. Harden and M. Hill (Eds.), *Breaking the rules: women in prison and feminist therapy* (pp. 29–45). New York: Harrington Park Press.

Holzkamp, K (1998). Den daglige livsførelse som subjektvidenskabeligt grundkoncept. *Nordiske udkast nr, 26*(2), 3–31.

Højdahl, T., Magnus, J. H., Hagen, R., Langeland, E. (2013). 'Vinn'—an accredited motivational program promoting convicted women's sense of coherence and coping. *Eurovista, 2*(3), 177–190.

ICPS. (2015). *World prison brief.* London: International Centre for Prison Studies. www.prisonstudies.org/world-prison-brief. Accessed 5 January 2015.

J van den Bergh, B., Gatherer, A., Fraser, A., Moller, L. (2011). Imprisonment and women's health: concerns about gender sensitivity, human rights and public health. *Bulletin of the World Health Organization, 89,* 689–694.

Kriminalforsorgen. (2011). Udvalget vedrørende fængslede kvinders vilkår—Indstilling. (2011, September 12). http://www.kriminalforsorgen.dk/Betænkninger-mv-1645.aspx. Accessed 11 October 2015.

Kriminalomsorgen. (2015, January). Likeverdige forhold for kvinner og menn under kriminalomsorgens ansvar, https://www.kriminalomsorgen.no/getfile.php/2970352.823.yrvxftvbae/Kvinnerapporten.pdf. Accessed 12 February 2016.

Kriminalforsorgens principprogram. (1998). København: Direktoratet for Kriminalforsorgen.

Kubiak, S. P., Hanna, J., Balton, M. (2005). I came to prison to do my time—not to get raped, coping within the institutional setting. *Stress, Trauma and Crisis, 8,* 157–177.

Lindstad, J. M. (2014). *Brugerundersøgelsen 2013. Indsatte I fængsler og arresthuse.* København: Kriminalforsorgen.

Leontjev, A. N. (1983). *Virksomhed, bevidsthed, personlighed.* USSR: Sputnik/Progres.

Loizidou, E. (2007). *Judith Butler: Ethics, law, politics.* New York: Cavendish publishing.

Lund-Sørensen, N., & Clausen, S. (2014). *Klientundersøgelsen. Delrapport om kvinder.* København: Kriminalforsorgen.

Maruna, S. (2001). *Making good. How ex-convicts reform and rebuild their lives.* Washington, DC: American Psychological Association.

Maruna, S., & Immarigeon, R. (2004). *After crime and punishment. Pathways to offender reintegration.* Devon: Willan Publishing.

Maruna, S., Immarigeon, R., & LeBel, T. (2004). Ex-offender reintegration: Theory and practice. In S. Maruna and R. Immarigeon (Eds.), *After crime and punishment: Pathways to ex-offender reintegration.* Devon: Willan Publishing.

Mathiassen, C. (2011). *Perspektiver på kvinders dagligdag i Danske fængsler. Erfaringer med kvinders og mænds fælles afsoning.* Emdrup: Aarhus Universitet, Danmarks Pædagogiske Universitetsskole.

Mathiassen, C. (2015a). Kvinder, køn og tilblivelser—i fængsler. *Psyke & Logos, 36*(1), 79–110.

Mathiassen, C. (2015b) Kvindefængsel—et relevant alternativ? En deskriptivt baseret fremstilling *Psyke & Logos, 36*(1), 50-79.

Mathiassen, C. (2016). Nothingness—imprisoned in existence—excluded from society. In J. Valsiner (Ed.), *Nothingness: and its importance to psychology* (pp. 169–191). New Jersey: Transaction Publishers.

Moore, L., & Scraton, P. (2016). Doing gendered time: The harms of women's incarceration. In Y. Jewkes, B. Crewe, J. Bennett (Eds.), *Handbook on prisons.* (pp. 549–567). New York: Routledge.

Nowak, M. (2009). Promotion and protection of all human rights, civil, political, economic, social and cultural rights, including the right to development. Report of the Special Rapporteur on torture and other cruel, inhuman or degrading treatment or punishment UN, Human Rights Council, Tenth session, Agenda item 3.

Olsen, S. (2014). *Da ligestillingspolitikken blev skrinlagt—En anlyse af de politiske kampe om ligestillingsbegrebetfra 1975–2013.* Roskilde: Roskilde University.

Pemberton, S. (2013). Enforcing gender: the constitution of sex and gender in prison regimes. *Women, Gender and Prison: National and Global Perspectives, 39*(1), 151–175.

Pollack, S. (2000). Reconceptualizing women's agency and empowerment. *Women & Criminal Justice, 12*(1), 75–89.

Schraube, E. (2013). First-person perspective in study of subjectivity and technology. *Subjectivity, 6*(1), 12–32.

Schraube, E., & Osterkamp, U. (2013). *Psychology from the standpoint of the subject: Selected writings of Klaus Holzkamp.* Basingstoke: Palgrave Macmillan.

Smoyer, A. B. (2015). Feeding relationships: foodways and social networks in a women's prison. *Journal of Women and Social Work, 30*(1), 26–39.

Sykes, G. M. (1958). *The society of captives: A study of a maximum security prison.* Princeton: Princeton University Press.

Udvalget vedrørende det fremtidige ligestillingsarbejde (Udvalget). (1999). Betænkning om det fremtidige ligestillingsarbejde og dets organisering. Copenhagen: Statsministeriet. http://stm.dk/publikationer/ligestillingsar bejde/kap01001.htm. Accessed 16 October 2015.

Ugelvik, T. (2016). Prisons as welfare institutions?: Punishment and the Nordic model. In Y. Jewkes, B. Crewe, J. Bennett (Eds.), *Handbook on prisons.* (pp. 386–399). New York: Routledge.

Valsiner, J., & Lawrence, J. A. (1997). Human development in culture across the LIFE Span. In J. W. Berry, P. R. Dasen, T. S. Saraswathi (Eds.), *Handbook of cross-cultural psychology: basic processes and human development* (Vol. 2). Boston: Allyn & Bacon.

Vygotsky, L. S. (1978). In M. Cole, V. John-Steiner, S. Scribner, E. Souberman (Eds.), *Mind in society. The development of higher psychological processes.* Cambridge, MA: Harvard University Press.

The Limits of the Welfare State? Foreign National Prisoners in the Norwegian Crimmigration Prison

Thomas Ugelvik

The publication of the annual State Budget is always a significant political event in Norway, and the 2013 budget[1] (released on 8 October 2012) was no exception. One of the major new developments made public that day was the fact that Kongsvinger prison, until then an unremarkable medium-sized prison with both high-security and low-security wings serving the larger Kongsvinger area, would soon reopen as Norway's first all-foreign prison.

About a month later, the North-Eastern regional office of the Norwegian Correctional Services received a letter from the central Correctional Services administration office in Oslo.[2] According to the

---

[1] The 2013 budget is available at http://www.statsbudsjettet.no/upload/Statsbudsjett_2013/doku
menter/pdf/jd.pdf.

[2] Letter 12/7475: *Oppdragsbrev – Opprettelse av utlendingsenhet ved Kongsvinger fengsel.*

T. Ugelvik (✉)
Department of Criminology and Sociology of Law, University of Oslo,
Oslo, Norway
e-mail: thomas.ugelvik@jus.uio.no

© The Author(s) 2017   **405**
P. Scharff Smith, T. Ugelvik (eds.), *Scandinavian Penal History,
Culture and Prison Practice,* Palgrave Studies in Prisons and
Penology, DOI 10.1057/978-1-137-58529-5_17

letter, the target group for this new kind of institution would be male prisoners who had received a final expulsion order from the immigration authorities, and who were going to be either deported from the country upon release, or transferred to a prison in their country of origin to serve out some portion of their sentence there. The letter emphasized that although prisoners would be provided with services targeted at their specific status and situation, these services would be of the same quality as those you would expect to find in a Norwegian prison. Kongsvinger prison was explicitly *not* going to be a second-class institution.

Critics soon manned their cannons.[3] Despite the manifest good intentions, many felt that it was likely that Kongsvinger prison would become something other, and less, than a Norwegian prison. An institution catering exclusively to a foreign national prison population sounded to many as an excellent way to save money. Studies from other jurisdictions have shown that foreign nationals may be excluded from rehabilitation-oriented activities in prisons. Such activities are often in short supply, and foreign nationals are not given priority (Kaufman 2015). For critics and sceptics, this was bound to happen at Kongsvinger prison as well.

So what actually happened at Kongsvinger prison? Is it still, despite the fact that it is filled with foreign nationals who lack formal rights to many welfare provisions, what one might call a Scandinavian welfare state prison (Ugelvik 2015)? This chapter will explore the developments that followed the 2012 transformation of Kongsvinger prison. It is based on 4 months of fieldwork about a year after the change happened.[4] In addition to the

---

[3] E.g. http://journalen.hioa.no/journalen/incoming/2014/03/21/fengsel.pdf1/BINARY/Fengsel. pdf; http://www.nrk.no/ho/kritisk-til-utlendingsfengsel-1.11627543.

[4] This chapter is a result of the larger ERC-funded research project 'Crime Control in the Borderlands of Europe' headed by professor Katja Franko at the University of Oslo. It reports the findings from a comparative study of the so-called Aliens Holding Centre at Trandum (a closed immigration detention centre), and Kongsvinger prison. In 2013, I spent 40 days over the course of 4 months in each institution for a total of 80 days of fieldwork. I drew keys in both institutions, and could come and go as I pleased and talk with anyone I wanted to—detainees/prisoners as well as staff—without securing prior approval. The chapter is based on the data collected at Kongsvinger prison only. My fieldwork there was conducted about a year after the transfer to all-foreign prison status. It was still a relatively recent

discussion of Kongsvinger prison as a specific case, I will also develop the two concepts, 'crimmigration prison' and 'welfare state prison', further.

What Is a Welfare State Prison?

Before I take on the specific case of Kongsvinger prison, I will have to make a slight detour to give readers not familiar with the Norwegian prison system some relevant context. In Norwegian law, as in many other legal systems, a prison sentence is defined as a form of punishment, and thus as a penalty that is supposed to be experienced as an evil by prisoners (Christie 2007). But in the Norwegian Correctional Services policy documents, a prison sentence is also described as much more than that (Ministry of Justice 2008; Ugelvik 2011). In the current correctional services white paper, a prison sentence is, first and foremost, described as an opportunity, a potential arena for rehabilitation and successful reintegration. A spell in prison is supposed to change prisoners in a way as to make it less likely that they will return to the institution in the future, and more likely that they will choose to lead a different, law-abiding, life upon finishing their sentence. All aspects of the everyday life in a prison are supposed to be tailored to this future goal: to create a well-oiled and harmonious society where people can live in peace and prosperity through the successful transformation of individual offenders.

If the Norwegian prisons are ambitious social engineering machines, the welfare state is supposed to be the engine. The point is, through cooperation between a complex assemblage of different welfare state agencies, policies and practices, to provide aid and give opportunities to prisoners as part of their punishment in order to make them able to turn their lives around and recreate themselves as productive members of society. Welfare logics and welfare state agencies are integrated parts of the operations of the Norwegian prison service. The prison system is shot through with welfare state optics,

---

development that was regularly on people's minds and lips, but the prison had gone through the change and was beginning to exhibit 'normal operations'.

logics and policies to the degree that it makes sense, I think, to say they are full-fledged welfare state institutions.

The very use of the term 'welfare state prison', of course, is one that sparks controversy. Whether the Norwegian prison system should be considered to be part of the welfare state proper is a contested issue. 'Punishment' and 'welfare' are often taken to describe two separate branches of government that operates according to very different logics. Some people would argue that a prison, in its very essence, represents the opposite of a welfare state: to provide help, support and opportunities to subjects in a way as to ensure that they can thrive and prosper collectively, as a population (Foucault 2007; Ugelvik 2012). They see the provision of welfare and the implementation of punishment as two radically different kinds of phenomena. In this paper, I will argue that such a stance may be premised on a slightly naive and simplified understanding of welfare agencies being inherently benevolent and good, and a negative understanding of prisons as institutions that are exclusively preoccupied with the application of evils.

In addition to the infliction of a court-appointed penalty, a Norwegian prison service is supposed to fulfil the needs and create new future options for prisoners. The Norwegian government actually believes so strongly that a prison sentence should have ambitious future goals that they have made it a guarantee. The so-called 'reintegration guarantee' was launched by the Norwegian government in 2005. It states that any prisoner shall, when relevant, upon release be offered employment, education, a suitable housing accommodation, medical services, addiction treatment services and debt counselling. The slogan for what is called the 'seamless sentence' is that 'the prisoner belongs to the municipality before, during and after imprisonment' (Fridhov 2013), meaning that prisoners' home municipalities—the local government running the area where they are likely to live post-release—need to consider them a part of the populations for which they are responsible also during their sentence. The main goal of the guarantee is to decrease recidivism by strengthening prisoners' ability to live a law-abiding life. A key element is interdepartmental, intersectorial and interdisciplinary cooperation (Dyb and Johannessen 2011). The guarantee provides no new legal rights, nor is it a guarantee in any legal sense. Rather, it is a political and interministerial acknowledgement that prisoners' rights vis-à-vis the welfare state system is the responsibility of the welfare state as a whole, not just the criminal justice sector.

Successful welfare states need to be strong states to be able to deliver the comprehensive and multi-faceted welfare services that Scandinavian citizens have come to expect (Østerud 2005). These states are ambitious when it comes to the kinds and levels of welfare provisions they offer citizens (Rugkåsa 2011), and they are also ambitious when it comes to the sort of social engineering that is deemed possible and appropriate for them to engage in. The goal is not only to provide people with an amount of money that is enough to support them, but also to provide skills and abilities that enable them to become full members of the society they live in through their own efforts. Scandinavian welfare states deal in potential and opportunity as much as financial support. Social, education and health services aim to give individuals the possibilities independent of their class background. According to Kangas and Kvist (2013), such welfare states exhibit what they call an institutional model; they have institutionalized and professionalized a wide variety of different tasks and services, compared with what they call the residual model where the state is a provider of welfare as a last resort; a safety net when all else fails.

The distribution of aid, the gathering of information and the execution of social control are interconnected parts of any successful welfare system.[5] Welfare agencies are always also collecting information (power/knowledge) and asserting control, and prisons are also (at least some of the time) an arena for constructive meetings between public welfare agencies and welfare recipients. My argument, then, is based on an understanding of the relationship between welfare and punishment as blurred, and of welfare provisions and punishment as parts—sometimes overlapping and interconnected parts—of the same governmental power

---

[5] The Foucauldian division between sovereign power, discipline and governmentality is obviously not one that is mutually exclusive. The transition from sovereign power to disciplinary power that is described in *Discipline and Punish* (Foucault 1977), and that leads to a further transformation into governmentality in Foucault's later works (Foucault 2007), is not a transition from one form of power to another. Rather, he is describing a process where new technologies of power are added to the old ones to create an increasingly complex tapestry of interconnected forms of power.

toolkit (Smith 2009). In the following, punishment and welfare are not seen as different and mutually exclusive phenomena. Rather, any Norwegian prison is a practical articulation of a (sometimes harmonious, sometimes awkward and uneasy) mix of penal and welfare-oriented logics.

The Norwegian Way: The Principle of Normality and the Import Model

A vital part of the rationale of the Norwegian welfare state prison system is the so-called principle of normality (Bronebakk 2012; Ministry of Justice 2008); Engbo, this volume). It states that all aspects of life inside a prison should resemble life in society outside the prison walls as much as possible, with the obvious exceptions of the security and control measures that are necessary in institutions like prisons. Any deviation from this principle has to be based on an explicit argument. It also states that no prisoner shall serve her or his sentence under a higher security regime than what is necessary. Differently put, one could say that the punishment element of a prison sentence is supposed to consist solely of the deprivation of liberty for a period specified by the courts.

There is a dual logic behind this principle. In the Norwegian system, no individual right has been removed by the prison sentence. Prisoner retain the right to vote in general elections and the right to the various welfare provisions offered by the Norwegian welfare state system, including the right to free healthcare, social services and a secondary education.

The prison is also for pedagogical purposes supposed to create a life that resembles as closely as possible a 'normal' life outside the prison walls, to better prepare prisoners for what awaits them when they are released. The transition from prison to society can be difficult; prisons should be designed to make this transition as easy and as smooth as possible.

In practice, this is solved through the so-called import model, the brainchild of the late and great Nils Christie (1970). This model is explicitly understood as a direct result of the principle of normality

(Ministry of Justice 2008, p. 22). The Correctional Services imports services such as healthcare, education and cultural and social services from the external public welfare system on the other side of the wall. The prison healthcare system is thus part of the public healthcare system of Norway; the education department is part of the public school system. The prison librarian is hired by the municipality where the prison is located, and the prison library is part of a national system of public libraries. The Correctional Services is, in short, seen as a fully integrated part of the wider national welfare state system. Together with the various relevant state and municipal welfare state agencies, prisons are supposed to provide prisoners with the same level of welfare services that are available outside.

An important by-product of this model is that Norwegian prisoners in important ways may be said to still be included in the community outside; they are still acknowledged as citizens with important citizen's rights, even when they are serving a custodial sentence. The prison is part of the society surrounding it. The model also gives these public service institutions regular access to the prison, making the prison accountable to a wide range of potential critics on an everyday basis.

What About Foreign National Prisoners?

At this point I return to Kongsvinger prison and its transformation process. The prison, located about 90 minutes drive North-east of Oslo, is medium-sized by Norwegian standards. It has the capacity to hold 117 prisoners in total; 69 in the high-security unit behind the concrete wall here, and 48 in the low-security part of the prison between the wall and a much more climbable fence.

The Norwegian welfare state (including its prisons) to a large degree operates according to a logic of specific individual legal rights to welfare provisions. In most countries, some rights and benefits are reserved for people who possess full citizenship status. Traditionally, citizenship rights within the nation-state is marked by the exclusion of non-citizens (Benhabib 2004; Bosniak 2006; Newman 2013). This means that individuals who lack citizenship status may be legitimately denied the full enjoyment of social, political and civil rights. From this perspective, the dual process of inclusion of citizens and exclusion of non-citizens may be seen as an important part of the continuous reconstruction or reimagining of any nation-state (Abrams 1988; Anderson 1983; Neocleous 2003). And like Fredrik Barth (1996) has persuasively argued, border control is always at least partly about self-making. The imprisonment of foreigners may therefore be seen as part of a wide variety of different nation-state border control activities. What, then, happens to foreign national prisoners who lack these legal rights?

According to official statistics, 34 % of the prisoners in the Norwegian system are currently foreign citizens. The numbers are even higher among the prisoners in pre-trial detention; around two-thirds of detainees are at any time foreign citizens. Foreign nationals also spend more time, on average, in prison pre-trial. The rapid increase of foreign nationals in prison is not particular to Norway (Ugelvik 2014). Across Western Europe, we can see a transformation of the relationship between two previously separate branches of government that seem to be more and more interconnected these days, namely crime control and immigration control. A similar development in the United States famously prompted legal scholar Juliet Stumpf (2006) to use the phrase 'crimmigration control': Routine border control is becoming more and more like police work, and the police are spending more and more resources on border-crossing crimes and border control. Migration control and crime control are becoming like two sides of the same social control coin (Aas 2011, 2013; Pakes 2013; Zedner 2010, 2013). This development is making its mark on European prison systems. The advent of what I have defined as 'crimmigration prisons' is just one example. A 'crimmigration prison' is a prison or prison-like institution where immigration control and border control either (1) replaces or (2) is added to the traditional purposes of the institution. So, on the one hand, the term refers to prison-like institutions like some closed immigration detention centres; institutions that may look like a prison, smell like a prison and sound like a prison, but that are not prisons in the strict legal sense. In these institutions, migration control has replaced the traditional purposes of the prison, like punishment, deterrence and rehabilitation. On the other hand, I am referring to the special prison wings and even entire special prison institutions specifically designed to hold foreign national citizens only, like Kongsvinger prison. These institutions are formally and legally prisons; however, immigration control and border control has been added to the traditional purposes of the prison.

The question raised initially in this chapter may thus be rephrased and specified: What happens in a prison when you make immigration control a priority either in addition to or instead of crime control? What happens when welfare state-oriented prisons are filled with foreign national prisoners who lack formal rights to welfare? This question can be divided further into two related sub-questions: (1) How does the fact that Kongsvinger prison is an all-foreign prison impact the everyday reintegration and rehabilitation work that is supposed to happen in a Norwegian prison? And (2) how does the fact that Kongsvinger prison is an all-foreign prison impact prisoners' lives post-release? I will answer the two questions in turn.

Everyday Welfare in the Crimmigration Prison

How has the transition to an all-foreign prison impacted the everyday delivery of welfare provisions at Kongsvinger prison? Despite the fact that many prisoners in Kongsvinger prison lacks the right to anything other than emergency medical assistance (Johansen 2013; Søvig 2013), the institution did not immediately stop providing more advanced specialist healthcare services for prisoners following the change to status as an all-foreign prison. The Norwegian government has decided that foreign prisoners, regardless of residence status, are entitled to the full resources of the Norwegian healthcare system in the same way as an imprisoned citizen would be *while they are imprisoned*. For some groups of non-citizen prisoners—the most marginalized groups—the situation is, legally speaking, actually better inside a prison than it would be in the society outside.[6]

---

[6] This is complicated by the fact that there does exist a number of pro bono/NGO providers of medical services that seem to go above and beyond the legal minimum in practice (Johansen 2013).

Although it should be said that it sometimes is difficult to provide some forms of specialist healthcare services to prisoners due to language problems, these problems have nothing to do with the special all-foreign status of Kongsvinger prison. Language problems exist in all Norwegian prisons.

The education department also continued more or less as before the change. It did not close down, even though the prison was filled with people who lack the right to a free public education. The education department was told to stop teaching prisoners 'skills that would give them further ties to Norwegian society'. So they stopped teaching them Norwegian language skills, but started spending more time teaching them English instead. And they stopped teaching prisoners the Norwegian building code, but they continued to teach them how to build a house.

The prison library budget, however, did change. The municipal library service decided that they had to replace most of the Norwegian language books with new books in a number of different languages. In addition to buying thousands of new volumes, the library service hired a second librarian with Lithuanian and Russian language skills in a 40 % position. In some ways, then, the library service actually improved after the change.

As for work assignments, the prison still provides prisoners with a variety of different kinds of work opportunity. In addition to the kind of work that is important for the successful running of any prison, like cleaning and kitchen duty, there is a woodshop, a textile shop, a metal shop and a firewood crew producing sacks of firewood that are sold to the local community—quite a common work assignment in Norwegian prisons. One could, of course, ask whether this work gives prisoners relevant experience for their life post-release, but at least there are still (more or less) meaningful daytime activities available just like there used to be before the prison turned all-foreign national. And importantly, in an all-foreign prison, foreign prisoners do not have to compete with Norwegian prisoners over work assignments. This might be seen as an argument in favour of an all foreign nationals' prison: It might be good for foreign national prisoners to be spared the competition. The same is true when it comes to being transferred to low-security regimes. In other prisons, foreign nationals often have to serve the length of their punishment in high-security regimes, because their very foreignness makes them seem like escape risks.

Because Kongsvinger prison has its own low-security unit, foreign national prisoners here are not denied the opportunity to serve the last part of their sentence in a low-security regime.

What does the principle of normality entail for foreign national prisoners, the majority of which will be arrested and deported immediately after completing their sentence? Should the prison try to create conditions that resemble the life prisoners enjoyed in the Norwegian society prior to conviction? Or should the Correctional Services try to make the everyday life in prison resemble the many different future situations that foreigners from different countries around the world will experience post-release and post-deportation? Both seem like difficult (and potentially problematic) goals in practice. Although any Norwegian prison today will count foreign nationals among their prison populations, the range of different situations and lifestyles both pre- and post-release is wider in Kongsvinger prison than what is common in other comparable prisons. Some prisoners have been Norwegian residents for years. They may have completed an education from the Norwegian school system, or they may have a steady job. Some of them may have partners and children who are Norwegian citizens. Others may have only spent weeks or even just days in Norway before being arrested. They may have come to Norway from (other[7]) European Union countries with a specific goal of supporting their families back home by committing property crimes in one of the wealthiest countries in the world. Others still are failed asylum seekers hailing from the so-called third countries with experiences of armed conflicts and war. They may have led an unstable existence in the Norwegian asylum reception centre system, and some for years going through various appeal processes, before finally being turned down. Based on prisoner quality of life studies (Friestad and Hansen 2004; Nilsson 2002; Skarðhamar 2002; Thorsen 2004), Norwegian penologists are used to seeing prisoners as individuals drawn from more or less the same population of people with roughly the same characteristics. This understanding does not really apply to Kongsvinger

---

[7] Norway is not formally an EU member. Through the Norway–EU EEA agreement, however, Norway has access to the EEA area. It is also part of the borderless EU Schengen area.

prison. The range of different backgrounds is larger, and the situation that prisoners face upon release defies easy categorization.

For this reason, Kongsvinger prison seems, in practice if not on paper, to have informally reconceptualized the principle of normality to fit its foreign national prisoner population. 'Normality' no longer seems to refer to a normal life outside prison walls, the kind of lifestyle that prisoners will (hopefully) lead post-release. Most prisoners in Kongsvinger will go back to countries like Afghanistan, Lithuania, Nigeria and Romania. The prison knows very little about what kind of life they will lead. Nor does 'normality' refer to the set of legal rights prisoners had pre-release, rights that they are supposed to retain throughout their prison experience. Some prisoners have some legal rights vis-à-vis the Norwegian state as EU citizens, but many are third country citizens and thus lack the legal rights to welfare provisions that are the building blocks of the Norwegian welfare state system. Such a conceptualization of 'normal' would, in fact, have made it possible to argue for turning the prison into a second-class institution.

In Kongsvinger prison today, 'normality' refers instead to the normal situation in other Norwegian prisons. The prison and the various welfare state agencies it cooperates closely with have decided to emulate and recreate the normal Norwegian prison experience as closely as possible, with a few rather minor changes. The prison healthcare and education departments are basically the same as they were before; there were small changes to operations, but no cuts to either budget. The library budget actually increased. All in all, when it comes to the everyday life behind bars, this welfare state crimmigration prison is still, by and large, being operated according to the principle of normality—understood in the sense that the prison still provides prisoners with most of the welfare-oriented services that would be considered 'normal' in Norwegian society, and in other Norwegian prisons.

The Production of Future Welfare

But something did change for the worse with the opening of the first Norwegian crimmigration prison. Following the change, the explicit default assumption is that the foreign national prisoners will be deported upon release. Some rehabilitation-oriented programmes were seen as directly connected to the welfare system *outside* the prison walls and were therefore not seen as appropriate or relevant for prisoners who will not be part of that society anyway. This goes especially for programmes offered by the social services. Of course, working to provide newly released prisoners with suitable accommodation in Norway upon release seems like a waste of time, given that they are being deported. Norwegian studies have shown that employment post-release significantly lowers the recidivism risk (Skardhamar and Telle 2012). But the Norwegian social services currently has no programme to help prisoners find work or a place to live in another country.

In short, the question of deportability (De Genova 2002) has taken centre-stage when prison officers in Kongsvinger are making everyday decisions. From the perspective of prison officials, foreign nationals are increasingly being seen more like potential deportees than potentially rehabilitated members of society; as risks to manage and expel, rather than individuals with individual needs. This goes for all crimmigration prisons: prisoners are not supposed to be reintegrated back into society outside the prison walls. The whole point of a crimmigration prison is that the temporary exclusion in prison will be followed by a more permanent exclusion from the country or even from the entire Schengen area. Crimmigration prisons are thus part of the 'deportation machine' (Fekete 2005) more than they are part of any national correctional services rehabilitation machine.

This change affects prisoner–officer relationships in many ways. The 'model prisoner' is not any more just low-risk, readily governable and a good worker; he is also in practice deportable and ideally also motivated to leave the country voluntarily because voluntary return is cheaper than forced deportation. Furthermore, model prisoners in Kongsvinger prison hail from countries that are willing to accept them, and have helpful embassies that will provide the prison with new travel documents when these are missing or have been destroyed. Prisoner may be undeportable in practice for different reasons. Some countries refuse to issue travel documents, others simply take a very long time doing so. Communication between the criminal justice and immigration systems may also be poor, meaning that even in cases where prison officers are willing to help prisoners prepare for life post-release, relevant information may still be unavailable. As always, one arm of the state does not always know what the other is doing.

Studies from other jurisdictions have shown that foreign nationals are unlikely to be given release on temporary licence, regardless of the fact that they often have very good prison records (Bhui 2009; Kalmthout et al. 2007). This is not the case in Kongsvinger prison: the foreign national prisoners there seem to get early release as often as domestic prisoners. Unlike Norwegian prisoners, however, when foreign prisoners are released on licence, they are simply in most cases moved—often against their will—to a different country like a package and then just dropped. The ideal of a gradual release into the community under supervision by the probation service is seen as unattainable for foreign nationals. For the Norwegian correctional officers responsible for preparing prisoners for release, 'the whole rest of the world' seems to be an unknown and unknowable terra incognita. The result is that newly released prisoners are out of sight, and out of mind; somebody else's responsibility until they once again stray onto our territory. This might be a good or a bad thing, depending on your perspective on the usefulness of probation supervision, but is certainly not the kind of release process described by the welfare-oriented Norwegian prison system as ideal. From such a perspective, the Norwegian crimmigration prison does indeed seem like a second-class option.

Welfare State Crimmigration Prisons?

Are crimmigration prisons inevitably second-class institutions? Is the transformation of Kongsvinger prison an example of a more general tendency where a separate criminal justice system for foreigners is created (Fekete and Webber 2010), a system characterized by harsher sentencing practices and worse prison conditions? Is Kongsvinger prison today an institution where individual rights vis-à-vis the state are seen as irrelevant, and where prisoners are turned into what Agamben (1998), in contrast to politically and socially included nation-state citizens, described as 'bare life'? Following my 2013 fieldwork at Kongsvinger, I have had to admit that my fears were at least partly unfounded. When it comes to the everyday life behind bars, prisoners in Kongsvinger are still, as a rule, seen as the responsibility of the Norwegian welfare state. And the welfare state has, by and large, decided to not discriminate, but provide prisoners with the full force of the welfare regime available in other prisons. In a context where crimmigration control in general is expanding, this may actually result in some vulnerable migrants being exposed to welfare providers as well as punishment providers, or, as in this case, they may be given welfare provisions that would otherwise be unavailable as part of and intrinsically connected to serving a sentence. In some cases, prisons are sites where welfare agencies can reach hard to reach groups.

An important exception is some of the various programmes directed at providing prisoners with future welfare post-release. Even though the Council of Europe's European Prison Rules explicitly states that 'all prisoners should have the benefit of arrangements designed to assist them in returning to free society after release' (EPR §33.3), including foreign nationals, the Norwegian correctional services has not created alternative systems that would make it possible to help provide prisoners with suitable accommodation and a steady wage post-deportation.

The ties between the here-and-now in the prison and the post-release future are severed in the crimmigration prison. Prison officers' work revolves around the here-and-now. It is all about making it work, taking the edge off the pains of imprisonment. However, the long-term goals of rehabilitation and constructive social (re)integration are simply bracketed. The prison is no longer an ambitious piece of social engineering machinery. That does not mean that Kongsvinger prison has deteriorated into an Agambenian (1998) camp where all rights are forfeited and fellow human beings are turned into 'bare life'. The prison is still welfare-oriented; it still includes prisoners in the community of equal welfare recipients, but only temporarily. The point is to create a decent and humane institution *here-and-now*, not to create the future utopia any welfare system in the classical sense strives for on a global scale. Such a goal would, to be fair, perhaps seem a bit too ambitious for a single nation-state prison institution.

Strong welfare states are high-intensity information producers and consumers. Modern statistical techniques and the modern social sciences, in general, have to a large degree grown out of an increased governmental 'will to know'; a modern welfare state depends on the successful production and application of power/knowledge (Foucault 1980, 2007). What actually happens to foreign national prisoners on the long run? How do they manage, post-deportation? Has the stay in the Norwegian crimmigration prison experience been constructive somehow, or has the sentence left them worse off? The only possible answer at this time is that we do not know. Furthermore, it does not seem to be a priority for the Norwegian welfare state prison system to find out. It might in fact be the case that it suits the criminal justice system *not* to know. Part of 'seeing like a state' (Scott 1998) is deciding what *not* to see, what to overlook, and when to look in the other direction; what Mathews (2005) has called, with a Foucualdian paraphrase, power/ignorance.

In conclusion, is the Norwegian crimmigration prison still a welfare state prison, or has the change turned it into a different kind of institution? The answer is, as with all important and interesting questions, yes *and* no. When it comes to providing prisoners with a decent and humane prison environment and the welfare provisions one would expect in a Norwegian prison, Kongsvinger is, by and large, on par with other comparable institutions. But when it comes to the long-term rehabilitation and reintegration of prisoners, Kongsvinger prison has decided to not even try.

References

Aas, K. F. (2011). "Crimmigrant" bodies and bona fide travelers: surveillance, citizenship and global governance. *Theoretical Criminology, 15*(3), 331–346.

Aas, K. F. (2013). *Globalization & crime.* London and Thousand Oaks: Sage.

Abrams, P. (1988). Notes on the difficulty of studying the state. *Journal of Historical Sociology, 1*(1), 58–89.

Agamben, G. (1998). *Homo Sacer: sovereign power and bare life.* Stanford, CA: Stanford University Press.

Anderson, B. (1983). *Imagined communities: reflections on the origin and spread of nationalism.* London: Verso.

Barth, F. (1996). Ethnic groups and boundaries. In J. Hutchinson and A. D. Smith (Eds.), *Ethnicity*. Oxford and New York: Oxford University Press.

Benhabib, S. (2004). *The rights of others: aliens, residents and citizens*. Cambridge: Cambridge University Press

Bhui, H. S. (2009). Foreign national prisoners: issues and debates. In H. S. Bhui (Ed.), *Race and criminal justice* (pp. 154–169). London and Thousand Oaks: Sage.

Bosniak, L. (2006). *The citizen and the alien: dilemmas of contemporary membership*. Princeton: Princeton University Press

Bronebakk, K. B. (2012). Hvis det var mitt barn. In Y. Hammerlin and B. Johnsen (Eds.), *Festskrift til Inger Marie Fridhov*. Oslo: KRUS.

Christie, N. (1970). Modeller for fengselsorganisasjonen. In R. Østensen (Ed.), *I Stedet for fengsel*. Oslo: Pax.

Christie, N. (2007). *Limits to pain*. Eugene: Wipf & Stock.

De Genova, N. P. (2002). Migrant "illegality" and deportability in everyday life. *Annual Review of Anthropology, 31*, 419–447.

Dyb, E., & Johannessen, K. (2011). *Tilbakeføring av straffedømte*. Oslo: NIBR.

Fekete, L., & Webber, F. (2010). Foreign nationals, enemy penology and the criminal justice system. *Race & Class, 51*(4), 1–25.

Fekete, L. (2005). The deportation machine: Europe, asylum and human rights. *Race & Class, 47*(1), 64–78.

Foucault, M. (1977). *Discipline and punish: the birth of the prison*. London and New York: Penguin.

Foucault, M. (1980). Truth and power. In C. Gordon (Ed.), *Power/knowledge: selected interviews and other writings 1972–1977*. (pp. 109–133). New York: Pantheon Books.

Foucault, M. (2007). *Security, territory, population: lectures at the Collège De France 1977–1978*. Basingstoke and New York: Palgrave Macmillan.

Fridhov, I. M. (2013). Norge: Tilbakeføringsgarantien og forvaltningssamarbeid. In A. Storgaard (Ed.), *Løsladelse: Planlægning og samarbeid i Danmark, Norge og Sverige*. (pp. 26–33). Aarhus: Nordisk Samarbejdsråd for Kriminologi. 26–33

Friestad, C., & Hansen, I. L. S. (2004). *Levekår blant innsatte*. Oslo: Fafo.

Johansen, N. B. (2013). Governing the funnel of expulsion: Agamben, the dynamics of force, and minimalist biopolitics. In K. F. Aas and M. Bosworth (Eds.), *The borders of punishment: migration, citizenship, and social exclusion*. (pp. 256–272). Oxford: Oxford University Press.

Kalmthout, Av., Meulen, F.H.-vd, Dünkel, F. (Eds.) (2007). Comparative overview, conclusions and recommendations. In *Foreigners in European prisons*. Nijmegen: Wolf Legal Publishers.

Kangas, O., & Kvist, J. (2013). Nordic welfare states. In B. Greve (Ed.), *Routledge handbook of the welfare state*. (pp. 148–160). Abingdon: Routledge.

Kaufman, E. (2015). *Punish and expel: Border control, nationalism, and the new purpose of the prison*. Oxford: Oxford University Press.

Mathews, A. S. (2005). Power/knowledge, power/ignorance: forest fires and the state in Mexico. *Human Ecology, 33*(6), 795–820.

Ministry of Justice (2008). Straff som virker – Mindre kriminalitet – Tryggere samfunn. *St.meld. nr, 37*, 2007–2008.

Neocleous, M. (2003). *Imagining the state*. Maidenhead and Philadelphia: Open University Press.

Newman, J. (2013). Citizenship. In B. Greve (Ed.), *Routledge handbook of the welfare state*. (pp. 40–46). Abingdon: Routledge.

Nilsson, A. (2002). *Fånge i marginalen: Uppväxtilkor, levnadsförhållanden och återfall i brott bland fångar*. Stockholm: Stockholms universitet.

Østerud, Ø. (2005). Introduction: the peculiarities of Norway. *West European Politics, 28*(4), 705–720.

Pakes, F. J. (2013). *Globalisation and the challenge to criminology*. Abingdon and New York: Routledge.

Recommendation on the European Prison Rules (Rec(2006)2). (2006). Strasbourg: Council of Europe, Committee of Ministers.

Rugkåsa, M. (2011). Velferdsambisiøsitet - sivilisering og normalisering: statlig velferdspolitikks betydning for forming av borgeres subjektivitet. *Norsk antropologisk tidsskrift, 22*(3–4), 245–255.

Scott, J. C. (1998). *Seeing like a state: how certain schemes to improve the human condition have failed*. New Haven: Yale University Press.

Skarðhamar, T. (2002). *Levekår og livssituasjon blant innsatte i norske fengsler*. Oslo: IKRS, UiO.

Skardhamar, T., & Telle, K. (2012). Post-release employment and recidivism in Norway. *Journal of Quantitative Criminology, 28*(4), 629–649.

Smith, M. J. (2009). *Power and the state*. Basingstoke: Palgrave.

Søvig, K. H. (2013). Straffansvar og straffeforfølgning av humanitære hjelpere ved ulovlig opphold. In N. B. Johansen, T. Ugelvik, K. F. Aas (Eds.), *Krimmigrasjon? Den nye kontrollen av de fremmede*. (pp. 139–155). Oslo: Universitetesforlaget.

Stumpf, J. (2006). The crimmigration crisis: immigrants, crime, and sovereign power. *American University Law Review, 56*(2), 367–419.

Thorsen, L. R. (2004). *For mye av ingenting...: Straffedes levekår og sosiale bakgrunn.* Oslo: IKRS, UiO.

Ugelvik, T. (2011). Hva er et fengsel? En analyse av manualen til en sosial teknologi. *Retfærd, 34*(1), 85–100.

Ugelvik, T. (2012). Imprisoned on the border: subjects and objects of the state in two Norwegian prisons. In B. Hudson and S. Ugelvik (Eds.), *Justice and security in the 21st century: risks, rights and the rule of law.* (pp. 64–82). Abingdon: Routledge.

Ugelvik, T. (2014). The incarceration of foreigners in European prisons. In S. Pickering and J. Ham (Eds.), *The Routledge handbook on crime and international migration.* (pp. 107–120). New York: Routledge.

Ugelvik, T. (2015). Prisons as welfare state institutions? Punishment and the Nordic Model. In Y. Jewkes, B. Crewe, and J. Bennett (Eds.), *Handbook on prisons.* (pp. 388–402). New York: Routledge.

Zedner, L. (2010). Security, the state and the citizen: the changing architecture of crime control. *New Criminal Law Review, 13*(2), 379–403.

Zedner, L. (2013). Is the criminal law only for citizens? A problems at the borders of punishment. In K. F. Aas and M. Bosworth (Eds.), *The borders of punishment: migration, citizenship, and social exclusion.* (pp. 40–57). Oxford: Oxford University Press.

Part V

A View from
the Outside—Scandinavian Penal
Practice Under Foreign Scrutiny

In Search of Norwegian Penal Exceptionalism: A Prison Tourist's Perspective

Tom Vander Beken

Introduction

Between May 2013 and November 2014, I had visited 15 prisons in the United Kingdom, Norway, France, the Netherlands, Italy and Azerbaijan. These prison visits were the backbone of a project inspired by the travels and work of John Howard (1726–1790). Anyone interested in prisons ought to know who John Howard was. His countless visits to institutions of correction and of confinement all over Europe, and his books describing with exacting precision what he found (see, e.g. Howard 1791, 1792), were an eye-opener for 18th-century society and set people thinking about what prisons were like and what they should (or should not) be. Although he was a man of rather limited personal ambition or skill in

T. Vander Beken (⊠)
Department of Criminologie, Criminal Law and Social Law,
Faculty of Law, Universiteitstraat, Ghent, Belgium
e-mail: Tom.vanderbeken@ugent.be

© The Author(s) 2017
P. Scharff Smith, T. Ugelvik (eds.), *Scandinavian Penal History,
Culture and Prison Practice,* Palgrave Studies in Prisons and
Penology, DOI 10.1057/978-1-137-58529-5_18

427

terms of policymaking, his activities and publications had a great impact, which often ended up placing him in the foreground as a major philanthropist and prison reformer. In his books he describes and analyses detention and conditions of detention in a way that can be seen as an embryo of the work of national and international monitoring bodies of our day (Smith 2016).

This chapter is based on what I have learned from my prison visits in Norway. While John Howard has never visited Norway—and had no specific reasons to do this in his time—this country needed to be on my *State of the Prisons* list. In discussions about prisons and penal policies, Scandinavia, and Norway in particular, holds a special position. It is a part of the world where highly remarkable and even unique aspects are said to be in evidence. In an age in which prison numbers are swelling in almost every corner of the world, Norway has been considered a beacon of stability and less vulnerable to overcrowding problems. Besides this, the quality of prison life is said to be exceptionally good. Inmates are reported to enjoy outstanding detention conditions and are held in modern, often very small-scale prisons which in many cases have the character of open prisons. Especially the work of John Pratt, who also believes in prison tourism as a research method (Pratt and Eriksson 2012, pp. 236–237) and has put the Scandinavian exceptionalism on the table (Pratt 2008a, b, 2011; Pratt and Eriksson 2011, 2012, 2013; Ugelvik and Dullum 2012), has been the trigger for my journey to Norway.

Methodology and Design

The main idea of my project was to learn about the roles and functions of prison in today's Europe (Vander Beken 2016). I did this through reading, looking, listening, talking and writing throughout. The most valuable aspect of the process remained the travelling, however. In essence, this was the method that Howard used for *State of the Prisons* (Howard 1792): he washed around Europe, knocking on prison doors and stepping inside to see how prisons were run and what life was like there. He took note of what he saw and heard and later compiled it into thick volumes with the help of a few associates (England 1993; West 2011).

Since Loïc Wacquant concluded in 2002 that prison researchers (in the United States) were making too few forays in prison, carceral tours have become a real bone of contention. Some (Dey 2009; Huckelbury 2009; Minogue 2009; Nagelsen and Huckelbury 2009; Piché and Walby 2009, 2010, 2012) find that Wacquant was underestimating the limitations and disadvantages of visiting prisons: there is hardly a prison tour that is not essentially scripted, so that the visitor only gets to see that which is on-message. Nor should the many ethical dilemmas around prison visiting be disregarded (Minogue 2009; Piché and Walby 2012). There are also advocates of carceral tours, who insist that much can be learned from ethical designs of prison visiting (Pakes 2015; Wilson et al. 2011). They refer to the valuable insights gained from such prison tourists as John Howard, David Downes (1988), John Pratt (2008a, b) and Sharon Shalev (2013). I share the conviction of those believers in the potential of a prison tourism design that even in relatively brief visits, the prison visitor can form impressions and collate information that would be difficult to obtain in any other way. The visitor in person can use his own five senses to understand the world of prison, as well as being in a position to piece together much of value about the scene-setting that has gone on before his arrival and about which aspects it is that he has not been shown.

The foregoing view of prison tourism has strongly influenced the style and layout of the study. It is narrated as sort of a travelogue that digests visits to prisons in six European countries and is written up in the first person. This is not only very similar to the way Howard did it in his times, it is also my way of suppressing the ephemerality, superficiality and impersonalness that are otherwise part and parcel of the prison tourism format, or at the least my way of highlighting the inherent limitations of that format. This includes ethical considerations. Although carceral tours are largely about visiting particular locations, one cannot ignore the fact that they are, of course, also visits to specific people. Since the human contact possible during short visits tends to be of a passing nature and cannot be unpacked in the way that an ethnographer could manage in a monograph, the temptation is great in studies in the prison tourism mould to be highly vague in reporting on the actual people encountered, or even to draw the veil of silence over them altogether. Conscious of this, I have done my best to give the people I met, however briefly and superficially, an accredited place in the descriptions I have provided, together with an account of the experiences and emotions that meeting them evoked (Crewe 2015; Crewe and Ievins 2015; Liebling 2014, 2015). Nor are my rendezvous with my local guides, their interventions or the debates I had with them blurred into some general analysis or conclusions; they are explicitly presented as they happened, or as they were experienced.

For this paper, however, it was not possible to keep that level of depth and detail. The following sections only summarize some of the findings and conclusions on my visit to Norway (for a detailed account, see Vander Beken 2016, pp. 51–82).

A Land of Equality and Solidarity?

In John Howard's day, Norway had been subjugated to the Kingdom of Denmark for long centuries. Just like the other Scandinavian countries, it was thinly populated and for the most part not very fertile. People lived in small communities and there was no real social domination by any one group. The feudal structures that had imprinted most other European countries had barely been known in Norway. Life was organized in local structures, with prominence given to *likhet* (literally 'likeness' with a meaning sliding between 'equality', 'similarity' and 'sameness', see Ugelvik 2012, p. 125), the concept of equality and community-mindedness. The Norwegian aristocracy was abolished as early as the beginning of the 19th century. Solidarity and cohesion were the hallmarks of this society, which lacked any really great distinctions between its inhabitants. Like the rest of Scandinavia, Norway in Howard's time was not coping with an influx of foreigners; rather, it was experiencing emigration (Pratt 2008a, pp. 125–126; Ugelvik and Ugelvik 2013).

Until 1905, the crown of Norway was in a personal union with the crown of Sweden. Since then, the country has been an independent parliamentary monarchy with a preoccupation for equality, solidarity and fair sharing. When the country was plunged into the Great Depression in the early 1930s, it opted for a model of which social bargaining, government investment and a growing welfare state formed the central planks. This (costly) social welfare model worked, but from the 1970s onwards it came under pressure. Both ideologically and economically, the country's policy began to be readjusted towards the thinking dominant elsewhere in Europe (Christensen 2003). However, more than its Nordic neighbours, Norway was at liberty to carry on along its own trajectory. The huge oil reserves discovered in the North Sea, and later also in the Barentz Sea, made the country far less susceptible to external economic vicissitudes, so that only a minimal revisiting of policy was necessary in the 1980s and 1990s. Norway is a country keen to do a lot on its own, and is well able to do so. It has repeatedly chosen not to join the European Union, for instance, although it is a member of the European Free Trade Association (EFTA), the European Economic Area (EEA) and the open-border Schengen Agreement. As in other Scandinavian countries, political decision-making in Norway is largely consensual, rational and highly transparent (Bondeson 2005). Minority governments are very common.

However, recent years have seen palpable changes. Norway is no longer the paragon of equality that it was. Even in Norway, the gaps between income categories, and the levels of individualism, are on the rise (Pratt 2008b, p. 282). The Norwegians are beginning to look less of a homogeneous people, with gulfs opening up between the few and the many. A country with a long history of people seeking their fortunes elsewhere, it has now become a major immigration destination. On 1 January 2015, 32 % of the population of Oslo was of non-Norwegian origin (Statistics Norway 2015). This is giving rise to tensions and is putting the tradition of *likhet* under pressure. Immigration has become a massive political issue.

Bastøy Prison Tourist Island

In late March 2014, I end up in the town of Horten, a hundred kilometres South-west of Oslo to visit Bastøy. This is a prison island high on the agenda of prison tourists, often in a combined visit with the ultra-modern and exceptionally well-appointed prison of Halden. There is no shortage of reading matter about these prisons, and one can easily make a virtual visit, thanks to all the film clips available.

Around 115 prisoners live on Bastøy, some of whom have been sentenced for very severe crimes. The small *Vederøy* ferry boat, chugging back and forth, is the only link to the outside world. It is a waterborne prison gate. At night, the *Vederøy* remains moored on the island. Most of the prison staff are ashore overnight, leaving the inmates more or less to their own devices on the island.

At Horten quayside, I am immediately spotted and hailed by a prison staff member who will be my guide for the day. After about 15 minutes, we reach the island's pier. From there we make the trek on foot to the interior of the island. The first thing we come across to our left is a wooden cottage that serves as a visiting centre. Here, and here alone, inmates can enjoy a few hours relatively undisturbed with visitors from outside, 3 days a week. It has several rooms fitted out with furniture suites and kitchen facilities. It is very much reminiscent of a modest and not particularly well-maintained holiday home. Toys are strewn on the lawn at the back. From there, inmates can take their visitors to the beach at the north end. This is the only public corner of the island, and locals also come here on their own boats. Inmates are only allowed over here, in fact, if they are accompanied by visitors.

After a bracing walk past fields and woods, we reach the village. A sizeable building beside the church turns out to be the prison administration, the operating base for the staff. The reception desk itself would not look out of place in a minor post office. It is the place where new inmates are required to register when they first show up on the island. Sometimes, they have to twiddle their thumbs for a while or are directed to take a walk outside while their papers are put in order. It is typically a very surprising and memorable experience for those arriving from other prisons with stricter security regimes (Shammas 2014, p. 112).

As we walk around, I am told that Bastøy is chiefly a prison for those coming to the end of their sentences, who are transferred here from less open-type prisons. The aim is for them to relearn as well as possible how life is in the outside world. For some, however, Bastøy is the first prison they are dispatched to after trial. They arrive here straight from freedom, often a long time after sentencing. It would not be the last time during my journey that I would hear about inmates self-presenting, or about the waiting list for places to become free for inmates to turn up and serve out their sentences. A decade ago, there were almost as many convicts on the national waiting list as there were in the prisons (Shishkin 2003). In May 2012, there were 784 convicts on the waiting list (Council of Europe 2012, p. 14). While Norway is a country with just 72 people per 100,000 incarcerated as of 2013, the prisons there are pretty full up. Between 1992 and 2013, the prison population grew from 2,477 to 3,649, although the rate of increase slowed down in the last few years (International Centre for Prison Studies 2014). There is little exotic or exceptional about Norway in that respect. Even their plans to rent spare prison space in Sweden or the Netherlands or to repurpose old army bases as prisons sound very familiar to me (Alter 2013; Orange 2013). We Belgians rent prison capacity from the Dutch as well.

There are no cells on this island, my guide tells me. When unruliness does occur, they have to make do with handcuffs, and if things really get out of hand, the police are summoned by boat. I am told that the administration building has a room for 'unwell' prisoners, but I do not get to see it. On our way to the interior of the island, I saw a little medical services building and heard that any inmate on the island can be required to provide a urine sample for drug testing. My guides are quite taken aback that I find this unusual, and by my remark that there are plenty of countries where such a thing would not be permissible just like that. On Bastøy, there are isolation cells, one of whose functions is to hold inmates for a few hours who are unwilling or unable to provide urine. They are called 'solar cells', evidently because they allow generous sunlight in. The brochure at reception euphemistically calls these facilities 'individual recreation rooms' (Shammas 2014, p. 117). While it is not in the least surprising that there should be rooms of this kind in a prison context, I regret not being able to view them. Perhaps I should have read up more in advance—though I did not find reliable statistics on this afterwards either—and set out more clearly what I wished to see. Prison tourists who only form (or who only *can* form) their opinions on the basis of what they get to see and hear are liable to gain the wrong impression (Minogue 2009; Pakes 2015).

My guide and I walk outside for our tour of the island. First, we visit two buildings in which new arrivals are held. They are right beside the central facilities and have room for about 15 inmates. Typically sleeping several to a room, they have dedicated living rooms and a kitchen of their own. This is the first, but not the last, kitchen that I will see in a Norwegian prison on this visit. It is a Scandinavian tradition to let inmates cook for themselves if they want to. Throughout Norway, even in higher-security prisons than Bastøy, prisons have well-equipped kitchens for inmates. I spot large knives hanging from the wall that inmates would have no trouble in using—or in taking elsewhere.

Leaving the new arrivals' wing, we stroll past the church to the farmstead a little further down the track. The inmates working on this farm are dressed as farmers, too. One of them makes straight for us and shakes my hand. He launches into a passionate diatribe about animals, their care and the farm organization. We also call in at a horse stall, where a few more people are at work. Horses are essential to the running of the island and are looked after painstakingly. Outside, I can hear the whine of band saws. The trees growing in the woods are sawn down in the area around the farm. We call in at a fantastically well kitted-out woodwork studio, with a pair of inmates plying their craft, and a laundry.

It is time to visit the inmates in their living environment. Near the central complex, there are wooden cottages all along the dirt tracks, where the inmates live and where they are obliged to be between 11 pm and 7 am. During the day, they are supposed to be working and are free to move around at will. Roll-call is done four times a day. After work and domestic chores are done, inmates may do what they want. There is a great deal of fishing, and in summer they swim plenty in the fjord. This generates the photos of sunbathing and swimming prisoners that have gained notoriety all over the internet. My guide is of the opinion that it is as it should be that prisoners are allowed to do all that, but that people's image of this place has got out of all proportion. He tells me that things are being done nowadays to make sure that visitors do not merely document that aspect of life on Bastøy.

Five or six inmates share each cottage. I see lots of bicycles, the standard mode of transport on the island. My guide knocks on the door of one of the cottages and walks straight in. The television is on, and the wood-burning stove is making it quite toasty in the living room. Each inmate has his own bedroom, and there is a common room and of course a kitchen to supplement the canteen fare. The only inmate at home comes out of his room to meet us. We shake hands and talk about life on Bastøy. The conversation does not flow very well—and perhaps that's largely down to me. For some reason or other, I feel much more of an interloper, a voyeur even, than I ever have in the many prisons I have previously visited.

My visit to this prison has come to an end. It is with mixed feelings that I return to Horten. Naturally, I have seen and heard things remarkable for a prison, and of course Bastøy is a special case where inmates life in exceptional circumstances of confinement. But what have I really learnt from this visit about prisons and penal policy in Norway?

Kroksrud and Ullersmo

My next prison to visit is Kroksrud. This outstation of a larger entity, Ullersmo Prison, is a lower-security prison with a couple of dozen warders and around 60 inmates. Kroksrud is one of the country's open prisons at which convicts can serve out the final months of their sentences. Norwegian policy is geared towards housing prisoners nearing the end of their term in less heavily guarded settings, or even in completely open settings, so that the focus can gradually shift to the Return to Society agenda. In fact, Kroksrud does not even look much like a prison. The grounds are situated on the outskirts of a forest and are surrounded by a fence less than ten feet high.

The main building contains a little administrative office, an attractive kitchen and a canteen-cum-chapel. The kitchen contains a big freezer with an individually locked drawer for each inmate. Here, too, inmates can cook their own meals, though what there is not is a prison shop. Here, you simply go into town to do your shopping: two warders will drive a prisoner to the regular shops.

The inmates' cells are located in another single-level housing block. We find rather small rooms without their own toilets; those are down the corridor. Consequently, the cell doors are never locked from the outside, though inmates can lock themselves away from other inmates. In other respects, they come and go just as they please. We see no-one in the cell block: everyone is at work, whether onsite or offsite.

Opposite the cell block, we visit the dog kennels. Here, prisoners provide the initial training to dogs subsequently destined to be trained by the army in specialist tasks. The governor says that inmates love this work and put their all into it. The industrial building houses a large workshop in which inmates produce all manner of commodities in wood—right up to complete kitchens—which are sold in a shop in town. It also boasts a mechanics workshop and a quiet room for inmates whose work is clumsier or slower-tempo than the others'. These are wonderfully well-equipped workspaces. On the floor above the workshops, training courses and programmes are provided.

The governor tells us that many inmates find this comparative freedom hard to handle: they have to reconcile their permission to do quite a lot with the fact that they are still prisoners and subject to a prison regime. To be able to resist the tempting call of the world beyond, and to use responsibly the measure of freedom that one is given, is not a gift possessed by everyone (Neumann 2012). In prisons of this kind, the traditionally described 'pains of imprisonment', the prisoner's suffering his loss of liberty, goods and services, relations with the opposite sex, autonomy and security (Crewe 2011; Sykes 1958), are less keenly felt than in a traditional prison setup. On the other hand, the more open a prison is, the more its inmates experience other pains: new pains such as confusion, anxiety, ambiguity, a relative deprivation and an unaccustomed degree of individual responsibility (Shammas 2014). That said, I do find this a highly peaceful place. As we take our leave, the governor says that calm is vital and that it is the enabler of so many other good things. I believe him.

Not far from Kroksrud is Ullersmo, the main prison in the area. It bears a totally different appearance. Put otherwise, with its high walls, fences and copious use of concrete, it actually looks altogether like a prison. Ullersmo was built in the 1970s and is one of the country's maximum-security prisons. Its 220 staff currently guard 190 men who are either on remand or serving long sentences. Ullersmo is one of the country's larger prisons. The average length of custodial sentence of an inmate here is in excess of 6 years. Two-thirds of Ullersmo inmates are foreigners, and a very large share of the inmates are there for drugs-related crimes. Drug trafficking is treated as an extremely severe crime in Norway, punished in the most serious cases with life sentences. The number of remanded prisoners is continually on the rise. Like the waiting-list for places to serve sentences, this aspect is one that is not unfamiliar to me.

Before we begin our visit, we are taken off by one of the prison management team for a talk and lunch in the administration building. I am given information about the inmates here and the workings of the prison. We talk about the dedicated wing established for prisoners who pose a danger to themselves or others, also used to hold prisoners who were made subject to a judicial restraining order while on remand. I am told that such restraining orders are quite common practice among Norwegian judges, and that the prison is struggling to cope with all the remand prisoners (Smith 2012; Shalev 2015). Even remand is a stage of prison life that can often be protracted in Norway, but the trouble is that prisoners on remand cannot always be readily integrated into the wealth of resocialization projects on offer.

We do, of course, also come on to the topic of the many foreigners held at Ullersmo. It is an issue that is causing problems here as elsewhere. Since it is common for foreigners with serious convictions to be expelled from the country at the end of their prison term, they typically sit out their sentences here almost to the very last day. For them, parole and early release are impermissible. It is also foreign prisoners who typically spend the longest periods on remand. I had already read a compelling article about these remanded foreigners as background material before coming to Norway (Ugelvik 2012).

The issue of foreigners and the deportation policy in Norway keeps on puzzling me. Shortly before I left for Norway, I had read that 5,198 foreigners were deported from the country in 2013, arising in almost half of cases from a criminal conviction. This is an absolute record and substantially higher than the figures for 2012 (3,958) and 2011 (3,142). The budgeting for each deportation (currently equivalent to around 20,000 euros) has been augmented further (Berglund 2014).

Foreigners are provided with equivalent, but not necessarily identical, facilities. For instance, while Norwegian inmates have a legal entitlement to pursue further education in prison just as they could in the outside world, that right does not extend to foreigners, who are only given access to basic-level courses. Medical services cannot be faulted and are provided to everyone in prison. They are comparable to what would be on offer in Norwegian society at large. Even dental care, which on the outside is inevitably a high-cost service, is provided at a reasonably good standard and entirely free of charge. Both the bodily and the religious diet are Norwegian through and through. Inmates are given predominantly traditional Nordic food, and—as is customary in Scandinavia—plenty of milk to drink. Foreigners often find it very strange fare (Ugelvik 2011). The religious experience in the prisons seems also hammered on a Norwegian anvil. Ministers of the established Lutheran Church are everywhere. I hear that prison chapels have been reconfigured as multi-faith spaces or rooms for silent reflection, but there is no imam at Ullersmo.

It is time to visit the prison itself. One of the hallmarks of Ullersmo is the warren of underground corridors connecting the various buildings. The large central courtyard, which even contains an open-air swimming pool (currently empty), is only for outdoor activities as far as the prisoners themselves are concerned.

We first visit the wing for drug-addicted prisoners. Recently established, it is for prisoners not just from Ullersmo but from the whole area. I am taken aback to hear that there is a maximum of ten places available here. The same building houses a wing for older prisoners who want a bit more peace and quiet. We proceed to the wing where prisoners can be isolated, and here I see some security cells, as typically spartan as they would be in other countries. There is a cell with a plastic bag-bottomed toilet for prisoners suspected of having ingested drugs, and even a cell where a prisoner can be bound to a bed with straps. This confinement room does not actually look any different from what is found elsewhere if you are accustomed to visiting prisons.

The workshops are impressive, differing nothing from a modern factory or workshop in the outside world. The spacious rooms house big new machines, with inmates busily making a variety of wooden articles. In the mechanics workshop, men are milling objects. Inmates are also given proper vocational training so that they can leave prison with a qualification in hand. In Norwegian prisons, work is no mere pastime or some contrivance to give the inmates pocket money; it is a central pillar of the whole penal policy and receives inordinate amounts of attention and resources.

On the drive back to Oslo, I tell my guides how impressed I am by the huge efforts being made to provide inmates with worthwhile work and to prepare them for their return to society. Of course, I don't know to what extent this also provides results in terms of job participation and education in a context where many prisoners serve a short prison sentence (see below). But what I have seen serves to confirm the positive assertions, and perhaps the claims to exceptionalism, that I had read about Norwegian prisons. I have also seen plenty of pride and belief in people's innate capabilities and in the potential for reform of a criminal. Also, I have seen aspects of prison life that are far less exceptional on an international scale. Prisons in Norway can just as well look humdrum as they can look amazing, and struggle with the same or similar problems as prisons in many other countries. I am led to conclude that there is not really much of a vision or policy for the large numbers of foreign prisoners. Moreover, the regularity with which lengthy remand detentions have to be undergone, largely in solitary confinement in many cases, is not really congruent with the image with which Norway tends to be credited. However, it is too early in my trip to draw my conclusions. Two more prisons are on the agenda for tomorrow.

Small Is Beautiful? Eidsberg and Trøgstad

Today, our first destination is Eidsberg, one of Norway's smallest prisons. Eidsberg Prison is a high-security prison that houses a mere 17 inmates. It looks like an oversized wooden house with some outbuildings around it. Eidsberg contains almost exclusively prisoners on remand. The great majority of them were caught smuggling drugs over the nearby Swedish border. The only two men on site who are serving custodial sentences were sent here for the peace and quiet. Of the 17 inmates, only five are Norwegian citizens.

We walk through to the back of the house, where the workshop is situated. Inmates are seen doing their woodwork. The small mechanics workshop beside this room is occupied by an inmate repairing an old tractor. Making our way upstairs, we find four prisoners awaiting us in a small kitchen. Supervised by a professional chef, they draw up the prison menu and cook for the inmates and staff. The whole place is decked out like a genuine restaurant, with the inmates even doing the book-keeping. One of the African prisoners tells us that he is happy enough to have ended up working in the kitchen, but that he would much prefer being in a larger prison like Ullersmo. He would have far more scope to do things and mix with people there. We proceed to the cells, which are on the top floor of the main building. It is nothing more than a corridor with ten rooms along it. Everything is made of wood, even the doors, though they are reinforced a little. Carrying on through the house, we come back downstairs and encounter a nurse in the surgery. It is all very human-scale here, and wherever we walk, the planks creak comfortingly underfoot.

I have to say that my visit to this mini-prison leaves me unconvinced. I see too little potential in this format, particularly for higher-security confinements. More to the point, it seems to be an expensive option. However, a Norwegian study claims that the quality of life in smaller prisons is markedly better than in larger ones (Johnsen et al. 2011).

We leave this remarkable institution and drive to the wing at Trøgstad, an open prison. Although this is a prison with a low-security regime, it does have a proper gate and fence. There are 90 inmates held here at the moment. Once again, the prison buildings here are mostly quite low, and their exteriors entirely of wood just like most other Norwegian exteriors. They house mostly sentenced prisoners. Some of them are serving the last portion of a longer sentence; others are sitting out the whole of a shorter term here. The latter category is something I find really remarkable about the Norwegian system. Short custodial sentences are imposed very frequently in Norway and typically they actually have to be served, although it can sometimes take quite a while before a place becomes available at a prison to do so. In 2011, fully 87.3 % of custodial sentences imposed were for a period of less than a year. Even more surprisingly, 67.5 % of prison sentences were for less than 3 months (Statistics Norway 2013a). Of the 8,635 people released from Norwegian prisons in 2010, 3,683 had spent fewer than 30 days in custody, and a further 2,152 between 30 and 60 days (Statistics Norway 2012). I had already had animated discussions with my guides about these short sentences. To me, in Norway prison remains a punishment that is still held to be highly important, whether the crime be a felony or a misdemeanour. While it is true that the proportion of custodial sentences that were for a term of more than 3 years increased by 9 % between 2010 and 2011 (Statistics Norway 2013b), short sentences remain an essential tool in this country. Of course, fines and community service do exist, and tagging is increasingly practised, but they have not yet got off the ground as full-fledged alternatives to prison (Lappi-Seppälä 2012). I had it told to me that the three objectives of prison sentences in Norway were the protection of society, the reduction of reoffending and the reintegration of offenders. So which of these three objectives is actually met when there is such an emphasis on short custodial sentences, I wonder?

We finally call in at an office that coordinates the provision of various services outside the prison. Prison life in Norway, which has been governed by a dedicated directorate since 2013, has in-house rules only for the security aspects of detention and for the basic terms and conditions of reintegration work. For all other aspects of life, such as health and work, inmates are governed by rules emanating from beyond the Prisons Directorate. One consequence of this is that there are plenty of prisoners working, and services provided, that are not paid for by the Ministry of Justice and Security. There is a strong push to ensure that these services are adequately represented within the prisons, not least as part of preparing the prisoners for reintegration into society. The last government even announced that prisoners (at least, the Norwegian ones) would have a 'guarantee of reintegration', and made this aim concrete by providing a robust system of work, training and residence schemes (Norwegian Ministry of Justice and Police 2008).

Conclusion

It is time to weigh up my experiences and to form an overall opinion of Norwegian prisons. I certainly have seen some quite remarkable things on my trip, that is for sure. Norway is investing copiously in its policy of reintegration. The prison labour schemes are sensible ones. I find the strategy of running projects for long-term prisoners involving guaranteed reintegration, and whose final stages are relatively open institutions, a convincing one. This could qualify Norway an outlier, but in my judgement not necessarily a one-off. Besides, I have seen great differences between prisons within the country: some prisons that are highly remarkable to my mind, but others that are quite run-of-the-mill. For reasons such as these, it is not really possible to form a general impression and pronouncement on prisons in a whole country (Crewe and Liebling 2012).

Be that as it may, I have certainly seen plenty that I found anything but unconventional. For me, the notion holds little water that we should view Norway as an exotic land bristling with thoroughgoing historical, political, social and cultural exceptionalism. Obviously, John Pratt was quite right that the Scandinavian countries have remarkably low levels of social polarisation and that in every domain of life they are highly geared towards equality and inclusion, and they will likely remain substantially so. This also explains in part why the region's prison system is different (Pratt 2008a; Pratt and Eriksson 2011, 2012, 2013). However, despite what is often asserted (Pratt 2008b), I am far from convinced that the uniquely Nordic social constructions can serve to disprove the changed context, whichever way they might be spun. I have also heard and seen many causes for doubt. Contrary to what many had been expecting, Norwegian prisons (at least, the closed-regime ones) overall turned out not to score much higher on quality of prison life than England and Wales (Johnsen and Granheim 2012, p. 204). Also, it is not necessarily the case that small-scale means high quality in Norway, nor that the Norwegians themselves believe that that is so. The Norwegian prison system's newest policy showpiece is Halden, and with a capacity of 252 inmates, it is actually one of the country's largest prisons.

In addition, the frequency and length of pre-trial detention is as far as I am concerned something inimical to what the Norwegian system is supposed to be all about, and the plethora of foreign detainees is putting the traditional model under pressure. The vigorous deportation policy reveals a determination to keep Norway Norwegian, indeed to keep Norway above all for the Norwegians. But how can that desire sit with the reality of prisons receiving more and more non-Norwegians? And what kind of reintegration into society should be invested in by the country's prisons? There is very much a punitive and retributive aim to prisons in Norway. Foreign convicts are only released once they have served out their sentences in full, and those found guilty of relatively minor offences—whether Norwegians or foreigners—can have custodial sentences dished out to them that they actually have to serve. In Norway, if you are guilty, you must pay, and this will often be by going to prison. Just as in Sweden (Barker 2012), I see a many-facetted penal policy in Norway (Shammas 2015).

I have a strong suspicion that John Howard would be greatly taken with what he would see if he could visit modern Norway. As a staunch Protestant, he would doubtless have endorsed the strict application of punishment and the emphasis on guilt in the penal climate. He would surely have been greatly impressed by the smooth running of the system and by the often outstandingly good prison conditions. Moreover, I dare say he would have been delighted by the stress laid on worthy and sensible prison work, and even that he might have recognized in this prison system a nigh-perfect outworking of the trends he saw developing in the prisons of his day.

Yet, based on what I have seen, read and heard about prisons in Norway, I see ripples on the surface which hint that society and the penal system are not immune to challenges being seen elsewhere. Even in Norwegian society, it seems the golden age of equality is over, as a result of which we see a range of problems rearing their heads in the domain of rehabilitation. What to do with the growing group of foreigners who have no place in Norwegian society but who nevertheless end up in one of its prisons? What kind of return should these people be prepared for, seeing that they are likely to be kicked out of the country as soon as their sentence is up? As long as Norwegian prisons can busy themselves preparing inmates for a return to Norwegian society, everything seems just fine. But what does return to society mean in this age of increasingly multicultural societies and intensifying globalization? And is that not causing major inequalities between the group of prisoners regarded as worth working on and those who are written off as not worth the investment because the country will gain no benefit from them after the sentence has expired anyway? These are questions that now seem to confront even Norway, and to which there are no obvious answers. They may also cause a shift in the functions of prisons and punishment. I believe, based on what I have taken from my prison tours to six European countries, that in social contexts where some form of equality is a totem, or where there are paradigms of mutual respect and consensus-based politics, prisons seem to have a much easier time of it acquiring a rehabilitating function. In such countries, a lawbreaker is not automatically locked away (or at least not further excluded from the mainstream than he already was), but is temporarily locked up pending his resumption at some future time of a role in society. In societies where there is a substantial degree of inequality, on the other hand, prisons can far more readily become depots for undesirables seen by the dominant social groups as a threat. In those social contexts, it is much harder to construct genuine rehabilitation programmes, because those who are in prison are no longer regarded as being part of society, if they ever were. Such countries' prisons lock people up and lock them away. Very often, this inequality has seeped into the very prisons, so that a distinction is maintained between those inmates who deserve to be rehabilitated (and who justify that expense) and the rest of the convict crowd. The uses to which prisons are put have much to do with the triad of locking people up, locking them away and locking them in. This third concept, which is to say the policy of managing wrongdoers in the community, is the hardest to get right and there is hardly a country that does not seem to have major challenges when attempting such an approach. And Norway is no exception to that.

References

Alter, C. (2013). Norway asks Sweden to rent vacant prisons. Sweden has closed some prisons as incarceration rate has fallen. *Time*. http://world.time.com/2013/12/10/norway-asks-sweden-to-rent-vacant-prisons/ Retrieved 14 July 2015.

Barker, V. (2012). Nordic exceptionalism revisited: Explaining the paradox of Janus-faced penal regime. *Theoretical Criminology, 17*(1), 5–15.

Berglund, N. (2014, 27 January 2014). Record number of foreigners deported, *NewsinEnglish.no*. Retrieved 14 July 2015, from http://www.newsinenglish.no/2014/01/27/record-number-of-foreigners-deported/

Bondeson, U. V. (2005). Crime and criminals in Nordic countries. *Society, 42*(2), 62–70.

Council of Europe. (2012). *Response of the Norwegian government to the report of the European committee for the prevention of torture and inhuman and degrading treatment or punishment (CPT) on its visits to Norway from 18 to 27 May 2011* (p. 33). Strasbourg: Council of Europe.

Christensen, T. (2003). Narratives of Norwegian governance: elaborating the strong state tradition. *Public Administration, 81*(1), 163–190.

Crewe, B. (2011). Depth, weight, tightness: revisiting the pains of imprisonment. *Punishment & Society, 13*(5), 509–529.

Crewe, B. (2015). Inside the belly of the penal beast: understanding the experience of imprisonment. *International Journal for Crime, Justice and Social Democracy, 4*(1), 50–65.

Crewe, B., & Ievins, A. (2015). Closeness, distance and honesty in prison ethnography. In D. Drake, R. Earle, J. Sloan (Eds.), *The Palgrave handbook on prison ethnography* (pp. 124–142). Basingstoke: Palgrave Macmillan.

Crewe, B., & Liebling, A. (2012). Are liberal-humanitarian penal values and practices exceptional? In T. Ugelvik and J. Dullum (Eds.), *Penal exceptionalism? Nordic prison policy and practice* (pp. 175–198). Abingdon and New York: Routledge.

Dey, E. (2009). Prison tours as a research tool in the Golden Gulag. *Journal of Prisoners on Prisons, 18*(1–2), 119–125.

Downes, D. (1988). *Contrasts in tolerance: post-war penal policy in the Netherlands and England and Wales*. Oxford: Clarendon.

England, R. W. (1993). Who wrote John Howard's text? The state of the prisons as a dissenting enterprise. *British Journal of Criminology, 33*(2), 203–214.

Howard, J. (1791). *An account of the principal lazarettos in Europe. With various papers relative to the plague: Together with further observations on some foreign prisons and hospitals; and additional remarks on the present state of those in Great Britain and Ireland.* London: Johnson, Dilly and Cadell Reprint, 1973.

Howard, J. (1792). *The state of the prisons in England and Wales with preliminary observations, and an account of some foreign prisons and hospitals* (4th ed.). London: Johnson, Dilly and Cadell Reprint, 1973.

Huckelbury, C. (2009). Tour de farce. *Journal of Prisoners on Prisons, 18*, 126–128.

International Centre for Prison Studies. (2014). Norway. *World prison brief.* http://www.prisonstudies.org/country/norway. Retrieved 14 July 2015.

Johnsen, B., & Granheim, P. K. (2012). Prison size and quality of life in Norwegian closed prisons in late modernity. In T. Ugelvik and J. Dullum (Eds.), *Penal exceptionalism? Nordic prison policy and practice* (pp. 199–214). Abingdon and New York: Routledge.

Johnsen, B., Granheim, P. K., Helgesen, J. (2011). Exceptional prison conditions and the quality of prison life: prison size and prison culture in Norwegian closed prisons. *European Journal of Criminology, 8*(6), 515–529.

Lappi-Seppälä, T. (2012). Penal policies in the Nordic countries 1960–2010. *Journal of Scandinavian Studies in Criminology and Crime Prevention, 13*(1), 85–111.

Liebling, A. (2014). Postscript: integrity and emotion in prison research. *Qualitative Inquiry, 20*(4), 481–486.

Liebling, A. (2015). Description at the edge? I-It/I-Thou relations and action in prisons research. *International Journal for Crime, Justice and Social Democracy, 4*(1), 18–32.

Minogue, C. (2009). The engaged specific intellectual: resisting unethical prison tourism and the hubries of objectifying modality of the universal intellectual. *Journal of prisoners on prisons, 18*(1–2), 129–142.

Nagelsen, S., & Huckelbury, C. (2009). The prisoner's role in ethnographic examinations of the carceral state. *Journal of Prisoners on Prisons, 18*, 111–118.

Neumann, C. B. (2012). Imprisoning the soul. In T. Ugelvik and J. Dullum (Eds.), *Penal exceptionalism? Nordic prison policy and practice* (pp. 139–155). Abingdon and New York: Routledge.

Norwegian Ministry of Justice and Police. (2008). Punishment that works—less crime—a safer society. Report to the Storting on the Norwegian Correctional Services (p. 16). Norwegian Ministry of Justice and the Police.

Orange, R. (2013, November 18). Norway gov mulls Arctic prisons for foreigners, *The Local. Norway's News in English.* http://www.thelocal.no/20131118/norway-gov-mulls-arctic-prisons-for-foreigners. Retrieved 14 July 2015.

Pakes, F. (2015). Howard, Pratt and beyond: assessing the value of carceral tours as a comparative method. *The Howard Journal of Criminal Justice, 54*(3), 265–275.

Piché, J., & Walby, K. (2009). Dialogue on the status of prison ethnography and carceral tours: an introduction. *Journal of Prisoners on Prisons, 18*(1–2), 88–90.

Piché, J., & Walby, K. (2010). Problematizing carceral tours. *British Journal of Criminology, 50*(3), 570–581.

Piché, J., & Walby, K. (2012). Carceral tours and the need for reflexivity: a response to Wilson, Spina and Canaan. *The Howard Journal of Criminal Justice, 51*(4), 411–418.

Pratt, J. (2008a). Scandinavian exceptionalism in an era of penal excess. Part I: the nature and roots of Scandinavian exceptionalism. *British Journal of Criminology, 48*(2), 119–137.

Pratt, J. (2008b). Scandinavian exceptionalism in an era of penal excess. Part II: does Scandinavian exceptionalism have a future? *British Journal of Criminology, 48*(3), 275–292.

Pratt, J. (2011). The international diffusion of punitive penalty: or, penal exceptionalism in the United States? Wacquant v Whitman. *Australian & New Zealand Journal of Criminology, 44*(1), 116–128.

Pratt, J., & Eriksson, A. (2011). "Mr. Larsson is walking out again". The origins and development of Scandinavian prison systems. *Australian & New Zealand Journal of Criminology, 44*(1), 7–23.

Pratt, J., & Eriksson, A. (2012). In defence of Scandinavian exceptionalism. In T. Ugelvik and J. Dullum (Eds.), *Penal exceptionalism? Nordic prison policy and practice* (pp. 235–260). Abingdon and New York: Routledge.

Pratt, J., & Eriksson, A. (2013). *Contrasts in punishment. An explanation of Anglophone excess and Nordic exceptionalism.* Abindon: Routledge.

Shalev, S. (2013). *Supermax. Controlling risk through solitary confinement.* Abingdon: Routlegde.

Shalev, S. (2015). Solitary confinement: the view from Europe. *Canadian Journal of Human Rights, 4*(1), 143–165.

Shammas, V. L. (2014). The pains of freedom: assessing the ambiguity of Scandinavian penal exceptionalism on Norway's prison island. *Punishment & Society, 16*(1), 104–123.

Shammas, V. L. (2015, August 21). The rise of a more punitive state: on the attenuation of Norwegian penal exceptionalism in an era of welfare state transformation. *Critical Criminology*, doi: 10.1007/s10612-015-9296-1.

Shishkin, P. (2003). In Norway, criminals wait a long time to serve time. *The Wall Street Journal*. http://online.wsj.com/news/articles/SB105476716745428400. Retrieved 14 July 2015.

Smith, P. S. (2012). A critical look at Scandinavian exceptionalism. Welfare state theories, penal populism and prison conditions in Denmark and Scandinavia. In T. Ugelvik and J. Dullum (Eds.), *Penal exceptionalism? Nordic prison policy and practice* (pp. 38–57). Abingdon and New York: Routledge.

Smith, P. S. (2016). Prisons and human rights—past present and future challenges. In L. Weber, E. Fishwick, M. Marmo (Eds.), *The Routledge handbook of criminology and human rights* (pp. 525–535). Abingdon and New York: Routledge.

Statistics Norway. (2012). 58 Discharges, by prison time, type of sanction and age 2010. http://www.ssb.no/a/english/kortnavn/a_krim_tab_en/tab/tab-2012-03-08-58-en.html. Retrieved 14 July 2015.

Statistics Norway. (2013a, April 16). 43 Sentences to imprisonment, by terms of imprisonment, sex and age 2011. http://www.ssb.no/a/english/kortnavn/a_krim_tab_en/tab/tab-2013-01-24-43-en.html. Retrieved 14 July 2014.

Statistics Norway. (2013b). Imprisonments 2011. http://www.ssb.no/en/fengsling/. Retrieved 14 July 2015.

Statistics Norway. (2015, January 1). Immigrants and Norwegian-born to immigrant parents. https://www.ssb.no/en/befolkning/statistikker/innvbef. Retrieved 4 December 2015.

Sykes, G. (1958). *The society of captives: a study of a maximum security prison*. Princeton: Princeton University Press.

Ugelvik, T. (2011). The hidden food: mealtime resistance and identity work in a Norwegian prison. *Punishment & Society, 13*(1), 47–63.

Ugelvik, T. (2012). The dark side of a culture of equality. Reimagining communities in a Norwegian remand prison. In T. Ugelvik and J. Dullum (Eds.), *Penal exceptionalism? Nordic prison policy and practice* (pp. 121–138). Abingdon and New York: Routledge.

Ugelvik, T., & Dullum, J. (Eds.). (2012). *Penal exceptionalism? Nordic prison policy and practice*. Abindon and New York: Routlegde.

Ugelvik, S., & Ugelvik, T. (2013). Immigration control in Ultima Thule: detention and exclusion, Norwegian style. *European Journal of Criminology, 10*(6), 709–724.

Vander Beken, T. (2016). *The role of prison in Europe. Travelling in the footsteps of John Howard.* Abingdon: Palgrave Macmillan.

Wacquant, L. (2002). The curious eclipse of prison ethnography in the age of mass incarceration. *Ethnography, 3*(4), 371–397.

West, T. (2011). *The curious Mr. Howard. Legendary prison reformer.* Hook: Waterside Press.

Wilson, D., Spina, R., Canaan, J. E. (2011). In praise of the carceral tour: learning from the Grendon experience. *The Howard Journal of Criminal Justice, 50*(4), 345–355.

The View from Elsewhere: Scandinavian Penal Practices and International Critique

Malcolm Langford, Aled Dilwyn Fisher,
Johan Karlsson Schaffer, and Frida Pareus

Introduction

Periodic assessments by United Nations bodies offer an alternative window through which to assess the nature and origins of Scandinavian detention practices. International treaty bodies review rights performance regularly

M. Langford (✉)
Department of Public and International Law, University of Oslo and Co-Director, Centre on Law and Social Transformation, University of Bergen and Chr. Michelsen Institute, Oslo, Norway
e-mail: malcolm.langford@jus.uio.no

A.D. Fisher
Department of Public and International Law, University of Oslo, Oslo, Norway
e-mail: a.d.fisher@jus.uio.no

J.K. Schaffer · F. Pareus
Norwegian Centre for Human Rights, University of Oslo, Oslo, Norway
e-mail: j.k.schaffer@nchr.uio.no; f.m.pareus@nchr.uio.no

© The Author(s) 2017   451
P. Scharff Smith, T. Ugelvik (eds.), *Scandinavian Penal History, Culture and Prison Practice,* Palgrave Studies in Prisons and Penology, DOI 10.1057/978-1-137-58529-5_19

and while one may dispute their objectivity, their access to relevant information has risen significantly in recent years. Through this material, we have engaged in a longitudinal, comparative analysis of penal exceptionalism in Scandinavia. We contrast in particular the findings of the UN Committee against Torture (CAT) for Norway, Sweden and Denmark against four Western European states (Belgium, United Kingdom, Germany and Italy). In other words, we compare the Scandinavian states with countries with similar economic development and determine to what extent there are differences in detention conditions.

The international human rights organs provide a useful alternative lens on the question of Scandinavian penal exceptionalism. They represent an epistemic community that is qualitatively distinct from that of comparative criminology and public policy in two salient, albeit contradictory, ways. First, the logic of human rights orients practitioners towards implementation of universal minimum standards rather than a comparative search (whether explicit or implicit) for best practices or some other criterion of justice or fairness. The second is that human rights monitoring is often geared towards the exposure of violations, focusing on the more problematic aspects of state practice. Thus, the narrative of detention conditions in international human rights discourse may diverge significantly from that acquired through a comparative snapshot. A human rights review may be more positive towards states in areas that, as criminologists would suggest, need greater improvement. Contrariwise, it may be more critical in areas that are shrouded by the comparativist search for progressive detention models (see e.g. Pratt 2008; for a critique, see Scharff Smith 2011). In any case, our chapter seeks to provide a 'view from elsewhere', possibly that of an 'impartial spectator' immune from the impulse of parochialism (cf. Sen 2009). Indeed, international human rights treaty bodies are designed to play precisely this role (Buchanan 2008).

This international material may also permit us to investigate the causes of any Scandinavian exceptionalism(s). The editors challenged us to explore the hypothesis that any differences, whether positive or negative, in detention conditions in the Scandinavian region may be explained by a strong social welfare state. In our view, this supposition is both important and problematic. Our departure point in studying the Scandinavian exceptionalism is that the field must move beyond the cultural essentialism that pervades much of the scholarship (Langford and Schaffer 2014; cf. Scharff Smith 2011, p. 42). Vast swathes of public policy with all their variations cannot be explained simply by 'distinctive domestic social values, including that of solidarity' (cf. Bergman 2007; Lawler 1997). Thus, we agree that a focus on the Scandinavian social welfare model and its underlying ideology is crucial. The reciprocal nature of the Scandinavian social contract may exclude and marginalize certain groups, particularly those groups perceived as unable to make a contribution (Langford and Schaffer 2014). Travellers and Roma, Sami, person with disabilities, certain juveniles have been historically met with repressive or assimilatory measures (e.g. Minde 2003; Sköld 2013). Moreover, we agree with the editors that the coercive power and the ambition of the welfare states may have unintended consequences in the field of punishment: 'the fact that Scandinavian welfare states are large, powerful and arguably often trusted by the public, can lead both towards humane policies on the one hand and effective social control on the other hand' (Scharff Smith 2011, p. 41).

However, a singular focus on the welfare state and its ideologies risks falling into a new form of essentialist exceptionalism and conflating analytically distinct factors. Values, ideas, culture or mentalities do not automatically translate into actions, decisions and policy—it requires the active work of purposive agents, who hold certain beliefs and act on them, as also argued by ideational scholars in comparative politics and international relations (Beland 2005; Berman 2001). In order to assert the centrality of national values for policy, existing essentialist accounts of exceptionalism tend to focus on hegemonic discourses and dominant norms in Scandinavian societies (Brysk 2009, p. 60f.), despite the fact that such discourses are usually produced through processes of political contestation (Schmidt 2008). We therefore worry that agents and contestation can be too easily lost in orienting the explanatory focus strongly towards the form of the state and its ideologies, in this case social welfarism. Comparative analysis of Scandinavian exceptionalism needs also to compare the politics, structures and incentives that guide and shape detention policy.

In this chapter, we attempt to provide a greater handle on this explanatory question by examining two dimensions of our primary material. First, we examine whether the Scandinavian states in their argumentation to these UN committees use a discourse and justificatory rhetoric that reflects a social welfare model or ideology, which we have supplemented through a brief analysis of the more detailed response to the European Committee for the Prevention of Torture (CPT). Second, we analyse variation in the Scandinavian states. If the Scandinavian model or ideology is a paramount explanation, we should expect similar approaches to detention conditions across time and space. If not, it would suggest that domestic politics and structures may be more salient.

A Broad Picture: The UN Treaty Bodies

Our primary sources of information come from the UN human rights treaty bodies. These independent expert committees are charged with monitoring the core international human rights conventions. For example, the UN Human Rights Committee (HRC) is responsible for the International Covenant on Civil and Political Rights; and the CAT monitors the convention against torture. The principal function of these committees is to periodically review the performance of states (they also issue general inter-pretive statements and most of them adjudicate, in a quasi-judicial fashion, individual complaints). They do so through a dialogue with states (roughly every 5 years), based on a report issued by a state, which is increasingly supplemented by information submitted by non-governmental organizations (NGOs) or acquired from intergovernmental organizations. At the conclusion of the review, concluding observations (COs) are issued by the committee. Some describe this as the most important activity of human rights treaty bodies; it 'provides an opportunity for the delivery of an authoritative over-view of the state of human rights in a country and . . . advice which can stimulate systematic improvements' (O'Flaherty 2006, p. 35).

The regular and independent nature of these COs offers a useful insight into evaluating Scandinavian penal practices. However, there are several methodological conundrums to be addressed. Treaty body periodic review developed recently, with different committees developing different practices. For example, the CAT's practice can be divided into eras. Until the early 1990s, the emphasis was on 'constructive dialogue' (Kälin 2012, p. 35), including a few general observations that did not distinguish between commendations and concern. COs in their monitoring-orientated form only emerged in the mid-to-late 1990s (Kälin 2012, p. 36), distinguishing between 'positive aspects' and 'subjects of concern'; nevertheless, COs remained short, lacking detail. In the early 2000s, the committee introduced an informal distinction between very positive commendations and more general ones, noted 'with satisfaction', and established a clearer link between concerns and specific recommendations. These trends continued into the most recent reporting era, coinciding with the 'Harmonised Guidelines' for treaty bodies issued in 2006 (Kälin 2012, pp. 21–23). 'Principal subjects of concern and recommendation' now link concerns and recommendations directly, ensuring at least one recommendation per concern, and are listed thematically. The List of Issues to be addressed by states during their reports adds a further source for gauging committee views. In some instances, 1-year follow-up requests are attached to pressing recommendations, suggesting the CAT's priorities.

A related challenge is the partial lack of institutional memory in the process. Commenting on the HRC, Kälin notes that 'while the majority of concerns addressed in the most recent Concluding Observations remain the same as those raised during the previous examination, there are always several points that are no longer mentioned' (Kälin 2012, p. 67f.). This may reflect that the state has implemented a recommendation, but could equally reflect 'an oversight' or that other concerns have emerged (Kälin 2012, p. 66f.). Likewise, repetition may imply that the state is conducting reforms to which the committee wishes to contribute. Nonetheless, O'Flaherty found the CAT to be among those 'least inclined to even loosely refer to previous concluding observations' (O'Flaherty 2006, p. 27).

With these points in mind, we firstly take a look at how five human rights treaty bodies have reviewed the Scandinavian states over time in relation to detention practices. These bodies are the HRC; CAT; Committee on the Elimination of Racial Discrimination; Committee of the Rights of the Child (CRC); and Committee on Economic, Social and Cultural Rights (CESCR).

We have reviewed all 53 COs between 1986 and 2015 from these bodies. Detention sites were defined to include police stations and prisons and we examined the review of a broad spectrum of practices: solitary confinement, placement of juveniles with adults, visitor rights, etc. Across these COs, we have specifically coded whether the committees refer positively and negatively to detention practices.[1] While the language is occasionally ambiguous, it is usually clear when a committee is affirmatory or critical. Note that positive and negative comments sometimes occur in a single observation while some committees almost never addressed detention conditions (CESCR).

In Fig. 1, we divide the COs into six periods of 5-year blocks. There were 7 to 11 observations in each period with the exception of the period 1986–1990, which had only 5 observations. Strikingly, in the first three periods, negative evaluations by UN committees of Scandinavian states is relatively rare and the differential is generally in favour of positive comments (i.e. the gap between the percentage of positive and negative comments). However, in the latter three periods, there is a rise in the presence of negative reviews; and by 2015 the differential is inverse.

We also coded whether the observation was general in nature or referred to a specific practice concerning detention. An index was created whereby a specific observation was weighted twice that of a general observation. As Fig. 2 shows, negative observations were on average more specific and decidedly more negative in the most recent period.

This longitudinal perspective across different committees therefore provides us with a different lens on the Scandinavian states. The trend suggests that Scandinavian states are not simply (or no longer) viewed as positive models for others to emulate. Rather, the focus is on eliminating certain problematic practices. An illustrative example comes from the CRC in relation to Sweden. The early reviews raise concerns but suggest a high level of trust between this state and Committee. In 1993, the Committee raised direct concerns about detention:

> The Committee is concerned that the Government does not ensure that children in detention are separated from adults. The Committee is also concerned by the practice of taking foreign children into custody under

---

[1] The coding manual is available on request from the authors.

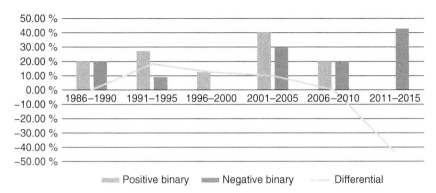

Fig. 1 UN Concluding Observations: Detention in Scandinavian States, 1986–2015

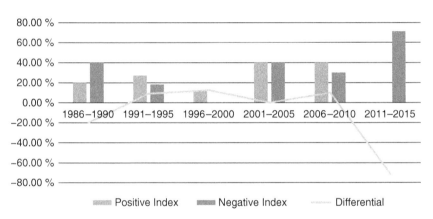

Fig. 2 UN Concluding Observations Specificity of Observations on Scandinavian States, 1986–2015

the Aliens Act and notes that this practice is discriminatory in so far as Swedish children generally cannot be placed in custody until after the age of 18. (Committee on the Rights of the Child 1993, para. 9)

In 1999, there is a positive comment made in relation to the concern expressed in 1993, under the heading concerning follow-up measures.

The Committee appreciates the efforts of the State party to implement the recommendations of the Committee … and welcomes progress achieved in reviewing legislation and taking appropriate measures to improve the compatibility of the juvenile justice system with the Convention, especially articles 37, 39 and 40, as well as other relevant international standards in this area, such as the Beijing Rules, the Riyadh Guidelines and the United Nations Rules for the Protection of Juveniles Deprived of their Liberty. (Committee on the Rights of the Child 1999, para. 4)

It was another decade until Sweden faced negative evaluation on penal practices from this Committee. When it came, the concern was more specific, directed at the use solitary confinement, and made reference to independently acquired information:

The Committee welcomes various achievements made by the State party in the area of juvenile justice. However, the Committee expresses its concern that under current rules … it is possible to isolate children in youth detention centres if they display violent behaviour or are affected by drugs to the extent that they jeopardize the general order. In addition, the Committee expresses its concern at reports that this treatment is also used as punishment. The Committee is of the view that solitary confinement should not be used unless it is judged to be absolutely necessary and the period of isolation may not exceed 24 hours. (Committee on the Rights of the Child 2009, para. 70, recommendation at 71)

A similar trend can also be seen in the HRC's evaluation of Norway. In 1989, the Committee (1989, para. 68–69) expressed a wish to receive more information on, inter alia, time limits governing resort by prison authorities to solitary confinement or the use of security cells; clarification as regards to detention in mental health institutions; time limits for preventative detention; and the placing under special observation. However, in 2006, the Committee gives much more detailed accounts of their concerns in direct relation to Norway's penal practices, expressing 'concern':

[A]bout provisions of solitary confinement and the possibility of unlimited prolongation of such pre-trial confinement, which might be combined with far-reaching restrictions on the possibility to receive visits and other contact with the outside world . . . [and] the continued use of pre-trial detention for excessive periods of time. (Human Rights Committee 2006, para. 13–14, see also 16)

and in 2011:

[A]t reports of excessive use of coercive force on psychiatric patients and the poor mechanisms of the Control Commissions for monitoring mental health-care institutions . . . the increased use of pretrial detention and solitary pretrial detention, as well as post-conviction incommunicado detention, in the State party . . . the excessive length and conditions of pretrial detention of juveniles . . . [and] that the State party maintains a reservation to article 10, paragraphs 2 (b) and 3, of the Covenant and that juveniles are not segregated from adult prisoners. (Human Rights Committee 2011, para. 10, 12, 13)

A Comparative Method

The above UN assessments may suggest particular problems with the humanitarian narrative of Scandinavian penal practices. However, an isolated reading of COs risks conflating the rise in critique of Scandinavian practices with a more critical approach by the committees to all states. Any change may be simply accounted by shifts in committee practice. Indeed, as the level of detail (Kälin 2012, p. 63) and diversity of issues covered have generally increased, a mere longitudinal perspective is insufficient. In order to address whether the Scandinavians present exceptionalism, we therefore compare over time the Scandinavian states to four European states: Belgium, Germany, Italy and United Kingdom, representing the other two categories of welfare state regimes in Esping-Andersen's (1990) typology: corporatist and liberal. We have also decided to use data from the CAT periodic review process. It is a convention devoted to one right (protection from cruel, degrading and inhuman treatment), thus making comparison between states easier, and it is oriented towards domestic detention conditions.[2] Moreover, recent research suggests there has been a gradual improvement in state reporting to the CAT (Creamer and Simmons 2015).

Still, there are limitations to using COs for this purpose. The first is prioritization. It can be difficult to interpret the seriousness CAT attaches to recommendations as there is no formal practice in differentiating between particular positives and negatives. The second is accuracy. Some argue that these committees are no longer impartial; becoming more critical, particularly towards supposed better performers, including the Scandinavian states. Recent work finds no correlation between good performance on torture indexes and state responsiveness in reporting; indeed, there is a weak correlation in the other direction, although this disappears when controlling for recent democratization (Creamer and Simmons 2015). Despite these limitations, COs provide a basis for comparative qualitative analysis. Certain themes repeatedly return in COs and, in later reporting eras, the Committee specifically categorizes concerns and recommendations. These categories can be projected effectively backwards, and the nature of concerns raised under each theme can be discussed based on: frequency of repetition; tone, length and detail; whether previous recommendations are followed up; whether they are outcome or process orientated; whether they relate to positive or negative obligations; which articles of the treaty they relate to; and whether they relate to minimum or developmental standards. Moreover, for the Scandinavian and comparator states, there has been largely consistent reporting from the early 1990s, which provides a more secure basis for comparison. In addition, we have checked the more skeletal CAT reports against the more fulsome reports of the European CPT. Using these sources, we can analyse the Scandinavian states to determine if COs reflect superior human rights practices.

---

[2] Although it is not always clear which article(s) CAT grounds such discussions in, Article 11 stands out: 'Each State Party shall keep under systematic review interrogation rules, instructions, methods and practices as well as arrangements for the custody and treatment of persons subjected to any form of arrest, detention or imprisonment in any territory under its jurisdiction, with a view to preventing any cases of torture'.

Scandinavian States

Denmark

While the Committee has raised various detention-related issues in Denmark, solitary confinement (recently given a separate section in COs) is the most consistently addressed topic, constituting a familiar pattern in international institutionalised expert assessments of Scandinaviqan states (Barker 2012; Smith 2007). This concern is first raised in 1989 (Committee Against Torture 1989, para. 103). The state representative responded that access to media, exercise and 'contact with prison staff...distinct from police officials' meant 'such confinement could not be considered...true solitary confinement', adding that stricter rules were introduced to ensure it was proportional to sentences and did not exceed 8 weeks (Committee Against Torture 1989, para. 116).

This did not prevent the Committee returning to the issue in 1996, although it is grouped with other miscellaneous concerns, without a corresponding recommendation. However, a year later, the Committee (1997a, para. 181, 186) highlights 'the institution of solitary confinement, particularly as a preventive measure during pre-trial detention, but also as a disciplinary measure', including a recommendation that 'except in exceptional circumstances... solitary confinement [should] be abolished, particularly during pre-trial detention, or at least that it should be strictly and specifically regulated by law... and that judicial supervision should be introduced' (Committee Against Torture 1997a, para. 11). Other detention-related concerns and recommendations are made regarding police treatment of detainees and demonstrators, including use of dogs for crowd control, and 'the real degree of independence' of detainee complaint mechanisms.

In 2002, the CAT (2002a, para. 5(a), (b), 6(b), 7(c)–(d)) implies progress, noting 'with satisfaction' new controls regarding solitary confinement, the decrease of its use and the provision for judicial control in addition to progress on earlier family access, mandatory medical examinations, and access to lawyers and interpreters'. However, concerns linger about 'lack of effective recourse procedures against decisions imposing solitary confinement'. This leads to recommendations to 'continue to monitor the effects of solitary confinement... and... of the new bill', and to 'establish adequate review mechanisms relating to... [its] determination and duration' (Ibid, para. 7(c)).

In 2007, solitary confinement still has its own section, but the tone is tempered by the report's first positive aspect welcoming 'ongoing efforts to improve conditions in prisons', and 'in particular... efforts to introduce alternative measures to custodial ones' (Committee Against Torture 2007a, para. 4). The Committee also starts its specific concern on solitary confinement by appreciating the reduction of the upper limit for under-18s to 4 weeks and concludes by observing the judicial review mechanism to review continued confinement (citing Article 11). However, the CAT (2007a, para. 11) 'remains concerned' about 'prolonged' confinement, 'with particular concern' that suspects, including under-18s, 'may be held indefinitely in solitary confinement during... pre-trial detention'.

The Committee recommended that Denmark continue to monitor the effects of solitary confinement, and amendments restricting its grounds and duration; Denmark is urged to make confinement 'a measure of last resort, for as short a time as possible under strict supervision... with a possibility of judicial review', including restricting it to 'very exceptional cases' for under-18 s, and to 'aim at its eventual abolition', with a direct reference to the same points in Denmark's 2005 CRC report. Regarding indefinite pre-trial detention, Denmark is urged to 'respect... the principle of proportionality and establish strict limits', and 'increase the level of psychologically meaningful social contact' (Committee Against Torture 2007a, p. 14).

These recommendations are not considered pressing enough for 1-year follow-up. Still, committee members, while encouraging progressive restriction, are not satisfied that solitary confinement continues and develop increasingly detailed and clear COs.

Sweden

Turning to Sweden, the Committee (1989, para. 48, 66) requests information on time limits for 'incommunicado detention' already in the state's 1989 report. Yet, the Committee does not follow up the clarification in the same report or in 1993. The 1993 COs instead reflect a glowing report, concluding that Sweden's 'legal and administrative regimes ... were *models* to which most other countries should aspire' (Committee Against Torture 1993a, para. 374, 386).

However, in 1997, '"restrictions", some leading to solitary confinement for a prolonged period ... in pre-trial detention', emerge as the second subject of concern, alongside worries about police methods for detainees and demonstrators (Committee Against Torture 1997b, para. 220, 222). While the Committee welcomed that these 'restrictions' were 'under review', it recommended 'that the institution of solitary confinement be abolished, particularly during ... pre-trial detention, other than in exceptional cases ... and the measure is applied, in accordance with the law and under judicial control' (Committee Against Torture 1997b, para. 225). The next COs list among issues that 'also' concern the Committee 'several cases of the excessive use of force by police personnel and prison guards'; however, solitary confinement is not mentioned (Committee Against Torture 2002b, para. 5(c), 7(f)).

By 2008, detention issues return. One issue is 'fundamental safeguards', where the Committee (2008a, para. 11) notes 'with appreciation' new legislation concerning access to a lawyer and notification of custody; nonetheless, the CAT is concerned about how fundamental safeguards are administered, and recommends 'effective measures' to ensure they are secured 'in practice'. There is also a concern regarding 'imposition of restrictions on remand prisoners' affecting 40–50 % of remand prisoners, while remand prisoners are unable 'to effectively challenge and appeal decisions'. The Committee (2008a, para. 16) 'also regrets the lack of official statistics on ... such restrictions', but positively notes proposed 'regulatory changes aimed at securing a uniform and legally secure use of restrictions'. All detention-related paragraphs are subject to a 1-year follow-up (Committee Against Torture 2008a, para. 30).

Thus, like Denmark, the CAT gives Sweden's detention issues, particularly isolation, considerable attention, with gradual reforms unable to allay concerns.

Norway

In Norway's 1993 report, the CAT (1993b, para. 73) 'congratulates' the country regarding its 'rules and practices' for detention and treatment of prisoners. Solitary confinement is first raised in 1998, particularly its 'preventive' use during pre-trial detention, and includes a recommendation almost identical to the corresponding recommendation in Denmark's 1997 report (Committee Against Torture 1998, para. 154, 156).

In 2002, the Committee (2002c, para. 84–86) 'continues to be concerned' about pre-trial solitary confinement – the sole concern listed – recommending 'information on steps taken to respond to the Committee's ongoing concern . . . be included in the . . . next periodic report'. However, it notes developments 'with satisfaction' regarding 'proposals . . . for an amendment to the Criminal Procedure Act to reduce . . . overall use of solitary confinement and to strengthen . . . judicial supervision', and guidelines on family notification, lawyers and healthcare access.

In 2008, the Committee (2008b, para. 3(b)) notes with satisfaction that the amendment has been adopted, alongside 'abolition of solitary confinement as a sanction', although this appears in a somewhat parenthetical 'as well as' clause. Worries persist about 'lack of adequate statistics validating the effectiveness of these measures'. The Committee (2008b, para. 8, 18) instructs Norway to 'compile detailed statistics' on these measures, and 'application of recent amendments to the Immigration Act concerning . . . detention of foreign nationals', with this requiring 1-year follow-up.

This concern with immigration is reflected in the rest of the detention section, where the CAT (2008b, para. 18, 9), 'while welcoming the recent . . . legislative act to regulate the rights of persons staying at the Trandum Alien Holding Centre, notes that the supervisory board . . . has yet to be established', with a corresponding recommendation (requiring a 1-year follow-up). Furthermore, the Committee (2008b, para. 10) 'remains concerned about reports on the use of unnecessary force . . . and . . . discriminatory treatment based on ethnicity', and requests the government to 'ensure that all appropriate measures are taken', although this recommendation does not require a 1-year follow-up. Thus, after perceiving that some progress has been made on solitary confinement and other detention-related issues, the Committee's focus has turned to implementation and a disaggregated, discrimination-based approach.

Comparator States

Belgium

How does the CAT's reporting of the Scandinavian states compare with other European states? We first examine Belgium. In Belgium's first report in 2003, the positive aspects the Committee (2003, para. 4(e), 5(h–l), 6 (g–l)) mentions include the repeal of a law allowing minors to be placed in detention centres for up to 15 days and efforts to solve problems of overcrowding in juvenile detention, but the Committee raises concerns regarding deficient legislation on rights of persons under arrest, prison violence, inadequate information about access to medical care in prisons, and the possibility of isolation of juvenile delinquents over 12 years for up to 17 days, with detailed corresponding recommendations. The report concludes with a uniquely pointed prioritization, requesting the next report 'contain detailed information on the practical implementation of the Convention and all of the points raised in the present conclusions' (Ibid, para. 133).

In 2009, the Committee [2009, para. 4(a), 5(a), 16, 17] notes steps forward 'on principles governing ... prison establishments and the legal status of detainees' and 'minimum standards for places of detention'. However, there is a long list of detention-related concerns, dominating the latter COs. The Committee begins these with children. It is 'deeply concerned' that the requirements that legal counsel or trusted adults be present during interrogation of minors 'is rarely respected', and 'remains concerned' under-18s can be tried as adults—a concern expressed with reference to CRC's 2002 COs.

Additionally, the Committee (Committee Against Torture 2009, para. 16–19) is concerned about prison overcrowding, conditions and violence. It recommends establishing a national organ for 'conducting regular visits' to detention facilities, and to consider alternatives to detention. The Committee also raises concerns about the 'special individual security regime'.

Despite noting with satisfaction certain improvements, the Committee is concerned about the lack of a right to appeal, and 'allegations that the mandated procedure is not followed, that detainees are not able to challenge the appropriateness of such measures and that hearings are conducted without an interpreter or lawyer'. Yet further detention-related worries are expressed about the 'register of detainees'; again, the positives regarding legislative changes are tempered by the CAT's focus on implementation.

Moreover, the Committee (Committee Against Torture 2009, para. 20–23, 31) 'regrets' lack of recognition of detainees' rights to legal assistance and that 'the draft Code of Criminal Procedure mandates access to legal assistance only eight hours after detention', explicitly referring to 'previous recommendations'. The final concerns regard conditional release and committal of mentally ill offenders. Of these detention-related concerns, only two – on protection of minors and the detainee register – require a 1-year follow-up. Nonetheless, the volume and variety of concerns, with the increasingly detailed and disaggregated focus that does not take legislation at face value, suggest that the CAT is significantly worried about detention in Belgium.

Italy

The assessment of Italy is not so different. In 1992, Italian representatives stressed isolation was allowed only 'for health reasons and normally involved exclusion from communal activities for . . . up to two weeks', and that incommunicado detention was limited to 24 hours. Committee members expressed concern that Italy had no system for compensating victims of ill treatment in detention, mentioning specific cases (Committee Against Torture 1992, para. 332, 337, 338).

By 1995, detention becomes the subject of two of the three concerns [Committee Against Torture 1995, para. 154–156, 157(c)]. These detention-related concerns were 'serious acts of torture', reports of inmate deaths by NGOs, with penalties imposed on state officials 'not commensurate with the seriousness of these acts'; and a broader 'matter of some concern' regarding 'the number of unconvicted prisoners . . . overcrowding in prisons and the suspension, even temporary, of humanitarian rules' on prisoners' treatment. While recommendations do not reflect the same weighting towards custody-related issues, one recommendation 'suggests' Italy 'should... monitor effective compliance with safeguards during preliminary custody', particularly legal and medical access.

The Committee [1999a, para. 165(b), 167] finds progress in its 1999 report, praising modification of 'precautionary measures to protect arrested persons and detainees from ill-treatment or torture', including audiovisual documentation of questioning outside court. Nevertheless, one of just two concerns is prison overcrowding and 'facilities which [make] the overall conditions of detention not conducive to the efforts of preventing inhuman or degrading treatment or punishment', with lingering 'cases of ill-treatment... many of them involv[ing] foreigners'.

Again, recommendations return to other issues, but both the 1995 and 1999 reports list, among 'Factors and difficulties impeding the application of the provisions of the Convention', attitudes towards foreigners (Committee Against Torture 1995, para. 153). The relative dominance of detention-related issues continues in 2007, where, after the principal concern regarding domestic incorporation of a definition of torture, preventative detention and 'fundamental safeguards' take centre stage (Committee Against Torture 2007b, para. 6, 7). The Committee is also 'concerned at allegations that fundamental legal safeguards for persons detained by the police... are not being observed in all situations', and is further concerned over how 'an accused person may be held in detention for five days... before being allowed to contact an attorney'.

These concerns are subject to a 1-year follow-up. Later concerns also address detention of asylum seekers and non-citizens. One final concern, which is also subject to 1-year follow-up, relates to 'continuing overcrowding and understaffing in prisons', noting improved penitentiary health care, but expressing concern about reported ill-treatment, 'unsuitable infrastructures and unhygienic living conditions, in CPTAs and identification centres', and the lack of an 'independent organization' to 'systematically monitor' these centres (Committee Against Torture 2007b, para. 29, 9, 16). The CAT makes two recommendations regarding these issues. Detention-related issues in Italy are closely linked to broader concerns about non-citizens and immigrants, once more reflecting an increasingly disaggregated assessment.

Germany

In terms of the expressed level of concern, CAT's assessments of Germany are the closest to the Scandinavin states. However, solitary confinement is not a major detention-related issue for Germany. The first mention of it comes in 1990, where the Committee (1990, para. 185, 193) requests specific information, eliciting a response that 'confinement was a disciplinary measure . . . could not exceed 21 days, before which a medical check was undertaken; if illness occurred during confinement it had to be discontinued; visits were not prohibited'.

The Committee members (1990, para. 166, 183, 191, 193, 195) were particularly concerned with 'incommunicado detention', and sought 'clarification on the concept of "remand custody"' and police use of force. The government representative emphasized 'that, although there was no incommunicado detention . . . detainees could be held in separate quarters for health or personal reasons or, in cases of violence or attempted escape, could be isolated for not more than 15 days, when an attorney had to be informed', while stressing that 'treatment in such circumstances was the same as for other prisoners' (Ibid. para. 193). The Committee praised Germany for 'abolition of incommunicado detention'.

In 1993, Committee members (1993c, pp. 166, 189) ask again about incommunicado detention but the state representative does not respond. Related concerns are raised in 1998 regarding 'open-ended legal provisions permitting, under certain circumstances, the discretionary but significant reduction of the legal guarantees of those detained', although there are no related recommendations.

Preventative detention is raised in 2011. The Committee (2011, para. 5(b), 16, 17) praises Germany for limiting preventive detention, yet notes 'with regret . . . that more than 500 persons remain in preventive detention, some of them having been in preventive detention for more than twenty years'. Beyond this, the Committee's concerns regard specific ill treatment, especially related to delayed investigation, raised in 2004 [Committee Against Torture 2004a, para. 4(a)], foreigners and use of physical restraints at state level. Thus, while there is less of a clear pattern to detention-related concerns for Germany, there is also a trend towards more disaggregated analysis.

United Kingdom

Detention-related concerns regarding the United Kingdom focus in earlier reports on Northern Ireland, with detailed questions and answers regarding terror detainees (Committee Against Torture 1992, para. 99, 111, 105, 119). In (somewhat unusually for early CAT reports) specific queries regarding other detention issues, the Committee members wondered what standards were applied to detainees, whether the Government was concerned about the reported 100 % increase from 1980 to 1990 in detainee suicides, and whether using strip cells to house suicidal prisoners was appropriate. In response, state representatives informed the Committee that prison rules reflected the United Nations Standard Minimum Rules for the Treatment of Prisoners, where 'exceptions related to budgetary or technical problems'. The representative also 'gave statistics' and explained 'proposals to reform the prison system'.

The committee (1992, para. 125) concludes that 'except for the situation existing in Northern Ireland . . . the United Kingdom met in virtually every respect the obligations . . . in the Convention'. The Committee [1996, p. 60 (b–c, d, g, k)] continues this focus in 1996, noting improved interrogation practices and conditions in the detention centres located in Northern Ireland. However, under Factors and Difficulties Impeding the Application of the Convention, the CAT [1996, para. 61, 64(a, c), 65(a, e)] notes that 'maintenance of the emergency legislation and of separate detention or holding centres will inevitably continue to create conditions leading to breach of the Convention' in Northern Ireland, and that 'this is particularly so because . . . permitting legal counsel to consult with their clients at their interrogations is not yet permitted'. This is further reflected in concerns about 'vigorous interrogation of detainees . . . which may sometimes breach the Convention', with a recommendation regarding 'abolishing detention centres in Northern Ireland . . . repealing . . . emergency legislation', taping interrogations and permitting access to lawyers. Again, the general concern relates to suicide and detention facilities.

In 1999, again, Northern Ireland is the only listed impediment to the Convention. However, many issues raised previously do not feature, with concerns related to 'deaths in police custody and the apparent failure . . . to provide an effective investigative mechanism'; and 'the retention of detention centres in Northern Ireland' (Committee Against Torture 1999b, para. 75, 76(a, c)).

The 2004 report also provides little continuity between reports, with a long, new concern detailing 'reports of unsatisfactory conditions in ... detention facilities', including deaths in custody, violence overcrowding, 'slopping out' and 'unacceptable conditions for female detainees' in one prison. However, terrorism-related themes continue to dominate, both regarding Northern Ireland and new antiterror legislation, including operations under the 'war of terror' [Committee Against Torture 2004b, para. 4(g, c)].

Summary

Does the above review of COs reveal penal exceptionalism? Partly yes, partly no. Table 4 summarizes changes over time in the COs. Overall, the Committee finds *fewer issues* of concern in the Scandinavian states than in some comparator states, particularly Belgium, Italy and the United Kingdom. However, Germany's COs suggest that there are no qualitatively substantive differences even if the topics are different; and all states, including the Scandinavian states are facing probing questions on treatment of migrants in detention.

Yet Scandinavian reporting is, to varying degrees, somewhat dominated by *solitary confinement*. This is a difficult issue to weigh in comparative analysis. It might be thought to be a singular issue particular to the long history of this practice in the Scandinavian countries. Conversely, there is significant evidence that prolonged solitary confinement has deeply harmful psychological and physical effects (Smith 2006). Moreover, in our material, almost all Scandinavian states are persistently unresponsive to calls from the Committee to address the problem, even when the 1-year follow-up is established. At most, we can identify a certain positive exceptionalism (Scandinavians outperform most comparator states on detention conditions generally) and negative exceptionalism (regarding solitary confinement). However, the picture becomes slightly more complicated once we disaggregate and examine particular countries and practices.

In order to check the reliability of CAT reports we have compared their conclusions with those of the European CPT using Sweden and Germany as

Table 4 Detention conditions

State	Early COs	Late COs
Denmark	Solitary confinement—'institution'	Nods to progress but increasingly detailed
Sweden	Solitary confinement not major issue	Becomes central ('institution'), disappears, then returns
Norway	Similar to Denmark	Progress, attention turns to foreign nationals
Belgium	Uniquely long, detailed concerns, including isolation	Even more detailed, disaggregated concerns
Italy	Police discrimination and treatment in custody	Preventative detention and basic safeguards, focus on foreign nationals
Germany	Few concerns beyond exceptions to legal safeguards	Preventative detention, increasingly disaggregated focus
United Kingdom	Terrorism (Northern Ireland)	Terrorism (Northern Ireland, antiterror legislation)

a small sample. First, we compared reports on Sweden and found that the emphasis at different points in time is not overly dissimilar. The CPT (1992, para. 63–69) raises the issue of solitary confinement in the 1990s (although 4 years earlier) and becomes more critical over time. Interestingly, the COs from CAT (2008a) detail concern about a wide range of restrictions (including solitary confinement) on remand prisoners that largely resembles the later CPT report (2009) in both language and substance. Obviously, the voluminous CPT reports examine a wider range of issues.[3] Some issues are more serious than other. One notable omission from the CAT COs is police misconduct and the adequacy of follow-up investigation of individual police

[3] The CPT report in 1993 voiced concern over the following issues: Too small cubicles [six cubicles each measuring 1.65 m × 0.88 m (1.45 m²)] found in the Central Police Station in Stockholm) (§18); Lack of arrangements for providing food to persons in custody (§19); Notification of custody (§22–24); Access to a lawyer (§25); Information as to rights: medical care; conduct of interrogation; custody records (§29–37); Cellular accommodation (§42–48); Food for inmates (§49); Outdoor exercise (§50–53); Regime activities (§54–62); Induction unit (§82–83); Reinforced security measures (§88); Watchdog procedures (§135–137); Closed psychiatric wards (§144–147); Closed unit, refugee centre (§148–150).

and systemic problems. The CPT (2009, para. 10–17) places particular emphasis on this issue, which is arguably relevant in all Nordic states (see e.g. Nasjonal institusjon for menneskerettigheter 2015). However, this omission does little to weaken the reliability of the CAT's reports. Instead, it might strengthen scepticism over Scandinavian exceptionalism.

For comparison, we have chosen to look at Germany given that it was the most similar to the Nordic states in terms of the tenor of the CAT review. We hypothesized that CAT may have been too gentle with Germany and that the CPT might have displayed a more critical stance. Interestingly, this was not borne out by the CPT report and any differences between Sweden and Germany seem to narrow considerably when the two reports are placed side by side. Of particular interest, is that the 1993 CPT report strongly criticizes Germany for the extensive use of solitary confinement in:

> the situation of prisoners placed in solitary confinement or under a segregation regime in the establishments visited (in particular Straubing and Tegel Prisons) is of concern to the CPT. Its delegation found that the regime applied to prisoners undergoing prolonged periods of non-voluntary isolation did not provide the stimulation required to avert damaging changes in their social and mental faculties. In this respect, the CPT has recommended immediate changes to the solitary confinement arrangements in order to provide the prisoners concerned with purposeful activity and guarantee them appropriate human contact... (European Committee for the Prevention of Torture 1993, para. 216)

Yet, in its more recent reports, the CPT (2014) directs less criticism against Germany and it appears the state has taken steps to address solitary confinement. Instead, the most critical remarks concern the overuse of preventive detention and certain security measures.[4] It is thus notable that Germany seems more responsive to concerns on solitary confinement than Sweden, although read together the reports do not provide evidence for any assertion that detention practices are

---

[4] For example, (§40); use of broad metal handcuffs and legs being immobilized with leather belt (§43); 'specially secured rooms' (§45); and the use of surgical castration in the context of treatment of sexual offenders (§49).

more humane in Germany than in Sweden. Rather, this comparison suggests that strong Scandinavian exceptionalism, as it pertains to humane treatment, is difficult to substantiate.

Conclusion: Strong State Social Welfarism as Explanation?

This chapter sets out the view from elsewhere on Scandinavian penal exceptionalism. The comparative analysis of four European states with three Scandinavian states suggests that the general idea that Scandinavians are relatively strong positive performers on detention conditions finds some support. However, the analysis across all committees also reveals a negative exceptionalism on some issues (such as solitary confinement) but also that the degree of positive exceptionalism depends on the choice of comparator state (e.g. Germany vs. Italy). Notably, a state like Germany seems more receptive to critique on the practice of solitary confinement when compared to Sweden.

To the extent that there is exceptionalism, how does strong state social welfarism feature in the material we have amassed? In a very preliminary fashion, we have sought to address the challenge, but the answers point in three different directions. First, we have reviewed the responses by Scandinavian states to criticisms from the CAT and have found no use of an explicitly social welfare discourse. The responses are characterized by a strong orientation to factual descriptions and an acceptance of the discursive playing field created by the conventions. Thus, social welfarism is not so pervasive an ideology that Scandinavian states find it difficult to employ other forms of discourse. There seems to be at least a recognition that it is not a discourse that can be easily mobilized by these states to justify poor performance or negative exceptionalism.

Second, in order to corroborate these findings, the analytical framework we have developed in this chapter could usefully be applied to provide a more detailed, qualitative analysis of other treaty bodies dealing with human rights in the penal area. Among these, the European CPT would again be a natural candidate. An initial review of German and Swedish government responses to reports between 1993 and 2014 suggest some subtle differences even though the Swedish responses do not invoke social welfarism as a justification: In the German response there is a slightly more frequent and engaged invocation of *principles* (e.g. rule of law, human rights and proportionality) and the noting of more rights-inflected policies like *monitoring and accountability* (Government of Germany 2012, 2014). In the Swedish responses, principles are sometimes mentioned but practices are more likely to be defended reports are more likely to defend its response by reference to its 'systems' for addressing certain problems (Government of Sweden 2010, 2004). Moreover, Swedish responses are significantly more terse than their German counterparts and engage less with the Committee's concerns.

Can these differences be ascribed to a social welfarist ideology? Possibly. However, further research would obviously be necessary across a wider group of states to test whether these differences are constant and significant. Moreover, even if it was, it is not axiomatically clear whether this discursive variation reveals a social welfarist *ideology* or an exceptionalist *mythology*. Thus, the Swedish reports could be read as containing an attitude that the CPT has little right to criticize Sweden since it is exceptional and a world leader in detention conditions. In other words, it is not that the Swedish state is completely infused by social welfarist frame but rather the government is convinced of the fact that its social welfare state has been exceptionally successful and that foreign critics have little to contribute to its improvement. This may also explain why Sweden has been more resistant to criticism on solitary confinement but a state like Germany has been more reflexive.

Third, while there are many similarities between the Scandinavian states, they respond somewhat differently to the committees. We see this partly with the issue of detention conditions and even more so with other issues in the CAT such as defining torture in domestic law (Fisher et al. 2015). Norway has exhibited more responsiveness than Sweden and Denmark. This suggests that domestic politics and configurations of actors and interests also need to be taken into consideration. In order to test the social welfarist hypothesis properly, we need to analyse how and why the Scandinavian states differ from one another. It is likely that domestic configurations of actors and discourses and background structures and incentives are of particular importance in shaping the trajectories of the practice of detention in strong social welfare states.

References

Barker, V. (2012). Nordic exceptionalism revisited: explaining the paradox of a Janus-faced penal regime. *Theoretical Criminology, 17*, 5–25. doi: 10.1177/1362480612468935.

Beland, D. (2005). Ideas and social policy: an institutionalist perspective. *Social Policy and Administration Journal, 39*, 1–18. doi: 10.1111/j.1467-9515.2005.00421.x.

Bergman, A. (2007). Co-constitution of domestic and international welfare obligations: the case of Sweden's social democratically inspired internationalism. *Cooperation and Conflict Journal, 42*, 73–99. doi: 10.1177/0010836707073477.

Berman, S. (2001). Ideas, norms, and culture in political analysis. *Comparative Politics, 33*, 231–250.

Brysk, A. (2009). *Global good Samaritans: human rights as foreign policy*. Oxford: Oxford University Press.

Buchanan, A. (2008). Human rights and the legitimacy of the international order. *Legal Theory, 14*, 39–70. doi: 10.1017/S1352325208080038.

Committee Against Torture. (1989). Report of the committee against torture (No. A/44/46).

Committee Against Torture. (1990). Report of the committee against torture (No. A/45/44).

Committee against Torture. (1992). Report of the Committee against Torture (No. A/47/44).

Committee against Torture. (1993a). Report of the Committee against Torture (No. A/48/44).

Committee against Torture. (1993b). Concluding observations: Norway (No. A/48/44(SUPP)).

Committee against Torture. (1993c). Conclusions and recommendations of the Committee against Torture: Germany (No. A/48/44).

Committee against Torture. (1995). Report of the Committee against Torture (No. A/50/44).

Committee against Torture. (1996). Report of the Committee against Torture (No. A/51/44).

Committee against Torture. (1997a). Conclusions and recommendations of the Committee against Torture: Denmark (No. A/52/44).

Committee against Torture. (1997b). Report of the Committee against Torture (No. A/52/44).

Committee against Torture. (1998). Report of the Committee against Torture (No. A/53/44).

Committee against Torture. (1999a). Report of the Committee against Torture (No. A/54/44).

Committee against Torture. (1999b). Conclusions and recommendations of the Committee against Torture: UK and Northern Ireland (No. A/54/44).

Committee against Torture. (2002a). Conclusions and recommendations of the Committee against Torture: Denmark (No. CAT/C/CR/28/1).

Committee against Torture. (2002b). Conclusions and recommendations of the Committee against Torture: Sweden (No. CAT/C/CR/28/6).

Committee against Torture. (2002c). Concluding observations: Norway (No. CAT/C/CR/28/3).

Committee against Torture. (2003). Conclusions and recommendations of the Committee against Torture: Belgium (No. CAT/C/CR/30/6).

Committee against Torture. (2004a). Conclusions and recommendations of the Committee against Torture: Germany (No. CAT/C/CR/32/7).

Committee against Torture. (2004b). Conclusions and recommendations of the Committee against Torture: United Kingdom and Northern Ireland (No. CAT/C/CR/33/3).

Committee against Torture. (2007a). Conclusions and recommendations of the Committee against Torture: Denmark (No. CAT/C/DNK/CO/5).

Committee against Torture. (2007b). Conclusions and recommendations of the Committee against Torture: Italy (No. CAT/C/ITA/CO/4).

Committee against Torture. (2008a). Concluding observations: Sweden (No. CAT/C/SWE/CO/5).

Committee against Torture. (2008b). Concluding observations: Norway (No. CAT/C/NOR/CO/5).

Committee against Torture. (2009). Concluding observations: Belgium (No. CAT/C/BEL/CO/2).

Committee against Torture. (2011). Concluding observations: Germany (No. CAT/C/DEU/CO/5).

Committee on the Rights of the Child. (1993). Concluding observations of the Committee on the Rights of the Child: Sweden (No. CRC/C/15/Add.2).

Committee on the Rights of the Child. (1999). Concluding observations: Sweden (No. CRC/C/15/Add.101).

Committee on the Rights of the Child. (2009). Concluding observations of the Committee on the Rights of the Child: Sweden (No. CRC/C/SWE/CO/4).

Creamer, C.D., Simmons, B.A. (2015). Ratification, reporting, and rights: Quality of participation in the convention against torture. *Human Rights Quarterly*, 37, 579–608. doi:10.1353/hrq.2015.0041.

Esping-Andersen, G. (1990). *The three worlds of welfare capitalism*. Princeton, N.J.: Princeton University Press.

European Committee for the Prevention of Torture. (1992). Report to the Swedish Government on the visit to Sweden carried out by the European Committee for the Prevention of Torture and Inhuman or Degrading Treatment or Punishment (CPT) from 5 to 14 May 1991 (No. CPT/Inf (92) 4). Council of Europe, Strasbourg.

European Committee for the Prevention of Torture. (1993). Report to the Government of the Federal Republic of Germany on the visit to Germany carried out by the European Committee for the Prevention of Torture and Inhuman or Degrading Treatment or Punishment (CPT) from 8 to 20 December 1991 (No. CPT/Inf (93) 13). Council of Europe, Strasbourg.

European Committee for the Prevention of Torture. (2009). Report to the Swedish Government on the visit to Sweden carried out by the European Committee for the Prevention of Torture and Inhuman or Degrading Treatment or Punishment (CPT) from 9 to 18 June 2009 (No. CPT/Inf (2009) 34). Council of Europe, Strasbourg.

European Committee for the Prevention of Torture. (2014). Report to the German Government on the visit to Germany carried out by the European Committee for the Prevention of Torture and Inhuman or Degrading Treatment or Punishment (CPT) from 25 November to 2 December 2013 (No. CPT/Inf (2014) 23). Council of Europe, Strasbourg.

Fisher, A.D., Langford, M., Schaffer, J.K. (2015). Compliance with the Convention against Torture: Testing Nordic exceptionalism (SSRN Scholarly Paper No. ID 2585377). Social Science Research Network, Rochester, NY.

Government of Germany. (2012). Response of the German Government to the report of the European Committee for the Prevention of Torture and Inhuman or Degrading Treatment or Punishment (CPT) on its visit to Germany from 25 November to 2 December 2010 (No. CPT/Inf (2012) 7). Council of Europe, Strasbourg.

Government of Germany. (2014). Response of the German Government to the report of the European Committee for the Prevention of Torture and Inhuman or Degrading Treatment or Punishment (CPT) on its visit to Germany from 25 November to 2 December 2013 (CPT/Inf (2014) 24). Council of Europe, Strasbourg.

Government of Sweden. (2004). Response of the Swedish Government to the report of the European Committee for the Prevention of Torture and Inhuman or Degrading Treatment or Punishment (CPT) on its visit to Sweden from 27 January to 5 February 2003 (No. CPT/Inf (2004) 33). Council of Europe, Strasbourg.

Government of Sweden. (2010). Response of the Swedish Government to the report of the European Committee for the Prevention of Torture and Inhuman or Degrading Treatment or Punishment (CPT) on its visit to Sweden from 9 to 18 June 2009, (No. CPT/Inf (2010) 18). Council of Europe, Strasbourg.

Human Rights Committee. (1989). Report of the Human Rights Committee (No. A/44/40).

Human Rights Committee. (2006). Concluding observations of the Human Rights Committee: Norway (No. CCPR/C/NOR/CO/5).

Human Rights Committee. (2011). Concluding observations of the Human Rights Committee: Norway.

Kälin, W. (2012). Examination of state reports. In UN Human Rights Treaty Bodies, *Studies on human rights conventions*. Cambridge: Cambridge University Press.

Langford, M., Schaffer, J.K. (2014). The Nordic Human Rights Paradox (SSRN Scholarly Paper No. ID 2275905). Social Science Research Network, Rochester, NY.

Lawler, P. (1997). Scandinavian exceptionalism and European Union. *Journal of Common Market Studies*, 35, 565–594. doi:10.1111/1468-5965.00089.

Minde, H. (2003). Assimilation of the Sami – implementation and consequences. *Acta Borealia*, 20, 121–146. doi:10.1080/08003830310002877.

Nasjonal institusjon for menneskerettigheter. (2015). *Criminalisation of homelessness in Oslo: An investigation*. Oslo: Norsk senter for menneskerettigheter.

O'Flaherty, M. (2006). The concluding observations of United Nations Human Rights Treaty Bodies. *Human Rights Law Review*, 6, 27–52. doi:10.1093/hrlr/ngi037.

Pratt, J. (2008). Scandinavian exceptionalism in an era of penal excess part I: The nature and roots of Scandinavian exceptionalism. *British Journal of Criminology*, 48, 119–137. doi:10.1093/bjc/azm072.

Scharff Smith, P. (2011). A critical look at Scandinavian penal exceptionalism. In T. Ugelvik, J. Dullum (Eds.), *Penal Exceptionalism?: Nordic Prison Policy and Practice* (pp. 38–57). Abingdon, Oxon: Routledge.

Schmidt, V.A. (2008). Discursive institutionalism: The explanatory power of ideas and discourse. *Annual Review of Political Science, 11,* 303–326. doi:10.1146/annurev.polisci.11.060606.135342.

Sen, A. (2009). *The idea of justice.* London: Allen Lane.

Sköld, J. (2013). Historical abuse—a contemporary issue: Compiling inquiries into abuse and neglect of children in out-of-home care worldwide. *Journal of Scandinavian Studies in Criminology and Crime Prevention,* 14, 5–23. doi:10.1080/14043858.2013.771907.

Smith, P. S. (2006). The effects of solitary confinement on prison inmates: a brief history and review of the literature. *Crime Justice, 34,* 441–528. doi:10.1086/500626.

Smith, P.S. (2007). Prisons and human rights: The case of solitary confinement in Denmark and the US from the 1820s until today. In S. Lagoutte, H.-O. Sano (Eds.), *Human rights in Turmoil: Facing threats, consolidating achievements* (pp. 221–248). Boston: Martinus Nijhoff Publishers.

Negotiating Imperfect Humanity in the Danish Penal System

Keramet Reiter, Lori Sexton, and Jennifer Sumner

American prison experts are increasingly looking to Europe, and especially to Nordic countries, for examples of a better prison system. In 2014, a retired New York State Prison warden visited Norway's Halden prison, and a video of the warden's shock at seeing the tools and knives to which prisoners had access went viral on the Internet in the United States (Sterbenz 2014). In 2015, the Vera Institute of Justice, an American think tank focused on criminal justice issues, led a group of prison scholars,

---

K. Reiter (✉)
Department of Criminology, Law & Society and at the School of Law at the University of California, Irvine, USA
e-mail: reiterk@uci.edu

L. Sexton
Department of Criminal Justice and Criminology at the, University of Missouri-Kansas City, Missouri, USA

J. Sumner
Department of Public Administration at California State University, Dominguez Hills, California, USA

481
P. Scharff Smith, T. Ugelvik (eds.), *Scandinavian Penal History, Culture and Prison Practice,* Palgrave Studies in Prisons and Penology, DOI 10.1057/978-1-137-58529-5_20

policy makers, and wardens on a tour of European prisons. Upon their return, two of these scholars published an opinion piece in the *New York Times* lauding the values of dignity and rehabilitation they saw in action in German prisons especially (Turner and Travis 2015). Although Americans (and Brits) are both shocked and impressed by the humane prison conditions they see in prisons in Germany and Scandinavia, they are also quick to acknowledge the influence of differing social contexts. As Turner and Travis said in their *New York Times* opinion piece, "America's criminal justice system was constructed in slavery's long shadow and is sustained today by the persistent forces of racism" (2015). Nordic prisons, by contrast, grew out of "cultures of equality" and the robust Scandinavian welfare state (Pratt 2008a, p. 124). Slavery and racism produce one kind of system, and equality and welfare produce another.

As American prison scholars who recently initiated an empirical study of Danish prison policy, practice, and culture, we have gathered data that complicates this Scandinavian exceptionalism thesis. By drawing on data collected during 6 weeks of fieldwork in Denmark, including ethnographic observations in Danish prisons and interviews with prison officials, guards, and prisoners, we examine what happens below the flashy surface of Scandinavian prisoners' apparent freedoms.

First, we complicate the oversimplified characterization of Scandinavian prison conditions as consistently humane and relatively lenient. We build on the work of many in this volume who have argued that Scandinavian prisons fail to achieve their lofty humanitarian ideals, whether by forcing individuals to conform to a dominant concept of the normal (Fredwall), stripping pretrial prisoners of their rights and isolating them (Smith), or failing to provide adequate transitional and community services to former prisoners (Olesen). But instead of focusing on failures per se, in this chapter we examine the tensions of adhering to the values of dignity and normalization in an inherently coercive institution. Indeed, our observations reveal that in some ways Danish prisons are not necessarily any less restrictive, coercive, or punitive than prisons in any other social and geographic context. As Jefferson (2012) and Liebling and Arnold (2004) have argued, certain aspects of prison culture are fundamental.

Second, we focus not on whether the Scandinavian welfare state produces exceptionally humane prison conditions, but on how the conditions that do exist are negotiated and implemented on a daily basis by staff who work in Danish prisons and by prisoners confined there. Whereas Pratt and Eriksson argue that Scandinavian prisons tend to implement "soft" policies as a result of the equality and welfare supports structuring the larger social system in which the prisons operate (2013), Danish prisons are actually the site of constant and intentional negotiation of a balance between *both* "hard" and "soft" policies and practices. Official Danish Prison and Probation Service (DPPS) documents describe a commitment to the principle of normalization and a "value" of "the art of balancing a strict and soft approach" in carrying out their mission to "contribute to reducing criminality" (Kriminal Forsorgen 2015, p. 2). In other words, Danish prison officials consciously understand and explicitly frame prison work as a deliberate balance of hard and soft. In doing so, prison staff and officials simultaneously reveal a commitment to internal operational goals of order and security (e.g., forbidding drugs or building prisons with ample provisions for solitary confinement) and more externally oriented goals of resocialization of prisoners through normalization (e.g., permitting family apartment visits, personal clothing, and prisoners cooking for themselves). Others have written about this balance in the Scandinavian context, including analyzing how prisoners exchange drugs and how guards overlook the exchanges (Mjåland 2014), and how staff control prisoners through informal rewards (Ibsen 2013), or by compromising rules, walking a fine line between being strict and steadfast, but also flexible (Ugelvik 2014, pp. 61–63). Building on this work, we identify mechanisms by which prison officials and prisoners negotiate the balance between "soft" and "hard," sometimes favoring "soft" values and other times building "hard" institutions.

Third, our research reveals a key mechanism affecting the hard-soft negotiation in Danish prisons: acceptance of error. Where Danish prisons appear soft, humane, or relatively materially comfortable, this often also represents an acceptance of imperfect results, such as escapes or the pervasiveness of drug use, even if those imperfect results undermine harder security goals. Prison officials' acceptance of the inevitability of making mistakes, as well as their acknowledgement of the potential futility of punishment writ large, work to both mitigate the hard and to accentuate the soft in punishment. On the other hand, inasmuch as the system seeks to completely prevent error (e.g., by designing escape-proof prisons) it hardens, and the ideal of normalization weakens.

Methods

This essay draws on 6 weeks of ethnographic observation and interviews conducted by 3 US scholars within the DPPS. During the summer of 2015, our research team visited 6 Danish prisons and jails, and conducted in-depth qualitative interviews and focus groups with 56 prisoners, 26 prison staff members, and 12 senior-level Danish prison administrators and prison policy experts. Our most sustained observations, along with prisoner and staff interviews, were conducted at two facilities: a maximum-security "closed" prison facility and a minimum-security "open" prison facility, both in the Jutland region of Denmark. We each spent between 8 and 12 hours per day, for a total of 5 days, at each facility. In addition to our formal interviews, we also observed prisoner activity, workshop, classroom, and living spaces and ate meals, interacted, and conversed with prisoners and staff as they went about their daily routines. For this chapter, we draw on these data in order to both convey a general sense of the workings of each facility and to more specifically explain mechanisms through which prisoners and staff negotiate the hard–soft balance described earlier.

Supplemental ethnographic data are drawn from observations and conversations during day-long visits to four additional facilities, including three closed prisons and one jail (or remand facility) where prisoners await trial, as well as numerous interviews with experts and managers at the DPPS headquarters. These daylong visits at select prisons may arguably be characterized as "carceral tours" of the sort criticized by Piché and Walby (2010, 2012), as well as Adams (2001), Brown (2009), and Dey (2009). We are aware that, especially on these shorter tours, we may have only seen "the 'front stage' of imprisonment" (Goffman 1961; Piché and Walby 2010, p. 571). Yet, understanding and describing the "front stage" presented by Danish prison officials on tours given to outsiders is key to making sense of the larger values upon which Danish punishment policy and practice are based. Moreover, Pakes has argued that prison tourism can play an especially important role in comparative work, to orient foreign visitors to a new system (2015, p. 266).

Our position as US visitors to Danish prisons certainly influenced the field and how it was presented to us. Each of our research sites was well prepared for our arrival, extending great courtesy to us in terms of dedicating staff and prisoner time and resources, space and accommodations, and often even meals. In choosing whether to speak with us, what information to share, and how to frame this information to us as outsiders, participants shaped the data in particular ways (as is the case in all field research). Before we arrived at each prison, prisoners and staff alike were notified of our visit via e-mail and signs announcing our research; they volunteered to participate by approaching us directly, obviating the fears described by Piché and Walby (2010) and Nagelsen and Huckelbury (2009) that prison authorities would select the individuals most likely to "represent[] nothing more than the talking points of their captors" (Piché and Walby 2010, p. 573). Together these approaches helped to reduce the ways in which the research may be "limiting the participant knowledge to the aspects of incarceration to which [a prison service] permits access" (Piché and Walby 2012, p. 412).[1] To be sure, some participants likely did represent the talking points of their captors (or supervisors), but the variety of data we collected from a large number of participants at multiple sites provided myriad opportunities for variation to emerge where it existed.

We approached all of our data collection from daylong visits, to interviews and focus groups, to ethnographic observation from a constructivist standpoint, taking into consideration that the facts and perspectives presented to us were a function of institutional and individual

---

[1] One example that affirms we were able to accomplish what was intended along these lines is one particular interview with a prisoner at the open prison. At the end of the interview, the respondent told of a group that recently visited the facility from South Korea "doing some kind of movie or research as well, some weeks ago."

Respondent: And they actually—they instructed the inmates on what to do in the movie, and act. And could you please look like you're reading this book now? But it's not the same that you are doing. Like, it felt like they had all the answers, and they just needed to bag it up with material.

Interviewer: Oh. And what does this feel like.

Respondent: It feels like- stupid. I don't know. But they- Yeah. They had the conclusion before coming here.

Interviewer: And does this feel- Does this feel the same way?

Respondent: No, not at all.

Interviewer: How does this feel?

Respondent: Well, you're just asking a lot of questions.

presentation of self, and acknowledging that participants are not immune from the power relations that constitute prison dynamics more generally (Piché and Walby 2010), even when "power relations are less obvious" (Pakes 2015, p. 271). We examined not only how Danish prisons operate, but how people living and working in these prisons present their experiences to outsiders like us, following the premise that "performance (for Goffman) or performativity (for Butler), is, in general, central to the presentation or production of the self" (Wilson et al. 2011, p. 344). In this case, our multiple data collection methods and constructivist approach to data collection and analysis allowed us to view multiple "stages" presented, including that which the system purports to value, or what it expects outsiders to *want* to see, and also how staff and prisoners alike experience these values.

Exceptional Conditions and a Danish Commitment to Normalization

In their analyses of Nordic exceptionalism, Pratt and Eriksson identify five dimensions along which Nordic prisons can be distinguished from Anglophone prisons: prison size, officer–inmate relations, quality of prison life, prison officer training, and prisoner work and education programs (2013, p. 9). In drawing their conclusions, they focus on prisons in Finland, Sweden, and Norway. In Danish prisons, we observed many of the same distinctive characteristics highlighted by Pratt and Eriksson. However, as we describe in this and subsequent sections, these "exceptional" characteristics were neither uniformly present nor consistently implemented across the Danish prison facilities we studied. These varieties in exceptional characteristics within and across institutions reveal the ongoing tensions between "hard" and "soft" policies, which are present throughout Danish prisons.

In terms of size, the Danish prison facilities we visited were small—housing a few hundred prisoners at most—compared to the few thousand prisoners housed in many US prisons, as well as in Anglophone prisons identified by Pratt and Eriksson. Beyond the distinguishing features of prison scale, Pratt and Eriksson described a social interactional milieu characterized by collegial officer-inmate relations, in which officers and prisoners call each other by their first names, refer to "clients" as well as to "inmates," officers knock on prisoners' doors before entering their cells, and prisoners and officers have "more routine social interaction and less social distance" than in Anglophone prisons (2013, p. 10). To some degree, our data confirm Danish prisons' divergence from Anglophone prisons in scale and structure of social interactions, especially in light of the many mutually polite day-to-day interactions we observed. However, we also observed fairly limited social interaction between prisoners and officers, particularly in the higher security, closed prisons that we visited, but also in the open prisons. In closed prison facilities, we talked with and observed officers as they spent hours at a time in staff-designated kitchens, or in office spaces sealed off from the prison common areas by locked doors. Even in open prisons, we observed that officers spent much of the day behind a desk, away from the common areas in which prisoners congregated. In open prison workshops, "workmasters" spent entire days working with prisoners in various assembly and production tasks. However, these workmasters were not uniformed guards; they were trained craftsman who participated in only a few weeks of the guard-training program and performed a role more akin to civilian teachers than prison guards.

Despite differences in the extent of their interactions, guards and work-masters alike emphasized the importance of interacting with prisoners. Similarly, prison officials noted the importance of designing prison institutions that facilitate, rather than hinder, prisoner–guard interaction. As the president of the prison officer's union explained, staff in higher security units "can use security as an excuse" to avoid interacting with prisoners. He expressed concern with "buildings that make it so staff do not have to be" with the prisoners and said that because a "main goal is to get them [prisoners] out of high security," staff should be out working with and among the prisoners in order to facilitate this. Where Pratt and Eriksson saw routine interactions between prisoners and staff, we observed a tension between the stated goal of frequent, normalized interaction and (1) our observations of frequently limited interactions and (2) prison administrators' ongoing concerns about this reality.

Pratt and Eriksson's observations about the generally high quality of life in Scandinavian facilities resonated more with our observations (2013, p. 11).

Adherence to the principle of normalization, the first of six principles guiding the DPPS, entails providing prisoners with many freedoms consistent with those of the outside world; this is the aspect of Danish incarceration generally emphasized in traditional portrayals of Scandinavian exceptionalism, including Pratt and Eriksson's work. For instance, today Danish prisoners wear their own personal clothing rather than state-issued uniforms.

As prisoners go about their daily routines in this context, they have varying degrees of freedom to move around the facility, depending on their individual security classification and the security level of the facility. In open prisons, prisoners are largely free to traverse the grounds, and in many instances even leave the prison entirely for home visits with family, to see a doctor, or just to go to work or school. Even in the far more constrained closed prisons, groups like Hells Angels and Banditos (two of Denmark's largest and allegedly most violent motorcycle gangs) are still given a fair range of movement within their designated living areas. Each section contains numerous wings that are set up suite-style and provide all of the daily necessities for the prisoners who live within them, including a kitchen and a small living area with a television, coffee table, and cushioned seating. Each section also houses shared recreational space where prisoners can play darts or billiards and use fitness training equipment. In the communal kitchens, prisoners prepare their own meals individually or cooperatively with food that they have purchased at the prison store, using money from their personal accounts—a system known as "self-catering" that was implemented in 1976 (Minke 2014). Each kitchen has a full-sized refrigerator, oven, and stove, with drawers and cabinets for tableware and cookware. The sole indicator that any kitchen is in a prison is the steel cables tethering the butcher knives and, in some prisons, the vegetable peeler, to the wall above the counter.

These observations support Pratt and Eriksson's image of Scandinavian prison life as both high quality and surprisingly normalized relative to Anglophone prison life. However, some scholars have suggested that these very freedoms can create confusion and anxiety, a sense of relative deprivation and uncomfortable processes of self-disciplining, which together produce "pains of freedom" in Scandinavian prisons (Shammas 2014), or that the gap between expectations and experiences of punishment can be as salient to the degree of punishment experienced as the absolute harsh-ness of the punishment in prisons more generally (Sexton 2015).

Moreover, even the "normalized" prison conditions Pratt and Eriksson characterize as high quality were not uniformly implemented across the Danish prison system. Prisoners in pretrial detention and prisoners in short-term segregation are not permitted to move about the institution freely, prepare their own meals, or leave prison facilities for home visits. Pratt and Eriksson (2013, p. 18) do acknowledge the use of solitary confinement in Nordic prison systems in their work, but they describe it as a blip in the overall humanity of the system, an "exception" to the general exceptionalism. Both Smith (2012) and Barker (2013), however, have argued that these exceptions to the exceptionally high quality of prison life raise fundamental questions about whether Scandinavian pris-ons are as humane and lenient as they at first seem. As Smith notes in this volume, the use of isolation in remand facilities is more than a blip in the system; one-third of Danish prisoners are in remand facilities, under harsh conditions of confinement, sometimes isolated in their cells for 23 hours a day. Moreover, over the course of the 2000s, Denmark opened a number of new facilities designed to institutionalize solitary confinement of sen-tenced prisoners for at least a few weeks, if not months, at a time. Politigården is a Copenhagen facility that was renovated in 2004 to maintain 25 dangerous prisoners at a time in total isolation 22–23 hours per day; Østjylland (now Enner Mark), opened in 2006 and has a few dozen cells for short and long-term isolation; and Denmark plans to open another new prison, Nordfalster (now Storstrøm), in 2016, which will have an additional 36 cells for short and long-term isolation. The practice of keeping a subset of Danish prisoners in long-term isolation seems not like an exception, but like an integral practice within the national prison system.

In sum, Danish prisons, like the other Nordic prisons that Pratt and Eriksson observed, certainly have characteristics that appear generally more humane, normalized, and even facilitative of prisoner–guard interactions, than corresponding conditions in Anglophone prisons, particularly the prisons in the United States, Canada, and the United Kingdom which have faced widespread criticism for overcrowding, lack of health-care provision, lack of programming, and conditions that have been frequently cited as violating international human rights standards (e.g., Reiter and Koenig 2015). However, in our 6 weeks of intensive observations and interviews, these characteristics were neither consistently apparent across all units and prison facilities, nor were they unchallenged by the daily operational realities of prison. Below the surface of Denmark's humane prisons, prison staff and prisoners are constantly negotiating a tension between "soft" and "hard" conditions of confinement, balancing and re-balancing the allocation of privileges and punishments.

Balancing Hard and Soft

As discussed earlier, the DPPS's mission to reduce criminality through the enforcement of sanctions is a "dual primary task" that encompasses control and security as well as support and motivation, a balance between "a strict and a soft approach" (Kriminal Forsorgen 2015, p. 2). The achievement of these goals is guided—and constrained—by a program of six principles. First among these principles is a commitment to normalization. The subsequent five principles are: openness, responsibility, security, least possible intervention, and optimum use of resources (Kriminal Forsorgen 2015, p. 2). The commitment to normalization within a punitive setting requires prison staff to ensure that proximate, operational goals of control and security are met while simultaneously pursuing long-term resocialization goals through support and motivation.

In interviews, Prison Service staff of all levels described this balancing act as engaging in a constant negotiation between "hard" and "soft" elements of incarceration. In defining "hard" elements, prison staff identified control-oriented aspects of incarceration such as physical (or "static") security, including shatterproof glass, locked doors on housing units and cells, and live-pulse fingerprint scanning to access restricted areas of the prison, as well as behavioral interventions (or "dynamic" security), including reprimands, privilege restrictions, and other administrative sanctions. Crewe's (2011) research on prisons in the United Kingdom provides another way of conceptualizing this blend of static and dynamic security, as the "depth," "weight," and "tightness" of punishments, which he argues affect both carceral regimes and prisoners' experiences of these regimes. Indeed, Crewe argues that even attempts to balance the hard of something like a "stick" with the soft of something like a "carrot" can actually be both "coercive and instrumental," as well as "punitive and restrictive" in its overall effect (Crewe 2007, p. 258). "Soft" elements of incarceration, in contrast, consist of the normalization-oriented aspects of incarceration, such as prison guards chatting informally while sitting alongside prisoners on the drive to a home visit or, in select housing units, sharing a meal with them. These "soft" elements both help to normalize life in prison and serve to counteract the negative, punitive impact of the hard elements. In the United States, Sexton (2015) has demonstrated how even relatively soft elements of incarceration—often provided under the guise of the "direct supervision" style of inmate management—can have unintentionally punitive effects. At times, the subtle failings of soft elements can actually eclipse the impact of traditionally hard carceral elements (e.g., restrictions on freedom of movement) by increasing the salience of punishment.

Prison work in Denmark necessarily entails an ongoing negotiation between hard and soft that appears in other Scandinavian contexts (and in any prison context, for that matter). Not only does the DPPS acknowledge this tension in its own summaries of goals and missions, but scholars of Scandinavian punishment have documented that "deprivations do exist" in prisons throughout the region (Shammas 2014, p. 119), detailing everything from compulsory treatment of drug addicts (Barker 2013), to exclusionary policies that target non-citizens for drug policing and deportation (Aas 2015), to the overuse of solitary confinement (Barker 2013; Smith 2012). We argue that paying closer attention to the day-to-day negotiation of the explicitly articulated balance between hard and soft principles of confinement is critical to understanding whether and how Danish prisons are truly exceptional.

Our findings do reveal many instances of Scandinavian softness that, upon first glance, appear to fit squarely within the Scandinavian exceptionalism thesis. One prisoner, upon learning that our research team hailed from the United States, explained to us:

> In Denmark, we have it good here. This is jail. In America, what do you call this? Kindergarten. There you have no freedom. You have—they take

your clothes, they take everything. And you're in lockdown and you eat together the same food. We can go down and buy our own food, and we make it ourselves, and we have a room with a toilet and bathroom. It's a party here, compared to [the US].

The particular "party" described by this respondent is in Østjylland, Denmark's most secure and, by many accounts, "hardest" prison. In spite of the Danish commitment to normalization and the associated attempts to soften prisoners' experiences of imprisonment, however, the hard aspects of incarceration are omnipresent, continually challenging the softness, the normalization, and the exceptionalism of Danish incarceration. The influence of hard elements can be seen even in the lowest security, most open prisons, while the influence of soft elements can be detected even in the highest security, closed prisons, where prisoners are isolated 23 hours a day—perhaps the ultimate Danish embodiment of hard incarceration.

The balancing act between hard and soft principles of confinement is immediately visible upon entry into a Danish prison on the heels of the morning guard shift, and remains evident until the goodnight routines that signal the end of each day. We experienced this interplay upon arrival at Østjylland, Denmark's highest security prison as of 2015, one morning, as a smiling guard, accompanied by a drug-sniffing dog on a short leash, greeted us. Drug searches of this kind are a common demonstration orchestrated for outsiders entering prison facilities (Pakes 2015), but what loomed large in this example was the friendly, nonthreatening nature of the dog, unlike the drug dogs in the United States—even those in ostensibly non-punitive settings like airport security areas. The guard handling the dog explained that the dog is not just for use on prisoners and other adults, but also on children. For this reason, the dog needs to be friendly and approachable, instead of menacing, while doing her job. The guard proceeded to demonstrate the dog's effectiveness at sniffing out contraband by planting decoy drugs on some members of our research team, who were then seated comfortably in a chair while the drug dog, tail wagging, sniffed around our pockets, licked our hands, placed her paws on our laps for a thorough search, and nibbled gently at the pocket where she found the hidden contraband. On the one hand, the friendly drug dog demonstrated her effectiveness as a security measure, while retaining a soft touch. On the other, the presence of the dog contributed to a characterization of the prisoners as frequent, and even sneaky, drug users (Pakes 2015). And the drug dog represented increasing attention to identifying drug users and prosecuting drug possession in Denmark. Throughout the first decade of the 2000s, the number of people charged with drug crimes in Denmark increased 50 % (National Board of Health 2012, p. 75). People convicted of selling drugs in Denmark face sentences as long as 16 years, and Danish lawmakers have resisted trends (spreading across the United States in particular) to legalize cannabis and reduce the penalties for possessing and selling it (National Board of Health 2005, pp. 7–8; 2012, p. 74).

This persistent negotiation between hard and soft in Danish prisons is ongoing over the course of the day. For instance, one prisoner housed in a drug and alcohol treatment unit at Østjylland described his friendly relationships with the guards in his section, and how this relationship benefited both prisoners and guards:

Yeah, because they know you more. They know you more deep inside. Otherwise only like this, but you show them. Here they see what they want to see. So it's more good for us. And it's more good for them too. Because they come—they don't have to go stress in the job. Over in the other section, people make too much trouble, fight, drugs, alcohol, telephone. Here it's not like that. There is nothing about it. They just play billiards with us, table tennis in the hall; play football and this in the gym. It's good for them and it's good for us.

While this particular housing unit was exceptional—it was the only section where prisoners and staff ate lunch together on a routine basis—it is by no means the only site of softness at Østjylland.

Even when we interviewed prisoners housed in solitary confinement in that same facility (in that other section where "people make too much trouble"), in some of the most secure cells in Denmark, we could see the balance between the hard and the soft aspects of confinement. On the one hand, the prisoners spent 23 hours or more per day locked in their cells; at least two guards escorted each prisoner to an interview; and the interviews took place in a locked room with a live video camera (without sound recording) fixed on the isolated prisoner. In stark contrast to these high-security precautions, one of the prisoners we interviewed was granted time in the kitchen the day before the interview to prepare crepes for us. The next day, prison officers permitted him to reheat the crepes before his scheduled interview, carry them to the interview room, and set places for us with paper plates, plastic forks and knives, and cups of milk. Another prisoner in this unit was permitted to leave mid-interview for a cigarette break, returning with coffee he had made to share with us. He described some of the other "soft" allowances within this setting. For example, although he is usually alone in his cell, he is allowed to cook some meals with his friend, another prisoner in the same section. In addition to cooking they also spend their "yard time" together. He explained that, depending on the guard working, he and his friend might be allowed extra time outside. "The rules are you are not—you are only allowed to have one and a half hour, but I've been here so many years, and also this guy, he have been here many years also. So, we do like this. The other people go out first, and when they are finished, normally about 5:00 or 6:00, we go out 6:00, and we stay out until 9:00."

One veteran guard in this unit explained the value of this kind of balance between the hard conditions of segregation with soft flexibility around degree of freedom to move (or make crepes). Although prisoners are supposed to be confined to their cells 23 hours a day, he said, "if we have the time for extra . . . we can invite them to go play badminton or something" to allow them more time out of their cells. "The more time we can have them out, the more relaxed and civil they become for us." He then explained the importance of establishing a relationship with the prisoners, in contrast to just "knock[ing] them down." Developing a relationship "helps us in our work with them because . . . when we have done something good for them, they don't want to hurt us. And so, then they are listening more to what we say." Ugelvik has described a similar mindset among prison guards in Norwegian prisons, whom prisoners respect for communicating sympathy, and who make small compromises to maintain broader structures of control (2011, pp. 91, 59–60). The apparent softness inherent in permitting one of the highest security prisoners in Denmark to prepare crepes for his interviewers or to leave his cell for extra badminton time—at the guard's discretion—must be weighed against the hardness of 23 hours per day in isolation for months, and sometimes years, at a time, at the mercy of guards who have absolute control over whether any one prisoner warrants "extra" time out of the cell.

Prisoners at the open Møgelkær prison, in contrast to the prisoners in the high security Østjylland prison, moved throughout the facility much more freely. But even as we observed prisoners moving from housing unit to workplace without escort, congregating outside housing units at tables with benches to talk and smoke, and meeting at the church for a social hour, there were also many subtle indications of the potential for hard securitization. For instance, as visitors, we were issued phones with prominent alarm buttons on the top and warned not to hit the button twice in quick succession, because all of the staff would come running.

The balance between hard and soft prison practices loomed especially large in a poignant example reported to us by both prisoners and staff in a unit at Møgelkær: a combined guard and prisoner jog through the woods. Two interviewers and two female guards, who worked in a unit designated for sex offenders—the only section of the otherwise open facility that enclosed prisoners within a secure perimeter, primarily for their safety, describe the jog:

Interviewer 1: Do you think it's any different for you [doing your job] as a woman?

Respondent 1: No. Easier than a man. I was running with them [prisoners] in the woods. I have 8–9 person group.

Interviewer 1: From this unit? And you feel safe?

Respondent 1: Yeah.

Interviewer 1: I feel I've interviewed many prisoners in the U.S., but running in the woods, I don't know. (Laughing)

Respondent 2: The reason we do that is because you have eight [prisoners] with you, if one wants to hurt you, the seven left want to help you.

Respondent 1: Once I took a trip to the woods, at night, I had a headlamp. I had seven inmates with me in the dark.

Interviewer 2: [to Respondent 2] Do you do that?
Respondent 2: No I don't do that (laughing).
Interviewer 1: So you are brave. . . .
Respondent 1: I think we are open-minded. We smile a lot. We do things
with them. We are polite. I think that is a lot of connection
here that the prison guards in the USA do not have. . . .

The softness of a guard leading as many as nine prisoners from a specially secured sex offender unit on a jog through the woods stands in stark contrast to the relative hardness of the small prison within a prison in which those same guards and prisoners spend the majority of their time. Respondent 2 in the exchange above simultaneously acknowledged the danger inherent in such an outing, laughingly noting that she would not "do that" (go on a run alone with eight prisoners convicted of sex offenses), while supporting her colleague's assertion that being alone with a group of eight to nine prisoner sex offenders in the woods after dark is not quite the threatening situation that we, the interviewers, envisioned.

Respondent 1's explanation of her approach to prisoners revealed that, for her, running in the woods with prisoners is not a show of bravery in the face of potential threat, but rather an example of the open-minded attitude that staff have toward prisoners—an element of softness to counter the hardness that this group of prisoners experiences in relative isolation, within an otherwise open prison. While this example may be extreme—by no means do all Danish prison guards run in the woods with prisoners—it nonetheless demonstrates one of the myriad ways that guards could temper the hardness of prison by drawing upon the ethic of normalization that undergirds Danish prisons. It might also be an example of prison staff presenting a particularly dramatic story to us as American researchers, but it remains an important example of how these staff choose to present the work of guarding prisoners, unimaginable in the US context in which the presentation of prisoners would more commonly focus on the potential dangers of being with prisoners in uncontrolled environments.

Another example of softness beyond the bounds of the prison facility can be seen in "home visits": supervised visits in the community between prisoners and their families. On these visits, a guard dressed in plain clothes, rather than a blue Prison Service uniform, drives the prisoner to his home, sometimes hours away from the prison, and stays with the prisoner for the duration of the visit. During the car ride, one prison guard explained, he would have a prisoner ride up front alongside him. In response to a question about what they would talk about during the ride, the guard explained: "Just like normal friends. If you can say it like that. And I would say the rules for him. No drinking, and stuff like that. And not time too much cell phone, if it is there. And who is coming on the visit. Stuff like that." Sitting together in the front seat of the car, chatting "like normal friends"—alongside the practice of shedding the prison uniform for plain clothes for the occasion—softens the delivery of state-sanctioned guidelines still at play in this community setting.

Officers described using different approaches in managing the inter-action once at the prisoner's home. Although some preferred to remain on the periphery, simply standing guard to be sure the prisoner adheres to the restrictions in place for the visit, interacting minimally with the prisoner's family, others accepted invitations to participate in the visit more inclusively, sharing meals and conversation. All have to manage a balance between correctional control and normalization. The same prison guard, who discussed chatting like friends on the car ride to the visit, highlighted this tension in recounting his experiences on two home visits. He explained that the families had been nice to him and engaged him in conversation, but this can be strange. "I just try to be myself, as a person who's not judging the family. And just say, okay, it's maybe your son, your father, that has done something wrong. But still, your father, your son, have done some wrong but he's still a human. And we have to make the best out of it. But I also control their escape routes, if there is any one." When asked *how* he controls it, he explained he does this "discreetly" through observation. Of the 60,000 home leaves granted to Danish prisoners annually, only 0.1 % result in reoffending and 3 % result in some other form of abuse: failure to return, returning late, or returning intoxicated, so these situations rarely do need to be controlled (Kriminal Forsorgen 2015, p. 9). Still, as Ugelvik notes, there is the "omnipresent potential crisis" in prison work (2014, p. 59).

Thus, in the car and in the home, the prison guard is challenged—perhaps even more so than while inside prison walls—to manage a tricky balance between hard and soft. He must maintain *discreet* control, without the buttressing of hard structural elements (physical perimeters, lock and key, and colleagues ready to run at the push of a button) that he is used to on a daily basis on prison grounds, within a primarily *normalized* (i.e., non-carceral) setting. This stands in direct contrast to his daily routine in which he must do the reverse: soften or normalize an otherwise "hard" (i.e., controlled carceral) setting.

When guard and prisoner return to the prison grounds, the interplay between soft and hard in Danish prisons remains evident even in the very last moments of the day, when guards close down the housing units for the evening with their goodnight routine. We accompanied guards on their nightly routine in a special security wing at Østjylland—a space reserved for members of Denmark's street gangs and other prisoners who posed a greater-than-average risk to the facility. We walked through the quiet halls alongside prison guards, moving slowly and patiently down the wing as they stopped by each prisoner's cell for at least a brief face-to-face interaction. During this routine, the guards we observed took the opportunity to chat with the prisoners for a minute or two, ensure that no problems or issues had gone unresolved that day, administer medication, and lock each prisoner into the cell for the night the old fashioned way, with a key turned in each and every lock, by hand. (Another prisoner on a different special security unit at Østjylland noted that guards also come around at the start of the day and "say good morning... you can get your hot water, medicine or something if you need this.")

One officer explained the goodnight routine as a way to check in with the prisoner, make sure that any earlier conflicts had been put to rest, and even reckon with the effects of his own actions, apologizing if necessary, in order to ensure that no one went to sleep with a chip on his shoulder. He emphasized the importance of standing face-to-face and looking another person in the eye, on equal footing as a human being. An exchange from an interview with this guard affirms his commitment to these evening interactions:

> Respondent: Yeah, we can start to argue, have a little verbal fight with the prisoners, and then handle it, so that when we go home, we are friends again. That's possible.

Interviewer: Friends again with the prisoners.

Respondent: Yeah, yeah, we can I think can say that.

Interviewer: Yeah, I know what you mean. So, it's possible to be friends again, even after you have a verbal conflict.

Respondent: Of course, of course. If you do it in the right way, they also know when they make a mistake.

Not all of the goodnight interactions we observed were substantive, but all were polite, and many were individualized. Some prisoners seemed uninterested in chatting with the guards, instead issuing a brief goodnight and retiring to their bed—a clear signal that the interaction was over. Regardless of the content or tenor of each particular interaction, the guards we watched would conclude by saying "good night, sleep tight" thereby softening the hard practice of closing and locking the cell door. When one member of the research team expressed surprise that prisoners are bid goodnight and put to bed in such a gentle fashion, one guard responded "What would you have us do, stand at the end of the hall and flip a big switch to lock them all in?"[2]

The Role of Imperfection and Leaving Room for Error

In observing how both individual guards and institutional policies managed the delicate balance between hard and soft prison policies—during drug searches, in isolation or sex offender units, on supervised home visits, and during evening lockup routines—we noticed one key factor that facilitated the privileging of soft policies and practices over hard: acceptance of imperfection. Specifically, when guards and institutions prioritized humanizing policies oriented toward resocialization, whether through access to kitchen knives, or letting prisoners in isolation bring coffee or homemade crepes to an interview, they did so with the explicit knowledge that these practices might actually compromise

---

[2] Unrecorded conversation with guard, captured verbatim to the best of our ability in field notes.

harder goals of maintaining institutional safety and security. In this section, we examine when and how individual guards acknowledged, or institutional policies and practices revealed, this willingness to accept imperfection and leave room for error.

Creating a system centered around normalization and resocialization required embracing not only the potential for reform, but also the messiness of humanity—the knowledge that not everything can be predicted or controlled. For prison officials who embraced these imperfections, they were not indicative of institutional failure, but simply inherent to negotiating humanity in a coercive institution. For each of the examples described in the previous section, there was an acceptance of a potential for error built into the negotiation of hard and soft. Where guards and institutions accepted messiness and unpredictability, we observed that they more readily cultivated softer policies. Where they resisted imperfection or prioritized eliminating errors, we observed policies and practices quickly hardening.

In the case of the tail-wagging drug dog that sniffed us happily as we entered a high-security prison, prison officials made an explicit choice to use not only a friendly and nonthreatening dog, but also a minimally invasive means of searching for drugs. Danish prison officials have explicitly refused to implement cavity searches of either prisoners or visitors, even though they know that many drugs are smuggled into the prison inside body cavities. Here, the willingness to allow some drugs to make their way inside prison walls is key to maintaining the softer policy of using a friendly drug dog, rather than an invasive body cavity search.

Still, prison officials are not immune to the threat of drugs making their way into the prison. In addition to the drug dog, they also described to us how some prisoners suspected of smuggling contraband inside body cavities might be required to sit in an empty room until they "go to the toilet in a tray," either revealing contraband, or proving that there is none. This harsher response to the possible existence of smuggled drugs is a perfect example of how, as prison officials seek to minimize possible error (like letting drugs into the prison), policies become harsher, more oriented toward safety and security, and less oriented toward normalization and resocialization.

Just as enforcing drug policies requires accepting the possibility for error, so too does maintaining the "self-catering" regime. When prisoners cook for themselves, staff accept the possibility that they might hurt other prisoners or staff with some of the cooking implements. In one prison, we learned that a prisoner stabbed another prisoner with a potato peeler. Instead of removing the potato peeler from the kitchen entirely, prison staff simply decided to anchor the peeler to the wall with a steel cord, along with the knives. This minimized, though certainly did not eliminate, the possibility that the kitchen utensil could be repurposed as a weapon. A similar sense that prisoners should be able not only to cook for themselves, but to share meals with others, seemed to motivate guards to allow prisoners in isolation to bring food, and even plastic knives, to their interviews with us. Accepting the possibility that kitchen implements might be dangerously repurposed—and responding to such incidents on a case-by-case basis with a narrowly tailored institutional response—allowed prison staff to maintain normalizing self-catering regimes even in the face of potential threats to safety and security.

This willingness to accept microlevel mistakes—some drugs might be smuggled into the prison, or some knives might be misused—corresponds to an acceptance of more macro-level imperfections as well. In some cases, this included an acknowledgment of the futility of punishment. Guards accepted that some prisoners would fail to be resocialized and would return again and again to prison, or even again and again to isolation. This exchange with a guard working on an isolation unit illustrates this perspective:

Interviewer: How often do you see the same people [in the isolation unit]?

Respondent: All the time. It's the same people all the time. I think 70 % of them.
Have they been once, they come back. It's more because the gang they are in, and they are high rank in the gangs and they end up here. And some of the new known crazy people like the one I told you about now. Yeah.

Interviewer: Does it feel frustrating?

Respondent: No. No. It's kind of seeing a family member you only see sometimes. Once a year or something. Yeah.

This guard describes knowing that once a prisoner has been in isolation, he is likely to return to isolation. While this guard, like others working in isolation, described going out of his way to talk with prisoners in isolation and taking specific steps to mitigate the harshness of their confinement, he knows that these efforts might be futile. Acknowledging the futility, however, seems to mitigate this guard's frustration; futility is humanizing, too, and the prisoner becomes "like a family member you only see sometimes."

For the guard who described negotiating the hard-soft balance while supervising a prisoner on a home visit, the guard also acknowledged that error—in the form of escape—was a distinct possibility:

> Respondent: Yeah. That's the risk to be on a home visit, that they can escape.
> Interviewer: Are you watching him the whole time?
> Respondent: Not the whole time. Mostly. If he's in another room and I'm the next room, it's okay for me. I take it easy. Because I always have like, if he is escaping, then he is escaping. And Denmark is a little country. So, there is high risk that he's going to be found again. And it's only to – And it's not to his benefit if he escapes and comes in again. So.

This exchange reveals how a willingness to accept the small possibility of escape allows this guard to consciously choose to prioritize a soft resocialization policy, giving a prisoner a bit of space alone with his family during a supervised home visit, over a hard security policy of constant surveillance. As with the rarity of prisoners abusing family leave policies, escapes from the Danish prisons are also relatively rare; only one prisoner escaped from a closed Danish prison in 2014, and an additional 71 escaped from local and open prisons that year (where static control measures are nearly nonexistent) (Kriminal Forsorgen 2015, p. 9).

The guard who casually told us about donning a single head lamp on a nighttime jogging expedition in the woods with eight or nine prisoners could easily have faced a different possibility for error: the potential for danger to herself, rather than the community. What she described as "open-mindedness" rather than "bravery" seemed to facilitate a broad conceptualization of her role as a prison guard and a willingness to enter uncontrolled settings without getting caught up in the preoccupation of what-ifs and worst-case scenarios.

Not all negotiation of hard and soft carried a substantially increased possibility of error. Sometimes the introduction of soft elements into an otherwise hard moment—such as the nightly goodnight routine for locking down prisoners in a special security wing—carried with it no increased risk or room for error. Sometimes softness is simply soft.

In the cases we have examined, the degree of risk invited by the introduction of softness varies considerably. With each step along this blurry line between hard and soft, an acknowledgement of the possibility of error went hand-in-hand with policy decisions to prioritize softer, more normalized, resocialization-oriented practices. However, where the possibility of mistakes was foreclosed, or prison officials attempted to reduce errors (such as contraband, violence, or escapes), harder, more security oriented practices tended to be favored.

Danish prison officials often describe this balance as part of a "dynamic security" system that integrates hard and soft practices. For instance, the Project Manager overseeing the building of Denmark's newest closed prison, Nordfalster, explained that the prison design seeks to balance "static and dynamic security." The wall around the prison, he explained, represents the static security, but designers and staff seek to "normalize as much as possible inside the wall." This requires "dynamic security," where staff interact with prisoners, not surveilling them, but preventing any tension or unrest before it arises. You "secure the outside so you can normalize the inside," he said. While prison officials focused on how static security can facilitate dynamic security, we noted that the focus on security—especially static security infrastructure—contributed to an overall hardening of prison practices.

When Mistakes Cease to Be Acceptable

In writing about the future of Scandinavian exceptionalism, Pratt argued that, as "homogeneity and solidarity" erode in Scandinavia, the system is becoming less exceptional, or, functionally, harder (2008b, p. 277).

Others have also acknowledged this hardening of punishment practices in Scandinavia, documenting public opinions that existing policies are too lenient (Balvig et al. 2015), describing a "security turn" in prison design following four prison escapes in Sweden (Bruhn et al. 2016, p. 107), and pointing to increasingly harsh drug and deportation policies, again in Sweden (Barker 2013; Aas 2015). While these authors tend to disagree with Pratt's characterizations of Scandinavian exceptionalism, they also point to broader social characteristics as key explanatory factors in understanding the hardening of punishment and the "security turn." For instance, Brugh, Nylander, and Lindberg describe a turn away from social welfarism and toward neoliberalism, and both Barker and Aas describe the othering and exclusion of foreign nationals.

We observed a different mechanism of hardening within and around Danish prisons, one based on microlevel hard–soft negotiations rather than macro-level political or social negotiations. Specifically, we noted that prisons seemed to get harder as room for error decreased. For instance, the new closed prisons at Østjylland and Nordfalster, as well as Politigården (the retrofitted 25-bed isolation facility in Copenhagen), all represent increased investment in extremely secure, closed prison facilities. Prison officials described these facilities as simply replacing older, outdated facilities, or as cultivating external, static security, so as to facilitate internal, dynamic security. Politigården was a retrofitted Copenhagan jail site. Østjylland replaced the older Horsens prison, built in the middle of the 19th century, and, in 2016, Nordfalster will replace Vridsløselille, also built in the mid-19th century. The head of the DPPS Planning Unit explained that the newest facilities include "quite an element of future-proofing" in their design, so they can be sustainably updated as prison design and policies change in the future. The new prisons, then, do not represent expansions in the overall bed capacity of the Danish prison system, but rather maintenance of the existing scale of incarceration.

However, many of the design features of the new facilities suggest a movement toward harder prison designs and policies, stemming at least in part from a decreasing acceptance of the possibility for mistakes, whether fights between prisoners, attacks on staff, or escapes. Although the Project Manager noted that the new prison design at Nordfalster was meant to balance the competing hard and soft goals of "order and security; motivation and support," he also explained that the Nordfalster prison includes many new design touches that are even more restrictive than those at Østjylland. These include an underground walkway to the prison's isolation unit, to minimize visibility of who enters and exits the facility, and prison cell windows that face the perimeter wall, rather than the internal yard, again to minimize visibility between self-contained prison units. (At the same time, the windows do provide unobstructed views of nature.) He also described how staff increasingly carry pepper spray in the newer, closed prison facilities like Østjylland. Likewise, an architectural consultant to DPPS noted that, in practice, the day-to-day regime at Østjylland is stricter than the designers envisioned. "Lots of opportunities have been lost there" for normalization, he explained, describing the "sectioning" of prisoners in self-contained units, and noting the limited interaction staff have with prisoners. This combination of design innovations and practical implementation of restrictive policies in these new, state-of-the-art facilities suggests both a movement toward minimizing the possibility of dangerous errors, and an associated tendency to prioritize hard policies over soft policies, thereby constraining efforts to normalize.

We examine prison policy and practice in order to make sense of DPPS's negotiation of hard and soft, and examine how an acceptance of imperfection informs and shapes this balance in an ongoing, dynamic interaction. Our empirical examples explore this balance by examining the liminal and looking to the edges of correctional practice, both physically and temporally. We recount a morning encounter with a friendly drug dog at the entry point to Denmark's most secure prison to demonstrate the prison's prioritization of human dignity over the total elimination of drugs from the facility. We present a nighttime jaunt shared by guards and prisoners as they jog at the boundaries of controlled prison grounds and uncontrolled forest, in order to demonstrate how prison guards engage in practices with considerable room for error and possibilities of imperfection, in furtherance of normalization and resocialization. We describe home visits that allow prisoners and guards to traverse the bounds of the prison together in plain clothes, challenging guards to rely minimally on hard procedures in the soft setting of a prisoner's own home. And finally, we tell of the individualized goodnight routines in which guards attempt to do just the opposite—inject a modicum of softness into the quintessentially hard moment that finalizes each day with prisoners locked alone in their cells and guards retreating to their quarters.

In each of these microlevel negotiations, we see tensions between security and humanity that are fundamental to punishment in any context. Where we observed softness and humanity, which scholars like Pratt argue make the Scandinavian context exceptional, we saw it stemming not simply from a broad social context of welfarism but from a specific institutional context of accepting imperfections and a willingness to leave room for potential errors. However, we also saw examples of hardening associated with attempts to reduce error and minimize imperfection.

Acknowledgements This material is based upon work supported by the National Science Foundation under Grant Nos. 1455971, 1455413, 1455091.

References

Aas, K. F. (2015). Bordered penalty: precarious membership and abnormal justice. *Punishment & Society, 16*(5), 520–541.

Adams, J. (2001). "The wildest show in the south": tourism and incarceration at Angola. *Drama Review, 45*, 94–108.

Balvig, F., Gunnlaugsson, H., Jerre, K., Tham, H., Kinnuen, A. (2015). The public sense of justice in Scandinavia: a study of attitudes towards punishment. *European Journal of Criminology, 12*(3), 342–361.

Barker, V. (2013). Nordic exceptionalism revisited: explaining the paradox of a Janus-faced penal regime. *Theoretical criminology, 17*(1), 5–25.

Brown, M. (2009). *The culture of punishment: prison, society, and spectacle*. New York: New York University Press.

Bruhn, A., Nylander, P., Lindberg, O. (2016). Swedish "prison exceptionalism" in decline: trends toward distantiation and objectification of the Other. In A. Eriksson (Ed.), *Punishing the other: production of immorality revisited.* (pp. 101–123). New York, NY: Routledge.

Crewe, B. (2007). Power, adaptation and resistance in a late-modern men's prison. *British Journal of Criminology, 47*, 256–275.

Crewe, B. (2011). Depth, weight, tightness: revisiting the pains of imprison-ment. *Punishment & Society, 13*(5), 509–529.

Dey, E. (2009). Prison tours as a research tool in the golden gulag. *Journal of Prisoners on Prisons, 18*, 119–125.

Goffman, E. (1961). *Asylums: essays on the social situation of mental patients and other inmates*. New York: Doubleday.

Ibsen, A. Z. (2013). Ruling by favors: prison guards' informal exercise of institutional control. *Law & Social Inquiry, 38*(2), 342–363.

Jefferson, A. M. (2012). Comparison at work: exporting "exceptional norms". In T. Ugelvik and J. Dullum (Eds.), *Penal exceptionalism? Nordic prison policy and practice* (pp. 100–118). New York: Routledge.

Kriminal Forsorgen. (2015). Danish Prison and Probation Service—in brief. Report on file with authors.

Liebling, A., & Arnold, H. (2004). *Prisons and their moral performance: a study of values, quality and prison life*. Cambridge: Cambridge University Press.

Minke, L. K. (2014). Cooking in prison—from crook to cook. *International Journal of Prison Health, 10*(4), 228–238.

Mjåland, K. (2014). "A culture of sharing": drug exchange in a Norwegian prison. *Punishment & Society, 16*(3), 336–352.

Nagelsen, S., & Huckelbury, C. (2009). The prisoner's role in ethno-graphic examinations of the Carceral state. *Journal of Prisoners on Prisons, 18*, 111–118.

National Board of Health (Sundhedsstyrelsen). (2005). 2005 national report to the EMCDDA by the Reitox national focal point: Denmark: new develop-ment, trends and in-depth information on selected issues. Lisbon, Portugal: EMCDDA. http://www.drugwarfacts.org/cms/Denmark#sthash.3FvguPZm.dpuf. Accessed 2 September 2016.

National Board of Health (Sundhedsstyrelsen). (2012). 2011 National report (2010 data) to the European Monitoring Centre for Drugs and Drug Addiction (EMCDDA) by the Reitox National Focal Point: Denmark: new development, trends and in-depth information on selected issues. Lisbon, Portugal: EMCDDA. http://www.drugwarfacts.org/cms/Denmark#sthash.3FvguPZm.dpuf. Accessed 2 September 2016.

Pakes, F. (2015). Howard, Pratt and beyond: assessing the value of Carceral tours as a comparative method. *Howard Journal of Criminal Justice, 54*(3), 265–276.

Piché, J., & Walby, K. (2010). Problematizing Carceral tours. *British Journal of Criminology, 50*, 570–581.

Piché, J., & Walby, K. (2012). Carceral tours and the need for reflexivity: a response to Wilson, Spina and Canaan. *Howard Journal of Criminal Justice, 51*(4), 411–418.

Pratt, J. (2008a). Scandinavian exceptionalism in an era of penal excess: Part I: the nature and roots of Scandinavian exceptionalism. *British Journal of Criminology, 48*, 119–137.

Pratt, J. (2008b). Scandinavian exceptionalism in an era of penal excess: Part II: does Scandinavian exceptionalism have a future. *British Journal of Criminology, 48*, 275–292.

Pratt, J., & Eriksson, A. (2013). *Contrasts in punishment: an explanation of Anglophone excess and Nordic exceptionalism.* New York: Routledge.

Reiter, K., & Koenig, A. (2015). *Extreme punishment: comparative studies in detention, incarceration, and solitary confinement.* New York: Palgrave MacMillan.

Sexton, L. (2015). Penal subjectivities: developing a theoretical framework for penal consciousness. *Punishment & Society, 17*(1), 114–136.

Shammas, V. L. (2014). The pains of freedom: Assessing the ambiguity of Scandinavian penal exceptionalism on Norway's Prison Island. *Punishment & Society, 16*(1), 104–123.

Smith, P. S. (2012). A critical look at Scandinavian Exceptionalism: Welfare state theories, penal populism, and prison conditions in Denmark and Scandinavia. In T. Ugelvik and J. Dullum (Eds.), *Penal exceptionalism? Nordic prison policy and practice* (pp. 38–57). New York: Routledge.

Sterbenz, C. (2014, October 20). An American prison warden visited a Norwegian prison, and he couldn't believe what he saw. *Business Insider.* http://www.businessinsider.com/anamerican-warden-visited-a-norwegian-prison–and-he-couldnt-believe-what-he-saw-2014-10. Accessed 2 September 2016.

Turner, N., & Travis, J. (2015, August 6). What we learned from German prisons. *New York Times.* http://www.nytimes.com/2015/08/07/opinion/what-we-learned-from-german-prisons.html. Accessed 2 September 2016.

Ugelvik, T. (2011). The hidden food: mealtime resistance and identity work in a Norwegian prison. *Punishment & Society, 13*(1), 47–63.

Ugelvik, T. (2014). *Power and resistance in prison: doing time, doing freedom.* New York: Palgrave MacMillan.

Wilson, D., Spina, R., Canaan, J. E. (2011). In praise of the Carceral tour: learning from the Grendon experience. *Howard Journal of Criminal Justice, 50*(4), 343–355.

Part VI

Conclusion

Punishment and Welfare in Scandinavia

Peter Scharff Smith and Thomas Ugelvik

Are Scandinavian Prisons Welfare Institutions?

Analytically, one could argue that the literature on Scandinavian or Nordic exceptionalism has been characterised by a logic of juxtaposition where specific prisons in specific countries have been used as stand-ins for two ideal types:

1. Punitive penal state prisons, with high prison population rates and punitive and coercive regimes that lack any proper focus on rehabilitation;
2. Egalitarian welfare state prisons, where punishment is humane, rehabilitative, supportive, inclusive and future-oriented, and where imprisonment is an intervention which is ultimately designed to empower

P.S. Smith (✉) · T. Ugelvik
Department of Criminology and Sociology of Law, University of Oslo, Oslo, Norway
e-mail: p.s.smith@jus.uio.no; thomas.ugelvik@jus.uio.no

P. Scharff Smith, T. Ugelvik (eds.), *Scandinavian Penal History, Culture and Prison Practice,* Palgrave Studies in Prisons and Penology, DOI 10.1057/978-1-137-58529-5_21

prisoners to increase their chances of returning to society and living a good life post release.

Much of the exceptionalism literature has been based on an analysis where specific institutions have been seen as representations of one or the other ideal type—and the decisive factor has generally been whether a penal practice has been found to be 'punitive' or not. In real life, we should probably not expect any state or any prison system to fall solely and completely into one of these categories. Nevertheless, we certainly seem to have states and prison systems which put a lot of effort into aligning as much as possible with the first model, while it might be more difficult to find countries that can be placed firmly in the latter model. If any states have been said to systematically approach the second model it is certainly the Scandinavian/Nordic states. But when reading through the chapters in this book it seems that we need a more complex analytical framework to discuss the Scandinavian prison practice. In our opinion, the analysis risk becoming to one-dimensional when everything becomes a question of measuring much or less punitiveness and then attempt to explain these differences as a result of higher or lower welfare ambitions and welfare state models. As Minke and Smoyer point out (in this volume), the Nordic prison models are first and foremost 'different strategies of confinement' and should be analysed as such. There are clearly different ways of broadening our understanding of the connection between punishment and welfare, as we have seen in this book. One possible way forward would be to expand on the system with two ideal types. Adding a third one might allow us to escape the one-sided use of the 'more or less punitiveness' measure. Here we find inspiration in David Garlands 1985 book on 'Punishment and Welfare' where he identified how the British 'penal welfare strategies' adopted during a period from late 19th century and well into the 20th century involved, for example, a significant expansion and diversification of the available penal sanctions and the establishment of an extended apparatus of state control. However, the Scandinavian welfare states of the 21st century are obviously much more expansive and stronger than their British counterpart around a century ago and we should expect the penal strategies of these states to be more forceful and capable of producing more social control (and potentially more welfare) as, indeed, several chapters in this book illustrate. Hence, we call our third ideal type 'The Big Mother penal welfare state model'.

In the Big Mother penal welfare state, imprisonment and treatment programs are powerful interventions in the private life of citizens, which often constitute attempts not only to punish but also to rehabilitate, change and 'normalise' citizens according to the normative and often unquestioned value sets these states are built upon. These arrangements might clearly benefit a large group of citizens who are initially labelled as criminals as they stand a relatively good chance of becoming re-socialised and returning to society. But one could also argue that such inclusive policies come with a price where use of state power against those deemed to be deviant may sometimes be deployed very brusquely and intrusively, because the norm is seen as self-explanatory and the intervention labelled as benign, fair and benevolent. This might be the case when punishment is justified by the same core values that support the welfare state in general. In that sense these states have perhaps developed a culture of intervention (Andersson, in this volume) which can leave the individual and his or her private life very vulnerable. In short, being embraced by Big Mother can be something of a mixed blessing. Her embrace is simultaneously loving and forceful, and she both wants and knows what is best for you.

In addition, if the Big Mother welfare state finally loses confidence in her citizens she will frequently opt for the 'othering' and exclusion of deviants. The result may be a process of producing outsiders which in some ways might be much harsher compared to other types of states since the vast majority of individuals in Scandinavian welfare states are included and part of the norm while the excluded truly are a minority and therefore much more different and deviant than in most other types of states and communities, where more people can be said to live on the fringe of society. Close-knitted, 'tight', and egalitarian societies might treat scapegoats particularly harshly. As we have seen in some of the chapters in this book, the Scandinavian states are often not afraid to deploy their powers whether those deprived of their liberty have been found guilty or not. In such a society, characterised by very high levels of trust in the state and its justice system, as well as a rather smug self-image of being inclusive and human rights-oriented, it can be very difficult to question the authorities and their use of power.

It seems clear that penal policies and practices in many jurisdictions in recent decades have moved in the direction of the first penal model. Some describe this as a rise of neoliberal influences and the introduction of policies associated with New Public Management including a focus on risk, self-sufficiency, 'responsibilisation', cost-benefit, self-help incentives, and of course more punishment and more punitive practices. This is a development that several authors in this book describe as having had a significant impact on Scandinavian prison policy during recent years. The question remains, then: to what degree does Scandinavian prison practice reflect any of the above models and in what direction are these prisons currently developing? In order to answer these questions, we need to dig a level deeper and look at the way that the apparently different discourses and techniques of rehabilitation, welfare and punishment mix and sometimes work together.

Rehabilitation, Welfare, Rights and Power

Whether one finds the above models useful as analytical tools or not, a crucial discussion when trying to understand Scandinavian prison practice has to do with the nexus of rehabilitation, welfare, rights and power. For example, is rehabilitation of prisoners a priority and, if so, how is this handled by the state and what does this means in terms of social control and welfare policies? This is a complicated issue and history has taught us that rehabilitative programmes in prison (and elsewhere) are not necessarily benign, nor always especially humane. Even when (or perhaps if) rehabilitation is truly in the best interest of those on the receiving end, a prison might not exactly be the best place to instigate such an effort. Indeed, as Ploeg points out (in this volume) the contradiction between simultaneously executing a punishment and implementing rehabilitation measures in the work of correctional officers is well known and much discussed. In that sense, we have punishment and security on the one hand, and rehabilitative work on the other, and some argue that you cannot expect the same staff to be able to do both. If this is true perhaps we are talking about an awkward mix of fundamentally incompatible logics; a philosophical equivalent of trying to mix oil and water? Are there any reasons that Scandinavian states should be better at this than others? On the other hand, one could also argue that the strong Scandinavian welfare states and their cultures of intervention make rehabilitative work natural in a prison context. This still leaves the question open to what degree such work may benefit prisoners and if it is truly aimed at empowering individuals or whether it is rather the result of a strong state trying protect itself. Of course, the two are not mutually exclusive.

If we adopt the latter approach, it would in fact make sense to expect Scandinavian welfare states to use their relatively unquestioned practices and value base (inclusiveness, equality, extensive social welfare policies etc.) as part of a strategy to neutralise deviant behaviour. In other words, such a state would employ not only punitive measures but also rehabilitative efforts as a natural element in its social control efforts. Indeed, history has taught us that rehabilitative programs can easily be punitive as well. Nevertheless, one would arguably expect a truly humane state to focus more on empowerment of its citizens than on rehabilitation as social control. Here the principle of normalisation and the question of prisoners' rights also comes into play, and potentially take up a central role in the discussion, as a way to balance the scales between state power and rehabilitative programming on the one hand, and the autonomy of the individual on the other.

The question we have raised and discussed in this book has been whether it makes sense to say that there is a specifically Scandinavian way of trying to reconcile the different projects of security, power, welfare, punishment, social control, rights and rehabilitation. In other words, how do Scandinavian welfare states approach and handle the nexus of rehabilitation, welfare, rights and power in a prison context? All the individual chapters have, each in their own way, addressed this issue. Drawing on a wide range of relevant literature and a variety of different perspectives, the chapters have put their spotlight on different aspects of prison history, policy and practice in the three Scandinavian countries.

By way of conclusion, we will in the following collect and re-examine selected insights from the various chapters in order try to move the discussion even further along.

Drug Treatment

Several chapters touch on issues surrounding drug treatment in custodial settings. The question of drug treatment in prisons may be one of the best and most pregnant examples of the both expansive and yet uneasy mix of punishment and welfare, of coercion and help, in Scandinavian prisons.

The dilemma is how to strike a working balance between the sometimes conflicting objectives of protecting people from imprisoned criminals on the one hand, and rehabilitating prisoners on the other. Security and individual treatment does indeed frequently seem to be at odds with each other in everyday life on the wings in Scandinavian prisons. According to Bruhn, Lindberg and Nylander, in the case of Sweden, an increasingly repressive prison service chooses security over constructive rehabilitative relationships in many cases. Furthermore, the increase in prison-based drug treatment in Sweden in recent years can be described as a perverse mirror image of the decrease of non-custodial treatment methods in the same period (Bruhn, Lindberg and Nylander, this volume). If prisons are becoming major centres for drug treatment, it could mean that prisons are becoming more welfare oriented, but also, at the same time, that the Swedish state is diverting more resources *from* the welfare system and *into* the penal system; an important reminder that prisons should not be studied in isolation from the rest of society. These changes, at first glance self-contradictory, do in fact seem to be compatible. One could perhaps call such a process a development from social welfare to prison welfare? In any case such practices can be understood first and foremost as traditional social control – in this case imprisonment of drug users lacking support in their communities – although with a somewhat more humane face than purely punitive prison practices. Indeed, while rehabilitation in prisons has often been portrayed as a force that opposes punitive policies, in the Big Mother's authoritarian welfare prisons, rehabilitation programmes arguably fit hand in glove with the framework of a late modern managerial penal strategy, which focuses on risk management and exclusionary politics.

Kolind finds a more or less similar situation in the Danish context. From the point of view of Danish prison treatment wings, the difference between welfare and punishment has become muddled to a degree that it is now difficult to keep the two apart, according to Kolind. Compared with the drug treatment schemes that are currently in vogue in Denmark in general, which are rights-based, community-based and based on voluntary participation, the Danish prison-based treatment schemes are based on control and coercion. According to Kolind, the prison context with its innate penal logic transforms a welfare-oriented programme designed to help individuals and turns it into a tool for efficient control and administration of a problem population. Several chapters in this book note how such a blurring of the line between help and social control has had terrible consequences in Scandinavia's past.

Normalisation

Normalisation is a core value of all Scandinavian prison systems, but it is also a European human rights principle codified in the European prison rules. This means that technically all the 47 Council of Europe member states should follow the principle of normalisation, but this is clearly not always the case. In Scandinavia, however, we expect normalisation to play an important role. What that exactly means in practice and what the results are on the ground in a Scandinavian prison wings is, however, far from clear. There are considerable differences between the Scandinavian countries, and also between prisons within the three jurisdictions, and sometimes between separate prison wings and even from one staff shift to another.

Engbo introduces a useful distinction between defensive and proactive normalisation concepts. The defensive concept states that authorities must not interfere with prisoners' lives more than what is necessary in a prison environment. A prison is a prison, but from this perspective, prisons should be as normal and non-intrusive as possible. The proactive aspect, on the other hand, requires authorities to actively create conditions which approach conditions on the outside whenever possible, and even, in some interpretations of the concept, to actively encourage prisoners to lead normal lives. According to Engbo, however, the latter utilitarian argument – to normalise people and not only prison conditions – runs contrary to the very ethos of normalisation, which 'is not a tool or a strategy for social reintegration' but rather 'an essential element of a democratically based prison regime' (p. 341). This is in complete opposition to 'totalitarian prison regimes in which inmates only have the rights and conditions of life (…) that the powerful prison management opts to bestow on them' (p. 341).

Langelid's chapter describes the history of prison education in Norway as closely connected to the development of the principle of normalisation. All Norwegians have a right to a free secondary education according to the Norwegian Education Act. Prisoners bring this right with them into prison. It is observed in policy documents and vision statements that education in prison might impact positively on reconviction rates, but that is in a sense, from the point of view of normalisation, beside the point. Education is an individual right, and as a right, it corresponds with concomitant duties of the correctional and education services: The prison and public school systems have a duty to cooperate efficiently in order to provide prisoners with the education services they need. The principle of normalisation, then, is not in itself a rehabilitation tool (although the difference is sometimes unclear in key policy texts, according to Engbo), but one might say that normalisation is an important part – perhaps an indispensable part – of the equation when Scandinavian prison systems set out to reintegrate prisoners in practice. The welfare systems outside the prison gates for a large part run according to a logic of legal rights to welfare provisions. According to the principle of normalisation, prisoners keep all such rights when incarcerated. It is the duty of the prison to ensure that prisoners are generally able to make practical use of these rights even while they are serving a custodial sentence. A theoretical right is not much use to anyone. The principle of normalisation may therefore be seen as a necessary condition of any welfare-oriented prison in practice.

For a large part thanks to their ambitious welfare schemes, the Scandinavian societies are among the most gender equal in the world. Gender equality is seen as a fundamental value. A specifically Scandinavian take on gender issues can be said to be at the core of Scandinavians' self-image. In Denmark (and unlike Norway and Sweden), a result is that there are no women's prisons. Instead incarcerated men and women mix in certain prisons and on certain wings. In Denmark mixed gender prisons are seen to reflect both the principle of normalisation, and the gender-equal society on the other side of the prison walls. As Mathiassen observes, however, forcing a tiny minority of women to live in total institutions that are almost exclusively male does not seem to reflect normal life in Danish society. Mathiassen's study deftly points to an insight that is shared by several of the authors in this book: the principle of normalisation is just that, a principle. For it to be put to actual use, it must be translated into actual practice in real institutions where real-life people interact. In this case, what appears to be non-intervention (choosing not to separate men and women to create a gender-equal prison to match the gender-equal Danish society outside) actually amounts to the active creation of very exceptional and not in any sense 'normal' living conditions for female prisoners in the Danish system. Nevertheless, as Mathiassen also notes, many women *do* prefer to have male company in prison, but many are clearly also placed in a very vulnerable situation and their relationships subjected to the logic of the prison and the power of their male counterparts.

The food provided to prisoners in Danish remand centres, described by Minke and Smoyer is another example of what we might call abnormal normalisation. The prisoners who actually have to eat it, do not experience the food produced to mimic a 'normal' Danish diet outside the prison, as anything close to 'normal'. In fact, even the self-cooking regime often ends up producing situations that prisoners experience as being far from normal, although they clearly prefer this model compared to the food handed out in remand prisons. Ploeg makes a related point: As the forces of globalisation are changing the world around us, making new goods and services (including social media) from around the globe readily available, prisons are lagging behind, making prison life less and less 'normal' every day. Especially when it comes to the growing importance of Internet access in almost all areas of life we are clearly faced with a massive challenge which all prison systems have to handle in the future. How the Scandinavian systems with their reliance on the principle of normalisation will deal with this is a most interesting question.

Security Levels and Regimes

Security decisions are vital parts of the management of any prison and any prison system. Empirically, we know that Scandinavian prisons exhibit a large variety of very different institutions. Among the prisons in these countries, one can find a small number of high-security institutions and special security wings that rival the maximum-security facilities one can find in jurisdictions far removed – geographically as well as culturally – from Scandinavia. One can also find prison regimes that are among the most open and least prison-like regimes in the world; institutions that according to some international commentators look more like hotels or college dorms than prisons. This variety does in some ways make it difficult to say anything at all about Scandinavian prisons in general. It is probably right, though, that compared to other prison systems in other countries, a larger proportion of prisoners spend their prison time in more open, lower security regimes.

In the cases of Denmark and Norway, the aftermath of the Second World War resulted in similar experiences which helped create novel uses of imprisonment, as described by both Fransen (Denmark) and Shammas (Norway). In both countries, the end of the war saw the new governments taking over after German capitulation faced with the problem of what to do with large numbers of convicted collaborators. There were so many in fact that they could not possibly be housed in the prison facilities that were available at the time. Both countries were forced to quickly build a number of low-security penal camps to resolve the situation, in many cases transforming army barracks and camps established by the German forces. Fransen describes how, in the case of Denmark, the result was the creation of open prisons and thereby a new tradition of low-security imprisonment. The experiences gathered from the immediate post-war ad hoc solutions were promising enough (and the open camps made enough economic sense) that when things started to return back to normal in the 1950s, the open prison had been introduced as a constructive low-cost alternative.

One should, however, remember that not all Scandinavian prisons are open places where prisoners can move around and express themselves freely all the time. Paradoxically, in many cases the least open and most restrictive conditions are reserved for prisoners who have not yet been convicted of any crime. Smith describes a number of very intrusive and essentially punitive Scandinavian pre-trial practices including the exceptionally high rate of pre-trial solitary confinement still found in Sweden. This particular Scandinavian problem is well known but Smith venture beyond this and looks at different pre-trial practices including ordinary conditions in Danish remand prisons. Here he finds some of the harshest prison conditions and toughest regimes in the entire Danish prison estate. According to Smith, such forceful state interventions against those still presumed innocent can be understood within the framework of the strong Scandinavian welfare state and alongside 'other well-known examples of extensive social control and social engineering' in these states (p. 143). Langford, Fisher, Schaffer and Pareus describe how the issue of solitary confinement in Scandinavian prisons in itself has challenged the human rights record of these states. In their comparative analysis, it is sometimes difficult to see how the Scandinavian countries differ from the German example in particular, although they generally seem to fare better than the other European countries in the comparative analysis.

One should also remember that even open prisons are prisons. The openness of Bastøy prison in Norway, a farm prison on an island where prisoners can roam more or less freely, for instance, is predicated on the ever-present threat of being sent back to a closed, high-security prison if one fails to behave according to Bastøy's house rules. As Reiter, Sexton and Sumner points out even relatively soft prison regimes can be experienced as punitive. Furthermore, there is no guarantee that the openness of the Scandinavian systems will continue. According to Fransen, the Danish open prisons today are hardly as open as their earlier counterparts. Fences have been built where previously there were none. CCTV cameras and other similar static control measures have been introduced. He argues that the term 'open' today perhaps should be replaced by 'not fully closed' and further finds that in Denmark 'there has been a failure to drive the liberal and humanistic treatment of prisoners beyond that of the 1970s' (p. 96). Bruhn, Lindberg and Nylander describe a similar 'security turn' that has changed the Swedish system in the wake of a series of spectacular prison escapes in 2004. Higher fences and stronger walls were built, additional security officers were hired, and risk assessment – always a factor in any prison – has now been elevated to a core part of everything that goes on in the Swedish prison estate. This improved security has created increased distance between prisoners and staff, impacting negatively on the rehabilitation goals of the Swedish system. Reiter, Sexton, and Sumner describe a similar process where design innovations in newly built state-of-the-art Danish prisons represent a movement towards the situational reduction of risks and an associated tendency to prioritise hard policies over soft ones, constraining efforts to normalise the prison experience in the process.

Individualised Treatment

Individually tailored solutions are generally seen as all-important for a successful rehabilitation and re-entry process. According to this logic, there is no one size fits all solution in the world of Scandinavian correctional intervention; the ideal is bespoke schemes and solutions, not *prêt-à-porter*. This view is in fact at the core of the Scandinavian welfare model in general: What is right for one client is not necessarily right for another. Individuals should be seen and treated on an individual basis by experts who know how to identify the main challenges and possibilities in the specific case at hand, and choose between different possible interventions accordingly. Lundeberg concludes that the many different rehabilitative approaches available to staff in the Norwegian prison system do warrant use of the term 'exceptional'. She describes how the wider range of approaches and extensive use of discretion make prisoners feel that their individual needs are often taken into consideration. In a legal context focused on the rule of law and predictable sentences, individualised treatment may look a lot like discrimination, however. This is another example of the everyday, local clashes between penal considerations, welfare logics and prisoner rights. On the one hand, prisoners should be treated fairly and according to the rules—what goes for one prisoner should also go for the prisoners in the next cell over. On the other hand, these two individuals may be seen to have very different individual needs, and they should thus be treated differently. Lundeberg's study shows that prisoner agree that staff should use their discretionary powers to make individual decisions. As long as the point is to help individual prisoners, fellow prisoners will tolerate a certain level of discrimination. Decisions that are seen as arbitrary and unjust, however, are never suffered lightly.

Individually tailored services may sound well and good, but it has a potential dark side. There is a fine line between rehabilitation and authoritarian intervention, and in a Big Mother state it may be hard to spot any difference between these two approaches as they can sometimes merge into a coordinated strategy. Indeed, when services are tailored to the individual's needs they are always based on some sort of ideal. According to Lundeberg, the individualisation of welfare services may improve prisoners' chances, but it may also lead to paternalism. Remembering Engbo's distinction between defensive and proactive normalisation, when authorities actively set out to create 'normal' lives for prisoners, it inevitably involves the more or less coercive use of a norm, and to make matters worse, a norm that is frequently left implicit. What is a 'normal' life and who should be allowed to set the standard? In Fredwall's analysis, Norwegian prison officers have different opinions when it comes to this question. His distinction between a guiding and a transformational officer ideal points to the difference between officers who try to provide prisoners with a range of constructive opportunities to choose from, and officers who want to decide for prisoners, because they think they know what is best for them, and for society in general.

Paternalism is not necessarily a problem, however. Even the most well thought-out and benevolent welfare system will have a paternalistic side more or less deeply hidden in its conception of a 'good life'. But when decisions are systematically taken on the behalf of prisoners who feel that they are not included in the decision-making process, even the best-intended schemes may turn out to be counterproductive. In any case, such programmes are certainly more a matter of paternalistic moral education of incarcerated individuals than they are strategies of empowerment. Nilsson describes how the work assignments in Swedish prisons historically were designed to change prisoners into good industrial workers, not simply disciplined pawns in a capitalist economy. In Sweden, prisons were to produce not only 'law abiding workers' but also 'industrious, "respectable" citizens loyal to the welfare state, its laws and moral underpinnings' (p. 51). The idea that regular wage labour is a fundamental part of any 'normal' life can be found in the organisational make-up of most Scandinavian prison to this day. The fact that the work assignments offered to prisoners often are very different from the jobs that may be available to them on release is however rarely recognised.

The result of active normalisation attempts may sometimes even be outright destructive. Andersson's chapter gives several historical examples of the injustices that may result when strong welfare-oriented Big Mother states decide to intervene in the lives of individuals for the good of all. According to Andersson, in a welfare state like Sweden, with a strong culture of intervention, the development of a just and egalitarian welfare society has gone hand in hand with the use of invasive, coercive and intrusive measures against 'clients' that refuse to better themselves, all for their own good. According to Shammas, the same was certainly true in Norway. In the inter-war years, Norway, like many other countries, passed a new sterilisation law on the basis of eugenic principles. Unlike many other European societies, however, the Norwegian turn to eugenics took place as part of a democratic social reform agenda rather than being part of a politically conservative or openly anti-liberal agenda. Similarly, in Denmark and Sweden eugenics and sterilisation was also part of a social and democratic welfare project. When paternalism thus combines with moralism and the pair takes the guise of legitimate and benevolent interventions, history tells us that the results risk becoming totalitarian and authoritarian in nature and should be watched very closely.

Release, Re-entry and Inclusion

The fundamental long-term goal of a prison sentence in Scandinavia is, on paper at least, always inclusion. A prison sentence excludes, but it is supposed to be a temporary exclusion suffered in order to include. This makes sense given that Scandinavian prisoners (with a few possible exceptions, including prisoners serving the Norwegian indeterminate *forvaring* sentence or the Swedish life sentence) are all going to be released at some point. Any prisoner might end up as your next-door neighbour in the future, and given the Scandinavian sentencing levels, in the majority of cases, the not-so-distant future. According to Vander Beken, for this reason, the rehabilitation focus of the Scandinavian systems is deeply connected to the inclusive, high-trust, and consensus-based Scandinavian societies they are part of. Scandinavian prisoners are often given opportunities and responsibilities they are not trusted with in other jurisdictions. An example can be found in Minke and Smoyer's chapter. The ethos of normalisation in the Danish prison system is reflected by the fact that prisoners are trusted to shop and cook for themselves even in high-security institutions. This contributes to create and strengthen prisoners' sense of autonomy and allows them to express themselves through the food they choose to prepare and eat, which ideally also help them prepare for successful release and re-entry into society. Similarly, we find in Engbo's interpretation of the normalisation principle – an interpretation by a Scandinavian prison governor – a deep-rooted respect for the rights and autonomy of prisoners.

Ploeg describes the various community-based sanctions that are available in the Norwegian system. These alternatives are explicitly designed to be more inclusionary and carry less of a negative impact than a traditional prison sentence. Community sanctions will almost by default comply better with the principle of normalisation than even the most open-prison regime. In many jurisdictions, community-based alternatives will have a weak legitimacy among the general public; they are seen as too lax and 'soft on crime'. This is not the case in Norway, according to Ploeg; here community sanctions alternatives enjoy a strong acceptance among the general public. It is therefore a paradox that the use of community sanctions are in decline in Norway. Ploeg argues that this is mainly due to a decrease in property and youth crime, but one might then ask why the decrease has not been accompanied by a decrease in the daily Norwegian prison population rate. One might also ask, following Vander Beken, why short-term prison sentences have such a strong standing in the Norwegian system when inclusionary, low-cost and low-impact community sanctions are losing ground?

Several chapters argue that there are limits to the inclusionary Scandinavian correctional systems. As long as Norwegian prisons busy themselves with returning Norwegian citizens to Norwegian society, everything is just fine, according to Vander Beken. But what about the large number of foreign nationals going through the system? The Norwegian prison system has yet to solve the dilemma of what an inclusionary and rehabilitation-oriented prison system should do with people who are not going to be returned to Norwegian society on release. Ugelvik describes how prisoners in Kongsvinger prison, Norway's only prison designed to hold an all-foreign population, actually by and large are given access to the same welfare benefits and rehabilitation-oriented schemes that are available to Norwegian citizens while they are in prison. This is true for a large part also in cases when foreigners lack an individual right to welfare provision; the prison system and the relevant welfare agencies cooperating with the prisons choose to treat foreign national prisoners as if they had these rights. However, when it comes to the preparation for release and through care schemes that are seen as vital for a successful re-entry process by the Norwegian correctional services, this situation changes. When the release date approaches and the plan is to put prisoners on a plane and send them off to Lithuania, Romania or Nigeria, Kongsvinger prison simply capitulates. Unlike the ideal in other Norwegian prisons, their responsibilities in practice stop at the gates. According to Shammas, this lack of interest in the future of foreign national prisoners is an example of a wider tendency where the criminal justice system bifurcates along ethnonational lines. He argues, in some ways *contra* Ugelvik, that the result should be described as a split between a welfare-oriented and rehabilitative system reserved for citizens, and another, more punitive alternative system designed for outsiders.

A different kind of de facto exclusionary policy is described in Olesen's chapter. In the Danish system prisoners are expected to pay for all the expenses incurred by their court cases when they are released from prison. The result is that most Danish prisoners are released with a considerable economic debt to the state, which can sometimes run into the millions of *kroner*. Although it does seem like more of a penal-oriented than a welfare-oriented policy, expecting prisoners to pay for their old sins may sound like a sensible thing to do. For newly released prisoners, however, many of which lack resources and some actually live from hand to mouth, repaying their debts is simply impossible. The best or in some cases only possible solution may be to continue a life of crime, according to Olesen. This one policy may in some cases in one stroke cancel out all the rehabilitation and welfare oriented efforts of the Danish system.

A Scandinavian Way of Doing Things?

Vander Beken describes a wide variety of very different prison regimes within just one of the Scandinavian countries. The question is whether it makes sense at all to say something in general about all prisons in all three Scandinavian countries. The question is difficult, and any answer needs to be based on a strong empirical foundation. Based on the analyses presented in this book, we would have to conclude that it seems difficult or even impossible to identify something that is uniquely Scandinavian in the sense that it can be found in all three Scandinavian countries, and nowhere else. Langford, Fisher, Schaffer and Pareus as well as Minke and Smoyer ask whether Scandinavian exceptionalism is in fact fiction rather than fact. We agree that there is a mythical quality to the exceptionalism literature, but we also do think that one may find some shared characteristics of the Scandinavian systems and (many of) the Scandinavian prisons that makes it relevant to at least discuss whether something like a Scandinavian correctional model exists.

Most importantly, one can find a certain level of commitment to a set of shared values. The principle of normalisation has a strong standing in all three countries, albeit in slightly different ways. The philosophy that prisons should ultimately be places of inclusion and that even prisoners are members of society that retain important citizens' rights can be said to constitute an important part of such a model. But many differences come into play when these values are put into practice in specific prisons. The level of paternalism and the extent to which prisons, policy makers and prison officers think it is appropriate to intervene in prisoners lives Big Mother-style will differ and this can create practices where notions of welfare and rehabilitation becomes more authoritarian than empowering. Furthermore, the culture and regimes will also sometimes differ from prison to prison and from one policy area to another, which can create prison practices that are de facto much more excluding and punitive than anything else. In some cases, such as the use of pre-trial solitary confinement and the remand regimes described by Smith, the Scandinavian countries are liberal in their use of power and seem to have very little interest in welfare and reintegration of prisoners. In other words, although Scandinavian prison practice will probably tend to lie mostly in the vicinity of the two latter of the three ideal types mentioned in the beginning of this concluding chapter, we nevertheless find elements of all three in prisons in Norway, Sweden and Denmark.

Make no mistake, Scandinavian prisons are still prisons. Some of them seem exceptional and even strange and outlandish to international visitors. Some visitors may be fooled into thinking that they are witnessing something entirely different; prisons from some sort of parallel humane and social–democratic universe. Other Scandinavian prisons are, like Vander Beken discovered, instantly recognisable as what they are. Like all prisons in democratic countries, Scandinavian prisons have to find an uneasy balance between security concerns, punishment, prisoner rights, rehabilitation and welfare ambitions. Mixing punishment and welfare is sometimes like trying to mix oil and water. But like any chef would tell you, mixing oil and water is actually possible. The result is called an emulsion. Emulsions are difficult, however. The result is unstable; it will revert back to its constituent parts if you heat it too quickly or if you forget about it and leave it to sit by itself out on the counter. It is in a sense kitchen magic; something that should not exist, but does. It needs know-how, attention and care to work. When you do get it to work, however, you know that you have created something special. The best Scandinavian prison practices are good examples of what is possible when you have the ideas, the resources, the values and the will to create truly welfare-oriented regimes. The bad ones are every bit as unappetising and sad as a bowl of split Hollandaise, and even less constructive. Because in the end, prisons are institutions with officers and inmates, where the former are placed in a position of power over the latter and where history as well as social psychology has taught us that harmful practices may result. Perhaps, where Scandinavian prisons are most exceptional is when they focus not so much on rehabilitation but on the principle of normalisation as a way to respect the rights and autonomy of the individual prisoner? In such places respect, dignity and empowerment of individuals will be the first priority to the degree that attaining these qualities are, in fact, possible in a prison.

Index

© The Author(s) 2017
P. Scharff Smith, T. Ugelvik (Eds.), *Scandinavian Penal History,
Culture and Prison Practice,* Palgrave Studies in Prisons and
Penology, DOI 10.1057/978-1-137-58529-5